Citroën Xsara Picasso
Service and Repair Manual

John S. Mead MISTC

Models covered

(3944 - 336 - 2AJ1)

All Citroën Xsara Picasso MPV models with petrol and diesel engines

1.6 litre (1587cc) and 1.8 litre (1749cc) petrol engines
2.0 litre (1997cc) turbo-diesel engines

© Haynes Publishing 2005

A book in the **Haynes Service and Repair Manual Series**

ABCDE
FGHIJ
KLMN

Printed in the USA

ISBN **1 85960 944 9**

British Library Cataloguing in Publication Data
A catalogue record for this book is available from the British Library.

Haynes Publishing
Sparkford, Yeovil, Somerset BA22 7JJ, England

Haynes North America, Inc
861 Lawrence Drive, Newbury Park, California 91320, USA

Editions Haynes
4, Rue de l'Abreuvoir
92415 COURBEVOIE CEDEX, France

Haynes Publishing Nordiska AB
Box 1504, 751 45 UPPSALA, Sverige

Contents

LIVING WITH YOUR CITROEN XSARA PICASSO

MAINTENANCE

Routine maintenance and servicing

Contents

Advanced driving

Many people see the words 'advanced driving' and believe that it won't interest them or that it is a style of driving beyond their own abilities. Nothing could be further from the truth. Advanced driving is straightforward safe, sensible driving - the sort of driving we should all do every time we get behind the wheel.

An average of 10 people are killed every day on UK roads and 870 more are injured, some seriously. Lives are ruined daily, usually because somebody did something stupid. Something like 95% of all accidents are due to human error, mostly driver failure. Sometimes we make genuine mistakes - everyone does. Sometimes we have lapses of concentration. Sometimes we deliberately take risks.

For many people, the process of 'learning to drive' doesn't go much further than learning how to pass the driving test because of a common belief that good drivers are made by 'experience'.

Learning to drive by 'experience' teaches three driving skills:

☐ Quick reactions. (Whoops, that was close!)
☐ Good handling skills. (Horn, swerve, brake, horn).
☐ Reliance on vehicle technology. (Great stuff this ABS, stop in no distance even in the wet...)

Drivers whose skills are 'experience based' generally have a lot of near misses and the odd accident. The results can be seen every day in our courts and our hospital casualty departments.

Advanced drivers have learnt to control the risks by controlling the position and speed of their vehicle. They avoid accidents and near misses, even if the drivers around them make mistakes.

The key skills of advanced driving are **concentration,** effective all-round **observation, anticipation** and **planning.** When **good vehicle handling** is added to these skills, all driving situations can be approached and negotiated in a safe, methodical way, leaving nothing to chance.

Concentration means applying your mind to safe driving, completely excluding anything that's not relevant. Driving is usually the most dangerous activity that most of us undertake in our daily routines. It deserves our full attention.

Observation means not just looking, but seeing and seeking out the information found in the driving environment.

Anticipation means asking yourself what is happening, what you can reasonably expect to happen and what could happen unexpectedly. (One of the commonest words used in compiling accident reports is 'suddenly'.)

Planning is the link between seeing something and taking the appropriate action. For many drivers, planning is the missing link.

If you want to become a safer and more skilful driver and you want to enjoy your driving more, contact the Institute of Advanced Motorists at www.iam.org.uk, phone 0208 996 9600, or write to IAM House, 510 Chiswick High Road, London W4 5RG for an information pack.

Working on your car can be dangerous. This page shows just some of the potential risks and hazards, with the aim of creating a safety-conscious attitude.

General hazards

Scalding

• Don't remove the radiator or expansion tank cap while the engine is hot.
• Engine oil, automatic transmission fluid or power steering fluid may also be dangerously hot if the engine has recently been running.

Burning

• Beware of burns from the exhaust system and from any part of the engine. Brake discs and drums can also be extremely hot immediately after use.

Crushing

• When working under or near a raised vehicle, always supplement the jack with axle stands, or use drive-on ramps. *Never venture under a car which is only supported by a jack.*
• Take care if loosening or tightening high-torque nuts when the vehicle is on stands. Initial loosening and final tightening should be done with the wheels on the ground.

Fire

• Fuel is highly flammable; fuel vapour is explosive.
• Don't let fuel spill onto a hot engine.
• Do not smoke or allow naked lights (including pilot lights) anywhere near a vehicle being worked on. Also beware of creating sparks (electrically or by use of tools).
• Fuel vapour is heavier than air, so don't work on the fuel system with the vehicle over an inspection pit.
• Another cause of fire is an electrical overload or short-circuit. Take care when repairing or modifying the vehicle wiring.
• Keep a fire extinguisher handy, of a type suitable for use on fuel and electrical fires.

Electric shock

• Ignition HT voltage can be dangerous, especially to people with heart problems or a pacemaker. Don't work on or near the ignition system with the engine running or the ignition switched on.

• Mains voltage is also dangerous. Make sure that any mains-operated equipment is correctly earthed. Mains power points should be protected by a residual current device (RCD) circuit breaker.

Fume or gas intoxication

• Exhaust fumes are poisonous; they often contain carbon monoxide, which is rapidly fatal if inhaled. Never run the engine in a confined space such as a garage with the doors shut.
• Fuel vapour is also poisonous, as are the vapours from some cleaning solvents and paint thinners.

Poisonous or irritant substances

• Avoid skin contact with battery acid and with any fuel, fluid or lubricant, especially antifreeze, brake hydraulic fluid and Diesel fuel. Don't syphon them by mouth. If such a substance is swallowed or gets into the eyes, seek medical advice.
• Prolonged contact with used engine oil can cause skin cancer. Wear gloves or use a barrier cream if necessary. Change out of oil-soaked clothes and do not keep oily rags in your pocket.
• Air conditioning refrigerant forms a poisonous gas if exposed to a naked flame (including a cigarette). It can also cause skin burns on contact.

Asbestos

• Asbestos dust can cause cancer if inhaled or swallowed. Asbestos may be found in gaskets and in brake and clutch linings. When dealing with such components it is safest to assume that they contain asbestos.

Special hazards

Hydrofluoric acid

• This extremely corrosive acid is formed when certain types of synthetic rubber, found in some O-rings, oil seals, fuel hoses etc, are exposed to temperatures above 400°C. The rubber changes into a charred or sticky substance containing the acid. *Once formed, the acid remains dangerous for years. If it gets onto the skin, it may be necessary to amputate the limb concerned.*
• When dealing with a vehicle which has suffered a fire, or with components salvaged from such a vehicle, wear protective gloves and discard them after use.

The battery

• Batteries contain sulphuric acid, which attacks clothing, eyes and skin. Take care when topping-up or carrying the battery.
• The hydrogen gas given off by the battery is highly explosive. Never cause a spark or allow a naked light nearby. Be careful when connecting and disconnecting battery chargers or jump leads.

Air bags

• Air bags can cause injury if they go off accidentally. Take care when removing the steering wheel and/or facia. Special storage instructions may apply.

Diesel injection equipment

• Diesel injection pumps supply fuel at very high pressure. Take care when working on the fuel injectors and fuel pipes.

⚠ *Warning: Never expose the hands, face or any other part of the body to injector spray; the fuel can penetrate the skin with potentially fatal results.*

Remember...

DO

• Do use eye protection when using power tools, and when working under the vehicle.

• Do wear gloves or use barrier cream to protect your hands when necessary.

• Do get someone to check periodically that all is well when working alone on the vehicle.

• Do keep loose clothing and long hair well out of the way of moving mechanical parts.

• Do remove rings, wristwatch etc, before working on the vehicle – especially the electrical system.

• Do ensure that any lifting or jacking equipment has a safe working load rating adequate for the job.

DON'T

• Don't attempt to lift a heavy component which may be beyond your capability – get assistance.

• Don't rush to finish a job, or take unverified short cuts.

• Don't use ill-fitting tools which may slip and cause injury.

• Don't leave tools or parts lying around where someone can trip over them. Mop up oil and fuel spills at once.

• Don't allow children or pets to play in or near a vehicle being worked on.

The Citroën Xsara Picasso was launched in June 2000 as a five-door mini-MPV version of the Citroën Xsara. The Picasso range is available with three engine options comprising 1.6 litre (1587 cc) and 1.8 litre (1749 cc) petrol engines and 2.0 litre (1997 cc) high-pressure diesel injection (HDi) engine. The engines are all of four-cylinder single- or double-overhead camshaft design, mounted transversely at the front of the vehicle, with a five-speed manual transmission mounted on the left-hand side.

All models have fully-independent front suspension. The rear suspension is semi-independent, with torsion bars and trailing arms.

A wide range of standard and optional equipment is available within the Xsara Picasso range to suit most tastes, including power steering, central locking, engine immobiliser, electric windows, electric sunroof, and air bags. An anti-lock braking system and air conditioning system are available as standard or optional equipment depending on model.

Provided that regular servicing is carried out in accordance with the manufacturer's recommendations, the Citroën Xsara Picasso should prove reliable and very economical. The engine compartment is well-designed, and most of the items requiring frequent attention are easily accessible.

Your Citroën Xsara Picasso Manual

The aim of this manual is to help you get the best value from your vehicle. It can do so in several ways. It can help you decide what work must be done (even should you choose to get it done by a garage), provide information on routine maintenance and servicing, and give a logical course of action and diagnosis when random faults occur. However, it is hoped that you will use the manual by tackling the work yourself. On simpler jobs it may even be quicker than booking the car into a garage and going there twice, to leave and collect it. Perhaps most important, a lot of money can be saved by avoiding the costs a garage must charge to cover its labour and overheads.

The manual has drawings and descriptions to show the function of the various components so that their layout can be understood. Tasks are described and photographed in a clear step-by-step sequence.

References to the 'left' and 'right' of the vehicle are in the sense of a person in the driver's seat facing forward.

Acknowledgements

Thanks are due to Draper Tools Limited, who provided some of the workshop tools, and to all those people at Sparkford who helped in the production of this Manual.

We take great pride in the accuracy of information given in this manual, but vehicle manufacturers make alterations and design changes during the production run of a particular vehicle of which they do not inform us. No liability can be accepted by the authors or publishers for loss, damage or injury caused by errors in, or omissions from, the information given.

The following pages are intended to help in dealing with common roadside emergencies and breakdowns. You will find more detailed fault finding information at the back of the manual, and repair information in the main chapters.

Car won't start

Starter motor doesn't turn

☐ Lift the front passenger's seat, take off the battery cover and make sure that the battery terminals are clean and tight.

☐ Switch on the headlights and try to start the engine. If the headlights go very dim when you're trying to start, the battery is probably flat. Get out of trouble by jump starting (see below) using a friend's car.

Starter motor turns as normal

☐ Is there fuel in the tank?

☐ Remove the engine cover (where fitted) and spray all visible electrical connectors with a water-dispersant spray like WD40 if you suspect a problem due to damp.

Jump starting

When jump-starting a car using a booster battery, observe the following precautions:

✔ Before connecting the booster battery, make sure that the ignition is switched off.

✔ Ensure that all electrical equipment (lights, heater, wipers, etc) is switched off.

✔ Take note of any special precautions printed on the battery case.

✔ Make sure that the booster battery is the same voltage as the discharged one in the vehicle.

✔ If the battery is being jump-started from the battery in another vehicle, the two vehicles MUST NOT TOUCH each other.

✔ Make sure that the transmission is in neutral (or PARK, in the case of automatic transmission).

 HAYNES HiNT *Jump starting will get you out of trouble, but you must correct whatever made the battery go flat in the first place. There are three possibilities:*

1 *The battery has been drained by repeated attempts to start, or by leaving the lights on.*

2 *The charging system is not working properly (alternator drivebelt slack or broken, alternator wiring fault or alternator itself faulty).*

3 *The battery itself is at fault (electrolyte low, or battery worn out).*

1 Lift up the cover over the flat battery's positive (+) cable terminal box located behind the air cleaner and connect one end of the red jump lead to the terminal stud.

2 Connect the other end of the red lead to the positive (+) terminal of the booster battery.

3 Connect one end of the black jump lead to the negative (–) terminal of the booster battery.

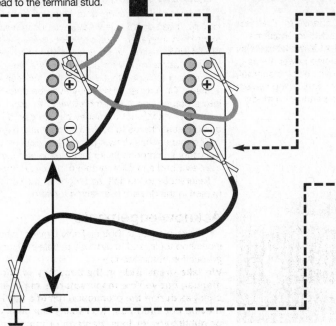

4 Connect the other end of the black jump lead to a bolt or bracket on the engine block on the vehicle to be started.

5 Make sure that the jump leads will not come into contact with the fan, drivebelts or any other moving parts of the engine.

6 Start the engine using the booster battery and run it at idle speed. Disconnect the jump leads in the reverse order of connection.

Wheel changing

 Warning: *Do not change a wheel in a situation where you risk being hit by other traffic. On busy roads, try to stop in a lay-by or a gateway. Be wary of passing traffic while changing the wheel – it is easy to become distracted by the job in hand.*

Preparation

- ☐ When a puncture occurs, stop as soon as it is safe to do so.
- ☐ Park on firm level ground, if possible, and well out of the way of other traffic.

- ☐ If you have one, use a warning triangle to alert other drivers of your presence.
- ☐ Apply the handbrake and engage first or reverse gear.

- ☐ Use hazard warning lights if necessary.
- ☐ If the ground is soft, use a flat piece of wood to spread the load under the foot of the jack.

Changing the wheel

1 Lift up the lid on the under floor storage box behind the front seat and take out the wheelbrace.

From inside the boot area, use the wheel-brace to lower the spare wheel cradle.

2 From inside the boot area, use the wheel-brace to lower the spare wheel cradle.

3 Slide the spare wheel and tool kit out from the underside of the car.

4 Open the box and take out the jack. Use the chock supplied to chock the wheel diagonally opposite the one being removed.

5 Slacken each wheel bolt by a half turn.

6 Locate the jack below the reinforced jacking point and on firm ground (don't jack the car at any other point on the sill). Turn the jack handle clockwise until the wheel is raised clear of the ground, remove the bolts and wheel trim (where applicable), then lift the wheel clear.

7 Position the space-saver spare wheel and fit the wheel bolts. Tighten the bolts moderately with the wheelbrace, then lower the car to the ground. Tighten the wheel bolts in a diagonal sequence, then secure the punctured wheel in the spare wheel cradle.

Finally...

- ☐ Remove the wheel chocks. Stow the jack and tools in the appropriate locations in the car.

- ☐ Check the tyre pressure on the wheel just fitted. If it is low, or if you don't have a pressure gauge with you, drive slowly to the nearest garage and inflate the tyre to the correct pressure. Have the damaged tyre or wheel repaired, or renew it, as soon as possible.

- ☐ Don't leave the spare wheel cradle empty and unsecured – it could drop onto the ground while the car is moving.

Identifying leaks

Puddles on the garage floor or drive, or obvious wetness under the bonnet or underneath the car, suggest a leak that needs investigating. It can sometimes be difficult to decide where the leak is coming from, especially if the engine bay is very dirty already. Leaking oil or fluid can also be blown rearwards by the passage of air under the car, giving a false impression of where the problem lies.

 Warning: Most automotive oils and fluids are poisonous. Wash them off skin, and change out of contaminated clothing, without delay.

HAYNES HINT *The smell of a fluid leaking from the car may provide a clue to what's leaking. Some fluids are distinctively coloured. It may help to clean the car carefully and to park it over some clean paper overnight as an aid to locating the source of the leak.*
Remember that some leaks may only occur while the engine is running.

Sump oil

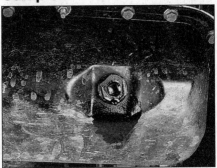

Engine oil may leak from the drain plug...

Oil from filter

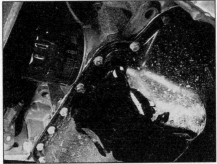

...or from the base of the oil filter.

Gearbox oil

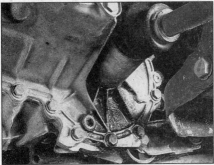

Gearbox oil can leak from the seals at the inboard ends of the driveshafts.

Antifreeze

Leaking antifreeze often leaves a crystalline deposit like this.

Brake fluid

A leak occurring at a wheel is almost certainly brake fluid.

Power steering fluid

Power steering fluid may leak from the pipe connectors on the steering rack.

Towing

When all else fails, you may find yourself having to get a tow home – or of course you may be helping somebody else. Long-distance recovery should only be done by a garage or breakdown service. For shorter distances, DIY towing using another car is easy enough, but observe the following points:
☐ Use a proper tow-rope – they are not expensive. The vehicle being towed must display an ON TOW sign in its rear window.
☐ Always turn the ignition key to the 'on'

position when the vehicle is being towed, so that the steering lock is released, and that the direction indicator and brake lights will work.
☐ Only attach the tow-rope to the towing eyes provided. These are located in or below the bumpers at the front and rear.
☐ Before being towed, release the handbrake and select neutral on the transmission.
☐ Note that greater-than-usual pedal pressure will be required to operate the brakes, since the vacuum servo unit is only operational with the engine running.

☐ Greater-than-usual steering effort will also be required.
☐ The driver of the car being towed must keep the tow-rope taut at all times to avoid snatching.
☐ Make sure that both drivers know the route before setting off.
☐ Only drive at moderate speeds and keep the distance towed to a minimum. Drive smoothly and allow plenty of time for slowing down at junctions.

Introduction

There are some very simple checks which need only take a few minutes to carry out, but which could save you a lot of inconvenience and expense.

These 'Weekly checks' require no great skill or special tools, and the small amount of time they take to perform could prove to be very well spent, for example;

☐ Keeping an eye on tyre condition and pressures, will not only help to stop them wearing out prematurely, but could also save your life.

☐ Many breakdowns are caused by electrical problems. Battery-related faults are particularly common, and a quick check on a regular basis will often prevent the majority of these.

☐ If your car develops a brake fluid leak, the first time you might know about it is when your brakes don't work properly. Checking the level regularly will give advance warning of this kind of problem.

☐ If the oil or coolant levels run low, the cost of repairing any engine damage will be far greater than fixing the leak, for example.

Underbonnet check points

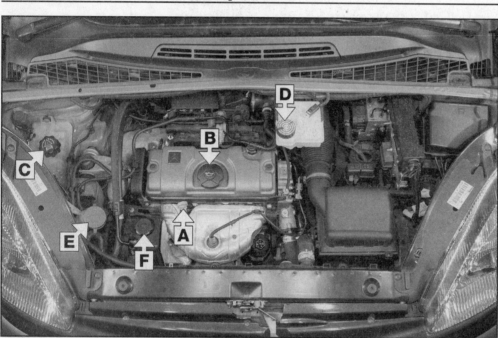

◀ 1.6 litre petrol

A *Engine oil level dipstick*

B *Engine oil filler cap*

C *Coolant expansion tank*

D *Brake fluid reservoir*

E *Screen washer fluid reservoir*

F *Power steering fluid reservoir*

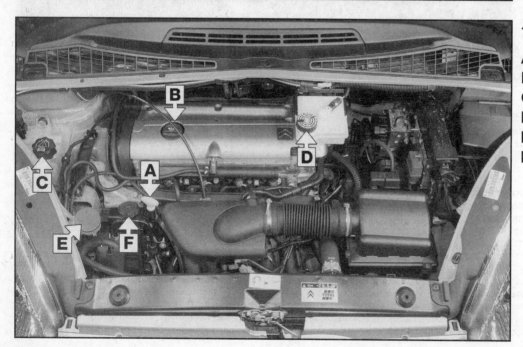

◀ 1.8 litre petrol

A *Engine oil level dipstick*

B *Engine oil filler cap*

C *Coolant expansion tank*

D *Brake fluid reservoir*

E *Screen washer fluid reservoir*

F *Power steering fluid reservoir*

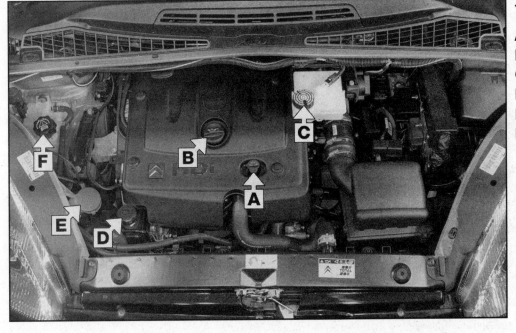

A *Engine oil level dipstick*

B *Engine oil filler cap*

C *Brake fluid reservoir*

D *Power steering fluid reservoir*

E *Screen washer fluid reservoir*

F *Coolant expansion tank*

Engine oil level

Before you start

✔ Make sure that your car is on level ground.
✔ Check the oil level before the car is driven, or at least 5 minutes after the engine has been switched off.

 If the oil is checked immediately after driving the vehicle, some of the oil will remain in the upper engine components, resulting in an inaccurate reading on the dipstick!

The correct oil

Modern engines place great demands on their oil. It is very important that the correct oil for your car is used (See 'Lubricants and fluids').

Car Care

● If you have to add oil frequently, you should check whether you have any oil leaks. Place some clean paper under the car overnight, and check for stains in the morning. If there are no leaks, the engine may be burning oil.

● Always maintain the level between the upper and lower dipstick marks (see photo 3). If the level is too low severe engine damage may occur. Oil seal failure may result if the engine is overfilled by adding too much oil.

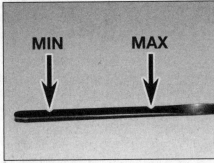

1 The dipstick is often brightly coloured for easy identification. Withdraw the dipstick.

3 Note the oil level on the end of the dipstick, which should be between the upper (MAX) mark and lower (MIN) mark. Approximately 1.25 litres of oil will raise the level from the lower mark to the upper mark.

2 Using a clean rag or paper towel, wipe all the oil from the dipstick. Insert the clean dipstick into the tube as far as it will go, then withdraw it again.

4 Oil is added through the filler cap. Unscrew the cap and top-up the level; a funnel may help to reduce spillage. Add the oil slowly, checking the level on the dipstick often. Don't overfill (see *Car Care*).

Power steering fluid level

Before you start:
✔ Park the vehicle on level ground.
✔ Set the steering wheel straight-ahead.
✔ The engine should be turned off.

HAYNES HiNT *For the check to be accurate, the steering must not be turned once the engine has been stopped.*

Safety First!
● The need for frequent topping-up indicates a leak, which should be investigated immediately.

1 The power steering fluid reservoir is integral with the power steering pump located at the front of the engine. With the engine stopped, wipe clean the area around the reservoir filler neck and unscrew the filler cap/dipstick from the reservoir.

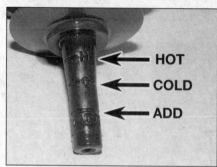

← HOT
← COLD
← ADD

2 Dip the fluid with the filler cap/dipstick. When the engine is cold, the fluid level should be between the ADD mark and the COLD mark; when hot it should be between the ADD and HOT marks. Top-up when the fluid is at the ADD mark.

3 When topping-up use the specified type of fluid and do not overfill the reservoir. When the level is correct, securely refit the cap.

Coolant level

 Warning: DO NOT attempt to remove the expansion tank pressure cap when the engine is hot, as there is a very great risk of scalding. Do not leave open containers of coolant about, as it is poisonous.

Car Care
● With a sealed-type cooling system, adding coolant should not be necessary on a regular basis. If frequent topping-up is required, it is likely there is a leak. Check the radiator, all hoses and joint faces for signs of staining or wetness, and rectify as necessary.

● It is important that antifreeze is used in the cooling system all year round, not just during the winter months. Don't top-up with water alone, as the antifreeze will become too diluted.

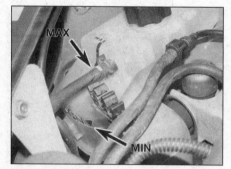

MAX

MIN

1 The coolant level varies with engine temperature. The level is checked in the expansion tank, which is located at the rear, right-hand side of the engine compartment. When the engine is cold, the coolant level should be between the MAX and MIN marks on the side of the tank.

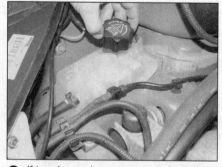

2 If topping-up is necessary, **wait until the engine is cold** then turn the expansion tank cap slowly anti-clockwise, and pause until any pressure remaining in the system is released. Unscrew the cap and lift off.

3 Add a mixture of water and antifreeze to the expansion tank, until the coolant level is up to the MAX level mark. Refit the cap, turning it clockwise as far as it will go until it is secure.

Screen washer fluid level

Screenwash additives not only keep the winscreen clean during foul weather, they also prevent the washer system freezing in cold weather - which is when you are likely to need it most. Don't top up using plain water as the screenwash will become too diluted, and will freeze during cold weather. *On no account use coolant antifreeze in the washer system - this could discolour or damage paintwork.*

1 The windscreen/tailgate washer fluid reservoir is located at the front right-hand side of the engine compartment. If topping-up is necessary, open the cap.

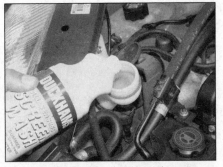

2 When topping-up the reservoir, a screen-wash additive should be added in the quantities recommended on the bottle.

Brake and clutch fluid level

Note: *Not all models have a hydraulic clutch.*

Warning:
● *Brake fluid can harm your eyes and damage painted surfaces, so use extreme caution when handling and pouring it.*
● *Do not use fluid that has been standing open for some time, as it absorbs moisture from the air, which can cause a dangerous loss of braking effectiveness.*

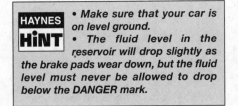

HAYNES HINT
● *Make sure that your car is on level ground.*
● *The fluid level in the reservoir will drop slightly as the brake pads wear down, but the fluid level must never be allowed to drop below the DANGER mark.*

Safety First!

● If the reservoir requires repeated topping-up this is an indication of a fluid leak somewhere in the system, which should be investigated immediately.

● If a leak is suspected, the car should not be driven until the braking system has been checked. Never take any risks where brakes are concerned.

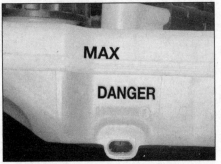

1 The MAX and DANGER marks are indicated on the edge of the reservoir, which is located at the rear of the engine compartment, just to the left of centre. The fluid level must be kept between these two marks.

2 If topping-up is necessary, first wipe the area around the filler cap with a clean rag before removing the cap. When adding fluid, it's a good idea to inspect the reservoir. The system should be drained and refilled if dirt is seen in the fluid (see Chapter 9).

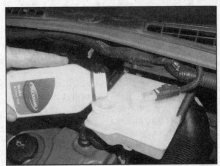

3 Carefully add fluid, avoiding spilling it on surrounding paintwork. Use only the specified hydraulic fluid; mixing different types of fluid can cause damage to the system and/or a loss of braking effectiveness. After filling to the correct level, refit the cap securely and wipe off any spilt fluid.

Tyre condition and pressure

It is very important that tyres are in good condition, and at the correct pressure - having a tyre failure at any speed is highly dangerous. Tyre wear is influenced by driving style - harsh braking and acceleration, or fast cornering, will all produce more rapid tyre wear. As a general rule, the front tyres wear out faster than the rears. Interchanging the tyres from front to rear ("rotating" the tyres) may result in more even wear. However, if this is completely effective, you may have the expense of replacing all four tyres at once!

Remove any nails or stones embedded in the tread before they penetrate the tyre to cause deflation. If removal of a nail does reveal that the tyre has been punctured, refit the nail so that its point of penetration is marked. Then immediately change the wheel, and have the tyre repaired by a tyre dealer.

Regularly check the tyres for damage in the form of cuts or bulges, especially in the sidewalls. Periodically remove the wheels, and clean any dirt or mud from the inside and outside surfaces. Examine the wheel rims for signs of rusting, corrosion or other damage. Light alloy wheels are easily damaged by "kerbing" whilst parking; steel wheels may also become dented or buckled. A new wheel is very often the only way to overcome severe damage.

New tyres should be balanced when they are fitted, but it may become necessary to re-balance them as they wear, or if the balance weights fitted to the wheel rim should fall off. Unbalanced tyres will wear more quickly, as will the steering and suspension components. Wheel imbalance is normally signified by vibration, particularly at a certain speed (typically around 50 mph). If this vibration is felt only through the steering, then it is likely that just the front wheels need balancing. If, however, the vibration is felt through the whole car, the rear wheels could be out of balance. Wheel balancing should be carried out by a tyre dealer or garage.

1 *Tread Depth - visual check*
The original tyres have tread wear safety bands (B), which will appear when the tread depth reaches approximately 1.6 mm. The band positions are indicated by a triangular mark on the tyre sidewall (A).

2 *Tread Depth - manual check*
Alternatively, tread wear can be monitored with a simple, inexpensive device known as a tread depth indicator gauge.

3 *Tyre Pressure Check*
Check the tyre pressures regularly with the tyres cold. Do not adjust the tyre pressures immediately after the vehicle has been used, or an inaccurate setting will result. Tyre pressures are shown on page 0•18.

Tyre tread wear patterns

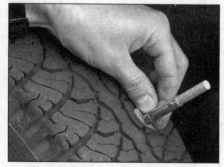

Shoulder Wear

Underinflation (wear on both sides)
Under-inflation will cause overheating of the tyre, because the tyre will flex too much, and the tread will not sit correctly on the road surface. This will cause a loss of grip and excessive wear, not to mention the danger of sudden tyre failure due to heat build-up.
Check and adjust pressures
Incorrect wheel camber (wear on one side)
Repair or renew suspension parts
Hard cornering
Reduce speed!

Centre Wear

Overinflation
Over-inflation will cause rapid wear of the centre part of the tyre tread, coupled with reduced grip, harsher ride, and the danger of shock damage occurring in the tyre casing.
Check and adjust pressures

If you sometimes have to inflate your car's tyres to the higher pressures specified for maximum load or sustained high speed, don't forget to reduce the pressures to normal afterwards.

Uneven Wear

Front tyres may wear unevenly as a result of wheel misalignment. Most tyre dealers and garages can check and adjust the wheel alignment (or "tracking") for a modest charge.
Incorrect camber or castor
Repair or renew suspension parts
Malfunctioning suspension
Repair or renew suspension parts
Unbalanced wheel
Balance tyres
Incorrect toe setting
Adjust front wheel alignment
Note: *The feathered edge of the tread which typifies toe wear is best checked by feel.*

Battery

Caution: Before carrying out any work on the vehicle battery, read the precautions given in 'Safety first' at the start of this manual.

✔ Make sure that the battery tray is in good condition, and that the clamp is tight. Corrosion on the tray, retaining clamp and the battery itself can be removed with a solution of water and baking soda, after removing the affected components from the car (see Chapter 5A). Thoroughly rinse all cleaned areas with water. Any metal parts damaged by corrosion should be covered with a zinc-based primer, then painted.

✔ Periodically (approximately every three months), check the charge condition of the battery as described in Chapter 5A.

✔ If the battery is flat, and you need to jump start your vehicle, see *Roadside Repairs*.

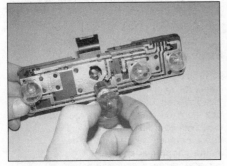

Battery corrosion can be kept to a minimum by applying a layer of petroleum jelly to the clamps and terminals after they are reconnected.

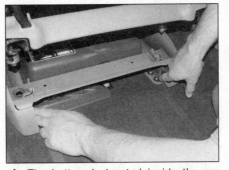

1 The battery is located inside the car under the front passenger's seat. To gain access, move the front seat fully rearward then depress the locking catches located at the rear of the seat on each side.

2 Tip the seat forward then release the locking clip on the top of the battery cover. Lift off the cover for access to the battery.

3 Check the tightness of the battery cable clamps to ensure good electrical connections. You should not be able to move them. Also check each cable for cracks and frayed conductors.

4 If corrosion (white, fluffy deposits) is evident, remove the cables from the battery terminals, clean them with a small wire brush, then refit them. Automotive stores sell a useful tool for cleaning the battery post and terminals

---

Electrical systems

✔ Check all external lights and the horn. Refer to the appropriate Sections of Chapter 12 for details if any of the circuits are found to be inoperative.

✔ Visually check all accessible wiring connectors, harnesses and retaining clips for security, and for signs of chafing or damage.

HAYNES HINT *If you need to check your brake lights and indicators unaided, back up to a wall or garage door and operate the lights. The reflected light should show if they are working properly.*

1 If a single indicator light, brake light or headlight has failed, it is likely that a bulb has blown and will need to be renewed. Refer to Chapter 12 for details. If both brake lights have failed, it is possible that the brake light switch operated by the brake pedal has failed. Refer to Chapter 9 for details.

2 If more than one indicator light or tail light has failed it is likely that either a fuse has blown or that there is a fault in the circuit (see Chapter 12). The main fuses are located in the fuse/relay boxes situated behind the cover in the facia on the driver's side, and in the engine compartment (refer to Chapter 12).

3 To renew a blown fuse, remove it, where applicable, using the plastic tool provided. Fit a new fuse of the same rating, available from car accessory shops. It is important that you find the reason that the fuse blew (see *Electrical fault finding* in Chapter 12).

Wiper blades

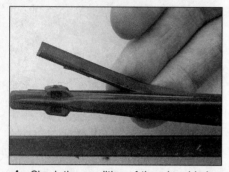

1 Check the condition of the wiper blades; if they are cracked or show any signs of deterioration, or if the glass swept area is smeared, renew them. Wiper blades should be renewed annually.

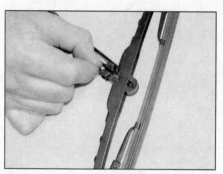

2 To remove a windscreen wiper blade, pull the arm fully away from the screen until it locks. Swivel the blade through 90º, then depress the locking clip at the base of the mounting block.

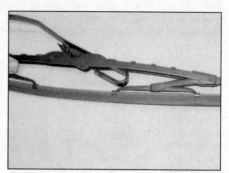

3 Move the blade down the arm to disengage the mounting block, then slide the blade from the arm. Don't forget to check the tailgate wiper blade as well.

Lubricants and fluids

Engine:

Petrol . . . . Multigrade engine oil, viscosity SAE 5W/40 to 10W/40, to API SJ or SJ-EC and ACEA-A3.98

Diesel . . . . Multigrade engine oil, viscosity SAE 5W/40 to 10W/40, to API CF or CF-EC and ACEA-B3.98

Cooling system . . . . Ethylene glycol-based antifreeze and soft water

Transmission . . . . Total BV 75W/80 gear oil

Braking system . . . . Hydraulic fluid to SAE J1703F or DOT 4

Power steering . . . . Dexron type II ATF

Choosing your engine oil

Engines need oil, not only to lubricate moving parts and minimise wear, but also to maximise power output and to improve fuel economy.

HOW ENGINE OIL WORKS

• *Beating friction*

Without oil, the moving surfaces inside your engine will rub together, heat up and melt, quickly causing the engine to seize. Engine oil creates a film which separates these moving parts, preventing wear and heat build-up.

• *Cooling hot-spots*

Temperatures inside the engine can exceed 1000° C. The engine oil circulates and acts as a coolant, transferring heat from the hot-spots to the sump.

• *Cleaning the engine internally*

Good quality engine oils clean the inside of your engine, collecting and dispersing combustion deposits and controlling them until they are trapped by the oil filter or flushed out at oil change.

OIL CARE - FOLLOW THE CODE

To handle and dispose of used engine oil safely, always:

OIL CARE

OIL BANK LINE
0800 66 33 66
www.oilbankline.org.uk

• *Avoid skin contact with used engine oil. Repeated or prolonged contact can be harmful.*
• *Dispose of used oil and empty packs in a responsible manner in an authorised disposal site. Call 0800 663366 to find the one nearest to you. Never tip oil down drains or onto the ground.*

Tyre pressures (cold)

Note 1: *The latest tyre pressure recommendations are marked on a label attached to the driver's door pillar. The following pressures are included as a guide, and apply to original-equipment tyres. The pressures may vary if any other make or type of tyre is fitted; check with the tyre manufacturer or supplier for correct pressures if necessary.*

Note 2: *If the space-saver emergency spare tyre is fitted, it should be inflated to a pressure of 3.0 bar (44 psi).*

	Front	Rear
Petrol engine models:		
Normal use	2.2 bar (32 psi)	2.2 bar (32 psi)
Fully laden	2.5 bar (36 psi)	3.0 bar (44 psi)
Diesel engine models:		
Normal use	2.3 bar (33 psi)	2.3 bar (33 psi)
Fully laden	2.5 bar (36 psi)	3.0 bar (44 psi)

Chapter 1 Part A:
Routine maintenance and servicing – petrol engine models

Contents

Degrees of difficulty

| **Easy,** suitable for novice with little experience | | **Fairly easy,** suitable for beginner with some experience | | **Fairly difficult,** suitable for competent DIY mechanic | | **Difficult,** suitable for experienced DIY mechanic | | **Very difficult,** suitable for expert DIY or professional | |

Lubricants and fluids .... Refer to end of *Weekly checks* on page 0•17

Capacities

Engine oil (including filter)
1.6 litre engines .... 3.50 litres
1.8 litre engines .... 4.25 litres
Difference between MAX and MIN dipstick marks (approx) .... 1.25 litres

Cooling system (approximate)
1.6 litre engines .... 5.8 litres
1.8 litre engines .... 6.5 litres

Transmission .... 1.8 litres

Fuel tank .... 55.0 litres

Engine

Auxiliary drivebelt tension (for use with electronic tension checking tool – see text):
  1.6 litre engines:
    With air conditioning .... Controlled by automatic tensioner
    Without air conditioning .... 120 SEEM units
  1.8 litre engines .... Controlled by automatic tensioner

Cooling system

Antifreeze mixture:
  28% antifreeze .... Protection down to –15°C
  50% antifreeze .... Protection down to –30°C
Note: *Refer to antifreeze manufacturer for latest recommendations*

Ignition system

Spark plugs:
  1.6 litre engines .... Bosch FR7KDC
  1.8 litre engines .... Bosch FR8ME
Spark plug electrode gap:
  1.6 litre engines .... 0.9 mm
  1.8 litre engines .... 1.0 mm

Brakes

Brake pad friction material minimum thickness .... 2.0 mm
Brake shoe friction material minimum thickness .... 1.5 mm

Tyre pressures .... Refer to end of *Weekly checks* on page 0•18

Torque wrench settings

	Nm	lbf ft
Oil filter cover (later 1.6 litre engines)	25	18
Roadwheel bolts	85	63
Spark plugs	25	18
Transmission oil filler/level plug	20	15

The maintenance intervals in this manual are provided with the assumption that you, not the dealer, will be carrying out the work. These are the minimum maintenance intervals recommended for vehicles driven daily. If you wish to keep your vehicle in peak condition at all times, you may wish to perform some of these procedures more often. We encourage frequent maintenance, because it enhances the efficiency, performance and resale value of your vehicle.

If the vehicle is driven in dusty areas, used to tow a trailer, or driven frequently at slow speeds (idling in traffic) or on short journeys, more frequent maintenance intervals are recommended.

When the vehicle is new, it should be serviced by a factory-authorised dealer service department, in order to preserve the factory warranty.

Valve clearance adjustment is hydraulic on 1.8 litre models, and on 1.6 litre model checking is no longer specified as part of the routine maintenance schedule. Check the valve clearances if there is any tapping or rattling from the top of the engine, or in the event of an unexplained lack of performance. The prudent owner may wish to check the clearances more often, perhaps at 25 000 mile (40 000 km) or two-yearly intervals.

Every 250 miles (400 km) or weekly

☐ Refer to *Weekly checks*

Every 12 500 miles (20 000 km) or 12 months – whichever comes first

☐ Renew the engine oil and filter (Section 3)*.
☐ Check all underbonnet/underbody components for fluid leaks (Section 4).
☐ Check the condition of the auxiliary drivebelt (Section 5).
☐ Check the clutch control mechanism (Section 6).
☐ Renew the pollen filter (Section 7).
☐ Check the condition of the driveshaft rubber gaiters (Section 8).
☐ Check the steering and suspension components (Section 9).
☐ Check the condition of the front brake pads (Section 10).
☐ Check the condition of the exhaust system (Section 11).
☐ Check the condition of the rear brake shoes (Section 12).
☐ Operate and lubricate all hinges and locks (Section 13).
☐ Road test (Section 14).

*Note: *The engine oil renewal interval shown is based on the use of either a semi-synthetic or fully synthetic engine oil. If a mineral oil is used, the interval should be reduced. Consult your Citroën dealer for further information.*

Every 25 000 miles (40 000 km) or 2 years – whichever comes first

In addition to all the items listed above, carry out the following:
☐ Renew the brake fluid (Section 15)*.
*Note: *Also renew the fluid on models with a hydraulic clutch.*

Every 37 500 miles (60 000 km) or 3 years – whichever comes first

In addition to all the items listed above, carry out the following:
☐ Renew the spark plugs (Section 16).
☐ Renew the air filter (Section 17).
☐ Check the manual transmission oil level (Section 18).
☐ Check the condition and operation of the braking system components (Section 19).
☐ Check the operation of the handbrake (Section 20).
☐ Renew the fuel filter (Section 21).
☐ Renew the timing belt (Section 22).

Note: *Although the normal interval for timing belt renewal is 75 000 miles (120 000 km), it is strongly recommended that the interval is halved to 37 500 miles (60 000 km) on vehicles which are subjected to intensive use, ie, mainly short journeys or a lot of stop-start driving. The actual belt renewal interval is therefore very much up to the individual owner, but bear in mind that severe engine damage will result if the belt breaks.*

Every 75 000 miles (120 000 km) or 5 years – whichever comes first

n addition to all the items listed above, carry out the following:
☐ Renew the coolant (Section 23).

Every 10 years – regardless of mileage

☐ Renew the air bag(s) and seat belt pretensioners (Section 24).

Underbonnet view of a 1.6 litre engine (later model)

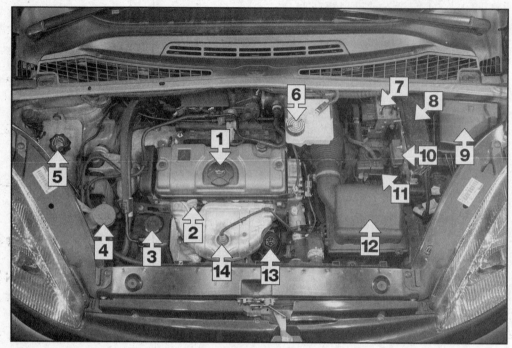

1 Engine oil filler cap
2 Engine oil dipstick
3 Power steering fluid reservoir filler cap
4 Windscreen/tailgate washer fluid reservoir filler cap
5 Coolant expansion tank filler cap
6 Brake master cylinder fluid reservoir
7 ABS hydraulic modulator
8 Engine management ECU
9 Engine compartment fuse/relay box
10 Injection double relay
11 Battery positive cable terminal box
12 Air cleaner housing
13 Oil filter housing
14 Lambda sensor

Underbonnet view of a 1.8 litre engine

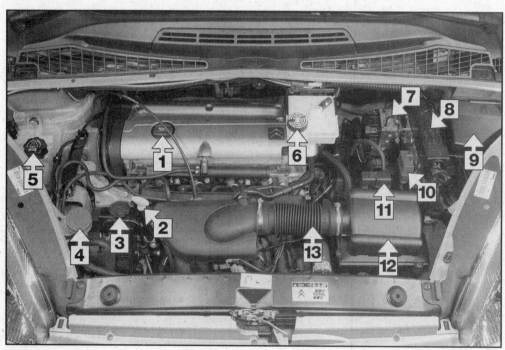

1 Engine oil filler cap
2 Engine oil dipstick
3 Power steering fluid reservoir filler cap
4 Windscreen/tailgate washer fluid reservoir filler cap
5 Coolant expansion tank filler cap
6 Brake master cylinder fluid reservoir
7 ABS hydraulic modulator
8 Engine management ECU
9 Engine compartment fuse/relay box
10 Injection double relay
11 Battery positive cable terminal box
12 Air cleaner housing
13 Air inlet duct

Front underbody view (1.6 litre model)

1 Alternator
2 Exhaust front pipe
   (catalytic converter)
3 Clutch slave cylinder
4 Radiator bottom hose
5 Air cleaner air inlet duct
6 Transmission oil drain plug
7 Driveshaft
8 Sump drain plug
9 Engine/transmission rear
   mounting
10 Rack and pinion steering
    gear
11 Front suspension subframe
12 Front anti-roll bar
13 Track rod balljoint
14 Front suspension lower
    arm
15 Front brake caliper

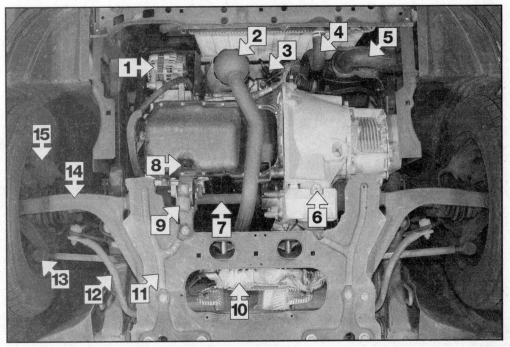

Front underbody view (1.8 litre model)

1 Air conditioning
   compressor
2 Engine oil filter
3 Power steering fluid hoses
4 Radiator bottom hose
5 Air cleaner air inlet duct
6 Transmission oil drain plug
7 Sump drain plug
8 Driveshaft
9 Engine/transmission rear
   mounting
10 Rack and pinion steering
    gear
11 Front suspension subframe
12 Front anti-roll bar
13 Track rod balljoint
14 Front suspension lower
    arm
15 Front brake caliper

Rear underbody view (1.6 litre model – 1.8 similar)

1 Rear silencer
2 Spare wheel
3 Rear shock absorber
4 Rear suspension trailing
   arm
5 Rear suspension tubular
   crossmember
6 Rear suspension torsion
   bar
7 Handbrake cable
8 Fuel tank

Maintenance procedures

1 General information

This Chapter is designed to help the home mechanic maintain his/her vehicle for safety, economy, long life and peak performance.

The Chapter contains a master maintenance schedule, followed by Sections dealing specifically with each task in the schedule. Visual checks, adjustments, component renewal and other helpful items are included. Refer to the accompanying illustrations of the engine compartment and the underside of the vehicle for the locations of the various components.

Servicing your vehicle in accordance with the mileage/time maintenance schedule and the following Sections will provide a planned maintenance programme, which should result in a long and reliable service life. This is a comprehensive plan, so maintaining some items but not others at the specified service intervals will not produce the same results.

As you service your vehicle, you will discover that many of the procedures can – and should – be grouped together, because of the particular procedure being performed, or because of the proximity of two otherwise-unrelated components to one another. For example, if the vehicle is raised for any reason, the exhaust can be inspected at the same time as the suspension and steering components.

The first step in this maintenance programme is to prepare yourself before the actual work begins. Read through all the Sections relevant to the work to be carried out, then make a list and gather all the parts and tools required. If a problem is encountered, seek advice from a parts specialist, or a dealer service department.

Service interval display

Certain models are equipped with a service interval display indicator in the instrument panel. When the ignition is initially switched on, a spanner appears in the display window and the total number of miles remaining until the next service is due is also shown.

The display should not necessarily be used as a definitive guide to the servicing needs of your Xsara, but it is useful as a reminder, to ensure that servicing is not accidentally overlooked. Owners of older cars, or those covering a small annual mileage, may feel inclined to service their car more often, in which case the service interval display is perhaps less relevant.

The display should be reset whenever a service is carried out, and this is achieved using the trip meter reset button on the instrument panel as follows.

With the ignition switched off, press and hold down the trip meter reset button. Switch the ignition on and the mileage remaining until the next service will flash. Continue to hold the button down for a further ten seconds. The spanner symbol will disappear and the mileage will return to zero.

2 Regular maintenance

1 If, from the time the vehicle is new, the routine maintenance schedule is followed closely, and frequent checks are made of fluid levels and high-wear items, as suggested throughout this manual, the engine will be kept in relatively good running condition, and the need for additional work will be minimised.
2 It is possible that there will be times when the engine is running poorly due to the lack of regular maintenance. This is even more likely if a used vehicle, which has not received regular and frequent maintenance checks, is purchased. In such cases, additional work

may need to be carried out, outside of the regular maintenance intervals.

3 If engine wear is suspected, a compression test (refer to relevant Part of Chapter 2) will provide valuable information regarding the overall performance of the main internal components. Such a test can be used as a basis to decide on the extent of the work to be carried out. If, for example, a compression test indicates serious internal engine wear, conventional maintenance as described in this Chapter will not greatly improve the performance of the engine, and may prove a waste of time and money, unless extensive overhaul work is carried out first.

4 The following series of operations are those most often required to improve the performance of a generally poor-running engine:

Primary operations

a) *Clean, inspect and test the battery (See 'Weekly checks').*
b) *Check all the engine-related fluids (See 'Weekly checks').*
c) *Check the condition of all hoses, and check for fluid leaks (Section 4).*
d) *Check the condition and tension of the auxiliary drivebelt (Section 5).*
e) *Renew the spark plugs (Section 16).*

f) *Check the condition of the air filter, and renew if necessary (Section 17).*
g) *Renew the fuel filter (Section 21).*

5 If the above operations do not prove fully effective, carry out the following secondary operations:

Secondary operations

All items listed under *Primary operations*, plus the following:

a) *Check the valve clearances – 1.6 litre engines (Chapter 2A)*
b) *Check the charging system (Chapter 5A).*
c) *Check the ignition system (Chapter 5B).*
d) *Check the fuel system (Chapter 4A).*

Every 12 500 miles (20 000 km) or 12 months

3 Engine oil and filter renewal

Note: *A suitable square-section wrench will be required to undo the sump drain plug. These wrenches can be obtained from most motor factors.*

1 Frequent oil and filter changes are the most important preventative maintenance procedures which can be undertaken by the DIY owner. As engine oil ages, it becomes

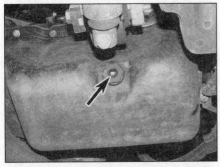

3.3a Sump drain plug location (arrowed) – 1.6 litre engines

3.3b Sump drain plug location (arrowed) – 1.8 litre engines

diluted and contaminated, which leads to premature engine wear.

2 Before starting this procedure, gather together all the necessary tools and materials. Also make sure that you have plenty of clean rags and newspapers handy, to mop up any spills. Ideally, the engine oil should be warm, as it will drain better, and any impurities suspended in the oil will be removed with it. Take care, however, not to touch the exhaust or any other hot parts of the engine when working under the vehicle. To avoid any possibility of scalding, and to protect yourself from possible skin irritants and other harmful contaminants in used engine oils, it is advisable to wear rubber gloves when carrying out this work. Access to the underside of the vehicle will be greatly improved if it can be raised on a lift, driven onto ramps, or jacked up and supported on axle stands (see *Jacking and vehicle support*).

3 Remove the engine undertray, then slacken the sump drain plug about half a turn **(see illustrations)**. Position the draining container

HAYNES HiNT

As the drain plug releases from the threads, move it away sharply so the stream of oil issuing from the sump runs into the container, not up your sleeve.

under the drain plug, then remove the plug completely. If possible, try to keep the plug pressed into the sump while unscrewing it by hand the last couple of turns **(see Haynes Hint)**. Recover the sealing ring from the drain plug.

4 Allow some time for the old oil to drain, noting that it may be necessary to reposition the container as the oil flow slows to a trickle.

5 After all the oil has drained, wipe off the drain plug with a clean rag, and fit a new sealing washer. Clean the area around the drain plug opening, and refit the plug. Tighten the plug securely.

6 Move the container into position under the oil filter, which is located on the front facing side of the cylinder block.

7 On early 1.6 litre engines, and all 1.8 litre engines, the oil filter is of the disposable metal canister type screwed into the front of the cylinder block or into the oil filter housing on the front of the cylinder block. On later 1.6 litre engines, the oil filter consists of a separate disposable paper element contained in a plastic housing. The housing is located on the front of the cylinder block adjacent to the radiator hoses **(see illustration)**. Proceed as follows according to filter type.

3.7 Cartridge type oil filter housing location (arrowed) – later 1.6 litre engines

3.8 Using an oil filter removal tool to slacken the canister type oil filter

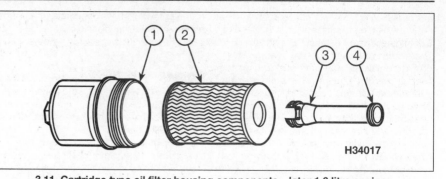

3.11 Cartridge type oil filter housing components – later 1.6 litre engines

| 1 Oil filter cover | 2 Oil filter cartridge | 3 Plunger tube | 4 Plunger tube O-ring |

Metal canister type filter

8 Using an oil filter removal tool if necessary, slacken the filter initially, then unscrew it by hand the rest of the way **(see illustration)**. Empty the oil in the old filter into the container. To ensure that the old filter is completely empty before disposal, puncture the filter dome in at least two places and allow any remaining oil to drain through the punctures and into the container.

9 Use a clean rag to remove all oil and dirt from the filter sealing area on the engine. Check the old filter to make sure that the rubber sealing ring hasn't stuck to the engine. If it has, carefully remove it.

10 Apply a light coating of clean engine oil to the sealing ring on the new filter, then screw it into position on the engine. Tighten the filter firmly by hand only – do not use any tools.

Paper element type filter

11 Using a 27 mm socket or spanner, slacken the oil filter cover initially, then unscrew it by hand the rest of the way. As the cover is unscrewed, the plunger tube located internally in the housing will be lifted off its seat allowing the oil remaining in the housing to drain back into the sump **(see illustration)**.

12 Lift the filter cover off the housing and remove the paper element. Withdraw the plunger tube from the oil filter cover. Note that a new plunger tube should always be fitted when renewing the oil filter. The tube should be supplied together with the new oil filter, but if this is not the case, obtain a new plunger tube from your Citroën dealer.

13 Use a clean rag to remove all oil and dirt from the oil filter housing and clean the filter cover inside and out using a suitable solvent.

14 Place the new oil filter on the filter housing then insert the new plunger tube into its location in the cover. Lightly lubricate the seal in the filter cover and the O-ring on the end of the plunger tube with clean engine oil.

15 Screw the filter cover onto the housing and tighten it to the specified torque.

All engines

16 Refit the engine undertray then remove the old oil and all tools from under the car. Lower the car to the ground (if applicable).

17 Remove the dipstick, then unscrew the oil filler cap from the cylinder head cover. Fill the engine, using the correct grade and type of oil (see *Weekly checks*). An oil can spout or funnel may help to reduce spillage. Pour in half the specified quantity of oil first, then wait a few minutes for the oil to fall to the sump. Continue adding oil a small quantity at a time until the level is up to the lower mark on the dipstick. Adding approximately 1.25 litres will bring the level up to the upper mark on the dipstick. Refit the filler cap.

18 Start the engine and run it for a few minutes; check for leaks around the oil filter seal and the sump drain plug. Note that there may be a delay of a few seconds before the oil pressure warning light goes out when the engine is first started, as the oil circulates through the engine oil galleries and the new oil filter before the pressure builds-up.

19 Switch off the engine, and wait a few minutes for the oil to settle in the sump once more. With the new oil circulated and the filter completely full, recheck the level on the dipstick, and add more oil as necessary.

20 Dispose of the used engine oil and filter safely, with reference to *General repair procedures* at the rear of this manual. Do not discard the old filter with domestic household waste. The facility for waste oil disposal provided by many local council refuse tips generally has a filter receptacle alongside.

HAYNES HiNT

A leak in the cooling system will usually show up as white- or rust-coloured deposits on the area adjoining the leak.

4 Underbonnet/ underbody component/ hose fluid leak check

⚠ *Warning: Refer to the safety information given in 'Safety First!' and Chapter 3 before disturbing any of the cooling system components.*

1 Carefully check the radiator and heater coolant hoses along their entire length. Renew any hose which is cracked, swollen or which shows signs of deterioration. Cracks will show up better if the hose is squeezed. Pay close attention to the clips that secure the hoses to the cooling system components. Hose clips that have been over-tightened can pinch and puncture hoses, resulting in cooling system leaks.

2 Inspect all the cooling system components (hoses, joint faces, etc) for leaks. Where any problems of this nature are found on system components, renew the component or gasket with reference to Chapter 3 **(see Haynes Hint)**.

Fuel

⚠ *Warning: Refer to the safety information given in 'Safety First!' and Part A of Chapter 4 before disturbing any of the fuel system components.*

3 Petrol leaks are difficult to pinpoint, unless the leakage is significant and hence easily visible. Fuel tends to evaporate quickly once it comes into contact with air, especially in a hot engine bay. Small drips can disappear before you get a chance to identify the point of leakage. If you suspect that there is a fuel leak from the area of the engine bay, leave the vehicle overnight then start the engine from cold, with the bonnet open. Metal components tend to shrink when they are cold, and rubber seals and hoses tend to harden, so any leaks will be more apparent whilst the engine is warming-up from a cold start.

4 Check all fuel lines at their connections to the fuel rail, fuel pressure regulator and fuel filter. Examine each rubber fuel hose along its length for splits or cracks. Check for leakage from the crimped joints between rubber and metal fuel lines. Examine the unions on the metal fuel lines and check the area around the fuel injectors for signs of O-ring leakage.

5 To identify fuel leaks between the fuel tank and the engine bay, the vehicle should be raised and securely supported on axle stands (see *Jacking and vehicle support*). Inspect the petrol tank and filler neck for punctures, cracks and other damage. The connection between the filler neck and tank is especially critical. Sometimes a rubber filler neck or connecting hose will leak due to loose retaining clamps or deteriorated rubber.

6 Carefully check all rubber hoses and metal fuel lines leading away from the petrol tank. Check for loose connections, deteriorated hoses, kinked lines, and other damage. Pay particular attention to the vent pipes and hoses, which often loop up around the filler neck and can become blocked or kinked, making tank filling difficult. Follow the fuel supply and return lines to the filter, then to the front of the vehicle, carefully inspecting them all the way for signs of damage or corrosion. Renew damaged sections as necessary.

Engine oil

7 Inspect the area around the cylinder head cover, cylinder head, oil filter and sump joint faces. Bear in mind that, over a period of time, some very slight seepage from these areas is to be expected – what you are really looking for is any indication of a serious leak caused by gasket failure. Engine oil seeping from the base of the timing belt cover or the transmission bellhousing may be an indication of crankshaft or transmission input shaft oil seal failure. Should a leak be found, renew the failed gasket or oil seal by referring to the appropriate Chapter in this manual.

Power steering fluid

8 Examine the power steering fluid feed and return hoses and pipes running between the power steering pump and the steering rack. To identify any problems where the pipes run under the engine, the vehicle should be raised and securely supported on axle stands (see *Jacking and vehicle support*).

9 Check the condition of each pipe and hose carefully. Look for deterioration caused by corrosion and damage from grounding, or debris thrown up from the road surface.

10 Pay particular attention to crimped unions, and the area surrounding the hoses that are secured with adjustable worm drive clips. Power steering fluid is a thin oil, and is usually red in colour.

Air conditioning refrigerant

⚠️ **Warning: Refer to the safety information given in 'Safety First!' and Chapter 3, regarding the dangers of disturbing any of the air conditioning system components.**

11 The air conditioning system is filled with a liquid refrigerant, which is retained under high pressure. If the air conditioning system is opened and depressurised without the aid of specialised equipment, the refrigerant will immediately turn into gas and escape into the atmosphere. If the liquid comes into contact with your skin, it can cause severe frostbite. In addition, the refrigerant contains substances which are environmentally damaging; for this reason, it should *never* be allowed to escape into the atmosphere.

12 Any suspected air conditioning system leaks should be immediately referred to a Citroën dealer or air conditioning specialist. Leakage will be shown up as a steady drop in the level of refrigerant in the system.

13 Note that water may drip from the condenser drain pipe, underneath the car, immediately after the air conditioning system has been in use. This is normal, and should not be cause for concern.

Hydraulic fluid

⚠️ **Warning: Refer to the safety information given in 'Safety First!' and Chapter 9, regarding the dangers of handling brake fluid.**

14 With reference to Chapter 9, examine the area surrounding the brake pipe unions at the master cylinder for signs of leakage. Check the area around the base of fluid reservoir, for signs of leakage caused by seal failure. Also examine the brake pipe unions at the ABS hydraulic unit.

15 If fluid loss is evident, but the leak cannot be pinpointed in the engine bay, the brake calipers/wheel cylinders and underbody brake lines should be carefully checked with the vehicle raised and supported on axle stands (see *Jacking and vehicle support*). Leakage of fluid from the braking system is a serious fault that must be rectified immediately.

16 Hydraulic fluid is a toxic substance with a watery consistency. New fluid is almost colourless, but it becomes darker with age and use.

17 On models with a hydraulically-operated clutch, the hydraulic system is supplied with fluid from the brake master cylinder reservoir. Inspect all the clutch hydraulic pipes and connections at the master and slave cylinders in the same way as for the brake fluid checks, referring to Chapter 6 for additional information.

Unidentified fluid leaks

18 If there are signs that a fluid of some description is leaking from the vehicle, but you cannot identify the type of fluid or its exact origin, park the vehicle overnight and slide a large piece of card underneath it. Providing that the card is positioned in roughly the right location, even the smallest leak will show up on the card. Not only will this help you to pinpoint the exact location of the leak, it should be easier to identify the fluid from its colour. Bear in mind, though, that the leak may only be occurring when the engine is running.

Vacuum hoses

19 Although the braking system is hydraulically-operated, the brake servo unit amplifies the effort applied at the brake pedal, by making use of the vacuum in the inlet manifold, generated by the engine. Vacuum is ported to the servo by means of a medium-bore plastic hose. Any leaks that develop in this hose will reduce the effectiveness of the braking system, and may affect the running of the engine.

20 In addition, a number of the underbonnet components, particularly the emission control components, are driven by vacuum supplied from the inlet manifold via narrow-bore rubber hoses. A leak in a vacuum hose means that air is being drawn into the hose (rather than escaping from it) and this makes leakage very difficult to detect. One method is to use an old length of vacuum hose as a kind of stethoscope – hold one end close to (but not in) your ear and use the other end to probe the area around the suspected leak. When the end of the hose is directly over a vacuum leak, a hissing sound will be heard clearly through the hose. Care must be taken to avoid contacting hot or moving components, as the engine must be running when testing in this manner. Renew any vacuum hoses that are found to be defective.

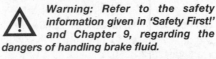

5 Auxiliary drivebelt check and renewal

Note: *Citroën specify the use of an electronic tension checking tool (SEEM 4122-T) to accurately check the auxiliary drivebelt tension on 1.6 litre engines not equipped with air conditioning. If access to this equipment (or suitable alternative equipment calibrated to display belt tension in SEEM units) cannot be obtained, an approximate setting can be achieved as described below. If an approximate setting method is used, the tension must be checked using the electronic tool at the earliest possible opportunity.*

1 A single, multi-ribbed auxiliary drivebelt is used on all models. The belt drives the alternator, power steering pump and air conditioning compressor according to equipment fitted. On 1.6 litre engines without air conditioning, the belt is adjusted manually, whereas on all other engines, adjustment is by means of an automatic spring-loaded tensioning mechanism.

Checking the drivebelt condition

2 Chock the rear wheels then jack up the front of the vehicle and support it on axle stands (see *Jacking and vehicle support*). Remove the right-hand front roadwheel.

3 To gain access to the right-hand end of the engine, the centre section of the wheelarch plastic liner must be removed. The liner is secured by stud-type plastic clips along its

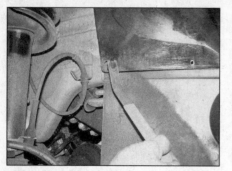

5.3a Using a forked type tool, extract the wheelarch liner upper . . .

5.3b . . . and lower retaining clips . . .

5.3c . . . then remove the liner centre section from under the front wing

upper and front edges. These clips can be removed using a forked type tool, or alternatively, with a large screwdriver (although there is a risk of breakage if the screwdriver method is used). Extract all the clips, then remove the liner centre section from under the front wing **(see illustrations)**. It will be necessary to ease back the front liner section slightly to allow the front edge of the centre section to be released. Note how the two sections overlap as you do this to aid refitting.

4 Using a suitable socket and extension bar fitted to the crankshaft pulley bolt, rotate the crankshaft so that the entire length of the drivebelt can be examined. Examine the drive-belt for cracks, splitting, fraying or damage. Check also for signs of glazing (shiny patches) and for separation of the belt plies. Renew the belt if worn or damaged.

5 If the condition of the belt is satisfactory, on engines where the belt is adjusted manually, check the drivebelt tension as described below, bearing in mind the Note at the start of this Section. On engines with an automatic spring-loaded tensioner, there is no need to check the drivebelt tension.

Drivebelt with manual adjuster

6 If not already done, proceed as described in paragraphs 2 and 3.

7 Slacken the tensioner pulley retaining nut then rotate the pulley using a suitable Torx spanner until there is sufficient slack for the drivebelt to be removed from the pulleys.

8 If the belt is being renewed, ensure that the correct type is used. Fit the belt around the pulleys, ensuring that the ribs on the belt are correctly engaged with the grooves in the

pulleys, and that the drivebelt is correctly routed **(see illustration)**. Tension the belt as follows.

9 If not already done, proceed as described in paragraphs 2 and 3.

10 If the electronic tool is not being used, the belt should be tensioned so that, under firm thumb pressure, there is about 5.0 mm of free movement at the mid-point between the pulleys on the longest belt run. If the electronic tool is being used, the tool sensor should be positioned on the belt midway between the crankshaft pulley and power steering pump pulley

11 To adjust the tension, with the tensioner pulley retaining nut slackened, rotate the pulley until the correct hand tension is achieved, or the specified number of SEEM units are displayed on the electronic tool. Refer to the Specifications for the SEEM unit tension settings. Hold the pulley in this position and tighten the retaining nut.

12 Remove the tool (if used), and rotate the crankshaft through four complete revolutions in the normal direction of rotation.

13 Recheck the belt tension using firm thumb pressure or the electronic tool and, if necessary, readjust.

14 Clip the coolant hoses into position (where necessary), then refit the wheelarch liner. Refit the roadwheel, and lower the vehicle to the ground.

Drivebelt with automatic adjuster

1.6 litre engines

15 If not already done, proceed as described in paragraphs 2 and 3.

16 Move the tensioner pulley away from the drivebelt, using a ratchet handle or extension bar with 3/8 inch square-section end engaged in the square hole in the automatic tensioner arm. Once the tensioner is released, retain it in the released position by inserting a 6.0 mm Allen key or similar in the hole provided.

17 Disengage the drivebelt from all the pulleys and remove the belt from the engine.

18 If the belt is being renewed, ensure that the correct type is used. Fit the belt around the pulleys, ensuring that the ribs on the belt are correctly engaged with the grooves in the pulleys, and that the drivebelt is correctly routed **(see illustration)**.

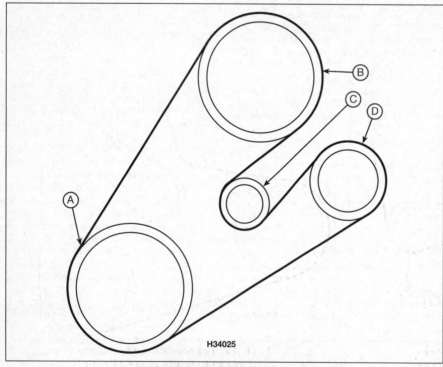

H34025

5.8 Auxiliary drivebelt configuration – 1.6 litre engines without air conditioning

A Crankshaft pulley
B Power steering pump pulley
C Manual tensioner pulley
D Alternator pulley

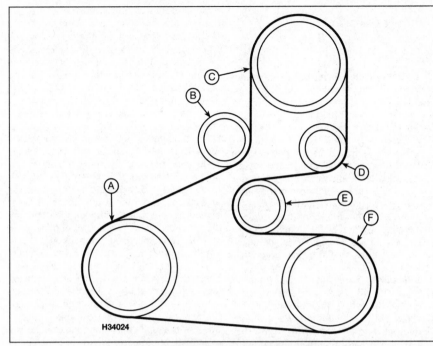

5.22 Rotate the tensioner pulley anti-clockwise using a spanner, and slip the belt off the pulleys – 1.8 litre engines

liner. Refit the roadwheel, and lower the vehicle to the ground.

1.8 litre engines

21 If not already done, proceed as described in paragraphs 2 and 3.
22 From under the wheelarch, rotate the tensioner pulley anti-clockwise, against spring tension, using a spanner on the tensioner pulley retaining bolt. Hold the tensioner pulley in this position and slip the belt off the pulleys **(see illustration)**. Release the tensioner pulley and remove the belt from the engine.
23 If the belt is being renewed, ensure that the correct type is used. Fit the belt around all the pulleys, except the tensioner pulley, ensuring that the ribs on the belt are correctly engaged with the pulley grooves, and that the drivebelt is correctly routed **(see illustrations)**.

5.18 Auxiliary drivebelt configuration – 1.6 litre engines with air conditioning

A Crankshaft pulley
B Automatic tensioner pulley
C Power steering pump pulley
D Alternator pulley
E Idler pulley
F Air conditioning compressor pulley

19 Take the load off the tensioner arm and remove the Allen key or similar retaining tool. Release the tensioner arm and allow the assembly to automatically tension the belt.
20 Clip the coolant hoses into position (where necessary), then refit the wheelarch

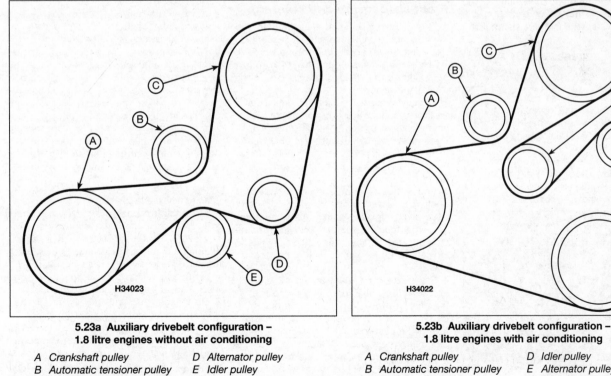

5.23a Auxiliary drivebelt configuration – 1.8 litre engines without air conditioning

A Crankshaft pulley
B Automatic tensioner pulley
C Power steering pump pulley
D Alternator pulley
E Idler pulley

5.23b Auxiliary drivebelt configuration – 1.8 litre engines with air conditioning

A Crankshaft pulley
B Automatic tensioner pulley
C Power steering pump pulley
D Idler pulley
E Alternator pulley
F Air conditioning compressor pulley

8.1 Check the condition of the driveshaft gaiters (arrowed)

24 Rotate the tensioner pulley anti-clockwise, hold it in this position and slide the belt around it. Release the tensioner and allow the assembly to automatically tension the belt.
25 Clip the coolant hoses into position (where necessary), then refit the wheelarch liner. Refit the roadwheel, and lower the vehicle to the ground.

6 Clutch control mechanism check

1 Check that the clutch pedal moves smoothly and easily through its full travel, and that the clutch itself functions correctly, with no trace of slip or drag.
2 On models with a cable-operated clutch, if excessive effort is required to operate the clutch, check first that the cable is correctly routed and undamaged, then remove the pedal and check that its pivot is properly greased. See Chapter 6 for more information.

7 Pollen filter renewal

1 Working in the engine compartment, undo the plastic nuts securing the filter access cover to the centre of the engine compartment bulkhead.
2 Remove the cover and withdraw the filter from its location. Clean the filter housing and the access cover, then fit the new filter using a reversal of the removal procedure.

9.4 Check for wear in the hub bearings by grasping the wheel and trying to rock it

8 Driveshaft gaiter check

1 With the vehicle raised and securely supported on axle stands (see *Jacking and vehicle support*), and the undertray removed, turn the steering onto full lock, then slowly rotate the roadwheel. Inspect the condition of the outer constant velocity (CV) joint rubber gaiters, squeezing the gaiters to open out the folds **(see illustration)**. Check for signs of cracking, splits or deterioration of the rubber, which may allow the grease to escape, and lead to water and grit entry into the joint. Also check the security and condition of the retaining clips. Repeat these checks on the inner CV joints. If any damage or deterioration is found, the gaiters should be renewed (see Chapter 8).
2 At the same time, check the general condition of the CV joints themselves by first holding the driveshaft and attempting to rotate the wheel. Repeat this check by holding the inner joint and attempting to rotate the driveshaft. Any appreciable movement indicates wear in the joints, wear in the driveshaft splines, or a loose driveshaft retaining nut.

9 Steering and suspension check

Front suspension and steering

1 Firmly apply the handbrake, then jack up the front of the car and support it securely on axle stands (see *Jacking and vehicle support*). Remove the engine undertray, then refit it again after completing all the checks at the front of the vehicle.
2 Visually inspect the balljoint dust covers and the steering rack-and-pinion gaiters for splits, chafing or deterioration. Any wear of these components will cause loss of lubricant, together with dirt and water entry, resulting in rapid deterioration of the balljoints or steering gear.
3 Check the power steering fluid hoses for chafing or deterioration, and the pipe and hose unions for fluid leaks. Also check for signs of fluid leakage under pressure from the steering gear rubber gaiters, which would indicate failed fluid seals within the steering gear.
4 Grasp the roadwheel at the 12 o'clock and 6 o'clock positions, and try to rock it **(see illustration)**. Very slight free play may be felt, but if the movement is appreciable, further investigation is necessary to determine the source. Continue rocking the wheel while an assistant depresses the footbrake. If the movement is now eliminated or significantly reduced, it is likely that the hub bearings are at fault. If the free

play is still evident with the footbrake depressed, then there is wear in the suspension joints or mountings.
5 Now grasp the wheel at the 9 o'clock and 3 o'clock positions, and try to rock it as before. Any movement felt now may again be caused by wear in the hub bearings or the steering track rod balljoints. If the inner or outer balljoint is worn, the visual movement will be obvious.
6 Using a large screwdriver or flat bar, check for wear in the suspension mounting bushes by levering between the relevant suspension component and its attachment point. Some movement is to be expected as the mountings are made of rubber, but excessive wear should be obvious. Also check the condition of any visible rubber bushes, looking for splits, cracks or contamination of the rubber.
7 With the vehicle standing on its wheels, have an assistant turn the steering wheel back-and-forth about an eighth of a turn each way. There should be very little, if any, lost movement between the steering wheel and roadwheels. If this is not the case, closely observe the joints and mountings previously described, but in addition, check the steering column universal joints for wear, and the rack-and-pinion steering gear itself.

Suspension strut and shock absorber

8 Check for any signs of fluid leakage around the suspension strut/shock absorber body, or from the rubber gaiter around the piston rod. Should any fluid be noticed, the suspension strut/shock absorber is defective internally, and should be renewed. **Note:** *Suspension struts/shock absorbers should always be renewed in pairs on the same axle.*
9 The efficiency of the suspension strut/shock absorber may be checked by bouncing the vehicle at each corner. Generally speaking, the body will return to its normal position and stop after being depressed. If it rises and returns on a rebound, the suspension strut/shock absorber is probably suspect. Examine also the suspension strut/shock absorber upper and lower mountings for any signs of wear.

10 Front brake pad condition check

1 Firmly apply the handbrake, then jack up the front of the vehicle and support it securely on axle stands (see *Jacking and vehicle support*). Remove the front roadwheels.
2 It is now possible to check the thickness of the pad friction material **(see Haynes Hint)**. If any pad's friction material is worn to the specified thickness or less, *all four pads must be renewed as a set*. Note: *If any pad is approaching the minimum thickness, consider renewal as a precautionary measure in case the pads wear out before the next service.*

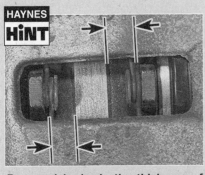

For a quick check, the thickness of friction material on each brake pad can be measured through the aperture in the caliper body.

3 For a comprehensive check, the brake pads should be removed and cleaned. The operation of the caliper can then be checked, and the brake disc itself can be fully examined on both sides. Refer to Chapter 9 for details.

11 Exhaust system check

1 With the engine cold (at least an hour after the vehicle has been driven), check the complete exhaust system from the engine to the end of the tailpipe. The exhaust system is most easily checked with the vehicle raised on a hoist, or suitably supported on axle stands, so that the exhaust components are readily visible and accessible (see *Jacking and vehicle support*).
2 Check the exhaust pipes and connections for evidence of leaks, severe corrosion and damage. Make sure that all brackets and mountings are in good condition, and that all relevant nuts and bolts are tight. Leakage at

any of the joints or in other parts of the system will usually show up as a black sooty stain in the vicinity of the leak.
3 Rattles and other noises can often be traced to the exhaust system, especially the brackets and mountings. Try to move the pipes and silencers. If the components are able to come into contact with the body or suspension parts, secure the system with new mountings. Otherwise separate the joints (if possible) and twist the pipes as necessary to provide additional clearance.

12 Rear brake shoe condition check

1 Chock the front wheels then jack up the rear of the vehicle and support it on axle stands (see *Jacking and vehicle support*).
2 For a quick check, the thickness of friction material remaining on one of the brake shoes can be measured through the slot in the brake backplate that is exposed by prising out its sealing grommet **(see illustrations)**. If a rod of the same diameter as the specified minimum thickness is placed against the shoe friction material, the amount of wear can quickly be assessed – a small mirror may help observation. If any shoe's friction material is worn to the specified thickness or less, all four shoes must be renewed as a set. **Note***: If any shoe is approaching the minimum thickness, consider renewal as a precautionary measure in case the shoes wear out before the next service.*
3 For a comprehensive check, the brake drums should be removed and cleaned. This will permit the wheel cylinders to be checked and the condition of the brake drum itself to be fully examined. Refer to Chapter 9 for further information.

13 Hinge and lock operation and lubrication

1 Work around the vehicle, and lubricate the hinges of the bonnet, doors and tailgate with a small amount of general-purpose oil.
2 Lightly lubricate the bonnet release mechanism and exposed section of inner cable with a smear of grease.
3 Check carefully the security and operation of all hinges, latches and locks, adjusting them where required. Check the operation of the central locking system.
4 Check the condition and operation of the tailgate struts, renewing them if they are leaking or no longer able to support the tailgate securely when raised.

14 Road test

Instruments/ electrical equipment

1 Check the operation of all instruments and electrical equipment.
2 Make sure that all instruments read correctly, and switch on all electrical equipment in turn to check it functions properly.

Steering and suspension

3 Check for any abnormalities in the steering, suspension, handling or road 'feel'.
4 Drive the vehicle, and check that there are no unusual vibrations or noises.
5 Check that the steering feels positive, with no excessive 'sloppiness', or roughness, and check for any suspension noises when cornering, or when driving over bumps.

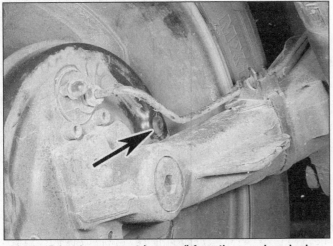

12.2a Prise the grommet (arrowed) from the rear drum brake backplate

12.2b Viewing the thickness of the brake shoe lining using a small mirror

Drivetrain

6 Check the performance of the engine, clutch, transmission and driveshafts.

7 Listen for any unusual noises from the engine, clutch and transmission.

8 Make sure that the engine runs smoothly when idling, and that there is no hesitation when accelerating.

9 Check that the clutch action is smooth and progressive, that the drive is taken up smoothly, and that the pedal travel is not excessive. Also listen for any noises when the clutch pedal is depressed.

10 Check that all gears can be engaged smoothly without noise, and that the gear lever action is smooth and not abnormally vague or 'notchy'.

11 Listen for a metallic clicking sound from the front of the vehicle, as the vehicle is driven slowly in a circle with the steering on full lock. Carry out this check in both directions. If a clicking noise is heard, this indicates lack of lubrication or wear in a driveshaft constant velocity joint (see Chapter 8).

Braking system

12 Make sure that the vehicle does not pull to one side when braking, and that the wheels do not lock prematurely when braking hard (models without ABS).

13 Check that there is no vibration through the steering when braking.

14 Check that the handbrake operates correctly, without excessive movement of the lever, and that it holds the vehicle on a slope.

15 Test the operation of the brake servo unit as follows. With the engine off, depress the footbrake four or five times to exhaust the vacuum. Start the engine, holding the brake pedal depressed. As the engine starts, there should be a noticeable 'give' in the brake pedal as vacuum builds-up. Allow the engine to run for at least two minutes, and then switch it off. If the brake pedal is depressed now, it should be possible to detect a hiss from the servo as the pedal is depressed. After about four or five applications, no further hissing should be heard, and the pedal should feel considerably firmer.

Every 25 000 miles (40 000 km) or 2 years

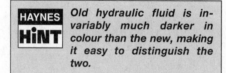

15 Brake fluid renewal

⚠ **Warning: Brake hydraulic fluid can harm your eyes and damage painted surfaces, so use extreme caution when handling and pouring it. Do not use fluid that has been standing open for some time, as it absorbs moisture from the air. Excess moisture can cause a dangerous loss of braking effectiveness.**

Note: *Also renew the fluid on models fitted with a hydraulic clutch, with reference to Chapter 6.*

1 The procedure is similar to that for the bleeding of the hydraulic system as described in Chapter 9, except that the brake fluid reservoir should be emptied by syphoning, using a clean poultry baster or similar before starting, and allowance should be made for the old fluid to be expelled when bleeding a section of the circuit.

2 Alternatively, to empty the reservoir, working as described in Chapter 9, open the first bleed screw in the sequence, and pump the brake pedal gently until nearly all the old fluid has been emptied from the master cylinder reservoir.

> **HAYNES HiNT** *Old hydraulic fluid is invariably much darker in colour than the new, making it easy to distinguish the two.*

3 Top-up to the MAX level with new fluid, and continue pumping until only the new fluid remains in the reservoir, and new fluid can be seen emerging from the bleed screw. Tighten the screw, and top the reservoir level up to the MAX level line.

4 Work through all the remaining bleed screws in the sequence until new fluid can be seen at all of them. Be careful to keep the master cylinder reservoir topped-up to above the DANGER level at all times, or air may enter the system and increase the length of the task.

5 When the operation is complete, check that all bleed screws are securely tightened, and that their dust caps are refitted. Wash off all traces of spilt fluid, and recheck the master cylinder reservoir fluid level.

6 Check the operation of the brakes before taking the car on the road.

Every 37 500 miles (60 000 km) or 3 years

16 Spark plug renewal

1 The correct functioning of the spark plugs is vital for the correct running and efficiency of the engine. It is essential that the plugs fitted

16.4 Unscrew the spark plugs using a spark plug spanner or a deep socket and extension bar

are appropriate for the engine (a suitable type is specified at the start of this Chapter). If this type is used and the engine is in good condition, the spark plugs should not need attention between scheduled replacement intervals. Spark plug cleaning is rarely necessary, and should not be attempted unless specialised equipment is available, as damage can easily be caused to the firing ends.

2 Remove the ignition coil module/unit as described in Chapter 5B.

3 It is advisable to remove the dirt from the spark plug recesses using a clean brush, vacuum cleaner or compressed air before removing the plugs, to prevent dirt dropping into the cylinders.

4 Unscrew the plugs using a spark plug spanner, suitable box spanner or a deep socket and extension bar **(see illustration)**. Keep the socket aligned with the spark plug – if it is forcibly moved to one side, the ceramic insulator may be broken off. As each plug is removed, examine it as follows.

5 Examination of the spark plugs will give a good indication of the condition of the engine. If the insulator nose of the spark plug is clean and white, with no deposits, this is indicative of a weak mixture or too hot a plug (a hot plug transfers heat away from the electrode slowly, a cold plug transfers heat away quickly).

6 If the tip and insulator nose are covered with hard black-looking deposits, then this is indicative that the mixture is too rich. Should the plug be black and oily, then it is likely that the engine is fairly worn, as well as the mixture being too rich.

7 If the insulator nose is covered with light tan to greyish-brown deposits, then the mixture is correct and it is likely that the engine is in good condition.

8 The spark plug electrode gap is of considerable importance as, if it is too large or too small, the size of the spark and its efficiency will be seriously impaired.

9 Measure the gap with a feeler blade, and then bend open, or closed, the outer plug electrode(s) until the correct gap is achieved

(see illustration). The centre electrode should never be bent, as this may crack the insulator and cause plug failure, if nothing worse. If using feeler blades, the gap is correct when the appropriate-size blade is a firm sliding fit.

10 Special spark plug electrode gap adjusting tools are available from most motor accessory shops, or from spark plug manufacturers.

11 Check that the threaded connector sleeves are tight, and that the plug exterior and threads are clean, then insert the spark plugs into their locations **(see Haynes Hint)**.

12 Remove the rubber hose (if used), and tighten the plug to the specified torque using the spark plug socket and a torque wrench. Refit the remaining spark plugs in the same manner.

13 Refit the ignition coil module/unit as described in Chapter 5B.

17 Air filter renewal

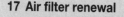

1 Undo the screws securing the lid to the air filter housing. Lift the lid up and take out the air filter element **(see illustrations)**.

2 Wipe clean the inside of the filter housing and fit the new element.

3 Locate the air filter lid in position and secure with the retaining screws.

18 Transmission oil level check

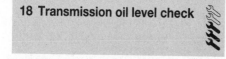

Note: *A suitable square-section wrench will be required to undo the transmission filler/level plug. These wrenches can be obtained from most motor factors or your Citroën dealer. A new sealing washer will also be required when refitting the transmission filler/level plug.*

> **HAYNES HINT**
>
> *It may be possible to use the square end fitting on a ratchet handle (as found in a typical socket set) to undo the plug.*

1 The manual transmission oil does not need to be renewed as part of the regular maintenance schedule, but the oil level must be checked and if necessary topped-up at the interval specified here. To drain the transmission as part of a repair procedure, refer to the information given in Chapter 7.

2 The oil level must be checked before the car is driven, or at least 5 minutes after the engine has been switched off. If the oil is checked immediately after driving the car, some of the oil will remain distributed around the transmission components, resulting in an inaccurate level reading.

3 With the car on level ground, firmly apply the handbrake, then jack up the front and rear

16.9 Measuring the spark plug gap with a feeler blade

of the car and support it securely on axle stands (see *Jacking and vehicle support*). Note that the car must be level, to ensure accuracy, when checking the oil level.

4 For improved access to the filler/level plug, the centre section of the left-hand wheelarch plastic liner can be removed after removing the roadwheel. The liner is secured by stud-type plastic clips along it upper and front edges which can be removed using a forked type tool. Extract all the clips, and remove the liner centre section from under the front wing **(see illustration)**. It will be necessary to ease back the front section slightly to allow the front edge of the centre section to be released. Note how the two sections overlap, as you do this, to aid refitting.

5 Wipe clean the area around the filler/level plug, which is on the left-hand end of the transmission. Unscrew the plug and clean it; discard the sealing washer.

17.1a Undo the air filter housing lid retaining screws . . .

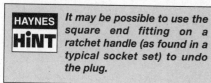

18.4 Extract the clips and remove the wheelarch liner centre section for access to the transmission filler/level plug

It is very often difficult to insert spark plugs into their holes without cross-threading them. To avoid this possibility, fit a short length of 5/16 inch internal diameter rubber hose over the end of the spark plug. The flexible hose acts as a universal joint to help align the plug with the plug hole. Should the plug begin to cross-thread, the hose will slip on the spark plug, preventing thread damage to the cylinder head.

6 The oil level should reach the lower edge of the filler/level hole. A certain amount of oil will have gathered behind the filler/level plug, and will trickle out when it is removed; this does **not** necessarily indicate that the level is correct. To ensure that a true level is established, wait until the initial trickle has stopped, then add oil as necessary until a trickle of new oil can be seen emerging **(see illustration)**. The level will be correct when

17.1b . . . lift the lid up and take out the air filter element

18.6 Top-up the transmission until a trickle of new oil can be seen emerging from the filler/level plug

the flow ceases; use only good-quality oil of the specified type (refer to *Lubricants and fluids*).

7 If the transmission has been overfilled so that oil flows out as soon as the filler/level plug is removed, check that the car is completely level (front-to-rear and side-to-side), and allow the surplus to drain off into a container.

8 When the level is correct, fit a new sealing washer to the filler/level plug, refit the plug and tighten it to the specified torque.

9 Refit the wheelarch liner and roadwheel, then lower the car to the ground. Tighten the roadwheel bolts to the specified torque.

19 Braking system check

Front brakes

1 Firmly apply the handbrake, then jack up the front of the car and support it securely on axle stands (see *Jacking and vehicle support*).

2 Inspect the area around both brake calipers for signs of brake fluid leakage, either from the piston seals, the brake pipe union or the bleed screw.

3 Examine the brake hoses leading to each caliper and check for signs of cracking, chafing or damage. Renew a hose which shows signs of deterioration without delay.

4 Ensure that the transmission is in neutral, then grasp each front wheel hub and turn it by hand. Slight resistance is normal, but if the hub is difficult to turn smoothly, this indicates that the brake pads are binding, possibly due to a seized or partially-seized brake caliper piston; refer to Chapter 9 for details of caliper removal and overhaul.

5 Remove the front brake pads as described in Chapter 9. Examine the brake pads and measure the depth of the remaining friction material. Renew all four pads, if any are worn below their minimum limit.

6 Using proprietary brake cleaning fluid and a stiff brush, wash all traces of dirt and brake dust from the brake calipers – take care to avoid inhaling any of the airborne brake dust. Examine the piston dust seal for signs of damage or deterioration and check that it is securely seated in its retaining groove.

7 Check the condition of the brake disc with reference to the information given in Chapter 9.

8 Refit the front brake pads as described in Chapter 9, then refit the roadwheels and lower the front of the car to the ground. Tighten the roadwheel bolts to the specified torque.

Rear brakes

9 Chock the front wheels then jack up the rear of the car and support it on axle stands (see *Jacking and vehicle support*).

10 Ensure that the handbrake is released, then grasp each rear roadwheel and turn it by hand. Slight resistance is normal, but if the wheel is difficult to turn smoothly, this could be due to a seized or partially-seized wheel cylinder, or incorrect handbrake adjustment; refer to Chapter 9 for further details.

11 Remove the rear roadwheels, then with reference to Chapter 9, remove the rear brake shoes. Examine the brake shoes and measure the depth of the remaining friction material. Renew all four brake shoes, if any are worn below their minimum limit.

12 Check the brake drums for wear and damage and check the area around the wheel cylinder piston seals for signs of fluid leakage. Check at the rear of the brake backplate for evidence of fluid leakage from the brake pipe union or bleed screw. Renew the wheel cylinder without delay if it shows signs of leakage; see Chapter 9 for details.

13 Using proprietary brake cleaning fluid and a stiff brush, wash all traces of dirt and brake dust from the wheel cylinders and backplates – take care to avoid inhaling any of the airborne brake dust.

14 On completion, refit the brake shoes, brake drums and roadwheels, then lower the car to the ground. Tighten the roadwheel bolts to the specified torque.

20 Handbrake check and adjustment

Refer to Chapter 9.

21 Fuel filter renewal

⚠ **Warning: Before carrying out the following operation, refer to the precautions given in 'Safety first!' at the beginning of this manual, and follow them implicitly. Petrol is a highly-dangerous and volatile liquid, and the precautions necessary when handling it cannot be overstressed.**

1 The fuel filter is situated underneath the rear of the vehicle, on the side of the fuel tank. To gain access to the filter, chock the front wheels then jack up the rear of the car and support it on axle stands (see *Jacking and vehicle support*).

21.3 Unclip the retaining strap (arrowed) to release the fuel filter from the fuel tank

2 Seal off the fuel hoses leading to and from the filter, using proprietary hose clamps, with rounded jaws – do not use G-clamps, self-locking grips, or similar with flat or square jaws as these could damage the hose internally, causing leakage later.

3 Unclip the filter retaining strap from the fuel tank **(see illustration)**.

4 Noting the direction of the arrow marked on the filter body, release the quick-release fittings and disconnect the fuel hoses from the filter.

5 Remove the filter from the car. Dispose of the old filter safely; it will be highly flammable, and may explode if thrown on a fire.

6 Slide the new filter into position and clip the filter strap back onto the fuel tank. Ensure that the arrow on the filter body is pointing in the direction of the fuel flow, as noted when removing the old filter. The flow direction can otherwise be determined by tracing the fuel hoses back along their length.

7 Connect the fuel hoses to the filter by pressing each hose onto its respective filter port until it 'snaps' into position. Remove the hose clamps.

8 Start the engine, check the filter hose connections for leaks, then lower the vehicle to the ground.

22 Timing belt renewal

Refer to Chapter 2A or 2B as applicable.
Note: *Although the normal interval for timing belt renewal is 75 000 miles (120 000 km), it is strongly recommended that the interval is halved to 37 500 miles (60 000 km) on vehicles which are subjected to intensive use, ie, mainly short journeys or a lot of stop-start driving. The actual belt renewal interval is therefore very much up to the individual owner, but bear in mind that severe engine damage will result if the belt breaks.*

23.4a Cooling system bleed screws are located in the heater matrix outlet hose (arrowed) . . .

23.4b . . . and in the coolant outlet housing (arrowed) – 1.6 litre engine

Every 75 000 miles (120 000 km) or 5 years

23 Coolant renewal

⚠️ **Warning: Wait until the engine is cold before starting this procedure. Do not allow antifreeze to come in contact with your skin, or with the painted surfaces of the vehicle. Rinse off spills immediately with plenty of water. Never leave antifreeze lying around in an open container, or in a puddle in the driveway or on the garage floor. Children and pets are attracted by its sweet smell, but antifreeze can be fatal if ingested.**

Cooling system draining

Note: *Later models are filled with a 'long-life' coolant during vehicle assembly which is claimed to be suitable for ten years use before renewal is required. If you are sure that the vehicle is filled with this type of coolant, then renewal may not be necessary at this service interval. Consult your Citroën dealer for details of coolant specification and renewal recommendations.*

1 With the engine completely cold, remove the expansion tank filler cap. Turn the cap slowly anti-clockwise, wait until any pressure remaining in the system is released, then fully unscrew the cap.

2 Firmly apply the handbrake, then jack up the front of the vehicle and support it securely on axle stands (see *Jacking and vehicle support*). Remove the engine undertray.

3 Position a suitable container beneath the bottom hose connection on the radiator. Release the retaining clip, then disconnect the hose and allow the coolant to drain into the container.

4 To assist draining, open the cooling system bleed screws which are located in the heater matrix outlet hose union on the engine compartment bulkhead, and on the coolant outlet housing on the left-hand end of the cylinder head **(see illustrations)**.

5 The manufacturers do not specify a requirement to drain the cylinder block at the time of routine coolant renewal. If, however, the coolant is being drained as part of an engine repair procedure (such as cylinder head gasket renewal), then it is advisable to drain the cylinder block also. Note that the cylinder block drain plugs are virtually inaccessible and it may be necessary to move certain cables, brackets or hoses to one side for access.

6 To drain the cylinder block, reposition the container below the drain plug located at the front left-hand side of the cylinder block on 1.6 litre engines, and at the rear left-hand side of the cylinder block on 1.8 litre engines. Remove the drain plug, and allow the coolant to drain into the container.

7 On completion of draining, refit the radiator bottom hose and cylinder block drain plugs (where applicable). Refit any components disturbed for access, then refit the engine undertray and lower the vehicle to the ground.

Cooling system flushing

8 If coolant renewal has been neglected, or if the antifreeze mixture has become diluted, then in time, the cooling system may gradually lose efficiency, as the coolant passages become restricted due to rust, scale deposits, and other sediment. The cooling system efficiency can be restored by flushing the system clean.

9 The radiator should be flushed separately from the engine, to avoid excess contamination.

Radiator flushing

10 To flush the radiator, disconnect the top and bottom hoses and any other relevant hoses from the radiator, with reference to Chapter 3.

11 Insert a garden hose into the radiator top inlet. Direct a flow of clean water through the radiator, and continue flushing until clean water emerges from the radiator bottom outlet.

12 If after a reasonable period, the water still does not run clear, the radiator can be flushed with a suitable proprietary cleaning agent, suitable for radiators of plastic/aluminium construction. It is important that the instructions provided with the product are followed carefully. If the contamination is particularly bad, insert the hose in the radiator bottom outlet, and reverse-flush the radiator.

Engine flushing

13 To flush the engine, tighten the cooling system bleed screws, then remove the thermostat (see Chapter 3). Temporarily refit the thermostat cover, without the thermostat.

14 With the top and bottom hoses disconnected from the radiator, insert a garden hose into the radiator top hose. Direct a clean flow of water through the engine, and continue flushing until clean water emerges from the radiator bottom hose.

15 When flushing is complete, refit the thermostat and reconnect the hoses with reference to Chapter 3.

Cooling system filling

16 Before attempting to fill the cooling system, make sure that all hoses and clips are in good condition, and that the clips are tight. Note that an antifreeze mixture must be used all year round, to prevent corrosion of the engine components (see the following sub-Section).

17 If not already done, remove the expansion tank filler cap and open all the cooling system bleed screws (see paragraph 4).

18 To provide the required 'head' of coolant necessary to force all trapped air from the system, a 'header tank' must be used when refilling. Although Citroën dealers use a special header tank, the same effect can be achieved by using a suitable bottle, with a seal between the bottle and the expansion tank **(see Haynes Hint)**.

19 Fit the 'header tank' to the expansion tank and slowly fill the system. Coolant will emerge from each of the bleed screws in turn, starting with the lowest screw. As soon as coolant free from air bubbles emerges from the lowest screw, tighten that screw, and watch the next bleed screw in the system. Repeat the procedure until the coolant is emerging from the highest bleed screw in the cooling system and all bleed screws are securely tightened.

20 Ensure that the 'header tank' is full (at least 0.5 litres of coolant). Start the engine, and run it at a fast idle speed (do not exceed 2000 rpm) until the cooling fan cuts in, and then cuts out three times. Stop the engine. **Note:** *Take great care not to scald yourself.*

21 Allow the engine to cool, then remove the 'header tank'.

22 When the engine has cooled, check the

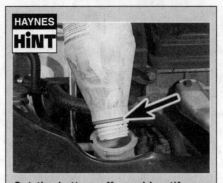

Cut the bottom off an old antifreeze container to make a 'header tank' for use when refilling the cooling system. The seal at the point arrowed must be as airtight as possible.

coolant level with reference to *Weekly checks*. Top-up the level if necessary, and refit the expansion tank cap.

Antifreeze mixture

23 The antifreeze should always be renewed at the specified intervals (see the note at the beginning of this Section). This is necessary not only to maintain the antifreeze properties, but also to prevent corrosion which would otherwise occur as the corrosion inhibitors become progressively less effective.

24 Always use an ethylene-glycol based antifreeze which is suitable for use in mixed-metal cooling systems. A general guide to the quantity of antifreeze and levels of protection is given in the Specifications, but follow the instructions provided by the antifreeze manufacturer for exact requirements.

25 Before adding antifreeze, the cooling system should be completely drained, preferably flushed, and all hoses checked for condition and security.

26 After filling with antifreeze, a label should be attached to the expansion tank, stating the type and concentration of antifreeze used, and the date installed. Any subsequent topping-up should be made with the same type and concentration of antifreeze.

27 Do not use engine antifreeze in the windscreen/tailgate washer system, as it will damage the vehicle paintwork. A screenwash additive should be added to the washer system in the quantities stated on the bottle.

Every 10 years – regardless of mileage

24 Air bag(s) and seat belt pretensioner renewal

Due to the safety critical nature of the air bag and seat belt pretensioner components, these operations must be carried out by a Citroën dealer.

Chapter 1 Part B:
Routine maintenance and servicing – diesel engine models

Contents

Degrees of difficulty

Easy, suitable for novice with little experience	**Fairly easy,** suitable for beginner with some experience	**Fairly difficult,** suitable for competent DIY mechanic	**Difficult,** suitable for experienced DIY mechanic	**Very difficult,** suitable for expert DIY or professional

Lubricants and fluids . . . . Refer to end of *Weekly checks* on page 0•17

Capacities

Engine oil (including filter) . . . . 4.5 litres
Difference between MAX and MIN dipstick marks (approx) . . . . 1.25 litres
Cooling system (approximate) . . . . 11.0 litres
Transmission . . . . 1.8 litres
Fuel tank . . . . 60.0 litres

Cooling system

Antifreeze mixture:
   28% antifreeze . . . . Protection down to –15ºC
   50% antifreeze . . . . Protection down to –30ºC
Note: *Refer to antifreeze manufacturer for latest recommendations*

Preheating system

Glow plugs . . . . Bosch 2 250 202 032

Brakes

Brake pad friction material minimum thickness . . . . 2.0 mm
Brake shoe friction material minimum thickness . . . . 1.5 mm

Tyre pressures . . . . Refer to end of *Weekly checks* on page 0•18

Torque wrench settings

	Nm	lbf ft
Auxiliary drivebelt eccentric tensioner pulley bolt	44	32
Auxiliary drivebelt tensioner pulley arm retaining bolt	95	70
Roadwheel bolts	85	63
Transmission oil filler/level plug	20	15

The maintenance intervals in this manual are provided with the assumption that you, not the dealer, will be carrying out the work. These are the minimum maintenance intervals recommended for vehicles driven daily. If you wish to keep your vehicle in peak condition at all times, you may wish to perform some of these procedures more often. We encourage frequent maintenance, because it enhances the efficiency, performance and resale value of your vehicle.

If the vehicle is driven in dusty areas, used to tow a trailer, or driven frequently at slow speeds (idling in traffic) or on short journeys, more frequent maintenance intervals are recommended.

When the vehicle is new, it should be serviced by a factory-authorised dealer service department, in order to preserve the factory warranty.

Valve clearance adjustment is hydraulic.

Every 250 miles (400 km) or weekly

- [ ] Refer to Weekly checks

Every 12 500 miles (20 000 km) or 12 months – whichever comes first

- [ ] Renew the engine oil and filter (Section 3)*.
- [ ] Drain any water from the fuel filter (Section 4).
- [ ] Check all underbonnet/underbody components for fluid leaks (Section 5).
- [ ] Check the condition of the auxiliary drivebelt (Section 6).
- [ ] Check the clutch control mechanism (Section 7).
- [ ] Renew the pollen filter (Section 8).
- [ ] Check the condition of the driveshaft rubber gaiters (Section 9).
- [ ] Check the steering and suspension components (Section 10).
- [ ] Check the condition of the front brake pads (Section 11).
- [ ] Check the condition of the exhaust system (Section 12).
- [ ] Check the condition of the rear brake shoes (Section 13).
- [ ] Operate and lubricate all hinges and locks (Section 14).
- [ ] Road test (Section 15).

*Note: The engine oil renewal interval shown is based on the use of either a semi-synthetic or fully synthetic engine oil. If a mineral oil is used, the interval should be reduced. Consult your Citroën dealer for further information.

Every 25 000 miles (40 000 km) or 2 years – whichever comes first

In addition to all the items listed above, carry out the following:
- [ ] Renew the brake fluid (Section 16).

Every 37 500 miles (60 000 km) or 3 years – whichever comes first

In addition to all the items listed above, carry out the following:
- [ ] Renew the fuel filter (Section 17).
- [ ] Renew the air filter (Section 18).
- [ ] Check the manual transmission oil level (Section 19).
- [ ] Check the condition and operation of the braking system components (Section 20).
- [ ] Check the operation of the handbrake (Section 21).
- [ ] Renew the timing belt (Section 22).

Note: Although the normal interval for timing belt renewal is 75 000 miles (120 000 km), it is strongly recommended that the interval is halved to 37 500 miles (60 000 km) on vehicles which are subjected to intensive use, ie, mainly short journeys or a lot of stop-start driving. The actual belt renewal interval is therefore very much up to the individual owner, but bear in mind that severe engine damage will result if the belt breaks.

Every 75 000 miles (120 000 km) or 5 years – whichever comes first

In addition to all the items listed above, carry out the following:
- [ ] Renew the coolant (Section 23).

Every 10 years – regardless of mileage

- [ ] Renew the air bag(s) and seat belt pretensioners (Section 24).

Underbonnet view

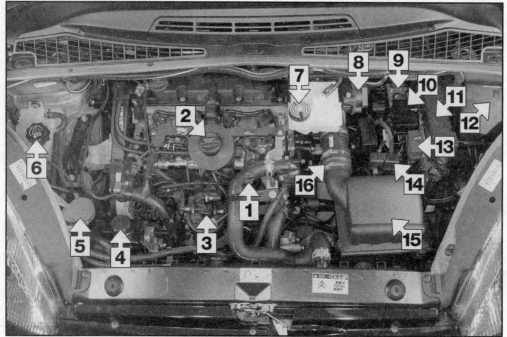

1 Engine oil dipstick
2 Engine oil filler cap
3 Fuel filter
4 Power steering fluid reservoir filler cap
5 Windscreen/tailgate washer fluid reservoir filler cap
6 Coolant expansion tank filler cap
7 Brake master cylinder fluid reservoir
8 Accelerator pedal position sensor
9 ABS hydraulic modulator
10 Diesel preheating system control unit
11 Engine management ECU
12 Engine compartment fuse/relay box
13 Injection double relay
14 Battery positive cable terminal box
15 Air cleaner housing
16 Air mass meter

Front underbody view

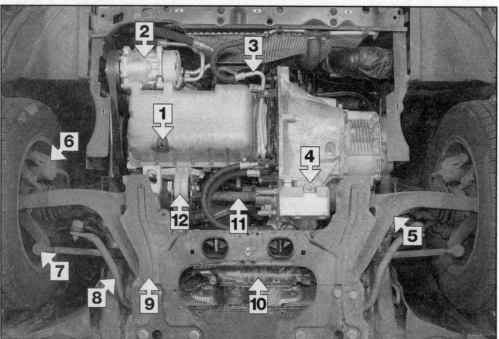

1 Sump drain plug
2 Alternator
3 Power steering pipe
4 Transmission oil drain plug
5 Front suspension lower arm
6 Front brake caliper
7 Track rod balljoint
8 Front anti-roll bar
9 Front suspension subframe
10 Steering gear assembly
11 Right-hand driveshaft
12 Engine/transmission rear mounting

Rear underbody view

1 Spare wheel
2 Rear silencer
3 Fuel tank
4 Handbrake cable
5 Rear suspension torsion bar
6 Rear suspension tubular crossmember
7 Rear shock absorber
8 Rear suspension trailing arm

Maintenance procedures

1 General information

This Chapter is designed to help the home mechanic maintain his/her vehicle for safety, economy, long life and peak performance.

The Chapter contains a master maintenance schedule, followed by Sections dealing specifically with each task in the schedule. Visual checks, adjustments, component renewal and other helpful items are included. Refer to the accompanying illustrations of the engine compartment and the underside of the vehicle for the locations of the various components.

Servicing your vehicle in accordance with the mileage/time maintenance schedule and the following Sections will provide a planned maintenance programme, which should result in a long and reliable service life. This is a comprehensive plan, so maintaining some items but not others at the specified service intervals will not produce the same results.

As you service your vehicle, you will discover that many of the procedures can – and should – be grouped together, because of the particular procedure being performed, or because of the proximity of two otherwise-unrelated components to one another. For example, if the vehicle is raised for any reason, the exhaust can be inspected at the same time as the suspension and steering components.

The first step in this maintenance programme is to prepare yourself before the actual work begins. Read through all the Sections relevant to the work to be carried out, then make a list and gather all the parts and tools required. If a problem is encountered, seek advice from a parts specialist, or a dealer service department.

Service interval display

Certain models are equipped with a service interval display indicator in the instrument panel. When the ignition is initially switched on, a spanner appears in the display window and the total number of miles remaining until the next service is due is also shown.

The display should not necessarily be used as a definitive guide to the servicing needs of your Xsara, but it is useful as a reminder, to ensure that servicing is not accidentally overlooked. Owners of older cars, or those covering a small annual mileage, may feel inclined to service their car more often, in which case the service interval display is perhaps less relevant.

The display should be reset whenever a service is carried out, and this is achieved using the trip meter reset button on the instrument panel as follows.

With the ignition switched off, press and hold down the trip meter reset button. Switch the ignition on and the mileage remaining until the next service will flash. Continue to hold the button down for a further ten seconds. The spanner symbol will disappear and the mileage will return to zero.

2 Regular maintenance

1 If, from the time the vehicle is new, the routine maintenance schedule is followed closely, and frequent checks are made of fluid levels and high-wear items, as suggested throughout this manual, the engine will be kept in relatively good running condition, and the need for additional work will be minimised.
2 It is possible that there will be times when the engine is running poorly due to the lack of regular maintenance. This is even more likely if a used vehicle, which has not received regular and frequent maintenance checks, is purchased. In such cases, additional work

may need to be carried out, outside of the regular maintenance intervals.

3 If engine wear is suspected, a compression test or leakdown test (refer to Chapter 2C) will provide valuable information regarding the overall performance of the main internal components. Such a test can be used as a basis to decide on the extent of the work to be carried out. If, for example, a compression or leakdown test indicates serious internal engine wear, conventional maintenance as described in this Chapter will not greatly improve the performance of the engine, and may prove a waste of time and money, unless extensive overhaul work is carried out first.

4 The following series of operations are those most often required to improve the performance of a generally poor-running engine:

Primary operations

a) Clean, inspect and test the battery (See 'Weekly checks').
b) Check all the engine-related fluids (see 'Weekly checks').
c) Check the fuel filter (Sections 4 and 17).
d) Check the condition of all hoses, and check for fluid leaks (Section 5).

e) Check the condition of the auxiliary drivebelt (Section 6).
f) Check the condition of the air filter, and renew if necessary (Section 18).

5 If the above operations do not prove fully effective, carry out the following secondary operations:

Secondary operations

All items listed under *Primary operations*, plus the following:
a) Check the charging system (Chapter 5A).
b) Check the preheating system (Chapter 5C).
c) Check the fuel system (Chapter 4B).

Every 12 500 miles (20 000 km) or 12 months

3 Engine oil and filter renewal

1 Frequent oil and filter changes are the most important preventative maintenance procedures which can be undertaken by the DIY owner. As engine oil ages, it becomes diluted and contaminated, which leads to premature engine wear.

2 Before starting this procedure, gather together all the necessary tools and materials. Also make sure that you have plenty of clean rags and newspapers handy, to mop up any spills. Ideally, the engine oil should be warm, as it will drain better, and any impurities suspended in the oil will be removed with it. Take care, however, not to touch the exhaust or any other hot parts of the engine when working under the vehicle. To avoid any possibility of scalding, and to protect yourself from possible skin irritants and other harmful contaminants in used engine oils, it is advisable to wear rubber gloves when carrying out this work. Access to the underside of the vehicle will be greatly improved if it can be raised on a lift, driven onto ramps, or jacked up and supported on axle stands (see *Jacking and vehicle support*). Whichever method is chosen, make sure that the vehicle remains level, or if it is at an angle, that the drain plug is at the lowest point.

3 Remove the engine undertray, then slacken the sump drain plug about half a turn (see illustration). Position the draining container under the drain plug, then remove the plug completely. If possible, try to keep the plug pressed into the sump while unscrewing it by hand the last couple of turns (see Haynes Hint). Recover the sealing ring from the drain plug.

4 Allow some time for the old oil to drain, noting that it may be necessary to reposition the container as the oil flow slows to a trickle.

5 After all the oil has drained, wipe off the drain plug with a clean rag, and fit a new sealing washer. Clean the area around the drain plug opening, and refit the plug. Tighten the plug securely.

6 Release the four plastic fasteners and lift off the engine cover (see illustrations).

7 Move the container into position under the oil filter, which is located on the front facing side of the cylinder block (see illustration).

8 Using an oil filter removal tool if necessary, slacken the filter initially, then unscrew it by hand the rest of the way. Empty the oil in the old filter into the container. To ensure that the old filter is completely empty before disposal, puncture the filter dome in at least two places and allow any remaining oil to drain through the punctures and into the container.

9 Use a clean rag to remove all oil and dirt from the filter sealing area on the engine. Check the old filter to make sure that the rubber sealing ring hasn't stuck to the engine. If it has, carefully remove it.

3.3 Engine oil sump drain plug location (arrowed)

HAYNES HINT

As the drain plug releases from the threads, move it away sharply so the stream of oil issuing from the sump runs into the container, not up your sleeve.

3.6a Release the four plastic fasteners . . .

3.6b . . . and lift off the engine cover

3.7 Engine oil filter location (arrowed)

10 Apply a light coating of clean engine oil to the sealing ring on the new filter, then screw it into position on the engine. Tighten the filter firmly by hand only – do not use any tools.

11 Refit the engine undertray then remove the old oil and all tools from under the vehicle. Lower the vehicle to the ground (if applicable).

12 Remove the dipstick, then unscrew the oil filler cap from the oil filler/breather neck. Fill the engine, using the correct grade and type of oil (see *Lubricants and fluids*). An oil can spout or funnel may help to reduce spillage. Pour in half the specified quantity of oil first, then wait a few minutes for the oil to fall to the sump. Continue adding oil a small quantity at a time until the level is up to the lower mark on the dipstick. Adding approximately 1.25 litres will bring the level up to the upper mark on the dipstick. Refit the filler cap.

13 Start the engine and run it for a few minutes; check for leaks around the oil filter seal and the sump drain plug. Note that there may be a delay of a few seconds before the oil pressure warning light goes out when the engine is first started, as the oil circulates through the engine oil galleries and the new oil filter before the pressure builds-up.

14 Switch off the engine, and wait a few minutes for the oil to settle in the sump once more. With the new oil circulated and the filter completely full, recheck the level on the dipstick, and add more oil as necessary.

15 Refit the engine cover and secure with the four fasteners.

16 Dispose of the used engine oil and filter safely, with reference to *General repair procedures* at the rear of this manual. Do not discard the old filter with domestic household waste. The facility for waste oil disposal provided by many local council refuse tips generally has a filter receptacle alongside.

4 Fuel filter water draining

1 Release the four plastic fasteners and remove the engine cover from the top of the engine.

2 Firmly apply the handbrake, then jack up the front of the vehicle and support it securely on axle stands (see *Jacking and vehicle support*). Remove the engine undertray.

3 Place a container beneath the fuel filter housing on the front of the engine. Note that there is a drain tube extending down to the underside of the engine, below the filter housing

4 Open the drain tap, located at the base of the filter, by turning it anti-clockwise **(see illustration)**.

5 Allow fuel and water to drain until fuel, free from water, emerges from the drain tube. Close the drain tap, and tighten it securely.

6 Dispose of the drained fuel safely.

7 Refit the engine undertray and lower the vehicle to the ground.

8 Refit the engine cover and start the engine. Priming is not required as the fuel system is self-bleeding.

5 Underbonnet/underbody component/hose fluid leak check

> ⚠️ **Warning: Refer to the safety information given in 'Safety First!' and Chapter 3 before disturbing any of the cooling system components.**

1 Release the four plastic fasteners and remove the engine cover from the top of the engine.

2 Carefully check the radiator and heater coolant hoses along their entire length. Renew any hose which is cracked, swollen or which shows signs of deterioration. Cracks will show up better if the hose is squeezed. Pay close attention to the clips that secure the hoses to the cooling system components. Hose clips that have been over-tightened can pinch and puncture hoses, resulting in cooling system leaks.

3 Inspect all the cooling system components (hoses, joint faces, etc) for leaks. Where any problems of this nature are found on system components, renew the component or gasket with reference to Chapter 3 **(see Haynes Hint)**.

Fuel

> ⚠️ **Warning: Refer to the safety information given in 'Safety First!' and Chapter 4B before disturbing any of the fuel system components.**

4 Unlike petrol leaks, diesel leaks are fairly easy to pinpoint; diesel fuel tends to settle on the surface around the point of leakage collecting dirt, rather than evaporate. If you suspect that there is a fuel leak from the area of the engine bay, leave the vehicle overnight then start the engine from cold, and allow it to idle with the bonnet open. Metal components tend to shrink when they are cold, and rubber seals and hoses tend to harden, so any leaks may be more apparent whilst the engine is warming-up from a cold start.

5 Check all fuel lines at their connections to the high pressure fuel pump, and fuel filter. Examine each rubber fuel hose along its length for splits or cracks. Check for leakage from the crimped joints between rubber and metal fuel lines. Examine the unions between the metal fuel lines and the fuel filter housing. Also check the area around the fuel injectors for signs of leakage.

6 To identify fuel leaks between the fuel tank and the engine bay, the vehicle should be raised and securely supported on axle stands (see *Jacking and vehicle support*). Inspect the fuel tank and filler neck for punctures, cracks and other damage. The connection between the filler neck and tank is especially critical. Sometimes a rubber filler neck or connecting hose will leak due to loose retaining clamps or deteriorated rubber.

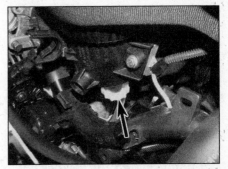

4.4 Fuel filter water drain tap location (arrowed)

7 Carefully check all rubber hoses and metal fuel lines leading away from the fuel tank. Check for loose connections, deteriorated hoses, kinked lines, and other damage. Pay particular attention to the vent pipes and hoses, which often loop up around the filler neck and can become blocked or kinked, making tank filling difficult. Follow the fuel supply and return lines to the front of the vehicle, carefully inspecting them all the way for signs of damage or corrosion. Renew damaged sections as necessary.

Engine oil

8 Inspect the area around the cylinder head cover, cylinder head, oil filter and sump joint faces. Bear in mind that, over a period of time, some very slight seepage from these areas is to be expected – what you are really looking for is any indication of a serious leak caused by gasket failure. Engine oil seeping from the base of the timing belt cover or the transmission bellhousing may be an indication of crankshaft or transmission input shaft oil seal failure. Should a leak be found, renew the failed gasket or oil seal by referring to the appropriate Chapter in this manual.

Power steering fluid

9 Examine the power steering fluid feed and return hoses and pipes running between the power steering pump and the steering rack. To identify any problems where the pipes run under the engine, the vehicle should be raised

A leak in the cooling system will usually show up as white- or rust-coloured deposits on the area adjoining the leak.

and securely supported on axle stands (see *Jacking and vehicle support*). The engine undertray should also be removed.

10 Check the condition of each hose carefully. Look for deterioration caused by corrosion and damage from grounding, or debris thrown up from the road surface.

11 Pay particular attention to crimped unions, and the area surrounding the hoses that are secured with adjustable worm drive clips. Power steering fluid is a thin oil, and is usually red in colour.

Air conditioning refrigerant

⚠️ **Warning: Refer to the safety information given in 'Safety First!' and Chapter 3, regarding the dangers of disturbing any of the air conditioning system components.**

12 The air conditioning system is filled with a liquid refrigerant, which is retained under high pressure. If the air conditioning system is opened and depressurised without the aid of specialised equipment, the refrigerant will immediately turn into gas and escape into the atmosphere. If the liquid comes into contact with your skin, it can cause severe frostbite. In addition, the refrigerant contains substances which are environmentally damaging; for this reason, it should not be allowed to escape into the atmosphere.

13 Any suspected air conditioning system leaks should be immediately referred to a Citroën dealer or air conditioning specialist. Leakage will be shown up as a steady drop in the level of refrigerant in the system.

14 Note that water may drip from the condenser drain pipe, underneath the vehicle, immediately after the air conditioning system has been in use. This is normal, and should not be cause for concern.

Hydraulic fluid

⚠️ **Warning: Refer to the safety information given in 'Safety First!' and Chapter 9, regarding the dangers of handling brake fluid.**

15 With reference to Chapter 9, examine the area surrounding the brake pipe unions at the master cylinder for signs of leakage. Check the area around the base of fluid reservoir, for signs of leakage caused by seal failure. Also

examine the brake pipe unions at the ABS hydraulic unit.

16 If fluid loss is evident, but the leak cannot be pinpointed in the engine bay, the brake calipers/wheel cylinders and underbody brake lines should be carefully checked with the vehicle raised and supported on axle stands (see *Jacking and vehicle support*). Leakage of fluid from the braking system is a serious fault that must be rectified immediately.

17 Hydraulic fluid is a toxic substance with a watery consistency. New fluid is almost colourless, but it becomes darker with age and use.

18 On models with a hydraulically-operated clutch, the hydraulic system is supplied with fluid from the brake master cylinder reservoir. Inspect all the clutch hydraulic pipes and connections at the master and slave cylinders in the same way as for the brake fluid checks, referring to Chapter 6 for additional information.

Unidentified fluid leaks

19 If there are signs that a fluid of some description is leaking from the vehicle, but you cannot identify the type of fluid or its exact origin, park the vehicle overnight and slide a large piece of card underneath it. Providing that the card is positioned in roughly the right location, even the smallest leak will show up on the card. Not only will this help you to pinpoint the exact location of the leak, it should be easier to identify the fluid from its colour. Bear in mind, though, that the leak may only be occurring when the engine is running.

Vacuum hoses

20 Although the braking system is hydraulically-operated, the brake servo unit amplifies the effort applied at the brake pedal, by making use of the vacuum generated by the engine-driven vacuum pump. Vacuum is ported to the servo by means of a medium-bore hose. Any leaks that develop in this hose will seriously reduce the effectiveness of the braking system.

21 In addition, a number of the underbonnet components, particularly the emission control components, are driven by vacuum supplied from the vacuum pump via narrow-bore

hoses. A leak in a vacuum hose means that air is being drawn into the hose (rather than escaping from it) and this makes leakage very difficult to detect. One method is to use an old length of vacuum hose as a kind of stethoscope – hold one end close to (but not in) your ear and use the other end to probe the area around the suspected leak. When the end of the hose is directly over a vacuum leak, a hissing sound will be heard clearly through the hose. Care must be taken to avoid contacting hot or moving components, as the engine must be running, when testing in this manner. Renew any vacuum hoses that are found to be defective.

---

6 Auxiliary drivebelt check and renewal

1 A single, multi-ribbed auxiliary drivebelt is fitted. The belt drives the alternator, power steering pump and air conditioning compressor according to equipment fitted, and is adjusted by means of an automatic spring-loaded tensioning mechanism.

Checking the drivebelt condition

2 Chock the rear wheels then jack up the front of the vehicle and support it on axle stands (see *Jacking and vehicle support*). Remove the right-hand front roadwheel.

3 To gain access to the right-hand end of the engine, the centre section of the wheelarch plastic liner must be removed. The liner is secured by stud-type plastic clips along its upper and front edges. These clips can be removed using a forked type tool, or alternatively, with a large screwdriver (although there is a risk of breakage if the screwdriver method is used). Extract all the clips, then remove the liner centre section from under the front wing **(see illustrations)**. It will be necessary to ease back the front liner section slightly to allow the front edge of the centre section to be released. Note how the two sections overlap as you do this to aid refitting. Unclip the coolant hoses from under the wing to improve access further.

4 Using a suitable socket and extension bar fitted to the crankshaft pulley bolt, rotate the crankshaft so that the entire length of the drivebelt can be examined. Examine the drivebelt for cracks, splitting, fraying or damage. Check also for signs of glazing (shiny patches) and for separation of the belt plies. Renew the belt if worn or damaged.

Removal

Note: *The following procedure is applicable to engines with and without air conditioning.*

5 If not already done, proceed as described in paragraphs 2 and 3.

6 Using a suitable spanner engaged with the hexagonal stud in the centre of the automatic tensioner pulley, move the pulley toward the rear of the vehicle to release the tension on

6.3a Using a forked type tool, extract the wheelarch liner retaining studs . . .

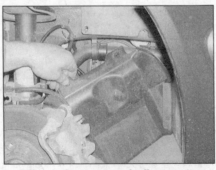
6.3b . . . then remove the liner centre section from under the front wing

the drivebelt, then slip the belt off the pulleys **(see illustration)**. Note that considerable effort will be needed to move the pulley against spring tension and it may be necessary to use some form of extension piece on the spanner to exert sufficient leverage.

Refitting and tensioning

7 Using the spanner on the hexagonal stud of the automatic tensioner pulley, move the pulley toward the rear of the vehicle until the hole in the pulley arm is aligned with the hole in the mounting bracket behind. When the holes are aligned, slide a suitable locking tool (a bolt or cranked length of bar of approximately 4.0 mm diameter) through the hole in the arm and into the mounting bracket **(see illustrations)**. It is useful to have a small mirror available to enable the alignment of the locking holes to be more easily seen in the limited space available.

8 Working under the wheelarch, slacken the retaining bolt located in the centre of the eccentric tensioner pulley **(see illustration)**.

9 If the belt is being renewed, ensure that the correct type is used. Fit the belt around the pulleys, ensuring that the ribs on the belt are correctly engaged with the grooves in the pulleys, and that the drivebelt is correctly routed **(see illustrations)**.

10 Turn the eccentric tensioner pulley to apply tension to the drivebelt, until the load is released from the locking tool in the automatic tensioner. Without altering the position of the eccentric tensioner pulley, tighten its retaining bolt to the specified torque.

11 Remove the locking tool from the automatic tensioner, then rotate the crank-

6.6 Using a spanner, move the automatic tensioner pulley rearwards, then slip the drivebelt off the pulleys

6.7b . . . then insert a 4.0 mm locking tool through the hole and into the mounting bracket

6.7a Turn the tensioner pulley until the hole in the pulley arm (arrowed) is aligned with the hole in the mounting bracket . . .

6.8 Slacken the retaining bolt (arrowed) located in the centre of the eccentric tensioner pulley

shaft through four complete revolutions in the normal direction of rotation.

12 Check that the holes in the automatic adjuster and the mounting bracket are still aligned, and that it is now possible to insert a setting tool of 2.0 mm diameter through both holes. If the setting tool will not slide in easily,

slacken the eccentric tensioner pulley retaining bolt and repeat the entire tensioning procedure.

13 On completion, clip the coolant hoses into position (where necessary), then refit the wheelarch liner. Refit the roadwheel and lower the vehicle to the ground.

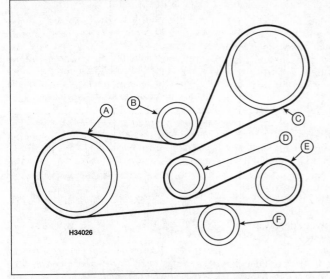

6.9a Auxiliary drivebelt configuration – engines without air conditioning

A Crankshaft pulley
B Automatic tensioner pulley
C Power steering pump pulley
D Eccentric tensioner pulley
E Alternator pulley
F Idler pulley

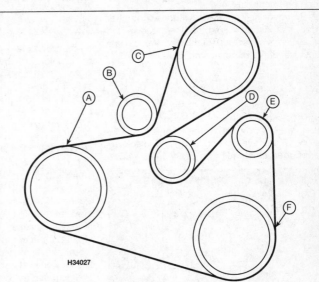

6.9b Auxiliary drivebelt configuration – engines with air conditioning

A Crankshaft pulley
B Automatic tensioner pulley
C Power steering pump pulley
D Eccentric tensioner pulley
E Alternator pulley
F Air conditioning compressor pulley

9.1 Check the condition of the driveshaft gaiters (arrowed)

7 Clutch control mechanism check

1 Check that the clutch pedal moves smoothly and easily through its full travel, and that the clutch itself functions correctly, with no trace of slip or drag.
2 On models with a cable-operated clutch, if excessive effort is required to operate the clutch, check first that the cable is correctly routed and undamaged, then remove the pedal and check that its pivot is properly greased. See Chapter 6 for more information.

8 Pollen filter renewal

1 Working in the engine compartment, undo the plastic nuts securing the filter access cover to the centre of the engine compartment bulkhead.
2 Remove the cover and withdraw the filter from its location. Clean the filter housing and the access cover, then fit the new filter using a reversal of the removal procedure.

9 Driveshaft gaiter check

1 With the vehicle raised and securely supported on stands (see *Jacking and vehicle*

10.4 Check for wear in the hub bearings by grasping the wheel and trying to rock it

support), and the undertray removed, turn the steering onto full lock, then slowly rotate the roadwheel. Inspect the condition of the outer constant velocity (CV) joint rubber gaiters, squeezing the gaiters to open out the folds **(see illustration)**. Check for signs of cracking, splits or deterioration of the rubber, which may allow the grease to escape, and lead to water and grit entry into the joint. Also check the security and condition of the retaining clips. Repeat these checks on the inner CV joints. If any damage or deterioration is found, the gaiters should be renewed (see Chapter 8).
2 At the same time, check the general condition of the CV joints themselves by first holding the driveshaft and attempting to rotate the wheel. Repeat this check by holding the inner joint and attempting to rotate the driveshaft. Any appreciable movement indicates wear in the joints, wear in the driveshaft splines, or a loose driveshaft retaining nut.

10 Steering and suspension check

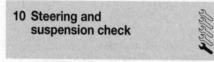

Front suspension and steering

1 Firmly apply the handbrake, then jack up the front of the vehicle and support it securely on axle stands (see *Jacking and vehicle support*). Remove the engine undertray, then refit it again after completing all the checks at the front of the vehicle.
2 Visually inspect the balljoint dust covers and the steering rack-and-pinion gaiters for splits, chafing or deterioration. Any wear of these components will cause loss of lubricant, together with dirt and water entry, resulting in rapid deterioration of the balljoints or steering gear.
3 Check the power steering fluid hoses for chafing or deterioration, and the pipe and hose unions for fluid leaks. Also check for signs of fluid leakage under pressure from the steering gear rubber gaiters, which would indicate failed fluid seals within the steering gear.
4 Grasp the roadwheel at the 12 o'clock and 6 o'clock positions, and try to rock it **(see illustration)**. Very slight free play may be felt, but if the movement is appreciable, further investigation is necessary to determine the source. Continue rocking the wheel while an assistant depresses the footbrake. If the movement is now eliminated or significantly reduced, it is likely that the hub bearings are at fault. If the free play is still evident with the footbrake depressed, then there is wear in the suspension joints or mountings.
5 Now grasp the wheel at the 9 o'clock and 3 o'clock positions, and try to rock it as before. Any movement felt now may again be caused by wear in the hub bearings or the steering track rod balljoints. If the inner or outer balljoint is worn, the visual movement will be obvious.

6 Using a large screwdriver or flat bar, check for wear in the suspension mounting bushes by levering between the relevant suspension component and its attachment point. Some movement is to be expected as the mountings are made of rubber, but excessive wear should be obvious. Also check the condition of any visible rubber bushes, looking for splits, cracks or contamination of the rubber.
7 With the vehicle standing on its wheels, have an assistant turn the steering wheel back-and-forth about an eighth of a turn each way. There should be very little, if any, lost movement between the steering wheel and roadwheels. If this is not the case, closely observe the joints and mountings previously described, but in addition, check the steering column universal joints for wear, and the rack-and-pinion steering gear itself.

Suspension strut/shock absorber

8 Check for any signs of fluid leakage around the suspension strut/shock absorber body, or from the rubber gaiter around the piston rod. Should any fluid be noticed, the suspension strut/shock absorber is defective internally, and should be renewed. **Note:** *Suspension struts/shock absorbers should always be renewed in pairs on the same axle.*
9 The efficiency of the suspension strut/shock absorber may be checked by bouncing the vehicle at each corner. Generally speaking, the body will return to its normal position and stop after being depressed. If it rises and returns on a rebound, the suspension strut/shock absorber is probably suspect. Examine also the suspension strut/shock absorber upper and lower mountings for any signs of wear.

11 Front brake pad condition check

1 Firmly apply the handbrake, then jack up the front of the vehicle and support it securely on axle stands (see *Jacking and vehicle support*). Remove the front roadwheels.

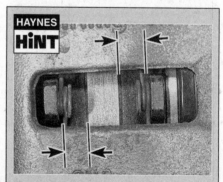

For a quick check, the thickness of friction material remaining on each brake pad can be measured through the aperture in the caliper body.

2 It is now possible to check the thickness of the pad friction material (**see Haynes Hint**). If any pad's friction material is worn to the specified thickness or less, *all four pads must be renewed as a set*. **Note**: *If any pad is approaching the minimum thickness, consider renewal as a precautionary measure in case the pads wear out before the next service.*

3 For a comprehensive check, the brake pads should be removed and cleaned. The operation of the caliper can then be checked, and the brake disc itself can be fully examined on both sides. Refer to Chapter 9 for details.

12 Exhaust system check

1 With the engine cold (at least an hour after the vehicle has been driven), check the complete exhaust system from the engine to the end of the tailpipe. The exhaust system is most easily checked with the vehicle raised on a hoist, or suitably supported on axle stands, so that the exhaust components are readily visible and accessible (see *Jacking and vehicle support*).

2 Check the exhaust pipes and connections for evidence of leaks, severe corrosion and damage. Make sure that all brackets and mountings are in good condition, and that all relevant nuts and bolts are tight. Leakage at any of the joints or in other parts of the system will usually show up as a black sooty stain in the vicinity of the leak.

3 Rattles and other noises can often be traced to the exhaust system, especially the brackets and mountings. Try to move the pipes and silencers. If the components are able to come into contact with the body or suspension parts, secure the system with new mountings. Otherwise separate the joints (if possible) and twist the pipes as necessary to provide additional clearance.

13 Rear brake shoe condition check

1 Chock the front wheels then jack up the rear of the vehicle and support it on axle stands (see *Jacking and vehicle support*).

2 For a quick check, the thickness of friction material remaining on one of the brake shoes can be measured through the slot in the brake backplate that is exposed by prising out its sealing grommet (**see illustrations**). If a rod of the same diameter as the specified minimum thickness is placed against the shoe friction material, the amount of wear can quickly be assessed – a small mirror may help observation. If any shoe's friction material is worn to the specified thickness or less, all four shoes must be renewed as a set. **Note**: *If any shoe is approaching the minimum thickness, consider renewal as a precautionary measure*

13.2a Prise the grommet (arrowed) from the rear drum brake backplate

in case the shoes wear out before the next service.

3 For a comprehensive check, the brake drums should be removed and cleaned. This will permit the wheel cylinders to be checked and the condition of the brake drum itself to be fully examined. Refer to Chapter 9 for further information.

14 Hinge and lock operation and lubrication

1 Work around the vehicle, and lubricate the hinges of the bonnet, doors and tailgate with a small amount of general-purpose oil.

2 Lightly lubricate the bonnet release mechanism and exposed section of inner cable with a smear of grease.

3 Check carefully the security and operation of all hinges, latches and locks, adjusting them where required. Check the operation of the central locking system.

4 Check the condition and operation of the tailgate struts, renewing them if they are leaking or no longer able to support the tailgate securely when raised.

15 Road test

Instruments/ electrical equipment

1 Check the operation of all instruments and electrical equipment.

2 Make sure that all instruments read correctly, and switch on all electrical equipment in turn to check that it works properly.

Steering and suspension

3 Check for any abnormalities in the steering, suspension, handling or road 'feel'.

4 Drive the vehicle, and check that there are no unusual vibrations or noises.

5 Check that the steering feels positive, with no excessive 'sloppiness', or roughness, and check for any suspension noises when cornering, or when driving over bumps.

13.2b Viewing the thickness of the brake shoe lining using a small mirror

Drivetrain

6 Check the performance of the engine, clutch, transmission and driveshafts.

7 Listen for any unusual noises from the engine, clutch and transmission.

8 Make sure that the engine runs smoothly when idling, and that there is no hesitation when accelerating.

9 Check that the clutch action is smooth and progressive, that the drive is taken up smoothly, and that the pedal travel is not excessive. Also listen for any noises when the clutch pedal is depressed.

10 Check that all gears can be engaged smoothly, without noise, and that the gear lever action is smooth and not abnormally vague or 'notchy'.

11 Listen for a metallic clicking sound from the front of the vehicle, as the vehicle is driven slowly in a circle with the steering on full lock. Carry out this check in both directions. If a clicking noise is heard, this indicates lack of lubrication or wear in a driveshaft constant velocity joint (see Chapter 8).

Braking system

12 Make sure that the vehicle does not pull to one side when braking, and that the wheels do not lock prematurely when braking hard (models without ABS).

13 Check that there is no vibration through the steering when braking.

14 Check that the handbrake operates correctly, without excessive movement of the lever, and that it holds the vehicle stationary on a slope.

15 Test the operation of the brake servo unit as follows. With the engine off, depress the footbrake four or five times to exhaust the vacuum. Start the engine, holding the brake pedal depressed. As the engine starts, there should be a noticeable 'give' in the brake pedal as vacuum builds-up. Allow the engine to run for at least two minutes, and then switch it off. If the brake pedal is depressed now, it should be possible to detect a hiss from the servo as the pedal is depressed. After about four or five applications, no further hissing should be heard, and the pedal should feel considerably firmer.

Every 25 000 miles (40 000 km) or 2 years

16 Brake fluid renewal

⚠️ *Warning: Brake hydraulic fluid can harm your eyes and damage painted surfaces, so use extreme caution when handling and pouring it. Do not use fluid that has been standing open for some time, as it absorbs moisture from the air. Excess moisture can cause a dangerous loss of braking effectiveness.*

Note: *Also renew the fluid on models fitted with a hydraulic clutch, with reference to Chapter 6.*

1 The procedure is similar to that for the bleeding of the hydraulic system as described in Chapter 9, except that the brake fluid reservoir should be emptied by syphoning, using a clean poultry baster or similar before starting, and allowance should be made for the old fluid to be expelled when bleeding a section of the circuit.

2 Alternatively, to empty the reservoir, working as described in Chapter 9, open the first bleed screw in the sequence, and pump the brake pedal gently until nearly all the old fluid has been emptied from the master cylinder reservoir.

> **HAYNES HiNT** *Old hydraulic fluid is invariably much darker in colour than the new, making it easy to distinguish the two.*

3 Top-up to the MAX level with new fluid, and continue pumping until only the new fluid remains in the reservoir, and new fluid can be seen emerging from the bleed screw. Tighten the screw, and top the reservoir level up to the MAX level line.

4 Work through all the remaining bleed screws in the sequence until new fluid can be seen at all of them. Be careful to keep the master cylinder reservoir topped-up to above the DANGER level at all times, or air may enter the system and increase the length of the task.

5 When the operation is complete, check that all bleed screws are securely tightened, and that their dust caps are refitted. Wash off all traces of spilt fluid, and recheck the master cylinder reservoir fluid level.

6 Check the operation of the brakes before taking the vehicle on the road.

Every 37 500 miles (60 000 km) or 3 years

17 Fuel filter renewal

⚠️ *Warning: Refer to the safety information given in 'Safety First!' and Chapter 4B before disturbing any of the fuel system components.*

Early type filter assembly

Note: *The early type filter assembly can be recognised by the absence of an electrical connector on the filter housing cover.*

1 Firmly apply the handbrake, then jack up the front of the vehicle and support it securely on axle stands (see *Jacking and vehicle support*). Remove the engine undertray.

2 Release the four plastic fasteners and remove the engine cover from the top of the engine.

3 The fuel filter is located in a plastic housing at the front of the engine.

4 Cover the area below the filter housing with rags or a piece of plastic sheeting, to protect against fuel spillage.

5 Thoroughly clean the exterior of filter housing, paying particular attention to the fuel hose unions and the area around the cover-to-housing joint.

6 Position a suitable container under the fuel filter drain outlet. Open the drain screw on the base of the filter housing, and allow the fuel to drain completely. Securely tighten the drain screw when the fuel has completely drained.

7 At the connections on the filter housing cover, disconnect the fuel supply and return hose quick-release fittings using a small screwdriver to release the locking clip **(see illustration)**. Suitably plug or cover the open hose unions to prevent dirt entry.

8 Using a suitable socket engaged with the hexagonal moulding on the filter housing cover, turn the cover approximately a quarter turn anti-clockwise to release the locking lugs **(see illustration)**.

9 Lift off the housing cover, and collect the metal sealing ring and the O-ring seal, then lift out the filter element **(see illustrations)**.

10 Remove all traces of dirt or debris from inside the filter housing then fit the new fuel filter element.

17.7 Disconnect the fuel supply and return hose quick-release fittings . . .

17.8 . . . then turn the filter housing cover anti-clockwise to release the locking lugs – early type filter assembly

17.9a Lift off the filter housing cover . . .

17.9b . . . remove the metal sealing ring . . .

17.9c . . . and the sealing O-ring . . .

17.9d . . . then lift out the filter element – early type filter assembly

17.12 Refit the filter housing cover and turn it clockwise until the arrow is in line with the drain outlet – early type assembly

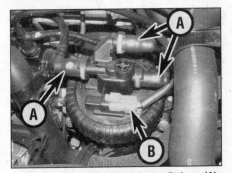

17.16 Fuel hose quick-release fittings (A) and wiring connector (B) – later type filter assembly

11 Locate the O-ring seal in position, followed by the metal sealing ring.

12 Refit the housing cover and turn it clockwise until the arrow on the housing cover is in line with the filter drain outlet (see illustration).

13 Reconnect the fuel supply and return hoses, then start the engine and check for fuel leaks.

14 On completion, refit the engine cover and engine undertray and lower the vehicle to the ground.

Later type filter assembly

Note: *The later type filter assembly incorporates a fuel heating element and can be recognised by the presence of an electrical connector on the filter housing cover.*

15 Carry out the operations described previously in paragraphs 1 to 5.

16 At the connections on the filter housing cover, disconnect the fuel hose quick-release fittings using a small screwdriver to release the locking clip (see illustration). Suitably plug or cover the open hose unions to prevent dirt entry.

17 Disconnect the wiring connector from the fuel heating element.

18 Unscrew the locking ring securing the filter housing cover to the filter housing.

19 Lift off the housing cover, collect the seals and lift out the filter element.

20 Remove all traces of dirt or debris from inside the filter housing then fit the new fuel filter element.

21 Locate the new seals in position and place the housing cover on the filter housing.

22 Screw the locking ring onto the housing and tighten it securely.

23 Reconnect the fuel hoses, then start the engine and check for fuel leaks.

24 On completion, refit the engine cover and engine undertray and lower the vehicle to the ground.

18 Air filter renewal

1 Disconnect the wiring connector from the underside of the air mass meter (see illustration).

2 Slacken the hose clip securing the air mass meter inlet duct to the filter housing lid.

3 Undo the screws securing the lid to the air filter housing.

4 Lift up the lid and detach the air mass meter inlet duct, then withdraw the filter element from the housing.

5 Wipe clean the inside of the filter housing, then fit the new filter element.

6 Refit the lid to the inlet duct and filter housing. Tighten the hose clip and secure the lid with the retaining screws.

7 Reconnect the air mass meter wiring connector.

19 Transmission oil level check

Note: *A suitable square-section wrench may be required to undo the transmission filler/level plug. These wrenches can be obtained from most motor factors or your Citroën dealer. A new sealing washer will also be required when refitting the transmission filler/level plug.*

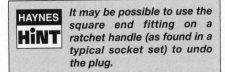

HAYNES HINT *It may be possible to use the square end fitting on a ratchet handle (as found in a typical socket set) to undo the plug.*

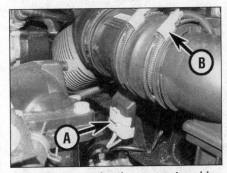

18.1 Disconnect the air mass meter wiring connector (A), then slacken the inlet duct retaining clip (B)

1 The manual transmission oil does not need to be renewed as part of the regular maintenance schedule, but the oil level must be checked and if necessary topped-up at the interval specified here. To drain the transmission as part of a repair procedure, refer to the information given in Chapter 7.

2 The oil level must be checked before the vehicle is driven, or at least 5 minutes after the engine has been switched off. If the oil is checked immediately after driving the vehicle, some of the oil will remain distributed around the transmission components, resulting in an inaccurate level reading.

3 With the vehicle on level ground, firmly apply the handbrake, then jack up the front and rear of the vehicle and support it securely on axle stands (see *Jacking and vehicle support*). Note that the vehicle must be level, to ensure accuracy, when checking the oil level.

4 For improved access to the filler/level plug, the centre section of the left-hand wheelarch plastic liner can be removed after removing the roadwheel. The liner is secured by stud-type plastic clips along it upper and front edges which can be removed using a forked type tool. Extract all the clips, and remove the liner centre section from under the front wing (see illustration). It will be necessary to ease back the front section slightly to allow the front edge of the centre section to be released. Note how the two sections overlap, as you do this, to aid refitting.

5 Wipe clean the area around the filler/level

19.4 Extract the clips and remove the wheelarch liner centre section for access to the transmission filler/level plug

plug, which is on the left-hand end of the transmission. Unscrew the plug and clean it; discard the sealing washer.

6 The oil level should reach the lower edge of the filler/level hole. A certain amount of oil will have gathered behind the filler/level plug, and will trickle out when it is removed; this does **not** necessarily indicate that the level is correct. To ensure that a true level is established, wait until the initial trickle has stopped, then add oil as necessary until a trickle of new oil can be seen emerging **(see illustration)**. The level will be correct when the flow ceases; use only good-quality oil of the specified type (refer to *Lubricants and fluids*).

7 If the transmission has been overfilled so that oil flows out as soon as the filler/level plug is removed, check that the vehicle is completely level (front-to-rear and side-to-side), and allow the surplus to drain off into a container.

8 When the level is correct, fit a new sealing washer to the filler/level plug, refit the plug and tighten it to the specified torque.

9 Refit the wheelarch liner and roadwheel, then lower the vehicle to the ground. Tighten the roadwheel bolts to the specified torque.

20 Braking system check

Front brakes

1 Firmly apply the handbrake, then jack up the front of the vehicle and support it securely on axle stands (see *Jacking and vehicle support*).

2 Inspect the area around both brake calipers for signs of brake fluid leakage, either from the piston seals, the brake pipe union or the bleed screw.

3 Examine the brake hoses leading to each caliper and check for signs of cracking, chafing or damage. Renew a hose which shows signs of deterioration without delay.

4 Ensure that the transmission is in neutral, then grasp each front wheel hub and turn it by

19.6 Top-up the transmission until a trickle of new oil can be seen emerging from the filler/level plug

hand. Slight resistance is normal, but if the hub is difficult to turn smoothly, this indicates that the brake pads are binding, possibly due to a seized or partially-seized brake caliper piston; refer to Chapter 9 for details of caliper removal and overhaul.

5 Remove the front brake pads as described in Chapter 9. Examine the brake pads and measure the depth of the remaining friction material. Renew all four pads, if any are worn below their minimum limit.

6 Using proprietary brake cleaning fluid and a stiff brush, wash all traces of dirt and brake dust from the brake calipers – take care to avoid inhaling any of the airborne brake dust. Examine the piston dust seal for signs of damage or deterioration and check that it is securely seated in its retaining groove.

7 Check the condition of the brake disc with reference to the information given in Chapter 9.

8 Refit the front brake pads as described in Chapter 9, then refit the roadwheels and lower the front of the vehicle to the ground. Tighten the roadwheel bolts to the specified torque.

Rear brakes

9 Chock the front wheels then jack up the rear of the vehicle and support it on axle stands (see *Jacking and vehicle support*).

10 Ensure that the handbrake is released, then grasp each rear roadwheel and turn it by hand. Slight resistance is normal, but if the wheel is difficult to turn smoothly, this could

be due to a seized or partially-seized wheel cylinder, or incorrect handbrake adjustment; refer to Chapter 9 for further details.

11 Remove the rear roadwheels, then with reference to Chapter 9, remove the rear brake shoes. Examine the brake shoes and measure the depth of the remaining friction material. Renew all four brake shoes, if any are worn below their minimum limit.

12 Check the brake drums for wear and damage and check the area around the wheel cylinder piston seals for signs of fluid leakage. Check at the rear of the brake backplate for evidence of fluid leakage from the brake pipe union or bleed screw. Renew the wheel cylinder without delay if it shows signs of leakage; see Chapter 9 for details.

13 Using proprietary brake cleaning fluid and a stiff brush, wash all traces of dirt and brake dust from the wheel cylinders and backplates – take care to avoid inhaling any of the airborne brake dust.

14 On completion, refit the brake shoes, brake drums and roadwheels, then lower the vehicle to the ground. Tighten the roadwheel bolts to the specified torque.

21 Handbrake check and adjustment

Refer to Chapter 9.

22 Timing belt renewal

Refer to Chapter 2C.

Note: *Although the normal interval for timing belt renewal is 75 000 miles (120 000 km), it is strongly recommended that the interval is halved to 37 500 miles (60 000 km) on vehicles which are subjected to intensive use, ie, mainly short journeys or a lot of stop-start driving. The actual belt renewal interval is therefore very much up to the individual owner, but bear in mind that severe engine damage will result if the belt breaks.*

Every 75 000 miles (120 000 km) or 5 years

23 Coolant renewal

Cooling system draining

⚠ **Warning: Wait until the engine is cold before starting this procedure. Do not allow antifreeze to come in contact with your skin, or with the painted surfaces of the vehicle. Rinse off spills immediately with plenty of water. Never leave antifreeze lying around**

in an open container, or in a puddle in the driveway or on the garage floor. Children and pets are attracted by its sweet smell, but antifreeze can be fatal if ingested.

Note: *Later models are filled with a 'long-life' coolant during vehicle assembly which is claimed to be suitable for ten years use before renewal is required. If you are sure that the vehicle is filled with this type of coolant, then renewal may not be necessary at this service interval. Consult your Citroën dealer for details of coolant specification and renewal recommendations.*

1 With the engine completely cold, remove

the expansion tank filler cap. Turn the cap slowly anti-clockwise, wait until any pressure remaining in the system is released, then fully unscrew the cap. Release the four plastic fasteners and lift off the engine cover

2 Firmly apply the handbrake, then jack up the front of the vehicle and support it securely on axle stands (see *Jacking and vehicle support*). Remove the engine undertray.

3 Position a suitable container beneath the bottom hose connection on the radiator. Release the retaining clip, then disconnect the hose and allow the coolant to drain into the container.

4 To assist draining, open the cooling system bleed screws which are located in the heater matrix outlet hose union on the engine compartment bulkhead, and on the thermostat cover.

5 The manufacturers do not specify a requirement to drain the cylinder block at the time of routine coolant renewal. If, however, the coolant is being drained as part of an engine repair procedure (such as cylinder head gasket renewal), then it is advisable to drain the cylinder block also. Note that the cylinder block drain plug is virtually inaccessible and it may be necessary to move certain cables, brackets or hoses to one side for access.

6 To drain the cylinder block, reposition the container below the drain plug located at the rear left-hand side of the cylinder block. Remove the drain plug, and allow the coolant to drain into the container.

7 On completion of draining, refit the radiator bottom hose and cylinder block drain plug (where applicable). Refit any components disturbed for access then, unless the system is to be flushed, refit the engine undertray and lower the vehicle to the ground.

Cooling system flushing

8 If coolant renewal has been neglected, or if the antifreeze mixture has become diluted, then in time, the cooling system may gradually lose efficiency, as the coolant passages become restricted due to rust, scale deposits, and other sediment. The cooling system efficiency can be restored by flushing the system clean.

9 The radiator should be flushed separately from the engine, to avoid excess contamination.

Radiator flushing

10 To flush the radiator, disconnect the top and bottom hoses and any other relevant hoses from the radiator, with reference to Chapter 3.

11 Insert a garden hose into the radiator top inlet. Direct a flow of clean water through the radiator, and continue flushing until clean water emerges from the radiator bottom outlet.

12 If after a reasonable period, the water still does not run clear, the radiator can be flushed with a suitable proprietary cleaning agent, suitable for radiators of plastic/aluminium construction. It is important that the instructions provided with the product are

followed carefully. If the contamination is particularly bad, insert the hose in the radiator bottom outlet, and reverse-flush the radiator.

Engine flushing

13 To flush the engine, tighten the cooling system bleed screws, then remove the thermostat (see Chapter 3). Temporarily refit the thermostat cover, without the thermostat.

14 With the top and bottom hoses disconnected from the radiator, insert a garden hose into the radiator top hose. Direct a clean flow of water through the engine, and continue flushing until clean water emerges from the radiator bottom hose.

15 When flushing is complete, refit the thermostat and reconnect the hoses with reference to Chapter 3.

Cooling system filling

16 Before attempting to fill the cooling system, make sure that all hoses and clips are in good condition, and that the clips are tight. Note that an antifreeze mixture must be used all year round, to prevent corrosion of the engine components (see the following sub-Section).

17 If not already done, remove the expansion tank filler cap and open all the cooling system bleed screws (see paragraph 4).

18 To provide the required 'head' of coolant necessary to force all trapped air from the system, a 'header tank' must be used when refilling. Although Citroën dealers use a special header tank, the same effect can be achieved by using a suitable bottle, with a seal between the bottle and the expansion tank **(see Haynes Hint)**.

19 Fit the 'header tank' to the expansion tank and slowly fill the system. Coolant will emerge from each of the bleed screws in turn, starting with the lowest screw. As soon as coolant free from air bubbles emerges from the lowest screw, tighten that screw, and watch the next bleed screw in the system. Repeat the procedure until the coolant is emerging from the highest bleed screw in the cooling system and all bleed screws are securely tightened.

20 Ensure that the 'header tank' is full (at least 0.5 litres of coolant). Start the engine, and run it at a fast idle speed (do not exceed 2000 rpm) until the cooling fan cuts in, and then cuts out three times. Stop the engine.
Note: *Take great care not to scald yourself.*

21 Allow the engine to cool, then remove the 'header tank'.

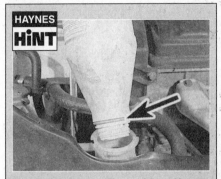

Cut the bottom off an old antifreeze container to make a 'header tank' for use when refilling the cooling system. The seal at the point arrowed must be as airtight as possible.

22 When the engine has cooled, check the coolant level with reference to *Weekly checks*. Top-up the level if necessary, and refit the expansion tank cap and engine cover.

Antifreeze mixture

23 The antifreeze should always be renewed at the specified intervals (see the note at the beginning of this Section). This is necessary not only to maintain the antifreeze properties, but also to prevent corrosion which would otherwise occur as the corrosion inhibitors become progressively less effective.

24 Always use an ethylene-glycol based antifreeze which is suitable for use in mixed-metal cooling systems. A general guide to the quantity of antifreeze and levels of protection is given in the Specifications, but follow the instructions provided by the antifreeze manufacturer for exact requirements.

25 Before adding antifreeze, the cooling system should be completely drained, preferably flushed, and all hoses checked for condition and security.

26 After filling with antifreeze, a label should be attached to the expansion tank, stating the type and concentration of antifreeze used, and the date installed. Any subsequent topping-up should be made with the same type and concentration of antifreeze.

27 Do not use engine antifreeze in the windscreen/tailgate washer system, as it will damage the vehicle paintwork. A screenwash additive should be added to the washer system in the quantities stated on the bottle.

Every 10 years – regardless of mileage

24 Air bag(s) and seat belt pretensioner renewal

Due to the safety critical nature of the air bag and seat belt pretensioner components, these operations must be carried out by a Citroën dealer.

Notes

Chapter 2 Part A:
TU series petrol engine in-car repair procedures

Contents

Degrees of difficulty

Easy, suitable for novice with little experience	**Fairly easy,** suitable for beginner with some experience	**Fairly difficult,** suitable for competent DIY mechanic	**Difficult,** suitable for experienced DIY mechanic	**Very difficult,** suitable for expert DIY or professional

Specifications

Engine (general)

Designation	TU5
Capacity	1587 cc (1.6 litre)
Engine codes*:	
Up to 2001 model year	NFZ (TU5JP+/L3)
2001 model year onward	NFV (TU5JP/L4)
Bore	78.50 mm
Stroke	82.00 mm
Direction of crankshaft rotation	Clockwise (viewed from right-hand side of vehicle)
No 1 cylinder location	At transmission end of block
Compression ratio (typical):	
NFZ (TU5JP+/L3)	9.6 : 1
NFV (TU5JP/L4)	10.5 : 1

The engine code is situated on front left-hand end of the engine, stamped directly on the cylinder block

Timing belt

Tension setting (see text – Section 6):	
Initial setting	44 SEEM units
Final setting	29 to 33 SEEM units

Camshaft

Drive	Toothed belt
Number of bearings	5
Camshaft bearing journal diameter (outside diameter):	
No 1	36.950 to 36.925 mm
No 2	40.650 to 40.625 mm
No 3	41.250 to 41.225 mm
No 4	41.850 to 41.825 mm
No 5	42.450 to 42.425 mm
Cylinder head bearing journal diameter (inside diameter):	
No 1	37.000 to 37.039 mm
No 2	40.700 to 47.739 mm
No 3	41.300 to 41.339 mm
No 4	41.900 to 41.939 mm
No 5	42.500 to 42.539 mm

Valve clearances (engine cold)

Inlet .... 0.20 mm
Exhaust .... 0.40 mm

Lubrication system

Oil pump type .... Gear-type, chain-driven off the crankshaft
Minimum oil pressure at 90ºC .... 4 bars at 4000 rpm
Oil pressure warning switch operating pressure .... 0.8 bars

Torque wrench settings

	Nm	lbf ft
Big-end bearing cap nuts	38	28
Camshaft sprocket retaining bolt	80	59
Camshaft thrust fork retaining bolt	16	12
Crankshaft pulley retaining bolts	8	6
Crankshaft sprocket retaining bolt	110	81
Cylinder head bolts:		
Stage 1	20	15
Stage 2	Angle-tighten a further 120º	
Stage 3	Angle-tighten a further 120º	
Cylinder head cover nuts	16	12
Engine-to-transmission fixing bolts	50	37
Engine/transmission left-hand mounting:		
Mounting bracket-to-body bolts	25	18
Mounting bracket-to-transmission bolts	65	48
Rubber mounting centre nut	65	48
Rubber mounting-to-bracket nuts	22	16
Engine/transmission rear mounting:		
Connecting link-to-mounting bracket bolt	55	41
Connecting link-to-subframe bolt	55	41
Mounting bracket-to-cylinder block bolts	40	30
Engine/transmission right-hand mounting:		
Lower support brace-to-engine	26	19
Upper mounting bracket-to-engine bolts	45	33
Upper mounting bracket-to-mounting rubber nut	32	24
Upper support brace-to-engine	26	19
Upper support brace-to-upper mounting bracket	45	33
Flywheel retaining bolts	65	48
Main bearing cap bolts:		
Stage 1	20	15
Stage 2	Angle-tighten a further 50º	
Oil pump retaining bolts	8	6
Piston oil jet spray tube bolts	10	7
Sump drain plug	30	22
Sump retaining nuts and bolts	8	6
Timing belt cover bolts	8	6
Timing belt tensioner pulley nut	23	17

1 General information

Using this Chapter

This Part of Chapter 2 is devoted to in-vehicle repair procedures for the TU series petrol engines. Similar information covering the EW series petrol engines, and the diesel engine will be found in Chapters 2B and 2C. All procedures concerning engine removal and refitting, and engine block/cylinder head overhaul for petrol and diesel engines can be found in Chapters 2D and 2E as applicable.

Most of the operations included in Chapter 2A are based on the assumption that the engine is still installed in the vehicle. Therefore, if this information is being used during a complete engine overhaul, with the engine already removed, many of the steps included here will not apply.

TU series engine description

The TU series engine is a well-proven unit which has been fitted to many previous Citroën and Peugeot vehicles. The engine is of the in-line four-cylinder, single overhead camshaft (SOHC) type, mounted transversely at the front of the vehicle, with the transmission attached to its left-hand end.

The crankshaft runs in five main bearings. Thrustwashers are fitted to No 2 main bearing (upper half) to control crankshaft endfloat.

The connecting rods rotate on horizontally-split bearing shells at their big-ends. The pistons are attached to the connecting rods by gudgeon pins, which are an interference fit in the connecting rod small-end eyes. The aluminium-alloy pistons are fitted with three piston rings – two compression rings and an oil control ring.

The inlet and exhaust valves are each closed by coil springs, and operate in guides pressed into the cylinder head; the valve seat inserts are also pressed into the cylinder head, and can be renewed separately if worn.

The camshaft rotates directly in the cylinder head, is driven by a toothed timing belt, and operates the eight valves via rocker arms. Valve clearances are adjusted by a screw-and-locknut arrangement. The timing belt also drives the coolant pump.

Lubrication is by means of an oil pump, which is driven (via a chain and sprocket) off the right-hand end of the crankshaft. It draws oil through a strainer located in the sump, and then forces it through an externally-mounted filter into galleries in the cylinder block/crankcase. From there, the oil is distributed to the crankshaft (main bearings) and camshaft. The big-end bearings are supplied with oil via internal drillings in the crankshaft, while the camshaft bearings also receive a pressurised supply. The camshaft lobes and valves are lubricated by splash, as are all other engine components.

Throughout this manual, it is often necessary to identify the engines not only by their capacity, but also by their engine code which is incorporated in the engine number. This can be found stamped on a machined surface on the front face of the cylinder block at the flywheel end. The first part of the engine number gives the engine code – eg, NFZ **(see illustration)**.

Repair operations possible with the engine in the vehicle

The following work can be carried out with the engine in the vehicle:
a) *Compression pressure – testing.*
b) *Cylinder head cover – removal and refitting.*
c) *Timing belt covers – removal and refitting.*
d) *Timing belt – removal, refitting and adjustment.*
e) *Timing belt tensioner and sprockets – removal and refitting.*
f) *Camshaft oil seal(s) – renewal.*
g) *Camshaft and rocker arms – removal, inspection and refitting.* *
h) *Cylinder head – removal and refitting.*
i) *Cylinder head and pistons – decarbonising.*
j) *Sump – removal and refitting.*
k) *Oil pump – removal, overhaul and refitting.*
l) *Crankshaft oil seals – renewal.*
m) *Engine/transmission mountings – inspection and renewal.*
n) *Flywheel – removal, inspection and refitting.*

The cylinder head must be removed for the successful completion of this work. Refer to Section 10 for details.

2 Compression test – description and interpretation

1 When engine performance is down, or if misfiring occurs which cannot be attributed to the ignition or fuel systems, a compression

1.9 Engine code is stamped on a plate (arrowed) attached to the front of the cylinder block – viewed from above

test can provide diagnostic clues as to the engine's condition. If the test is performed regularly, it can give warning of trouble before any other symptoms become apparent.
2 The engine must be fully warmed-up to normal operating temperature, the battery must be fully charged, and all the spark plugs must be removed (see Chapter 1A). The aid of an assistant will also be required.
3 Referring to Chapter 12, disable and depressurise the fuel system by identifying and removing the fuel pump fuse from the engine compartment fusebox. Start the engine, and run it until it cuts out.
4 Disable the ignition system by disconnecting the LT wiring connector from the ignition coil module, referring to Chapter 5B for further information.
5 Fit a compression tester to the No 1 cylinder spark plug hole – the type of tester which screws into the plug thread is to be preferred.
6 Have the assistant hold the throttle wide open, and crank the engine on the starter motor; after one or two revolutions, the compression pressure should build up to a maximum figure, and then stabilise. Record the highest reading obtained.
7 Repeat the test on the remaining cylinders, recording the pressure in each.
8 All cylinders should produce very similar pressures; a difference of more than 2 bars between any two cylinders indicates a fault. Note that the compression should build-up quickly in a healthy engine; low compression on the first stroke, followed by gradually-increasing pressure on successive strokes, indicates worn piston rings. A low compression reading on the first stroke, which does not build-up during successive strokes, indicates leaking valves or a blown head gasket (a cracked head could also be the cause). Deposits on the undersides of the valve heads can also cause low compression.
9 Although Citroën do not specify exact compression pressures, as a guide, any cylinder pressure of below 10 bars can be considered as less than healthy. Refer to a Citroën dealer or other specialist if in doubt as to whether a particular pressure reading is acceptable.

10 If the pressure in any cylinder is low, carry out the following test to isolate the cause. Introduce a teaspoonful of clean oil into that cylinder through its spark plug hole, and repeat the test.
11 If the addition of oil temporarily improves the compression pressure, this indicates that bore or piston wear is responsible for the pressure loss. No improvement suggests that leaking or burnt valves, or a blown head gasket, may be to blame.
12 A low reading from two adjacent cylinders is almost certainly due to the head gasket having blown between them; the presence of coolant in the engine oil will confirm this.
13 If the compression reading is unusually high, the combustion chambers are probably coated with carbon deposits. If this is the case, the cylinder head should be removed and decarbonised.
14 On completion of the test, refit the spark plugs and fuel pump fuse, and reconnect the ignition coil module wiring connector.

3 Engine assembly/ valve timing holes – general information and usage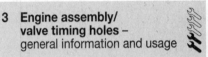

Note: *Do not attempt to rotate the engine whilst the crankshaft/camshaft are locked in position. If the engine is to be left in this state for a long period of time, it is a good idea to place warning notices inside the vehicle, and in the engine compartment. This will reduce the possibility of the engine being accidentally cranked on the starter motor, which is likely to cause damage with the locking pins in place.*

1 On all engines, timing holes are drilled in the camshaft sprocket and in the flywheel. The holes are used to ensure that the crankshaft and camshaft are correctly positioned when assembling the engine (to prevent the possibility of the valves contacting the pistons when refitting the cylinder head), or refitting the timing belt. When the timing holes are aligned with access holes in the cylinder head and the cylinder block, suitable diameter pins or bolts can be inserted to lock both the camshaft and crankshaft in position, preventing them from rotating. Proceed as follows.
2 Remove the timing belt upper cover as described in Section 5.
3 The crankshaft must now be turned until the timing hole in the camshaft sprocket is aligned with the corresponding hole in the cylinder head. The holes are aligned when the camshaft sprocket hole is in the 2 o'clock position, when viewed from the right-hand end of the engine. The crankshaft can be turned by using a spanner on the crankshaft sprocket bolt, noting that it should always be rotated in a clockwise direction (viewed from the right-hand end of the engine).
4 With the camshaft sprocket hole correctly positioned, insert a 6 mm diameter bolt or drill bit through the hole in the front, left-hand

3.4 Insert a 6 mm bolt (arrowed) through the hole in cylinder block flange and into the timing hole in the flywheel . . .

3.5 . . . then insert a 10 mm bolt through the camshaft sprocket timing hole, and locate it in the cylinder head

flange of the cylinder block, and locate it in the timing hole in the flywheel **(see illustration)**. Note that it may be necessary to rotate the crankshaft slightly, to get the holes to align.

5 With the flywheel correctly positioned, insert a 10 mm diameter bolt or drill bit through the timing hole in the camshaft sprocket, and locate it in the hole in the cylinder head **(see illustration)**.

6 The crankshaft and camshaft are now locked in position, preventing unnecessary rotation.

4.2 Disconnect the breather hose from the cylinder head cover

4 Cylinder head cover – removal and refitting

Removal

1 Disconnect the battery negative terminal (refer to *Disconnecting the battery* in the Reference Chapter).

2 Release the quick-release fitting and withdraw the breather assembly from the cylinder head cover **(see illustration)**.

3 Undo the two retaining nuts, and remove the washer from each of the cylinder head cover studs.

4 Lift off the cylinder head cover, and remove it along with its rubber seal. Examine the seal for signs of damage and deterioration, and if necessary, renew it.

5 Remove the spacer from each stud, and lift off the oil baffle plate.

Refitting

6 Carefully clean the cylinder head and cover mating surfaces, and remove all traces of oil.

7 Fit the rubber seal over the edge of the cylinder head cover, ensuring that it is correctly located along its entire length.

8 Refit the oil baffle plate to the engine, and locate the spacers in their recesses in the baffle plate.

9 Carefully refit the cylinder head cover to the engine, taking great care not to displace the rubber seal.

10 Check that the seal is correctly located, then refit the washers and cover retaining nuts, and tighten them to the specified torque.

11 Refit the breather assembly to the stub on the cylinder head cover, pushing it down until it locks into place.

12 Reconnect the battery negative terminal on completion.

5 Timing belt covers – removal and refitting

Removal

Upper cover

1 Unclip the hose from the top of the upper cover. Slacken and remove the two retaining bolts (one at the front and one at the rear), and remove the upper timing cover from the cylinder head **(see illustrations)**.

5.1a Unclip the hose from the upper timing belt cover . . .

5.1b . . . undo the front mounting bolt . . .

5.1c . . . and rear mounting bolt . . .

5.1d . . . then lift off the upper cover

Lower cover

2 Remove the auxiliary drivebelt as described in Chapter 1A.

3 Remove the upper cover as described previously.

4 Slacken and remove the three retaining bolts (one at the rear of the cover, beneath the engine mounting plate, and two directly above the crankshaft pulley).

5 Undo the three crankshaft pulley retaining bolts and remove the pulley, noting which way round it is fitted.

6 Slacken and remove the remaining retaining bolt(s), and slide the lower cover off the end of the crankshaft.

Refitting

Upper cover

7 Refit the cover, ensuring it is correctly located with the lower cover, and tighten its retaining bolts. Locate the hose in its retaining clip on the cover.

Lower cover

8 Locate the lower cover over the timing belt sprocket, and tighten its retaining bolt(s).

9 Fit the pulley to the end of the crankshaft, ensuring it is fitted the correct way round, and tighten its bolts to the specified torque.

10 Refit the upper cover as described above, then refit and tension the auxiliary drivebelt as described in Chapter 1A.

---

6 Timing belt –
  general information,
  removal and refitting

Note: *Citroën specify the use of an electronic belt tension checking tool (SEEM 4122-T), and valve rocker contact plate (4533-T.Z.) to correctly set the timing belt tension. The following procedure assumes that this equipment (or suitable alternatives) is available. Accurate tensioning of the timing belt is essential, and if access to this equipment cannot be obtained, it is recommended that the work is entrusted to a Citroën dealer or suitably-equipped garage.*

General information

1 The timing belt drives the camshaft and

coolant pump from a toothed sprocket on the right-hand end of the crankshaft. If the belt breaks or slips in service, the pistons are likely to hit the valve heads, resulting in extensive (and expensive) damage.

2 The timing belt should be renewed at the specified intervals (see Chapter 1A), or earlier if it is contaminated with oil or if it is at all noisy in operation (a 'scraping' noise due to uneven wear).

3 If the timing belt is being removed, it is a wise precaution to check the condition of the coolant pump at the same time (check for signs of coolant leakage). This may avoid the need to remove the timing belt again at a later stage, should the coolant pump fail.

Removal

4 Disconnect the battery negative terminal (refer to *Disconnecting the battery* in the Reference Section of this manual).

5 Align the engine assembly/valve timing holes as described in Section 3, and lock both the camshaft sprocket and the flywheel in position. *Do not* attempt to rotate the engine whilst the locking tools are in position.

6 Remove the timing belt upper and lower covers as described in Section 5.

7 Loosen the timing belt tensioner pulley retaining nut. Allow the pulley to pivot in a clockwise direction, to relieve the tension from the timing belt. Retighten the tensioner pulley retaining nut to secure it in the slackened position.

8 If the timing belt is to be re-used, use white paint or similar to mark the direction of rotation on the belt (if markings do not already exist) **(see illustration)**. Slip the belt off the sprockets.

9 Check the timing belt carefully for any signs of uneven wear, splitting, or oil contamination. Pay particular attention to the roots of the teeth. Renew the belt if there is the slightest doubt about its condition. If the engine is undergoing an overhaul, renew the belt as a matter of course, regardless of its apparent condition. The cost of a new belt is nothing when compared to the cost of repairs, should the belt break in service. If signs of oil contamination are found, trace the source of the oil leak, and rectify it. Wash down the engine timing belt area and all related components, to remove all traces of oil.

Refitting

10 Prior to refitting, thoroughly clean the timing belt sprockets. Check that the tensioner pulley rotates freely, without any sign of roughness. If necessary, renew the tensioner pulley as described in Section 7. Make sure that the locking tools are still in place, as described in Section 3.

11 Manoeuvre the timing belt into position, ensuring that the arrows on the belt are pointing in the direction of rotation (clockwise, when viewed from the right-hand end of the engine).

12 Do not twist the timing belt sharply while

6.8 Mark the direction of rotation on the belt, if it is to be re-used

refitting it. Fit the belt over the crankshaft and camshaft sprockets. Make sure that the 'front run' of the belt is taut – ie, ensure that any slack is on the tensioner pulley side of the belt. Fit the belt over the coolant pump sprocket and tensioner pulley. Ensure that the belt teeth are seated centrally in the sprockets.

13 Slacken the tensioner pulley retaining nut and insert a short length of 8.0 mm square bar into the square hole on the front face of the tensioner pulley **(see Tool Tip 1)**. Using the square bar and a spanner, pivot the pulley anti-clockwise to remove all free play from the timing belt, then retighten the nut.

14 The timing belt must now be accurately tensioned using electronic belt tension measuring equipment as follows.

Tensioning

15 Fit the sensor head of the belt tensioning measuring equipment to the 'front run' of the timing belt, approximately midway between the camshaft and crankshaft sprockets.

16 Slacken the tensioner pulley retaining nut, then using the square bar and spanner, pivot the tensioner pulley anti-clockwise until an initial setting of 44 SEEM units is displayed on

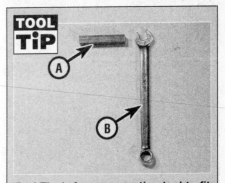

Tool Tip 1: A square section tool to fit the timing belt tensioner pulley can be made from a length of standard 8 mm door handle rod (A), obtained from a DIY shop, and then cut to size. Once the rod has been fitted to the tensioner, the timing belt can be tensioned by turning the rod with an 8 mm spanner (B).

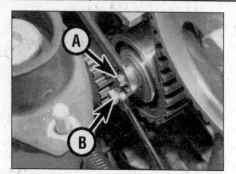

6.16 Slacken the tensioner centre nut, then pivot the tensioner pulley anti-clockwise using the 8 mm bar and a spanner

    A *Tensioner centre nut*
    B *8 mm bar*

the tensioning measuring equipment **(see illustration)**. Hold the tensioner pulley in that position and retighten the retaining nut.

17 Remove the locking tools from the camshaft sprocket and flywheel, and remove the tension measuring equipment from the belt.

18 Using a suitable socket and extension bar on the crankshaft sprocket bolt, rotate the crankshaft through four complete rotations in a clockwise direction (viewed from the right-hand end of the engine). *Do not* at any time rotate the crankshaft anti-clockwise. Refit the locking tool to the flywheel and check that the camshaft sprocket timing hole is aligned.

19 To enable an accurate belt tension final setting to be achieved, all the load exerted on the camshaft lobes through the action of the valve springs and rocker arms must be removed. To do this, Citroën mechanics use a valve rocker contact plate (special tool 4533-T.Z.) which is simply a steel plate fitted over the rocker arms in place of the cylinder head cover, and secured using the cylinder head cover retaining nuts. Eight studs and suitable locknuts are fitted to the plate, with each stud located directly over the valve stem end of each rocker arm. The studs are then screwed down until they just lift the rocker arms away from the camshaft lobes

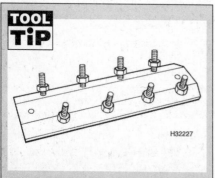

Tool Tip 2: A valve rocker contact plate can be made from steel sheet with eight studs and locknuts to contact the rocker arms.

and are then secured in that position with the locknuts. This has the effect of removing all the load from the camshaft, allowing it to move very slightly as the belt tension is adjusted. If this is not done, the tension reading shown on the belt tension measuring equipment will be inaccurate. If the special tool cannot be obtained, a suitable alternative can be fabricated **(see Tool Tip 2)**.

20 Remove the cylinder head cover (see Section 4). Slacken the eight rocker arm contact bolts in the valve rocker contact plate and fit the contact plate to the cylinder head, observing the correct fitted direction. Tighten each rocker arm contact bolt until the rockers are just free of the camshaft lobes. Do not over-tighten the contact bolts otherwise the valves will contact the pistons.

21 Ensure that the flywheel locking tool is in place, but the camshaft sprocket locking tool is removed.

22 Refit the tension measuring equipment to the belt, slacken the tensioner pulley retaining nut, and turn the tensioner pulley until a setting of between 29 and 33 SEEM units is indicated on the measuring equipment. Hold the tensioner pulley in this position and tighten the retaining nut to the specified torque.

23 Remove the measuring equipment from the belt, the valve rocker contact plate from the cylinder head, and the locking tool from the flywheel. Rotate the crankshaft through another two complete rotations in a clockwise direction and check that both the camshaft sprocket and flywheel timing holes are realigned, and that the locking tools can be inserted. *Do not* at any time rotate the crankshaft anti-clockwise. If the locking tools cannot be inserted, repeat the refitting and tensioning procedure. If all is satisfactory, remove the locking tools.

24 With the belt tension correctly set, refit the cylinder head cover and timing belt covers, and reconnect the battery negative terminal.

---

7   Timing belt tensioner and sprockets – removal, inspection and refitting

Note 1: *This Section describes the removal and refitting of the components concerned as individual operations. If more than one of them is to be removed at the same time, start by removing the timing belt as described in Section 6; remove the component as described below, ignoring the preliminary dismantling steps.*

Note 2: *The following operations entail the slackening and then retensioning of the timing belt. Refer to Section 6 and ensure that the necessary equipment to accurately tension the timing belt is available, before proceeding.*

Removal

1 Disconnect the battery negative terminal (refer to *Disconnecting the battery* in the Reference Chapter).

2 Position the engine assembly/valve timing holes as described in Section 3, and lock both the camshaft sprocket and flywheel in position. *Do not* attempt to rotate the engine whilst the locking tools are in position.

Camshaft sprocket

3 Remove the timing belt upper and lower covers as described in Section 5.

4 Loosen the timing belt tensioner pulley retaining nut. Rotate the pulley in a clockwise direction, using a suitable square-section bar fitted to the hole in the pulley hub (see **Tool Tip 1** in Section 6). Retighten the retaining nut to hold the pulley in the slackened position.

5 Disengage the timing belt from the sprocket, and move the belt clear, taking care not to bend or twist it sharply. Remove the locking tool from the camshaft sprocket.

6 Slacken the camshaft sprocket retaining bolt and remove it, along with its washer. To prevent the camshaft rotating as the bolt is slackened, a sprocket-holding tool will be required. In the absence of the special Citroën tool, an acceptable substitute can be easily fabricated **(see Tool Tip)**. *Do not* attempt to use the locking tool inserted into the engine assembly/valve timing hole to prevent the sprocket from rotating whilst the bolt is slackened.

7 With the retaining bolt removed, slide the sprocket off the end of the camshaft. If the locating peg is a loose fit in the rear of the sprocket, remove it for safe-keeping. Examine the camshaft oil seal for signs of oil leakage and, if necessary, renew it as described in Section 8.

To make a camshaft sprocket holding tool, obtain two lengths of steel strip about 6 mm thick by 30 mm wide or similar, one 600 mm long, the other 200 mm long (all dimensions approximate). Bolt the two strips together to form a forked end, leaving the bolt slack so that the shorter strip can pivot freely. At the end of each 'prong' of the fork, secure a bolt with a nut and a locknut, to act as the fulcrums; these will engage with the cut-outs in the sprocket, and should protrude by about 30 mm.

7.10 Lock the flywheel ring gear to prevent the crankshaft rotating

7.11a Remove the crankshaft sprocket bolt . . .

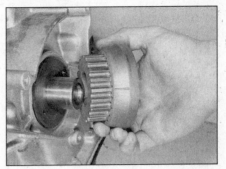

7.11b . . . then slide off the sprocket

Crankshaft sprocket

8 Remove the upper and lower timing belt covers as described in Section 5.

9 Loosen the timing belt tensioner pulley retaining nut. Rotate the pulley in a clockwise direction, using a suitable square-section bar fitted to the hole in the pulley hub (see **Tool Tip 1** in Section 6). Retighten the retaining nut to hold the pulley in the slackened position.

10 To prevent crankshaft rotation whilst the sprocket retaining bolt is slackened, select top gear and have an assistant apply the brakes firmly. Alternatively, the flywheel ring gear can be locked using a suitable tool made from steel angle; remove the cover plate from the base of the transmission bellhousing and bolt the tool to the bellhousing flange so it engages with the ring gear teeth. If the engine has been removed from the vehicle, lock the flywheel ring gear, using an arrangement similar to that shown **(see illustration)**. *Do not be tempted to use the flywheel locking tool described in Section 3 to prevent the crankshaft from rotating;* temporarily remove the locking tool from the flywheel prior to slackening the pulley bolt, then refit it once the bolt has been slackened.

11 Unscrew the retaining bolt and washer, then slide the sprocket off the end of the crankshaft **(see illustrations)**. Refit the locking tool to the flywheel.

12 If the Woodruff key is a loose fit in the crankshaft, remove it and store it with the sprocket for safe-keeping. If necessary, also slide the flanged spacer off the end of the crankshaft **(see illustration)**. Examine the crankshaft oil seal for signs oil leakage and, if necessary, renew as described in Section 14.

Tensioner pulley

13 Remove the timing belt upper and lower covers as described in Section 5.

14 Slacken and remove the timing belt tensioner pulley retaining nut, and slide the pulley off its mounting stud. Examine the mounting stud for signs of damage and, if necessary, renew it.

Inspection

15 Clean the sprockets thoroughly, and renew any that show signs of wear, damage or cracks. If any of the sprockets are to be

renewed, the timing belt should also be renewed as a matter of course.

16 Clean the tensioner assembly, but do not use any strong solvent which may enter the pulley bearing. Check that the pulley rotates freely about its hub, with no sign of stiffness or of free play. Renew the tensioner pulley if there is any doubt about its condition, or if there are any obvious signs of wear or damage.

Refitting

Camshaft sprocket

17 Refit the locating peg (where removed) to the rear of the sprocket, then locate the sprocket on the end of the camshaft. Ensure that the locating peg is correctly engaged with the cut-out in the camshaft end.

18 Refit the sprocket retaining bolt and washer. Tighten the bolt to the specified torque, whilst retaining the sprocket with the holding tool.

19 Realign the timing hole in the camshaft sprocket (see Section 3) with the corresponding hole in the cylinder head, and refit the locking tool.

20 Refit the timing belt to the camshaft sprocket. Ensure that the 'front run' of the belt is taut – ie, ensure that any slack is on the tensioner pulley side of the belt. Do not twist the belt sharply while refitting it, and ensure that the belt teeth are seated centrally in the sprockets.

21 Loosen the tensioner pulley retaining nut. Using the square-section bar and a spanner, rotate the pulley anti-clockwise to remove all

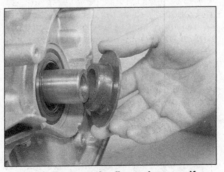

7.12 Remove the flanged spacer if necessary

free play from the timing belt, then retighten the nut.

22 Tension the timing belt as described in Section 6.

23 Refit the timing belt covers as described in Section 5.

Crankshaft sprocket

24 Where removed, locate the Woodruff key in the crankshaft end, then slide on the flanged spacer, aligning its slot with the Woodruff key.

25 Align the crankshaft sprocket slot with the Woodruff key, and slide it onto the end of the crankshaft.

26 Temporarily remove the locking tool from the flywheel, then refit the crankshaft sprocket retaining bolt and washer. Tighten the bolt to the specified torque, whilst preventing crankshaft rotation using the method employed on removal. Refit the locking tool to the flywheel.

27 Relocate the timing belt on the crankshaft sprocket. Ensure that the 'front run' of the belt is taut – ie, ensure that any slack is on the tensioner pulley side of the belt. Do not twist the belt sharply while refitting it, and ensure that the belt teeth are seated centrally in the sprockets.

28 Loosen the tensioner pulley retaining nut. Using the square-section bar and a spanner, rotate the pulley anti-clockwise to remove all free play from the timing belt, then retighten the nut.

29 Tension the timing belt as described in Section 6.

30 Refit the timing belt covers as described in Section 5.

Tensioner pulley

31 Refit the tensioner pulley to its mounting stud, and fit the retaining nut.

32 Ensure that the 'front run' of the belt is taut – ie, ensure that any slack is on the pulley side of the belt. Check that the belt is centrally located on all its sprockets. Rotate the pulley anti-clockwise to remove all free play from the timing belt, then tighten the pulley retaining nut securely.

33 Tension the belt as described in Section 6.

34 Refit the timing belt covers as described in Section 5.

8.2 Carefully prise the camshaft oil seal from its housing with a flat-bladed screwdriver

8 Camshaft oil seal – renewal

Note: *If the camshaft oil seal is to be renewed with the timing belt still in place, check first that the belt is free from oil contamination. (Renew the belt as a matter of course if signs of oil contamination are found; see Section 6.) Cover the belt to protect it from oil contamination while work is in progress. Ensure that all traces of oil are removed from the area before the belt is refitted.*

1 Remove the camshaft sprocket as described in Section 7.

2 Punch or drill two small holes opposite each other in the oil seal. Screw a self-tapping screw into each, and pull on the screws with pliers to extract the seal. Alternatively, carefully prise the seal from its housing with a flat-bladed screwdriver **(see illustration)**. Take great care to avoid scoring the cylinder head and camshaft sealing surfaces.

3 Clean the seal housing, and polish off any burrs or raised edges, which may have caused the seal to fail in the first place.

4 Lubricate the lips of the new seal with clean engine oil, and drive it into position until it seats on its locating shoulder. Use a suitable tubular drift, such as a socket, which bears only on the hard outer edge of the seal. Take care not to damage the seal lips during fitting. Note that the seal lips should face inwards.

5 Refit the camshaft sprocket as described in Section 7.

10.4 Remove the circlip, and slide the components off the end of the rocker arm

9 Valve clearances – checking and adjustment

Note: *The valve clearances must be checked and adjusted only when the engine is cold.*

1 The importance of having the valve clearances correctly adjusted cannot be overstressed, as they vitally affect the performance of the engine. If the clearances are too big, the engine will be noisy (characteristic rattling or tapping noises) and engine efficiency will be reduced, as the valves open too late and close too early. A more serious problem arises if the clearances are too small, however. If this is the case, the valves may not close fully when the engine is hot, resulting in serious damage to the engine (eg, burnt valve seats and/or cylinder head warping/cracking). The clearances are checked and adjusted as follows.

2 Remove the cylinder head cover as described in Section 4.

3 The engine can now be turned using a suitable socket and extension bar fitted to the crankshaft sprocket/pulley bolt.

> **HAYNES HINT** *Turning the engine will be easier if the spark plugs are removed first – see Chapter 1A.*

4 It is important that the clearance of each valve is checked and adjusted only when the valve is fully closed, with the rocker arm resting on the heel of the cam (directly opposite the peak). This can be ensured by carrying out the adjustments in the following sequence, noting that No 1 cylinder is at the transmission end of the engine. The correct valve clearances are given in the Specifications at the start of this Chapter. The valve locations can be determined from the position of the manifolds.

Valve fully open	Adjust valves
No 1 exhaust	No 3 in. and No 4 ex.
No 3 exhaust	No 4 in. and No 2 ex.
No 4 exhaust	No 2 in. and No 1 ex.
No 2 exhaust	No 1 in. and No 3 ex.

5 Start by turning the crankshaft in the normal direction of rotation until the exhaust valve for No 1 cylinder is fully open. The clearances for No 3 cylinder inlet valve and No 4 cylinder exhaust valve can now be checked. The clearances are checked by inserting a feeler blade of the correct thickness between the valve stem and the rocker arm adjusting screw. The feeler blade should be a light, sliding fit, similar to a knife through butter. If adjustment is necessary, slacken the adjusting screw locknut, and turn the screw as necessary. Once the correct clearance is obtained, hold the adjusting screw and securely tighten the locknut. Recheck the valve clearance, and adjust again if necessary.

6 Rotate the crankshaft until the next valve in the sequence is fully open, and check the clearances of the next two specified valves.

7 Repeat the procedure until all eight valve clearances have been checked (and if necessary, adjusted), then refit the cylinder head cover as described in Section 4.

10 Camshaft and rocker arms – removal, inspection and refitting

General information

1 The rocker arm assembly is secured to the top of the cylinder head by the cylinder head bolts. Although in theory it is possible to undo the head bolts and remove the rocker arm assembly without removing the head, in practice, this is not recommended. Once the bolts have been removed, the head gasket will be disturbed, and the gasket will almost certainly leak or blow after refitting. For this reason, removal of the rocker arm assembly cannot be done without removing the cylinder head and renewing the head gasket.

2 The camshaft is slid out of the right-hand end of the cylinder head, and it therefore cannot be removed without first removing the cylinder head, due to a lack of clearance.

Removal

Rocker arm assembly

3 Remove the cylinder head as described in Section 11.

4 To dismantle the rocker arm assembly, carefully prise off the circlip from the right-hand end of the rocker shaft; retain the rocker pedestal, to prevent it being sprung off the end of the shaft. Slide the various components off the end of the shaft, keeping all components in their correct fitted order **(see illustration)**. Make a note of each component's correct fitted position and orientation as it is removed, to ensure it is fitted correctly on reassembly.

5 To separate the left-hand pedestal and shaft, first unscrew the cylinder head cover retaining stud from the top of the pedestal; this can be achieved using a stud extractor, or two nuts locked together. With the stud removed, unscrew the grub screw from the top of the pedestal, and withdraw the rocker shaft **(see illustrations)**.

Camshaft

6 Remove the cylinder head as described in Section 11.

7 With the head on a bench, remove the sprocket locking tool, then remove the camshaft sprocket as described in Section 7.

8 Unbolt the coolant housing from the left-hand end of the cylinder head. Undo the retaining bolt, and remove the camshaft thrust fork from the cylinder head **(see illustration)**.

9 Using a large flat-bladed screwdriver, carefully prise the oil seal out of the right-hand

10.5a To remove the left-hand pedestal, lock two nuts together and unscrew the stud ...

10.5b ... then remove the grub screw

10.8 Undo the retaining bolt, and remove the camshaft thrust fork (arrowed) ...

end of the cylinder head, then slide out the camshaft **(see illustrations)**. Discard the seal – a new one must be used on refitting.

Inspection

Rocker arm assembly

10 Roller rocker arms are used incorporating a roller bearing at the camshaft lobe contact point. Check for any sign of excess play of the roller bearing or any roughness as it is rotated. Renew worn components as necessary. If a rocker arm roller bearing contact surface is badly scored, also examine the corresponding lobe on the camshaft for wear, as both will likely be worn.

11 Inspect the ends of the (valve clearance) adjusting screws for signs of wear or damage, and renew as required.

12 If the rocker arm assembly has been dismantled, examine the rocker arm and shaft bearing surfaces for wear ridges and scoring. If there are obvious signs of wear, the relevant rocker arm(s) and/or the shaft must be renewed.

Camshaft

13 Examine the camshaft bearing surfaces and cam lobes for signs of wear ridges and scoring. Renew the camshaft if any of these conditions are apparent. Examine the condition of the bearing surfaces, both on the camshaft journals and in the cylinder head. If the head bearing surfaces are worn excessively, the cylinder head will need to be renewed. If the necessary measuring equipment is available, camshaft bearing journal wear can be checked by direct measurement, noting that No 1 journal is at the transmission end of the head.

14 Examine the thrust fork for signs of wear or scoring, and renew as necessary.

Refitting

Rocker arm assembly

15 If the rocker arm assembly was dismantled, refit the rocker shaft to the left-hand pedestal, aligning its locating hole with the pedestal threaded hole. Refit the grub screw, and tighten it securely. With the grub screw in position, refit the cylinder head cover mounting stud to the pedestal, and tighten it securely. Apply a smear of clean engine oil to

the shaft, then slide on all removed components, ensuring each is correctly fitted in its original position. Once all components are in position on the shaft, compress the right-hand pedestal and refit the circlip. Ensure that the circlip is correctly located in its groove on the shaft.

16 Refit the cylinder head and rocker arm assembly as described in Section 11.

Camshaft

17 Ensure that the cylinder head and camshaft bearing surfaces are clean, then liberally oil the camshaft bearings and lobes. Slide the camshaft back into position in the cylinder head.

18 Locate the thrust fork with the left-hand end of the camshaft. Refit the fork retaining bolt, tightening it to the specified torque setting.

19 Ensure that the coolant housing and cylinder head mating surfaces are clean and dry, with all traces of old sealant removed. Using RTV sealant, refit the coolant housing to the left-hand end of the cylinder head. Tighten the retaining bolts securely in a progressive sequence.

20 Lubricate the lips of the new seal with clean engine oil, then drive it into position until it seats on its locating shoulder. Use a suitable tubular drift, such as a socket, which bears only on the hard outer edge of the seal. Take care not to damage the seal lips during fitting. Note that the seal lips should face inwards.

21 Refit the camshaft sprocket as described in Section 7.

22 Refit the cylinder head as described in Section 11.

11 Cylinder head – removal and refitting

Note: *The following operations entail the slackening and then retensioning of the timing belt. Refer to Section 6 and ensure that the necessary equipment to accurately tension the timing belt is available, before proceeding.*

Removal

1 Disconnect the battery negative terminal (refer to *Disconnecting the battery* in the Reference Chapter).

2 Drain the cooling system as described in Chapter 1A.

3 Remove the cylinder head cover as described in Section 4.

4 Align the engine assembly/valve timing holes as described in Section 3, and lock both the camshaft sprocket and flywheel in position. *Do not* attempt to rotate the engine whilst the locking tools are in position.

5 Note that the following text assumes that the cylinder head will be removed with both inlet and exhaust manifolds attached; this is easier, but makes it a bulky and heavy assembly to handle. If it is wished to remove the manifolds first, proceed as described in Chapter 4A.

6 Working as described in Chapter 4A, disconnect the exhaust system front pipe from the manifold. Disconnect or release the

10.9a ... prise out the oil seal ...

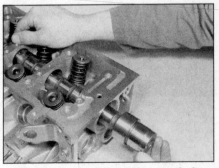

10.9b ... and slide out the camshaft

lambda sensor wiring, so that it is not strained by the weight of the exhaust.

7 Remove the air cleaner housing and inlet duct assembly as described in Chapter 4A.

8 Carry out the following operations as described in Chapter 4A:

a) *Depressurise the fuel system, and disconnect the fuel feed hose from the fuel rail (plug all openings, to prevent loss of fuel and entry of dirt into the fuel system).*

b) *Disconnect the accelerator cable.*

c) *Disconnect the relevant electrical connectors from the throttle housing, fuel injectors and the idle speed stepper motor.*

d) *Disconnect the vacuum servo unit hose, coolant hose(s) and all the other relevant/breather hoses from the manifold.*

9 Remove the lower timing belt cover as described in Section 5.

10 Loosen the timing belt tensioner pulley retaining nut. Pivot the pulley in a clockwise direction, using an 8.0 mm square-section bar fitted to the hole in the pulley hub (see Section 6), then retighten the retaining nut.

11 Disengage the timing belt from the camshaft sprocket, and position the belt clear of the sprocket. Ensure that the belt is not bent or twisted sharply.

12 Slacken the retaining clips, and disconnect the coolant hoses from the thermostat housing (on the left-hand end of the cylinder head).

13 Depress the retaining clip(s), and disconnect the wiring connector(s) from the electrical switch and/or sensor(s) which are screwed into the thermostat housing/cylinder head (as appropriate).

14 Disconnect the wiring connector from the ignition coil module. If the cylinder head is to be dismantled for overhaul, remove the ignition coil module as described in Chapter 5B.

15 Slacken and remove the bolt securing the engine oil dipstick tube to the cylinder head.

16 Working in the *reverse* of the sequence shown in illustration 11.33, progressively slacken the ten cylinder head bolts by half a turn at a time, until all bolts can be unscrewed by hand.

17 With all the cylinder head bolts removed, lift the rocker arm assembly off the cylinder head. Note the locating pins which are fitted to the base of each rocker arm pedestal. If any pin is a loose fit in the head or pedestal, remove it for safe-keeping.

18 Carefully lift the cylinder head off the engine. Seek assistance if possible, as it is a heavy assembly, especially if it is being removed complete with the manifolds.

19 Remove the gasket from the top of the block, noting the two locating dowels. If the locating dowels are a loose fit, remove them and store them with the head for safe-keeping.

20 If the cylinder head is to be dismantled for overhaul, remove the camshaft as described in Section 10, then refer to Part D of this Chapter.

Preparation for refitting

21 The mating faces of the cylinder head and cylinder block/crankcase must be perfectly clean before refitting the head. Citroën recommend the use of a scouring agent for this purpose, but acceptable results can be achieved by using a hard plastic or wood scraper to remove all traces of gasket and carbon. The same method can also be used to clean the piston crowns. Take particular care to avoid scoring or gouging the cylinder head/cylinder block mating surfaces during the cleaning operations, as aluminium alloy is easily damaged. Also, make sure that the carbon debris is not allowed to enter the oil and water passages – this is particularly important for the lubrication system, as carbon could block the oil supply to the engine's components. Using adhesive tape and paper, seal the water, oil and bolt holes in the cylinder block/crankcase.

> **HAYNES HiNT** *To prevent carbon debris entering the gap between the pistons and bores, smear a little grease in the gap. After cleaning each piston, use a small brush to remove all traces of grease and carbon from the gap, then wipe away the remainder with a clean rag.*

22 Check the mating surfaces of the cylinder block and the cylinder head for nicks, deep scratches and other damage. If slight, they may be removed carefully with a file, but if excessive, machining may be the only alternative to renewal.

23 Thoroughly clean the threads of the cylinder head bolt holes in the cylinder block. Ensure that the bolts run freely in their threads, and that all traces of oil and water are removed from each bolt hole.

24 If warpage of the cylinder head gasket surface is suspected, use a straight-edge to check it for distortion. Refer to Part D of this Chapter if necessary.

25 When purchasing a new cylinder head gasket, it is essential that a gasket of the correct thickness is obtained. At the time of writing, only one thickness of gasket was available, but confirm that this is still the case with your dealer or parts supplier. If you have any doubts, take the old gasket along to your dealer or parts supplier, and have him confirm the type of replacement gasket required.

26 Check the condition of the cylinder head bolts, and particularly their threads, whenever they are removed. Wash the bolts in a suitable solvent, and wipe them dry. Check each bolt for any sign of visible wear or damage, renewing them if necessary. Measure the length of each bolt from the underside of its head to the end of the bolt. The bolts may be re-used if their length does not exceed 175.5 mm. If any one bolt is longer than the specified length, *all* of the bolts should be renewed as a complete set. Considering the stress which the cylinder head bolts are under, it is highly recommended that they are renewed, regardless of their apparent condition.

Refitting

27 Wipe clean the mating surfaces of the cylinder head and cylinder block/crankcase. Check that the two locating dowels are in position at each end of the cylinder block/crankcase surface.

28 Position a new gasket on the cylinder block surface, ensuring that the manufacturer's identification markings face upwards **(see illustrations)**.

29 Check that the flywheel and camshaft sprocket are still correctly locked in position with their respective locking tools then, with the aid of an assistant, carefully refit the cylinder head assembly to the block, aligning it with the locating dowels.

30 Ensure that the locating pins are in position in the base of each rocker pedestal, then refit the rocker arm assembly to the cylinder head **(see illustration)**.

31 Apply a smear of grease to the threads, and to the underside of the heads, of the cylinder head bolts **(see illustration)**. Citroën specify Molykote G Rapid Plus grease (available from your Citroën dealer – a sachet may supplied with the top-end gasket set).

32 Carefully enter each bolt into its relevant

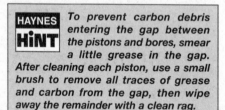

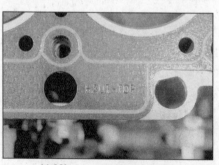

11.28a Position a new gasket on the cylinder block surface . . .

11.28b . . . ensuring that the manufacturers identification markings (HAUT – TOP) face upwards

hole (*do not drop them in*) and screw in, by hand only, until finger-tight.

33 Working progressively and in the sequence shown, tighten the cylinder head bolts to their Stage 1 torque setting, using a torque wrench and suitable socket **(see illustration)**.

34 Once all the bolts have been tightened to their Stage 1 setting, working again in the given sequence, angle-tighten the bolts through the specified Stage 2 angle, then the Stage 3 angle, using a socket and extension bar. It is recommended that an angle-measuring gauge is used during this stage of the tightening, to ensure accuracy.

35 With the cylinder head bolts correctly tightened, refit the dipstick tube retaining bolt and tighten it securely.

36 Refit the timing belt to the camshaft sprocket. Ensure that the 'front run' of the belt is taut – ie, ensure that any slack is on the tensioner pulley side of the belt. Do not twist the belt sharply while refitting it, and ensure that the belt teeth are seated centrally in the sprockets.

37 Loosen the tensioner pulley retaining nut. Pivot the pulley anti-clockwise to remove all free play from the timing belt, then retighten the nut.

38 Tension the belt as described in Section 6, then refit the timing belt covers as described in Section 5.

39 If removed, refit the ignition coil module, as described in Chapter 5B, or alternatively reconnect the wiring connector.

40 Reconnect the wiring connector(s) to the coolant switch/sensor(s) on the left-hand end of the head.

41 Reconnect the coolant hoses to the thermostat housing, securely tightening their retaining clips.

42 Working as described in Chapter 4A, carry out the following tasks:
a) *Refit all disturbed wiring, hoses and control cable(s) to the inlet manifold and fuel system components.*
b) *Reconnect and adjust the accelerator cable.*
c) *Reconnect the exhaust system front pipe to the manifold. If applicable, reconnect the lambda sensor wiring connector.*

11.30 Refit the rocker arm assembly to the cylinder head

d) *Refit the air cleaner housing and inlet duct.*

43 Check and, if necessary, adjust the valve clearances as described in Section 9.

44 On completion, reconnect the battery, and refill the cooling system as described in Chapter 1A.

12 Sump – removal and refitting

Removal

1 Disconnect the battery negative terminal (refer to *Disconnecting the battery* in the Reference Chapter). Chock the rear wheels then jack up the front of the vehicle and support it on axle stands (see *Jacking and vehicle support*).

2 Drain the engine oil, then clean and refit the engine oil drain plug, tightening it to the specified torque. If the engine is nearing its service interval when the oil and filter are due for renewal, it is recommended that the filter is also removed, and a new one fitted. After reassembly, the engine can then be refilled with fresh oil. Refer to Chapter 1A for further information.

3 Remove the exhaust system front pipe as described in Chapter 4A.

4 Progressively slacken and remove all the sump nuts and bolts. It may be necessary to unbolt the flywheel cover plate from the

11.31 Apply a smear of the grease supplied with the gasket set to the threads, and to the underside of the heads, of the cylinder head bolts

transmission to gain access to the left-hand sump fasteners.

5 Try to break the joint by striking the sump with the palm of your hand, then lower and withdraw the sump from under the vehicle **(see illustration)**. If the sump is stuck (which is quite likely) use a putty knife or similar, carefully inserted between the sump and block. Ease the knife along the joint until the sump is released.

6 While the sump is removed, take the opportunity to check the oil pump pick-up/strainer for signs of clogging or splitting. If necessary, remove the pump as described in Section 13, and clean or renew the strainer.

Refitting

7 Clean all traces of sealant from the mating surfaces of the cylinder block and sump, then use a clean rag to wipe out the sump and the engine's interior.

8 Ensure that the sump and cylinder block mating surfaces are clean and dry, then apply a coating of suitable sealant to the sump mating surface.

9 Offer up the sump, locating it on its retaining studs, and refit its retaining nuts and bolts. Tighten the nuts and bolts evenly and progressively to the specified torque.

10 Refit the exhaust front pipe as described in Chapter 4A.

11 Replenish the engine oil as described in Chapter 1A.

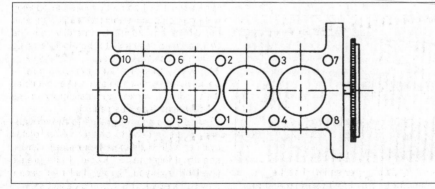

11.33 Cylinder head bolt tightening sequence

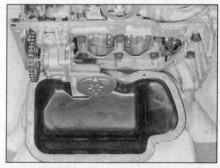

12.5 Slacken and remove the sump nuts and bolts, then remove the sump from the engine

13.2 Oil pump is retained by three bolts

13 Oil pump –
removal, inspection
and refitting

Removal

1 Remove the sump as described in Section 12.
2 Slacken and remove the three bolts securing the oil pump in position **(see illustration)**. Disengage the pump sprocket from the chain, and remove the oil pump. If the pump locating dowel is a loose fit, remove and store it with the bolts for safe-keeping.

Inspection

3 Examine the oil pump sprocket for signs of damage and wear, such as chipped or missing teeth. If the sprocket is worn, the pump assembly must be renewed, as the sprocket is not available separately. It is also recommended that the chain and drive sprocket, fitted to the crankshaft, are renewed at the same time. The drive sprocket and chain can be removed with the engine *in situ*, once the crankshaft sprocket has been removed and the crankshaft oil seal housing has been unbolted.
4 Slacken and remove the bolts securing the strainer cover to the pump body, then lift off the strainer cover. Remove the relief valve piston, spring and guide pin, noting which way round they are fitted.
5 Examine the pump rotors and body for signs of wear ridges and scoring. If worn, the complete pump assembly must be renewed.
6 Examine the relief valve piston for signs of

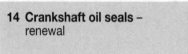

14.2 Using a screwdriver to lever out the crankshaft right-hand oil seal

wear or damage, and renew if necessary. The condition of the relief valve spring can only be measured by comparing it with a new one; if there is any doubt about its condition, it should also be renewed. Both the piston and spring are available individually.
7 Thoroughly clean the oil pump strainer with a suitable solvent, and check it for signs of clogging or splitting. If the strainer is damaged, the strainer and cover assembly must be renewed.
8 Locate the relief valve spring, piston and guide pin in the strainer cover, then refit the cover to the pump body. Align the relief valve piston with its bore in the pump. Refit the cover retaining bolts, tightening them securely.

Refitting

9 Ensure that the locating dowel is in position, then engage the pump sprocket with its drive chain. Locate the pump on its dowel, and refit the pump retaining bolts, tightening them to the specified torque setting.
10 Refit the sump as described in Section 12.

14 Crankshaft oil seals –
renewal

Right-hand oil seal

1 Remove the crankshaft sprocket and flanged spacer as described in Section 7. Secure the timing belt clear of the working area, so that it cannot be contaminated with oil. Make a note of the correct fitted depth of the seal in its housing.
2 Punch or drill two small holes opposite each other in the seal. Screw a self-tapping screw into each, and pull on the screws with pliers to extract the seal. Alternatively, the seal can be levered out of position using a suitable flat-bladed screwdriver, taking great care not to damage the crankshaft shoulder or seal housing **(see illustration)**.
3 Clean the seal housing, and polish off any burrs or raised edges, which may have caused the seal to fail in the first place.
4 Lubricate the lips of the new seal with clean engine oil, and carefully locate the seal on the end of crankshaft. Note that its sealing lip must face inwards. Take care not to damage the seal lips during fitting.
5 Using a suitable tubular drift (such as a socket) which bears only on the hard outer edge of the seal, tap the seal into position, to the same depth in the housing as the original was prior to removal. The inner face of the seal must be flush with the inner wall of the crankcase.
6 Wash off any traces of oil, then refit the crankshaft sprocket as described in Section 7.

Left-hand oil seal

7 Remove the flywheel as described in Section 15.
8 Make a note of the correct fitted depth of

the seal in its housing. Punch or drill two small holes opposite each other in the seal. Screw a self-tapping screw into each, and pull on the screws with pliers to extract the seal.
9 Clean the seal housing, and polish off any burrs or raised edges, which may have caused the seal to fail in the first place.
10 Lubricate the lips of the new seal with clean engine oil, and carefully locate the seal on the end of the crankshaft.
11 Using a suitable tubular drift, which bears only on the hard outer edge of the seal, drive the seal into position, to the same depth in the housing as the original was prior to removal.
12 Wash off any traces of oil, then refit the flywheel as described in Section 15.

15 Flywheel –
removal, inspection
and refitting

Removal

1 Remove the transmission as described in Chapter 7, then remove the clutch assembly as described in Chapter 6.
2 Prevent the flywheel from turning by locking the ring gear teeth with a similar arrangement to that shown in illustration 7.10. Alternatively, bolt a strap between the flywheel and the cylinder block. *Do not* attempt to lock the flywheel in position using the locking tool described in Section 3.
3 Slacken and remove the flywheel retaining bolts, and remove the flywheel from the end of the crankshaft. Be careful not to drop it; it is heavy. If the flywheel locating dowel is a loose fit in the crankshaft end, remove it and store it with the flywheel for safe-keeping. Discard the flywheel bolts; new ones must be used on refitting.

Inspection

4 Examine the flywheel for scoring of the clutch face, and for wear or chipping of the ring gear teeth. If the clutch face is scored, the flywheel may be surface-ground, but renewal is preferable. Seek the advice of a Citroën dealer or engine reconditioning specialist to see if machining is possible. If the ring gear is worn or damaged, the flywheel must be renewed, as it is not possible to renew the ring gear separately.

Refitting

5 Clean the mating surfaces of the flywheel and crankshaft. Remove any remaining locking compound from the threads of the crankshaft holes, using the correct size of tap, if available.

HAYNES HINT *If a suitable tap is not available, cut two slots along the threads of one of the old flywheel bolts, and use the bolt to remove the locking compound from the threads.*

6 If the new flywheel retaining bolts are not supplied with their threads already pre-coated, apply a suitable thread-locking compound to the threads of each bolt.

7 Ensure that the locating dowel is in position. Offer up the flywheel, locating it on the dowel, and fit the new retaining bolts.

8 Lock the flywheel using the method employed on dismantling, and tighten the retaining bolts to the specified torque.

9 Refit the clutch as described in Chapter 6. Remove the flywheel locking tool, and refit the transmission as described in Chapter 7.

16 Engine/transmission mountings – inspection and renewal

Inspection

1 If improved access is required, firmly apply the handbrake, then jack up the front of the vehicle and support it securely on axle stands (see *Jacking and vehicle support*).

2 Check the mounting rubber to see if it is cracked, hardened or separated from the metal at any point; renew the mounting if any such damage or deterioration is evident.

3 Check that all the mountings' fasteners are securely tightened; use a torque wrench to check if possible **(see illustration)**.

4 Using a large screwdriver or a crowbar, check for wear in the mounting by carefully levering against it to check for free play. Where this is not possible, enlist the aid of an assistant to move the engine/transmission back-and-forth, or from side-to-side, while you watch the mounting. While some free play is to be expected even from new components,

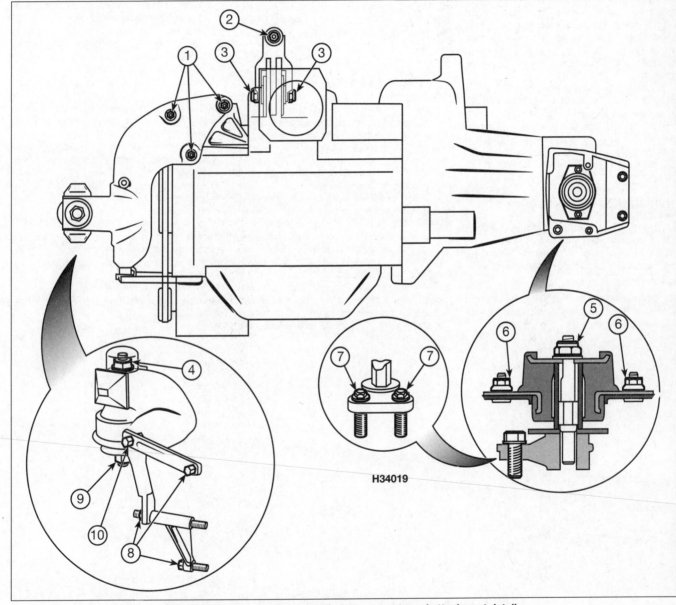

H34019

16.3 Engine/transmission mounting components and attachment details

1 *Upper mounting bracket-to-engine bolts*
2 *Rear mounting connecting link-to-subframe bracket bolt*
3 *Rear mounting connecting link-to-cylinder block bracket bolt*
4 *Right-hand rubber mounting centre nut*
5 *Left-hand rubber mounting centre nut*
6 *Left-hand rubber mounting-to-bracket nuts*
7 *Left-hand mounting bracket-to-transmission bolts*
8 *Right-hand mounting support brace-to-engine bolts/nuts*
9 *Right-hand rubber mounting*
10 *Right-hand mounting support brace-to-upper mounting bracket bolt*

excessive wear should be obvious. If excessive free play is found, check first that the fasteners are secure, then renew any worn components as described below.

Renewal

Right-hand mounting

5 Disconnect the battery negative terminal (refer to *Disconnecting the battery* in the Reference Chapter).

6 Place a jack beneath the engine, with a block of wood on the jack head. Raise the jack until it is supporting the weight of the engine.

7 Slacken and remove the three nuts securing the right-hand engine mounting upper bracket to the bracket on the cylinder block. Unscrew the single nut securing the bracket to the rubber mounting, and lift off the bracket.

8 Unscrew the rubber mounting from the body. A strap wrench or similar may be used to unscrew the mounting, or alternatively fabricate a tool from suitable metal tube with projections to engage in the cut-outs in the mounting.

9 Check for signs of wear or damage on all components, and renew as necessary.

10 On reassembly, securely tighten the rubber mounting in the body, then install the mounting bracket.

11 Tighten the mounting bracket retaining nuts to the specified torque wrench setting.

12 Remove the jack from under the engine, and reconnect the battery negative terminal.

Left-hand mounting

13 Disconnect the battery negative terminal (refer to *Disconnecting the battery* in the Reference Chapter).

14 Remove the air cleaner assembly and intake ducting as described in Chapter 4A.

15 Lift up the covers on the battery positive cable terminal box and unscrew the nuts securing the battery cables to the terminal studs. Lift the cables off the studs and suitably label them for correct refitting.

16 Withdraw the engine management ECU from its location on the support tray and move it to one side.

17 Release the wiring harness from the retaining clips on the ECU support tray, then undo the retaining bolts and lift out the support tray.

18 Place a jack beneath the transmission, with a block of wood on the jack head. Raise the jack until it is supporting the weight of the transmission.

19 Slacken and remove the centre nut and washer from the left-hand mounting, then undo the nuts securing the mounting to the mounting bracket. Lift off the mounting and remove it from the engine compartment.

20 If necessary, slide the spacer (where fitted) off the mounting stud, then unscrew the stud from the top of the transmission housing, and remove it along with its washer. If the mounting stud is tight, a universal stud extractor can be used to unscrew it.

21 Check all components carefully for signs of wear or damage, and renew as necessary.

22 Clean the threads of the mounting stud, and apply a coat of thread-locking compound to its threads. Refit the stud and washer to the top of the transmission, and tighten it to the specified torque setting.

23 Slide the spacer (where fitted) onto the mounting stud, then refit the rubber mounting. Tighten both the mounting-to-bracket nuts and the mounting centre nut to their specified torque settings, and remove the jack from underneath the transmission.

24 Refit the ECU support tray, and clip the wiring harness back into position.

25 Refit the ECU to the support tray and reconnect the battery positive cables to their respective terminal studs.

26 Refit the air cleaner assembly and intake ducting as described in Chapter 4A, then reconnect the battery negative terminal.

Rear mounting

27 If not already done, firmly apply the handbrake, then jack up the front of the vehicle and support it securely on axle stands (see *Jacking and vehicle support*).

28 Unscrew and remove the bolt securing the rear mounting connecting link to the mounting on the rear of the cylinder block.

29 Remove the bolt securing the connecting link to the bracket on the subframe. Withdraw the link.

30 To remove the mounting assembly it will first be necessary to remove the right-hand driveshaft as described in Chapter 8.

31 With the driveshaft removed, undo the retaining bolts and remove the mounting from the rear of the cylinder block.

32 Check carefully for signs of wear or damage on all components, and renew them where necessary.

33 On reassembly, fit the rear mounting assembly to the rear of the cylinder block, and tighten its retaining bolts to the specified torque. Refit the driveshaft as described in Chapter 8.

34 Refit the rear mounting connecting link, and tighten both its bolts to their specified torque settings.

35 Lower the vehicle to the ground.

Chapter 2 Part B:
EW series petrol engine in-car repair procedures

Contents

Degrees of difficulty

Easy, suitable for novice with little experience	**Fairly easy,** suitable for beginner with some experience	**Fairly difficult,** suitable for competent DIY mechanic	**Difficult,** suitable for experienced DIY mechanic	**Very difficult,** suitable for expert DIY or professional

Specifications

Engine (general)

Designation	EW7
Capacity	1749 cc (1.8 litre)
Engine code*	6FZ (EW7J4)
Bore	82.7 mm
Stroke	81.4 mm
Direction of crankshaft rotation	Clockwise (viewed from the right-hand side of vehicle)
No 1 cylinder location	At the transmission end of block
Compression ratio	10.8 : 1

The engine code is stamped onto the right-hand front face of the cylinder block, adjacent to the engine mounting bracket

Camshafts

Drive	Toothed belt
No of bearings	5

Camshaft bearing journal diameter (nominal):
No 1 (transmission end)	28.0 – 0.020; – 0.041 mm
No 2	28.5 – 0.020; – 0.041 mm
No 3	29.0 – 0.020; – 0.041 mm
No 4	29.5 – 0.020; – 0.041 mm
No 5	30.0 – 0.020; – 0.041 mm

Cylinder head bearing journal diameter (nominal):
No 1 (transmission end)	28.0 – 0; + 0.033 mm
No 2	28.5 – 0; + 0.033 mm
No 3	29.0 – 0; + 0.033 mm
No 4	29.5 – 0; + 0.033 mm
No 5	30.0 – 0; + 0.033 mm

Lubrication system

Oil pump type	Rotor-type, driven directly off the crankshaft
Minimum oil pressure at 90°C	6.3 bars at 4000 rpm

Torque wrench settings

	Nm	lbf ft
Ancillary components mounting bracket	19	14
Auxiliary drivebelt tensioner pulley bolt	20	15
Auxiliary drivebelt idler pulley	37	27
Big-end bearing cap bolts*:		
Stage 1	10	7
Stage 2	Slacken by 180°	
Stage 3	23	17
Stage 4	Angle-tighten a further 46°	
Camshaft bearing cap housing bolts:		
Stage 1	5	4
Stage 2	10	7
Camshaft sprocket retaining bolt:		
Stage 1	30	22
Stage 2	75	55
Crankshaft bearing cap housing:		
Stage 1:		
M11 bolts	10	7
M6 bolts	2	1
Stage 2:		
M11 bolts	Fully slacken	
Stage 3:		
M11 bolts	20	15
Stage 4:		
M11 bolts	Angle-tighten a further 70°	
Stage 5:		
M6 bolts	10	7
Crankshaft pulley-to-sprocket retaining bolts:		
Stage 1	15	11
Stage 2	20	15
Crankshaft sprocket centre bolt:		
Stage 1	40	30
Stage 2	Angle-tighten a further 53°	
Cylinder head bolts:		
Stage 1	15	11
Stage 2	50	37
Stage 3	Slacken by 360° then tighten to:	
Stage 4	20	15
Stage 5	Angle-tighten a further 285°	
Cylinder head cover bolts:		
Stage 1	5	4
Stage 2	11	8
Engine-to-transmission fixing bolts	50	37
Engine/transmission left-hand mounting:		
Mounting bracket-to-body bolts	22	16
Mounting bracket-to-transmission bolts	60	44
Rubber mounting centre nut	65	48
Rubber mounting-to-bracket nuts	22	16
Engine/transmission rear mounting:		
Connecting link-to-mounting bracket bolt	55	41
Connecting link-to-subframe bolt	55	41
Mounting bracket-to-cylinder block bolts	45	33
Engine/transmission right-hand mounting:		
Rubber mounting centre nut	45	33
Rubber mounting-to-body	22	16
Upper mounting bracket-to-lower (engine) bracket nuts	61	45
Flywheel retaining bolts*:		
Stage 1	25	18
Stage 2	Fully slacken then tighten to:	
Stage 3	8	6
Stage 4	20	15
Stage 5	Angle-tighten a further 21°	
Oil pump retaining bolts	8	6
Sump retaining bolts	8	6
Timing belt idler pulley bolt	37	27
Timing belt tensioner pulley bolt	20	15

*New nuts/bolts must be used.

1 General information

Using this Chapter

This Part of Chapter 2 is devoted to in-car repair procedures for the EW series petrol engine. Similar information covering the TU series petrol engine, and the diesel engine will be found in Chapters 2A and 2C. All procedures concerning engine removal and refitting, and engine block/cylinder head overhaul for petrol and diesel engines can be found in Chapters 2D and 2E as applicable.

Most of the operations included in Chapter 2B are based on the assumption that the engine is still installed in the car. Therefore, if this information is being used during a complete engine overhaul, with the engine already removed, many of the steps included here will not apply.

EW series engine description

The EW series engine is of the DOHC 16-valve, in-line four-cylinder type, mounted transversely at the front of the car with the clutch and transmission attached to its left-hand end.

The aluminium alloy cylinder block/crank-case is of modular construction consisting of three sections – the cylinder block itself, the crankshaft bearing cap housing and the sump. The cylinder block incorporates four cast iron dry cylinder liners which are cast into the block and cannot be renewed.

The crankshaft is supported in five shell-type main bearings with thrustwashers fitted to No 2 main bearing, to control crankshaft endfloat.

The connecting rods are attached to the crankshaft by horizontally-split shell-type big-end bearings, and to the pistons by gudgeon pins which are an interference fit in the connecting rod small-end eyes. The aluminium alloy pistons are of the slipper type, and are fitted with three piston rings – two compression rings and a scraper-type oil control ring.

The cylinder head is of the crossflow type, the inlet ports being at the front of the engine and the exhaust ports at the rear. The camshafts run in plain bearings integral with the cylinder head and with the two camshaft bearing cap housings. The inlet and exhaust valves are each closed by single coil springs, and operate in guides pressed into the cylinder head. Valve actuation is by self-adjusting hydraulic tappets acted upon directly by the camshaft lobes.

Drive to the camshafts is by a toothed timing belt and sprockets and incorporating an automatic tensioning mechanism. The timing belt also drives the coolant pump. All accessories are driven from the crankshaft pulley by a single multi-ribbed auxiliary drivebelt.

The lubrication system is of the full-flow, pressure-feed type. Oil is drawn from the sump by a rotor type pump, driven directly from the front of the crankshaft. The pump draws oil through a strainer located in the sump and then forces it through an externally-mounted filter into galleries in the cylinder block. From there, the oil is distributed to the crankshaft (main bearings) and camshafts. The big-end bearings are supplied with oil via internal drillings in the crankshaft; the camshaft bearings also receive a pressurised supply. The camshaft lobes and valves are lubricated by splash, as are all other engine components.

Throughout this manual, it is often necessary to identify the engines not only by their capacity, but also by their engine code which is incorporated in the engine number. This can be found stamped onto the right-hand front face of the cylinder block, adjacent to the engine mounting bracket. The first part of the engine number gives the engine code – eg, 6FZ.

Repair operations possible with the engine in the vehicle

The following work can be carried out with the engine in the vehicle:
a) Compression pressure – testing.
b) Cylinder head covers – removal and refitting.
c) Crankshaft pulley – removal and refitting.
d) Timing belt covers – removal and refitting.
e) Timing belt – removal, refitting and adjustment.
f) Timing belt tensioner and sprockets – removal and refitting.
g) Camshaft oil seals – renewal.
h) Camshafts and tappets – removal, inspection and refitting.
i) Cylinder head – removal and refitting.
j) Cylinder head and pistons – decarbonising.
k) Sump – removal and refitting.
l) Crankshaft oil seals – renewal.
m) Engine/transmission mountings – inspection and renewal.
n) Flywheel – removal, inspection and refitting.

2 Compression test – description and interpretation

Refer to Chapter 2A, Section 2.

3 Engine assembly/ valve timing holes – general information and usage

Note 1: *The following procedure entails the use of Citroën special tool (-).0189.B (camshaft setting rods). If the Citroën tool is not available, details for fabricating suitable alternatives are given in the text.*

Note 2: *Do not attempt to rotate the engine whilst the crankshaft/camshafts are locked in position. If the engine is to be left in this state for a long period of time, it is a good idea to place suitable warning notices inside the vehicle, and in the engine compartment. This will reduce the possibility of the engine being accidentally cranked on the starter motor, which is likely to cause damage with the locking pins in place.*

1 Timing holes are drilled in the crankshaft sprocket end plate and in the two camshaft sprockets. The holes are used to ensure that the crankshaft and camshafts are correctly positioned when assembling the engine (to prevent the possibility of the valves contacting the pistons when refitting the cylinder head), or refitting the timing belt. When the timing holes are aligned with corresponding holes in the cylinder head and oil pump housing, suitable diameter pins or bolts can be inserted to lock both the camshafts and crankshaft in position, preventing them from rotating. To set the engine in the timing position, proceed as follows.

2 Remove the crankshaft pulley as described in Section 5.

3 Remove the timing belt upper (outer) and lower covers as described in Section 6.

4 Using a socket and extension bar fitted to the crankshaft sprocket centre bolt, turn the crankshaft in the normal direction of rotation until the timing holes in both camshaft sprockets are aligned with their corresponding holes in the cylinder head. The holes are aligned when the inlet camshaft sprocket hole is in approximately the 5 o'clock position and the exhaust camshaft sprocket hole is in approximately the 7 o'clock position, when viewed from the right-hand end of the engine. Use a small mirror to accurately observe the position of the holes.

5 With the camshaft sprocket holes correctly positioned, insert an 8.0 mm diameter drill bit or bolt through the timing hole in the crankshaft sprocket end plate, and locate it in the corresponding hole in the oil pump housing **(see illustration)**.

6 The camshaft sprockets can now be locked

3.5 8.0 mm diameter drill bit inserted through the crankshaft sprocket end plate timing hole, and engaged in the corresponding hole in the oil pump housing

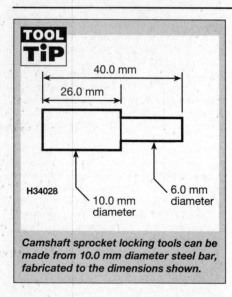

TOOL TiP

H34028

40.0 mm
26.0 mm
10.0 mm diameter
6.0 mm diameter

Camshaft sprocket locking tools can be made from 10.0 mm diameter steel bar, fabricated to the dimensions shown.

in position using the Citroën camshaft setting rods, or suitable home-made alternatives (**see Tool Tip**). With the crankshaft locked in position, insert the Citroën special tools, or alternatives, through the timing hole in each camshaft sprocket and locate it in the corresponding hole in the cylinder head (**see illustration**).

7 The crankshaft and camshafts are now locked in position, preventing rotation. In this position the crankshaft is at 90° BTDC and all the pistons are positioned half way down their cylinder bores.

3.6 Camshaft sprocket locking tools inserted through the timing hole in each sprocket

4 Cylinder head covers – removal and refitting

Removal

1 Disconnect the battery negative terminal (refer to *Disconnecting the battery* in the Reference Chapter).
2 Undo the six screws and lift off the engine cover.
3 Disconnect the crankcase breather hose at the quick-fit connector on the rear cylinder head cover (**see illustration**).
4 Disconnect the wiring connector at the camshaft position sensor, then undo the bolt and remove the sensor from the rear cylinder head cover (**see illustrations**).

5 Working in the reverse sequence to that shown in illustration 4.10, progressively slacken, then remove the eleven retaining bolts from each cylinder head cover.
6 Lift off each cover in turn and remove it (**see illustrations**). The cover seal should remain attached as the cover is removed – do not try to remove it, unless it is obviously damaged.

Refitting

7 Clean the cylinder head and cylinder head cover mating surfaces, and remove all traces of oil.
8 Check the condition of the rubber seal attached to each cover. The seal is designed to be re-usable, and so should not automatically be renewed unless its condition is suspect. If renewal is necessary, locate the seal in the cover groove, ensuring that it is fully seated along its entire length (**see illustration**).
9 Carefully refit the cylinder head cover(s) to the engine.
10 Refit the cover retaining bolts and, working in the sequence shown, tighten them to the specified torque in the two Stages given in the Specifications (**see illustration**).
11 Check the condition of the O-ring seal on the camshaft position sensor and renew the seal if it is in any way suspect.
12 Refit the camshaft position sensor and secure with the retaining bolt. Reconnect the sensor wiring connector.

4.3 Disconnect the crankcase breather hose from the rear cylinder head cover

4.4a Disconnect the camshaft position sensor wiring connector . . .

4.4b . . . then undo the bolt and remove the sensor from the rear cylinder head cover

4.6a Undo the retaining bolts and lift off the front . . .

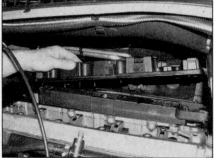

4.6b . . . and rear cylinder head covers

4.8 Locate the cylinder head cover seal in the groove, ensuring that it is fully seated along its entire length

4.10 Cylinder head cover bolt tightening sequence (rear cover shown)

13 Reconnect the breather hoses to the rear cover.
14 Refit the engine cover then reconnect the battery negative terminal.

5 Crankshaft pulley – removal and refitting

Removal

1 Remove the auxiliary drivebelt as described in Chapter 1A.
2 Undo the four crankshaft pulley retaining

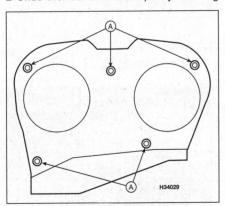

6.2a Undo the upper timing belt cover retaining bolts (A) . . .

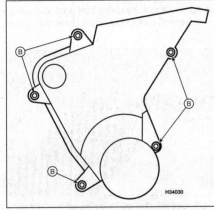

6.5 Undo the lower timing belt cover retaining bolts (B) . . .

5.2a Undo the four crankshaft pulley retaining bolts . . .

bolts and remove the pulley from the crank-shaft sprocket end plate **(see illustrations)**.

Refitting

3 Locate the pulley on the crankshaft sprocket end plate, refit the four retaining bolts and tighten them to the specified torque.
4 Refit and tension the auxiliary drivebelt as described in Chapter 1A.

6 Timing belt covers – removal and refitting

Removal

Upper (outer) cover

1 Release the retaining clip, and free the fuel inlet hose from the rear of the upper (outer) cover.

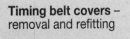

6.6 . . . and manipulate the cover up and out from between the engine and bulkhead

5.2b . . . and remove the pulley from the crankshaft sprocket end plate

2 Using a suitable Allen key, undo the five retaining bolts and withdraw the cover from the cylinder head **(see illustrations)**.

Lower cover

3 Remove the upper (outer) cover as described previously.
4 Remove the crankshaft pulley as described in Section 5.
5 Undo the five cover retaining bolts and release the cover from the locating dowels **(see illustration)**.
6 Manipulate the cover clear of the crankshaft sprocket then twist it round so that it can be withdrawn upwards from between the engine and bulkhead **(see illustration)**. Clearance is extremely limited and considerable patience will be needed.

Upper (inner) cover

7 Remove the timing belt as described in Section 7.
8 Remove both camshaft sprockets as described in Section 8.
9 Undo the five bolts securing the cover to the cylinder head and remove the cover from the engine **(see illustration)**.

Refitting

10 Refitting is a reversal of the relevant removal procedure, ensuring that each cover section is correctly located, and that the cover retaining bolts are securely tightened. When refitting the upper (inner) cover, apply thread locking compound to the retaining bolts.

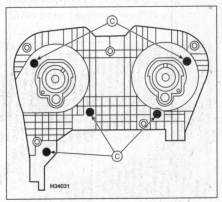

6.9 Upper (inner) timing belt cover retaining bolts (C)

7.8 Using an Allen key in the hole (arrowed) on the tensioner pulley, rotate the pulley clockwise to relieve the tension from the timing belt

11 Refit the camshaft sprockets and timing belt as described in Sections 8 and 7 after refitting the upper (inner) cover.
12 Refit the crankshaft pulley as described in Section 5 after refitting the lower cover.

7 Timing belt – general information, removal and refitting

Note: *The following procedure entails the use of Citroën special tool 6310-T to prevent the crankshaft rotating when the sprocket retaining bolt is slackened and tightened. If the Citroën tool is not available, details for fabricating a suitable alternative are given in the text.*

General information

1 The timing belt drives the camshafts and coolant pump from a toothed sprocket on the right-hand end of the crankshaft. If the belt breaks or slips in service, the pistons are likely to hit the valve heads, resulting in extensive (and expensive) damage.
2 The timing belt should be renewed at the specified intervals (see Chapter 1A), or earlier if it is contaminated with oil or if it is at all noisy in operation (a 'scraping' noise due to uneven wear).
3 If the timing belt is being removed, it is a wise precaution to check the condition of the coolant pump at the same time (check for signs of coolant leakage). This may avoid the need to remove the timing belt again at a later stage, should the coolant pump fail.
4 The crankshaft sprocket is a two-piece

7.14a Retain the belt on the crankshaft sprocket and feed it over the idler pulley . . .

7.9 With the tensioner released, slip the timing belt off the sprockets and pulleys

assembly consisting of the toothed sprocket itself and an outer end plate. The end plate is locked to the crankshaft by means of a conventional Woodruff key. When the sprocket retaining bolt is slackened, the sprocket is free to turn on the crankshaft within the limits afforded by an additional keyway within the end plate. When the sprocket retaining bolt is tightened the complete assembly is locked to the crankshaft. This arrangement allows accurate tensioning of the timing belt when refitting, provided that the procedures contained in this Section are strictly adhered to.

Removal

5 Disconnect the battery negative terminal (refer to *Disconnecting the battery* in the Reference Chapter).
6 Remove the upper (outer) and lower timing belt covers as described in Section 6.
7 Align the engine assembly/valve timing holes as described in Section 3, and lock the crankshaft sprocket and camshaft sprockets in position. *Do not* attempt to rotate the engine whilst the locking tools are in position.
8 Loosen the timing belt tensioner pulley retaining bolt. Using an Allen key in the hole provided on the front of the pulley, rotate the pulley in a clockwise direction, to relieve the tension from the timing belt **(see illustration)**. Retighten the tensioner pulley retaining bolt to secure it in the slackened position.
9 If the timing belt is to be re-used, use white paint or chalk to mark the direction of rotation on the belt (if markings do not already exist), then slip the belt off the sprockets and pulleys

7.14b . . . inlet camshaft sprocket . . .

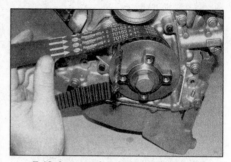

7.13 Locate the timing belt on the crankshaft sprocket, with the arrows on the belt pointing in the direction of rotation

(see illustration). Note that the crankshaft must not be rotated whilst the belt is removed.
10 Check the timing belt carefully for any signs of uneven wear, splitting, or oil contamination. Pay particular attention to the roots of the teeth. Renew it if there is the slightest doubt about its condition. If the engine is undergoing an overhaul, it is advisable to renew the belt as a matter of course, regardless of its apparent condition. The cost of a new belt is nothing compared with the cost of repairs, should the belt break in service. If signs of oil contamination are found, trace the source of the oil leak and rectify it. Wash down the engine timing belt area and all related components, to remove all traces of oil.

Refitting

11 Before refitting, thoroughly clean the timing belt sprockets. Check that the tensioner and idler pulleys rotate freely, without any sign of roughness. If necessary, renew the relevant pulley as described in Section 8.
12 Ensure that the crankshaft and camshaft sprocket locking tools are still in position.
13 Locate the timing belt on the crankshaft sprocket, ensuring that any arrows on the belt are pointing in the direction of rotation (clockwise when viewed from the right-hand end of the engine) **(see illustration)**.
14 Retain the timing belt on the crankshaft sprocket then, keeping it taut, feed the belt over the remaining sprockets and pulleys in the following order **(see illustrations)**:
    a) Idler pulley.

7.14c exhaust camshaft sprocket . . .

7.14d ... coolant pump and tensioner pulley

7.16a Using an Allen key, turn the tensioner pulley anti-clockwise ...

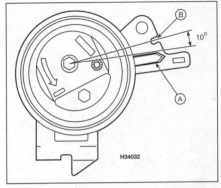

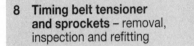

7.16b ... until the upper edge of the index pointer (A) is positioned approximately 10° past the slot (B) in the backing plate

b) Inlet camshaft.
c) Exhaust camshaft.
d) Coolant pump.
e) Tensioner pulley.

15 Remove the locking tool from the exhaust camshaft sprocket.

16 Slacken the tensioner pulley retaining bolt and turn the tensioner pulley anti-clockwise, by means of the Allen key, so that the upper edge of the index pointer is positioned approximately 10° past the slot in the backing plate **(see illustrations)**. Note that if the index pointer will not attain a position of at least 10° past the backing plate slot, then the tensioner pulley, or both the tensioner pulley and the timing belt must be renewed.

17 Now rotate the tensioner pulley clockwise until the index pointer is exactly aligned with the slot in the backing plate **(see illustration)**. Hold the pulley in this position and tighten the retaining bolt to the specified torque. With the timing belt tensioned and the tensioner pulley retaining bolt tightened, the Allen key slot in the pulley should be below the cylinder head gasket level. If this is not the case, then the tensioner pulley, or both the tensioner pulley and the timing belt must be renewed.

18 Remove the remaining camshaft and crankshaft locking tools and rotate the crankshaft through ten complete rotations in a clockwise direction (viewed from the right-hand end of the engine). Realign the engine assembly/valve timing holes and refit the inlet camshaft sprocket locking tool.

19 Check that the tensioner pulley index

pointer is still aligned with the slot in the backing plate. If not repeat the tensioning operation from paragraph 16 onward.

20 With the inlet camshaft sprocket locking tool in place, it should now also be possible to fit the crankshaft sprocket locking tool. If so, continue with the refitting procedure from paragraph 24 onward. If the crankshaft sprocket locking tool will not engage, then the crankshaft sprocket end plate must be repositioned as follows.

21 Slacken the crankshaft sprocket retaining bolt while holding the sprocket end plate stationary using Citroën special tool 6310-T or a suitable home-made alternative (see **Tool Tip** in Section 8). *Do not* attempt to use only the sprocket locking tools inserted in the engine assembly/valve timing holes to prevent rotation whilst the bolt is slackened.

22 With the sprocket retaining bolt slackened, turn the end plate until the sprocket locking tool can be fully inserted through the end plate and into the hole in the oil pump housing.

23 Hold the end plate with the holding tool and tighten the sprocket retaining bolt to the specified torque, then through the specified angle **(see illustrations)**.

24 Remove the camshaft and crankshaft locking tools and refit the lower and upper (outer) timing belt covers as described in Section 6.

25 Refit the crankshaft pulley as described in Section 5.

8 Timing belt tensioner and sprockets – removal, inspection and refitting

Removal

Note: The following procedures entail the use of certain Citroën special tools. If the Citroën tools are not available, details for fabricating suitable alternative are given in the text.

Camshaft sprockets

1 Remove the timing belt as described in Section 7.

2 The camshafts must now be prevented from rotating to allow the sprocket retaining bolts to be slackened. If working on the exhaust camshaft sprocket, it will be necessary to remove the rear cylinder head cover (see Section 4) to allow a spanner to be engaged with a square section of the camshaft, provided for this purpose. This is because the sprocket contains a rubber vibration damper incorporated into the sprocket hub. If the sprocket itself is held as the bolt is slackened, the rubber hub will be damaged. The inlet camshaft sprocket is conventional and can be held using Citroën tool 6016-T, or an acceptable substitute can be fabricated at home **(see Tool Tip)**.

7.17 Now rotate the pulley clockwise until the index pointer is exactly aligned with the slot in the backing plate

7.23a Hold the crankshaft sprocket end plate with the holding tool and tighten the retaining bolt to the specified torque ...

7.23b ... then through the specified angle

8.3 The camshafts can be held with a spanner engaged with the square section adjacent to No 8 cam lobe

8.4a Remove the previously slackened sprocket retaining bolt and washer . . .

HAYNES HINT

To make a sprocket holding tool, obtain two lengths of steel strip about 6 mm thick by about 30 mm wide or similar, one 600 mm long, the other 200 mm long (all dimensions approximate). Bolt the two strips together to form a forked end, leaving the bolt slack so that the shorter strip can pivot freely. At the other end of each 'prong' of the fork, drill a suitable hole and fit a nut and bolt to engage with the spokes or holes in the sprocket. The same tool can be used to hold both the camshaft sprocket and crankshaft sprocket.

Alternatively, remove the front cylinder head cover and hold the camshaft with a spanner as described for the exhaust camshaft. *Do not* attempt to use the engine assembly/valve timing hole locking tools to prevent the sprockets from rotating whilst the bolts are slackened.

8.4b . . . and withdraw the relevant sprocket from the end of the camshaft

3 Remove the engine assembly/valve timing hole locking tool from the relevant sprocket, then slacken the centre retaining bolt. If a spanner is being used to prevent camshaft rotation, the spanner should be engaged with

8.6 Hold the crankshaft sprocket end plate with the home-made tool while the retaining bolt is slackened

the square section of the camshaft adjacent to No 8 cam lobe **(see illustration)**.
4 Remove the previously slackened sprocket retaining bolt and washer, and withdraw the relevant sprocket from the end of the camshaft **(see illustrations)**.

Crankshaft sprocket

5 Remove the timing belt as described in Section 7.
6 Remove the crankshaft sprocket locking tool and slacken the crankshaft sprocket retaining bolt. Prevent the crankshaft from turning while the bolt is slackened using Citroën special tool 6310-T or a suitable home-made alternative, such as that described in the previous sub-Section, bolted to the sprocket end plate **(see illustration)**. *Do not* attempt to use only the sprocket locking tools inserted in the engine assembly/valve timing holes to prevent rotation whilst the bolt is slackened.
7 Unscrew the retaining bolt and slide the sprocket end plate and the sprocket itself off the end of the crankshaft. If loose, remove the Woodruff key from the crankshaft, and store it with the sprocket components for safe-keeping **(see illustrations)**.
8 Examine the crankshaft oil seal for signs of oil leakage and, if necessary, renew it as described in Section 13.

Tensioner and idler pulleys

9 Remove the timing belt as described in Section 7.
10 Undo the tensioner and idler pulley retaining bolts and remove the relevant pulley from the engine **(see illustrations)**.

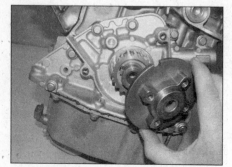

8.7a Withdraw the crankshaft sprocket end plate . . .

8.7b . . . the sprocket itself . . .

8.7c . . . and the Woodruff key from the end of the crankshaft

8.10a Removing the timing belt tensioner pulley . . .

8.10b . . . and idler pulley

Inspection

11 Clean the camshaft/crankshaft sprockets thoroughly, and renew any that show signs of wear, damage or cracks. Check the condition of the rubber vibration damper in the exhaust camshaft sprocket and renew the sprocket if there is any sign of deterioration of the rubber.
12 Clean the tensioner/idler pulleys, but do not use any strong solvent which may enter the pulley bearings. Check that the pulleys rotate freely, with no sign of stiffness or free play. Renew them if there is any doubt about their condition, or if there are any obvious signs of wear or damage.

Refitting

Camshaft sprockets

13 Locate the relevant sprocket on the end of the camshaft, engaging the lug in the sprocket hub with the slot in the end of the camshaft.
14 Refit the sprocket retaining bolt and washer, and tighten it to the specified torque. Prevent the sprocket from turning as the bolt is tightened using the method employed for removal.
15 Realign the hole in the camshaft sprocket with the corresponding hole in the cylinder head, and refit the locking tool. Check that the crankshaft pulley locking tool is still in position.
16 Where removed, refit the cylinder head cover(s) as described in Section 4.
17 Refit and tension the timing belt as described in Section 7.

Crankshaft sprocket

18 Refit the Woodruff key (if removed) to its slot in the crankshaft end.
19 Slide on the crankshaft sprocket followed by the sprocket end plate, then refit the retaining bolt.
20 Hold the end plate with the holding tool and tighten the sprocket retaining bolt to the specified torque, then through the specified angle.
21 Realign the hole in the sprocket end plate with the corresponding hole in the oil pump housing, and refit the locking tool. Check that the camshaft sprocket locking tools are still in position.
22 Refit and tension the timing belt as described in Section 7.

Tensioner and idler pulleys

23 Refit the tensioner and idler pulleys, ensuring that the slot on the tensioner pulley body correctly engages with the projecting web on the cylinder block **(see illustration)**.
24 Secure the pulleys with the retaining bolts tightened to the specified torque.
25 Refit and tension the timing belt as described in Section 7.

9 Camshaft oil seal(s) – renewal

1 Remove the timing belt as described in Section 7.
2 Remove the camshaft sprocket(s) as described in Section 8.
3 Punch or drill a small hole in the face of the oil seal. Screw a self-tapping screw into the hole, and pull on the screw with pliers to extract the seal **(see illustration)**.
4 Clean the seal housing, and polish off any burrs or raised edges, which may have caused the seal to fail in the first place.
5 Lubricate the lips of the new seal with clean engine oil, and locate it in position with the seal lips facing inwards **(see illustration)**.
6 Using a block of wood, tap the seal into place initially, then finish using a suitable drift until the seal is fully seated **(see illustrations)**. Take care not to damage the seal lips during fitting.
7 Refit the camshaft sprocket(s) as described in Section 8.

9.3 Using pliers and a self-tapping screw to extract the inlet camshaft oil seal

9.6a Using a block of wood, tap the new seal into place initially . . .

8.23 Ensure that the slot (arrowed) on the tensioner pulley body engages with the web on the cylinder block when refitting

8 Refit and tension the timing belt as described in Section 7.

10 Camshafts and tappets – removal, inspection and refitting

Removal

1 Disconnect the battery negative terminal (refer to *Disconnecting the battery* in the Reference Chapter).
2 Remove both cylinder head covers as described in Section 4.
3 Refer to Section 8 and remove both camshaft sprockets.
4 Remove the timing belt upper (inner) cover as described in Section 6.
5 Progressively slacken, by a few turns at a

9.5 Locate the new seal in position with the seal lips facing inwards

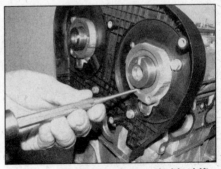

9.6b . . . then finish using a suitable drift until the seal is fully seated

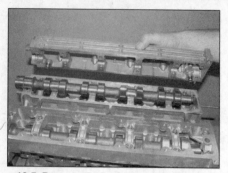

10.5 Progressively slacken and remove the retaining bolts, then lift off camshaft bearing cap housing(s)

10.7 Carefully lift the camshaft(s) up and out of their locations

10.8 Use a rubber sucker to withdraw the hydraulic tappets

time, the twelve bolts securing each camshaft bearing cap housing to the cylinder head. Release the bearing cap housings from their dowels and cylinder head locations. When each housing is free, remove the bolts completely, and lift off the housings **(see illustration)**.

6 As both camshafts are visually identical, suitably mark them inlet and exhaust, or front and rear before removal.

7 Tilt the camshafts by pressing them down at their transmission end to release the centralising bearing at the timing belt end. Carefully lift the camshafts up and out of their locations and slide the oil seal off each camshaft end **(see illustration)**.

8 Obtain sixteen small, clean plastic containers, and number them inlet 1 to 8 and exhaust 1 to 8; alternatively, divide a larger container into sixteen compartments and

number each compartment accordingly. Using a rubber sucker, withdraw each hydraulic tappet in turn, and place it in its respective container **(see illustration)**. Do not interchange the tappets, or the rate of wear will be much increased.

Inspection

9 Thoroughly clean the sealant from the mating surfaces of the cylinder head and bearing cap housings. Use a suitable liquid gasket dissolving agent (available from Citroën dealers) together with a soft putty knife; do not use a metal scraper or the faces will be damaged. As there is no conventional gasket used, the cleanliness of the mating faces is of the utmost importance.

10 Examine the camshaft bearing surfaces and cam lobes for signs of wear ridges and scoring. Renew the camshaft if any of these

conditions are apparent. Examine the condition of the bearing surfaces, both on the camshaft journals and in the cylinder head/bearing cap housings. If the head bearing surfaces are worn excessively, the cylinder head will need to be renewed. If suitable measuring equipment is available, camshaft bearing journal wear can be checked by direct measurement, noting that No 1 journal is at the transmission end of the head.

11 Examine the hydraulic tappet bearing surfaces which contact the camshaft lobes for wear ridges and scoring. Renew any tappet on which these conditions are apparent. If a tappet bearing surface is badly scored, also examine the corresponding lobe on the camshaft for wear, as it is likely that both will be worn. Renew worn components as necessary.

Refitting

12 Prior to refitting, remove all traces of oil from the bearing cap housing retaining bolt holes in the cylinder head, using a clean rag. Also ensure that both the cylinder head and bearing cap housing mating faces are clean and free from oil.

13 Liberally oil the cylinder head hydraulic tappet bores and the tappets. Carefully refit the tappets to the cylinder head, ensuring that each tappet is refitted to its original bore **(see illustrations)**. Some care will be required to enter the tappets squarely into their bores. Check that each tappet rotates freely in its bore.

14 Ensure that the four locating dowels are in position, one at each corner of the cylinder head.

15 Apply a bead of anaerobic jointing compound around the perimeter of the cylinder head mating faces **(see illustration)**.

16 Liberally oil the camshaft bearings in the cylinder head and the camshaft lobes, then lay the camshafts in the cylinder head, ensuring that they are in their correct locations **(see illustration)**. Turn the camshafts so that the cam lobes are in the best position to facilitate the seating of the bearing cap housings.

17 Liberally oil the camshaft bearings and carefully locate the bearing cap housings over

10.13a Lubricate the hydraulic tappet bores and the tappets . . .

10.13b . . . then refit the tappets ensuring that each is refitted to its original bore

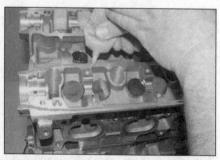

10.15 Apply a bead of anaerobic jointing compound around the perimeter of the cylinder head mating faces

10.16 Liberally oil the camshaft bearings and lobes, then lay the camshafts in the cylinder head

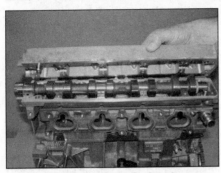

10.17 Carefully locate the bearing cap housings over the camshafts

the camshafts **(see illustration)**. Refit the retaining bolts and progressively tighten them finger tight only at this stage.

18 Working in the order shown, progressively tighten the bearing cap housing retaining bolts to the Stage 1 torque setting then to the Stage 2 setting **(see illustration)**.

19 Refit the timing belt upper (inner) cover as described in Section 6.

20 Fit a new oil seal to each camshaft, using the information given in Section 9, then refit the camshaft sprockets as described in Section 8.

21 Refit the cylinder head covers as described in Section 4.

11 Cylinder head –
removal and refitting

Removal

1 Disconnect the battery negative terminal (refer to *Disconnecting the battery* in the Reference Chapter).

2 Drain the cooling system as described in Chapter 1A.

3 Remove the timing belt as described in Section 7.

4 Remove the cylinder head covers as described in Section 4.

5 Remove the air cleaner assembly and intake ducting as described in Chapter 4A.

6 Remove the inlet manifold as described in Chapter 4A.

7 Working as described in Chapter 4A,

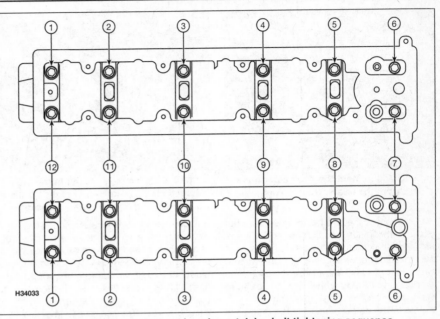

10.18 Camshaft bearing cap housing retaining bolt tightening sequence

disconnect the catalytic converter from the exhaust manifold. Where necessary, disconnect or release the lambda sensor wiring, so that it is not strained by the weight of the exhaust.

8 Disconnect the radiator hoses from the coolant outlet housing and thermostat cover.

9 Disconnect the air inlet hose from the secondary air injection valve at the left-hand end of the cylinder head **(see illustration)**.

10 Disconnect the wiring connector from the

left-hand end of the ignition coil unit **(see illustration)**.

11 Disconnect the wiring connectors from the EGR valve and coolant temperature sensor **(see illustrations)**.

12 Undo the nuts securing the wiring harness support bracket to the studs on the coolant outlet housing. Release any additional cable ties and clips then move the support bracket, wiring harness and hoses clear of the cylinder head **(see illustration)**.

11.9 Disconnect the air inlet hose from the secondary air injection valve

11.10 Disconnect the wiring connector from the ignition coil unit

11.11a Disconnect the wiring connectors from the EGR valve . . .

11.11b . . . and coolant temperature sensor

11.12 Undo the wiring harness support bracket nuts, release the cable ties and clips then move the bracket, wiring harness and hoses clear of the cylinder head

11.13 Disconnect the two heater hose from the heater matrix pipes

11.14 Remove the bolt and horseshoe-shaped clamp plate securing the coolant pipe to the coolant outlet housing

13 Disconnect the two heater hose from the heater matrix pipes **(see illustration)**.

14 Undo the bolt and remove the horseshoe-shaped clamp plate securing the coolant pipe to the rear of the coolant outlet housing **(see illustration)**. Withdraw the coolant pipe from the housing and recover the sealing O-ring.

15 Undo the bolt securing the lower (engine) mounting bracket to the cylinder head **(see illustration)**. Ensure that the bolt is fully unscrewed but note that there is insufficient clearance to completely remove the bolt from its location.

16 Undo the nuts securing the brake master cylinder reservoir support bracket to the body panel and move the reservoir and bracket to one side.

17 Check that all vacuum/breather hoses, pipes, and electrical connectors likely to impede removal have been disconnected from the cylinder head.

18 Working in the *reverse* of the sequence shown in illustration 11.37, progressively slacken the ten cylinder head bolts by half a turn at a time, until all bolts can be unscrewed by hand. Remove the bolts along with their washers.

19 Connect an engine hoist or suitable lifting gear to the two lifting brackets on the cylinder head.

20 Release the joint between the cylinder head and gasket using two L-shaped metal bars which fit into the cylinder head bolt holes. Using the bars, gently 'rock' the cylinder head free towards the front of the vehicle. *Do not* try to swivel the head on the

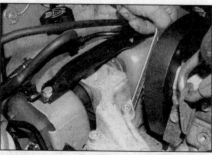

11.15 Undo the bolt securing the lower (engine) mounting bracket to the cylinder head

cylinder block as it is located by dowels.

21 When the joint is broken, obtain the help of an assistant and slowly raise the hoist to lift the cylinder head off the block **(see illustration)**. At the same time, support the head at the rear as it will tend to tip backwards due to the offset position of the lifting brackets. Take care as the head is lifted as it is very easy to break the lower rear projecting corner of the upper (inner) timing belt cover. Try to keep the head as level as possible until it is raised sufficiently to clear the cylinder block.

22 During removal, check that the camshaft oil supply non-return valve (located in the underside of the cylinder head at the timing belt end) does not drop out; it is easily lost if it does.

23 When sufficient clearance exists, move the hoist forward, raise it further and lift the cylinder head out of the engine compartment.

24 Remove the gasket from the top of the block, noting the two locating dowels. If the locating dowels are a loose fit, remove them and store them with the head for safe-keeping. Do not discard the gasket; it may be needed for identification purposes.

25 If the cylinder head is to be dismantled for overhaul, refer to Part D of this Chapter.

Preparation for refitting

26 The mating faces of the cylinder head and cylinder block must be perfectly clean before refitting the head. Citroën recommend the use of a scouring agent for this purpose, but acceptable results can be achieved by using a

11.21 Removing the cylinder head from the block

hard plastic or wood scraper to remove all traces of gasket and carbon. The same method can also be used to clean the piston crowns. Take particular care to avoid scoring or gouging the cylinder head/cylinder block mating surfaces during the cleaning operations, as aluminium alloy is easily damaged. Make sure that the carbon is not allowed to enter the oil and water passages – this is particularly important for the lubrication system, as carbon could block the oil supply to the engine's components. Using adhesive tape and paper, seal the water, oil and bolt holes in the cylinder block. To prevent carbon entering the gap between the pistons and bores, smear a little grease in the gap. After cleaning each piston, use a small brush to remove all traces of grease and carbon from the gap, then wipe away the remainder with a clean rag.

27 Check the mating surfaces of the cylinder block and the cylinder head for nicks, deep scratches and other damage. If slight, they may be removed carefully with a file, but if excessive, machining may be the only alternative to renewal. If warpage of the cylinder head gasket surface is suspected, use a straight-edge to check it for distortion. Refer to Part D of this Chapter if necessary.

28 Thoroughly clean the threads of the cylinder head bolt holes in the cylinder block. Ensure that the bolts run freely in their threads, and that all traces of oil and water are removed from each bolt hole.

29 When purchasing a new cylinder head gasket, it is essential that a gasket of the correct thickness is obtained. At the time of writing, there are two different thicknesses available – the standard gasket which is fitted at the factory, and a slightly thicker 'repair' gasket (+ 0.3 mm), for use once the head gasket face has been machined. If the cylinder head has been machined, it should be marked '-0.3' on the upper corner, on the inlet manifold side, at the timing belt end. Note that modifications to the cylinder head gasket material, type, and manufacturer are constantly taking place; seek the advice of a Citroën dealer as to the latest recommendations.

30 Check the condition of the cylinder head bolts, and particularly their threads, whenever they are removed. Wash the bolts in a suitable solvent, and wipe them dry. Check each bolt for any sign of visible wear or damage, renewing them if necessary. Measure the length of each bolt from the underside of its head to the end of the bolt **(see illustration)**. Two different lengths of cylinder head bolts may be encountered according to the date of manufacture of the engine. Early engines were fitted with bolts 127.5 mm in length, whereas on later engines the length was increased to 144.5 mm. The bolts may be re-used if their length does not exceed the following dimensions.

Early engines   129.0 mm
Later engines   147.0 mm

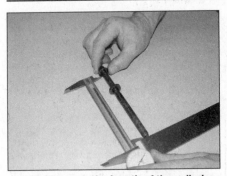

11.30 Measure the length of the cylinder head bolts from the underside of the head to the end of the bolt

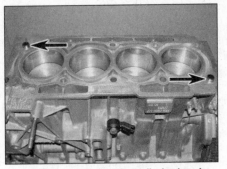

11.32a Check that the cylinder head locating dowels (arrowed) are in position in the block . . .

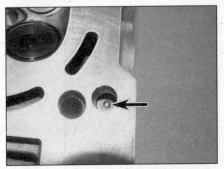

11.32b . . . and that the camshaft oil supply non-return valve (arrowed) is in place in the cylinder head

31 If any one bolt is longer than the specified length, *all* of the bolts should be renewed as a complete set. Considering the stress which the cylinder head bolts are under, it is highly recommended that they are renewed, regardless of their apparent condition.

Refitting

32 Wipe clean the mating surfaces of the cylinder head and cylinder block and check that the two locating dowels are in position at each diagonally opposite end of the block. Check also that the camshaft oil supply non-return valve is in place in the oil feed bore at the timing belt end of the cylinder head **(see illustrations)**.

33 Position a new gasket on the cylinder block surface, with the word TOP uppermost and toward the oil filter side of the block **(see illustration)**.

34 Check that the crankshaft pulley and camshaft sprockets are still locked in position with their respective locking tools. With the aid of an assistant, carefully refit the cylinder head assembly to the block, aligning it with the locating dowels.

35 Apply a smear of grease to the threads, and to the underside of the heads, of the cylinder head bolts. Citroën recommend the use of Molykote G Rapid Plus for this purpose.

36 Carefully enter each bolt and washer into its relevant hole (*do not drop it in*) and screw it in finger-tight.

37 Working in the sequence shown, tighten all the cylinder head bolts first to their Stage 1

torque setting, then to their Stage 2 torque setting using a torque wrench and a suitable socket **(see illustration)**.

38 Once all the bolts have been tightened to their Stage 2 torque setting, slacken all the head bolts by one complete turn, working in the reverse of the tightening sequence. Once the bolts are loose, and again working in the sequence shown, tighten all the bolts to the Stage 4 torque setting.

39 When all the bolts have been tightened to the Stage 4 torque setting, tighten each bolt in the sequence shown through the specified Stage 5 angle, using a socket and extension bar. It is recommended that an angle-measuring gauge is used during this stage of tightening, to ensure accuracy.

40 The remainder of the refitting procedure is a reversal of removal, noting the following points:

a) *Fit new O-ring seals to all applicable components.*

b) *Ensure that all wiring is correctly routed, and that all connectors are securely reconnected to the correct components.*

c) *Ensure that all coolant, vacuum and breather hoses are correctly reconnected, and that their retaining clips are securely tightened, where applicable.*

d) *Refit and tension the timing belt as described in Section 7.*

e) *Refit the cylinder head covers as described in Section 4.*

f) *Reconnect the catalytic converter to the exhaust manifold, refit the inlet manifold,*

air cleaner assembly and intake ducting as described in Chapter 4A.

g) *On completion, refill the cooling system as described in Chapter 1A, and reconnect the battery.*

12 Sump – removal and refitting

Removal

1 Disconnect the battery negative terminal (refer to *Disconnecting the battery* in the Reference Chapter).

2 Chock the rear wheels then jack up the front of the vehicle and support it on axle stands (see *Jacking and vehicle support*). Remove the engine undertray.

3 Drain the engine oil, then clean and refit the engine oil drain plug, tightening it securely. If the engine is nearing its service interval when the oil and filter are due for renewal, it is recommended that the filter is also removed, and a new one fitted. After reassembly, the engine can then be refilled with fresh oil. Refer to Chapter 1A for further information.

4 Withdraw the engine oil dipstick from the guide tube.

5 Undo the bolt securing the upper end of the dipstick guide tube to the ancillary components mounting bracket. Undo the bolt securing the base of the guide tube to the sump and remove the guide tube **(see illustration)**. Collect the two O-rings from the

11.33 Position the cylinder head gasket with the word TOP uppermost and toward the oil filter side of the block

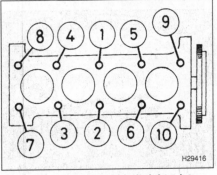

11.37 Cylinder head bolt tightening sequence

12.5 Undo the upper and lower retaining bolts and remove the dipstick guide tube

12.11a Oil pump pick-up tube retaining nuts and retaining bolt locations (arrowed)

12.11b Crankcase splash plate retaining bolt locations (arrowed)

base of the guide tube, noting that new O-rings will be required for refitting.

6 Release the retaining clamps securing the power steering fluid pipes to the sump. Move the pipes as far as possible towards the transmission and suitably retain them in this position.

7 Where fitted, disconnect the wiring connector from the oil temperature sender unit, which is screwed into the rear of the sump.

8 Undo the lower centre bolt securing the sump to the transmission bellhousing.

9 Progressively slacken and remove all the sump retaining bolts noting that there are nineteen short bolts and seven long bolts.

10 Carefully insert a putty knife or similar between the sump and cylinder block. Ease the knife along the joint to break the seal, carefully levering down at the same time. When the sump is released, lower it straight

down from its location and remove it from under the vehicle.

11 If access to the crankshaft components is required, undo the bolt and two nuts and remove the oil pump pick-up tube and gasket. Similarly, undo the four bolts and remove the crankcase splash plate **(see illustrations)**.

Refitting

12 Thoroughly clean all the removed components ensuring that all traces of sealant and gasket are removed from the mating surfaces of the sump, cylinder block, oil pump and oil pump pick-up tube, as applicable. Use a suitable liquid gasket dissolving agent (available from Citroën dealers) together with a soft putty knife; do not use a metal scraper or the faces will be damaged. As there is no conventional gasket used between the sump and cylinder block, the cleanliness of the mating faces is of the utmost importance.

13 If removed, locate the splash plate in position and secure with the four bolts securely tightened.

14 If the oil pump pick-up tube was removed, locate a new gasket over the oil pump studs then place the tube in position. Fit the retaining nuts and bolt and tighten them securely.

15 Ensure that the sump and cylinder block mating faces are clean and dry, then apply a thin bead of RTV sealant to the sump mating surface **(see illustration)**. Citroën recommend the use of Loctite Autojoint Noir for this purpose.

16 Check that the centring dowel is in place in the cylinder block then locate the sump in position. Refit the retaining bolts noting that four of the long bolts are fitted at the transmission end, and three at the timing belt end on the oil filter side of the engine **(see illustrations)**. Tighten the bolts finger tight only at this stage.

17 If the engine is in the vehicle with the transmission attached, refit the lower centre bolt securing the sump to the transmission bellhousing and tighten it sufficiently to hold the sump in contact with the bellhousing face. Tighten the sump to cylinder block retaining bolts evenly and progressively to the specified torque setting. When the sump retaining bolts have been tightened, tighten the sump to bellhousing bolt to the specified torque.

18 If the engine is out of the vehicle or the transmission has been removed, use a straight-edge to ensure that the rear faces of the cylinder block and sump are flush **(see illustration)**. Hold the sump in this position and tighten the retaining bolts evenly and progressively to the specified torque setting.

19 Lubricate the two new O-rings and locate them on the end of the dipstick guide tube. Engage the guide tube with the sump and fit the upper and lower retaining bolts. Tighten the bolts securely, then refit the dipstick.

20 Move the power steering fluid pipes back into position under the sump and secure with the retaining clamps.

21 Where fitted, reconnect the wiring connector to the oil temperature sender unit at the rear of the sump.

22 Refit the engine undertray, lower the vehicle to the ground, then refill the engine with oil as described in Chapter 1A.

12.15 Apply a thin bead of RTV sealant to the sump mating surface

12.16a Four of the long sump retaining bolts are fitted at the transmission end . . .

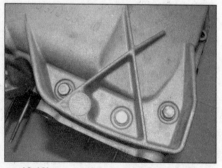

12.16b . . . and three are fitted at the timing belt end on the oil filter side

12.18 Use a straight-edge to ensure that the rear faces of the cylinder block and sump are flush

13 Crankshaft oil seals – renewal

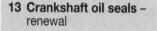

Right-hand oil seal

1 Remove the crankshaft sprocket as described in Section 8.

2 Make a note of the correct fitted depth of the seal in the oil pump housing, then punch or drill a small hole in the face of the seal. Screw a self-tapping screw into the hole and pull on the screw with pliers to extract the seal. Alternatively, the seal can be levered out of position. Use a flat-bladed screwdriver, and take great care not to damage the oil pump drive flange or seal housing.

3 Clean the seal housing, and polish off any burrs or raised edges on the pump drive flange, which may have caused the seal to fail in the first place.

4 Lubricate the lips of the new seal with clean engine oil, and carefully locate the seal over the oil pump drive flange. Note that its sealing lip must be facing inwards. Take care not to damage the seal lips during fitting.

5 Tap the seal into position, using a suitable drift, to the same depth in the housing as the original was prior to removal **(see illustration)**.

6 Wash off any traces of oil, then refit the crankshaft sprocket as described in Section 8.

Left-hand oil seal

7 Remove the flywheel as described in Section 14. Make a note of the correct fitted depth of the seal in its location.

8 Punch or drill two small holes opposite each other in the seal. Screw a self-tapping screw into each, and pull on the screws with pliers to extract the seal.

9 Clean the seal housing, and polish off any burrs or raised edges on the crankshaft, which may have caused the seal to fail in the first place.

10 The new seal will normally be supplied with a plastic fitting sleeve to protect the seal lips as the seal is fitted. If so, lubricate the fitting sleeve and locate it over the end of the crankshaft **(see illustration)**.

11 Lubricate the lips of the new seal with clean engine oil, and carefully locate the seal over the fitting sleeve and onto the end of the crankshaft **(see illustration)**.

12 Drive the seal into position, using a suitable tubular drift, to the same depth in the housing as the original was prior to removal.

13 Remove the fitting sleeve, wash off any traces of oil, then refit the flywheel as described in Section 14.

14 Flywheel –
removal, inspection and refitting

Removal

1 Remove the transmission as described in Chapter 7, then remove the clutch assembly as described in Chapter 6.

2 Prevent the flywheel from turning using a sturdy screwdriver inserted between the ring gear teeth and the cylinder block. Alternatively, bolt a strap between one of the clutch pressure plate mounting bolt holes and an adjacent hole on the cylinder block end face. *Do not* attempt to lock the flywheel in position using the crankshaft pulley locking tool described in Section 3.

3 Slacken and remove the flywheel retaining

13.5 Tap the crankshaft right-hand oil seal into position using a suitable drift

bolts, and remove the flywheel from the end of the crankshaft. Be careful not to drop it; it is heavy. If the flywheel locating dowel is a loose fit in the crankshaft end, remove it and store it with the flywheel for safe-keeping. Discard the flywheel bolts; new ones must be used on refitting.

Inspection

4 Examine the flywheel for scoring of the clutch face, and for wear or chipping of the ring gear teeth. If the clutch face is scored, the flywheel may be surface-ground, but renewal is preferable. Seek the advice of a Citroën dealer or engine reconditioning specialist to see if machining is possible. If the ring gear is worn or damaged, the flywheel must be renewed, as it is not possible to renew the ring gear separately.

Refitting

5 Clean the mating surfaces of the flywheel and crankshaft. Remove any remaining locking compound from the threads of the crankshaft holes, using the correct size of tap, if available.

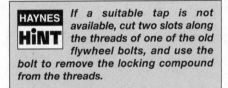

HAYNES HiNT *If a suitable tap is not available, cut two slots along the threads of one of the old flywheel bolts, and use the bolt to remove the locking compound from the threads.*

6 If the new flywheel retaining bolts are not supplied with their threads already pre-

coated, apply a suitable thread-locking compound to the threads of each bolt prior to fitting.

7 Ensure that the locating dowel is in position. Offer up the flywheel, locating it on the dowel, and fit the new retaining bolts.

8 Lock the flywheel using the method employed on removal, and tighten the retaining bolts to the specified torque and through the specified angle, in the stages given in the Specifications.

9 Refit the clutch as described in Chapter 6. Remove the flywheel locking tool, and refit the transmission as described in Chapter 7.

15 Engine/transmission
mountings –
inspection and renewal

Inspection

1 If improved access is required, firmly apply the handbrake, then jack up the front of the vehicle and support it securely on axle stands (see *Jacking and vehicle support*). Remove the engine undertray.

2 Check the mounting rubbers to see if they are cracked, hardened or separated from the metal at any point; renew the mounting if any such damage or deterioration is evident.

3 Check that all the mountings' fasteners are securely tightened; use a torque wrench to check if possible **(see illustration overleaf)**.

4 Using a large screwdriver or a crowbar, check for wear in each mounting by carefully levering against it to check for free play. Where this is not possible, enlist the aid of an assistant to move the engine/transmission back-and-forth, or from side-to-side, while you watch the mounting. While some free play is to be expected even from new components, excessive wear should be obvious. If excessive free play is found, check first that the fasteners are correctly secured, then renew any worn components as described below.

Renewal

Right-hand mounting

5 Disconnect the battery negative terminal

13.10 Lubricate the crankshaft left-hand oil seal fitting sleeve and locate it over the end of the crankshaft

13.11 Locate the oil seal over the fitting sleeve and onto the end of the crankshaft

(refer to *Disconnecting the battery* in the Reference Chapter). Release all the relevant hoses and wiring from their retaining clips, and position them clear of the mounting so that they do not hinder the removal procedure.

6 Undo the two bolts and remove the stiffener bracket located over the top of the mounting.

7 Place a jack beneath the engine, with a block of wood on the jack head. Raise the jack until it is supporting the weight of the engine.

8 Slacken and remove the three bolts, securing the upper mounting bracket to the lower (engine) bracket. Remove the single nut securing the upper bracket to the rubber mounting, and lift off the bracket.

9 Lift the rubber buffer plate off the rubber mounting stud, then remove the washer, unscrew the rubber mounting from the body, and remove it from the vehicle. A strap wrench or similar may be used to unscrew the mounting, or alternatively fabricate a tool from suitable metal tube with projections to engage in the cut-outs in the mounting.

10 Check all components carefully for signs of wear or damage, and renew them where necessary.

11 On reassembly, screw the mounting into the vehicle body, and tighten it securely.

12 Refit the rubber buffer plate to the rubber mounting stud, and install the upper mounting bracket. Tighten the retaining nuts/bolts to the specified torque setting.

13 Refit the stiffener bracket then secure all disturbed hoses and wiring in their relevant retaining clips.

14 Remove the jack from underneath the engine, and reconnect the battery negative terminal.

Left-hand mounting

15 Disconnect the battery negative terminal (refer to *Disconnecting the battery* in the Reference Chapter).

16 Remove the air cleaner assembly and intake ducting as described in Chapter 4A.

17 Lift up the covers on the battery positive cable terminal box and unscrew the nuts securing the battery cables to the terminal studs. Lift the cables off the studs and suitably label them for correct refitting.

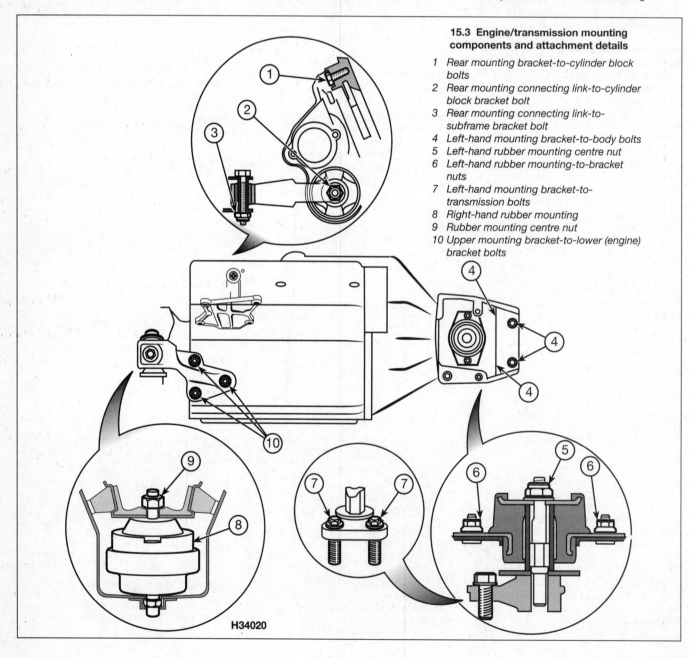

15.3 Engine/transmission mounting components and attachment details

1 *Rear mounting bracket-to-cylinder block bolts*
2 *Rear mounting connecting link-to-cylinder block bracket bolt*
3 *Rear mounting connecting link-to-subframe bracket bolt*
4 *Left-hand mounting bracket-to-body bolts*
5 *Left-hand rubber mounting centre nut*
6 *Left-hand rubber mounting-to-bracket nuts*
7 *Left-hand mounting bracket-to-transmission bolts*
8 *Right-hand rubber mounting*
9 *Rubber mounting centre nut*
10 *Upper mounting bracket-to-lower (engine) bracket bolts*

H34020

18 Withdraw the engine management ECU from its location on the support tray and move it to one side.

19 Release the wiring harness from the retaining clips on the ECU support tray, then undo the retaining bolts and lift out the support tray.

20 Place a jack beneath the transmission, with a block of wood on the jack head. Raise the jack until it is supporting the weight of the transmission.

21 Slacken and remove the centre nut and washer from the left-hand mounting, then undo the nuts securing the mounting to the mounting bracket. Lift off the mounting and remove it from the engine compartment.

22 If necessary, slide the spacer (where fitted) off the mounting stud, then unscrew the stud from the top of the transmission housing, and remove it along with its washer. If the mounting stud is tight, a universal stud extractor can be used to unscrew it.

23 Check all components carefully for signs of wear or damage, and renew as necessary.

24 Clean the threads of the mounting stud, and apply a coat of thread-locking compound to its threads. Refit the stud and washer to the top of the transmission, and tighten it to the specified torque setting.

25 Slide the spacer (where fitted) onto the mounting stud, then refit the rubber mounting. Tighten both the mounting-to-bracket nuts and the mounting centre nut to their specified torque settings, and remove the jack from underneath the transmission.

26 Refit the ECU support tray, and clip the wiring harness back into position.

27 Refit the ECU to the support tray and reconnect the battery positive cables to their respective terminal studs.

28 Refit the air cleaner assembly and intake ducting as described in Chapter 4A, then reconnect the battery negative terminal.

Rear mounting

29 If not already done, firmly apply the handbrake, then jack up the front of the vehicle and support it securely on axle stands (see *Jacking and vehicle support*). Remove the engine undertray.

30 Unscrew and remove the bolt securing the rear mounting connecting link to the mounting bracket on the rear of the cylinder block.

31 Remove the bolt securing the connecting link to the bracket on the subframe and withdraw the link.

32 To remove the mounting assembly it will first be necessary to remove the right-hand driveshaft as described in Chapter 8.

33 With the driveshaft removed, undo the retaining bolts and remove the mounting from the rear of the cylinder block.

34 Check carefully for signs of wear or damage on all components, and renew them where necessary.

35 On reassembly, fit the rear mounting assembly to the rear of the cylinder block, and tighten its retaining bolts to the specified torque. Refit the driveshaft as described in Chapter 8.

36 Refit the rear mounting connecting link, and tighten both its bolts to their specified torque settings.

37 Lower the vehicle to the ground.

Notes

Chapter 2 Part C:
Diesel engine in-car repair procedures

Contents

Degrees of difficulty

Easy, suitable for novice with little experience	**Fairly easy,** suitable for beginner with some experience	**Fairly difficult,** suitable for competent DIY mechanic	**Difficult,** suitable for experienced DIY mechanic	**Very difficult,** suitable for expert DIY or professional

Specifications

Engine (general)

Designation DW10
Capacity .... 1997 cc (2.0 litre)
Engine code* .... RHY (DW10TD)
Bore .... 85.00 mm
Stroke .... 88.00 mm
Direction of crankshaft rotation .... Clockwise (viewed from the right-hand side of vehicle)
No 1 cylinder location .... At the transmission end of block
Compression ratio .... 17.6 : 1
The engine code is stamped on a plate attached centrally to the lower front of the cylinder block

Compression pressures (engine hot, at cranking speed)

Normal .... 25 to 35 bars (363 to 508 psi)
Maximum difference between any two cylinders .... 5 bars (73 psi)

Timing belt

Tension setting (see text – Section 7):
   Initial setting .... 98 ± 2 SEEM units
   Final setting .... 54 ± 3 SEEM units

Camshaft

Drive .... Toothed belt
No of bearings 6

Lubrication system

Oil pump type .... Gear-type, chain-driven off the crankshaft right-hand end
Minimum oil pressure at 90°C .... 4.0 bars at 4000 rpm
Oil pressure warning switch operating pressure .... 0.8 bars

Torque wrench settings

	Nm	lbf ft
Big-end bearing cap nuts*:		
Stage 1	20	15
Stage 2	Tighten through a further 70°	
Camshaft bearing housing bolts	10	7
Camshaft sprocket hub-to-camshaft bolts	43	32
Camshaft sprocket-to-hub bolts	20	15
Crankshaft oil seal housing bolts	14	10
Crankshaft pulley bolt (see text – Section 5):		
Early type pulley without green paint mark:		
Stage 1	50	37
Stage 2	Tighten through a further 51°	
Later type pulley with green paint mark:		
Stage 1	70	52
Stage 2	Tighten through a further 82°	
Cylinder head bolts:		
Stage 1	20	15
Stage 2	60	44
Stage 3	Tighten through a further 220°	
Cylinder head cover bolts	8	6
Engine-to-transmission fixing bolts	45	33
Engine/transmission left-hand mounting:		
Mounting bracket-to-body bolts	22	16
Mounting bracket-to-transmission bolts	50	37
Mounting stud-to-transmission bracket	50	37
Rubber mounting centre nut	65	48
Rubber mounting-to-mounting bracket nuts	22	16
Engine/transmission rear mounting:		
Connecting link-to-mounting bracket nut/bolt	45	33
Connecting link-to-subframe nut/bolt	45	33
Mounting bracket-to-cylinder block bolts	45	33
Engine/transmission right-hand mounting:		
Lower (engine) bracket bolts	45	33
Rubber mounting domed buffer nut	22	16
Rubber mounting-to-body	45	33
Stiffener bracket bolts	20	15
Upper mounting bracket-to-lower (engine) bracket bolts	61	45
Upper mounting bracket-to-rubber mounting nut	45	33
Flywheel bolts*	50	37
High-pressure fuel pump sprocket nut	50	37
Main bearing cap bolts:		
Stage 1	25	18
Stage 2	Tighten through a further 60°	
Oil pump mounting bolts	18	13
Piston oil jet spray tube bolt	10	7
Sump bolts	16	12
Timing belt idler pulley bolt	25	18
Timing belt tensioner pulley bolt	25	18

*New nuts/bolts must be used.

1 General information and precautions

Using this Chapter

This Part of Chapter 2 is devoted to in-car repair procedures for the DW series diesel engine. Similar information covering the petrol engines will be found in Chapters 2A and 2B. All procedures concerning engine removal and refitting, and engine block/cylinder head overhaul for petrol and diesel engines can be found in Chapters 2D and 2E as applicable.

Most of the operations included in Chapter 2C are based on the assumption that the engine is still installed in the car. Therefore, if this information is being used during a complete engine overhaul, with the engine already removed, many of the steps included here will not apply.

DW series engine description

The DW series engine is a relatively new power unit based on the well-proven XUD series engine which has appeared in many Citroën and Peugeot vehicles. The engine is of four-cylinder single overhead camshaft design, mounted transversely, with the transmission mounted on the left-hand side.

A toothed timing belt drives the camshaft, high-pressure fuel pump and coolant pump. The camshaft operates the inlet and exhaust valves via rocker arms which are supported at their pivot ends by hydraulic self-adjusting tappets. The camshaft is supported by six bearings machined directly in the cylinder head and camshaft bearing housing.

The crankshaft runs in five main bearings of the usual shell type. Endfloat is controlled by thrustwashers either side of No 2 main bearing.

The pistons are selected to be of matching weight, and incorporate fully-floating gudgeon pins retained by circlips.

The oil pump is chain-driven from the end of the crankshaft and an oil cooler is fitted to all engines.

Throughout the manual, it is often necessary to identify the engines not only by their cubic capacity, but also by their engine code. The engine code, consists of four characters (eg, DW10). The code is stamped on a plate attached centrally to the lower front of the cylinder block.

Repair operations – precaution

The DW10 engine is a complex unit with numerous accessories and ancillary components. The design of the engine compartment is such that every conceivable space has been utilised, and access to virtually all of the engine components is extremely limited. In many cases, ancillary components will have to be removed, or moved to one side, and wiring, pipes and hoses will have to be disconnected or removed from various cable clips and support brackets.

When working on this engine, read through the entire procedure first, look at the vehicle and engine at the same time, and establish whether you have the necessary tools, equipment, skill and patience to proceed. Allow considerable time for any operation, and be prepared for the unexpected. Any major work on this engine is not for the faint-hearted!

Because of the limited access, many of the engine photographs appearing in this Chapter were, by necessity, taken with the engine removed from the vehicle.

⚠️ *Warning: It is essential to observe strict precautions when working on the fuel system components, particularly the high-pressure side of the system. Before carrying out any engine operations that entail working on, or near, any part of the fuel system, refer to the special information given in Chapter 4B, Section 2.*

Repair operations possible with the engine in the vehicle

The following work can be carried out with the engine in the vehicle:
a) Compression pressure – testing.
b) Cylinder head cover – removal and refitting.
c) Crankshaft pulley – removal and refitting.
d) Timing belt covers – removal and refitting.
e) Timing belt – removal, refitting and adjustment.
f) Timing belt tensioner and sprockets – removal and refitting.
g) Camshaft oil seal – renewal.
h) Camshaft, rocker arms and hydraulic tappets – removal, inspection and refitting.
i) Sump – removal and refitting.
j) Oil pump – removal and refitting.
k) Crankshaft oil seals – renewal.
l) Engine/transmission mountings – inspection and renewal.
m) Flywheel – removal, inspection and refitting.

Note: *Access between the cylinder head and engine compartment bulkhead, and to the rear underside of the engine is so restricted that it is impossible to remove the cylinder head with the engine in the car unless considerable*

additional dismantling is carried out first (eg, removal of the front suspension subframe and related components). Cylinder head removal and refitting procedures are therefore contained in Part E, assuming that the engine/transmission has been removed from the vehicle.

---

2 Compression and leakdown tests – description and interpretation

Compression test

Note: *A compression tester specifically designed for diesel engines must be used for this test.*

1 When engine performance is down, or if misfiring occurs which cannot be attributed to the fuel system, a compression test can provide diagnostic clues as to the engine's condition. If the test is performed regularly, it can give warning of trouble before any other symptoms become apparent.

2 A compression tester specifically intended for diesel engines must be used, because of the higher pressures involved. The tester is connected to an adapter which screws into the glow plug or injector hole. On these engines, an adapter suitable for use in the glow plug holes will be required, so as not to disturb the fuel system components. It is unlikely to be worthwhile buying such a tester for occasional use, but it may be possible to borrow or hire one – if not, have the test performed by a garage.

3 Unless specific instructions to the contrary are supplied with the tester, observe the following points:
a) The battery must be in a good state of charge, the air filter must be clean, and the engine should be at normal operating temperature.
b) All the glow plugs should be removed as described in Chapter 5C before starting the test.
c) The wiring connector on the engine management system ECU must be disconnected. Refer to Chapter 4B for further information.

4 The actual compression pressures measured are not so important as the balance between cylinders. Values are given in the Specifications.

5 The cause of poor compression is less easy to establish on a diesel engine than on a petrol one. The effect of introducing oil into the cylinders ('wet' testing) is not conclusive, because there is a risk that the oil will sit in the swirl chamber or in the recess on the piston crown instead of passing to the rings. However, the following can be used as a rough guide to diagnosis.

6 All cylinders should produce very similar pressures; any difference greater than that specified indicates the existence of a fault. Note that the compression should build-up

quickly in a healthy engine; low compression on the first stroke, followed by gradually-increasing pressure on successive strokes, indicates worn piston rings. A low compression reading on the first stroke, which does not build-up during successive strokes, indicates leaking valves or a blown head gasket (a cracked head could also be the cause). Deposits on the undersides of the valve heads can also cause low compression.

7 A low reading from two adjacent cylinders is almost certainly due to the head gasket having blown between them; the presence of coolant in the engine oil will confirm this.

8 If the compression reading is unusually high, the cylinder head surfaces, valves and pistons are probably coated with carbon deposits. If this is the case, the cylinder head should be removed and decarbonised (see Part E).

Leakdown test

9 A leakdown test measures the rate at which compressed air fed into the cylinder is lost. It is an alternative to a compression test, and in many ways it is better, since the escaping air provides easy identification of where pressure loss is occurring (piston rings, valves or head gasket).

10 The equipment needed for leakdown testing is unlikely to be available to the home mechanic. If poor compression is suspected, have the test performed by a suitably-equipped garage.

---

3 Engine assembly/ valve timing holes – general information and usage

General

Note: *Do not attempt to rotate the engine whilst the crankshaft and camshaft are locked in position. If the engine is to be left in this state for a long period of time, it is a good idea to place suitable warning notices inside the vehicle, and in the engine compartment. This will reduce the possibility of the engine being accidentally cranked on the starter motor, which is likely to cause damage with the locking tools in place.*

1 Timing holes or slots are located in the flywheel and in the camshaft sprocket or sprocket hub. The holes/slots are used to align the crankshaft and camshaft at the TDC position for Nos 1 and 4 pistons. This will ensure that the valve timing is maintained during operations that require removal and refitting of the timing belt and, on later engines, the crankshaft pulley. When the holes/slots are aligned with their corresponding holes in the cylinder block and cylinder head, suitable diameter bolts/pins can be inserted to lock the crankshaft and camshaft in position, preventing rotation. **Note:** *With the timing holes aligned, No 4 piston is at TDC on its compression stroke.*

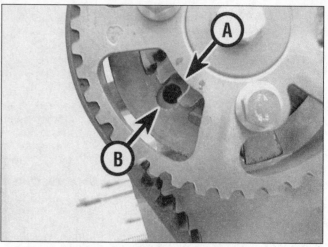

3.5a Use a mirror to observe the camshaft sprocket hub timing slot

3.5b Camshaft sprocket hub timing slot (A) aligned with the cylinder head timing hole (B)

2 The HDi type fuel system used on these engines does not have a conventional diesel injection pump, but instead uses a high-pressure fuel pump that does not have to be timed. The alignment of the fuel pump sprocket (and hence the fuel pump itself) with respect to crankshaft and camshaft position is therefore irrelevant.

3 To align the engine assembly/valve timing holes, proceed as follows.

4 Remove the upper timing belt cover as described in Section 6.

5 Using a suitable socket and extension bar, turn the crankshaft by means of the pulley bolt, until the timing slot in the camshaft sprocket hub is aligned with the corresponding hole in the cylinder head. Note that the crankshaft must always be turned in a clockwise direction (viewed from the right-hand side of vehicle). Use a small mirror so that the position of the sprocket hub timing slot can be observed **(see illustrations)**. When the slot is aligned with the corresponding hole in the cylinder head, the engine is positioned at TDC for Nos 1 and 4 pistons.

6 Insert an 8 mm diameter bolt, rod or drill through the hole in the left-hand flange of the cylinder block by the starter motor; if necessary, carefully turn the crankshaft a little either way until the rod enters the timing hole in the flywheel **(see illustration)**.

7 Insert an 8 mm bolt, rod or drill through the slot in the camshaft sprocket hub and into engagement with the cylinder head **(see illustration)**.

8 The crankshaft and camshaft are now locked in position, preventing unnecessary rotation.

---

4 Cylinder head cover – removal and refitting

Removal

1 Remove the timing belt upper cover as described in Section 6.

2 Slacken or release the clips securing the crankcase ventilation hoses to the centre and left-hand end of the cylinder head cover and disconnect the hoses.

3 Undo the bolts as necessary and move the engine cover and cable guide support bracket clear of the right-hand end of the cylinder head cover.

4 Disconnect the camshaft position sensor wiring connector.

5 Release the wiring harness from the clip on the cylinder head cover and move the harness to one side.

6 Undo the bolts securing the cylinder head cover to the camshaft carrier and collect the washers. Carefully lift off the cover taking care not to damage the camshaft position sensor as the cover is removed. Recover the seal from the cover.

Refitting

7 Refitting is a reversal of removal, bearing in mind the following points:
  a) *Examine the cover seal for signs of damage and deterioration, and renew if necessary.*
  b) *Tighten the cylinder head cover bolts to the specified torque.*
  c) *On early engines with a two-piece camshaft sprocket (see Section 7), adjust the camshaft position sensor air gap as described in Chapter 4B before refitting the upper timing belt cover.*

---

5 Crankshaft pulley – removal and refitting

Removal

1 Remove the auxiliary drivebelt as described in Chapter 1B.

2 It is now necessary to determine the type of pulley fitted, as there are two different removal and refitting procedures accordingly.

3 From under the wheelarch, observe the flat front face of the pulley. If there is a green paint mark on the pulley face it is of the later type. If no paint mark is present, the pulley is an early type. Proceed as described in the appropriate following sub-sections, according to pulley type.

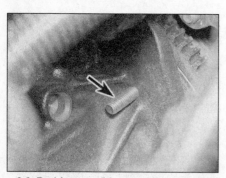

3.6 Rod (arrowed) inserted through the cylinder block into the flywheel timing hole

3.7 Insert an 8 mm bolt (arrowed) through the sprocket timing slot and into the cylinder head to lock the camshaft

Pulley without green paint mark

4 To prevent crankshaft rotation whilst the pulley retaining bolt is being slackened, the flywheel ring gear must be locked using a suitable tool made from steel angle (**see Tool Tip**). Release the power steering fluid pipes from the clamps on the cover plate at the base of the transmission bellhousing. Remove the cover plate from the bellhousing and bolt the tool to the lower bolt hole in the bellhousing flange so it engages with the ring gear teeth.

5 Using a suitable socket and extension bar, unscrew the retaining bolt, remove the washer, then slide the pulley off the end of the crankshaft (**see illustration**). If the pulley is a tight fit, it can be drawn off the crankshaft using a suitable puller. If a puller is being used, refit the pulley retaining bolt without the washer, to avoid damaging the crankshaft as the puller is tightened.

Pulley with green paint mark

6 Align the engine assembly/valve timing holes as described in Section 3, and lock the crankshaft and the camshaft sprocket in position. The crankshaft timing belt sprocket used with the later type pulley incorporates a wider keyway for the locating Woodruff key. When the pulley retaining bolt is slackened, the sprocket is free to turn on the crankshaft within the limits afforded by the wider keyway. This provides a certain degree of lateral movement of the sprocket for accurate adjustment of the timing belt tension. It is therefore essential that the flywheel and camshaft are locked in the engine assembly/valve timing position when the pulley bolt is slackened, otherwise the sprockets will turn slightly and the valve timing will be lost.

7 To prevent crankshaft rotation whilst the pulley retaining bolt is being slackened, make up and fit a flywheel ring gear locking tool as described in paragraph 4. *Do not* attempt to use only the engine assembly/valve timing locking tools to prevent rotation whilst the bolt is slackened.

8 Using a suitable socket and extension bar, unscrew the retaining bolt, remove the washer, then slide the pulley off the end of the

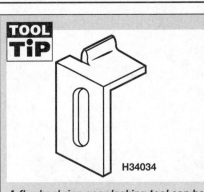

TOOL TiP

H34034

A flywheel ring gear locking tool can be made from a short strip of steel bent to form a right-angle. Cut a slot in the upper part and bend this part up to engage with the ring gear teeth. File the edges to form a tooth profile. Drill a hole in the lower part to enable the tool to be bolted to the bellhousing flange.

crankshaft. If the pulley is a tight fit, it can be drawn off the crankshaft using a suitable puller. If a puller is being used, refit the pulley retaining bolt without the washer, to avoid damaging the crankshaft as the puller is tightened.

Refitting

9 If working on the later type pulley, ensure that the engine assembly/valve timing holes are still aligned as described in Section 3, and the crankshaft and camshaft sprocket are locked in position.

10 Locate the pulley in position on the end of the crankshaft.

11 Thoroughly clean the threads of the pulley retaining bolt, then apply a coat of locking compound to the bolt threads. Citroën recommend the use of Loctite (available from your Citroën dealer); in the absence of this, any good-quality locking compound may be used.

12 Refit the crankshaft pulley retaining bolt and washer. Tighten the bolt to the specified torque, then through the specified angle, preventing the crankshaft from turning using the tool employed for removal (**see illustrations**). Note that different torque and

5.5 Removing the crankshaft pulley

angle settings are given in the Specifications, according to pulley type.

13 Remove the flywheel ring gear locking tool and, where applicable, the crankshaft and camshaft sprocket locking tools.

14 Refit the cover plate to the transmission bellhousing and secure the power steering fluid pipes in position.

15 If working on the later type pulley, refit the upper timing belt cover as described in Section 6.

16 Refit and tension the auxiliary drivebelt as described in Chapter 1B.

---

6 Timing belt covers – removal and refitting

Removal

⚠️ *Warning: Refer to the precautionary information contained in Section 1 before proceeding.*

Upper cover

1 Disconnect the battery negative terminal (refer to *Disconnecting the battery* in the Reference Chapter).

2 Release the four plastic fasteners and remove the engine cover from the top of the engine.

3 Firmly apply the handbrake, then jack up the front of the vehicle and support it securely on axle stands (see *Jacking and vehicle support*). Remove the right-hand front roadwheel.

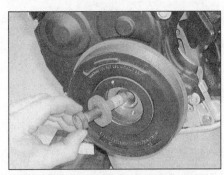

5.12a Refit the crankshaft pulley retaining bolt after applying locking compound to the threads

5.12b Tighten the pulley bolt to the specified Stage 1 torque . . .

5.12c . . . then through the specified Stage 2 angle

6.5 Disconnect the fuel supply and return hose quick-release fittings

6.6 Release the two fuel hoses from the retaining clips on the timing belt upper cover

4 Using a forked type removal tool, release the stud fasteners securing the centre section of the right-hand wheelarch liner. Withdraw the liner from under the front wing for access to the right-hand side of the engine. Unclip the coolant hoses from under the wing to improve access further.

5 At the connections above the fuel pump, disconnect the fuel supply and return hose quick-release fittings using a small screwdriver to release the locking clip **(see illustration)**. Cover the open unions to prevent dirt entry, using small plastic bags, or fingers cut from clean rubber gloves.

6 Release the two hoses from the retaining clips on the upper timing belt cover and move them to one side **(see illustration)**.

7 Release the EGR solenoid valve vacuum hose from the clip on the upper cover. If necessary for improved access, undo the EGR solenoid valve mounting bracket nuts and move the valve to one side.

8 Undo the bolt securing the upper cover to the cylinder head cover **(see illustration)**.

9 Undo the upper bolt on the edge of the cover nearest to the engine compartment bulkhead.

10 Undo the lower bolt on the bulkhead side of the cover, at the join between the upper and lower covers. Note that this bolt also retains the coolant pump. To avoid coolant leakage, after the upper cover is removed, refit the bolt fitted with a 17.0 mm spacer, and tighten it securely.

11 Undo the remaining bolt in the centre of the cover, just above the engine mounting bracket.

12 Disengage the upper cover from the intermediate cover and manipulate the upper cover from its location.

Intermediate cover

13 Remove the upper cover as described previously.

14 Connect an engine hoist or suitable lifting gear to the two lifting brackets on the cylinder head. Raise the hoist to just take the weight of the engine.

15 For additional stability, place a jack beneath the right-hand side of the engine, with a block of wood on the jack head. Raise the jack until it is just contacting the sump.

16 Slacken and remove the three bolts securing the right-hand engine/transmission mounting upper bracket to the lower (engine) bracket.

17 Undo the two bolts securing the right-hand mounting stiffener bracket to the body and lift off the bracket. Unscrew the domed buffer nut, then unscrew the single nut securing the upper bracket to the rubber mounting. Remove the upper bracket from the rubber mounting and lower (engine) bracket.

18 Undo the two nuts and remove the through bolts securing the rear engine/transmission mounting connecting link to the mounting bracket on the subframe and on the rear of the cylinder block. Release and remove the connecting link from the mounting brackets.

19 With the two engine mountings removed, alternatively raise and lower the lifting gear and the jack under the engine, as necessary, for access to the timing belt cover retaining bolts.

20 Undo the upper bolt on the top edge of the intermediate cover.

21 Undo the two remaining bolts at the join between the intermediate cover and lower cover, then manipulate the intermediate cover from its location.

Lower cover

22 Remove the crankshaft pulley as described in Section 5.

23 Remove the upper and intermediate covers as described previously.

24 Undo the two remaining bolts on the edge of the cover, one on either side of the crankshaft pulley location.

25 Lift the cover off the front of the engine and manipulate it from its location.

Refitting

26 Refitting of all the covers is a reversal of the relevant removal procedure, ensuring that each cover section is correctly located, and that the cover retaining bolts are securely tightened. Ensure that all disturbed hoses are reconnected and retained by their relevant clips, and that all nuts/bolts are tightened to their specified torque wrench settings (where given).

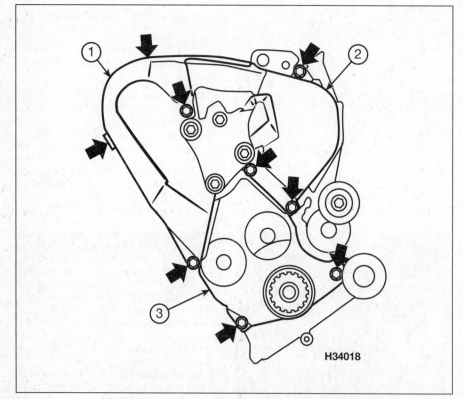

H34018

6.8 Timing belt cover retaining bolt locations (arrowed)

1 Upper cover   *2 Intermediate cover*   *3 Lower cover*

7 Timing belt – general information, removal and refitting

Note: *Citroën specify the use of an electronic belt tension checking tool (SEEM 4122–T) to correctly set the timing belt tension. The following procedure assumes that this equipment (or suitable alternative equipment calibrated to display belt tension in SEEM units) is available. Accurate tensioning of the timing belt is essential, and if the electronic equipment is not available, it is recommended that the work is entrusted to a Citroën dealer or suitably-equipped garage.*

General information

1 The timing belt drives the camshaft, high-pressure fuel pump, and coolant pump from a toothed sprocket on the end of the crankshaft. The belt also drives the brake servo vacuum pump indirectly via the flywheel end of the camshaft. If the belt breaks or slips in service, the pistons are likely to hit the valve heads, resulting in expensive damage.

2 The timing belt should be renewed at the specified intervals, or earlier if it is contaminated with oil, or at all noisy in operation (a 'scraping' noise due to uneven wear).

3 If the timing belt is being removed, it is a wise precaution to check the condition of the coolant pump at the same time (check for signs of coolant leakage). This may avoid the need to remove the timing belt again at a later stage, should the coolant pump fail.

4 Two types of timing belt sprocket arrangements may be encountered. On early engines, the camshaft sprocket is of the 'floating' type, secured to the sprocket hub with three bolts. The bolt holes are elongated and allow for a certain degree of lateral movement of the sprocket for accurate tensioning of the timing belt when refitting. On later engines, the camshaft sprocket is fixed, but the crankshaft sprocket becomes the 'floating' component. Lateral movement of the crankshaft sprocket is achieved by using a wider keyway for the locating Woodruff key. Timing belt removal procedures are the same for both types, but different procedures must be used when refitting.

Removal

5 Remove the crankshaft pulley as described in Section 5. Refit and tighten the pulley retaining bolt to allow the engine to be turned in subsequent operations.

6 Remove the upper, intermediate and lower timing belt covers as described in Section 6.

7 It is now necessary to identify the type of timing belt sprocket arrangement fitted by observing the design of the camshaft sprocket. On early engines the sprocket and hub is a two-piece assembly. The sprocket is secured to the sprocket hub by three retaining bolts, with the hub being secured to the camshaft by a single centre bolt. On later

7.9 Slacken the three camshaft sprocket-to-sprocket hub retaining bolts

engines the sprocket and hub are a single fixed assembly secured to the camshaft by a centre retaining bolt only. When refitting, proceed as described in the appropriate sub-Sections according to sprocket type.

8 If not already done, align the engine assembly/valve timing holes as described in Section 3, and lock the crankshaft and the camshaft sprocket in position. *Do not* attempt to rotate the engine whilst the locking pins are in position.

9 On early engines, slacken the three bolts securing the camshaft sprocket to the sprocket hub (see illustration).

10 Slacken the timing belt tensioner pulley retaining bolt and insert a short length of 8.0 mm square bar into the square hole on the front face of the tensioner pulley (see Tool Tip). Alternatively, although clearance is restricted, the square end of a 1/4 inch drive socket bar can also be used. Using the bar and a spanner, turn the pulley in a clockwise direction, to relieve the tension from the timing belt. Retighten the tensioner pulley retaining bolt to secure it in the slackened position.

11 If the timing belt is to be re-used, use white paint or chalk to mark the direction of rotation on the belt (if markings do not already exist), then slip the belt off the sprockets (see illustration). Note that the crankshaft must not be rotated whilst the belt is removed.

12 Check the timing belt carefully for any signs of uneven wear, splits or oil contamination. Pay particular attention to the roots of the teeth. Renew it if there is the slightest doubt about its condition. If the

7.11 Removing the timing belt

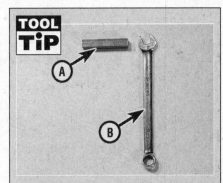

A square section tool to fit the timing belt tensioner pulley can be made from a length of standard 8 mm door handle rod (A), obtained from a DIY shop, and then cut to size. Once the rod has been fitted to the tensioner, the timing belt can be tensioned by turning the rod with an 8 mm spanner (B).

engine is undergoing an overhaul, renew the belt as a matter of course, regardless of its apparent condition. The cost of a new belt is nothing compared with the cost of repairs, should the belt break in service. If signs of oil contamination are found, trace the source of the oil leak and rectify it. Wash down the engine timing belt area and all related components, to remove all traces of oil. Check that the tensioner pulley and idler roller rotate freely, without any sign of roughness. If necessary, renew them as described in Section 8.

Refitting

Two-piece camshaft sprocket

13 Commence refitting by ensuring that the engine assembly/valve timing holes are still aligned as described in Section 3, and the crankshaft, and camshaft sprocket hub are locked in position.

14 Tighten the camshaft sprocket retaining bolts lightly so that the sprocket can still move within the elongated slots. Turn the sprocket fully clockwise to the ends of the slots.

15 Locate the timing belt on the crankshaft sprocket making sure that the direction of rotation arrow is facing the correct way.

16 Hold the belt on the crankshaft sprocket and, while keeping the 'lower run' of the belt taut (between the crankshaft and idler roller), feed the belt over the remaining sprockets and pulleys in the following order (see illustrations):

    a) Idler roller.
    b) High-pressure fuel pump.
    c) Camshaft.
    e) Coolant pump.
    d) Tensioner pulley.

17 Fit the sensor head of the electronic belt tension measuring equipment to the 'top run' of the timing belt, approximately midway between the camshaft and fuel pump sprockets.

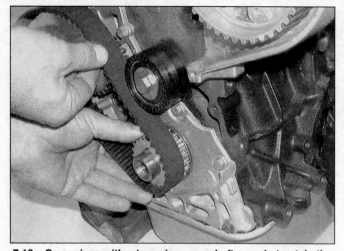

7.16a On engines with a two-piece camshaft sprocket, retain the timing belt on the crankshaft sprocket and feed it around the idler roller ...

7.16b ... high-pressure fuel pump sprocket ...

18 Slacken the tensioner pulley retaining bolt and, using the square bar and spanner, pivot the tensioner pulley anti-clockwise until an initial setting of 98 ± 2 SEEM units is displayed on the tension measuring equipment **(see illustrations)**. Hold the tensioner pulley in that position and retighten the retaining bolt.

19 Check that the camshaft sprocket retaining bolts are not at the ends of their slots (if necessary, remove one of the sprocket bolts to check this). If they are, repeat the refitting operation. If all is satisfactory, refit the removed bolt and tighten all three sprocket retaining bolts to the specified torque.

20 Remove the belt tension measuring equipment and the crankshaft, and camshaft sprocket hub locking tools.

21 Rotate the crankshaft through eight complete rotations in a clockwise direction (viewed from the right-hand end of the engine). Realign the engine assembly/valve timing holes and refit the crankshaft locking tool only.

22 Slacken the camshaft sprocket retaining bolts and refit the camshaft sprocket hub locking tool.

23 Slacken the tensioner pulley retaining bolt once more.

24 Refit the belt tension measuring equipment

to the top run of the belt, and turn the tensioner pulley to give a final setting of 54 ± 2 SEEM units on the tensioning gauge. Hold the tensioner pulley in this position and tighten the retaining bolt to the specified torque.

25 Retighten the camshaft sprocket retaining bolts to the specified torque.

26 Release the sensor head of the belt tension measuring equipment, then refit it again and check that a reading of 54 ± 3 SEEM units is indicated. Remove the tension measuring equipment.

27 Remove the locking tools, then rotate the crankshaft once again through two complete rotations in a clockwise direction. Realign the engine assembly/valve timing holes and refit the crankshaft locking tool.

28 Check that it is possible to insert the camshaft sprocket hub locking tool. If the tool cannot be inserted, check that the offset between the timing slot in the sprocket hub and the corresponding hole in the cylinder head is not greater than 1.0 mm. If it is, repeat the complete timing belt refitting and tensioning procedure.

29 Refit the lower, intermediate and upper timing belt covers as described in Section 6. Refit the crankshaft pulley as described in Section 5 after refitting the lower cover.

Fixed camshaft sprocket

30 Ensure that the engine assembly/valve timing holes are still aligned as described in Section 3, and the crankshaft and camshaft sprocket are locked in position.

31 Turn the crankshaft sprocket anti-clockwise to the limit of the movement afforded by the keyway. Lock the sprocket in this position by inserting a small screwdriver or similar implement down the left-hand side of the Woodruff key.

32 Locate the timing belt on the camshaft sprocket, making sure that the direction of rotation arrow is facing the correct way.

33 Retain the timing belt on the camshaft

7.16c ... camshaft sprocket ...

7.16d ... coolant pump and tensioner pulley

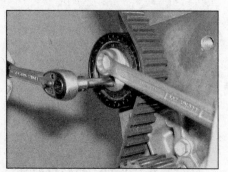

7.18a Pivot the tensioner pulley anti-clockwise, then tighten the retaining bolt ...

7.18b ... when the specified tension value is shown on the tensioning measuring equipment

sprocket using a cable tie to ensure that it does not jump a tooth. Keeping the 'top run' of the belt taut (between the camshaft and fuel pump sprockets), feed the belt over the remaining sprockets and pulleys in the following order:

a) *High-pressure fuel pump.*
b) *Idler roller.*
c) *Crankshaft.*
d) *Coolant pump.*
e) *Tensioner pulley.*

34 Cut off the cable tie securing the timing belt to the camshaft sprocket and remove the screwdriver from the crankshaft sprocket keyway.

35 Fit the sensor head of the electronic belt tension measuring equipment to the 'top run' of the timing belt, approximately midway between the camshaft and fuel pump sprockets.

36 Slacken the tensioner pulley retaining bolt and, using the square bar and spanner, pivot the tensioner pulley anti-clockwise until an initial setting of 98 ± 2 SEEM units is displayed on the tension measuring equipment. Hold the tensioner pulley in that position and retighten the retaining bolt.

37 If not already in place, refit the crankshaft pulley retaining bolt and washer and tighten the bolt to 70 Nm (52 lbf ft). Prevent the crankshaft from turning using the flywheel ring gear locking tool described for pulley removal in Section 5. *Do not* attempt to use only the engine assembly/valve timing locking tools to prevent rotation whilst the bolt is tightened.

38 Remove the belt tension measuring equipment, the flywheel ring gear locking tool and the engine assembly/valve timing locking tools.

39 Rotate the crankshaft through eight complete rotations in a clockwise direction (viewed from the right-hand end of the engine). Realign the engine assembly/valve timing holes and refit the crankshaft and camshaft sprocket locking tools.

40 Refit the flywheel ring gear locking tool and slacken the crankshaft pulley retaining bolt.

41 Slacken the tensioner pulley retaining bolt once more. Refit the belt tension measuring equipment to the top run of the belt, and turn the tensioner pulley to give a final setting of 54 ± 2 SEEM units on the tensioning gauge. Hold the tensioner pulley in this position and tighten the retaining bolt to the specified torque.

42 Release the sensor head of the belt tension measuring equipment, then refit it again and check that a reading of 54 ± 3 SEEM units is indicated. If not, repeat the complete tensioning procedure. If the reading is correct, remove the tension measuring equipment.

43 Remove all the locking tools, then rotate the crankshaft once again through two complete rotations in a clockwise direction. Realign the engine assembly/valve timing holes and refit the crankshaft and camshaft sprocket locking tools. If it is not possible to fit

both locking tools, repeat the complete tensioning procedure.

44 If all is satisfactory, locate the lower timing belt cover in position, refit the retaining bolts and tighten them securely.

45 With the engine assembly/valve timing holes aligned and the crankshaft and camshaft sprocket locking tools in place, refit the flywheel ring gear locking tool and unscrew the crankshaft pulley retaining bolt.

46 Locate the crankshaft pulley in position on the end of the crankshaft.

47 Thoroughly clean the threads of the pulley retaining bolt, then apply a coat of locking compound to the bolt threads. Citroën recommend the use of Loctite (available from your Citroën dealer); in the absence of this, any good-quality locking compound may be used.

48 Refit the crankshaft pulley retaining bolt and washer. Tighten the bolt to the specified torque, then through the specified angle.

49 Remove the flywheel ring gear locking tool and the crankshaft and camshaft sprocket locking tools.

50 Refit the intermediate and upper timing belt covers as described in Section 6, then refit and tension the auxiliary drivebelt as described in Chapter 1B.

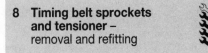

8 Timing belt sprockets and tensioner –
removal and refitting

Two-piece camshaft sprocket

Removal

1 Remove the timing belt as described in Section 7.

2 Remove the locking tool from the camshaft sprocket hub. Slacken the sprocket hub retaining bolt, and the three sprocket-to-hub retaining bolts. To prevent the camshaft rotating as the bolts are slackened, a sprocket holding tool will be required. In the absence of the special Citroën tool, an acceptable substitute can be fabricated at home **(see Tool Tip 1)**. *Do not* attempt to use the engine assembly/valve timing locking tool to prevent the sprocket from rotating whilst the bolt is slackened.

3 Remove the sprocket hub retaining bolt and washer, and slide the sprocket and hub off the end of the camshaft. Examine the camshaft oil seal for signs of oil leakage and, if necessary, renew it as described in Section 12.

4 If necessary, the sprocket can be separated from the hub after removing the three retaining bolts.

5 Clean the camshaft sprocket thoroughly, and renew it if there are any signs of wear, damage or cracks.

Refitting

6 If removed, refit the sprocket to the hub and secure with the three retaining bolts, moderately tightened only at this stage.

7 Refit the sprocket and hub to the camshaft, then refit the hub retaining bolt and washer. Tighten the bolt to the specified torque, preventing the camshaft from turning as during removal.

8 Align the engine assembly/valve timing slot in the camshaft sprocket hub with the hole in the cylinder head and refit the locking tool.

9 The air gap between the tip of the camshaft position sensor and the target plate at the rear of the camshaft sprocket hub must now be adjusted.

10 Slacken the camshaft position sensor retaining bolt and move the sensor away from the sprocket hub to the limit of its elongated retaining bolt slot.

11 Undo the three camshaft sprocket retaining bolts and remove the sprocket from the hub.

12 Select feeler blades to the value of 1.2 mm total thickness and insert them between the tip of the camshaft position sensor and the target plate inner face.

13 Move the sensor toward the sprocket until it just contacts the feeler blades. Hold the sensor in this position and tighten the retaining bolt.

14 With the gap correctly adjusted, refit the camshaft sprocket to the sprocket hub and secure with the three retaining bolts tightened finger tight only at this stage.

15 Refit the timing belt as described in Section 7.

Fixed camshaft sprocket

Removal

16 Remove the timing belt as described in Section 7.

17 Remove the locking tool from the camshaft sprocket. Slacken the sprocket retaining bolt while preventing the camshaft from rotating using the tool described in paragraph 2. *Do not* attempt to use the engine assembly/valve timing locking tool to prevent the sprocket from rotating whilst the bolt is slackened.

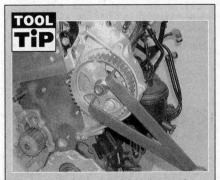

Tool Tip 1: A sprocket holding tool can be made from two lengths of steel strip bolted together to form a forked end. Bend the ends of the strip through 90° to form the fork 'prongs'.

8.24a Slide the crankshaft sprocket off the end of the crankshaft . . .

18 Remove the sprocket retaining bolt and washer, and slide the sprocket off the end of the camshaft. Examine the camshaft oil seal for signs of oil leakage and, if necessary, renew it as described in Section 12.

19 Clean the camshaft sprocket thoroughly, and renew it if there are any signs of wear, damage or cracks.

Refitting

20 Refit the sprocket to the camshaft, then refit the retaining bolt and washer. Tighten the bolt to the specified torque, preventing the camshaft from turning as during removal.

21 Align the engine assembly/valve timing hole in the camshaft sprocket with the hole in the cylinder head and refit the locking tool.

22 Refit the timing belt as described in Section 7.

Crankshaft sprocket

Removal

23 Remove the timing belt as described in Section 7.

24 Slide the sprocket off the end of the crankshaft and collect the Woodruff key (see illustrations).

25 Examine the crankshaft oil seal for signs of oil leakage and, if necessary, renew it as described in Section 12.

26 Clean the crankshaft sprocket thoroughly, and renew it if there are any signs of wear, damage or cracks.

Tool Tip 2: *Make a sprocket releasing tool from a short strip of steel. Drill two holes in the strip to correspond with the two holes in the sprocket. Drill a third hole just large enough to accept the flats of the sprocket retaining nut.*

8.24b . . . and collect the Woodruff key

Refitting

27 Refit the Woodruff key to the end of the crankshaft, then refit the crankshaft sprocket (with the flange nearest the cylinder block).

28 Refit the timing belt as described in Section 7.

Fuel pump sprocket

Removal

29 Remove the timing belt as described in Section 7.

30 Using a suitable socket, undo the pump sprocket retaining nut. The sprocket can be held stationary as the nut is slackened using a suitable forked tool engaged with the holes in the sprocket (see Tool Tip 1).

31 The pump sprocket is a taper fit on the pump shaft and it will be necessary to make up another tool to release it from the taper (see Tool Tip 2).

32 Partially unscrew the sprocket retaining nut, fit the home-made tool, and secure it to the sprocket with two suitable bolts. Prevent the sprocket from rotating as before, and unscrew the sprocket retaining nut (see illustration). The nut will bear against the tool as it is undone, forcing the sprocket off the shaft taper. Once the taper is released, remove the tool, unscrew the nut fully, and remove the sprocket from the pump shaft.

33 Clean the sprocket thoroughly, and renew it if there are any signs of wear, damage or cracks.

Refitting

34 Refit the pump sprocket and retaining nut, and tighten the nut to the specified torque.

8.32 Using the home-made tools to remove the fuel pump sprocket

Prevent the sprocket rotating as the nut is tightened using the sprocket holding tool.

35 Refit the timing belt as described in Section 7.

Coolant pump sprocket

36 The coolant pump sprocket is integral with the pump, and cannot be removed.

Tensioner pulley

Removal

37 Remove the timing belt as described in Section 7.

38 Remove the tensioner pulley retaining bolt, and slide the pulley off its mounting stud.

39 Clean the tensioner pulley, but do not use any strong solvent which may enter the pulley bearings. Check that the pulley rotates freely, with no sign of stiffness or free play. Renew the pulley if there is any doubt about its condition, or if there are any obvious signs of wear or damage.

40 Examine the pulley mounting stud for signs of damage and if necessary, renew it.

Refitting

41 Refit the tensioner pulley to its mounting stud, and fit the retaining bolt.

42 Refit the timing belt as described in Section 7.

Idler roller

Removal

43 Remove the timing belt as described in Section 7.

44 Undo the retaining bolt and withdraw the idler roller from the engine.

45 Clean the idler roller, but do not use any strong solvent which may enter the bearings. Check that the roller rotates freely, with no sign of stiffness or free play. Renew the idler roller if there is any doubt about its condition, or if there are any obvious signs of wear or damage.

Refitting

46 Locate the idler roller on the engine, and fit the retaining bolt. Tighten the bolt to the specified torque.

47 Refit the timing belt as described in Section 7.

9 Camshaft, tappets and rocker arms – removal, inspection and refitting

Removal

1 Remove the cylinder head cover as described in Section 4.

2 Remove the camshaft sprocket as described in Section 8.

3 Remove the braking system vacuum pump as described in Chapter 9.

4 Progressively slacken the camshaft bearing housing retaining bolts, working in a spiral pattern in the reverse order to that shown in illustration 9.25. When all the bolts have been

slackened, unscrew and remove them from their locations.

5 Carefully release the camshaft bearing housing from the cylinder head. The housing is likely to be initially tight to release as it is located by two dowels on the forward facing side of the cylinder head. If necessary, very carefully prise up the housing using a screwdriver inserted in the slotted lug adjacent to each dowel location.

6 Once the bearing housing is free, lift it squarely from the cylinder head **(see illustration)**. The camshaft will rise up slightly under the pressure of the valve springs – be careful it doesn't tilt and jam in the cylinder head or bearing housing section.

7 Lift the camshaft from the cylinder head and remove the oil seal **(see illustration)**. Discard the seal, a new one should be used on refitting.

8 Have ready a suitable box divided into eight segments, or some containers or other means of storing and identifying the rocker arms and hydraulic tappets after removal. The box or containers for the hydraulic tappets must be oil tight and deep enough to allow the tappets to be almost totally submerged in oil. Mark the segments in the boxes or the containers with the number for each rocker arm and tappet (ie, 1 to 8).

9 Lift out each rocker arm and release it from the spring clip on the tappet. Place the rocker arms in their respective positions in the box or containers **(see illustration)**.

10 Similarly lift out the tappets and place them in their respective positions in the box or containers **(see illustrations)**. Once all the tappets have been removed, add clean engine oil to the box or container so that the tappet is submerged.

Inspection

11 Inspect the cam lobes and the camshaft bearing journals for scoring or other visible evidence of wear. Once the surface hardening of the cam lobes has been eroded, wear will occur at an accelerated rate. **Note:** *If these symptoms are visible on the tips of the camshaft lobes, check the corresponding rocker arm, as it will probably be worn as well.*

12 Examine the condition of the bearing surfaces in the cylinder head and camshaft bearing housing. If wear is evident, the cylinder head and bearing housing will both have to be renewed, as they are a matched assembly.

13 Inspect the rocker arms and tappets for scuffing, cracking or other damage and renew any components as necessary. Also check the condition of the tappet bores in the cylinder head. As with the camshafts, any wear in this area will necessitate cylinder head renewal.

Refitting

14 Thoroughly clean the sealant from the mating surfaces of the cylinder head and camshaft bearing housing. Use a suitable liquid gasket dissolving agent (available from Citroën dealers) together with a soft putty

9.6 Remove the camshaft bearing housing from the cylinder head . . .

9.9 Lift out the rocker arms . . .

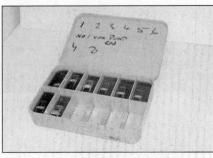

9.10b . . . and place all the components in their respective positions in a segmented box

knife; do not use a metal scraper or the faces will be damaged. As there is no conventional gasket used, the cleanliness of the mating faces is of the utmost importance.

15 Clean off any oil, dirt or grease from both components and dry with a clean lint free cloth. Ensure that all the oilways are completely clean.

16 To prevent any possibility of the valves contacting the pistons as the camshaft is refitted, remove the crankshaft locking tool and turn the crankshaft a quarter turn in the *opposite* direction to normal rotation, to position all the pistons at mid-stroke.

17 Liberally lubricate the tappet bores in the cylinder head with clean engine oil.

18 Insert the tappets into their original bores in the cylinder head unless they have been renewed.

19 Lubricate the rocker arms and place them over their respective tappets and valve stems.

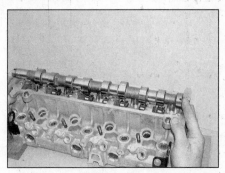

9.7 . . . then lift out the camshaft

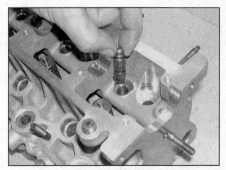

9.10a . . . followed by the hydraulic tappets . . .

Ensure that the ends of the rocker arms engage with the spring clips on the tappets.

20 Lubricate the camshaft bearing journals in the cylinder head sparingly with oil, taking care not to allow the oil to spill over onto the camshaft bearing housing contact areas.

21 Lay the camshaft in the cylinder head and temporarily locate the camshaft sprocket in position. Turn the camshaft so that the engine assembly/valve timing slot in the sprocket or sprocket hub is approximately aligned with the timing hole in the cylinder head. Remove the sprocket.

22 Ensure that the mating faces of the cylinder head and camshaft bearing housing are clean and free of any oil or grease.

23 Sparingly apply a bead of RTV sealant to the mating face of the camshaft bearing housing, taking care not to allow the product to contaminate the camshaft bearing journal areas **(see illustration)**.

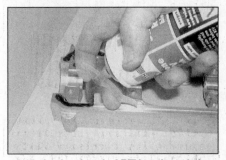

9.23 Apply a bead of RTV sealant to the mating face of the camshaft bearing housing

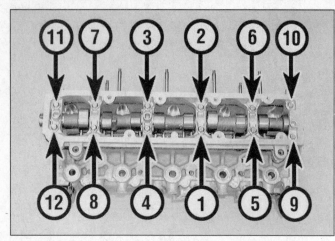

9.25 Camshaft bearing housing retaining bolt tightening sequence

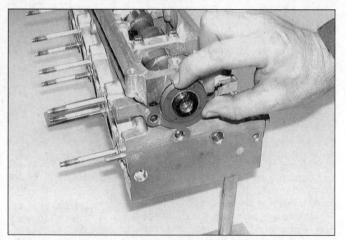

9.26a Locate a new oil seal over the camshaft, with its sealing lip facing inwards . . .

24 Locate the bearing housing over the camshaft and into position on the cylinder head.

25 Insert all the bearing housing retaining bolts and progressively tighten them to the specified torque, in the sequence shown **(see illustration)**.

26 Smear the lips of the new oil seal with clean engine oil and fit it over the camshaft, making sure its sealing lip is facing inwards. Press the seal into position until it is flush with the end face of the cylinder head. Use a suitable bolt (screwed into the end of the camshaft), washers and a tube or socket to press the seal into position **(see illustrations)**.

27 Refit the braking system vacuum pump as described in Chapter 9.

28 Again, temporarily locate the sprocket on the end of the camshaft, and make sure that the sprocket timing slot is aligned with the corresponding cut-out in the cylinder head.

29 Turn the crankshaft a quarter turn in the normal direction of rotation so that pistons 1 and 4 are again at TDC. Realign the engine assembly/valve timing hole and refit the crankshaft locking tool.

30 Refit the camshaft sprocket as described in Section 8.

31 Refit the cylinder head cover as described in Section 4.

9.26b . . . then use a bolt and socket or similar arrangement to press the seal into place

10 Sump –
removal and refitting

Removal

1 Disconnect the battery negative terminal (refer to *Disconnecting the battery* in the Reference Chapter).

2 Drain the engine oil, then clean and refit the engine oil drain plug, tightening it securely. If the engine is nearing its service interval when the oil and filter are due for renewal, it is recommended that the filter is also removed, and a new one fitted. After reassembly, the engine can then be refilled with fresh oil. Refer to Chapter 1B for further information.

3 Chock the rear wheels then jack up the front of the vehicle and support it on axle stands (see *Jacking and vehicle support*).

4 On models with air conditioning, where the compressor is mounted onto the side of the sump, remove the auxiliary drivebelt as described in Chapter 1B. Unbolt the compressor, and position it clear of the sump. Support the weight of the compressor by tying it to the vehicle, to prevent any excess strain being placed on the compressor lines. *Do not* disconnect the refrigerant lines from the compressor (refer to the warnings given in Chapter 3).

5 Where necessary, disconnect the wiring connector from the oil temperature sender unit, which is screwed into the sump.

6 Release the power steering fluid pipes from the clamps on the cover plate at the base of the transmission bellhousing. Remove the cover plate from the bellhousing for access to the sump rear retaining bolts.

7 Progressively slacken and remove all the sump retaining bolts. Since the sump bolts vary in length, remove each bolt in turn, and store it in its correct fitted order by pushing it through a clearly-marked cardboard template. This will avoid the possibility of installing the bolts in the wrong locations on refitting.

8 Try to break the joint by striking the sump with the palm of your hand, then lower and withdraw the sump from under the car. If the sump is stuck (which is quite likely) use a putty knife or similar, carefully inserted between the sump and block. Ease the knife along the joint until the sump is released. Remove the gasket (where fitted), and discard it; a new one must be used on refitting. While the sump is removed, take the opportunity to check the oil pump pick-up/strainer for signs of clogging or splitting. If necessary, remove the pump as described in Section 11, and clean or renew the strainer.

9 On some engines, a large spacer plate is fitted between the sump and the base of the cylinder block/crankcase. If this plate is fitted, undo the two retaining screws from diagonally-opposite corners of the plate. Remove the plate from the base of the engine, noting which way round it is fitted.

Refitting

10 Clean all traces of sealant/gasket from the mating surfaces of the cylinder block and sump, then use a clean rag to wipe out the sump and the engine's interior.

11 Where a spacer plate is fitted, remove all traces of sealant/gasket from the spacer plate, then apply a thin coating of suitable sealant to the plate upper mating surface. Offer up the plate to the base of the cylinder block/crankcase, and securely tighten its retaining screws **(see illustrations)**.

12 On engines where the sump was fitted without a gasket, ensure that the sump mating surfaces are clean and dry, then apply a thin coating of RTV sealant to the sump mating surface.

13 On engines where the sump was fitted with a gasket, ensure that all traces of the old gasket have been removed, and that the sump mating surfaces are clean and dry. Position the new gasket on the top of the sump, using a dab of grease to hold it in position.

14 Offer up the sump to the cylinder block. Refit its retaining bolts, ensuring that each is screwed into its original location. Tighten the bolts evenly and progressively to the specified torque setting.

15 Reconnect the wiring connector to the oil temperature sensor (where fitted).

16 Refit the cover plate to the transmission bellhousing and secure the power steering fluid pipes in position.

17 Where necessary, align the air conditioning compressor with its mountings on the sump, and insert the retaining bolts. Securely tighten the compressor retaining bolts, then refit the auxiliary drivebelt as described in Chapter 1B.

18 Lower the vehicle to the ground, then refill the engine with oil as described in Chapter 1B.

11 Oil pump and drive chain –
removal, inspection and refitting

Removal

1 Remove the sump as described in Section 10.

2 Where necessary, undo the two retaining screws, and slide the sprocket cover off the front of the oil pump.

3 Slacken and remove the three bolts securing the oil pump to the base of the cylinder block. Disengage the pump sprocket from the chain, and remove the oil pump **(see illustration)**. Where necessary, also remove the spacer plate which is fitted behind the oil pump.

Inspection

4 Examine the oil pump sprocket for signs of damage and wear, such as chipped or missing teeth. If the sprocket is worn, the pump assembly must be renewed, since the sprocket is not available separately. It is also recommended that the chain and drive sprocket, fitted to the crankshaft, be renewed at the same time. To renew the chain and drive sprocket, first remove the crankshaft timing belt sprocket as described in Section 8. Unbolt the oil seal carrier from the cylinder block. The sprocket, spacer (where fitted) and chain can then be slid off the end of the crankshaft.

5 Slacken and remove the bolts (along with the baffle plate, where fitted) securing the strainer cover to the pump body. Lift off the strainer cover, and take off the relief valve piston and spring, noting which way round they are fitted **(see illustrations)**.

6 Examine the pump rotors and body for signs of wear ridges or scoring. If worn, the complete pump assembly must be renewed.

7 Examine the relief valve piston for signs of wear or damage, and renew if necessary. The condition of the relief valve spring can only be measured by comparing it with a new one; if there is any doubt about its condition, it should also be renewed. Both the piston and spring are available individually.

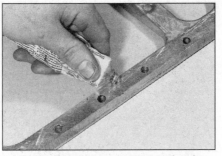

10.11a Where a sump spacer plate is fitted, apply sealant to the plate upper surface . . .

8 Thoroughly clean the oil pump strainer with a suitable solvent, and check it for signs of clogging or splitting. If the strainer is damaged, the strainer and cover assembly must be renewed.

9 Locate the relief valve spring and piston in the strainer cover. Refit the cover to the pump body, aligning the relief valve piston with its bore in the pump. Refit the baffle plate (where fitted) and the cover retaining bolts, and tighten them securely.

10 Prime the pump by filling it with clean engine oil before refitting.

Refitting

11 If removed, refit the drive sprocket, spacer (where fitted) and chain to the crankshaft, then refit the oil seal carrier using a new gasket. Refit the crankshaft timing belt sprocket as described in Section 8.

12 Offer up the spacer plate (where fitted),

11.3 Removing the oil pump

11.5b . . . then lift off the cover and remove the spring . . .

10.11b . . . then refit the plate to the base of the cylinder block

then engage the pump sprocket with its drive chain. Seat the pump on the base of the cylinder block. Refit the pump retaining bolts, and tighten them to the specified torque setting.

13 Where necessary, slide the sprocket cover into position on the pump. Refit its retaining bolts, tightening them securely.

14 Refit the sump as described in Section 10.

12 Oil seals –
renewal

Crankshaft

Right-hand oil seal

1 Remove the crankshaft sprocket as described in Section 8.

11.5a Remove the oil pump cover retaining bolts . . .

11.5c . . . and relief valve piston, noting which way round it is fitted

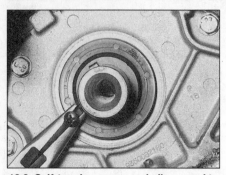

12.3 Self-tapping screw and pliers used to remove the crankshaft right-hand oil seal

2 Note the fitted depth of the oil seal.
3 Pull the oil seal from the housing using a hooked instrument. Alternatively, drill a small hole in the oil seal, and use a self-tapping screw and a pair of pliers to remove it **(see illustration)**.
4 Clean the oil seal housing and the crankshaft sealing surface.
5 Dip the new oil seal in clean engine oil, and press it into the housing (open end first) to the previously-noted depth, using a suitable tube or socket. A piece of thin plastic or tape wound around the front of the crankshaft is useful to prevent damage to the oil seal as it is fitted.
6 Where applicable, remove the plastic or tape from the end of the crankshaft.
7 Refit the crankshaft sprocket as described in Section 8.

Left-hand oil seal

8 Remove the flywheel as described in Section 13.
9 Proceed as described in paragraphs 2 to 6, noting that when fitted, the outer lip of the oil seal must point outwards; if it is pointing inwards, use a piece of bent wire to pull it out. Take care not to damage the oil seal.
10 Refit the flywheel as described in Section 13.

Camshaft

Right-hand oil seal

11 Remove the camshaft sprocket as described in Section 8.
12 Pull the oil seal from the housing using a hooked tool **(see illustration)**. Alternatively, drill a small hole in the oil seal and use a self-tapping screw and a pair of pliers to remove it.
13 Clean the oil seal housing and the camshaft sealing surface.
14 Smear the lips of the new oil seal with clean engine oil, then fit it over the end of the camshaft, open end first. A piece of thin plastic or tape wound round the front of the camshaft should prevent damage to the oil seal as it is fitted.
15 Press the seal into the housing until it is flush with the end face of the cylinder head. Use a suitable bolt (screwed into the end of the camshaft), washers and a tube or socket to press the seal into position.

12.12 Using a hooked tool to remove the camshaft oil seal

16 Refit the camshaft sprocket as described in Section 8.

Left-hand oil seal

17 No oil seal is fitted to the left-hand end of the camshaft. The sealing is provided by an O-ring fitted to the braking system vacuum pump flange. The O-ring can be renewed after unbolting the pump from the cylinder head (see Chapter 9). Note the smaller O-ring which seals the oil feed gallery to the pump – this may also cause leakage from the pump/cylinder head mating faces if it deteriorates or fails.

---

13 Flywheel –
removal, inspection
and refitting

Removal

1 Remove the transmission as described in Chapter 7, then remove the clutch assembly as described in Chapter 6.
2 Prevent the flywheel from turning using a sturdy screwdriver inserted between the ring gear teeth and the cylinder block. Alternatively, bolt a strap between one of the clutch pressure plate mounting bolt holes and an adjacent hole on the cylinder block end face. *Do not* attempt to lock the flywheel in position using the engine assembly/valve timing locking tools described in Section 3.
3 Slacken and remove the flywheel retaining bolts, and remove the flywheel from the end of the crankshaft. Be careful not to drop it; it is heavy. If the flywheel locating dowel is a loose fit in the crankshaft end, remove it and store it with the flywheel for safe-keeping. Discard the flywheel bolts; new ones must be used on refitting.

Inspection

4 Examine the flywheel for scoring of the clutch face, and for wear or chipping of the ring gear teeth. If the clutch face is scored, the flywheel may be surface-ground, but renewal is preferable. Seek the advice of a Citroën dealer or engine reconditioning specialist to see if machining is possible. If the ring gear is worn or damaged, the flywheel must be renewed, as it is not possible to renew the ring gear separately.

Refitting

5 Clean the mating surfaces of the flywheel and crankshaft. Remove any remaining locking compound from the threads of the crankshaft holes, using the correct size of tap, if available.

> **HAYNES HINT** *If a suitable tap is not available, cut two slots along the threads of one of the old flywheel bolts, and use the bolt to remove the locking compound from the threads.*

6 If the new flywheel retaining bolts are not supplied with their threads already pre-coated, apply a suitable thread-locking compound to the threads of each bolt prior to fitting.
7 Ensure that the locating dowel is in position. Offer up the flywheel, locating it on the dowel, and fit the new retaining bolts.
8 Lock the flywheel using the method employed on removal, and tighten the retaining bolts to the specified torque.
9 Refit the clutch as described in Chapter 6. Remove the flywheel locking tool, and refit the transmission as described in Chapter 7.

---

14 Engine/transmission mountings –
inspection and renewal

Inspection

1 If improved access is required, firmly apply the handbrake, then jack up the front of the vehicle and support it securely on axle stands (see *Jacking and vehicle support*).
2 Check the mounting rubbers to see if they are cracked, hardened or separated from the metal at any point; renew the mounting if any such damage or deterioration is evident.
3 Check that all the mounting's fasteners are securely tightened; use a torque wrench to check if possible **(see illustration)**.
4 Using a large screwdriver or a crowbar, check for wear in each mounting by carefully levering against it to check for free play. Where this is not possible, enlist the aid of an assistant to move the engine/transmission back-and-forth, or from side-to-side, while you watch the mounting. While some free play is to be expected even from new components, excessive wear should be obvious. If excessive free play is found, check first that the fasteners are correctly secured, then renew any worn components as described below.

Renewal

Right-hand mounting

5 Disconnect the battery negative terminal (refer to *Disconnecting the battery* in the Reference Chapter).
6 Release the four plastic fasteners and remove the engine cover from the top of the engine.

7 Release all the relevant hoses and wiring from their retaining clips. Place the hoses/wiring clear of the mounting so that the removal procedure is not hindered.

8 Place a jack beneath the engine, with a block of wood on the jack head. Raise the jack until it is supporting the weight of the engine.

9 Slacken and remove the three bolts securing the upper mounting bracket to the lower (engine) bracket.

10 Undo the two bolts securing the stiffener

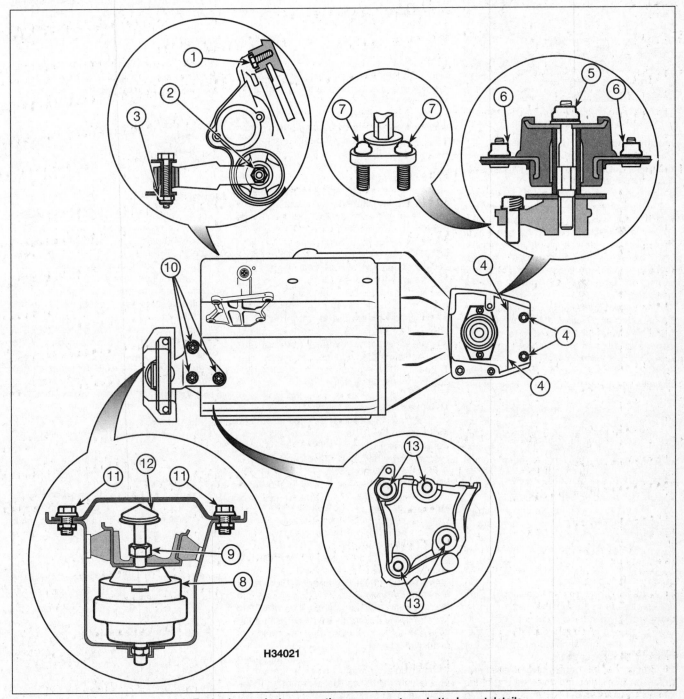

14.3 Engine/transmission mounting components and attachment details

1 Rear mounting bracket-to-cylinder block bolts
2 Rear mounting connecting link-to-cylinder block bracket nut
3 Rear mounting connecting link-to-subframe bracket nut
4 Left-hand mounting bracket-to-body bolts

5 Left-hand rubber mounting centre nut
6 Left-hand rubber mounting-to-bracket nuts
7 Left-hand mounting bracket-to-transmission bolts
8 Right-hand rubber mounting
9 Right-hand upper mounting bracket-to-rubber mounting nut

10 Right-hand upper mounting bracket-to-lower (engine) bracket bolts
11 Right-hand mounting stiffener bracket bolts
12 Right-hand rubber mounting domed buffer nut
13 Right-hand mounting lower (engine) bracket bolts

15.5 Oil cooler/oil filter mounting bolt (A) and locating notch (B)

bracket to the body and lift off the bracket. Unscrew the domed buffer nut, then unscrew the single nut securing the upper bracket to the rubber mounting.

11 Lift the upper bracket and the rubber buffer plate off the rubber mounting stud, then remove the washer, unscrew the rubber mounting from the body, and remove it from the vehicle. A strap wrench or similar may be used to unscrew the mounting, or alternatively fabricate a tool from suitable metal tube with projections to engage in the cut-outs in the mounting.

12 If required, the lower (engine) bracket can be unbolted and removed from the engine, but it will first be necessary to remove the upper and intermediate timing belt covers as described in Section 6.

13 Check all components carefully for signs of wear or damage, and renew them where necessary.

14 If removed, refit the lower (engine) bracket, apply a drop of locking compound to the retaining bolts and tighten them to the specified torque. Refit the intermediate and upper timing belt covers as described in Section 6.

15 Screw the rubber mounting into the vehicle body, and tighten it securely.

16 Refit the rubber buffer plate to the rubber mounting stud, and install the upper mounting bracket.

17 Tighten the upper mounting bracket retaining nuts/bolts to the specified torque setting.

18 Refit the domed buffer nut and stiffener bracket, then remove the jack from underneath the engine.

19 Refit all disturbed hoses and wiring, refit the engine cover and reconnect the battery.

Left-hand mounting

20 Disconnect the battery negative terminal (refer to *Disconnecting the battery* in the Reference Chapter).

21 Remove the air cleaner assembly and intake ducting as described in Chapter 4B.

22 Lift up the covers on the battery positive cable terminal box and unscrew the nuts securing the battery cables to the terminal studs. Lift the cables off the studs and suitably label them for correct refitting.

23 Withdraw the engine management ECU from its location on the support tray and move it to one side.

24 Release the wiring harness connectors and retaining clips on the ECU support tray, then undo the retaining bolts and lift out the support tray.

25 Place a jack beneath the transmission, with a block of wood on the jack head. Raise the jack until it is supporting the weight of the transmission.

26 Slacken and remove the centre nut and washer from the left-hand mounting, then undo the nuts securing the mounting to the mounting bracket. Lift off the mounting and remove it from the engine compartment.

27 If necessary, slide the spacer (where fitted) off the mounting stud, then unscrew the stud from the transmission bracket, and remove it along with its washer. If the mounting stud is tight, a universal stud extractor can be used to unscrew it.

28 Check all components carefully for signs of wear or damage, and renew as necessary.

29 Clean the threads of the mounting stud, and apply a coat of thread-locking compound to its threads. Refit the stud and washer to the transmission bracket, and tighten it to the specified torque setting.

30 Slide the spacer (where fitted) onto the mounting stud, then refit the rubber mounting. Tighten both the mounting-to-bracket nuts and the mounting centre nut to their specified torque settings, and remove the jack from underneath the transmission.

31 Refit the ECU support tray, reconnect and clip the wiring harness back into position.

32 Refit the ECU to the support tray and reconnect the battery positive cables to their respective terminal studs.

33 Refit the air cleaner assembly and intake ducting as described in Chapter 4B, then reconnect the battery negative terminal.

Rear mounting

34 If not already done, firmly apply the handbrake, then jack up the front of the vehicle and support it securely on axle stands (see *Jacking and vehicle support*). Remove the engine undertray.

35 Unscrew and remove the nut and through-bolt securing the rear mounting connecting link to the mounting on the rear of the cylinder block.

36 Unscrew and remove the nut and through-bolt securing the rear mounting connecting link to the bracket on the subframe. Withdraw the link.

37 To remove the mounting assembly it will first be necessary to remove the right-hand driveshaft as described in Chapter 8.

38 With the driveshaft removed, undo the retaining bolts and remove the mounting from the rear of the cylinder block.

39 Check carefully for signs of wear or damage on all components, and renew them where necessary.

40 On reassembly, fit the rear mounting assembly to the rear of the cylinder block, and tighten its retaining bolts to the specified torque. Refit the driveshaft as described in Chapter 8.

41 Refit the connecting link, and tighten both its nuts to their specified torque settings.

42 Refit the engine undertray and lower the vehicle to the ground.

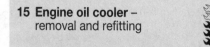

15 Engine oil cooler – removal and refitting

Removal

1 Firmly apply the handbrake, then jack up the front of the vehicle and support it securely on axle stands (see *Jacking and vehicle support*).

2 Drain the cooling system as described in Chapter 1B. Alternatively, clamp the oil cooler coolant hoses directly above the cooler, and be prepared for some coolant loss as the hoses are disconnected.

3 Position a suitable container beneath the oil filter. Unscrew the filter using an oil filter removal tool if necessary, and drain the oil into the container. If the oil filter is damaged or distorted during removal, it must be renewed. Given the low cost of a new oil filter relative to the cost of repairing the damage which could result if a re-used filter springs a leak, it is probably a good idea to renew the filter in any case.

4 Release the hose clips, and disconnect the coolant hoses from the oil cooler.

5 Unscrew the oil cooler/oil filter mounting bolt from the cylinder block, and withdraw the cooler. Note the locating notch in the cooler flange, which fits over the lug on the cylinder block **(see illustration)**. Discard the oil cooler sealing ring; a new one must be used on refitting.

Refitting

6 Fit a new sealing ring to the recess in the rear of the cooler, then offer the cooler to the cylinder block.

7 Ensure that the locating notch in the cooler flange is correctly engaged with the lug on the cylinder block, then refit the mounting bolt and tighten it securely.

8 Fit the oil filter, then lower the vehicle to the ground. Top-up the engine oil level as described in *Weekly checks*.

9 Refill or top-up the cooling system as described in Chapter 1B or *Weekly checks*. Start the engine, and check the oil cooler for signs of leakage.

Chapter 2 Part D:
Petrol engine removal and overhaul procedures

Contents

Degrees of difficulty

Easy, suitable for novice with little experience	Fairly easy, suitable for beginner with some experience	Fairly difficult, suitable for competent DIY mechanic	Difficult, suitable for experienced DIY mechanic	Very difficult, suitable for expert DIY or professional

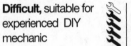

Specifications

Note: *At the time of writing, certain specifications were not available. Where the relevant specifications are not given here, refer to your Citroën dealer for further information*

Cylinder head
Maximum gasket face distortion .... 0.05 mm

Cylinder block
Cylinder bore diameter:
  1.6 litre engine:
    Standard size .... 78.00 mm
    Repair size .... Not available
  1.8 litre engine:
    Standard size .... 82.70 mm
    Repair size .... 83.30 mm

Valves
Valve head diameter:
  Inlet:
    1.6 litre engine .... 39.5 mm
    1.8 litre engine .... 29.8 mm
  Exhaust:
    1.6 litre engine .... 31.4 mm
    1.8 litre engine .... 27.2 mm
Valve stem diameter:
  Inlet:
    1.6 litre engine .... Not available
    1.8 litre engine .... 5.98 mm
  Exhaust:
    1.6 litre engine .... Not available
    1.8 litre engine .... 5.97 mm
Overall length:
  Inlet:
    1.6 litre engine .... Not available
    1.8 litre engine .... 104.17 mm
  Exhaust:
    1.6 litre engine .... Not available
    1.8 litre engine .... 104.10 mm

Valve springs

Free length:
1.6 litre engines . . . . Not available
1.8 litre engines . . . . 48.0 mm

Pistons

Piston diameter:
1.6 litre engine . . . . Not available
1.8 litre engine:
    Standard size . . . . 82.657 mm
    Repair size . . . . 83.257 mm

Piston rings

End gaps:
Top compression ring . . . . 0.20 to 0.45 mm
Second compression ring . . . . 0.20 to 0.40 mm

Crankshaft

Endfloat:
1.6 litre engine . . . . 0.07 to 0.32 mm
1.8 litre engine . . . . 0.06 to 0.15 mm
Main bearing journal diameter:
1.6 litre engine:
    Standard . . . . 49.965 to 49.981 mm
    Repair size . . . . 49.665 to 49.681 mm
1.8 litre engine:
    Standard . . . . 59.975 to 60.000 mm
    Repair size . . . . 59.675 to 59.700 mm
Big-end bearing journal diameter:
1.6 litre engine:
    Standard . . . . 44.992 to 45.008 mm
    Repair size . . . . 44.692 to 44.708 mm
1.8 litre engine:
    Standard . . . . 44.975 to 45.000 mm
    Repair size . . . . 44.675 to 44.700 mm
Maximum bearing journal out-of-round (all engines) . . . . 0.007 mm
Main bearing running clearance:
1.6 litre engine . . . . 0.023 to 0.048 mm
1.8 litre engine . . . . 0.019 to 0.049 mm
Big-end bearing running clearance (all engines) . . . . 0.030 to 0.054 mm

Torque wrench settings

1.6 litre (TU series) engines
Refer to Chapter 2A Specifications.

1.8 litre (EW series) engines
Refer to Chapter 2B Specifications.

1 General information

Included in this Part of Chapter 2 are details of removing the engine/transmission from the car and general overhaul procedures for the cylinder head, cylinder block and all other engine internal components.

The information given ranges from advice concerning preparation for an overhaul and the purchase of replacement parts, to detailed step-by-step procedures covering removal, inspection, renovation and refitting of engine internal components.

After Section 5, all instructions are based on the assumption that the engine has been removed from the vehicle. For information concerning in-car engine repair, as well as the removal and refitting of those external components necessary for full overhaul, refer to Part A or B of this Chapter (as applicable) and to Section 5. Ignore any preliminary dismantling operations described in Part A or B that are no longer relevant once the engine has been removed.

Apart from torque wrench settings, which are given at the beginning of Part A or B (as applicable), all available specifications relating to engine overhaul are at the beginning of this Part of Chapter 2.

2 Engine overhaul –
general information

It is not always easy to determine when, or if, an engine should be completely overhauled, as a number of factors must be considered.

High mileage is not necessarily an indication that an overhaul is needed, while low mileage does not preclude the need for an overhaul. Frequency of servicing is probably the most important consideration. An engine which has had regular and frequent oil and filter changes, as well as other required maintenance, should give many thousands of miles of reliable service. Conversely, a neglected engine may require an overhaul very early in its life.

Excessive oil consumption is an indication that piston rings, valve seals and/or valve guides are in need of attention. Make sure that oil leaks are not responsible before deciding that the rings and/or guides are worn. Perform a compression test, as described in Part A of this Chapter, to determine the likely cause of the problem.

Check the oil pressure with a gauge fitted in place of the oil pressure switch, and compare it with that specified in Part A or B of this Chapter. If it is extremely low, the main and big-end bearings, and/or the oil pump, are probably worn out.

Loss of power, rough running, knocking or metallic engine noises, excessive valve gear noise, and high fuel consumption may also point to the need for an overhaul, especially if they are all present at the same time. If a complete service does not remedy the situation, major mechanical work is the only solution.

An engine overhaul involves restoring all internal parts to the specification of a new engine. During an overhaul, the cylinder bores are rebored (where necessary), and the pistons and piston rings are renewed. New main and big-end bearings are generally fitted; if necessary, the crankshaft may be reground, to restore the journals. The valves are also serviced as well, since they are usually in less-than-perfect condition at this point. The end result should be an as-new engine that will give many trouble-free miles.

Note: *Critical cooling system components such as the hoses, thermostat and coolant pump should be renewed when an engine is overhauled. The radiator should be checked carefully, to ensure that it is not clogged or leaking. Also, it is a good idea to renew the oil pump whenever the engine is overhauled.*

Before beginning the engine overhaul, read through the entire procedure, to familiarise yourself with the scope and requirements of the job. Overhauling an engine is not difficult if you follow carefully all of the instructions, have the necessary tools and equipment, and pay close attention to all specifications. It can, however, be time-consuming. Plan on the car being off the road for a minimum of two weeks, especially if parts must be taken to an engineering works for repair or reconditioning. Check on the availability of parts and make sure that any necessary special tools and equipment are obtained in advance. Most work can be done with typical hand tools, although a number of precision measuring tools are required for inspecting parts to determine if they must be renewed. Often the engineering works will handle the inspection of parts and offer advice concerning reconditioning and renewal.

Always wait until the engine has been completely dismantled, and until all components (especially the cylinder block and the crankshaft) have been inspected, before deciding what service and repair operations must be performed by an engineering works. The condition of these components will be the major factor to consider when determining whether to overhaul the original engine, or to buy a reconditioned unit. Do not, therefore, purchase parts or have overhaul work done on other components until they have been thoroughly inspected. As a general rule, time is the primary cost of an overhaul, so it does not pay to fit worn or sub-standard parts.

As a final note, to ensure maximum life and minimum trouble from a reconditioned engine, everything must be assembled with care, in a spotlessly-clean environment.

3 Engine/transmission removal – methods and precautions

If you have decided that the engine must be removed for overhaul or major repair work, several preliminary steps should be taken.

Locating a suitable place to work is extremely important. Adequate work space, along with storage space for the vehicle, will be needed. If a workshop or garage is not available, at the very least, a flat, level, clean work surface is required.

Cleaning the engine compartment and engine/transmission before beginning the removal procedure will help keep tools clean and organised.

An engine hoist will also be necessary. Make sure the equipment is rated in excess of the combined weight of the engine and transmission. Safety is of primary importance, considering the potential hazards involved in removing the engine/transmission from the vehicle.

If this is the first time you have removed an engine, an assistant should ideally be available. Advice and aid from someone more experienced would also be helpful. There are many instances when one person cannot simultaneously perform all of the operations required during engine/transmission removal.

Plan the operation ahead of time. Before starting work, arrange for the hire of or obtain all of the tools and equipment you will need. Some of the equipment necessary to perform engine/transmission removal and installation safely (in addition to an engine hoist) is as follows: a heavy duty trolley jack, complete sets of spanners and sockets as described at the rear of this manual, wooden blocks, and plenty of rags and cleaning solvent for mopping-up spilled oil, coolant and fuel. If the hoist must be hired, make sure that you arrange for it in advance, and perform all of the operations possible without it beforehand. This will save you money and time.

Plan for the vehicle to be out of use for quite a while. An engineering works will be required to perform some of the work which the do-it-yourselfer cannot accomplish without special equipment. These places often have a busy schedule, so it would be a good idea to consult them before removing the engine, in order to accurately estimate the amount of time required to rebuild or repair components that may need work.

During the engine/transmission removal procedure, it is advisable to make notes of the locations of all brackets, cable ties, earthing points, etc, as well as how the wiring harnesses, hoses and electrical connections are attached and routed around the engine and engine compartment. An effective way of doing this is to take a series of photographs of the various components before they are disconnected or removed. A simple inexpensive disposable camera is ideal for this and the resulting photographs will prove invaluable when the engine is refitted.

Always be extremely careful when removing and refitting the engine/transmission. Serious injury can result from careless actions. Plan ahead and take your time, and a job of this nature, although major, can be accomplished successfully.

The engine and transmission assembly is removed downwards from the engine compartment on all models described in this manual.

4 Engine and transmission – removal, separation, reconnection and refitting

Removal

Note: *The engine is removed downwards from the engine compartment as a complete unit with the transmission; the two are then separated for overhaul.*

1 Disconnect the battery negative terminal (refer to *Disconnecting the battery* in the Reference Section of this manual).

2 Open and support the bonnet in its maximum height position.

3 Carry out the following operations, using the information given in Chapter 4A:

a) *Remove the air cleaner assembly and air inlet ducts.*

b) *Depressurise the fuel system, and disconnect the fuel feed hose at the fuel rail.*

c) *Disconnect the accelerator cable.*

4 On 1.8 litre engines, disconnect the air inlet hose from the secondary air injection valve, then disconnect the vacuum hoses and wiring connector at the EGR solenoid valve.

5 Disconnect the purge valve and/or braking system servo vacuum hoses from the inlet manifold (as applicable).

6 Lift off the engine compartment fuse/relay box cover and unscrew the nuts securing the two supply cables to the terminal studs **(see illustration)**. Lift the cables off the studs,

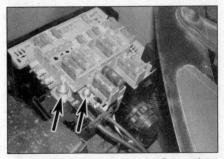

4.6 Unscrew the nuts (arrowed) securing the two supply cables to the fuse/relay box terminal studs

4.7 Disconnect the battery positive cables from the terminal box studs

4.9 Undo the retaining bolts (arrowed) and lift out the ECU support tray

release them from the fuse/relay box and suitably label them.

7 Similarly, lift up the covers on the battery positive cable terminal box and unscrew the nuts securing the battery cables to the terminal studs. Lift the cables off the studs and suitably label them for correct refitting **(see illustration)**.

8 Remove the engine management ECU as described in Chapter 4A, Section 13.

9 Release the wiring harness from the retaining clips and cable ties on the ECU support tray, then undo the retaining bolts and lift out the support tray **(see illustration)**.

10 Disconnect the main engine wiring harness at the connectors in front of the ECU support tray location.

11 Working as described in Chapter 6, on models with a cable-operated clutch, disconnect the clutch cable from the transmission, and position it clear of the working area. On models with a hydraulically-operated clutch, unbolt the slave cylinder from the front of the transmission. Release the hydraulic fluid supply pipe from the support brackets and move the pipe and cylinder assembly clear of the engine/transmission.

12 Working as described in Chapter 7, disconnect the gearchange selector cable end fittings from the transmission levers then release the cables from the support bracket.

13 Undo the bolt and release the transmission earth cable from body side-member.

14 Firmly apply the handbrake, then jack up the front of the vehicle and support it securely on axle stands (see *Jacking and vehicle support*). Note that the vehicle must be raised sufficiently high (approximately 500 mm) to enable the engine/transmission assembly to be withdrawn from under the front of the vehicle. Remove the front roadwheels.

15 Remove the auxiliary drivebelt as described in Chapter 1A.

16 If the engine is to be dismantled, drain the engine oil referring to Chapter 1A if necessary. Clean and refit the drain plug, tightening it securely.

17 Drain the cooling system as described in Chapter 1A.

18 Drain the transmission oil as described in Chapter 7. Refit the drain and filler plugs, and tighten them to their specified torque settings.

19 Remove the exhaust system front pipe as described in Chapter 4A.

20 Disconnect the radiator top and bottom hoses from the coolant outlet housing or coolant pipe, and thermostat cover.

21 Release the retaining clips and disconnect the heater matrix hoses from their connection on the engine compartment bulkhead.

22 Disconnect the wiring connector from the power steering pressure switch.

1.6 litre engines

23 Remove the heat shield from the rear of the power steering pump.

24 Position a suitable container beneath the power steering gear pump. Release the retaining clip and disconnect the power steering fluid return hose from the pump. Allow the power steering fluid to drain into the container. When the fluid has finished draining, suitably cover the hose end and the outlet on the pump.

25 Unscrew the union nut and disconnect the fluid supply pipe from the pump. Release the supply pipe and return hose from the retaining clamps and move the pipe and hose clear of the engine. Suitably cover the pipe end and pump orifice.

1.8 litre engines

26 Release the power steering fluid pipes from the clamps on each side of the transmission bellhousing.

27 Position a suitable container beneath the power steering gear assembly. Undo the bolt securing the fluid pipe flange plate to the rack housing and ease the flange plate from the

4.38 Lowering the engine/transmission from the engine compartment

rack. Allow the power steering fluid to drain into the container. When the fluid has finished draining, suitably cover the pipe ends and the orifices in the rack to prevent dirt ingress.

28 Slacken the retaining clip and disconnect the fluid return hose from the pipe connection below the radiator. Unscrew the union nut and disconnect the fluid supply hose from the pump. Release the pipe and hose assembly from the support bracket clamps and remove the pipes from under the vehicle. Suitably cover the pipe and hose ends and the orifices in the pump to prevent dirt ingress.

All engines

29 On models with air conditioning, disconnect the compressor wiring connector, then unbolt the compressor and position it clear of the engine. Support the weight of the compressor by tying it to the vehicle body, to prevent any excess strain being placed on the compressor lines whilst the engine is removed. *Do not* disconnect the refrigerant lines from the compressor (refer to the warnings given in Chapter 3).

30 Disconnect the wiring connector from the vehicle speed sensor.

31 Remove both driveshafts as described in Chapter 8.

32 Remove the front suspension subframe as described in Chapter 10.

33 Check that all the relevant wiring connectors have been disconnected, and that the harness is released from all the clips or ties, so that it is free to be removed with the engine/transmission.

34 Manoeuvre an engine hoist into position, and attach it to the engine lifting brackets. Raise the hoist until it is just supporting the weight of the engine.

35 Slacken and remove the centre nut and washer from the engine/transmission left-hand mounting. Undo the two nuts and washers securing the mounting to its bracket, remove the mounting from the engine com-partment and recover the washer and spacer.

36 Working on the right-hand engine/transmission mounting, on 1.8 litre engines, undo the two bolts securing the stiffener bracket to the body and lift off the bracket. Unscrew the nut securing the upper mounting bracket to the rubber mounting. Unscrew the three bolts securing the upper mounting bracket to the lower (engine bracket) and, on 1.6 litre engines, the additional bolt at the front securing the support brace to the upper mounting bracket. Remove the upper mounting bracket from the lower (engine) bracket.

37 Make a final check that any components which would prevent the removal of the engine/transmission from the vehicle have been removed or disconnected.

38 Carefully lower the engine/transmission assembly from the engine compartment, ensuring that nothing is trapped or damaged **(see illustration)**. Enlist the help of an assistant during this procedure, as it will be necessary to tilt and twist the assembly slightly to clear the body panels and adjacent components.

39 Ensure that the assembly is adequately supported using jacks or a suitable trolley, then disconnect the engine hoist and withdraw the engine/transmission out from under the front of the vehicle.

Separation

40 With the engine/transmission assembly removed, support the unit on suitable blocks of wood on a workbench (or failing that, on a clean area of the workshop floor).

41 Disconnect all the individual wiring connectors from the various components on the engine and transmission to enable the main engine wiring harness to be removed. Make notes or attach labels to each connector to aid reconnection.

42 With all wiring disconnected, detach the wiring harness support brackets and plastic ducting mountings, release the relevant cable ties and remove the complete harness assembly from the engine/transmission.

43 Where fitted, undo the retaining bolts, and remove the cover plate from the transmission bellhousing.

44 Slacken and remove the retaining bolts, and remove the starter motor from the transmission.

45 Ensure that both engine and transmission are adequately supported, then slacken and remove the remaining bolts securing the transmission housing to the engine. Note the correct fitted positions of each bolt (and the relevant brackets) as they are removed, to use as a reference on refitting.

46 Carefully withdraw the transmission from the engine, ensuring that the weight of the transmission is not allowed to hang on the input shaft while it is engaged with the clutch friction disc.

47 If they are loose, remove the locating dowels from the engine or transmission, and keep them in a safe place.

Reconnection

48 Apply a smear of high-melting-point grease (Citroën recommend the use of Molykote BR2 plus – available from your Citroën dealer) to the splines of the transmission input shaft. Do not apply too much, otherwise there is a possibility of the grease contaminating the clutch friction disc.

49 Ensure that the locating dowels are correctly positioned in the engine or transmission.

50 Carefully offer the transmission to the engine, until the locating dowels are engaged. Ensure that the weight of the transmission is not allowed to hang on the input shaft as it is engaged with the clutch friction disc.

51 Refit the transmission housing-to-engine bolts, ensuring that all the necessary brackets are correctly positioned, and tighten them securely.

52 Refit the starter motor, and securely tighten its retaining bolts.

53 Locate the main engine wiring harness on the engine and transmission and reconnect the relevant wiring connectors.

54 Where applicable, refit the cover plate to the transmission bellhousing, and securely tighten its retaining bolts.

Refitting

55 Manoeuvre the engine/transmission into position beneath the engine compartment and reconnect the hoist and lifting tackle to the engine lifting brackets. With the aid of an assistant, slowly lift the assembly into the engine compartment.

56 Manoeuvre the unit as necessary to clear the surrounding components, until it is possible to attach the engine mountings. Locate the right-hand mounting upper bracket onto the lower (engine) bracket and over the rubber mounting stud. Secure the bracket to the lower (engine) bracket with the bolts tightened to the specified torque. Refit the retaining nut to the stud on the rubber mounting and tighten it by hand only at this stage.

57 Working on the left-hand mounting, refit the rubber mounting, the mounting retaining nuts and washers, and the centre nut and washer, tightening them lightly only.

58 Rock the engine to settle it on its mountings, then go around and tighten all the mounting nuts and bolts to their specified torque settings. On 1.8 litre engines, refit the stiffener bracket to the right-hand mounting, tightening the retaining bolts securely.

59 It is advisable at this stage to refit the front suspension subframe as described in Chapter 10. The rear engine/transmission mounting connecting link can then be refitted, thus stabilising the power unit on its mountings. The hoist can then be detached from the engine and removed.

60 The remainder of the refitting procedure is a direct reversal of the removal sequence, noting the following points:

a) *Ensure that the wiring loom is correctly routed and retained by all the relevant retaining clips; all connectors should be correctly and securely reconnected.*

b) *Use new O-ring seals when refitting the power steering fluid pipes.*

c) *Prior to refitting the driveshafts to the transmission, renew the driveshaft oil seals as described in Chapter 7.*

d) *Ensure that all coolant hoses are correctly reconnected, and securely retained by their retaining clips.*

e) *Adjust the gearchange selector cables as described in Chapter 7 after reconnection.*

f) *Adjust the accelerator cable as described in Chapter 4A.*

g) *Refill the engine and transmission with the correct quantity and type of lubricant, as described in Chapters 1A and 7.*

h) *Refill the cooling system as described in Chapter 1A.*

i) *Bleed the power steering system as described in Chapter 10.*

j) *Bleed the hydraulic clutch system as described in Chapter 10.*

5 Engine overhaul – dismantling sequence

1 It is much easier to dismantle and work on the engine if it is mounted on a portable engine stand. These stands can often be hired from a tool hire shop. Before the engine is mounted on a stand, the flywheel should be removed, so that the stand bolts can be tightened into the end of the cylinder block.

2 If a stand is not available, it is possible to dismantle the engine with it blocked up on a sturdy workbench, or on the floor. Be extra careful not to tip or drop the engine when working without a stand.

3 If you are going to obtain a reconditioned engine, all the external components must be removed first, to be transferred to the replacement engine (just as they will if you are doing a complete engine overhaul yourself). These components include the following:

a) *Alternator (Chapter 5A).*
b) *Power steering pump (Chapter 10).*
c) *Power steering pump and air conditioning compressor bracket(s), as applicable.*
d) *Engine mounting brackets.*
e) *Coolant pump, thermostat and housing, and coolant outlet housing (Chapter 3).*
f) *Dipstick tube.*
g) *Fuel system components (Chapter 4A).*
h) *All electrical switches and sensors.*
i) *Inlet and exhaust manifolds (Chapter 4A).*
j) *Oil filter (Chapter 1A).*
k) *Flywheel (Chapter 2A or 2B).*

Note: *When removing the external components from the engine, pay close attention to details that may be helpful or important during refitting. Note the fitted position of gaskets, seals, spacers, pins, washers, bolts, and other small items.*

4 If you are obtaining a 'short' engine (cylinder block, crankshaft, pistons and connecting rods all assembled), then the cylinder head, sump, oil pump, and timing belt will have to be removed also.

5 If you are planning a complete overhaul, the engine can be dismantled, and the internal components removed, in the order given below, referring to Part A or B of this Chapter unless otherwise stated.

a) *Inlet and exhaust manifolds (Chapter 4A).*
b) *Timing belt, sprockets, tensioner and idler(s).*
c) *Coolant pump (Chapter 3).*
d) *Cylinder head.*
e) *Flywheel.*
f) *Sump.*
g) *Oil pump (Chapter 2A or Section 10 of this Chapter – as applicable).*
h) *Pistons/connecting rods (Section 9 of this Chapter).*
i) *Crankshaft (Section 11 of this Chapter).*
j) *All external brackets and housings.*

6.9a Compress the valve spring with a spring compressor . . .

6.9c . . . release the compressor and lift off the spring retainer . . .

6 Before beginning the dismantling and overhaul procedures, make sure that you have all of the tools necessary. Refer to *Tools and working facilities* for further information.

6.12a Secure a self-locking nut of suitable diameter to a long bolt . . .

6.12b . . . then use this tool to remove the valve stem oil seal – 1.8 litre engines

6.9b . . . remove the two split collets . . .

6.9d . . . and the valve spring

6 Cylinder head – dismantling

Note: *New and reconditioned cylinder heads are available from the manufacturer, and from engine overhaul specialists. Some specialist tools are required for dismantling and inspection, and new components may not be readily available. It may therefore be more practical and economical for the home mechanic to purchase a reconditioned head, rather than dismantle, inspect and recondition the original head.*

1.6 litre engines

1 Remove the cylinder head as described in Part A of this Chapter.
2 If not already done, remove the inlet and exhaust manifolds with reference to Chapter 4A.

6.13 Place each valve and its associated components in a labelled polythene bag

3 Remove the camshaft and rocker arms as described in Part A of this Chapter.
4 Using a valve spring compressor, compress each valve spring in turn until the split collets can be removed. Release the compressor, and lift off the spring retainer, spring and spring seat. Using a pair of pliers, carefully extract the valve stem oil seal from the top of the guide.
5 If, when the valve spring compressor is screwed down, the spring retainer refuses to free and expose the split collets, gently tap the top of the tool, directly over the retainer, with a light hammer. This will free the retainer.
6 Withdraw the valve through the combustion chamber.

1.8 litre engines

7 Remove the cylinder head as described in Part B of this Chapter.
8 Remove the following components from the cylinder head as described in the Chapters indicated:
a) *Camshafts and tappets (Part B of this Chapter).*
b) *Ignition coil module (Chapter 5B).*
c) *Exhaust manifold (Chapter 4B).*
d) *Coolant outlet housing (Chapter 3).*
9 Using a valve spring compressor, compress each valve spring in turn until the split collets can be removed. Release the compressor, and lift off the spring retainer and spring **(see illustrations)**.
10 If, when the valve spring compressor is screwed down, the spring retainer refuses to free and expose the split collets, gently tap the top of the tool, directly over the retainer, with a light hammer. This will free the retainer.
11 Withdraw the valve through the combustion chamber.
12 The valve stem oil seal also forms the spring seat and is deeply recessed in the cylinder head. It is also a tight fit on the valve guide making it difficult to remove with pliers or a conventional valve stem oil seal removal tool. It can be easily removed, however, using a self-locking nut of suitable diameter screwed onto the end of a bolt and locked with a second nut. Push the nut down onto the top of the seal; the locking portion of the nut will grip the seal allowing it to be withdrawn from the top of the valve guide **(see illustrations)**.

All engines

13 It is essential that each valve is stored together with its collets, retainer, spring, and spring seat. The valves should also be kept in their correct sequence, unless they are so badly worn that they are to be renewed. If they are going to be kept and used again, place each valve assembly in a labelled polythene bag or similar small container **(see illustration)**. Number the bags or containers 1 to 8, or 1 to 8 inlet, and 1 to 8 exhaust, as applicable. Note that No 1 valve is nearest to the transmission (flywheel) end of the engine.
14 Remove all the remaining valves in the same way.

7.6 Checking the cylinder head gasket surface for distortion

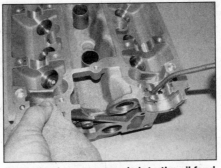

7.11a Apply compressed air to the oil feed bore of the inlet camshaft and seal the bore in the exhaust camshaft with a rag . . .

7.11b . . . the camshaft oil supply non-return valve will be ejected from the underside of the head

7 Cylinder head and valves – cleaning and inspection

1 Thorough cleaning of the cylinder head and valve components, followed by a detailed inspection, will enable you to decide how much valve service work must be carried out during the engine overhaul. **Note:** *If the engine has been severely overheated, it is best to assume that the cylinder head is warped – check carefully for signs of this.*

Cleaning

2 Remove all traces of old gasket material from the cylinder head. Citroën recommend the use of a scouring agent for this purpose, but acceptable results can be achieved by using a hard plastic or wood scraper to remove all traces of gasket and carbon.

3 Similarly, remove the carbon from the combustion chambers and ports, then wash the cylinder head thoroughly with paraffin or a suitable solvent.

4 Scrape off any heavy carbon deposits that may have formed on the valves, then use a power-operated wire brush to remove deposits from the valve heads and stems.

Inspection

Note: *Be sure to perform all the following inspection procedures before concluding that the services of a machine shop or engine overhaul specialist are required. Make a list of all items that require attention.*

Cylinder head

5 Inspect the head very carefully for cracks, evidence of coolant leakage, and other damage. If cracks are found, a new cylinder head should be obtained.

6 Use a straight-edge and feeler blade to check that the cylinder head gasket surface is not distorted **(see illustration)**. If it is, it may be possible to have it machined, provided that the cylinder head height is not significantly reduced.

7 Examine the valve seats in each of the combustion chambers. If they are severely pitted, cracked, or burned, they will need to

be renewed or recut by an engine overhaul specialist. If they are only slightly pitted, this can be removed by grinding-in the valve heads and seats with fine valve-grinding compound, as described below.

8 Check the valve guides for wear by inserting the relevant valve, and checking for side-to-side motion of the valve. A very small amount of movement is acceptable. If the movement seems excessive, remove the valve. Measure the valve stem diameter (see below), and renew the valve if it is worn. If the valve stem is not worn, the wear must be in the valve guide, and the guide must be renewed. The renewal of valve guides is best carried out by an engine overhaul specialist, who will have the necessary tools available. Where no valve stem diameter is specified, seek the advice of the specialist carrying out the work, or a Citroën dealer on the best course of action.

9 If renewing the valve guides, the valve seats should be recut or reground only *after* the guides have been fitted.

10 On 1.8 litre engines, examine the camshaft oil supply non-return valve in the oil feed bore at the timing belt end of the cylinder head. Check that the valve is not loose in the cylinder head and that the ball is free to move within the valve body. If the valve is a loose fit in its bore, or if there is any doubt about its condition, it should be renewed.

11 The non-return valve can be removed (assuming it is not loose), using compressed air, such as that generated by a tyre foot

7.14 Measuring a valve stem diameter

pump. Place the pump nozzle over the oil feed bore of the inlet camshaft No 4 bearing journal and seal the corresponding oil feed bore in the exhaust camshaft with a rag. Apply the compressed air and the valve will be forced out of its location in the underside of the cylinder head **(see illustrations)**.

12 Fit the new non-return valve to its bore on the underside of the head ensuring it is fitted the correct way. Oil should be able to pass upwards through the valve to the camshafts, but the ball in the valve should prevent the oil from returning back to the cylinder block. Use a thin socket or similar to push the valve fully into position.

Valves

13 Examine the head of each valve for pitting, burning, cracks, and general wear. Check the valve stem for scoring and wear ridges. Rotate the valve, and check for any obvious indication that it is bent. Look for pits or excessive wear on the tip of each valve stem. Renew any valve that shows any such signs of wear or damage.

14 If the valve appears satisfactory at this stage, measure the valve stem diameter at several points using a micrometer **(see illustration)**. Any significant difference in the readings obtained indicates wear of the valve stem. Should any of these conditions be apparent, the valve(s) must be renewed.

15 If the valves are in satisfactory condition, they should be ground (lapped) into their respective seats, to ensure a smooth, gas-tight seal. If the seat is only lightly pitted, or if it has been recut, fine grinding compound *only* should be used to produce the required finish. Coarse valve-grinding compound should *not* be used, unless a seat is badly burned or deeply pitted. If this is the case, the cylinder head and valves should be inspected by an expert, to decide whether seat recutting, or even the renewal of the valve or seat insert (where possible) is required.

16 Valve grinding is carried out as follows. Place the head upside-down on blocks, on a bench.

17 Smear a trace of (the appropriate grade of) valve-grinding compound on the seat face, and press a suction grinding tool onto the

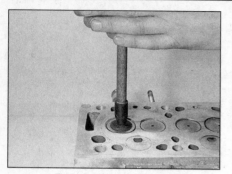

7.17 Grinding-in a valve

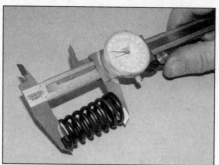

7.20 Measuring valve spring free length

valve head **(see illustration)**. With a semi-rotary action, grind the valve head to its seat, lifting the valve occasionally to redistribute the grinding compound. A light spring placed under the valve head will greatly ease this operation.

18 If coarse grinding compound is being used, work only until a dull, matt even surface is produced on both the valve seat and the valve, then wipe off the used compound, and repeat the process with fine compound. When a smooth unbroken ring of light grey matt finish is produced on both the valve and seat, the grinding operation is complete. *Do not grind-in the valves any further than absolutely necessary, or the seat will be prematurely sunk into the cylinder head.*

19 When all the valves have been ground-in, carefully wash off *all* traces of grinding compound using paraffin or a suitable solvent, before reassembling the cylinder head.

Valve components

20 Examine the valve springs for signs of damage and discoloration. Stand each spring on a flat surface, and check it for squareness noting that on 1.8 litre engines, the springs are tapered at the top. Measure the free length of the spring and compare it with the dimension given in the Specifications **(see illustration)**. On 1.6 litre engines, no minimum free length is specified by Citroën, so the only way of judging valve spring wear is by comparison with a new component.

21 If any of the springs are damaged, distorted or have lost their tension, obtain a complete new set of springs. It is normal to fit

new springs as a matter of course if a major overhaul is being carried out.

22 Renew the valve stem oil seals regardless of their apparent condition.

8 Cylinder head – reassembly

1.6 litre engines

1 Lubricate the stems of the valves, and insert the valves into their original locations. If new valves are being fitted, insert them into the locations to which they have been ground.

2 Refit the spring seat then, working on the first valve, dip the new valve stem oil seal in fresh engine oil. Carefully locate it over the valve and onto the guide. Take care not to damage the seal as it is passed over the valve stem. Use a suitable socket or tube to press the seal firmly onto the guide.

3 Locate the valve spring on top of its seat, then refit the spring retainer.

4 Compress the valve spring, and locate the split collets in the recess in the valve stem. Release the compressor, then repeat the procedure on the remaining valves.

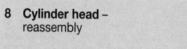 *Use a little dab of grease to hold the collets in position on the valve stem while the spring compressor is released.*

5 With all the valves installed, place the cylinder head on blocks on the bench and,

8.9a Place the valve stem oil seal over the valve guide . . .

8.9b . . . and use a suitable socket or tube to press the seal onto the guide

using a hammer and interposed block of wood, tap the end of each valve stem to settle the components.

6 Refit the camshaft and rocker arms as described in Part A of this Chapter.

7 Refit the inlet and exhaust manifolds with reference to Chapter 4A.

8 The cylinder head can then be refitted as described in Part A of this Chapter.

1.8 litre engines

9 Dip the new valve stem oil seal in fresh engine oil and place it in position over the valve guide. Use a suitable socket or tube to press the seal firmly onto the guide **(see illustrations)**.

10 Lubricate the stem of the valve, and insert the valve into the guide. Be sure to insert the valves into their original locations or, if new valves are being fitted, into the locations to which they have been ground.

11 Locate the valve spring on top of the oil seal/spring seat with its larger diameter towards the cylinder head.

12 Refit the spring retainer, compress the valve spring, and locate the split collets in the recess in the valve stem. Release the compressor, then repeat the procedure on the remaining valves.

13 With all the valves installed, place the cylinder head on blocks on the bench and, using a hammer and interposed block of wood, tap the end of each valve stem to settle the components.

14 Refit the following components to the cylinder head as described in the Chapters indicated:

a) *Camshafts and tappets (Part B of this Chapter).*

b) *Ignition coil module (Chapter 5B).*

c) *Exhaust manifold (Chapter 4B).*

d) *Coolant outlet housing (Chapter 3).*

15 The cylinder head can then be refitted as described in Part B of this Chapter.

9 Piston/connecting rod assembly – removal

1 On 1.6 litre engines, remove the cylinder head, sump and oil pump as described in Part A of this Chapter. On 1.8 litre engines, remove the cylinder head and sump as described in Part B of this Chapter.

2 If there is a pronounced wear ridge at the top of any bore, it may be necessary to remove it with a scraper or ridge reamer, to avoid piston damage during removal. Such a ridge indicates excess bore wear.

3 Using quick-drying paint or similar, mark each connecting rod and big-end bearing cap with its respective cylinder number on the flat machined surface provided; if the engine has been dismantled before, note carefully any identifying marks made previously **(see illustration)**. Note that No 1 cylinder is at the transmission (flywheel) end of the engine.

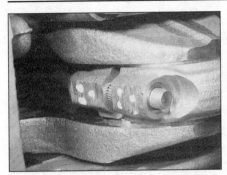

9.3 Connecting rod and big-end bearing cap identification marks (No 3 shown)

4 Turn the crankshaft to bring pistons 1 and 4 to BDC (bottom dead centre).
5 Unscrew the nuts or bolts, as applicable from No 1 piston big-end bearing cap. Take off the cap, and recover the bottom half bearing shell **(see illustration)**. If the bearing shells are to be re-used, tape the cap and the shell together.
6 On 1.6 litre engines, to prevent the possibility of damage to the crankshaft bearing journals, tape over the connecting rod stud threads.
7 Using a hammer handle, push the piston up through the bore, and remove it from the top of the cylinder block. Recover the bearing shell, and tape it to the connecting rod for safe-keeping.
8 Loosely refit the big-end cap to the connecting rod, and secure with the nuts/bolts – this will help to keep the components in their correct order.
9 Remove No 4 assembly in the same way.
10 Turn the crankshaft through 180° to bring pistons 2 and 3 to BDC (bottom dead centre), and remove them in the same way.

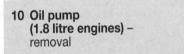

**10 Oil pump
(1.8 litre engines) –
removal**

1 Remove the crankshaft sprocket and the sump as described in Part B of this Chapter.
2 Undo the nine bolts and carefully ease the oil pump housing off the cylinder block and the locating dowels **(see illustration)**. Use a

10.2 Oil pump housing retaining bolt locations (arrowed) – 1.8 litre engines

9.5 Removing a big-end bearing cap and shell

screwdriver if necessary inserted in the recess at the rear of the housing to break the seal. With the pump housing removed, collect the O-ring seal from the outlet stub on the rear of the pump.
3 Slide the oil pump drive collar off the end of the crankshaft and collect the O-ring located behind the collar **(see illustrations)**.

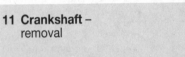

**11 Crankshaft –
removal**

1 On 1.6 litre engines, remove the crankshaft sprocket and the oil pump as described in Part A of this Chapter. On 1.8 litre engines, remove the oil pump as described in Section 10 of this Part.
2 Remove the pistons and connecting rods, as described in Section 9. If no work is to be done on the pistons and connecting rods, there is no need to remove the cylinder head, or to push the pistons out of the cylinder bores. The pistons should just be pushed far enough up the bores so that they are positioned clear of the crankshaft journals.
3 Check the crankshaft endfloat as described in Section 15, then proceed as follows.

1.6 litre engines

4 Unbolt and remove the crankshaft left- and right-hand oil seal housings from each end of the cylinder block, noting the correct fitted locations of the locating dowels. If the

10.3a Slide the oil pump drive collar off the crankshaft . . .

locating dowels are a loose fit, remove them and store them with the housings for safe-keeping.
5 Remove the oil pump drive chain, and slide the drive sprocket off the end of the crankshaft. Remove the Woodruff key, and store it with the sprocket for safe-keeping.
6 The main bearing caps should be numbered 1 to 5 from the transmission (flywheel) end of the engine. If not, mark them accordingly using quick-drying paint.
7 Unscrew and remove the main bearing cap retaining bolts, and withdraw the caps. Recover the lower main bearing shells, and tape them to their respective caps for safe-keeping.
8 Carefully lift out the crankshaft, taking care not to displace the upper main bearing shell.
9 Recover the upper bearing shells from the cylinder block, and tape them to their respective caps for safe-keeping. Remove the thrustwasher halves from the side of No 2 main bearing, and store them with the bearing cap.

1.8 litre engines

10 Working around the inner periphery of the crankcase, unscrew the 16 small (M6) bolts securing the crankshaft bearing cap housing to the base of the cylinder block. Note the correct fitted depth of the left-hand crankshaft oil seal in the cylinder block/bearing cap housing.
11 Working in the reverse of the sequence shown in illustration 19.48, evenly and progressively slacken the ten large (M11) bearing cap housing retaining bolts by a turn at a time. Once all the bolts are loose, remove them from the housing.
12 With all the retaining bolts removed, tap around the outer periphery of the bearing cap housing using a soft-faced mallet to break the seal between the housing and cylinder block. Once the seal is released and the housing is clear of the locating dowels, lift it up and off the crankshaft and cylinder block **(see illustration)**. Recover the lower main bearing shells, and tape them to their respective locations in the housing. If the two locating dowels are a loose fit, remove them and store them with the housing for safe-keeping.

10.3b . . . and collect the O-ring located behind the collar – 1.8 litre engines

11.12 Removing the crankshaft bearing cap housing – 1.8 litre engines

13 Lift out the crankshaft, and collect the left-hand oil seal.

14 Recover the upper main bearing shells, and store them along with the relevant lower bearing shell. Also recover the two thrustwashers (one fitted either side of No 2 main bearing) from the cylinder block.

12 Cylinder block/crankcase – cleaning and inspection

Cleaning

1 Remove all external components and electrical switches/sensors from the block.

2 Remove all traces of gasket/sealant from the cylinder block, and from the crankshaft bearing cap housing (1.8 litre engines), taking care not to damage the gasket/sealing surfaces.

3 If any of the castings are extremely dirty, all should be steam-cleaned.

4 After the castings are returned, clean all oil holes and oil galleries one more time. Flush all internal passages with warm water until the water runs clear. Dry thoroughly, and apply a light film of oil to the cylinder bores to prevent rusting. If you have access to compressed air, use it to speed up the drying process, and to blow out all the oil holes and galleries.

 Warning: Wear eye protection when using compressed air.

5 If the castings are not very dirty, you can do an adequate cleaning job with very hot, soapy water and a stiff brush. Take plenty of time, and do a thorough job. Regardless of the cleaning method used, be sure to clean all oil holes and galleries very thoroughly, and to dry all components well. Protect the cylinder bores as described above, to prevent rusting.

6 All threaded holes must be clean, to ensure accurate torque readings during reassembly. To clean the threads, run the correct-size tap into each of the holes to remove rust, corrosion, thread sealant or sludge, and to restore damaged threads **(see illustration)**. If possible, use compressed air to clear the holes of debris produced by this operation.

 Warning: Wear eye protection when using compressed air.

12.6 Cleaning a cylinder block threaded hole using a suitable tap

7 If the engine is not going to be reassembled right away, cover it with a large plastic bag to keep it clean; protect all mating surfaces and the cylinder bores as described above, to prevent rusting.

Inspection

8 Visually check the castings for cracks and corrosion. Look for stripped threads in the threaded holes. If there has been any history of internal water leakage, it may be worthwhile having an engine overhaul specialist check the cylinder block with special equipment. If defects are found, have them repaired if possible, or renew the assembly.

9 Check each cylinder bore for scuffing and scoring. Check for signs of a wear ridge at the top of the cylinder, indicating that the bore is excessively worn.

10 If the necessary measuring equipment is available, measure the bore diameter of each cylinder at the top (just under the wear ridge), centre, and bottom of the cylinder bore, parallel to the crankshaft axis.

11 Next, measure the bore diameter at the same three locations, at right-angles to the crankshaft axis. Compare the results with the figures given in the Specifications. Where no figures are stated by Citroën, if there is any doubt about the condition of the cylinder bores, seek the advice of an engine reconditioning specialist or Citroën dealer.

12 At the time of writing, it was not clear whether oversize pistons were available for all engines. Consult your Citroën dealer for the latest information on piston availability. If oversize pistons are available, then it may be

13.2 Removing a piston ring with the aid of a feeler blade

possible to have the cylinder bores rebored and fit the oversize pistons. If oversize pistons are not available, and the bores are worn, renewal of the block seems to be the only option.

13 Piston/connecting rod assembly – inspection

1 Before the inspection process can begin, the piston/connecting rod assemblies must be cleaned, and the original piston rings removed from the pistons.

2 Carefully expand the old rings over the top of the pistons. The use of two or three old feeler blades will be helpful in preventing the rings dropping into empty grooves **(see illustration)**. Be careful not to scratch the piston with the ends of the ring. The rings are brittle, and will snap if they are spread too far. They are also very sharp – protect your hands and fingers. Note that the third ring incorporates an expander. Always remove the rings from the top of the piston. Keep each set of rings with its piston if the old rings are to be re-used.

3 Scrape away all traces of carbon from the top of the piston. A hand-held wire brush (or a piece of fine emery cloth) can be used, once the majority of the deposits have been scraped away.

4 Remove the carbon from the ring grooves in the piston, using an old ring. Break the ring in half to do this (be careful not to cut your fingers – piston rings are sharp). Be careful to remove only the carbon deposits – do not remove any metal, and do not nick or scratch the sides of the ring grooves.

5 Once the deposits have been removed, clean the piston/connecting rod assembly with paraffin or a suitable solvent, and dry thoroughly. Make sure that the oil return holes in the ring grooves are clear.

6 If the pistons and cylinder bores are not damaged or worn excessively, and if the cylinder block does not need to be rebored, the original pistons can be refitted. Normal piston wear shows up as even vertical wear on the piston thrust surfaces, and slight looseness of the top ring in its groove. New piston rings should always be used when the engine is reassembled.

7 Carefully inspect each piston for cracks around the skirt, around the gudgeon pin holes, and at the piston ring 'lands' (between the ring grooves).

8 Look for scoring and scuffing on the piston skirt, holes in the piston crown, and burned areas at the edge of the crown. If the skirt is scored or scuffed, the engine may have been suffering from overheating, and/or abnormal combustion which caused excessively high operating temperatures. The cooling and lubrication systems should be checked thoroughly. Scorch marks on the sides of the pistons show that blow-by has occurred. A

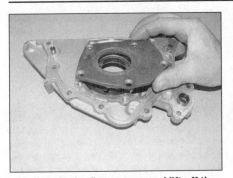

14.1 Undo the five screws and lift off the oil pump rear cover – 1.8 litre engines

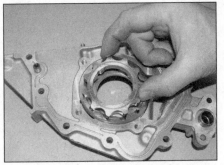

14.2a Remove the inner rotor . . .

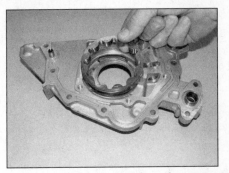

14.2b . . . and outer rotor from the pump housing – 1.8 litre engines

hole in the piston crown, or burned areas at the edge of the piston crown, indicates that abnormal combustion (pre-ignition, knocking, or detonation) has been occurring. If any of the above problems exist, the causes must be investigated and corrected, or the damage will occur again.

9 Corrosion of the piston, in the form of pitting, indicates that coolant has been leaking into the combustion chamber and/or the crankcase. Again, the cause must be corrected, or the problem may persist in the rebuilt engine.

10 Examine each connecting rod carefully for signs of damage, such as cracks around the big-end and small-end bearings. Check that the rod is not bent or distorted. Damage is highly unlikely, unless the engine has been seized or badly overheated. Detailed checking of the connecting rod assembly can only be carried out by an engine specialist or Citroën dealer with the necessary equipment.

11 On all engines, the gudgeon pins are an interference fit in the connecting rod small-end bearing. Therefore, piston and/or connecting rod renewal should be entrusted to an engine repair specialist who will have the necessary tooling to remove and install the gudgeon pins.

14 Oil pump (1.8 litre engines) – inspection

1 Undo the five screws and lift off the pump rear cover plate **(see illustration)**.

2 Lift out the inner and outer rotor, checking carefully for any identification markings indicating their fitted direction **(see illustrations)**.

3 Note the fitted depth of the crankshaft right-hand oil seal, then support the pump housing on blocks and tap out the seal using a suitable drift.

4 Thoroughly clean all the components, then inspect the rotors, pump housing and rear cover plate for any sign of wear or scoring. Oil pump clearances are not quoted by Citroën but if there is any doubt whatsoever as to the condition of the pump, the complete assembly should be renewed. Apart from the

oil seals, individual oil pump components are not available separately.

5 Prior to reassembly, obtain new O-rings and a new crankshaft right-hand oil seal.

6 Refit the inner and outer rotors to the pump body, respecting any identification markings noted during removal.

7 Liberally lubricate the rotors with clean engine oil then refit the rear cover plate. Refit the cover plate retaining screws and tighten them securely.

15 Crankshaft – inspection

Checking endfloat

1 If the crankshaft endfloat is to be checked, this must be done when the crankshaft is still installed in the cylinder block, but is free to move.

2 Check the endfloat using a dial gauge in contact with the end of the crankshaft. On 1.8 litre engines it may be necessary to bolt a suitable steel bracket to the rear of the cylinder block if the dial gauge incorporates a magnetic base. Push the crankshaft fully one way, and then zero the gauge. Push the crankshaft fully the other way, and check the endfloat. The result can be compared with the specified amount, and will give an indication as to whether new thrustwashers are required **(see illustration)**.

3 If a dial gauge is not available, feeler blades

15.2 Checking crankshaft endfloat using a dial gauge

can be used. First push the crankshaft fully towards the flywheel end of the engine, then use feeler blades to measure the gap between the web of No 2 crankpin and the thrustwasher.

Inspection

4 Clean the crankshaft using paraffin or a suitable solvent, and dry it, preferably with compressed air if available. Be sure to clean the oil holes with a pipe cleaner or similar probe, to ensure that they are not obstructed.

⚠ *Warning: Wear eye protection when using compressed air.*

5 Check the main and big-end bearing journals for uneven wear, scoring, pitting and cracking.

6 Big-end bearing wear is accompanied by distinct metallic knocking when the engine is running (particularly noticeable when the engine is pulling from low speed) and some loss of oil pressure.

7 Main bearing wear is accompanied by severe engine vibration and rumble – getting progressively worse as engine speed increases – and again by loss of oil pressure.

8 Check the bearing journal for roughness by running a finger lightly over the bearing surface. Any roughness (which will be accompanied by obvious bearing wear) indicates that the crankshaft requires regrinding (where possible) or renewal.

9 If the crankshaft has been reground, check for burrs around the crankshaft oil holes (the holes are usually chamfered, so burrs should not be a problem unless regrinding has been carried out carelessly). Remove any burrs with a fine file or scraper, and thoroughly clean the oil holes as described previously.

10 Using a micrometer, measure the diameter of the main and big-end bearing journals, and compare the results with the Specifications **(see illustration)**. By measuring the diameter at a number of points around each journal's circumference, you will be able to determine whether or not the journal is out-of-round. Take the measurement at each end of the journal, near the webs, to determine if the journal is tapered. Compare the results obtained with those given in the Specifications.

15.10 Measuring a crankshaft main bearing journal diameter

11 Check the oil seal contact surfaces on the crankshaft for wear and damage. If the seal has worn a deep groove in the surface of the crankshaft, consult an engine overhaul specialist; repair may be possible, but otherwise a new crankshaft will be required.

12 Citroën produce a set of oversize bearing shells for both the main and big-end bearings. Where oversize bearing shells are available, and if the crankshaft journals have not already been reground, it may be possible to have the crankshaft reconditioned, and to fit oversize shells. If the crankshaft has worn beyond the specified limits, it will have to be renewed. Consult your Citroën dealer or engine specialist for further information on parts availability.

16 Main and big-end bearings – inspection

1 Even though the main and big-end bearings should be renewed during the engine overhaul, the old bearings should be retained

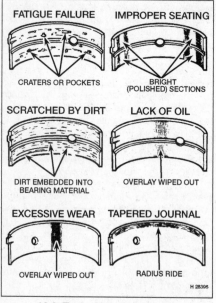

16.2 Typical bearing failures

for close examination, as they may reveal valuable information about the condition of the engine. The bearing shells are graded by thickness, the grade of each shell being indicated by the colour code, or size identification, marked on it.

2 Bearing failure can occur due to lack of lubrication, the presence of dirt or other foreign particles, overloading the engine, or corrosion **(see illustration)**. Regardless of the cause of bearing failure, the cause must be corrected (where applicable) before the engine is reassembled, to prevent it from happening again.

3 When examining the bearing shells, remove them from the cylinder block, the main bearing caps or cap housing (as appropriate), the connecting rods and the connecting rod big-end bearing caps. Lay them out on a clean surface in the same general position as their location in the engine. This will enable you to match any bearing problems with the corresponding crankshaft journal. *Do not touch any shell's bearing surface with your fingers while checking it, or the delicate surface may be scratched.*

4 Dirt and other foreign matter gets into the engine in a variety of ways. It may be left in the engine during assembly, or it may pass through filters or the crankcase ventilation system. It may get into the oil, and from there into the bearings. Metal chips from machining operations and normal engine wear are often present. Abrasives are sometimes left in engine components after reconditioning, especially when parts are not thoroughly cleaned using the proper cleaning methods. Whatever the source, these foreign objects often end up embedded in the soft bearing material, and are easily recognised. Large particles will not embed in the bearing, and will score or gouge the bearing and journal. The best prevention for this cause of bearing failure is to clean all parts thoroughly, and keep everything spotlessly-clean during engine assembly. Frequent and regular engine oil and filter changes are also recommended.

5 Lack of lubrication (or lubrication breakdown) has a number of interrelated causes. Excessive heat (which thins the oil), overloading (which squeezes the oil from the bearing face) and oil leakage (from excessive bearing clearances, worn oil pump or high engine speeds) all contribute to lubrication breakdown. Blocked oil passages, which usually are the result of misaligned oil holes in a bearing shell, will also oil-starve a bearing, and destroy it. When lack of lubrication is the cause of bearing failure, the bearing material is wiped or extruded from the steel backing of the bearing. Temperatures may increase to the point where the steel backing turns blue from overheating.

6 Driving habits can have a definite effect on bearing life. Full-throttle, low-speed operation (labouring the engine) puts very high loads on bearings, tending to squeeze out the oil film. These loads cause the bearings to flex, which produces fine cracks in the bearing face

(fatigue failure). Eventually, the bearing material will loosen in pieces, and tear away from the steel backing.

7 Short-distance driving leads to corrosion of bearings, because insufficient engine heat is produced to drive off the condensed water and corrosive gases. These products collect in the engine oil, forming acid and sludge. As the oil is carried to the engine bearings, the acid attacks and corrodes the bearing material.

8 Incorrect bearing installation during engine assembly will lead to bearing failure as well. Tight-fitting bearings leave insufficient bearing running clearance, and will result in oil starvation. Dirt or foreign particles trapped behind a bearing shell result in high spots on the bearing, which lead to failure.

9 *Do not* touch any shell's bearing surface with your fingers during reassembly; there is a risk of scratching the delicate surface, or of depositing particles of dirt on it.

10 As mentioned at the beginning of this Section, the bearing shells should be renewed as a matter of course during engine overhaul; to do otherwise is false economy. Refer to Sections 19 and 20 for details of bearing shell selection.

17 Engine overhaul – reassembly sequence

1 Before reassembly begins, ensure that all new parts have been obtained, and that all necessary tools are available. Read through the entire procedure to familiarise yourself with the work involved, and to ensure that all items necessary for reassembly of the engine are at hand. In addition to all normal tools and materials, thread-locking compound will be needed. A suitable tube of liquid sealant will also be required for the joint faces that are fitted without gaskets. It is recommended that Citroën's own products are used, which are specially formulated for this purpose; the relevant product names are quoted in the text of each Section where they are required.

2 In order to save time and avoid problems, engine reassembly can be carried out in the following order:
a) Crankshaft (See Section 19).
b) Piston/connecting rod assemblies (See Section 20).
c) Oil pump (See Part A or Section 21 of this Part – as applicable).
d) Sump (See Part A or B – as applicable).
e) Flywheel (See Part A or B – as applicable).
f) Cylinder head (See Part A or B – as applicable).
g) Timing belt tensioner and sprockets, and timing belt (See Part A or B – as applicable).
h) Engine external components.

3 At this stage, all engine components should be absolutely clean and dry, with all faults repaired. The components should be laid out (or in individual containers) on a completely clean work surface.

18 Piston rings – refitting

1 Before fitting new piston rings, the ring end gaps must be checked as follows.
2 Lay out the piston/connecting rod assemblies and the new piston ring sets, so that the ring sets will be matched with the same piston and cylinder during the end gap measurement and subsequent engine reassembly.
3 Insert the top ring into the first cylinder, and push it down the bore using the top of the piston. This will ensure that the ring remains square with the cylinder walls. Position the ring near the bottom of the cylinder bore, at the lower limit of ring travel. Note that the top and second compression rings are different. The second ring is easily identified by the step on its lower surface, and by the fact that its outer face is tapered.
4 Measure the end gap using feeler blades.
5 Repeat the procedure with the ring at the top of the cylinder bore, at the upper limit of its travel and compare the measurements with the figures given in the Specifications **(see illustration)**.
6 If the gap is too small (unlikely if genuine Citroën parts are used), it must be enlarged, or the ring ends may contact each other during engine operation, causing serious damage. Ideally, new piston rings providing the correct end gap should be fitted. As a last resort, the end gap can be increased by filing the ring ends very carefully with a fine file. Mount the file in a vice equipped with soft jaws, slip the ring over the file with the ends contacting the file face, and slowly move the ring to remove material from the ends. Take care, as piston rings are sharp, and are easily broken.
7 With new piston rings, it is unlikely that the end gap will be too large. If the gaps are too large, check that you have the correct rings for your engine and for the cylinder bore size.
8 Repeat the checking procedure for each ring in the first cylinder, and then for the rings in the remaining cylinders. Remember to keep rings, pistons and cylinders matched up.
9 Once the ring end gaps have been checked and if necessary corrected, the rings can be fitted to the pistons.
10 Fit the piston rings using the same technique as for removal. Fit the bottom (oil control) ring first, and work up. When fitting the oil control ring on 1.6 litre engines, first insert the expander (where fitted), then fit the ring with its gap positioned 180° from the expander gap. The oil control ring used on 1.8 litre engines is a one-piece type and does not have a gap.
11 Ensure that the second compression ring is fitted the correct way up, with its identification mark (either a dot of paint or the word TOP stamped on the ring surface) at the top, and the stepped surface at the bottom

18.5 Measuring a piston ring end gap

(see illustration). On 1.6 litre engines, arrange the gaps of the top and second compression rings 120° either side of the oil control ring gap. On 1.8 litre engines, position the rings so that the gaps are 180° apart and offset by 90° from the gudgeon pin centreline.
Note: *Always follow any instructions supplied with the new piston ring sets – different manufacturers may specify different procedures. Do not mix up the top and second compression rings, as they have different cross-sections.*

19 Crankshaft – refitting and main bearing running clearance check

Selection of bearing shells

1 There are two different sizes of main bearing shell available; the standard size shell for use with an original crankshaft and an oversize shell for use once the crankshaft has been reground. Within these two size classes there are additional thickness sizes (grades) for both the upper and lower shells, to allow the main bearing running clearance to be accurately set. The grades are indicated by a colour-coding marked on the edge of each

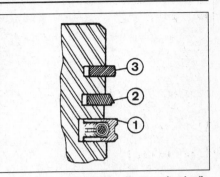

18.11 Piston ring fitting diagram (typical)

1 Oil control ring
2 Second compression ring
3 Top compression ring

shell, which denotes the shell's thickness.
2 The relevant set of bearing shells required can be obtained by measuring the diameter of the crankshaft main bearing journals (see Section 15). This will show if the crankshaft is original or whether its journals have been reground, identifying if either standard or oversize bearing shells are required.
3 The grade of the new bearing shells required (either standard size or oversize) is selected using the reference marks on the cylinder block and on the crankshaft. The cylinder block marks identify the diameter of the bearing bores in the block, and the crankshaft marks identify the diameter of the crankshaft journals.
4 On 1.6 litre engines, the cylinder block reference marks are on the right-hand (timing belt) end of the block, whereas on 1.8 litre engines they are on the front facing (oil filter) side adjacent to No 2 cylinder **(see illustration)**. On all engines, the crankshaft reference marks are on the right-hand (timing belt) end of the crankshaft, on the right-hand web of No 4 crankpin. These marks can be used for selection of bearing shells of the required thickness grade.

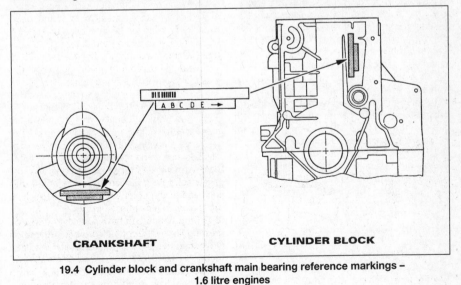

19.4 Cylinder block and crankshaft main bearing reference markings – 1.6 litre engines

19.13 Plastigauge in place on a crankshaft main bearing journal

19.16 Measure the width of the deformed Plastigauge using the scale on the card

5 Numerous grades of standard and oversize bearing shells are available, depending on the engine type, year of manufacture, and country of export. Using the cylinder block and crankshaft reference marks together with the crankshaft journal diameter, a Citroën dealer or engine overhaul specialist will be able to supply the correct bearing shells to give the required bearing running clearance for each journal.

6 Whether the original shells or new shells are being fitted, it is recommended that the running clearance is checked as follows prior to crankshaft installation.

Main bearing clearance check

1.6 litre engines

7 The running clearance check can be carried out using the original bearing shells. However, it is preferable to use a new set, since the results obtained will be more conclusive.

8 Clean the backs of the bearing shells, and the bearing locations in both the cylinder block and the main bearing caps.

9 Press the bearing shells into their locations, ensuring that the tab on each shell engages in the notch in the cylinder block or bearing cap. Take care not to touch any shell's bearing surface with your fingers. Note that the grooved bearing shells, both upper and lower, are fitted to Nos 2 and 4 main bearings. If the original bearing shells are being used for the check, ensure that they are refitted in their original locations. The clearance can be checked in either of two ways.

10 One method (which will be difficult to achieve without a range of internal micrometers or internal/external expanding calipers) is to refit the main bearing caps to the cylinder block, with bearing shells in place. With the cap retaining bolts tightened to the specified torque and through the specified angle, measure the internal diameter of each assembled pair of bearing shells. If the diameter of each corresponding crankshaft journal is measured and then subtracted from the bearing internal diameter, the result will be the main bearing running clearance.

11 The second (and more accurate) method is to use an American product known as Plastigauge. This consists of a fine thread of

perfectly-round plastic, which is compressed between the bearing shell and the journal. When the shell is removed, the plastic is deformed, and can be measured with a special card gauge supplied with the kit. The running clearance is determined from this gauge. Plastigauge should be available from your Citroën dealer; otherwise, enquiries at one of the larger specialist motor factors should produce the name of a stockist in your area. The procedure for using Plastigauge is as follows.

12 With the main bearing upper shells in place, carefully lay the crankshaft in position. Do not use any lubricant; the crankshaft journals and bearing shells must be perfectly clean and dry.

13 Cut several lengths of the appropriate-size Plastigauge (they should be slightly shorter than the width of the main bearings), and place one length on each crankshaft journal axis **(see illustration)**.

14 With the main bearing lower shells in position, refit the main bearing caps, tightening their retaining bolts to the specified torque and through the specified angle. Take care not to disturb the Plastigauge, and *do not* rotate the crankshaft at any time during this operation.

15 Remove the main bearing caps, again taking great care not to disturb the Plastigauge or rotate the crankshaft.

16 Compare the width of the crushed Plastigauge on each journal to the scale printed on the Plastigauge envelope, to obtain the main bearing running clearance **(see illustration)**. Compare the clearance

19.25 Fitting a thrustwasher to No 2 main bearing upper location – 1.6 litre engines

measured with that in the Specifications at the start of this Chapter.

17 If the clearance is significantly different from that expected, the bearing shells may be the wrong size (or excessively worn, if the original shells are being re-used). Before deciding that different-size shells are required, make sure that no dirt or oil was trapped between the bearing shells and the caps or block when the clearance was measured. If the Plastigauge was wider at one end than at the other, the crankshaft journal may be tapered.

18 Where necessary, obtain the required grades of bearing shell, and repeat the running clearance checking process described above.

19 On completion, carefully scrape away all traces of the Plastigauge material from the crankshaft and bearing shells. Use your fingernail, or a wooden or plastic scraper which is unlikely to score the bearing surfaces.

1.8 litre engines

20 The running clearance check can be carried out using the original bearing shells. However, it is preferable to use a new set, since the results obtained will be more conclusive.

21 Clean the backs of the bearing shells, and the bearing locations in both the cylinder block and in the crankshaft main bearing cap housing.

22 Press the bearing shells into their locations, ensuring that the tab on each shell engages in the notch in the cylinder block or crankshaft bearing cap housing location. Take care not to touch any shell's bearing surface with your fingers. Note that the grooved bearing shells are fitted to the cylinder block and the plain bearing shells are fitted to the bearing cap housing. If the original bearing shells are being used for the check, ensure that they are refitted in their original locations.

23 The clearance can now be checked using the procedures described in paragraphs 10 to 19, noting that the crankshaft bearing cap housing is removed as an assembly rather than the removal of each individual main bearing cap. When fitting the bearing cap housing for the running clearance check, tighten the retaining bolts to the specified torque settings, following the procedure and tightening sequence contained in paragraphs 47 to 51.

Final crankshaft refitting

1.6 litre engines

24 Carefully lift the crankshaft out of the cylinder block once more.

25 Using a little grease, stick the upper thrustwashers to each side of the No 2 main bearing upper location. Ensure that the oilway grooves on each thrustwasher face outwards (away from the cylinder block) **(see illustration)**.

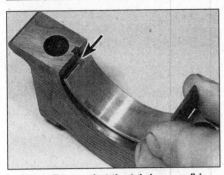

19.26 Ensure that the tab (arrowed) is correctly located in the cap when fitting the bearing shells – 1.6 litre engines

19.43 Lubricate the bearing shells and lower the crankshaft into the cylinder block – 1.8 litre engines

19.44 Insert the thrustwashers to either side of No 2 main bearing upper location – 1.8 litre engines

26 Place the bearing shells in their locations as described earlier **(see illustration)**. If new shells are being fitted, ensure that all traces of protective grease are cleaned off using paraffin. Wipe dry the shells and connecting rods with a lint-free cloth. Liberally lubricate each bearing shell in the cylinder block and cap with clean engine oil.

27 Lower the crankshaft into position so that Nos 2 and 3 cylinder crankpins are at TDC; Nos 1 and 4 cylinder crankpins will be at BDC, ready for fitting No 1 piston.

28 Lubricate the lower bearing shells in the main bearing caps with clean engine oil. Make sure that the locating lugs on the shells engage with the corresponding recesses in the caps.

29 Fit the main bearing caps to their correct locations, ensuring that they are fitted the correct way round (the bearing shell lug recesses in the block and caps must be on the same side). Insert the bolts loosely.

30 Tighten the main bearing cap bolts to the specified Stage 1 torque wrench setting. Once all the bolts have been tightened to the Stage 1 setting, angle-tighten the bolts through the specified Stage 2 angle, using a socket and extension bar. It is recommended that an angle-measuring gauge is used during this stage of the tightening, to ensure accuracy.

31 Check that the crankshaft rotates freely.

32 Refit the piston/connecting rod assemblies to the crankshaft as described in Section 20.

33 Refit the Woodruff key to the crankshaft groove, and slide on the oil pump drive sprocket. Locate the drive chain on the sprocket.

34 Ensure that the mating surfaces of the right-hand oil seal housing and cylinder block are clean and dry. Note the correct fitted depth of the oil seal then, using a large flat-bladed screwdriver, lever the seal out of the housing.

35 Apply a smear of RTV sealant to the oil seal housing mating surface (Citroën recommend the use of Loctite Autojoint Noir), and make sure that the locating dowels are in position. Slide the housing over the end of the crankshaft, and into position on the cylinder

block. Tighten the housing retaining bolts securely.

36 Repeat the operations in paragraphs 34 and 35, and fit the left-hand oil seal housing.

37 Fit a new right-hand and left-hand crankshaft oil seal as described in Part A of this Chapter.

38 Ensuring that the chain is correctly located on the drive sprocket, refit the oil pump and sump as described in Part A of this Chapter.

39 Refit the flywheel as described in Part A of this Chapter.

40 Refit the cylinder head and install the crankshaft sprocket and timing belt as described in Part A of this Chapter.

1.8 litre engines

41 Carefully lift the crankshaft out of the cylinder block once more.

42 Place the bearing shells in their locations as described earlier. If new shells are being fitted, ensure that all traces of protective grease are cleaned off using paraffin. Wipe dry the shells with a lint-free cloth.

43 Liberally lubricate each bearing shell in the cylinder block with clean engine oil then lower the crankshaft into position **(see illustration)**.

44 Insert the thrustwashers to either side of No 2 main bearing upper location and push them around the bearing journal until their edges are horizontal **(see illustration)**. Ensure that the oilway grooves on each thrustwasher face outwards (away from the bearing journal).

45 Thoroughly degrease the mating surfaces of the cylinder block and the crankshaft bearing cap housing. Apply a thin bead of RTV sealant to the bearing cap housing mating surface **(see illustration)**. Citroën recommend the use of Loctite Autojoint Noir for this purpose.

46 Lubricate the lower bearing shells with clean engine oil, then refit the bearing cap housing, ensuring that the shells are not displaced, and that the locating dowels engage correctly.

47 Install the ten M11, and sixteen M6 crankshaft bearing cap housing retaining bolts, and screw them in until they are just making contact with the housing.

48 Working in the sequence shown, tighten all the M11 bolts to the Stage 1 torque setting given in the Specifications **(see illustration)**. Now tighten all the M6 bolts to the Stage 1 torque setting (finger tight).

49 Fully slacken all the M11 bolts (Stage 2), then tighten them to the Stage 3 setting, working in the correct sequence.

50 Finally tighten all the M11 bolts, in the correct sequence, through the specified Stage 4 angle, using an angle tightening gauge.

51 The M6 bolts can now be tightened to the Stage 5 torque setting.

52 With the bearing cap housing in place, check that the crankshaft rotates freely.

53 Refit the piston/connecting rod assemblies to the crankshaft as described in Section 20.

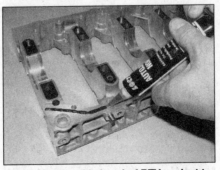

19.45 Apply a thin bead of RTV sealant to the bearing cap housing mating surface – 1.8 litre engines

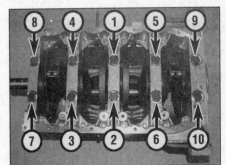

19.48 Crankshaft bearing cap housing retaining bolt tightening sequence – 1.8 litre engines

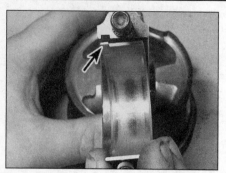

20.7 Ensure the bearing shell tab (arrowed) engages with the recess in the connecting rod

54 Refit the oil pump as described in Section 21 of this Part and the sump as described in Part B of this Chapter.

55 Fit a new crankshaft left-hand oil seal, then refit the flywheel as described in Part B.

56 Refit the cylinder head, crankshaft sprocket and timing belt also as described in Part B.

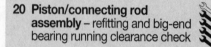

20 Piston/connecting rod assembly – refitting and big-end bearing running clearance check

Selection of bearing shells

1 There are two different sizes of big-end bearing shell available; the standard size shell for use with an original crankshaft and an oversize shell for use once the crankshaft has been reground. Within these two size classes there are additional thickness sizes (grades) for the lower bearing shells, to allow the big-end bearing running clearance to be accurately set. The grades are indicated by a colour-coding marked on the edge of each shell, which denotes the shell's thickness.

2 The relevant set of bearing shells required can be obtained by measuring the diameter of the crankshaft big-end bearing journals (see Section 15). This will show if the crankshaft is original or whether its journals have been reground, identifying if either standard or oversize bearing shells are required.

3 The grade of the new bearing shells required (either standard size or oversize) is selected using the reference marks on the

20.19 Tap the piston into the bore using a hammer handle – 1.6 litre engines

crankshaft. The reference marks are on the left-hand (flywheel) end of the crankshaft, on the left-hand web of No 1 crankpin. These marks can be used for selection of bearing shells of the required thickness grade.

4 Numerous grades of standard and oversize bearing shells are available, depending on the engine type, year of manufacture, and country of export. Using the crankshaft reference marks together with the crankshaft big-end bearing journal diameter, a Citroën dealer or engine overhaul specialist will be able to supply the correct bearing shells to give the required bearing running clearance for each journal.

5 Whether the original shells or new shells are being fitted, it is recommended that the running clearance is checked as follows.

Big-end bearing clearance check

6 Clean the backs of the bearing shells, and the bearing locations in both the connecting rod and bearing cap.

7 Press the bearing shells into their locations, ensuring that the tab on each shell engages in the notch in the connecting rod and cap. Take care not to touch any shell's bearing surface with your fingers **(see illustration)**. If the original bearing shells are being used for the check, ensure that they are refitted in their original locations. The clearance can be checked in either of two ways.

8 One method is to refit the big-end bearing cap to the connecting rod, ensuring that they are fitted the correct way around (see paragraph 20), with the bearing shells in place. With the cap retaining nuts/bolts correctly tightened, use an internal micrometer or vernier caliper to measure the internal diameter of each assembled pair of bearing shells. If the diameter of each corresponding crankshaft journal is measured and then subtracted from the bearing internal diameter, the result will be the big-end bearing running clearance.

9 The second, and more accurate method is to use Plastigauge (see Section 19).

10 Ensure that the bearing shells are correctly fitted. Place a strand of Plastigauge on each (cleaned) crankpin journal.

11 Refit the (clean) piston/connecting rod assemblies to the crankshaft, and refit the big-end bearing caps, using the marks made or noted on removal to ensure that they are fitted the correct way around.

12 Tighten the bearing cap nuts/bolts as described below in paragraph 21 or 29 (as applicable). Take care not to disturb the Plastigauge, nor rotate the connecting rod during the tightening sequence.

13 Dismantle the assemblies without rotating the connecting rods. Use the scale printed on the Plastigauge envelope to obtain the big-end bearing running clearance.

14 If the clearance is significantly different from that expected, the bearing shells may be the wrong size (or excessively worn, if the original shells are being re-used). Make sure

that no dirt or oil was trapped between the bearing shells and the caps or block when the clearance was measured. If the Plastigauge was wider at one end than at the other, the crankshaft journal may be tapered.

15 On completion, carefully scrape away all traces of the Plastigauge material from the crankshaft and bearing shells. Use your fingernail, or some other object which is unlikely to score the bearing surfaces.

Piston/connecting rod refitting

1.6 litre engines

16 Ensure that the bearing shells are correctly fitted as described earlier. If new shells are being fitted, ensure that all traces of the protective grease are cleaned off using paraffin. Wipe dry the shells and connecting rods with a lint-free cloth.

17 Lubricate the cylinder bores, the pistons, and piston rings, then lay out each piston/connecting rod assembly in its respective position.

18 Start with assembly No 1. Make sure that the piston rings are still spaced as described in Section 18, then clamp them in position with a piston ring compressor.

19 Insert the piston/connecting rod assembly into the top of cylinder No 1, ensuring that the arrow on the piston crown is pointing towards the timing belt end of the engine. Using a block of wood or hammer handle against the piston crown, tap the assembly into the cylinder bore until the piston crown is flush with the top of the cylinder block **(see illustration)**.

20 Ensure that the bearing shell is still correctly installed. Liberally lubricate the crankpin and both bearing shells. Taking care not to mark the cylinder bores, pull the piston/connecting rod assembly down the bore and onto the crankpin. Refit the big-end bearing cap, tightening the nuts finger-tight at first. Note that the faces with the identification marks must match (which means that the bearing shell locating tabs abut each other).

21 Tighten the bearing cap retaining nuts evenly and progressively to the specified torque setting.

1.8 litre engines

22 Ensure that the bearing shells are correctly fitted as described earlier. If new shells are being fitted, ensure that all traces of the protective grease are cleaned off using paraffin. Wipe dry the shells and connecting rods with a lint-free cloth.

23 Lubricate the cylinder bores, the pistons, and piston rings, then lay out each piston/connecting rod assembly in its respective position.

24 Due to the construction and small size of the oil control piston ring on these engines, it is very easy to damage the ring when fitting the piston/connecting rod assembly if a conventional piston ring compressor is used. The lower part of the ring slips out of the ring compressor just before it enters the cylinder bore and can easily be bent or distorted if the

To make a piston ring compressing tool for 1.8 litre engines, cut a strip of thin steel packing so that when it is wrapped tightly around the piston, the ends of the strip abut each other. Wrap the strip around the piston and secure with two large worm-drive hose clips to compress the rings.

fitting process continues. Citroën specify the use of a tapered cone type piston ring compressor tool, but a suitable alternative can easily be fabricated **(see Tool Tip)**.

25 Start with assembly No 1. Check that the piston rings are still spaced as described in Section 18, then liberally lubricate the piston and rings. Locate the Citroën ring compressor tool over the piston, or clamp the rings with the home-made alternative. If the home-made tool is being used, ensure that the oil control ring is fully compressed into its groove by the tool.

26 Insert the piston/connecting rod assembly into the top of cylinder No 1, ensuring that the arrow on the piston crown is pointing towards the timing belt end of the engine.

27 Hold the ring compressor tool hard against the top of the cylinder block (there must be no gap whatsoever between the bottom edge of the tool and the block face) then tap the assembly into the cylinder bore using a hammer handle against the piston crown. Continue until all the piston rings have entered the cylinder bore and the piston crown is flush with the top of the cylinder block.

28 Ensure that the upper bearing shell is still correctly installed. Liberally lubricate the crankpin and both bearing shells. Taking care not to mark the cylinder bores, pull the piston/connecting rod assembly down the bore and onto the crankpin. Refit the big-end

21.2 Locate a new O-ring over the oil pump outlet stub – 1.8 litre engines

bearing cap and insert the new retaining bolts tightened finger tight. Note that the faces with the identification marks must match (which means that the bearing shell locating tabs abut each other).

29 Tighten the bearing cap retaining bolts evenly and progressively to the specified torque setting, then through the specified angle using an angle tightening gauge.

All engines

30 Once the bearing cap retaining nuts/bolts have been correctly tightened, rotate the crankshaft. Check that it turns freely; some stiffness is to be expected if new components have been fitted, but there should be no signs of binding or tight spots.

31 Refit the other three piston/connecting rod assemblies in the same way.

32 Refit the cylinder head, oil pump and sump as described in Part A, Part B or Section 21 of this Chapter (as applicable).

21 Oil pump (1.8 litre engines) – refitting

1 Ensure that the mating surfaces of the oil pump housing and cylinder block are clean and free of oil.

2 Check that the locating dowels are in position on the pump flange then locate a new O-ring over the oil pump outlet stub **(see illustration)**.

3 Apply a thin bead of RTV sealant to the oil pump mating surface. Citroën recommend the

21.3 Apply a thin bead of RTV sealant to the oil pump mating surface – 1.8 litre engines

21.6 Position a new oil pump drive collar O-ring on the end of the crankshaft – 1.8 litre engines

use of Loctite Autojoint Noir for this purpose **(see illustration)**.

4 Prime the oil pump by injecting clean engine oil into the outlet stub, then place the pump in position on the cylinder block, engaging the locating dowels.

5 Apply thread locking compound to the threads of the nine oil pump retaining bolts, then refit the bolts and tighten them to the specified torque.

6 Position a new oil pump drive collar O-ring on the end of the crankshaft **(see illustration)**.

7 Lubricate the sealing lips of the new crankshaft right-hand oil seal and carefully fit the seal over the oil pump drive collar **(see illustrations)**. Note that the open part of the seal must be towards the shoulder of the drive collar.

8 Slide the drive collar over the end of the crankshaft and engage it with the oil pump inner rotor **(see illustration)**. As the collar

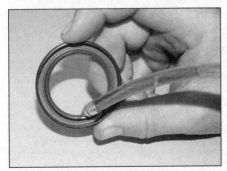

21.7a Lubricate the sealing lips of the new crankshaft right-hand oil seal . . .

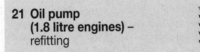

21.7b . . . and carefully fit the seal over the oil pump drive collar – 1.8 litre engines

21.8 Slide the drive collar onto the crankshaft and engage it with the oil pump inner rotor – 1.8 litre engines

engages with the pump inner rotor, push the oil seal initially into place in the oil pump housing. Tap the seal fully into position using a suitable drift.

9 Refit the sump and crankshaft sprocket as described in Part B of this Chapter.

22 Engine –
initial start-up after overhaul

1 With the engine refitted in the vehicle, double-check the engine oil and coolant levels. Make a final check that everything has been reconnected, and that there are no tools or rags left in the engine compartment.

2 Start the engine, noting that this may take a little longer than usual, due to the fuel system components having been disturbed. Make sure that the oil pressure warning light goes out then allow the engine to idle.

3 While the engine is idling, check for fuel, water and oil leaks. Don't be alarmed if there are some odd smells and smoke from parts getting hot and burning off oil deposits.

4 Assuming all is well, keep the engine idling until hot water is felt circulating through the top hose, then switch off the engine.

5 After a few minutes, recheck the oil and coolant levels as described in *Weekly checks*, and top-up as necessary.

6 Note that there is no need to retighten the cylinder head bolts once the engine has first run after reassembly.

7 If new pistons, rings or crankshaft bearings have been fitted, the engine must be treated as new, and run-in for the first 500 miles (800 km). *Do not* operate the engine at full-throttle, or allow it to labour at low engine speeds in any gear. It is recommended that the oil and filter be changed at the end of this period.

Chapter 2 Part E:
Diesel engine removal and overhaul procedures

Contents

Degrees of difficulty

Easy, suitable for novice with little experience	**Fairly easy,** suitable for beginner with some experience	**Fairly difficult,** suitable for competent DIY mechanic	**Difficult,** suitable for experienced DIY mechanic	**Very difficult,** suitable for expert DIY or professional

Specifications

Note: *At the time of writing, certain specifications were not available. Where the relevant specifications are not given here, refer to your Citroën dealer for further information*

Cylinder head
Maximum gasket face distortion . . . . 0.03 mm
Cylinder head height . . . . 133.0 mm
Swirl chamber protrusion . . . . 0 to 0.03 mm

Cylinder block
Cylinder bore diameter:
    Standard . . . . 85.000 to 85.018 mm

Pistons
Piston diameter:
    Standard . . . . 84.210 to 84.228 mm
Maximum weight difference between any two pistons . . . . 4.0 g

Piston rings
End gaps:
    Top compression ring . . . . 0.20 to 0.35 mm
    2nd compression ring . . . . 0.40 to 0.60 mm
    Oil control ring . . . . 0.25 to 0.50 mm

Crankshaft
Endfloat . . . . 0.07 to 0.32 mm
Main bearing journal diameter:
    Standard . . . . 59.977 to 60.000 mm
    Repair size . . . . 59.677 to 59.700 mm
Big-end bearing journal diameter:
    Standard . . . . 49.980 to 50.000 mm
Maximum bearing journal out-of-round . . . . 0.007 mm
Main bearing running clearance* . . . . 0.025 to 0.050 mm
Big-end bearing running clearance* . . . . 0.025 to 0.050 mm
These are suggested figures, typical for these types of engine – no exact values are stated by Citroën

Torque wrench settings
Refer to Chapter 2C Specifications.

1 General information

Included in this Part of Chapter 2 are details of removing the engine/transmission from the vehicle and general overhaul procedures for the cylinder head, cylinder block and all other engine internal components.

The information given ranges from advice concerning preparation for an overhaul and the purchase of replacement parts, to detailed step-by-step procedures covering removal, inspection, renovation and refitting of engine internal components.

After Section 4, all instructions are based on the assumption that the engine has been removed from the car. For information concerning in-car engine repair, as well as the removal and refitting of those external components necessary for full overhaul, refer to Part C of this Chapter and to Section 6. Ignore any preliminary dismantling operations described in Part C that are no longer relevant once the engine has been removed.

Apart from torque wrench settings, which are given at the beginning of Part C, all available specifications relating to engine overhaul are at the beginning of this Part of Chapter 2.

2 Engine overhaul – general information

It is not always easy to determine when, or if, an engine should be completely overhauled, as a number of factors must be considered.

High mileage is not necessarily an indication that an overhaul is needed, while low mileage does not preclude the need for an overhaul. Frequency of servicing is probably the most important consideration. An engine which has had regular and frequent oil and filter changes, as well as other required maintenance, should give many thousands of miles of reliable service. Conversely, a neglected engine may require an overhaul very early in its life.

Excessive oil consumption is an indication that piston rings, valve seals and/or valve guides are in need of attention. Make sure that oil leaks are not responsible before deciding that the rings and/or guides are worn. Perform a compression or leakdown test, as described in Part C of this Chapter, to determine the likely cause of the problem.

Check the oil pressure with a gauge fitted in place of the oil pressure switch, and compare it with that specified. If it is extremely low, the main and big-end bearings, and/or the oil pump, are probably worn out.

Loss of power, rough running, knocking or metallic engine noises, excessive valve gear noise, and high fuel consumption may also point to the need for an overhaul, especially if they are all present at the same time. If a complete service does not remedy the situation, major mechanical work is the only solution.

An engine overhaul involves restoring all internal parts to the specification of a new engine. During an overhaul, the cylinder bores are rebored (where necessary), and the pistons and the piston rings are renewed. New main and big-end bearings are generally fitted; if necessary, the crankshaft may be reground, to restore the journals. The valves are also serviced as well, since they are usually in less-than-perfect condition at this point. The end result should be an as-new engine that will give many trouble-free miles.

Note: *Critical cooling system components such as the hoses, thermostat and coolant pump should be renewed when an engine is overhauled. The radiator should be checked carefully, to ensure that it is not clogged or leaking. Also, it is a good idea to renew the oil pump whenever the engine is overhauled.*

Before beginning the engine overhaul, read through the entire procedure, to familiarise yourself with the scope and requirements of the job. Overhauling an engine is not difficult if you follow carefully all of the instructions, have the necessary tools and equipment, and pay close attention to all specifications. It can, however, be time-consuming. Plan on the vehicle being off the road for a minimum of two weeks, especially if parts must be taken to an engineering works for repair or reconditioning. Check on the availability of parts and make sure that any necessary special tools and equipment are obtained in advance. Most work can be done with typical hand tools, although a number of precision measuring tools are required for inspecting parts to determine if they must be renewed. Often the engineering works will handle the inspection of parts and offer advice concerning reconditioning and renewal.

Always wait until the engine has been completely dismantled, and until all components (especially the cylinder block and the crankshaft) have been inspected, before deciding what service and repair operations must be performed by an engineering works. The condition of these components will be the major factor to consider when determining whether to overhaul the original engine, or to buy a reconditioned unit. Do not, therefore, purchase parts or have overhaul work done on other components until they have been thoroughly inspected. As a general rule, time is the primary cost of an overhaul, so it does not pay to fit worn or sub-standard parts.

As a final note, to ensure maximum life and minimum trouble from a reconditioned engine, everything must be assembled with care, in a spotlessly-clean environment.

3 Engine/transmission removal – methods and precautions

If you have decided that the engine must be removed for overhaul or major repair work, several preliminary steps should be taken.

Locating a suitable place to work is extremely important. Adequate work space, along with storage space for the vehicle, will be needed. If a workshop or garage is not available, at the very least, a flat, level, clean work surface is required.

Cleaning the engine compartment and engine/transmission before beginning the removal procedure will help keep tools clean and organised.

An engine hoist will also be necessary. Make sure the equipment is rated in excess of the combined weight of the engine and transmission. Safety is of primary importance, considering the potential hazards involved in removing the engine/transmission from the vehicle.

If this is the first time you have removed an engine, an assistant should ideally be available. Advice and aid from someone more experienced would also be helpful. There are many instances when one person cannot simultaneously perform all of the operations required during engine/transmission removal.

Plan the operation ahead of time. Before starting work, arrange for the hire of or obtain all of the tools and equipment you will need. Some of the equipment necessary to perform engine/transmission removal and installation safely (in addition to an engine hoist) is as follows: a heavy duty trolley jack, complete sets of spanners and sockets as described at the rear of this manual, wooden blocks, and plenty of rags and cleaning solvent for mopping-up spilled oil, coolant and fuel. If the hoist must be hired, make sure that you arrange for it in advance, and perform all of the operations possible without it beforehand. This will save you money and time.

Plan for the vehicle to be out of use for quite a while. An engineering works will be required to perform some of the work which the do-it-yourselfer cannot accomplish without special equipment. These places often have a busy schedule, so it would be a good idea to consult them before removing the engine, in order to accurately estimate the amount of time required to rebuild or repair components that may need work.

During the engine/transmission removal procedure, it is advisable to make notes of the locations of all brackets, cable ties, earthing points, etc, as well as how the wiring harnesses, hoses and electrical connections are attached and routed around the engine and engine compartment. An effective way of doing this is to take a series of photographs of the various components before they are disconnected or removed. A simple inexpensive disposable camera is ideal for this and the resulting photographs will prove invaluable when the engine is refitted.

Always be extremely careful when removing and refitting the engine/transmission. Serious injury can result from careless actions. Plan ahead and take your time, and a job of this nature, although major, can be accomplished successfully.

The engine and transmission assembly is removed downwards from the engine compartment on all models described in this manual.

4 Engine and transmission –
removal, separation, reconnection and refitting

⚠️ **Warning: It is essential to observe strict precautions when working on the fuel system components.** Before carrying out any of the following operations, refer to the special information given in Chapter 4B, Section 2.

Removal

Note: *The engine is removed downwards from the engine compartment as a complete unit with the transmission; the two are then separated for overhaul.*

1 Disconnect the battery negative terminal (refer to *Disconnecting the battery* in the Reference Section of this manual).

2 Open and support the bonnet in its maximum height position.

3 Remove the air cleaner assembly and air inlet ducts as described in Chapter 4B.

4 Unbolt and remove the air cleaner support bracket.

5 Disconnect the vacuum hose from the braking system vacuum pump **(see illustration)**.

6 Disconnect the vacuum hoses and wiring connector at the EGR solenoid valve **(see illustration)**.

7 Referring to Chapter 4B, disconnect the fuel supply and return hose quick-release fittings at the connections above the fuel pump. Suitably plug or cover the open unions to prevent dirt entry. Release the fuel hoses from their retaining clips and move them clear of the engine.

8 Lift up the covers on the battery positive cable terminal box and unscrew the nuts securing the battery cables to the terminal studs. Lift the cables off the studs and suitably label them for correct refitting.

9 Similarly, lift off the fuse/relay box cover and unscrew the nuts securing the battery positive cables to the terminal studs. Lift the cables off the studs, release them from the fuse/relay box and suitably label them.

10 Disconnect the wiring connector from the accelerator pedal position sensor.

11 Remove the engine management ECU as described in Chapter 4B, Section 13.

12 Release the wiring harness from the retaining clips and cable ties on the ECU support tray, then undo the retaining bolts and lift out the support tray.

13 Disconnect the main engine wiring harness at the connectors in front of the fuse/relay box.

14 Working as described in Chapter 6, on models with a cable-operated clutch, disconnect the clutch cable from the

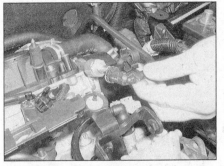

4.5 Disconnect the vacuum hose from the braking system vacuum pump

transmission, and position it clear of the working area. On models with a hydraulically-operated clutch, unbolt the slave cylinder from the front of the transmission. Release the hydraulic fluid supply pipe from the support brackets and move the pipe and cylinder assembly clear of the engine/transmission.

15 Working as described in Chapter 7, disconnect the gearchange selector cable end fittings from the transmission levers then release the cables from the support bracket.

16 Undo the bolt and release the transmission earth cable from body side-member.

17 Firmly apply the handbrake, then jack up the front of the vehicle and support it securely on axle stands (see *Jacking and vehicle support*). Note that the vehicle must be raised sufficiently high (approximately 500 mm) to enable the engine/transmission assembly to be withdrawn from under the front of the vehicle. Remove the front roadwheels.

18 Remove the auxiliary drivebelt as described in Chapter 1B.

19 If the engine is to be dismantled, drain the engine oil referring to Chapter 1B if necessary. Clean and refit the drain plug, tightening it securely.

20 Drain the cooling system as described in Chapter 1B.

21 Drain the transmission oil as described in Chapter 7. Refit the drain and filler plugs, and tighten them to their specified torque settings.

22 Disconnect the radiator top and bottom hoses from the coolant outlet housing and thermostat cover.

23 Disconnect the expansion tank hose from

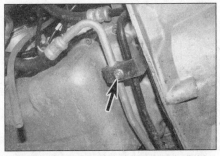

4.25a Release the power steering fluid pipes from the clamps (arrowed) on the front . . .

4.6 Disconnect the EGR solenoid valve vacuum hoses and wiring connector

the coolant outlet housing.

24 Release the retaining clip and disconnect the heater matrix hoses from their connection on the engine compartment bulkhead.

25 Release the power steering fluid pipes from the clamps on the cover plate at the base of the transmission bellhousing **(see illustrations)**.

26 Position a suitable container beneath the power steering gear assembly. Undo the bolt securing the fluid pipe flange plate to the rack housing and ease the flange plate from the rack. Allow the power steering fluid to drain into the container. When the fluid has finished draining, suitably cover the pipe ends and the orifices in the rack to prevent dirt ingress.

27 Slacken the retaining clip and disconnect the fluid return hose from the pipe connection below the radiator. Unscrew the union nut and disconnect the fluid supply hose from the pump. Release the pipe and hose assembly from the support bracket clamps and remove the pipes from under the vehicle. Suitably cover the pipe and hose ends and the orifices in the pump to prevent dirt ingress.

28 On models with air conditioning, disconnect the compressor wiring connector, then unbolt the compressor and position it clear of the engine. Support the weight of the compressor by tying it to the vehicle body, to prevent any excess strain being placed on the compressor lines whilst the engine is removed. *Do not* disconnect the refrigerant lines from the compressor (refer to the warnings given in Chapter 3).

29 Disconnect the exhaust system front pipe from the turbocharger.

4.25b . . . and rear of the transmission bellhousing cover plate

4.35 Remove the engine/transmission left-hand mounting

30 Disconnect the wiring connector from the vehicle speed sensor.

31 Remove both driveshafts as described in Chapter 8.

32 Remove the front suspension subframe as described in Chapter 10.

33 Check that all the relevant wiring connectors have been disconnected, and that the harness is released from all the clips or ties, so that it is free to be removed with the engine/transmission.

34 Manoeuvre an engine hoist into position, and attach it to the engine lifting brackets. Raise the hoist until it is just supporting the weight of the engine.

35 Slacken and remove the centre nut and washer from the engine/transmission left-hand mounting. Undo the two nuts and washers securing the mounting to its bracket, remove the mounting from the engine compartment and recover the washer and spacer **(see illustration).**

36 Working on the right-hand engine/transmission mounting, undo the two bolts securing the stiffener bracket to the body and lift off the bracket. Unscrew the domed buffer nut, then unscrew the single nut securing the upper bracket to the rubber mounting **(see illustrations).** Unscrew the three bolts and remove the upper bracket from the lower (engine) bracket.

37 Make a final check that any components which would prevent the removal of the engine/transmission from the vehicle have been removed or disconnected.

38 Carefully lower the engine/transmission assembly from the engine compartment,

ensuring that nothing is trapped or damaged. Enlist the help of an assistant during this procedure, as it will be necessary to tilt and twist the assembly slightly to clear the body panels and adjacent components.

39 Ensure that the assembly is adequately supported using jacks or a suitable trolley, then disconnect the engine hoist and withdraw the engine/transmission out from under the front of the vehicle.

Separation

40 With the engine/transmission assembly removed, support the unit on suitable blocks of wood on a workbench (or failing that, on a clean area of the workshop floor).

41 Disconnect all the individual wiring connectors from the various components on the engine and transmission to enable the main engine wiring harness to be removed. Make notes or attach labels to each connector to aid reconnection.

42 With all wiring disconnected, detach the wiring harness support brackets and plastic ducting mountings, release the relevant cable ties and remove the complete harness assembly from the engine/transmission.

43 Undo the retaining bolts, and remove the cover plate from the transmission bellhousing.

44 Slacken and remove the retaining bolts, and remove the starter motor from the transmission.

45 Undo the bolts and release the coolant heating housing from the transmission, noting the location of the earth leads and cable clips also secured by the housing retaining bolts.

46 Ensure that both engine and transmission are adequately supported, then slacken and remove the remaining bolts securing the transmission housing to the engine. Note the correct fitted positions of each bolt (and the relevant brackets) as they are removed, to use as a reference on refitting.

47 Carefully withdraw the transmission from the engine, ensuring that the weight of the transmission is not allowed to hang on the input shaft while it is engaged with the clutch friction disc.

48 If they are loose, remove the locating dowels from the engine or transmission, and keep them in a safe place.

Reconnection

49 Apply a smear of high-melting-point grease (Citroën recommend the use of Molykote BR2 plus – available from your Citroën dealer) to the splines of the transmission input shaft. Do not apply too much, otherwise there is a possibility of the grease contaminating the clutch friction disc.

50 Ensure that the locating dowels are correctly positioned in the engine or transmission.

51 Carefully offer the transmission to the engine, until the locating dowels are engaged. Ensure that the weight of the transmission is not allowed to hang on the input shaft as it is engaged with the clutch friction disc.

52 Refit the transmission housing-to-engine bolts, ensuring that all the necessary brackets are correctly positioned, and tighten them securely.

53 Locate the main engine wiring harness on the engine and transmission and reconnect the relevant wiring connectors.

54 Refit the coolant heating housing to the transmission, ensuring that the earth leads and cable clips are correctly attached.

55 Refit the starter motor, and securely tighten its retaining bolts.

56 Refit the cover plate to the transmission bellhousing, and securely tighten its retaining bolts.

Refitting

57 Manoeuvre the engine/transmission into position beneath the engine compartment and reconnect the hoist and lifting tackle to the engine lifting brackets. With the aid of an assistant, slowly lift the assembly into the engine compartment.

58 Manoeuvre the unit as necessary to clear the surrounding components, until it is possible to attach the engine mountings. Locate the right-hand mounting upper bracket onto the lower (engine) bracket and over the rubber mounting stud. Secure the bracket to the lower (engine) bracket with the three bolts tightened to the specified torque. Refit the retaining nut to the stud on the rubber mounting and tighten it by hand only at this stage.

59 Working on the left-hand mounting, refit the rubber mounting, the mounting retaining nuts and washers, and the centre nut and washer, tightening them lightly only.

60 Rock the engine to settle it on its mountings, then go around and tighten all the mounting nuts and bolts to their specified torque settings. Once the right-hand mounting bracket nut has been tightened, refit the domed buffer nut and stiffener bracket, tightening the retaining bolts to the specified torque.

61 It is advisable at this stage to refit the front suspension subframe as described in Chapter 10. The rear engine/transmission mounting connecting link can then be refitted, thus stabilising the power unit on its mountings. The hoist can then be detached from the engine and removed.

4.36a Remove the right-hand engine mounting stiffener bracket . . .

4.36b . . . then undo the domed buffer nut, and the upper bracket retaining nut

62 The remainder of the refitting procedure is a direct reversal of the removal sequence, noting the following points:
  a) *Ensure that the wiring loom is correctly routed and retained by all the relevant retaining clips; all connectors should be correctly and securely reconnected.*
  b) *Use new O-ring seals when refitting the power steering fluid pipes.*
  c) *Prior to refitting the driveshafts to the transmission, renew the driveshaft oil seals as described in Chapter 7.*
  d) *Ensure that all coolant hoses are correctly reconnected, and securely retained by their retaining clips.*
  e) *Adjust the gearchange selector cables as described in Chapter 7 after reconnection.*
  f) *Refill the engine and transmission with the correct quantity and type of lubricant, as described in Chapters 1B and 7.*
  g) *Refill the cooling system as described in Chapter 1B.*
  h) *Bleed the power steering system as described in Chapter 10.*
  i) *Bleed the hydraulic clutch system as described in Chapter 6.*

5 Cylinder head – removal and refitting

Note: *Due to the limited access at the rear of the engine, it is impossible to remove the cylinder head with the engine in the car unless considerable additional dismantling is carried out first (eg, removal of the front suspension subframe and related components). The following information describes the cylinder head removal and refitting procedure with the engine/transmission removed from the car.*

Removal

1 Remove the engine/transmission assembly as described in Section 4.
2 Remove the timing belt as described in Chapter 2C.
3 Carry out the following operations as described in Chapter 4B:
  a) *Remove the exhaust manifold and turbocharger.*
  b) *Remove the inlet manifold.*
  c) *Remove the fuel system accumulator rail.*
4 Undo the bolts securing the right-hand engine mounting lower (engine) bracket to the cylinder head and block and remove the bracket.
5 Remove the braking system vacuum pump as described in Chapter 9.
6 Disconnect the wiring connectors and coolant hoses at the coolant outlet housing on the left-hand end of the cylinder head.
7 Undo the bolts and release the wiring harness guide from the coolant outlet housing.
8 Undo the retaining nuts and bolts and remove the fuel injector wiring harness guide left-hand support bracket.

9 Undo the mounting bolt and release the dipstick tube from the cylinder head.
10 Move all the adjacent components clear, then undo the three bolts and two nuts securing the coolant outlet housing to the cylinder head. Lift off the hose and cable support bracket, then withdraw the housing. Recover the housing gasket.
11 Remove the cylinder head cover as described in Chapter 2C.
12 Progressively slacken the cylinder head bolts, in the reverse order to that shown in illustration 5.29.
13 When all the bolts are loose, unscrew them fully and remove them from the cylinder head.
14 Release the cylinder head from the cylinder block and location dowels by rocking it. The Citroën tool for doing this consists simply of two metal rods with 90-degree angled ends **(see illustration)**. Do not prise between the mating faces of the cylinder head and block, as this may damage the gasket faces.
15 Lift the cylinder head from the block, and recover the gasket.

Preparation for refitting

16 The mating faces of the cylinder head and cylinder block must be perfectly clean before refitting the head. Citroën recommend the use of a scouring agent for this purpose, but acceptable results can be achieved by using a hard plastic or wood scraper to remove all traces of gasket and carbon. The same method can be used to clean the piston crowns. Take particular care to avoid scoring or gouging the cylinder head/cylinder block mating surfaces during the cleaning operations, as aluminium alloy is easily damaged. Make sure that the carbon is not allowed to enter the oil and water passages – this is particularly important for the lubrication system, as carbon could block the oil supply to the engine's components. Using adhesive tape and paper, seal the water, oil and bolt holes in the cylinder block. To prevent carbon entering the gap between the pistons and bores, smear a little grease in the gap. After cleaning each piston, use a small brush to remove all traces of grease and carbon from the gap, then wipe away the remainder with a clean rag.
17 Check the mating surfaces of the cylinder block and the cylinder head for nicks, deep scratches and other damage. If slight, they may be removed carefully with a file, but if excessive, machining may be the only alternative to renewal. If warpage of the cylinder head gasket surface is suspected, use a straight-edge to check it for distortion. Refer to Section 8 if necessary.
18 Thoroughly clean the threads of the cylinder head bolt holes in the cylinder block. Ensure that the bolts run freely in their threads, and that all traces of oil and water are removed from each bolt hole.

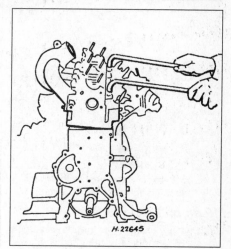

5.14 Freeing the cylinder head using angled rods

Gasket selection

19 Turn the crankshaft until pistons 1 and 4 are at TDC. Position a dial test indicator (dial gauge) on the cylinder block, and zero it on the block face. Transfer the probe to the edge of No 1 piston, then slowly turn the crankshaft back and forth past TDC, noting the highest reading on the indicator. Record this reading.
20 Repeat this measurement procedure on No 4 piston, then turn the crankshaft half a turn (180°) and repeat the procedure on Nos 2 and 3 pistons **(see illustration)**.
21 If a dial test indicator is not available, piston protrusion may be measured using a straight-edge and feeler blades or vernier calipers. However, this is much less accurate, and cannot therefore be recommended.
22 Note down the greatest piston protrusion measurement, and use this to determine the correct cylinder head gasket from the following table. The series of up to five notches on the side of the gasket are used for thickness identification **(see illustration)**.

Piston protrusion	Gasket identification
0.470 to 0.605 mm	*1 notch*
0.605 to 0.655 mm	*2 notches*
0.655 to 0.705 mm	*3 notches*
0.705 to 0.755 mm	*4 notches*
0.755 to 0.830 mm	*5 notches*

5.20 Measuring piston protrusion

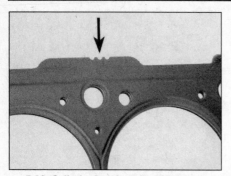

5.22 Cylinder head gasket thickness identification notches (arrowed)

Head bolt examination

23 Carefully examine the cylinder head bolts for signs of damage to the threads or head, and for any sign of corrosion. If the bolts are in a satisfactory condition, measure the length of each bolt from the underside of the head, to the end of the shank. The bolts may be re-used providing that the measured length does not exceed 133.3 mm. **Note:** *Considering the stress to which the cylinder head bolts are subjected, it is highly recommended that they are all renewed, regardless of their apparent condition.*

Refitting

24 Turn the crankshaft clockwise (viewed from the timing belt end) until Nos 1 and 4 pistons pass bottom dead centre (BDC) and begin to rise, then position them halfway up their bores. Nos 2 and 3 pistons will also be at their mid-way positions, but descending their bores.

25 Make sure that the locating dowels are in place, then fit the correct gasket the right way round on the cylinder block, with the identification notches toward the fuel pump side of the engine.

26 Lower the cylinder head onto the block.

27 Apply a smear of grease to the threads, and to the underside of the heads, of the cylinder head bolts. Citroën recommend the use of Molykote G Rapid Plus (available from your Citroën dealer).

28 Carefully enter each bolt into its relevant hole (*do not drop it in*) and screw it in finger-tight.

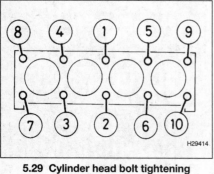

5.29 Cylinder head bolt tightening sequence

29 Working progressively and in the sequence shown, tighten the cylinder head bolts to their Stage 1 torque setting, using a torque wrench and suitable socket **(see illustration)**.

30 Once all the bolts have been tightened to their Stage 1 torque setting, working again in the specified sequence, tighten each bolt to the specified Stage 2 setting. Finally, angle-tighten the bolts through the specified Stage 3 angle. It is recommended that an angle-measuring gauge is used during this stage of tightening, to ensure accuracy.

31 Refit the cylinder head cover as described in Chapter 2C.

32 Ensure that the mating face of the cylinder head and coolant outlet housing are clean then refit the housing using a new gasket. Refit the hose and cable support bracket and the housing retaining nuts and bolts. Tighten the nuts and bolts securely.

33 Refit and tighten the dipstick tube retaining bolt.

34 Refit the wiring harness guide support brackets.

35 Reconnect the coolant hoses to the thermostat housing.

36 Refit the timing belt as described in Chapter 2C.

37 Refit the accumulator rail, inlet manifold, and the exhaust manifold and turbocharger, in strict accordance with the procedures described in Chapter 4B.

38 Refit the braking system vacuum pump as described in Chapter 9.

39 Refit the right-hand engine mounting bracket with reference to Chapter 2C.

40 Refit the engine/transmission assembly as described in Section 4.

6 Engine overhaul – dismantling sequence

1 It is much easier to dismantle and work on the engine if it is mounted on a portable engine stand. These stands can often be hired from a tool hire shop. Before the engine is mounted on a stand, the flywheel should be removed, so that the stand bolts can be tightened into the end of the cylinder block.

2 If a stand is not available, it is possible to dismantle the engine with it blocked up on a sturdy workbench, or on the floor. Be extra-careful not to tip or drop the engine when working without a stand.

3 If you are going to obtain a reconditioned engine, all the external components must be removed first, to be transferred to the replacement engine (just as they will if you are doing a complete engine overhaul yourself). These components include the following:

a) *Engine wiring harness and support brackets.*
b) *Alternator, power steering pump and air conditioning compressor mounting bracket.*
c) *Engine mounting brackets.*

d) *Coolant outlet housing.*
e) *Fuel filter housing.*
f) *Dipstick tube.*
g) *Fuel system components.*
h) *All electrical switches and sensors.*
i) *Inlet and exhaust manifolds and turbocharger.*
j) *Oil filter and oil cooler.*
k) *Flywheel.*

Note: *When removing the external components from the engine, pay close attention to details that may be helpful or important during refitting. Note the fitted position of gaskets, seals, spacers, pins, washers, bolts, and other small items.*

4 If you are obtaining a 'short' engine (cylinder block, crankshaft, pistons and connecting rods all assembled), then the cylinder head, sump, oil pump, and timing belt will have to be removed also.

5 If you are planning a complete overhaul, the engine can be dismantled, and the internal components removed, in the order given below, referring to Part C of this Chapter unless otherwise stated.

a) *Inlet and exhaust manifolds (Chapter 4B).*
b) *Timing belt, sprockets and tensioner.*
c) *Cylinder head (Section 5).*
d) *Flywheel.*
e) *Sump.*
f) *Oil pump.*
g) *Pistons/connecting rods (Section 10).*
h) *Crankshaft (Section 11).*

6 Before beginning the dismantling and overhaul procedures, make sure that you have all of the tools necessary. Refer to *Tools and working facilities* for further information.

7 Cylinder head – dismantling

Note: *New and reconditioned cylinder heads are available from the manufacturer, and from engine overhaul specialists. Some specialist tools are required for dismantling and inspection, and new components may not be readily available. It may therefore be more practical and economical for the home mechanic to purchase a reconditioned head, rather than dismantle, inspect and recondition the original head.*

1 Remove the cylinder head as described in Section 5.

2 If not already done, remove the inlet and exhaust manifolds with reference to Chapter 4B.

3 Remove the camshaft, rocker arms and hydraulic tappets as described in Part C of this Chapter.

4 Remove the glow plugs as described in Chapter 5C and the injectors as described in Chapter 4B.

5 Using a valve spring compressor, compress each valve spring in turn until the split collets can be removed. Release the compressor, and lift off the spring retainer, and spring **(see illustrations)**.

7.5a Compress the valve spring with a spring compressor and extract the split collets

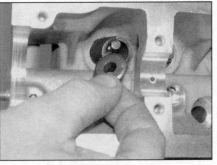

7.5b Remove the spring retainer . . .

7.5c . . . followed by the valve spring

7.7a Withdraw the valve through the combustion chamber . . .

7.7b . . . remove the valve stem oil seal . . .

7.7c . . . then lift out the spring seat

6 If, when the valve spring compressor is screwed down, the spring retainer refuses to free and expose the split collets, gently tap the top of the tool, directly over the retainer, with a light hammer. This will free the retainer.

7 Withdraw the valve through the combustion chamber, remove the valve stem oil seal from the top of the guide, then lift out the spring seat **(see illustrations)**.

8 It is essential that each valve is stored together with its collets, retainer, spring, and spring seat. The valves should also be kept in their correct sequence, unless they are so badly worn that they are to be renewed. If they are going to be kept and used again, place each valve assembly in a labelled polythene bag or similar small container **(see illustration)**. Note that No 1 valve is nearest to the transmission (flywheel) end of the engine.

8 Cylinder head and valves – cleaning and inspection

1 Thorough cleaning of the cylinder head and valve components, followed by a detailed inspection, will enable you to decide how much valve service work must be carried out during the engine overhaul. **Note:** *If the engine has been severely overheated, it is best to assume that the cylinder head is warped – check carefully for signs of this.*

Cleaning

2 Remove all traces of old gasket material

from the cylinder head. Citroën recommend the use of a scouring agent for this purpose, but acceptable results can be achieved by using a hard plastic or wood scraper to remove all traces of gasket and carbon.

3 Similarly, remove the carbon from the combustion chambers and ports, then wash the cylinder head thoroughly with paraffin or a suitable solvent.

4 Scrape off any heavy carbon deposits that may have formed on the valves, then use a power-operated wire brush to remove deposits from the valve heads and stems.

Inspection

Note: *Be sure to perform all the following inspection procedures before concluding that the services of a machine shop or engine overhaul specialist are required. Make a list of all items that require attention.*

Cylinder head

5 Inspect the head very carefully for cracks, evidence of coolant leakage, and other damage. If cracks are found, a new cylinder head should be obtained.

6 Use a straight-edge and feeler blade to check that the cylinder head gasket surface is not distorted **(see illustration)**. If it is, it may be possible to have it machined, provided that the cylinder head height is not significantly reduced.

7 Examine the valve seats in each of the combustion chambers. If they are severely pitted, cracked, or burned, they will need to be renewed or recut by an engine overhaul specialist. If they are only slightly pitted, this

7.8 Place each valve and its associated components in a labelled polythene bag

can be removed by grinding-in the valve heads and seats with fine valve-grinding compound, as described below.

8 Check the valve guides for wear by inserting the relevant valve, and checking for

8.6 Checking the cylinder head gasket surface for distortion

8.11 Measuring a valve stem diameter

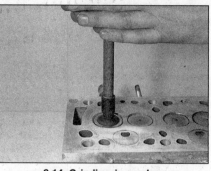

8.14 Grinding-in a valve

side-to-side motion of the valve. A very small amount of movement is acceptable. If the movement seems excessive, remove the valve. Measure the valve stem diameter (see below), and renew the valve if it is worn. If the valve stem is not worn, the wear must be in the valve guide, and the guide must be renewed. The renewal of valve guides is best carried out by an engine overhaul specialist, who will have the necessary tools available.

9 If renewing the valve guides, the valve seats should be recut or reground only *after* the guides have been fitted.

Valves

10 Examine the head of each valve for pitting, burning, cracks, and general wear. Check the valve stem for scoring and wear ridges. Rotate the valve, and check for any obvious indication that it is bent. Look for pits or excessive wear on the tip of each valve stem. Renew any valve that shows any such signs of wear or damage.

11 If the valve appears satisfactory at this stage, measure the valve stem diameter at several points using a micrometer **(see illustration)**. Any significant difference in the readings obtained indicates wear of the valve stem. Should any of these conditions be apparent, the valve(s) must be renewed.

12 If the valves are in satisfactory condition, they should be ground (lapped) into their respective seats, to ensure a smooth, gas-tight seal. If the seat is only lightly pitted, or if it has been recut, fine grinding compound *only* should be used to produce the required finish. Coarse valve-grinding compound should *not* be used, unless a seat is badly

burned or deeply pitted. If this is the case, the cylinder head and valves should be inspected by an expert, to decide whether seat recutting, or even the renewal of the valve or seat insert (where possible) is required.

13 Valve grinding is carried out as follows. Place the head upside-down on blocks, on a bench.

14 Smear a trace of (the appropriate grade of) valve-grinding compound on the seat face, and press a suction grinding tool onto the valve head **(see illustration)**. With a semi-rotary action, grind the valve head to its seat, lifting the valve occasionally to redistribute the grinding compound. A light spring placed under the valve head will greatly ease this operation.

15 If coarse grinding compound is being used, work only until a dull, matt even surface is produced on both the valve seat and the valve, then wipe off the used compound, and repeat the process with fine compound. When a smooth unbroken ring of light grey matt finish is produced on both the valve and seat, the grinding operation is complete. *Do not* grind-in the valves any further than absolutely necessary, or the seat will be prematurely sunk into the cylinder head.

16 When all the valves have been ground-in, carefully wash off *all* traces of grinding compound using paraffin or a suitable solvent, before reassembling the cylinder head.

Valve components

17 Examine the valve springs for signs of damage and discoloration. No minimum free length is specified by Citroën, so the only way of judging valve spring wear is by comparison with a new component.

18 Stand each spring on a flat surface, and check it for squareness. If any of the springs are damaged, distorted or have lost their tension, obtain a complete new set of springs. It is normal to fit new springs as a matter of course if a major overhaul is being carried out.

19 Renew the valve stem oil seals regardless of their apparent condition.

9 Cylinder head – reassembly

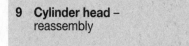

1 Working on the first valve assembly, refit the spring seat then dip the new valve stem oil seal in fresh engine oil. Locate the seal on the valve guide and press the seal firmly onto the guide using a suitable socket **(see illustrations)**.

2 Lubricate the stem of the first valve, and insert it in the guide **(see illustration)**.

3 Locate the valve spring on top of its seat, then refit the spring retainer.

4 Compress the valve spring, and locate the split collets in the recess in the valve stem. Release the compressor, then repeat the procedure on the remaining valves. Ensure that each valve is inserted into its original location. If new valves are being fitted, insert them into the locations to which they have been ground.

> **HAYNES HINT** *Use a little dab of grease to hold the collets in position on the valve stem while the spring compressor is released.*

5 With all the valves installed, place the cylinder head on blocks on the bench and, using a hammer and interposed block of wood, tap the end of each valve stem to settle the components.

6 Refit the camshaft, hydraulic tappets and rocker arms as described in Part C of this Chapter.

7 Refit the glow plugs as described in Chapter 5C.

8 Refit the inlet and exhaust manifolds and fuel injectors with reference to Chapter 4B.

9 The cylinder head can then be refitted as described in Section 5.

9.1a Locate the valve stem oil seal on the valve guide . . .

9.1b . . . and press the seal firmly onto the guide using a suitable socket

9.2 Lubricate the stem of the valve and insert it in the guide

10 Piston/connecting rod assembly – removal

1 Remove the cylinder head, sump and oil pump as described in this Part, or in Part C of this Chapter (as applicable).
2 If there is a pronounced wear ridge at the top of any bore, it may be necessary to remove it with a scraper or ridge reamer, to avoid piston damage during removal. Such a ridge indicates excess bore wear.
3 Using quick-drying paint, mark each connecting rod and big-end bearing cap with its respective cylinder number on the flat machined surface provided; if the engine has been dismantled before, note carefully any identifying marks made previously **(see illustration)**. Note that No 1 cylinder is at the transmission (flywheel) end of the engine.
4 Turn the crankshaft to bring pistons 1 and 4 to BDC (bottom dead centre).
5 Unscrew the nuts from No 1 piston big-end bearing cap. Take off the cap, and recover the bottom half bearing shell **(see illustration)**. If the bearing shells are to be re-used, tape the cap and the shell together.
6 To prevent the possibility of damage to the crankshaft bearing journals, tape over the connecting rod stud threads.
7 Using a hammer handle, push the piston up through the bore, and remove it from the top of the cylinder block. Recover the bearing shell, and tape it to the connecting rod for safe-keeping.

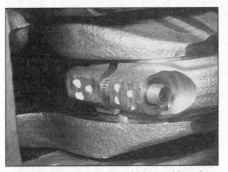

10.3 Connecting rod and big-end bearing cap identification marks (No 3 shown)

8 Loosely refit the big-end cap to the connecting rod, and secure with the nuts – this will help to keep the components in their correct order.
9 Remove No 4 assembly in the same way.
10 Turn the crankshaft through 180º to bring pistons 2 and 3 to BDC (bottom dead centre), and remove them in the same way.

11 Crankshaft – removal

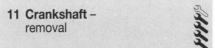

1 Remove the crankshaft sprocket and the oil pump as described in Part C of this Chapter.
2 Remove the pistons and connecting rods, as described in Section 10. If no work is to be done on the pistons and connecting rods,

10.5 Removing a big-end bearing cap and shell

there is no need to remove the cylinder head, or to push the pistons out of the cylinder bores. The pistons should just be pushed far enough up the bores so that they are positioned clear of the crankshaft journals.
3 Check the crankshaft endfloat as described in Section 14, then proceed as follows.
4 Slacken and remove the retaining bolts, and remove the oil seal carrier from the right-hand end of the cylinder block, along with its gasket (where fitted) **(see illustration)**.
5 Remove the oil pump drive chain, and slide the drive sprocket and spacer (where fitted) off the end of the crankshaft. Remove the Woodruff key, and store it with the sprocket for safe-keeping **(see illustrations)**.
6 The main bearing caps should be numbered 1 to 5, starting from the transmission (flywheel) end of the engine **(see illustration)**. If not, mark them accordingly using quick-drying paint. Also note the correct fitted depth of the left-hand crankshaft oil seal in the bearing cap.
7 Slacken and remove the main bearing cap retaining bolts, and lift off each bearing cap. Recover the lower bearing shells, and tape them to their respective caps for safe-keeping. Also recover the lower thrustwasher halves from the side of No 2 main bearing cap **(see illustration)**. Remove the sealing strips from the sides of No 1 main bearing cap, and discard them.
8 Lift out the crankshaft **(see illustration)**, and discard the left-hand oil seal.
9 Recover the upper bearing shells from the

11.4 Removing the oil seal carrier from the right-hand end of the block

11.5a Remove the oil pump drive chain . . .

11.5b . . . then slide off the drive sprocket . . .

11.5c . . . and remove the Woodruff key from the crankshaft

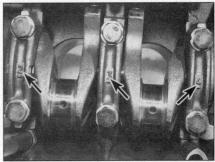

11.6 Main bearing cap identification markings (arrowed)

11.7 Removing No 2 main bearing cap. Note the thrustwasher (arrowed)

11.8 Lifting out the crankshaft

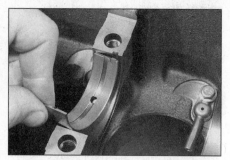

11.9 Remove the upper main bearing shells from the cylinder block, and store them with their lower shells

cylinder block **(see illustration)**, and tape them to their respective caps for safe-keeping. Remove the upper thrustwasher halves from the side of No 2 main bearing, and store them with the lower halves.

12 Cylinder block/crankcase – cleaning and inspection

Cleaning

1 Remove all external components and electrical switches/sensors from the block. For complete cleaning, the core plugs should ideally be removed **(see illustration)**. Drill a small hole in the plugs, then insert a self-tapping screw into the hole. Pull out the plugs by pulling on the screw with a pair of grips, or by using a slide hammer.

2 Undo the retaining bolt and remove the piston oil jet spray tube from inside the cylinder block.

3 Scrape all traces of gasket from the cylinder block, taking care not to damage the gasket/sealing surfaces.

4 Remove all oil gallery plugs (where fitted). The plugs are usually very tight – they may have to be drilled out, and the holes retapped. Use new plugs when the engine is reassembled.

5 If the cylinder block is extremely dirty, it should be steam-cleaned.

6 After steam-cleaning, clean all oil holes and oil galleries one more time. Flush all internal passages with warm water until the water runs

clear. Dry thoroughly, and apply a light film of oil to the cylinder bores and all mating surfaces, to prevent rusting. If you have access to compressed air, use it to speed up the drying process, and to blow out all the oil holes and galleries.

⚠️ **Warning: Wear eye protection when using compressed air.**

7 If the cylinder block is not very dirty, you can do an adequate cleaning job with very hot, soapy water and a stiff brush. Take plenty of time, and do a thorough job. Regardless of the cleaning method used, be sure to clean all oil holes and galleries very thoroughly, and to dry all components well. Protect the cylinder bores as described above, to prevent rusting.

8 All threaded holes must be clean, to ensure accurate torque readings during reassembly. To clean the threads, run the correct-size tap into each of the holes to remove rust, corrosion, thread sealant or sludge, and to restore damaged threads **(see illustration)**. If possible, use compressed air to clear the holes of debris produced by this operation.

⚠️ **Warning: Wear eye protection when using compressed air.**

9 Apply suitable sealant to the new oil gallery plugs, and insert them into the holes in the block. Tighten them securely.

10 Apply suitable sealant to the new core plugs, and insert them into the holes in the block. Tap them into place with a socket which just fits into the plugs.

11 On engines with a piston oil jet spray tube, clean the threads of the oil jet retaining bolt,

and apply a drop of thread-locking compound to the bolt threads. Refit the piston oil jet spray tube to the cylinder block, and tighten its retaining bolt to the specified torque setting.

12 If the engine is not going to be reassembled right away, cover it with a large plastic bag to keep it clean; protect all mating surfaces and the cylinder bores as described above, to prevent rusting.

Inspection

13 Visually check the block for cracks and corrosion. Look for stripped threads in the threaded holes. If there has been any history of internal water leakage, it may be worthwhile having an engine overhaul specialist check the cylinder block with special equipment. If defects are found, have them repaired if possible, or renew the assembly.

14 Check each cylinder bore for scuffing and scoring. Check for signs of a wear ridge at the top of the cylinder, indicating that the bore is excessively worn.

15 If the necessary measuring equipment is available, measure the bore diameter of each cylinder at the top (just under the wear ridge), centre, and bottom of the cylinder bore, parallel to the crankshaft axis.

16 Next, measure the bore diameter at the same three locations, at right-angles to the crankshaft axis. Compare the results with the figures given in the Specifications. If there is any doubt about the condition of the cylinder bores, seek the advice of an engine reconditioning specialist or Citroën dealer.

13 Piston/connecting rod assembly – inspection

1 Before the inspection process can begin, the piston/connecting rod assemblies must be cleaned, and the original piston rings removed from the pistons.

2 Carefully expand the old rings over the top of the pistons. The use of two or three old feeler blades will be helpful in preventing the rings dropping into empty grooves **(see illustration)**. Be careful not to scratch the piston with the ends of the ring. The rings are brittle, and will snap if they are spread too far.

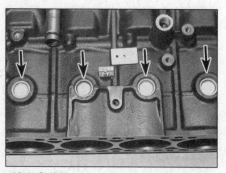

12.1 Cylinder block core plugs (arrowed)

12.8 Cleaning a cylinder block threaded hole using a suitable tap

13.2 Removing a piston ring with the aid of a feeler blade

13.14a Prise out the circlip . . .

13.14b . . . and withdraw the gudgeon pin

They are also very sharp – protect your hands and fingers. Note that the third ring incorporates an expander. Always remove the rings from the top of the piston. Keep each set of rings with its piston if the old rings are to be re-used.

3 Scrape away all traces of carbon from the top of the piston. A hand-held wire brush (or a piece of fine emery cloth) can be used, once the majority of the deposits have been scraped away.

4 Remove the carbon from the ring grooves in the piston, using an old ring. Break the ring in half to do this (be careful not to cut your fingers – piston rings are sharp). Be careful to remove only the carbon deposits – do not remove any metal, and do not nick or scratch the sides of the ring grooves.

5 Once the deposits have been removed, clean the piston/connecting rod assembly with paraffin or a suitable solvent, and dry thoroughly. Make sure that the oil return holes in the ring grooves are clear.

6 If the pistons and cylinder bores are not damaged or worn excessively, the original pistons can be refitted. Normal piston wear shows up as even vertical wear on the piston thrust surfaces, and slight looseness of the top ring in its groove. New piston rings should always be used when the engine is reassembled.

7 Carefully inspect each piston for cracks around the skirt, around the gudgeon pin holes, and at the piston ring 'lands' (between the ring grooves).

8 Look for scoring and scuffing on the piston skirt, holes in the piston crown, and burned areas at the edge of the crown. If the skirt is scored or scuffed, the engine may have been suffering from overheating, and/or abnormal combustion which caused excessively high operating temperatures. The cooling and lubrication systems should be checked thoroughly. Scorch marks on the sides of the pistons show that blow-by has occurred. A hole in the piston crown, or burned areas at the edge of the piston crown, indicates that abnormal combustion has been occurring. If any of the above problems exist, the causes must be investigated and corrected, or the damage will occur again.

9 Corrosion of the piston, in the form of

pitting, indicates that coolant has been leaking into the combustion chamber and/or the crankcase. Again, the cause must be corrected, or the problem may persist in the rebuilt engine.

10 Examine each connecting rod carefully for signs of damage, such as cracks around the big-end and small-end bearings. Check that the rod is not bent or distorted. Damage is highly unlikely, unless the engine has been seized or badly overheated. Detailed checking of the connecting rod assembly can only be carried out by an engine specialist with the necessary equipment.

11 Note that the big-end cap nuts and bolts must be renewed as a complete set prior to refitting. This should be done after the big-end bearing running clearance check has been carried out (see Section 19). The bolts can be simply tapped out of the connecting rods and new bolts fitted in the same way.

12 The gudgeon pins are of the floating type, secured in position by two circlips in each piston. The pistons and connecting rods can be separated as follows.

13 Before separating the piston and connecting rod, check the position of the valve recesses on the piston crown in relation to the connecting rod big-end bearing shell cut-outs and make a note of the orientation. On the new engine dismantled in the Haynes workshop during the preparation of this manual, the piston-to-connecting rod orientation did not agree with the manufacturer's technical documentation.

14 Using a small flat-bladed screwdriver, prise out the circlips, and push out the gudgeon pin **(see illustrations)**. Hand pressure should be sufficient to remove the pin. Identify the piston and rod to ensure correct reassembly. Discard the circlips – new ones *must* be used on refitting.

15 Examine the gudgeon pin and connecting rod small-end bearing for signs of wear or damage. Wear can be cured by renewing both the pin and bush. Bush renewal, however, is a specialist job – press facilities are required, and the new bush must be reamed accurately.

16 The connecting rods themselves should not be in need of renewal, unless seizure or some other major mechanical failure has occurred. Check the alignment of the

connecting rods visually, and if the rods are not straight, take them to an engine overhaul specialist for a more detailed check.

17 Examine all components, and obtain any new parts from your Citroën dealer. If new pistons are purchased, they will be supplied complete with gudgeon pins and circlips. Circlips can also be purchased individually.

18 Position the piston in relation to the connecting rod as noted during separation.

19 Apply a smear of clean engine oil to the gudgeon pin and slide it into the piston and through the connecting rod small-end. Check that the piston pivots freely on the rod, then secure the gudgeon pin in position with two new circlips. Ensure that each circlip is correctly located in its groove in the piston.

14 Crankshaft – inspection

Checking endfloat

1 If the crankshaft endfloat is to be checked, this must be done when the crankshaft is still installed in the cylinder block, but is free to move.

2 Check the endfloat using a dial gauge in contact with the end of the crankshaft. Push the crankshaft fully one way, and then zero the gauge. Push the crankshaft fully the other way, and check the endfloat. The result can be compared with the specified amount, and will give an indication as to whether new thrustwashers are required **(see illustration)**.

14.2 Checking crankshaft endfloat using a dial gauge

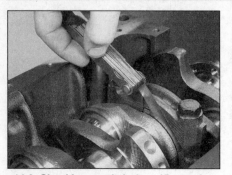

14.3 Checking crankshaft endfloat using feeler blades

14.10 Measuring a crankshaft big-end journal diameter

15 Main and big-end bearings – inspection

1 Even though the main and big-end bearings should be renewed during the engine overhaul, the old bearings should be retained for close examination, as they may reveal valuable information about the condition of the engine. The bearing shells are graded by thickness, the grade of each shell being indicated by the colour code, or size identification, marked on it.

2 Bearing failure can occur due to lack of lubrication, the presence of dirt or other foreign particles, overloading the engine, or corrosion **(see illustration)**. Regardless of the cause of bearing failure, the cause must be corrected (where applicable) before the engine is reassembled, to prevent it from happening again.

3 When examining the bearing shells, remove them from the cylinder block, the main bearing caps, the connecting rods and the connecting rod big-end bearing caps. Lay them out on a clean surface in the same general position as their location in the engine. This will enable you to match any bearing problems with the corresponding crankshaft journal. *Do not* touch any shell's bearing surface with your fingers while checking it, or the delicate surface may be scratched.

4 Dirt and other foreign matter gets into the engine in a variety of ways. It may be left in the engine during assembly, or it may pass through filters or the crankcase ventilation system. It may get into the oil, and from there into the bearings. Metal chips from machining operations and normal engine wear are often present. Abrasives are sometimes left in engine components after reconditioning, especially when parts are not thoroughly cleaned using the proper cleaning methods. Whatever the source, these foreign objects often end up embedded in the soft bearing material, and are easily recognised. Large particles will not embed in the bearing, and will score or gouge the bearing and journal. The best prevention for this cause of bearing failure is to clean all parts thoroughly, and keep everything spotlessly-clean during engine assembly. Frequent and regular engine oil and filter changes are also recommended.

5 Lack of lubrication (or lubrication breakdown) has a number of interrelated causes. Excessive heat (which thins the oil), overloading (which squeezes the oil from the bearing face) and oil leakage (from excessive bearing clearances, worn oil pump or high engine speeds) all contribute to lubrication breakdown. Blocked oil passages, which usually are the result of misaligned oil holes in a bearing shell, will also oil-starve a bearing, and destroy it. When lack of lubrication is the cause of bearing failure, the bearing material is wiped or extruded from the steel backing of

3 If a dial gauge is not available, feeler blades can be used. First push the crankshaft fully towards the flywheel end of the engine, then use feeler blades to measure the gap between the web of No 2 crankpin and the thrustwasher **(see illustration)**.

Inspection

4 Clean the crankshaft using paraffin or a suitable solvent, and dry it, preferably with compressed air if available. Be sure to clean the oil holes with a pipe cleaner or similar probe, to ensure that they are not obstructed.

 Warning: Wear eye protection when using compressed air.

5 Check the main and big-end bearing journals for uneven wear, scoring, pitting and cracking.

6 Big-end bearing wear is accompanied by distinct metallic knocking when the engine is running (particularly noticeable when the engine is pulling from low speed) and some loss of oil pressure.

7 Main bearing wear is accompanied by severe engine vibration and rumble – getting progressively worse as engine speed increases – and again by loss of oil pressure.

8 Check the bearing journal for roughness by running a finger lightly over the bearing surface. Any roughness (which will be accompanied by obvious bearing wear) indicates that the crankshaft requires regrinding (where possible) or renewal.

9 If the crankshaft has been reground, check for burrs around the crankshaft oil holes (the holes are usually chamfered, so burrs should not be a problem unless regrinding has been carried out carelessly). Remove any burrs with a fine file or scraper, and thoroughly clean the oil holes as described previously.

10 Using a micrometer, measure the diameter of the main and big-end bearing journals, and compare the results with the Specifications **(see illustration)**. By measuring the diameter at a number of points around each journal's circumference, you will be able to determine whether or not the journal is out-of-round. Take the measurement at each end of the journal, near the webs, to determine if the journal is

tapered. Compare the results obtained with those given in the Specifications.

11 Check the oil seal contact surfaces at each end of the crankshaft for wear and damage. If the seal has worn a deep groove in the surface of the crankshaft, consult an engine overhaul specialist; repair may be possible, but otherwise a new crankshaft will be required.

12 Citroën supply oversize bearing shells for the main bearings but not for the big-end bearings. It may, however, be possible to obtain oversize big-end bearing shells from an alternative source. Where oversize bearing shells are available, if the crankshaft journals have not already been reground, it may be possible to have the crankshaft reconditioned, and to fit the oversize shells. Where oversize shells are not available, or if the crankshaft has already been reconditioned, it will have to be renewed if worn beyond the specified limits. Consult your Citroën dealer or engine specialist for further information on parts availability.

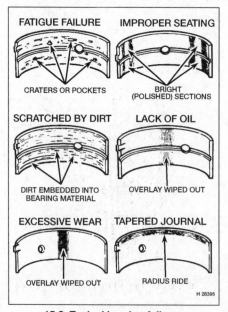

15.2 Typical bearing failures

the bearing. Temperatures may increase to the point where the steel backing turns blue from overheating.

6 Driving habits can have a definite effect on bearing life. Full-throttle, low-speed operation (labouring the engine) puts very high loads on bearings, tending to squeeze out the oil film. These loads cause the bearings to flex, which produces fine cracks in the bearing face (fatigue failure). Eventually, the bearing material will loosen in pieces, and tear away from the steel backing.

7 Short-distance driving leads to corrosion of bearings, because insufficient engine heat is produced to drive off the condensed water and corrosive gases. These products collect in the engine oil, forming acid and sludge. As the oil is carried to the engine bearings, the acid attacks and corrodes the bearing material.

8 Incorrect bearing installation during engine assembly will lead to bearing failure as well. Tight-fitting bearings leave insufficient bearing running clearance, and will result in oil starvation. Dirt or foreign particles trapped behind a bearing shell result in high spots on the bearing, which lead to failure.

9 Do not touch any shell's bearing surface with your fingers during reassembly; there is a risk of scratching the delicate surface, or of depositing particles of dirt on it.

10 As mentioned at the beginning of this Section, the bearing shells should be renewed as a matter of course during engine overhaul; to do otherwise is false economy.

16 Engine overhaul – reassembly sequence

1 Before reassembly begins, ensure that all new parts have been obtained, and that all necessary tools are available. Read through the entire procedure to familiarise yourself with the work involved, and to ensure that all items necessary for reassembly of the engine are at hand. In addition to all normal tools and materials, thread-locking compound will be needed. A suitable tube of liquid sealant will also be required for the joint faces that are fitted without gaskets. It is recommended that Citroën's own products are used, which are specially formulated for this purpose; the relevant product names are quoted in the text of each Section where they are required.

2 In order to save time and avoid problems, engine reassembly can be carried out in the following order:
a) Crankshaft (See Section 18).
b) Piston/connecting rod assemblies (See Section 19).
c) Oil pump (See Part C).
d) Sump (See Part C).
e) Flywheel (See Part C).
f) Cylinder head (See Section 5).
g) Timing belt tensioner and sprockets, and timing belt (See Part C).

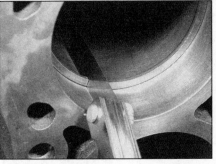

17.5 Measuring a piston ring end gap

h) Engine external components.

3 At this stage, all engine components should be absolutely clean and dry, with all faults repaired. The components should be laid out (or in individual containers) on a completely clean work surface.

17 Piston rings – refitting

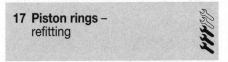

1 Before fitting new piston rings, the ring end gaps must be checked as follows.

2 Lay out the piston/connecting rod assemblies and the new piston ring sets, so that the ring sets will be matched with the same piston and cylinder during the end gap measurement and subsequent engine reassembly.

3 Insert the top ring into the first cylinder, and push it down the bore using the top of the piston. This will ensure that the ring remains square with the cylinder walls. Position the ring near the bottom of the cylinder bore, at the lower limit of ring travel. Note that the top and second compression rings are different. The second ring is easily identified by the fact that its outer face is tapered.

4 Measure the end gap using feeler blades.

5 Repeat the procedure with the ring at the top of the cylinder bore, at the upper limit of

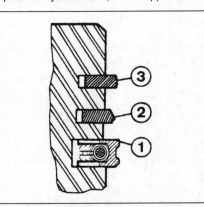

17.10 Piston ring fitting diagram (typical)

1 Oil control ring
2 Second compression ring
3 Top compression ring

its travel, and compare the measurements with the figures given in the Specifications (see illustration).

6 If the gap is too small (unlikely if genuine Citroën parts are used), it must be enlarged, or the ring ends may contact each other during engine operation, causing serious damage. Ideally, new piston rings providing the correct end gap should be fitted. As a last resort, the end gap can be increased by filing the ring ends very carefully with a fine file. Mount the file in a vice equipped with soft jaws, slip the ring over the file with the ends contacting the file face, and slowly move the ring to remove material from the ends. Take care, as piston rings are sharp, and are easily broken.

7 With new piston rings, it is unlikely that the end gap will be too large. If the gaps are too large, check that you have the correct rings for your engine and for the cylinder bore size.

8 Repeat the checking procedure for each ring in the first cylinder, and then for the rings in the remaining cylinders. Remember to keep rings, pistons and cylinders matched up.

9 Once the ring end gaps have been checked and if necessary corrected, the rings can be fitted to the pistons.

10 Fit the piston rings using the same technique as for removal. Fit the bottom (oil control) ring first, and work up. When fitting the oil control ring, first insert the expander (where fitted), then fit the ring with its gap positioned 180° from the expander gap. Ensure that the second compression ring is fitted the correct way up, with its identification mark (either a dot of paint or the word TOP stamped on the ring surface) at the top, and the stepped surface, or the larger diameter of the taper at the bottom (see illustration). Arrange the gaps of the top and second compression rings 120° either side of the oil control ring gap. **Note:** Always follow any instructions supplied with the new piston ring sets – different manufacturers may specify different procedures. Do not mix up the top and second compression rings, as they have different cross-sections.

18 Crankshaft – refitting and main bearing running clearance check

Note: It is recommended that new main bearing shells are fitted regardless of the condition of the original ones.

Selection of bearing shells

1 There are two different sizes of main bearing shell available; the standard size shell for use with an original crankshaft and an oversize shell for use once the crankshaft has been reground.

2 The relevant set of bearing shells required can be obtained by measuring the diameter of the crankshaft main bearing journals (see Section 14). This will show if the crankshaft is original or whether its journals have been

18.7a Fit the bearing shells, ensuring that the tab engages in the notch in the cylinder block . . .

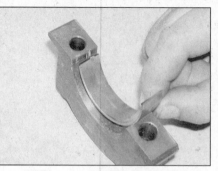

18.7b . . . and in the bearing cap

18.12 Plastigauge in place on a crankshaft main bearing journal

reground, identifying if either standard or oversize bearing shells are required.

3 If the access to the necessary measuring equipment cannot be gained, the size of the bearing shells can be identified by the markings stamped on the rear of each shell. Details of these markings should be supplied to your Citroën dealer who will then be able to identify the size of shell fitted.

4 Whether the original shells or new shells are being fitted, it is recommended that the running clearance is checked as follows prior to installation.

Main bearing clearance check

5 The running clearance check can be carried out using the original bearing shells. However, it is preferable to use a new set, since the results obtained will be more conclusive.

6 Clean the backs of the bearing shells, and the bearing locations in both the cylinder block and the main bearing caps.

7 Press the bearing shells into their locations, ensuring that the tab on each shell engages in the notch in the cylinder block or bearing cap **(see illustrations)**. Take care not to touch any shell's bearing surface with your fingers. Note that the upper bearing shells all have a grooved bearing surface, whereas the lower shells have a plain bearing surface. If the original bearing shells are being used for the check, ensure that they are refitted in their original locations.

8 The clearance can be checked in either of two ways.

9 One method (which will be difficult to achieve without a range of internal micrometers or internal/external expanding calipers) is to

refit the main bearing caps to the cylinder block, with bearing shells in place. With the cap retaining bolts tightened to the specified torque, measure the internal diameter of each assembled pair of bearing shells. If the diameter of each corresponding crankshaft journal is measured and then subtracted from the bearing internal diameter, the result will be the main bearing running clearance.

10 The second (and more accurate) method is to use an American product known as Plastigauge. This consists of a fine thread of perfectly-round plastic, which is compressed between the bearing shell and the journal. When the shell is removed, the plastic is deformed, and can be measured with a special card gauge supplied with the kit. The running clearance is determined from this gauge. Plastigauge should be available from your Citroën dealer; otherwise, enquiries at one of the larger specialist motor factors should produce the name of a stockist in your area. The procedure for using Plastigauge is as follows.

11 With the main bearing upper shells in place, carefully lay the crankshaft in position. Do not use any lubricant; the crankshaft journals and bearing shells must be perfectly clean and dry.

12 Cut several lengths of the appropriate-size Plastigauge (they should be slightly shorter than the width of the main bearings), and place one length on each crankshaft journal axis **(see illustration)**.

13 With the main bearing lower shells in position, refit the main bearing caps, tightening their retaining bolts to the specified

torque. Take care not to disturb the Plastigauge, and *do not* rotate the crankshaft at any time during this operation.

14 Remove the main bearing caps, again taking great care not to disturb the Plastigauge or rotate the crankshaft.

15 Compare the width of the crushed Plastigauge on each journal to the scale printed on the Plastigauge envelope, to obtain the main bearing running clearance **(see illustration)**. Compare the clearance measured with that in the Specifications at the start of this Chapter.

16 If the clearance is significantly different from that expected, the bearing shells may be the wrong size (or excessively worn, if the original shells are being re-used). Before deciding that different-size shells are required, make sure that no dirt or oil was trapped between the bearing shells and the caps or block when the clearance was measured. If the Plastigauge was wider at one end than at the other, the crankshaft journal may be tapered.

17 Note that Citroën do not specify a running clearance for these engines. The figure given in the Specifications is a guide figure which is typical for this type of engine. Before condemning the components concerned, seek the advice of your Citroën dealer or suitable engine repair specialist. They will also be able to inform as to the best course of action and whether it is possible to have the crankshaft journals reground (where possible) or whether renewal will be necessary.

18 Where necessary, obtain the correct size of bearing shell and repeat the running clearance checking procedure as described above.

19 On completion, carefully scrape away all traces of the Plastigauge material from the crankshaft and bearing shells using a fingernail or other object which is unlikely to score the bearing surfaces.

Final crankshaft refitting

20 Carefully lift the crankshaft out of the cylinder block once more.

21 Using a little grease, stick the upper thrust-washers to each side of the No 2 main bearing upper location. Ensure that the oilway grooves on each thrustwasher face outwards (away from the cylinder block) **(see illustration)**.

18.15 Measure the width of the deformed Plastigauge using the scale on the card

18.21 Fit the upper thrustwashers to No 2 main bearing location with the oilway grooves facing outwards

18.23 Lower the crankshaft into position in the cylinder block

18.26 Apply sealant to the No 1 main bearing cap mating face on the cylinder block, around the sealing strip holes and in the corners

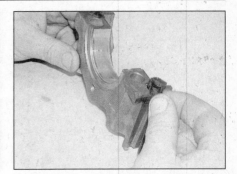

18.27 Fit the sealing strips to No 1 main bearing cap

22 Place the bearing shells in their locations as described earlier. If new shells are being fitted, ensure that all traces of protective grease are cleaned off using paraffin. Wipe dry the shells with a lint-free cloth. Liberally lubricate each bearing shell in the cylinder block and cap with clean engine oil.

23 Lower the crankshaft into position so that Nos 2 and 3 cylinder crankpins are at TDC; Nos 1 and 4 cylinder crankpins will be at BDC, ready for fitting No 1 piston **(see illustration)**. Check the crankshaft endfloat as described in Section 14.

24 Lubricate the lower bearing shells in the main bearing caps with clean engine oil. Make sure that the locating lugs on the shells engage with the corresponding recesses in the caps.

25 Fit main bearing caps Nos 2 to 5 to their correct locations, ensuring that they are fitted the correct way round (the bearing shell tab recesses in the block and caps must be on the same side). Insert the bolts, tightening them only loosely at this stage.

26 Apply a small amount of sealant to the No 1 main bearing cap mating face on the cylinder block, around the sealing strip holes and in the corners **(see illustration)**.

27 Locate the tab of each sealing strip over the pins on the base of No 1 bearing cap, and press the strips into the bearing cap grooves **(see illustration)**. It is now necessary to obtain two thin metal strips, of 0.25 mm thickness or less, in order to prevent the strips moving when the cap is being fitted. Metal strips, such as old feeler blades, can be used, provided all burrs which may damage the sealing strips are first removed.

28 Oil both sides of the metal strips, and hold them on the sealing strips. Fit the No 1 main bearing cap, insert the bolts loosely, then carefully pull out the metal strips in a horizontal direction, using a pair of pliers **(see illustration)**.

29 Tighten all the main bearing cap bolts evenly to the specified torque and through the specified angle. Using a sharp knife, trim off the ends of the No 1 bearing cap sealing strips, so that they protrude above the cylinder block mating surface by approximately 1 mm **(see illustrations)**.

30 Fit a new crankshaft left-hand oil seal as described in Part C of this Chapter.

31 Refit the piston/connecting rod assemblies to the crankshaft as described in Section 19.

32 Refit the Woodruff key, then slide on the oil pump drive sprocket and spacer (where fitted), and locate the drive chain on the sprocket.

33 Ensure that the mating surfaces of the right-hand oil seal carrier and cylinder block are clean and dry. Note the correct fitted depth of the oil seal then, using a large flat-bladed screwdriver, lever the old seal out of the housing.

34 Apply a smear of suitable sealant to the oil seal carrier mating surface. Ensure that the locating dowels are in position, then slide the carrier over the end of the crankshaft and into position on the cylinder block. Tighten the carrier retaining bolts securely.

35 Fit a new crankshaft right-hand oil seal as described in Part C of this Chapter.

36 Ensuring that the drive chain is correctly located on the sprocket, refit the oil pump and sump as described in Part C of this Chapter.

37 Where removed, refit the cylinder head as described in Section 5.

18.28 Use two metal strips (arrowed) to hold the sealing strips in place as the bearing cap is fitted

19 Piston/connecting rod assembly – refitting and big-end bearing running clearance check

Selection of bearing shells

1 Citroën supply only one size of big-end bearing shell for use with a standard size crankshaft, however it may be possible to obtain oversize big-end bearing shells from an alternative source.

18.29a Tighten all the main bearing cap bolts to the specified torque . . .

18.29b . . . and through the specified angle

18.29c Trim off the ends of No 1 bearing cap sealing strips, so that they protrude by approximately 1 mm

19.5a Fit the big-end bearing shells ensuring that the tab engages in the notch in the connecting rod . . .

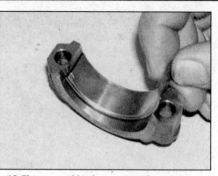

19.5b . . . and in the connecting rod cap

2 Consult your Citroën dealer or engine specialist for further information on parts availability. Always quote the diameter of the crankshaft big-end crankpins when ordering bearing shells.

3 Before refitting the piston/connecting rod assemblies, we recommend that the big-end bearing running clearance is checked as follows.

Big-end bearing clearance check

4 Clean the backs of the bearing shells, and the bearing locations in both the connecting rod and bearing cap.

5 Press the bearing shells into their locations, ensuring that the tab on each shell engages in the notch in the connecting rod and cap **(see illustrations)**. Take care not to touch any shell's bearing surface with your fingers. If the original bearing shells are being used for the check, ensure that they are refitted in their original locations. The clearance can be checked in either of two ways.

6 One method is to refit the big-end bearing cap to the connecting rod, ensuring that they are fitted the correct way around (see paragraph 20), with the bearing shells in place. With the cap retaining nuts correctly tightened, use an internal micrometer or vernier caliper to measure the internal diameter of each assembled pair of bearing shells. If the diameter of each corresponding crankshaft journal is measured and then subtracted from the bearing internal diameter,

the result will be the big-end bearing running clearance.

7 The second, and more accurate method is to use Plastigauge (see Section 18).

8 Ensure that the bearing shells are correctly fitted. Place a strand of Plastigauge on each (cleaned) crankpin journal.

9 Refit the (clean) piston/connecting rod assemblies to the crankshaft, and refit the big-end bearing caps, using the marks made or noted on removal to ensure that they are fitted the correct way around.

10 Tighten the bearing cap nuts to the specified torque, then through the specified angle. Take care not to disturb the Plastigauge, nor rotate the connecting rod during the tightening sequence.

11 Dismantle the assemblies without rotating the connecting rods. Use the scale printed on the Plastigauge envelope to obtain the big-end bearing running clearance.

12 If the clearance is significantly different from that expected, the bearing shells may be the wrong size (or excessively worn, if the original shells are being re-used). Make sure that no dirt or oil was trapped between the bearing shells and the caps or block when the clearance was measured. If the Plastigauge was wider at one end than at the other, the crankshaft journal may be tapered.

13 Note that Citroën do not specify a recommended big-end bearing running clearance. The figure given in the Specifications is a guide figure, which is typical for this type of engine. Before

condemning the components concerned, refer to your Citroën dealer or engine reconditioning specialist for further information on the specified running clearance. Their advice on the best course of action to be taken can then also be obtained.

14 On completion, carefully scrape away all traces of the Plastigauge material from the crankshaft and bearing shells. Use your fingernail, or some other object which is unlikely to score the bearing surfaces.

15 Fit the new bearing cap retaining bolts to the connecting rods as described in Section 13.

Piston/connecting rod refitting

16 Ensure that the bearing shells are correctly fitted as described earlier. If new shells are being fitted, ensure that all traces of the protective grease are cleaned off using paraffin. Wipe dry the shells and connecting rods with a lint-free cloth.

17 Lubricate the cylinder bores, the pistons, and piston rings, then lay out each piston/connecting rod assembly in its respective position.

18 Make sure that the piston rings are still spaced as described in Section 17, then clamp them in position with a piston ring compressor.

19 Insert the first piston/connecting rod assembly into the top of its corresponding cylinder. Ensure that the arrow on the piston crown is pointing towards the timing belt end of the engine. Using a block of wood or hammer handle against the piston crown, tap the assembly into the cylinder until the piston crown is flush with the top of the block **(see illustrations)**.

20 Ensure that the bearing shell is still correctly installed. Liberally lubricate the crankpin and both bearing shells. Taking care not to mark the cylinder bores, pull the piston/connecting rod assembly down the bore and onto the crankpin. Refit the big-end bearing cap, tightening the nuts finger-tight at first. Note that the faces with the identification marks must match (which means that the bearing shell locating tabs abut each other).

21 Tighten the bearing cap retaining nuts

19.19a Insert the piston/connecting rod assembly into the top of the relevant cylinder

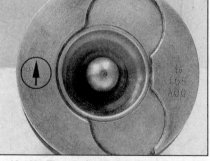

19.19b The arrow on the piston crown must point towards the timing belt end of the engine

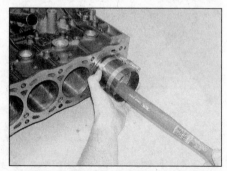

19.19c Tap the assembly into the cylinder bore until the piston crown is flush with the top of the block

evenly and progressively to the Stage 1 torque setting **(see illustration)**.

22 Once both nuts have been tightened to the Stage 1 setting, angle-tighten them through the specified Stage 2 angle, using a socket and extension bar. It is recommended that an angle-measuring gauge is used during this stage of the tightening, to ensure accuracy **(see illustration)**.

23 Once the bearing cap retaining nuts have been correctly tightened, rotate the crankshaft. Check that it turns freely; some stiffness is to be expected if new components have been fitted, but there should be no signs of binding or tight spots.

24 Refit the other three piston/connecting rod assemblies in the same way.

25 Refit the cylinder head and oil pump as described in Section 5 and in Part C of this Chapter.

20 Engine –
initial start-up after overhaul

1 With the engine refitted in the vehicle, double-check the engine oil and coolant levels. Make a final check that everything has been reconnected, and that there are no tools or rags left in the engine compartment.

19.21 Tighten the bearing cap retaining nuts evenly and progressively to the Stage 1 torque setting . . .

2 Turn the ignition key to position M, and wait for the preheating warning light to go out.

3 Start the engine, noting that this may take a little longer than usual, due to the fuel system components having been disturbed. Make sure that the oil pressure warning light goes out then allow the engine to idle.

4 While the engine is idling, check for fuel, water and oil leaks. Don't be alarmed if there are some odd smells and smoke from parts getting hot and burning off oil deposits.

5 Assuming all is well, keep the engine idling until hot water is felt circulating through the top hose, then switch off the engine.

19.22 . . . then angle-tighten them through the specified Stage 2 angle

6 After a few minutes, recheck the oil and coolant levels as described in *Weekly checks*, and top-up as necessary.

7 Note that there is no need to retighten the cylinder head bolts once the engine has first run after reassembly.

8 If new pistons, rings or crankshaft bearings have been fitted, the engine must be treated as new, and run-in for the first 500 miles (800 km). *Do not* operate the engine at full-throttle, or allow it to labour at low engine speeds in any gear. It is recommended that the oil and filter be changed at the end of this period.

Notes

Chapter 3
Cooling, heating and air conditioning systems

Contents

Degrees of difficulty

Easy, suitable for novice with little experience	**Fairly easy,** suitable for beginner with some experience	**Fairly difficult,** suitable for competent DIY mechanic	**Difficult,** suitable for experienced DIY mechanic	**Very difficult,** suitable for expert DIY or professional

Specifications

General
Maximum system pressure .... 1.4 bars

Thermostat
Opening temperature:
  Petrol engine models .... 89°C
  Diesel engine models .... 83°C

Torque wrench settings

	Nm	lbf ft
Coolant pump retaining bolts/nuts:		
1.6 litre petrol engines	15	11
1.8 litre petrol engines:		
Stage 1	3	2
Stage 2	8	6
Stage 3	14	10
Diesel engines	15	11
Coolant temperature sensors	18	13

1 General information and precautions

General information

The cooling system is of pressurised type, comprising a coolant pump driven by the timing belt, an aluminium crossflow radiator, expansion tank, electric cooling fan, a thermostat, heater matrix, and all associated hoses and switches.

The system functions as follows. Cold coolant in the bottom of the radiator passes through the bottom hose, through additional coolant pipes or housings (according to engine) to the coolant pump, where it is pumped around the cylinder block and head passages, and through the oil cooler (diesel engines). After cooling the cylinder bores, combustion surfaces and valve seats, the coolant reaches the underside of the thermostat, which is initially closed. The coolant passes through the heater, and is returned to the coolant pump.

When the engine is cold, the coolant circulates only through the cylinder block, cylinder head, and heater. When the coolant reaches a predetermined temperature, the thermostat opens, and the coolant passes through the top hose to the radiator. As the coolant circulates through the radiator, it is cooled by the in-rush of air when the car is in forward motion. The airflow is supplemented by the action of the electric cooling fan when necessary. Upon reaching the bottom of the radiator, the coolant has now cooled, and the cycle is repeated.

When the engine is at normal operating temperature, the coolant expands, and some of it is displaced into the expansion tank. Coolant collects in the tank, and is returned to the radiator when the system cools.

The electric cooling fan is mounted in a plastic housing located in front of the radiator. On early 1.6 litre petrol engine models, the fan is controlled by a thermostatic switch. On later 1.6 litre petrol engine models, and all other models, the fan is controlled by the engine management ECU. At a predetermined coolant temperature, the switch or the ECU actuates the fan.

Precautions

⚠️ **Warning: Do not attempt to remove the expansion tank filler cap, or to disturb any part of the cooling system, while the engine is hot, as there is a high risk of scalding. If the expansion tank filler cap must be removed before the engine and radiator have fully cooled (even though this is not recommended), the pressure in the cooling system must first be relieved. Cover the cap with a thick layer of cloth to avoid scalding, and slowly unscrew the filler cap until a hissing sound is heard. When the**

2.3 Releasing a radiator top hose spring clip

hissing has stopped, indicating that the pressure has reduced, slowly unscrew the filler cap until it can be removed; if more hissing sounds are heard, wait until they have stopped before unscrewing the cap. At all times, keep well away from the filler cap opening, and protect your hands.

⚠️ **Warning: Do not allow antifreeze to come into contact with your skin, or with the painted surfaces of the vehicle. Rinse off spills immediately, with plenty of water. Never leave antifreeze lying around in an open container, or in a puddle in the driveway or on the garage floor. Children and pets are attracted by its sweet smell, but antifreeze can be fatal if ingested.**

⚠️ **Warning: If the engine is hot, the electric cooling fan may start rotating even if the engine is not running. Be careful to keep your hands, hair, and any loose clothing well clear when working in the engine compartment.**

⚠️ **Warning: Refer to Section 11 for precautions to be observed when working on models equipped with air conditioning.**

2 Cooling system hoses – disconnection and renewal

Note: *Refer to the warnings given in Section 1 of this Chapter before proceeding. Hoses should only be disconnected once the engine has cooled sufficiently to avoid scalding.*

2.11 Using angled circlip pliers to spread the retaining clip and remove the heater hose – petrol engine models

General instructions

1 The number, routing and pattern of hoses will vary according to model, but the same basic procedure applies. Before commencing work, make sure that the new hoses are to hand, along with new hose clips if needed. It is good practice to renew the hose clips at the same time as the hoses.

2 Drain the cooling system, as described in Chapter 1A or 1B (as applicable), saving the coolant if it is fit for re-use. Squirt a little penetrating oil onto the hose clips if they are corroded.

3 Release the hose clips from the hose concerned. Two types of clip are used; worm drive and spring. The worm drive clip is released by turning its screw anti-clockwise. The spring clip is released by squeezing its tags together with pliers, at the same time working the clip away from the hose stub **(see illustration)**.

4 Unclip any wires, cables or other hoses which may be attached to the hose being removed. Make notes for reference when refitting if necessary.

5 Release the hose from its stubs, using a gentle twisting motion. Be careful not to damage the stubs on delicate components such as the radiator. If the hose is stuck fast, try carefully prising the end of the hose with a screwdriver or similar, taking care not to use excessive force. The best course is often to cut off a stubborn hose using a sharp knife, but again be careful not to damage the stubs.

6 Before fitting the new hose, smear the stubs with washing-up liquid or a suitable rubber lubricant to aid fitting. Do not use oil or grease, which may attack the rubber.

7 Fit the hose clips over the ends of the hose, then fit the hose over its stubs. Work the hose into position. When satisfied, locate and tighten the hose clips.

8 Refill the cooling system as described in Chapter 1A or 1B. Run the engine, and check that there are no leaks.

9 Recheck the tightness of the hose clips on any new hoses after a few hundred miles.

10 Top-up the coolant level if necessary.

Heater matrix connections

Note: *New O-rings should be used when reconnecting the hoses on diesel engine models.*

Removal – petrol models

11 Using angled circlip pliers engaged with the ends of the retaining spring clip, spread the clip and withdraw the relevant hose from the matrix pipe stub **(see illustration)**.

Removal – diesel models

12 The two hoses are connected to the matrix by means of a single connector.

13 Prise the metal retaining clip from the top of the connector **(see illustration)**.

14 Release the plastic retaining clip by pushing it towards the left-hand hose connection **(see illustration)**.

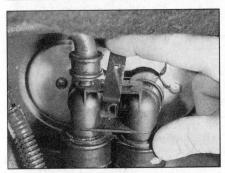

2.13 Remove the metal clip from the top of the heater matrix connector . . .

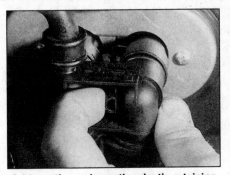

2.14 . . . then release the plastic retaining clip . . .

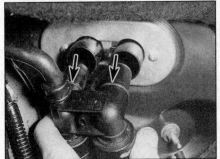

2.15 . . . and pull the connector off the pipes. Recover the O-rings (arrowed) – diesel engine models

15 Pull the connector assembly from the heater matrix. Recover the O-ring seals from the connector, and discard them; new ones should be used on refitting **(see illustration)**.

Refitting – all models

16 Refitting is a reversal of the removal procedure, using new O-rings on diesel engine models.
17 Refill the cooling system as described in Chapter 1A or 1B. Run the engine, and check that there are no leaks.

---

3 Radiator –
removal, inspection and refitting

Note: *If leakage is the reason for removing the radiator, bear in mind that minor leaks can often be cured using a radiator sealant with the radiator in situ.*

Removal

1 Disconnect the battery negative terminal (refer to *Disconnecting the battery* in the Reference Chapter).
2 Drain the cooling system as described in Chapter 1A or 1B as applicable.
3 Remove the air cleaner assembly and air inlet ducting as described in Chapter 4A or 4B as applicable.
4 Disconnect all the coolant hoses from the radiator with reference to Section 2.
5 Undo the nut and remove the washer securing the upper left-hand and right-hand corners of the cooling fan shroud to the front body panel **(see illustration)**.
6 Carefully ease the top of the radiator and fan shroud toward the engine.
7 Undo the screw and remove the washer securing each radiator upper mounting bracket to the fan shroud. Lift the brackets off the radiator mounting studs **(see illustrations)**.
8 Lift the radiator upward to disengage the lower locating lugs and remove the radiator from the engine compartment **(see illustration)**. Take care not to damage the radiator fins on surrounding components as it is lifted out.

Inspection

9 If the radiator has been removed due to suspected blockage, reverse flush it as described in Chapter 1A or 1B.
10 Clean dirt and debris from the radiator fins, using an air line (in which case, wear eye protection) or a soft brush. Be careful, as the fins are sharp, and easily damaged.
11 If necessary, a radiator specialist can perform a 'flow test' on the radiator, to establish whether an internal blockage exists.
12 A leaking radiator must be referred to a specialist for permanent repair. Do not attempt to weld or solder a leaking radiator, as damage to the plastic components may result.

13 Inspect the condition of the radiator mounting rubbers, and renew them if necessary.

Refitting

14 Refitting is a reversal of removal, bearing in mind the following points:
  a) *Ensure that the lower lugs on the radiator are correctly engaged with the mounting rubbers in the body panel.*
  b) *Reconnect the coolant hoses with reference to Section 2.*
  c) *Refit the air cleaner assembly and air inlet ducting as described in Chapter 4A or 4B.*
  d) *On completion, refill the cooling system as described in Chapter 1A or 1B.*

3.5 Remove the nut and washer securing the upper corners of the cooling fan shroud to the front body panel

3.7a Remove the screw and washer (arrowed) securing the radiator upper mounting brackets to the fan shroud . . .

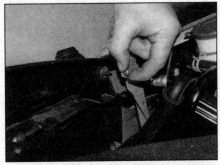

3.7b . . . then lift the brackets off the radiator mounting studs

3.8 Lift the radiator to disengage the lower lugs and remove it from the engine compartment

4.6a Lift off the thermostat cover and withdraw the thermostat . . .

4.6b . . . then remove the thermostat sealing ring

4 Thermostat –
removal, testing and refitting

Removal

1 On all engines, the thermostat is located in the coolant outlet housing at the left-hand end of the cylinder head.
2 Disconnect the battery negative terminal (refer to *Disconnecting the battery* in the Reference Chapter).
3 Drain the cooling system as described in Chapter 1A or 1B.
4 On 1.8 litre petrol engine models, remove the air cleaner assembly and air inlet ducting as described in Chapter 4A. On all models, where necessary, release any relevant wiring and hoses from their retaining clips, and

5.6 Undo the retaining screw and withdraw the fan from the fan motor spindle

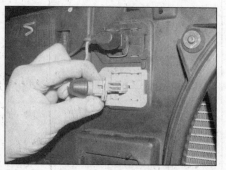

5.8a Disconnect the speed control resistor wiring plug . . .

position them clear of the coolant outlet housing to improve access.
5 Release the clip and disconnect the coolant hose from the thermostat cover.
6 Unscrew the retaining bolts, and carefully withdraw the thermostat cover to expose the thermostat. Lift the thermostat from the housing, noting which way round the thermostat is fitted, and recover the sealing ring **(see illustrations)**.

Testing

7 A rough test of the thermostat may be made by suspending it with a piece of string in a container full of water. Heat the water to bring it to the boil – the thermostat must open by the time the water boils. If not, renew it.
8 If a thermometer is available, the precise opening temperature of the thermostat may be determined; compare with the figures

5.7 Undo the three screws and withdraw the fan motor from the shroud

5.8b . . . undo the retaining screw . . .

given in the Specifications. The opening temperature is also marked on the thermostat.
9 A thermostat which fails to close as the water cools must also be renewed.

Refitting

10 Refitting is a reversal of removal, bearing in mind the following points:
  a) *Examine the sealing ring for damage or deterioration, and if necessary, renew.*
  b) *Ensure that the thermostat is fitted the correct way round as noted during removal.*
  c) *On 1.8 litre petrol engine models, refit the air cleaner assembly and air inlet ducting as described in Chapter 4A.*
  d) *On completion, refill the cooling system as described in Chapter 1A or 1B.*

5 Electric cooling fan –
removal and refitting

General information

1 On all models a single electric cooling fan is fitted, mounted in a shroud located between the front bumper and the radiator, or between the bumper and air conditioning condenser as applicable.
2 On vehicles without air conditioning, the fan is a single-speed unit on petrol engine models, and a two-speed unit on diesel engine models. On vehicles with air conditioning, initially a two-speed fan was used for petrol engine models, with a three-speed fan being fitted to diesels. From the 2001 model year, all models equipped with air conditioning were fitted with a three-speed fan.
3 On all except early 1.6 litre petrol engine models, the operation of the cooling fan is controlled by the engine management ECU (and air conditioning system control unit, where applicable) using coolant temperature information supplied by a coolant temperature sensor mounted in the coolant outlet housing. On early 1.6 litre petrol engine models, a separate thermal switch, mounted in the cylinder head was used to control the fan. From the 2001 model year, this arrangement was replaced by engine management ECU control, in line with all other models.

Removal

4 Disconnect the battery negative terminal (refer to *Disconnecting the battery* in the Reference Chapter).
5 Remove the front bumper assembly as described in Chapter 11.
6 Undo the retaining screw and withdraw the fan from the fan motor spindle **(see illustration)**. Note that the fan retaining screw has a **left-hand thread** and is unscrewed by turning it clockwise.
7 Undo the three screws and withdraw the fan motor from the shroud **(see illustration)**.
8 To remove the speed control resistor, disconnect the wiring plug, then undo the

retaining screw. Lift the retaining screw end of the resistor from the fan shroud, then disengage the locating lugs at the other end **(see illustrations)**.

Refitting

9 Refitting is a reversal of removal, bearing in mind the following points:
a) *Ensure that the fan motor wiring plug fully engages with the wiring socket on the shroud as the motor is refitted.*
b) *Refit the front bumper as described in Chapter 11.*

6 Cooling system electrical switches and sensors – removal and refitting

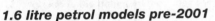

1.6 litre petrol models pre-2001

Cooling fan thermal switch

1 On models without air conditioning, the cooling fan thermal switch has a blue wiring connector and is located in the left-hand side of the cylinder head, below the coolant outlet housing.

2 On models with air conditioning, the cooling fans are controlled by the air conditioning system control unit in conjunction with a temperature sensor located in the left-hand side of the cylinder head, below the coolant outlet housing. The sensor can be identified by its blue or brown wiring connector.

Temperature warning light switch/gauge sensor

3 The coolant temperature warning light switch/temperature gauge sensor has a blue wiring connector and is located in the top of the coolant outlet housing at the left-hand end of the cylinder head **(see illustration)**.

Engine ECU temperature sensor

4 The engine management system coolant temperature sensor has a green wiring connector and is located above the thermostat in the coolant outlet housing at the left-hand end of the cylinder head.

1.6 litre petrol models from 2001

Engine ECU temperature sensor

5 On later engines, the coolant temperature sensor has a blue or green wiring connector and is located above the thermostat in the coolant outlet housing at the left-hand end of the cylinder head. The temperature signal from this sensor is used by the engine management ECU for fuel injection/ignition regulation and to control the operation of the cooling fan, air conditioning system and temperature warning light/gauge.

1.8 litre petrol models

Engine ECU temperature sensor

6 On 1.8 litre petrol engines the coolant temperature sensor has a green wiring

5.8c . . . and withdraw the resistor from the fan shroud

connector and is located in the coolant outlet housing at the left-hand end of the cylinder head **(see illustration)**. The temperature signal from this sensor is used by the engine management ECU for fuel injection/ignition regulation, and to control the operation of the exhaust gas recirculation, secondary air injection, cooling fan, air conditioning system and temperature warning light/gauge.

Diesel models

Engine ECU temperature sensor

7 On diesel engines the coolant temperature sensor has a green wiring connector and is mounted in the coolant outlet housing at the left-hand end of the cylinder head **(see illustration)**. The temperature signal from this sensor is used by the engine management ECU for diesel injection regulation and to control the operation of the exhaust gas recirculation, cooling fans, pre/post-heating control unit, air conditioning system and temperature warning light/gauge.

Removal

⚠️ **Warning: The engine should be cold before removing a cooling system switch or sensor.**

8 Disconnect the battery negative terminal (refer to *Disconnecting the battery* in the Reference Chapter).

9 Partially drain the cooling system to just below the level of the switch/sensor (as described in Chapter 1A or 1B). Alternatively, have ready a suitable bung to plug the switch aperture in the housing when the switch is

6.6 Engine management coolant temperature sensor (arrowed) – 1.8 litre petrol engine models

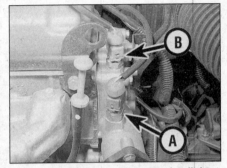

6.3 Coolant temperature warning light switch/temperature gauge sensor (A) and engine management coolant temperature sensor (B) – early 1.6 litre petrol engine models

removed. If this method is used, take care not to use anything which will allow foreign matter to enter the cooling system.

10 Where necessary, refer to Chapter 4A or 4B and remove the air cleaner and air inlet ducts for access to the switches/sensors located in the coolant outlet housing or cylinder head.

11 Unplug the wiring connector from the relevant switch/sensor.

12 Carefully unscrew the switch/sensor from its mounting and recover the sealing ring (where applicable). If the system has not been drained, plug the switch/sensor aperture to prevent further coolant loss.

Refitting

13 If the switch/sensor was originally fitted using sealing compound, clean the switch/sensor threads thoroughly, and coat them with fresh sealing compound. If the switch was originally fitted using a sealing ring, use a new sealing ring on refitting.

14 Fit the switch/sensor to its location, tighten it securely and reconnect the wiring connector.

15 Refill and bleed the cooling system as described in Chapter 1A or 1B. Follow the bleeding instructions carefully, to ensure that all air is expelled from the cooling system.

16 On completion, refit any components removed for access, then start the engine and run it until it reaches normal operating temperature. Continue to run the engine, and check that the component(s) controlled by the switch/sensor operate correctly.

6.7 Engine management coolant temperature sensor (arrowed) – diesel engine models

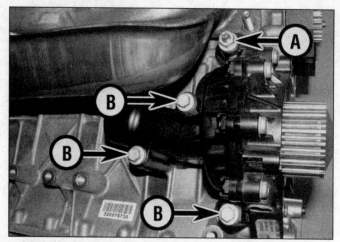

7.14 Coolant pump retaining nut (A) and retaining bolts (B) –
1.8 litre petrol engine models

7.16a Recover the rubber seal from the pump outlet aperture . . .

7 Coolant pump –
   removal and refitting

1.6 litre petrol models

Removal

Note: *A new pump assembly O-ring will be required on refitting.*

1 The coolant pump is driven by the timing belt and is located in the cylinder block at the timing belt end of the engine.
2 Drain the cooling system as described in Chapter 1A.
3 Remove the timing belt as described in the relevant Chapter 2A.
4 Remove the securing bolts, and withdraw the pump assembly from the cylinder block (access is most easily obtained from under the wheelarch). Recover the O-ring.

Refitting

5 Ensure that all mating faces are clean.
6 Refit the pump assembly to the cylinder block, using a new O-ring.
7 Refit the timing belt as described in Chapter 2A.
8 Refill the cooling system as described in Chapter 1A.

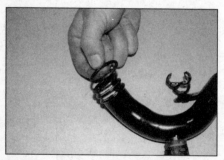

7.16b . . . and the O-ring from the end of
the coolant pipe –
1.8 litre petrol engine models

1.8 litre petrol models

General information

9 The coolant pump is driven by the timing belt and is bolted to the rear of the cylinder block at the timing belt end of the engine.
10 Although it is theoretically possible to remove and refit the coolant pump with the engine installed in the vehicle, access to the rear and left-hand side of the engine is virtually non-existent. Bearing in mind the tools, equipment and working facilities available to even the most competent of do-it-yourself mechanic, this operation will prove to be extremely difficult. For this reason, it has to be recommended that the engine/transmission be removed from the vehicle for removal and refitting of the coolant pump.
11 Read through the procedure first, then look at the engine compartment and coolant pump location. Establish whether you have the necessary tools, equipment, skill and patience to proceed with the engine installed. If not, either remove the engine/transmission assembly as described in Chapter 2D, or entrust the work to a Citroën dealer or suitably-equipped garage.

Removal

Note: *A new coolant pipe O-ring and pump outlet rubber seal will be required on refitting.*
12 If the engine/transmission have not been removed, drain the cooling system as described in Chapter 1A.
13 Remove the timing belt as described in Chapter 2B.
14 Undo the upper nut and the three lower bolts securing the coolant pump to the rear of the cylinder block (see illustration).
15 Unscrew the pump upper retaining stud, ease the pump off the locating dowels, then disengage the rear of the pump from the coolant pipe. Withdraw the pump assembly from the cylinder block.
16 Recover the rubber seal from the pump outlet aperture, and the O-ring from the end of the coolant pipe (see illustrations). A new

seal and O-ring must be obtained for refitting.
17 Note that only a complete pump assembly is available from Citroën parts stockists. Although the front and rear sections of the pump can be separated, they are not individually available.

Refitting

18 Ensure that the mating faces of the pump and cylinder block are clean.
19 Fit a new O-ring to the end of the coolant pipe and position a new rubber seal on the pump outlet. Check that the two locating dowels are in position in the cylinder block or in the pump.
20 Engage the pump with the coolant pipe then locate it on the cylinder block.
21 Refit the three retaining bolts tightening them finger tight only at this stage.
22 Screw the pump upper retaining stud into the cylinder block and tighten it securely. Fit the nut to the stud and tighten it finger tight only.
23 Starting with the lower retaining bolt and working in an anti-clockwise spiral pattern, tighten the retaining bolts and upper nut to the specified torque in the three stages given in the Specifications.
24 Refit the timing belt as described in Chapter 2B.
25 On completion of all other operations (depending on the pump removal/refitting method chosen), refill the cooling system as described in Chapter 1A.

Diesel models

26 The coolant pump removal and refitting procedures are the same as those given for 1.6 litre petrol engine models in paragraphs 1 to 8, substituting Chapter 1B and 2C for all references to Chapter 1A and 2A. Note, however, that working clearances in the engine compartment are extremely limited and the information contained in paragraphs 10 and 11 is equally applicable to diesel engine models. If the engine/transmission are to be removed, refer to the procedures contained in Chapter 2E.

8 Coolant outlet housing – removal and refitting

1.6 litre petrol models

Removal

1 Disconnect the battery negative terminal (refer to *Disconnecting the battery* in the Reference Chapter).
2 Drain the cooling system as described in Chapter 1A.
3 Remove the air cleaner assembly and air inlet ducts as described in Chapter 4A.
4 Disconnect and release the wiring connectors at the coolant outlet housing sensors, with reference to Section 6.
5 Disconnect the coolant hoses from the front and rear of the housing.
6 Undo the housing retaining bolts and move the wiring harness bracket or coolant pipe to one side.
7 Remove the housing from the side of the cylinder head and collect the gasket (where fitted). Obtain a new gasket, or a tube of RTV sealant (as applicable) for refitting.

Refitting

8 Clean all traces of old gasket/sealant from the mating faces of the coolant outlet housing and cylinder head mating faces.
9 Locate a new gasket in position on the housing, or apply a bead of RTV sealant to the housing mating face, as applicable.
10 Refit the housing to the cylinder head, locate the wiring harness bracket or coolant pipe in position and refit the retaining bolts, tightened securely.
11 Reconnect the coolant hoses to the housing.
12 Refit the air cleaner assembly and air inlet ducts as described in Chapter 4A.
13 Refill the cooling system as described in Chapter 1A then reconnect the battery negative terminal.

1.8 litre petrol models

Removal

14 Disconnect the battery negative terminal (refer to *Disconnecting the battery* in the Reference Chapter).
15 Drain the cooling system as described in Chapter 1A.
16 Remove the air cleaner assembly and air inlet ducts as described in Chapter 4A.
17 Disconnect the radiator hoses from the coolant outlet housing and thermostat cover. Disconnect the heater hose from the rear of the coolant outlet housing.
18 Disconnect the air inlet hose from the secondary air injection valve at the left-hand end of the cylinder head. Undo the two bolts and remove the air injection valve.
19 Disconnect the wiring connectors from the EGR valve and coolant temperature sensor.

20 Undo the nuts/bolts securing the wiring harness support bracket to the coolant outlet housing. Release any additional cable ties and clips then move the support bracket, wiring harness and hoses clear of the cylinder head.
21 Undo the bolt and remove the horseshoe-shaped clamp plate securing the coolant pipe to the rear of the coolant outlet housing. Withdraw the coolant pipe from the housing and recover the sealing O-ring.
22 Undo the remaining coolant outlet housing retaining bolts and the two stud nuts **(see illustration)**. Unscrew the two studs, then remove the coolant outlet housing from the cylinder head. Recover the housing gasket.
23 If required, the EGR valve can be removed from the housing after undoing the two retaining bolts.
24 Obtain new gaskets and O-rings for all disturbed components prior to refitting.

Refitting

25 Thoroughly clean the coolant outlet housing and cylinder head mating faces ensuring that all traces of old gasket are removed.
26 Where applicable, place a new EGR valve gasket on the housing, ensuring that the gasket is positioned with the word TOP uppermost. Refit the EGR valve and secure with the two bolts, tightened securely.
27 Using a new gasket, locate the coolant outlet housing on the cylinder head and refit the retaining bolts finger tight only at this stage.
28 Refit and tighten the two housing studs. Refit the nuts to the studs then progressively tighten all the retaining bolts/nuts securely.
29 Fit a new O-ring to the coolant pipe, then engage the pipe with the coolant outlet housing. Refit the horseshoe-shaped clamp plate and secure with the retaining bolt.
30 Position the wiring harness support bracket on the coolant outlet housing and secure with the retaining nuts/bolts. Ensure that the cable harness is secured with the retaining clips and new cable ties as necessary.
31 Reconnect the wiring connectors to the EGR valve and coolant temperature sensor.

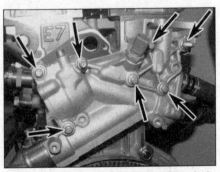

8.22 Coolant outlet housing retaining bolt and nut locations (arrowed) – 1.8 litre petrol engine models

32 Refit the secondary air injection valve to the cylinder head and secure with the two bolts. Refit the air inlet hose to the valve.
33 Reconnect the radiator hoses and heater hose.
34 Refit the air cleaner assembly and air inlet ducts as described in Chapter 4A.
35 Refill the cooling system as described in Chapter 1A then reconnect the battery negative terminal.

Diesel models

Removal

36 Disconnect the battery negative terminal (refer to *Disconnecting the battery* in the Reference Chapter).
37 Drain the cooling system as described in Chapter 1B.
38 Remove the air cleaner assembly and air inlet ducts as described in Chapter 4B.
39 Disconnect the radiator hoses, expansion tank hoses and oil cooler hoses from the coolant outlet housing and thermostat cover. Disconnect the heater hose from the rear of the coolant outlet housing.
40 Disconnect the wiring connector from the coolant temperature sensor.
41 Undo the nuts and bolts securing the wiring harness support bracket to the coolant outlet housing. Release any additional cable ties and clips then move the support bracket and wiring harness clear of the cylinder head.
42 Undo the remaining coolant outlet housing retaining bolts and the two stud nuts. Unscrew the two studs, then remove the coolant outlet housing from the cylinder head. Recover the housing gasket.
43 Obtain new gaskets for all disturbed components prior to refitting.

Refitting

44 Thoroughly clean the coolant outlet housing and cylinder head mating faces ensuring that all traces of old gasket are removed.
45 Using a new gasket, locate the coolant outlet housing on the cylinder head and refit the retaining bolts finger tight only at this stage.
46 Refit and tighten the two housing studs. Refit the nuts to the studs then progressively tighten all the retaining bolts/nuts securely.
47 Position the wiring harness support bracket on the coolant outlet housing and secure with the retaining nuts/bolts. Ensure that the cable harness is secured with the retaining clips and new cable ties as necessary.
48 Reconnect the wiring connectors to the coolant temperature sensor.
49 Reconnect the radiator, expansion tank and oil cooler hoses
50 Refit the air cleaner assembly and air inlet ducts as described in Chapter 4B.
51 Refill the cooling system as described in Chapter 1B then reconnect the battery negative terminal.

10.3 Undo the four screws (arrowed) securing the heater/ventilation control unit to the facia

10.4a Lift the control unit up to disengage the two lower lugs, then turn it over . . .

10.4b . . . for access to the control cables and wiring

9 Heating and ventilation system – general information

The heating/ventilation system consists of a four-speed blower motor (housed behind the facia), face level vents in the centre and at each end of the facia, and air ducts to the front and rear footwells.

The control unit is located in the facia, and the controls operate flap valves to deflect and mix the air flowing through the various parts of the heating/ventilation system. The flap valves are contained in the air distribution housing, which acts as a central distribution unit, passing air to the various ducts and vents.

Cold air enters the system through the grille at the rear of the engine compartment. If required, the airflow is boosted by the blower, and then flows through the various ducts, according to the settings of the controls. Stale air is expelled through ducts at the rear of the vehicle. If warm air is required, the cold air is passed over the heater matrix, which is heated by the engine coolant.

A recirculation switch enables the outside air supply to be closed off, while the air inside the vehicle is recirculated. This can be useful to prevent unpleasant odours entering from outside the vehicle, but should only be used briefly, as the recirculated air inside the vehicle will soon become stale.

10 Heater/ventilation components – removal and refitting

Heater/ventilation control unit

Removal

1 Disconnect the battery negative terminal (refer to *Disconnecting the battery* in the Reference Chapter).

2 Remove the facia upper centre panel as described in Chapter 11.

3 Undo the four screws securing the heater/ventilation control unit to the facia **(see illustration)**.

4 Lift the unit up to disengage the two lower locating lugs, feed it back into the aperture, then turn it over for access to the rear **(see illustrations)**.

5 Disconnect the wiring plug, then note the locations and correct fitted positions of the three control cables. Using a small screwdriver, release the outer cables from the support brackets, then disengage the inner cables from the operating levers.

6 Withdraw the control unit through the facia aperture and remove it from the car.

Refitting

7 Refitting is a reversal of removal, but ensure that the control cables are securely reconnected to their original locations.

Heater/ventilation control cables

Removal

8 Disconnect the cables from the heater/ventilation control unit, as described previously in this Section during the control unit removal procedure.

9 Working through the facia aperture or under the facia (it will be necessary to remove certain facia panels for access – see Chapter 11 – depending on which cable is to be removed), release the clips and disconnect the relevant cable from the air distribution housing. Note the routing of the cable to ensure correct refitting.

Refitting

10 Refitting is a reversal of removal, ensuring that the cables are correctly routed, and securely reconnected.

Heater matrix

Note: *New heater matrix connecting pipe O-rings must be used on refitting.*

Removal

11 Disconnect the battery negative terminal (refer to *Disconnecting the battery* in the Reference Chapter).

12 Drain the cooling system as described in Chapter 1A or 1B.

13 Working in the engine compartment, disconnect the heater hoses from the matrix pipes with reference to Section 2.

14 Undo the screw securing the cover plate over the matrix pipes bulkhead seal. Lift off the cover plate, and remove the rubber bulkhead seal **(see illustration)**.

15 Remove the facia lower centre panel as described in Chapter 11.

16 Working under the facia on the left-hand side, where applicable, release the wiring harness connector from its location above the front strengthening brace **(see illustration)**. Once the harness is released, disconnect the connector.

17 Undo the bolts securing the front and rear strengthening braces at the left-hand side of the air distribution housing **(see illustrations)**.

18 Undo the three screws and remove the air duct from the left-hand side of the air distribution housing **(see illustration)**.

10.14 Lift off the heater matrix pipe cover plate, and remove the rubber bulkhead seal

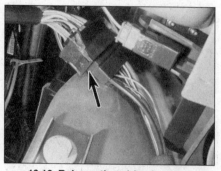

10.16 Release the wiring harness connector (arrowed) located above the facia front strengthening brace

10.17a Undo the bolts (arrowed) securing the front strengthening brace . . .

10.17b . . . and rear strengthening brace at the left-hand side of the air distribution housing

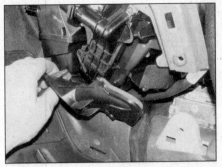

10.18 Undo the three screws and remove the air duct

19 Place suitable protective sheets on the carpet below the heater matrix and be prepared for coolant spillage.

20 Undo the retaining screw in the centre of the connecting pipe assembly **(see illustration)**.

21 Undo the remaining screw securing the flange of the connecting pipe assembly to the heater matrix. Collect the retaining nut from the rear of the connecting pipe flange **(see illustrations)**.

22 Unclip the matrix from the air distribution housing, then carefully withdraw the matrix until it can be released from the connecting pipe flange **(see illustrations)**.

23 Withdraw the matrix, then remove the connecting pipe assembly **(see illustrations)**.

24 Remove the O-ring seals from the connecting pipe assembly and obtain new seals for refitting **(see illustration)**.

Refitting

25 Refitting is a reversal of removal bearing in mind the following points.

a) *Fit new O-ring seals to the matrix connecting pipe assembly.*

b) *Reconnect the heater hoses to the matrix pipes with reference to Section 2.*

c) *Refit the facia lower centre panel as described in Chapter 11.*

d) *Refill the cooling system as described in Chapter 1A or 1B on completion.*

10.20 Undo the connecting pipe assembly centre retaining screw

10.21a Undo the screw securing connecting pipe flange to the heater matrix . . .

10.21b . . . and collect the retaining nut from the rear of the flange

10.22a Unclip the matrix from the air distribution housing . . .

10.22b . . . then release it from the connecting pipe flange

10.23a Withdraw the matrix . . .

10.23b . . . then remove the connecting pipe assembly

10.24 Recover the O-ring seals from the connecting pipe assembly

10.29 Disconnect the wiring connector from the front of the blower motor

Heater blower motor

Removal – right-hand drive models

26 Disconnect the battery negative terminal (refer to *Disconnecting the battery* in the Reference Chapter).
27 Remove the facia lower centre panel as described in Chapter 11.
28 Working under the facia on the left-hand side, release the wiring harness connector from its location above the front strengthening brace. Once the harness is released, disconnect the connector.
29 Disconnect the wiring connector from the front of the blower motor **(see illustration)**.
30 Rotate the motor assembly clockwise to release it from the retaining lugs, then withdraw the unit from the air distribution housing **(see illustration)**.

Refitting – right-hand drive models

31 Refitting the heater blower motor is a reversal of removal. Refer to Chapter 11 when refitting the facia lower centre panel.

Removal – left-hand drive models

32 Disconnect the battery negative terminal (refer to *Disconnecting the battery* in the Reference Chapter).
33 Remove the facia lower centre panel, and the lower side panel beneath the steering column as described in Chapter 11.
34 Set the roadwheels in the straight-ahead position and remove the ignition key to engage the steering lock.
35 Make alignment marks on the steering column upper universal joint and the intermediate shaft, then unscrew the universal joint pinch-bolt.
36 Separate the intermediate shaft from the universal joint and move the shaft away from the air distribution housing. Make sure that the steering lock remains engaged while the shaft is disconnected in order to maintain the position of the rotary connector.
37 Proceed as described for right-hand drive models in paragraphs 28 to 30.

Refitting – left-hand drive models

38 Refitting is a reversal of removal bearing

10.30 Rotate the motor clockwise and withdraw the unit from the air distribution housing

in mind the following points.
a) *Ensure that the marks made on removal are aligned when reconnecting the intermediate shaft to the steering column universal joint.*
b) *Tighten the universal joint pinch-bolt to the specified torque as given in Chapter 10.*
c) *Refit the facia panels as described in Chapter 11.*

11 Air conditioning system – general information and precautions

General information

An air conditioning system is available as standard or optional equipment on all models. It enables the temperature of incoming air to be lowered, and also dehumidifies the air, which makes for rapid demisting and increased comfort. On high specification models, a fully electronic version of the system is available, whereby the temperature and airflow through the vehicle are automatically regulated according to the temperature selected.

The cooling side of the system works in the same way as a domestic refrigerator. Refrigerant gas is drawn into a belt-driven compressor, and passes into a condenser mounted on the front of the radiator, where it loses heat and becomes liquid. The liquid passes through an expansion valve to an evaporator, where it changes from liquid under high pressure to gas under low pressure. This change is accompanied by a drop in temperature, which cools the evaporator. The refrigerant returns to the compressor, and the cycle begins again.

Air blown through the evaporator passes to the air distribution unit, where it is mixed with hot air blown through the heater matrix to achieve the desired temperature in the passenger compartment.

The heating side of the system works in the same way as on models without air conditioning (see Section 9).

The operation of the system is controlled by an electronic control unit, which controls the electric cooling fan, the compressor and the facia-mounted warning light. Any problems with the system should be referred to a Citroën dealer.

Precautions

When an air conditioning system is fitted, it is necessary to observe special precautions whenever dealing with any part of the system, or its associated components. If for any reason the system must be disconnected, entrust this task to your Citroën dealer or a refrigeration engineer.

⚠️ *Warning: The air conditioning system contains a liquid refrigerant, and it is therefore dangerous to disconnect any part of the system without specialised knowledge and equipment.*

The refrigerant is potentially dangerous, and should only be handled by qualified persons. If it is splashed onto the skin, it can cause frostbite. It is not itself poisonous, but in the presence of a naked flame (including a cigarette) it forms a poisonous gas. Uncontrolled discharging of the refrigerant is dangerous, and potentially damaging to the environment.

12 Air conditioning system components – removal and refitting

Note: *Do not operate the air conditioning system if it is known to be short of refrigerant, as this may damage the compressor.*
1 As the heating side of the system works in the same way as on models without air conditioning, the heater/ventilation control unit, control cables, heater matrix and heater blower motor removal and refitting procedures described in Section 10, are also applicable to models equipped with air conditioning. Note, however, that when working on the fully electronic version of the air conditioning system, there are no control cables to disconnect at the heater/ventilation control unit.
2 The only other operation which can be carried out without discharging the refrigerant is the renewal of the auxiliary (compressor) drivebelt. This is described in the relevant Part of Chapter 1. All other operations must be referred to a Citroën dealer or an air conditioning specialist.
3 If necessary, the compressor can be unbolted and moved aside, without disconnecting its flexible hoses, after removing the drivebelt.

⚠️ *Warning: Do not attempt to open the refrigerant circuit. Refer to the precautions given in Section 11.*

Chapter 4 Part A:
Fuel/exhaust systems – petrol engines

Contents

Degrees of difficulty

Easy, suitable for novice with little experience | **Fairly easy,** suitable for beginner with some experience | **Fairly difficult,** suitable for competent DIY mechanic | **Difficult,** suitable for experienced DIY mechanic | **Very difficult,** suitable for expert DIY or professional

Specifications

System type
1.6 litre engines:
  Pre-2001 models (engine code NFZ) . . . . Bosch Motronic MP7.2
  2001 models onward (engine code NFV) . . . . Bosch Motronic ME7.4.4
1.8 litre engines . . . . Sagem S2000

Fuel system data
Fuel pump type . . . . Electric, immersed in tank
Idle speed*:
  1.6 litre engines:
    Without air conditioning . . . . 850 ± 50 rpm
    With air conditioning . . . . 900 ± 50 rpm
  1.8 litre engines . . . . 700 ± 50 rpm
Idle mixture CO content* . . . . Less than 0.5%
*Not adjustable – controlled by ECU

Recommended fuel
Minimum octane rating . . . . 95 RON unleaded

Torque wrench settings
	Nm	lbf ft
Exhaust manifold nuts:		
1.6 litre engines	16	12
1.8 litre engines	35	26
Inlet manifold nuts/bolts	20	15

2.1 Slacken the clip and disconnect the air inlet duct from the air cleaner lid – 1.6 litre engines

2.2 Lift the air cleaner assembly upward off the support bracket and remove it from the engine compartment – 1.6 litre engines

2.3 Release the quick-release fitting and withdraw the breather hose from the air inlet duct – 1.6 litre engines

1 General information and precautions

The fuel supply system consists of a fuel tank (which is mounted under the centre of the vehicle, with an electric fuel pump immersed in it), a fuel filter and fuel feed lines. The fuel pump supplies fuel to the fuel rail, which acts as a reservoir for the four fuel injectors which inject fuel into the inlet tracts. The fuel filter incorporated in the feed line from the pump to the fuel rail ensures that the fuel supplied to the injectors is clean.

⚠️ *Warning: Many of the procedures in this Chapter require the removal of fuel lines and connections, which may result in some fuel spillage. Before carrying out any operation on the fuel system, refer to the precautions given in 'Safety first!' at the beginning of this manual, and follow them implicitly. Petrol is a highly dangerous and volatile liquid, and the precautions necessary when handling it cannot be overstressed.*

Refer to Section 6 for further information on the operation of each fuel injection system, and to Section 16 for information on the exhaust system.

Note: *Residual pressure will remain in the fuel lines long after the vehicle was last used. When disconnecting any fuel line, first depressurise the fuel system as described in Section 7.*

2.4 Slacken the clip and detach the duct from the throttle housing – 1.6 litre engines

2 Air cleaner assembly and air inlet ducts – removal and refitting

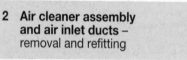

Removal

1.6 litre engines

1 Slacken the retaining clip securing the air inlet duct to the air cleaner lid and disconnect the duct **(see illustration)**.
2 Lift the air cleaner assembly upward to release it from the support bracket and remove it from the engine compartment **(see illustration)**.
3 To remove the air inlet duct, release the quick-release fitting and withdraw the breather hose from the duct **(see illustration)**.
4 Slacken the retaining clip and detach the duct from the throttle housing **(see illustration)**.

2.6 Slacken the clip and disconnect the air inlet flexible duct from the throttle housing fixed duct – 1.8 litre engines

5 If the air cleaner assembly is still in position, slacken the clip securing the inlet duct to the front of the air cleaner lid and remove the duct assembly from the engine compartment.

1.8 litre engines

6 Slacken the retaining clip securing the air inlet flexible duct to the air cleaner lid or the fixed duct on the throttle housing **(see illustration)**.
7 Disconnect the flexible duct and lift the air cleaner assembly upward to release it from the support bracket, then remove it from the engine compartment **(see illustration)**.
8 To remove the fixed duct on the throttle housing, release the quick-release fitting and withdraw the breather hose from the duct **(see illustration)**.
9 Insert a screwdriver through the aperture in the side of the duct and slacken the retaining clip **(see illustration)**.

2.7 Lift the air cleaner assembly upward off the support bracket and remove it from the engine compartment – 1.8 litre engines

2.8 Release the quick-release fitting and withdraw the breather hose from the throttle housing fixed duct – 1.8 litre engines

2.9 Insert a screwdriver through the aperture and slacken the retaining clip – 1.8 litre engines

2.10 Lift the fixed duct off the throttle housing – 1.8 litre engines

10 Lift the fixed duct off the throttle housing (see illustration).

Refitting

11 Refitting is a reversal of the removal procedure, ensuring that all air ducts are correctly seated and securely held by their retaining clips.

---

3 Accelerator cable – removal, refitting and adjustment

Removal

1 On 1.8 litre engines, remove the throttle housing fixed air inlet duct as described in Section 2.
2 Free the accelerator inner cable from the throttle housing cam, then pull the outer cable out from its mounting bracket rubber grommet. Remove the spring clip from its groove in the outer cable (see illustration).
3 Working back along the length of the cable, free it from any retaining clips or ties, noting its correct routing.
4 Extract the stud-type plastic clips, using a forked type tool, and remove the facia lower trim panel above the pedals on the driver's side.
5 Reach up under the facia, depress the ends of the cable end fitting, and detach the inner cable from the top of the accelerator pedal (see illustration).
6 Slide out the plastic retainer securing the outer cable to the bulkhead grommet.
7 Return to the engine compartment, pull the outer cable from the bulkhead grommet and withdraw the cable.

Refitting

8 Feed the accelerator cable through the bulkhead grommet, then return to the car and secure the outer cable with the plastic retainer. Locate the inner cable end fitting in the pedal and push it home until it locks in place.
9 From within the engine compartment, work along the cable, securing it in position with the retaining clips and ties, and ensuring that the cable is correctly routed.
10 Pass the outer cable through its throttle

3.2 Free the accelerator inner cable from the throttle cam, and pull the outer cable from its mounting bracket grommet

housing mounting bracket grommet, and reconnect the inner cable to the throttle cam. Adjust the cable as described below.

Adjustment

11 Ensuring that the throttle cam is fully against its stop, gently pull the cable out of its grommet until all free play is removed from the inner cable.
12 With the cable held in this position, refit the spring clip to the last exposed outer cable groove in front of the rubber grommet. When the clip is refitted and the outer cable is released, there should be only a small amount of free play in the inner cable.
13 Have an assistant depress the accelerator pedal, and check that the throttle cam opens fully and returns smoothly to its stop.
14 Refit the facia lower trim panel and, on 1.8 litre engines, refit the throttle housing fixed duct as described in Section 2.

---

4 Accelerator pedal – removal and refitting

Removal

1 Extract the stud-type plastic clips, using a forked type tool, and remove the facia lower trim panel above the pedals on the driver's side.
2 Reach up under the facia, depress the ends of the accelerator cable end fitting, and detach the inner cable from the top of the accelerator pedal.

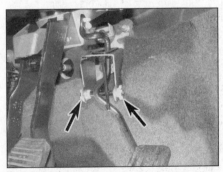

4.3 Accelerator pedal pivot retaining clips (arrowed)

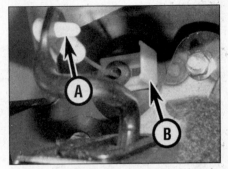

3.5 Accelerator cable end fitting (A) and outer cable plastic retainer (B)

3 Extract the pedal pivot retaining clips, slide the pedal out of the pivot bushes and manipulate it out of the pedal bracket (see illustration).
4 Examine the pivot bushes for signs of wear and, if necessary, renew the bushes.

Refitting

5 Refitting is a reversal of the removal procedure, applying a little multi-purpose grease to the pedal pivot. On completion, adjust the accelerator cable as described in Section 3.

---

5 Unleaded petrol – general information and usage

Note: *The information given in this Chapter is correct at the time of writing. If updated information is thought to be required, check with a Citroën dealer. If travelling abroad, consult one of the motoring organisations (or a similar authority) for advice on the fuel available.*
1 All Citroën Xsara Picasso petrol engines are designed to run on unleaded fuel with a minimum octane rating of 95 (RON). All engines have a catalytic converter, and so must be run on unleaded fuel **only**. Under no circumstances should leaded fuel, or lead replacement petrol (LRP) be used, as this will damage the catalytic converter.
2 The manufacturer's do state, however, that for improved vehicle performance (and possibly increased fuel economy), 98 (RON) unleaded petrol may be used, where this is available.

---

6 Fuel injection systems – general information

Note: *The fuel injection ECU is of the 'self-learning' type, meaning that as it operates, it also monitors and stores the settings which give optimum engine performance under all operating conditions. When the battery is disconnected, these settings are lost and the ECU reverts to the base settings programmed into its memory at the factory. On restarting,* *this may lead to the engine running/idling roughly for a short while, until the ECU has relearned the optimum settings. This process is best accomplished by taking the vehicle on a road test (for approximately 15 minutes), covering all engine speeds and loads, concentrating mainly in the 2500 to 3500 rpm region.*

On all engines, the fuel injection and ignition functions are combined into a single engine management system. The systems fitted are manufactured by Bosch and Sagem, and are very similar to each other in most respects, the only significant differences being in the software contained in the system ECU, and specific component location according to engine type. Each system incorporates a closed-loop catalytic converter and an evaporative emission control system, and complies with the latest emission control standards. Refer to Chapter 5B for information on the ignition side of each system; the fuel side of the system operates as follows.

The fuel pump supplies fuel from the tank to the fuel rail, via a replaceable cartridge filter mounted on the side of the fuel tank. The pump itself is mounted inside the tank, with the pump motor permanently immersed in fuel, to keep it cool. The fuel rail is mounted directly above the fuel injectors and acts as a fuel reservoir.

Fuel rail supply pressure is controlled by the pressure regulator, also located in the fuel tank. The regulator contains a spring-loaded valve, which lifts to allow excess fuel to recirculate within the tank when the optimum operating pressure of the fuel system is exceeded (eg, during low speed, light load cruising).

The fuel injectors are electromagnetic pintle valves, which spray atomised fuel into the combustion chambers under the control of the engine management system ECU. There are four injectors, one per cylinder, mounted in the inlet manifold close to the cylinder head. Each injector is mounted at an angle that allows it to spray fuel directly onto the back of the inlet valve(s). The ECU controls the volume of fuel injected by varying the length of time for which each injector is held open. The fuel injection systems are typically of the sequential type, whereby each injector operates individually in cylinder sequence.

The electrical control system consists of the ECU, along with the following sensors:

a) *Throttle potentiometer – informs the ECU of the throttle valve position, and the rate of throttle opening/closing.*
b) *Coolant temperature sensor – informs the ECU of engine temperature.*
c) *Inlet air temperature sensor – informs the ECU of the temperature of the air passing through the throttle housing.*
d) *Lambda sensors – inform the ECU of the oxygen content of the exhaust gases (explained in greater detail in Part C of this Chapter).*
e) *Manifold pressure sensor – informs the*

ECU of the load on the engine (expressed in terms of inlet manifold vacuum).
f) *Crankshaft sensor – informs the ECU of engine speed and crankshaft angular position.*
g) *Vehicle speed sensor – informs the ECU of the vehicle speed.*
h) *Knock sensor – informs the ECU of pre-ignition (detonation) within the cylinders.*
i) *Camshaft sensor – informs the ECU of which cylinder is on the firing stroke on systems with sequential injection.*

Signals from each of the sensors are compared by the ECU and, based on this information, the ECU selects the response appropriate to those values, and controls the fuel injectors (varying the pulse width – the length of time the injectors are held open – to provide a richer or weaker air/fuel mixture, as appropriate). The air/fuel mixture is constantly varied by the ECU, to provide the best settings for cranking, starting (with either a hot or cold engine) and engine warm-up, idle, cruising and acceleration.

The ECU also has full control over the engine idle speed, via a stepper motor fitted to the throttle housing. The stepper motor controls the amount of air passing through a bypass drilling at the side of the throttle. When the throttle valve is closed (accelerator pedal released), the ECU uses the motor to open or close an air passage, controlling the amount of air bypassing the throttle valve and so controlling the idle speed. The ECU also carries out 'fine tuning' of the idle speed by varying the ignition timing to increase or reduce the torque of the engine as it is idling. This helps to stabilise the idle speed when electrical or mechanical loads (such as headlights, air conditioning, etc) are switched on and off.

The throttle housing is also fitted with an electric heating element. The heater is supplied with current by the ECU, warming the throttle housing on cold starts to help prevent icing of the throttle valve.

The exhaust and evaporative loss emission control systems are described in more detail in Chapter 4C.

If there is any abnormality in any of the readings obtained from the coolant temperature sensor, the inlet air temperature sensor or the lambda sensor, the ECU enters its 'back-up' mode. If this happens, the erroneous sensor signal is overridden, and the ECU assumes a pre-programmed 'back-up' value, which will allow the engine to continue running, albeit at reduced efficiency. If the ECU enters this mode, the warning lamp on the instrument panel will be illuminated, and the relevant fault code will be stored in the ECU memory.

If the warning light illuminates, the vehicle should be taken to a Citroën dealer at the earliest opportunity. Once there, a complete test of the engine management system can be carried out, using a special electronic diagnostic test unit, which is plugged into the system's diagnostic connector.

7 Fuel injection system – depressurisation

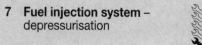

Note: *Refer to the warning note in Section 1 before proceeding.*

⚠ **Warning: The following procedure will merely relieve the pressure in the fuel system – remember that fuel will still be present in the system components and take precautions accordingly before disconnecting any of them.**

1 The fuel system referred to in this Section is defined as the tank-mounted fuel pump, the fuel filter, the fuel injectors, the fuel rail and the metal pipes and flexible hoses of the fuel lines between these components. All these contain fuel which will be under pressure while the engine is running, and/or while the ignition is switched on. The pressure will remain for some time after the ignition has been switched off, and must be relieved in a controlled fashion when any of these components are disturbed for servicing work.

2 Disconnect the battery negative terminal (refer to *Disconnecting the battery* in the Reference Chapter).

3 On 1.8 litre engines, remove the engine cover.

4 Place a container beneath the connection/union to be disconnected, and have a large rag ready to soak up any escaping fuel not being caught by the container.

5 Slowly loosen the connection or union nut to avoid a sudden release of pressure, and position the rag around the connection to catch any fuel spray which may be expelled. Once the pressure is released, disconnect the fuel line. Plug the pipe ends, to minimise fuel loss and prevent the entry of dirt into the fuel system.

6 On 1.8 litre engines a Schrader valve is fitted to the centre of the fuel rail and can, if desired, be used for depressurisation. The Schrader valve operates like a tyre valve, whereby on depressing the central plunger, the system pressure will be released. Ensure that the valve is protected with rags to soak up escaping fuel as this is done.

8 Fuel pump – removal and refitting

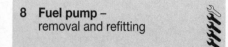

Note: *Refer to the warning note in Section 1 before proceeding.*

Removal

1 Remove the fuel tank as described in Section 10.

2 Wipe clean the area around the fuel pump external components located on the top of the fuel tank.

3 Disconnect the wiring connector from the centre of the fuel pump.

10.7 Fuel pump wiring harness connector (arrowed)

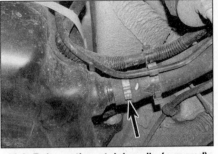

10.9 Release the retaining clip (arrowed) and disconnect the main filler neck hose from the fuel tank

10.11 Fuel tank support rod rear retaining bolt (arrowed)

4 Mark the hoses for identification purposes, then disconnect the quick-release fittings using a small screwdriver to release the locking clip. Disconnect both hoses from the top of the pump, and plug the hose ends.

5 Noting the alignment marks on the pump cover and the locking ring, unscrew the ring and remove it from the tank. This is best accomplished by making up a simple tool from two strips of metal, suitably drilled and joined together with two lengths of threaded bar and locknuts. Engage the tool with the raised ribs of the locking ring, and turn the ring anti-clockwise until it can be unscrewed by hand.

6 Lift the fuel pump and sender unit assembly out of the fuel tank, taking great care not to damage the float arm. Recover the sealing O-ring and discard it – a new one must be used on refitting.

7 Note that the fuel pump and sender unit is only available as a complete assembly – no components are available separately.

Refitting

8 Ensure the fuel pump pick-up filter is clean and free of debris, then locate the new sealing O-ring on the top of the fuel tank.

9 Carefully manoeuvre the pump and sender unit assembly into the fuel tank, aligning the notch on the pump body with the cut-out in the tank. Take care not to displace the O-ring as the pump is fitted.

10 Refit the locking ring and securely tighten it until the small raised arrow on the ring is aligned with the arrow on the top of the pump.

11 Reconnect the feed and return hoses to the top of the fuel pump, using the marks made on removal to ensure that they are correctly reconnected.

12 Reconnect the pump wiring connector.

13 Refit the fuel tank as described in Section 10.

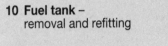

9 Fuel gauge sender unit – removal and refitting

The fuel gauge sender unit is integral with the fuel pump. Refer to the procedures contained in Section 8.

10 Fuel tank – removal and refitting

Note: *Refer to the warning note in Section 1 before proceeding.*

Removal

1 Before removing the fuel tank, all fuel must be drained from the tank. Since a fuel tank drain plug is not provided, it is therefore preferable to carry out the removal operation when the tank is nearly empty. Before proceeding, disconnect the battery negative terminal (refer to *Disconnecting the battery* in the Reference Chapter) and syphon or hand-pump the remaining fuel from the tank.

2 Chock the front wheels then jack up the rear of the vehicle and support it securely on axle stands (see *Jacking and vehicle support*). Remove the right-hand rear roadwheel.

3 For access to the filler neck and breather hose connections, remove the right-hand rear wheel arch liner. The liner is secured by a combination of screws and push-fit clips. Removal is self-evident and the clips can be released using a forked-shaped tool.

4 Disconnect the fuel tank breather hoses now accessible at their upper and lower quick-release connectors.

5 Remove the exhaust system and the heat shield below the fuel tank as described in Section 16.

6 Release the two handbrake cables from the plastic clips on the fuel tank, and from the wire retaining hooks on the underbody. Move

the cables away from the tank as far as possible.

7 Disconnect the wiring harness connector located in front of the tank on the right-hand side **(see illustration)**.

8 Disconnect the fuel filter outlet hose at the quick-release connector on the filter. Similarly, disconnect the fuel return hose (where fitted) at the quick-release connector just in front of the fuel filter.

9 Release the retaining clip and disconnect the main filler neck hose from the fuel tank **(see illustration)**. Suitably cover the end of the disconnected hose and the tank outlet.

10 Place a trolley jack with an interposed block of wood beneath the tank, then raise the jack until it is supporting the weight of the tank.

11 Undo and remove the two retaining bolts, then remove the support rod from the underside of the tank **(see illustration)**.

12 Undo and remove the fuel tank mounting bolt on each side of the tank **(see illustrations)**. Collect the large flat washers from each bolt.

13 Slowly lower the fuel tank out of position, and remove the tank from underneath the vehicle.

14 If the tank is contaminated with sediment or water, remove the fuel pump as described in Section 8, and swill the tank out with clean fuel. The tank is injection-moulded from a synthetic material – if seriously damaged, it should be renewed. However, in certain cases, it may be possible to have small leaks or minor damage repaired. Seek the advice of a specialist before attempting to repair the fuel tank.

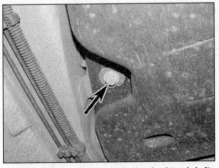

10.12a Undo and remove the fuel tank left-hand mounting bolt (arrowed) . . .

10.12b . . . and right-hand mounting bolt (arrowed)

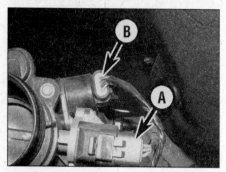

12.4 Throttle potentiometer (A) and stepper motor (B) wiring connectors – later 1.6 litre engines

Refitting

15 Refitting is the reverse of the removal procedure, noting the following points:
a) When lifting the tank back into position, take care to ensure that none of the hoses become trapped between the tank and vehicle body.
b) Ensure all pipes and hoses are correctly routed, and securely held in position with their retaining clips.
c) On completion, refill the tank with a small amount of fuel, and check for signs of leakage prior to taking the vehicle out on the road.

11 Fuel injection system – testing and adjustment

Testing

1 If a fault appears in the fuel injection/engine management system, first ensure that all the system wiring connectors are securely connected and free of corrosion. Ensure that the fault is not due to poor maintenance; ie, check that the air cleaner filter element is clean, the spark plugs are in good condition and correctly gapped, the cylinder compression pressures are correct, and that the engine breather hoses are clear and undamaged, referring to the relevant Parts of Chapters 1, 2 and 5 for further information.
2 If these checks fail to reveal the cause of

13.4 Accelerator cable mounting bracket retaining bolts (arrowed) – later 1.6 litre engines

the problem, the vehicle should be taken to a Citroën dealer or suitably-equipped garage for testing. A diagnostic socket is located adjacent to the passenger compartment fusebox in which a fault code reader or other suitable test equipment can be connected. By using the code reader or test equipment, the engine management ECU (and the various other vehicle system ECUs) can be interrogated, and any stored fault codes can be retrieved. This will allow the fault to be quickly and simply traced, alleviating the need to test all the system components individually, which is a time-consuming operation that carries a risk of damaging the ECU.

Adjustment

3 Experienced home mechanics with a considerable amount of skill and equipment (including a tachometer and an accurately calibrated exhaust gas analyser) may be able to check the exhaust CO level and the idle speed. However, if these are found to be outside the specified tolerance, the car must be taken to a suitably-equipped garage for further testing. Neither the mixture adjustment (exhaust gas CO level) nor the idle speed are adjustable, and should either be incorrect, a fault may be present in the engine management system.

12 Throttle housing – removal and refitting

Removal

1 Disconnect the battery negative terminal (refer to *Disconnecting the battery* in the Reference Chapter).

1.6 litre engines

2 Remove the air cleaner assembly and air inlet ducts as described in Section 2.
3 Disconnect the accelerator inner cable from the throttle cam, then withdraw the outer cable from the mounting bracket, along with its spring clip.
4 Disconnect the wiring connectors from the throttle potentiometer, stepper motor and, where applicable, from the inlet air temperature sensor and electric heating element on the throttle housing **(see illustration)**.
5 Slacken and remove the retaining screws, and remove the throttle housing from the inlet manifold. Recover the O-ring from manifold (where fitted) and discard it; a new one must be used when refitting.

1.8 litre engines

6 Remove the air inlet fixed duct from the throttle housing as described in Section 2.
7 Disconnect the accelerator inner cable from the throttle cam, then withdraw the outer cable from the mounting bracket along with its spring clip.
8 Depress the retaining clips, and disconnect the wiring connectors from the throttle

potentiometer, the electric heating element, the inlet air temperature sensor and idle speed stepper motor.
9 Disconnect the two breather hoses at the quick-release connectors behind the throttle housing.
10 Slacken and remove the retaining bolts, and remove the throttle housing from the inlet manifold. Remove the O-ring from the manifold, and discard it – a new one must be used on refitting.

Refitting

11 Refitting is a reversal of the removal procedure, noting the following points:
a) Fit a new O-ring to the manifold, then refit the throttle housing and securely tighten its retaining screws or bolts (as applicable).
b) Ensure all hoses are correctly reconnected and, where necessary, are securely held in position by the retaining clips.
c) Ensure all wiring is correctly routed, and that the connectors are securely reconnected.
d) Adjust the accelerator cable as described in Section 3.
e) Refit the air cleaner and air inlet components as described in Section 2.

13 Fuel injection system components – removal and refitting

1.6 litre engines

Fuel rail and injectors

Note: *Refer to the warning note in Section 1 before proceeding. If a faulty injector is suspected, before condemning the injector, it is worth trying the effect of one of the proprietary injector-cleaning treatments which are available from car accessory shops.*
1 Disconnect the battery negative terminal (refer to *Disconnecting the battery* in the Reference Chapter).
2 Remove the ignition coil unit as described in Chapter 5B.
3 Disconnect the accelerator inner cable from the throttle cam, then withdraw the outer cable from the mounting bracket along with its spring clip.
4 Undo the retaining bolts and remove the accelerator cable mounting bracket **(see illustration)**.
5 Bearing in mind the information given in Section 7, depress the catch on the fuel feed hose quick-release fitting, and disconnect the hose from the fuel rail **(see illustration)**. Suitably seal or plug the hose and the fuel rail union after disconnection.
6 Depress the retaining tangs and disconnect the wiring connectors from the four injectors.
7 Unclip the brake servo vacuum hose from the clips on the fuel rail (where applicable).
8 Slacken and remove the three fuel rail retaining bolts, then carefully ease the fuel rail

and injector assembly out from the inlet manifold and remove it from the engine. Remove the O-rings from the end of each injector and discard them; they must be renewed whenever they are disturbed.

9 Slide out the retaining clip(s) and remove the relevant injector(s) from the fuel rail. Remove the upper O-ring from each disturbed injector and discard; all disturbed O-rings must be renewed.

10 Refitting is a reversal of the removal procedure, noting the following points.

   a) Fit new O-rings to all disturbed injector unions.

   b) Apply a smear of engine oil to the O-rings to aid installation, then ease the injectors and fuel rail into position ensuring that none of the O-rings are displaced.

   c) Refit the ignition coil unit as described in Chapter 5B.

   d) Adjust the accelerator cable as described in Section 3.

   e) On completion, start the engine and check for fuel leaks.

Throttle potentiometer

11 Disconnect the battery negative terminal (refer to *Disconnecting the battery* in the Reference Chapter).

12 Depress the retaining clip and disconnect the wiring connector from the throttle potentiometer **(see illustration)**.

13 Slacken and remove the two retaining screws, then disengage the potentiometer from the throttle valve spindle and remove it from the engine.

14 Refit in the reverse order of removal. Ensure that the potentiometer is correctly engaged with the throttle valve spindle.

Electronic control unit (ECU)

Note: *If a new ECU is to be fitted, this work must be entrusted to a Citroën dealer. It is necessary to initialise the new ECU after installation which requires the use of dedicated Citroën diagnostic equipment.*

15 The ECU is located on the right-hand side of the engine compartment adjacent to the fuse/relay box. The ECU can be withdrawn from its location and moved to one side, without disconnecting its wiring connectors, if this is required for access to other components. To remove the ECU completely,

13.5 Fuel feed hose quick-release fitting (arrowed) at the fuel rail – later 1.6 litre engines

13.20a Drill out the pop rivets securing the metal cover over the ECU wiring connectors . . .

it will be necessary to drill out the pop rivets securing the metal tamperproof cover over the top of the wiring connectors. These rivets are larger than the standard type and it will be necessary to obtain new rivets and a suitable rivet gun for refitting.

16 Disconnect the battery negative terminal (refer to *Disconnecting the battery* in the Reference Chapter).

17 If necessary for improved access, remove the air cleaner assembly as described in Section 2.

18 Disconnect the wiring connector from the fuel injection double relay on the side of the ECU case.

19 Release the ECU wiring harness from the retaining clip at the base of the ECU support tray.

20 Lift the ECU up and out of the support tray, then drill out the pop rivets securing the

13.12 Disconnect the throttle potentiometer wiring connector – early 1.6 litre engines

13.20b . . . then lift the metal cover off the ECU – 1.6 litre engines

metal cover over the wiring connectors. Lift off the metal cover and release the protective boot over the connectors **(see illustrations)**.

21 Release the retaining clips on the connector locking catches using a small screwdriver. Rotate the locking catches and disconnect the three wiring connectors from the ECU.

22 If necessary the ECU can be unbolted and removed from its case.

23 To refit the ECU, first attach it to the case (if removed) and secure with the retaining bolts.

24 Locate the ECU in position in its engine compartment support tray.

25 Reconnect the three wiring connectors and lock them in place by rotating the retaining catches **(see illustration)**.

26 Refit the protective boot over the wiring connectors, then locate the metal cover in position. Secure the cover in position using new pop rivets **(see illustrations)**.

13.25 Reconnect the three ECU wiring connectors and lock them by rotating the retaining catches – 1.6 litre engines

13.26a Refit the protective boot over the ECU wiring connectors . . .

13.26b . . . locate the metal cover in position . . .

13.26c . . . and secure the cover using new pop rivets – 1.6 litre engines

13.32 Idle speed stepper motor securing screw (arrowed) – early 1.6 litre engines

13.36 Manifold pressure sensor securing screw (arrowed) – early 1.6 litre engines

27 Reconnect the injection double relay wiring connector and clip the ECU wiring harness to the support tray.

28 Refit the air cleaner assembly (if removed) and reconnect the battery.

Idle speed stepper motor

29 The idle speed stepper motor is located on the right-hand end of the inlet manifold on early engines, and on the side of the throttle housing assembly on later engines.

30 Disconnect the battery negative terminal (refer to *Disconnecting the battery* in the Reference Chapter).

31 Release the retaining clip and disconnect the wiring connector from the motor. On early engines, release the retaining clip and disconnect the air hose.

32 Slacken and remove the two retaining screws, and withdraw the motor from the manifold or throttle housing **(see illustration)**.

33 Refitting is a reversal of the removal procedure.

Manifold pressure sensor

34 The manifold pressure sensor is located on the front face of the inlet manifold.

35 Disconnect the battery negative terminal (refer to *Disconnecting the battery* in the Reference Chapter).

36 On early engines, remove the securing screw and withdraw the sensor from the manifold **(see illustration)**. Disconnect the wiring connector, and remove the sensor from the engine.

37 On later engines, disconnect the breather hose quick-release connector and move the hose to one side for improved access to the pressure sensor.

38 Disconnect the wiring connector, then undo the retaining bolt and withdraw the sensor from the manifold **(see illustrations)**.

39 Refitting is the reverse of the removal procedure but fit a new sealing O-ring to the sensor body.

Coolant temperature sensor

40 Refer to Chapter 3, Section 6.

Inlet air temperature sensor

41 On early engines, the inlet air temperature sensor is located on the underside of the throttle housing. On later engines the sensor is integral with the manifold pressure sensor.

42 Disconnect the battery negative terminal (refer to *Disconnecting the battery* in the Reference Chapter).

43 Disconnect the wiring connector, then unscrew the sensor and remove it from the manifold.

44 Refitting is the reverse of removal.

Crankshaft sensor

45 The crankshaft sensor is situated on the upper face of the transmission bellhousing and is virtually inaccessible.

46 Disconnect the battery negative terminal (refer to *Disconnecting the battery* in the Reference Chapter).

47 Release the cable clips, cable ties and coolant hose support clips for access to the sensor as necessary.

48 Disconnect the sensor to the wiring connector.

49 Slacken the sensor retaining bolt (there is no need to remove it completely) and rotate the sensor body to disengage it from the retaining bolt **(see illustration)**. Withdraw the sensor upward and out of its location.

50 Refitting is reverse of the removal procedure, ensuring that all wiring and hoses are correctly clipped back into place.

Knock sensor

51 Refer to Chapter 5B.

Vehicle speed sensor

52 The vehicle speed sensor is an integral part of the speedometer drive housing. Refer to Chapter 7 for removal and refitting details.

1.8 litre engines

Fuel rail and injectors

Note: *Refer to the warning note in Section 1 before proceeding. If a faulty injector is suspected, before condemning the injector, it is worth trying the effect of one of the proprietary injector-cleaning treatments which are available from car accessory shops.*

53 Disconnect the battery negative terminal (refer to *Disconnecting the battery* in the Reference Chapter).

54 Bearing in mind the information given in Section 7, depress the catch on the fuel feed hose quick-release fitting, and disconnect the hose from the fuel rail **(see illustration)**. Suitably seal or plug the hose and the fuel rail union after disconnection.

13.38a Disconnect the manifold pressure wiring connector . . .

13.38b . . . then undo the bolt and withdraw the sensor from the manifold – later 1.6 litre engines

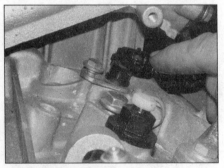

13.49 Rotate the crankshaft sensor body to disengage it from the retaining bolt – 1.6 litre engines

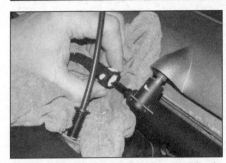

13.54 Depress the catch on the fuel feed hose quick-release fitting, and disconnect the hose from the fuel rail – 1.8 litre engines

13.55 Disconnect the wiring connectors from the four fuel injectors – 1.8 litre engines

13.56a Undo the two fuel rail retaining bolts (arrowed) . . .

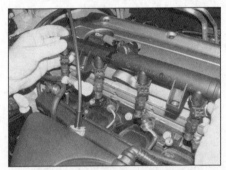

13.56b . . . then ease the fuel rail and injector assembly out from the inlet manifold – 1.8 litre engines

13.57a Slide out the retaining clip(s) . . .

13.57b . . . and remove the relevant injector(s) from the fuel rail – 1.8 litre engines

55 Using a small screwdriver, release the locking clip and disconnect the wiring connectors from the four fuel injectors **(see illustration)**.

56 Undo the two fuel rail retaining bolts, then carefully ease the fuel rail and injector assembly out from the inlet manifold and remove it from the engine **(see illustrations)**. Remove the O-rings from the end of each injector and discard them; they must be renewed whenever they are disturbed.

57 Slide out the retaining clip(s) and remove the relevant injector(s) from the fuel rail **(see illustrations)**. Remove the upper O-ring from each disturbed injector and discard; all disturbed O-rings must be renewed.

58 Refitting is a reversal of the removal procedure, noting the following points.

a) *Fit new O-rings to all disturbed injector unions.*

b) *Apply a smear of engine oil to the O-rings to aid installation, then ease the injectors and fuel rail into position ensuring that none of the O-rings are displaced.*

c) *On completion, start the engine and check for fuel leaks.*

Throttle potentiometer

59 Disconnect the battery negative terminal (refer to *Disconnecting the battery* in the Reference Chapter).

60 Remove the air inlet fixed duct from the throttle housing as described in Section 2.

61 Depress the retaining clip and disconnect the wiring connector from the throttle potentiometer, located on the side of the throttle housing **(see illustration)**.

62 Slacken and remove the two retaining screws, then disengage the potentiometer from the throttle valve spindle and remove it from the engine.

63 Refit in the reverse order of removal. Ensure that the potentiometer is correctly engaged with the throttle valve spindle.

Electronic control unit (ECU)

64 Refer to paragraphs 15 to 28.

Idle speed stepper motor

65 The idle speed stepper motor is located on the side of the throttle housing.

66 Disconnect the battery negative terminal (refer to *Disconnecting the battery* in the Reference Chapter).

67 Remove the air inlet fixed duct from the throttle housing as described in Section 2.

13.61 Throttle potentiometer wiring connector (arrowed) – 1.8 litre engines

68 Release the retaining clip and disconnect the wiring connector from the motor **(see illustration)**.

69 Slacken and remove the two retaining screws, and withdraw the motor from the throttle housing.

70 Refitting is a reversal of the removal procedure.

Manifold pressure sensor

71 The manifold pressure sensor is located on the front face of the inlet manifold, just below the throttle housing.

72 Disconnect the battery negative terminal (refer to *Disconnecting the battery* in the Reference Chapter).

73 Remove the air inlet fixed duct from the throttle housing as described in Section 2.

74 Disconnect the wiring connector, then undo the retaining bolt and withdraw the

13.68 Idle speed stepper motor wiring connector (arrowed) – 1.8 litre engines

13.74 Disconnect the manifold pressure sensor wiring connector – 1.8 litre engines

13.77 Inlet air temperature sensor location (arrowed) – 1.8 litre engines

90 The vehicle speed sensor is an integral part of the speedometer drive housing. Refer to Chapter 7 for removal and refitting details.

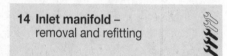

14 Inlet manifold – removal and refitting

Removal

Note: *Refer to the warning note in Section 1 before proceeding.*

1 Disconnect the battery negative terminal (refer to *Disconnecting the battery* in the Reference Chapter) then proceed as described under the relevant sub-heading.

1.6 litre engines

2 Remove the air cleaner assembly air inlet ducts as described in Section 2.
3 Remove the ignition coil unit as described in Chapter 5B.
4 Disconnect the accelerator inner cable from the throttle cam, then withdraw the outer cable from the mounting bracket, along with its spring clip.
5 Undo the retaining bolts and remove the accelerator cable mounting bracket.
6 Disconnect the wiring connectors from the throttle potentiometer, stepper motor, inlet air temperature sensor and electric heating element on the throttle housing.
7 Release the retaining clips (where fitted) and disconnect all the relevant vacuum and breather hoses from the manifold. Make identification marks on the hoses to ensure they are connected correctly on refitting.
8 Bearing in mind the information given in Section 7, depress the catch on the fuel feed hose quick-release fitting, and disconnect the hose from the fuel rail. Suitably seal or plug the hose and the fuel rail union after disconnection.
9 Depress the retaining tangs and disconnect the wiring connectors from the four injectors. Free the wiring from any relevant retaining clips and position it clear of the manifold.
10 Unclip the brake servo vacuum hose from the clips on the fuel rail (where applicable).
11 Undo the manifold retaining nuts and withdraw the manifold from the cylinder head. Recover the four manifold seals and discard them; new ones must be used on refitting.

1.8 litre engines

12 Remove the air inlet fixed duct from the throttle housing as described in Section 2.
13 Depress the retaining tangs and disconnect the wiring connectors from the four injectors.
14 Disconnect the accelerator inner cable from the throttle cam, then withdraw the outer cable from the mounting bracket along with its spring clip.
15 Depress the retaining clips, and disconnect the wiring connectors from the throttle potentiometer, the inlet air temperature

13.86a Disconnect the camshaft position sensor wiring connector . . .

13.86b . . . then undo the bolt and remove the sensor from the rear cylinder head cover – 1.8 litre engines

sensor from the manifold **(see illustration)**.
75 Refitting is the reverse of the removal procedure but fit a new sealing O-ring to the sensor body.

Coolant temperature sensor

76 Refer to Chapter 3, Section 6.

Inlet air temperature sensor

77 The inlet air temperature sensor is located on the front face of the throttle housing **(see illustration)**.
78 Disconnect the battery negative terminal (refer to *Disconnecting the battery* in the Reference Chapter).
79 Remove the air inlet fixed duct from the throttle housing as described in Section 2.
80 Disconnect the wiring connector, then withdraw the sensor from the manifold.
81 Refitting is the reverse of removal.

Camshaft position sensor

82 The camshaft position sensor is located at

the left-hand end of the exhaust camshaft cylinder head cover.
83 Disconnect the battery negative terminal (refer to *Disconnecting the battery* in the Reference Chapter).
84 Undo the six screws and lift off the engine cover.
85 Disconnect the crankcase breather hose at the quick-fit connector on the rear cylinder head cover.
86 Disconnect the wiring connector at the camshaft position sensor, then undo the bolt and remove the sensor from the rear cylinder head cover **(see illustrations)**.
87 Refitting is the reverse of removal but fit a new sealing O-ring to the sensor body.

Crankshaft sensor

88 Refer to paragraphs 45 to 50.

Knock sensor

89 Refer to Chapter 5B.

14.16a Disconnect the left-hand breather hose . . .

14.16b . . . and right-hand breather hose from their connections at the rear of the throttle housing – 1.8 litre engines

14.17 Disconnect the brake servo vacuum hose from below the throttle housing – 1.8 litre engines

14.18 Undo the two screws and release the wiring harness plastic duct from the inlet manifold – 1.8 litre engines

14.19 Release the locking clip and disconnect the EGR pipe from the cylinder head – 1.8 litre engines

14.20 Disconnect the fuel feed hose from the fuel rail – 1.8 litre engines

14.21 Undo the retaining bolts and the two nuts and withdraw the manifold from the cylinder head – 1.8 litre engines

14.22 Remove the manifold seals and use new ones when refitting – 1.8 litre engines

sensor the manifold pressure sensor and the idle speed stepper motor.

16 Depress the catches on the quick-release connectors and disconnect the two breather hoses at the rear of the throttle housing **(see illustrations)**. Disconnect the wiring connector located between the two breather hose connections.

17 Depress the catch on the quick-release connector and disconnect the brake servo vacuum hose from below the throttle housing **(see illustration)**.

18 Undo the two screws and release the wiring harness plastic duct from the inlet manifold. Move the duct and wiring harness to one side **(see illustration)**.

19 Using a small screwdriver, release the locking clip and disconnect the EGR pipe from the connection on the cylinder head **(see illustration)**.

20 Bearing in mind the information given in Section 7, depress the catch on the fuel feed hose quick-release fitting, and disconnect the hose from the fuel rail **(see illustration)**. Suitably seal or plug the hose and the fuel rail union after disconnection.

21 Undo the retaining bolts and the two nuts securing the manifold to the cylinder head. Withdraw the manifold from its location and remove it from the engine compartment **(see illustration)**.

22 Remove the four manifold seals and discard them; new ones must be used on refitting **(see illustration)**.

Refitting

23 Refitting is a reverse of the relevant removal procedure, noting the following points:

a) Ensure that the manifold and cylinder

head mating surfaces are clean and dry, then locate the new seals in their recesses in the manifold. Refit the manifold and tighten its retaining nuts and bolts to the specified torque.

b) Ensure that all relevant hoses are reconnected to their original positions and are securely held (where necessary) by the retaining clips.

c) Refit and reconnect all removed components as described in the Sections indicated in the removal procedure.

d) On completion, adjust the accelerator cable as described in Section 3.

15 Exhaust manifold – removal and refitting

Removal

1.6 litre engines

1 Disconnect the battery negative terminal (refer to *Disconnecting the battery* in the Reference Chapter).

2 Release the retaining catch and disconnect the lambda sensor wiring connector located on the side of the coolant outlet housing **(see illustration)**. Release the wiring from the clip and free it from the coolant outlet housing.

3 Release the lambda sensor wiring from the clip on the left-hand engine lifting bracket, then undo the retaining bolt and remove the lifting bracket **(see illustrations)**.

15.2 Disconnect the lambda sensor wiring connector at the side of the coolant outlet housing – 1.6 litre engines

15.3a Release the lambda sensor wiring from the clip on the engine lifting bracket . . .

15.3b . . . then undo the bolt and remove the lifting bracket – 1.6 litre engines

15.4 Undo the two bolts and lift the heat shield off the manifold – 1.6 litre engines

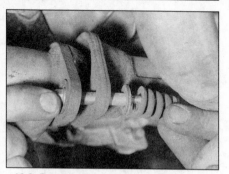

16.8 Remove the fasteners securing the exhaust front pipe to the catalytic converter – 1.6 litre engines

4 Undo the two bolts and lift the heat shield off the manifold, feeding the lambda sensor wiring through the hole in the centre of the shield as it is removed **(see illustration)**.

5 Firmly apply the handbrake, then jack up the front of the car and support it securely on axle stands (see *Jacking and vehicle support*).

6 Undo the nuts/bolts securing the exhaust front pipe to the manifold, then remove the bolt securing the front pipe to its mounting bracket. Disconnect the front pipe from the manifold, and recover the gasket. Support the front pipe on a block of wood.

7 Undo the eight retaining nuts securing the manifold to the cylinder head. Manoeuvre the manifold out of the engine compartment, and discard the manifold gaskets.

1.8 litre engines

8 Disconnect the battery negative terminal (refer to *Disconnecting the battery* in the Reference Chapter).

9 Remove the cylinder head cover over the exhaust camshaft as described in Chapter 2B.

10 Firmly apply the handbrake, then jack up the front of the vehicle and support it securely on axle stands (see *Jacking and vehicle support*).

11 Undo the nut and remove the through bolt, then spread the clamping ring securing the exhaust front pipe to the manifold. Withdraw the front pipe from the clamp.

12 Undo the ten nuts securing the exhaust manifold to the cylinder head. Withdraw the manifold from the cylinder head studs and manoeuvre it out from the rear of the engine with the gasket face uppermost.

13 Collect the gasket from the manifold studs.

Refitting

14 Refitting is the reverse of the removal procedure, noting the following points:

a) *Examine all the exhaust manifold studs for signs of damage and corrosion; remove all traces of corrosion, and repair or renew any damaged studs.*

b) *Ensure that the manifold and cylinder head sealing faces are clean and flat, and fit the new manifold gasket(s). Tighten the manifold retaining nuts to the specified torque.*

c) *Reconnect the front pipe to the manifold, using the information given in Section 16.*

d) *On 1.8 litre engines, refit the cylinder head cover as described in Chapter 2B.*

16 Exhaust system – general information, removal and refitting

General information

1 The exhaust system consists of three or four sections according to engine type, ie, the front pipe, the catalytic converter, the intermediate pipe and centre silencer, and the tailpipe and main silencer. All exhaust sections are secured by clamping rings, with a flexible section incorporated in the front pipe to cater for engine movement.

2 The system is suspended throughout its entire length by rubber mountings.

Removal – 1.6 litre engines

3 Each exhaust section can be removed individually, or alternatively, the complete system can be removed as a unit. Even if only one part of the system needs attention, it is often easier to remove the whole system and separate the sections on the bench.

4 To remove the system or part of the system, first jack up the front or rear of the car and support it on axle stands (see *Jacking and vehicle support*). Alternatively, position the car over an inspection pit or on car ramps.

5 On early engines, the catalytic converter is incorporated into the intermediate section, whereas on later engines the converter is part of the front pipe.

Front pipe/catalytic converter

6 On later engines, trace the wiring back from the downstream lambda sensor to the wiring connector and disconnect the connector.

7 Undo the nuts securing the front pipe flange joint to the manifold, and the single bolt securing the front pipe to its transmission mounting bracket. Separate the flange joint and collect the gasket.

8 According to the arrangement fitted, undo the nuts securing the front pipe flange joint to the intermediate pipe flange joint and recover the spring cups and springs **(see illustration)**. Alternatively, undo the nut and remove the through-bolt, then spread the clamping ring securing the front pipe flange joint to the intermediate pipe. Withdraw the front pipe from underneath the vehicle, and recover the gasket.

Intermediate pipe/catalytic converter

9 Slacken the clamping ring bolts or undo the flange joint nuts, as applicable and disengage the clamp(s) from the front and rear flange joints.

10 Unhook the intermediate pipe from its mounting rubber and remove it from underneath the vehicle.

Tailpipe

11 Slacken the tailpipe clamping ring nut and bolt and disengage the clamp from the flange joint.

12 Unhook the tailpipe from its mounting rubbers and remove it from the vehicle.

Complete system

13 Disconnect the lambda sensor wiring connectors from the main wiring harness.

14 Undo the nuts securing the front pipe flange joint to the manifold, and the single bolt securing the front pipe to its transmission mounting bracket. Separate the flange joint and collect the gasket. Free the system from all its mounting rubbers and lower it from under the vehicle.

Heat shield(s)

15 The heat shields are secured to the underside of the body by various nuts and bolts. Each shield can be removed once the relevant exhaust section has been removed. If a shield is being removed to gain access to a component located behind it, it may prove sufficient in some cases to remove the retaining nuts and/or bolts, and simply lower the shield, without disturbing the exhaust system.

Removal – 1.8 litre engines

16 Each exhaust section can be removed individually, or alternatively, the complete system can be removed as a unit. Even if only one part of the system needs attention, it is often easier to remove the whole system and separate the sections on the bench.

17 To remove the system or part of the system, first jack up the front or rear of the car and support it on axle stands (see *Jacking and vehicle support*). Alternatively, position the car over an inspection pit or on car ramps.

Front pipe/catalytic converter

18 Trace the wiring back from the lambda sensor to its wiring connector and disconnect the wiring from the main harness.
19 Undo the nut and remove the through-bolt, then spread the clamping ring securing the front pipe flange joint to the exhaust manifold.
20 Similarly, release the clamping ring securing the front pipe to the intermediate pipe. Separate the joints and remove the front pipe from underneath the vehicle.

Intermediate pipe

21 Undo the nuts and remove the through-bolts, then spread the clamping rings to disengage the front and rear flange joints.

22 Unhook the intermediate pipe from its mounting rubber and remove it from underneath the vehicle.

Tailpipe

23 Undo the nut and remove the through-bolt, then spread the clamping ring securing the intermediate section to the tailpipe.
24 Disengage the clamp from the flange joint, unhook the tailpipe from its mounting rubbers, and remove it from the vehicle.

Complete system

25 Disconnect the lambda sensor wiring connectors from the main wiring harness.
26 Undo the nut and remove the through-bolt, then spread the clamping ring securing the front pipe flange joint to the exhaust manifold.
27 Free the system from all its mounting rubbers and lower it from under the vehicle.

Heat shield(s)

28 Refer to paragraph 15.

Refitting – all engines

29 Each section is refitted by reversing the removal sequence, noting the following points:

   a) *Ensure that all traces of corrosion have been removed from the flanges and renew all necessary gaskets.*
   b) *Inspect the rubber mountings for signs of damage or deterioration, and renew as necessary.*
   c) *Where joints are secured together by a clamping ring, apply a smear of exhaust system jointing paste to the flange joint, to ensure a gas-tight seal.*
   d) *Prior to tightening the exhaust system fasteners, ensure that all rubber mountings are correctly located, and that there is adequate clearance between the exhaust system and vehicle underbody.*
   e) *Ensure that the lambda sensor wiring is reconnected correctly and secured to the underbody by the relevant retaining clips.*

Notes

Chapter 4 Part B:
Fuel/exhaust systems – diesel engines

Contents

Degrees of difficulty

| **Easy,** suitable for novice with little experience | ❀ | **Fairly easy,** suitable for beginner with some experience | ❀ | **Fairly difficult,** suitable for competent DIY mechanic | ❀ | **Difficult,** suitable for experienced DIY mechanic | ❀ | **Very difficult,** suitable for expert DIY or professional | ❀ |

Specifications

General

System type	HDi (High-pressure Diesel injection) with full electronic control, direct injection and turbocharger
Designation	Bosch EDC 15
Firing order	1-3-4-2 (No 1 at flywheel end)
Fuel system operating pressure	1350 bars

High-pressure fuel pump

Type	Bosch CP 1
Direction of rotation	Clockwise, viewed from sprocket end

Injectors

Type	Electromagnetic

Turbocharger

Type	Garrett GT15 or KKK K03
Boost pressure (approximate)	1 bar at 3000 rpm

Torque wrench settings

	Nm	lbf ft
Accumulator rail mounting bolts	23	17
Exhaust manifold nuts	20	15
Exhaust system fasteners:		
Front pipe-to-manifold nuts	10	7
Clamping ring nuts	20	15
Fuel injector clamp nuts	30	22
Fuel pressure sensor to accumulator rail	45	33
High-pressure fuel pipe union nuts*:		
Accumulator rail-to-fuel injector fuel pipe unions	25	18
Fuel pump-to-accumulator rail fuel pipe unions	20	15
High-pressure fuel pump front mounting bolts and nut	20	15
High-pressure fuel pump rear mounting bolt and nut	22	16
High-pressure fuel pump sprocket nut	50	37

These torque settings are base on the use of Citroën crow-foot adaptors – see Section 2

1 General information and system operation

General information

The fuel system consists of a centrally-mounted fuel tank and fuel lift pump, a fuel cooler mounted under the car, a fuel filter with integral water separator, and a turbocharged, electronically-controlled High-pressure Diesel injection (HDi) system.

The exhaust system is conventional, but to meet the latest emission levels an unregulated catalytic converter and an exhaust gas recirculation system are fitted to all models.

The HDi system (generally known as a 'common rail' system) derives its name from the fact that a common rail (also referred to as an accumulator rail) or fuel reservoir, is used to supply fuel to all the fuel injectors. Instead of an in-line or distributor type injection pump, which distributes the fuel directly to each injector, a high-pressure pump is used, which generates a very high fuel pressure (approximately 1350 bars) in the accumulator rail. The accumulator rail stores fuel, and maintains a constant fuel pressure, with the aid of a pressure control valve. Each injector is supplied with high-pressure fuel from the accumulator rail, and the injectors are individually controlled via signals from the system electronic control unit (ECU). The injectors are electromagnetically-operated.

In addition to the various sensors used on models with a conventional fuel injection pump, common rail systems also have a fuel pressure sensor. The fuel pressure sensor allows the ECU to maintain the required fuel pressure, via the pressure control valve.

System operation

For the purposes of describing the operation of a common rail injection system, the components can be divided into three sub-systems; the low-pressure fuel system, the high-pressure fuel system and the electronic control system.

Low-pressure fuel system

The low-pressure fuel system consists of the following components:
a) Fuel tank.
b) Fuel lift pump.
c) Fuel cooler.
d) Fuel filter/water trap.
e) Low-pressure fuel lines.

The low-pressure system (fuel supply system) is responsible for supplying clean fuel to the high-pressure fuel system.

High-pressure fuel system

The high-pressure fuel system consists of the following components:
a) High-pressure fuel pump with pressure control valve.
b) High-pressure accumulator rail.
c) Fuel injectors.
d) High-pressure fuel lines.

After passing through the fuel filter, the fuel reaches the high-pressure pump, which forces it into the accumulator rail, generating a pressure of 1350 bars. As diesel fuel has a certain elasticity, the pressure in the accumulator rail remains constant, even though fuel leaves the rail each time one of the injectors operates. Additionally, a pressure control valve mounted on the high-pressure pump ensures that the fuel pressure is maintained within pre-set limits.

The pressure control valve is operated by the ECU. When the valve is opened, fuel is returned from the high-pressure pump to the tank, via the fuel return lines, and the pressure in the accumulator rail falls. To enable the ECU to trigger the pressure control valve correctly, the pressure in the accumulator rail is measured by a fuel pressure sensor.

The electromagnetically-controlled fuel injectors are operated individually, via signals from the ECU, and each injector injects fuel directly into the relevant combustion chamber. The fact that high fuel pressure is always available allows very precise and highly flexible injection in comparison to a conventional injection pump: for example combustion during the main injection process can be improved considerably by the pre-injection of a very small quantity of fuel.

Electronic control system

The electronic control system consists of the following components:
a) Electronic control unit (ECU).
b) Crankshaft speed/position sensor.
c) Camshaft position sensor.
d) Accelerator pedal position sensor.
e) Coolant temperature sensor.
f) Fuel temperature sensor.
g) Air mass meter.
h) Fuel pressure sensor.
i) Fuel injectors.
j) Fuel pressure control valve.
k) Preheating control unit.
l) EGR solenoid valve.

The information from the various sensors is passed to the ECU, which evaluates the signals. The ECU contains electronic 'maps' which enable it to calculate the optimum quantity of fuel to inject, the appropriate start of injection, and even pre- and post-injection fuel quantities, for each individual engine cylinder under any given condition of engine operation.

Additionally, the ECU carries out monitoring and self-diagnostic functions. Any faults in the system are stored in the ECU memory, which enables quick and accurate fault diagnosis using appropriate diagnostic equipment (such as a suitable fault code reader).

System Components

Fuel lift pump

The fuel lift pump and integral fuel gauge sender unit is electrically-operated, and is mounted in the fuel tank.

High-pressure pump

The high-pressure pump is mounted on the engine in the position normally occupied by the conventional distributor fuel injection pump. The pump is driven at half engine speed by the timing belt, and is lubricated by the fuel which it pumps.

The fuel lift pump forces the fuel into the high-pressure pump chamber, via a safety valve.

The high-pressure pump consists of three radially-mounted pistons and cylinders. The pistons are operated by an eccentric cam mounted on the pump drive spindle. As a piston moves down, fuel enters the cylinder through an inlet valve. When the piston reaches bottom dead centre (BDC), the inlet valve closes, and as the piston moves back up the cylinder, the fuel is compressed. When the pressure in the cylinder reaches the pressure in the accumulator rail, an outlet valve opens, and fuel is forced into the accumulator rail. When the piston reaches top dead centre (TDC), the outlet valve closes, due to the pressure drop, and the pumping cycle is repeated. The use of multiple cylinders provides a steady flow of fuel, minimising pulses and pressure fluctuations.

As the pump needs to be able to supply sufficient fuel under full-load conditions, it will supply excess fuel during idle and part-load conditions. This excess fuel is returned from the high-pressure circuit to the low-pressure circuit (to the tank) via the pressure control valve.

The pump incorporates a facility to effectively switch off one of the cylinders to improve efficiency and reduce fuel consumption when maximum pumping capacity is not required. When this facility is operated, a solenoid-operated needle holds the inlet valve in the relevant cylinder open during the delivery stroke, preventing the fuel from being compressed.

Accumulator rail

As its name suggests, the accumulator rail acts as an accumulator, storing fuel and preventing pressure fluctuations. Fuel enters the rail from the high-pressure pump, and each injector has its own connection to the rail. The fuel pressure sensor is mounted in the rail, and the rail also has a connection to the fuel pressure control valve on the pump.

Pressure control valve

The pressure control valve is operated by the ECU, and controls the system pressure. The valve is integral with the high-pressure pump and cannot be separated.

If the fuel pressure is excessive, the valve opens, and fuel flows back to the tank. If the pressure is too low, the valve closes, enabling the high-pressure pump to increase the pressure.

The valve is an electromagnetically-operated ball valve. The ball is forced against its seat, against the fuel pressure, by a powerful spring, and also by the force provided by the electromagnet. The force generated by the electromagnet is directly proportional to the current applied to it by the ECU. The desired pressure can therefore be set by varying the current applied to the electromagnet. Any pressure fluctuations are damped by the spring.

Fuel pressure sensor

The fuel pressure sensor is mounted in the accumulator rail, and provides very precise information on the fuel pressure to the ECU.

Fuel injector

The injectors are mounted on the engine in a similar manner to conventional diesel fuel injectors. The injectors are electro-magnetically-operated via signals from the ECU, and fuel is injected at the pressure existing in the accumulator rail. The injectors are high-precision instruments and are manufactured to very high tolerances.

Fuel flows into the injector from the accumulator rail, via an inlet valve and an inlet throttle, and an electromagnet causes the injector nozzle to lift from its seat, allowing injection. Excess fuel is returned from the injectors to the tank via a return line. The injector operates on a hydraulic servo principle: the forces resulting inside the injector due to the fuel pressure effectively amplify the effects of the electromagnet, which does not provide sufficient force to open the injector nozzle directly. The injector functions as follows.

Five separate forces are essential to the operation of the injector.

a) A nozzle spring forces the nozzle needle against the nozzle seat at the bottom of the injector, preventing fuel from entering the combustion chamber.

b) In the valve at the top of the injector, the valve spring forces the valve ball against the opening to the valve control chamber. The fuel in the chamber is unable to escape through the fuel return.

c) When triggered, the electromagnet exerts a force which overcomes the valve spring force, and moves the valve ball away from its seat. This is the triggering force for the start of injection. When the valve ball moves off its seat, fuel enters the valve control chamber.

d) The pressure of the fuel in the valve control chamber exerts a force on the valve control plunger, which is added to the nozzle spring force.

e) A slight chamfer towards the lower end of the nozzle needle causes the fuel in the control chamber to exert a force on the nozzle needle.

When these forces are in equilibrium, the injector is in its rest (idle) state, but when a voltage is applied to the electromagnet, the forces work to lift the nozzle needle, injecting fuel into the combustion chamber. There are four phases of injector operation as follows:

a) Rest (idle) state – all forces are in equilibrium. The nozzle needle closes off the nozzle opening, and the valve spring forces the valve ball against its seat.

b) Opening – the electromagnet is triggered which opens the nozzle and triggers the injection process. The force from the electromagnet allows the valve ball to leave its seat. The fuel from the valve control chamber flows back to the tank via the fuel return line. When the valve opens, the pressure in the valve control chamber drops, and the force on the valve plunger is reduced. However, due to the effect of the input throttle, the pressure on the nozzle needle remains unchanged. The resulting force in the valve control chamber is sufficient to lift the nozzle from its seat, and the injection process begins.

c) Injection – within a few milliseconds, the triggering current in the electromagnet is reduced to a lower holding current. The nozzle is now fully open, and fuel is injected into the combustion chamber at the pressure present in the accumulator rail.

d) Closing – the electromagnet is switched off, at which point the valve spring forces the valve ball firmly against its seat, and in the valve control chamber, the pressure is the same as that at the nozzle needle. The force at the valve plunger increases, and the nozzle needle closes the nozzle opening. The forces are now in equilibrium once more, and the injector is once more in the idle state, awaiting the next injection sequence.

ECU and sensors

The ECU and sensors are described earlier in this Section – see *Electronic control system*.

---

2 High-pressure diesel injection system – special information

Warnings and precautions

1 It is essential to observe strict precautions when working on the fuel system components, particularly the high-pressure side of the system. Before carrying out any operations on the fuel system, refer to the precautions given in *Safety first!* at the beginning of this manual, and to the following additional information.

⚠️ **Warning: Do not carry out any repair work on the high-pressure fuel system unless you are competent to do so, have all the necessary tools and equipment required, and are aware of the safety implications involved.**

Before starting any repair work on the fuel system, wait at least 30 seconds after switching off the engine to allow the fuel circuit to return to atmospheric pressure.

Never work on the high-pressure fuel system with the engine running.

Keep well clear of any possible source of fuel leakage, particularly when starting the engine after carrying out repair work. A leak in the system could cause an extremely high-pressure jet of fuel to escape, which could result in severe personal injury.

Never place your hands or any part of your body near to a leak in the high-pressure fuel system.

Do not use steam cleaning equipment or compressed air to clean the engine or any of the fuel system components.

Repair procedures and general information

2 Strict cleanliness must be observed at all times when working on any part of the fuel system. This applies to the working area in general, the person doing the work, and the components being worked on.

3 Before working on the fuel system components, they must be thoroughly cleaned with a suitable degreasing fluid. Citroën recommend the use of a specific product (SODIMAC degreasing fluid – available from Citroën dealers). Alternatively, a suitable brake cleaning fluid may be used. Cleanliness is particularly important when working on the fuel system connections at the following components:

a) Fuel filter.

b) High-pressure fuel pump.

c) Accumulator rail.

d) Fuel injectors.

e) High-pressure fuel pipes.

4 After disconnecting any fuel pipes or components, the open union or orifice must be immediately sealed to prevent the entry of dirt or foreign material. Plastic plugs and caps in various sizes are available in packs from motor factors and accessory outlets, and are particularly suitable for this application **(see illustration)**. Fingers cut from disposable rubber gloves should be used to protect components such as fuel pipes, fuel injectors and wiring connectors, and can be secured in place using elastic bands. Suitable gloves of this type are available at no cost from most petrol station forecourts.

2.4 Typical plastic plug and cap set for sealing disconnected fuel pipes and components

2.7 Two crow-foot adaptors will be necessary for tightening the fuel pipe unions

5 Whenever any of the high-pressure fuel pipes are disconnected or removed, a new pipes must be obtained for refitting.

6 On the completion of any repair on the high-pressure fuel system, Citroën recommend the use of ARDROX 9D1 BRENT leak-detecting compound. This is a powder which is applied to the fuel pipe unions and connections and turns white when dry. Any leak in the system will cause the product to darken indicating the source of the leak.

7 The torque wrench settings given in the Specifications must be strictly observed when tightening component mountings and connections. This is particularly important when tightening the high-pressure fuel pipe unions. To enable a torque wrench to be used on the fuel pipe unions, two crow-foot adaptors are required (Citroën special tools -4220-T.D. and -4220-T.C.). Suitable alternatives are available from motor factors and accessory outlets **(see illustration)**.

3 Fuel system –
priming and bleeding

1 The fuel system is entirely self-bleeding because the fuel lift pump supplies fuel to the high-pressure pump whenever the ignition is switched on.

2 In the case of running out of fuel, or after disconnecting any part of the fuel supply system, ensure that there is fuel in the tank, then start the engine in the normal way.

4 Air cleaner assembly and air inlets ducts –
removal and refitting

Removal

Air cleaner and front air inlet ducts

1 Disconnect the battery negative terminal (refer to *Disconnecting the battery* in the Reference Chapter).

2 Undo the four plastic nuts and lift off the engine cover **(see illustration)**.

3 Disconnect the wiring connector from the underside of the air mass meter **(see illustration)**.

4 Slacken the hose clip securing the air mass meter inlet duct to the cleaner assembly lid.

5 Lift the air cleaner assembly upward to release it from the support bracket then detach the air mass meter inlet duct. Remove

the air cleaner assembly from the engine compartment.

6 To remove the air mass meter inlet duct, slacken the remaining clips (where applicable), and disconnect the duct from the turbocharger rigid inlet duct. Remove the inlet duct complete with air mass meter from the engine compartment. Suitably plug or cover the turbocharger rigid inlet duct, using clean rag to prevent any dirt or foreign material from entering.

Turbocharger inlet and outlet ducts

7 The rigid ducts at the rear of the engine, connecting the turbocharger to the flexible air inlet duct and to the inlet manifold are inaccessible with the engine in the car. To gain access it will be necessary to either remove the engine/transmission unit as described in Chapter 2E, or remove the front suspension subframe as described in Chapter 10.

8 Once access has been gained, begin removal of the turbocharger rigid inlet duct by disconnecting the crankcase ventilation hose at the top of the duct **(see illustration)**.

9 Undo the bolt securing the duct to the inlet manifold elbow **(see illustration)**.

10 At the lower end, undo the bolt securing the duct to the turbocharger **(see illustration)**. Lift off the duct and recover the seal from the lower end.

11 To remove the turbocharger-to-inlet manifold rigid plastic duct, slacken the retaining clip and release the connecting hose from the inlet manifold elbow **(see illustration)**.

4.2 Undo the four plastic nuts and lift off the engine cover

4.3 Air mass meter wiring connector (A) and inlet duct retaining clip (B)

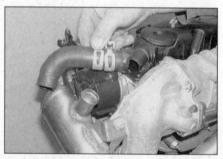

4.8 Disconnect the crankcase ventilation hose at the top of the turbocharger rigid inlet duct

4.9 Undo the bolt (arrowed) securing the rigid inlet duct to the inlet manifold elbow

4.10 Undo the bolt securing the rigid inlet duct to the turbocharger and remove the duct

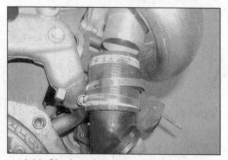

4.11 Slacken the clip and release the plastic duct connecting hose from the inlet manifold elbow

12 Slacken the clip securing the connecting hose at the lower end of the duct to the turbocharger. Release the attachment strap from the lug on the turbocharger and withdraw the duct from the engine (see illustration).

Refitting

13 Refitting is a reverse of the removal procedure. Examine the condition of the seals and retaining clips and renew if necessary.
14 Where applicable, refit the engine/transmission as described in Chapter 2E, or the front suspension subframe as described in Chapter 10.
15 Reconnect and adjust the accelerator cable as described in Section 5.

5 Accelerator cable – removal, refitting and adjustment

Removal

1 Undo the four plastic nuts and lift off the engine cover.
2 Undo the two bolts and lift the accelerator pedal position sensor off the master cylinder reservoir mounting bracket (see illustration).
3 Rotate the pedal position sensor quadrant, and release the inner cable from the quadrant (see illustration).
4 Withdraw the outer cable from the grommet in the pedal position sensor body, and remove the spring clip.
5 Release the cable from the remaining clips and brackets in the engine compartment, noting its routing.
6 Extract the stud-type plastic clips, using a forked type tool, and remove the facia lower trim panel above the pedals on the driver's side.
7 Reach up under the facia, depress the ends of the cable end fitting, and detach the inner cable from the top of the accelerator pedal (see illustration).
8 Slide out the plastic retainer securing the outer cable to the bulkhead grommet.
9 Return to the engine compartment, pull the outer cable from the bulkhead grommet and withdraw the cable.

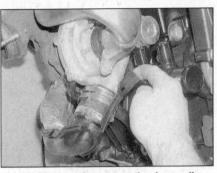

4.12 Slacken the connecting hose clip, release the attachment strap and withdraw the plastic duct from the engine

Refitting

10 Refitting is a reversal of removal, but ensure that the cable is routed as noted before removal and, on completion, adjust the cable as follows.

Adjustment

11 Remove the spring clip from the accelerator outer cable. Ensuring that the pedal position sensor quadrant is against its stop, gently pull the cable out of its grommet until all free play is removed from the inner cable.
12 With the cable held in this position, refit the spring clip to the last exposed outer cable groove in front of the rubber grommet. When the clip is refitted and the outer cable is released, there should be only a small amount of free play in the inner cable.
13 Have an assistant depress the accelerator pedal, and check that the pedal position sensor quadrant opens fully and returns smoothly to its stop.
14 Refit the engine cover and facia lower trim panel on completion.

6 Accelerator pedal – removal and refitting

Refer to Chapter 4A, Section 4, but adjust the accelerator cable as described above.

7 Fuel lift pump – removal and refitting

The diesel fuel lift pump is located in the same position as the conventional fuel pump on petrol models, and the removal and refitting procedures are virtually identical. Refer to Chapter 4A, Section 8.

8 Fuel gauge sender unit – removal and refitting

The fuel gauge sender unit is integral with the fuel lift pump. Refer to Chapter 4A, Section 8.

9 Fuel tank – removal and refitting

Refer to Chapter 4A, Section 10.

10 High-pressure fuel pump – removal and refitting

Removal

⚠️ *Warning: Refer to the information contained in Section 2 before proceeding.*

Note: *A new fuel pump-to-accumulator rail high-pressure fuel pipe will be required for refitting.*
1 Remove the timing belt as described in Chapter 2C. After removal of the timing belt, temporarily refit the right-hand engine mounting.
2 At the connections above the fuel pump, disconnect the fuel supply and return hose quick-release fittings using a small screwdriver to release the locking clip (see illustration). Suitably plug or cover the open unions to prevent dirt entry.
3 Similarly disconnect the supply and return

5.2 Undo the two bolts (arrowed) securing the pedal position sensor to the reservoir mounting bracket

5.3 Release the accelerator inner cable from the sensor quadrant

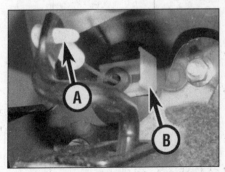

5.7 Accelerator cable end fitting (A) and outer cable plastic retainer (B)

10.2 Disconnect the fuel supply and return hose quick-release fittings at the connections above the fuel pump

10.8 Unscrew the unions and remove the high pressure fuel pipe

10.6 Undo the bolt (arrowed) to release the plastic wiring harness guide

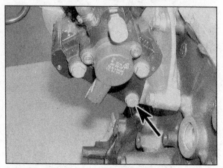

10.9 Undo the nut and bolt (arrowed) securing the fuel pump rear mounting to the mounting bracket

accumulator rail. Counterhold the unions on the pump and accumulator rail with a second spanner, while unscrewing the union nuts. Withdraw the high-pressure fuel pipe and plug or cover the open unions to prevent dirt entry **(see illustration)**. Note that a new high-pressure fuel pipe will be required for refitting.

9 Undo the nut and bolt securing the fuel pump rear mounting to the mounting bracket **(see illustration)**.

10 Using a suitable socket, undo the fuel pump sprocket retaining nut. The sprocket can be held stationary as the nut is slackened using a suitable forked tool engaged with the holes in the sprocket **(see Tool Tip 1)**.

11 The fuel pump sprocket is a taper fit on the pump shaft and it will be necessary to make up another tool to release it from the taper **(see Tool Tip 2)**.

12 Partially unscrew the sprocket retaining nut, fit the home-made tool, and secure it to the sprocket with two suitable bolts. Prevent the sprocket from rotating as before, and unscrew the sprocket retaining nut **(see illustration)**. The nut will bear against the tool as it is undone, forcing the sprocket off the shaft taper. Once the taper is released, remove the tool, unscrew the nut fully, and remove the sprocket from the pump shaft.

13 Undo the nut and two bolts securing the front of the fuel pump to the mounting bracket **(see illustrations)**. Withdraw the pump, complete with fuel supply and return hoses, rearwards, and lift it off the engine.

Caution: The high-pressure fuel pump is manufactured to extremely close

hose quick-release fittings at the fuel filter and plug or cover the open unions. Release the fuel hoses from the relevant retaining clips.

4 On early engines, lift the fuel filter out of its mounting bracket and move it slightly to one side, away from the pump. Undo the bolts and remove the filter mounting bracket from the engine.

5 On later engines, undo the two bolts and move fuel filter assembly slightly to one side, away from the pump

6 Undo the bolts securing the plastic wiring harness guide to the front of the engine **(see illustration)**. It will be necessary to lift up the

wiring harness as far as possible for access to the rear of the fuel pump. If necessary, disconnect the relevant wiring connectors to enable the harness and guide assembly to be moved further for additional access.

7 Disconnect the wiring connector at the pressure control valve on the rear of the fuel pump, and at the piston de-activator switch on the top of the pump.

8 Thoroughly clean the high-pressure fuel pipe unions on the fuel pump and accumulator rail. Using an open-ended spanner, unscrew the union nuts securing the high-pressure fuel pipe to the fuel pump and

10.12 Using the home-made tools to remove the fuel pump sprocket

Tool Tip 1: A sprocket holding tool can be made from two lengths of steel strip bolted together to form a forked end. Bend the ends of the strip through 90° to form the fork 'prongs'.

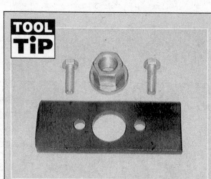

Tool Tip 2: Make a sprocket releasing tool from a short strip of steel. Drill two holes in the strip to correspond with the two holes in the sprocket. Drill a third hole just large enough to accept the flats of the sprocket retaining nut.

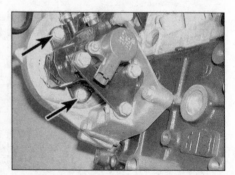

10.13a Fuel pump front mounting bolts (arrowed) . . .

tolerances and must not be dismantled in any way. Do not unscrew the fuel pipe male union on the rear of the pump, or attempt to remove the pressure control valve, piston de-activator switch, or the seal on the pump shaft. No parts for the pump are available separately and if the unit is in any way suspect, it must be renewed.

Refitting

14 Locate the pump on the mounting bracket, and refit the front retaining nut and the two bolts. Refit the nut and bolt securing the fuel pump rear mounting to the mounting bracket, then tighten all the mountings to the specified torque.

15 Refit the pump sprocket and retaining nut and tighten the nut to the specified torque. Prevent the sprocket rotating as the nut is tightened using the sprocket holding tool.

16 Remove the blanking plugs from the fuel pipe unions on the pump and accumulator rail. Locate a new high-pressure fuel pipe over the unions and screw on the union nuts finger tight at this stage.

17 Using a torque wrench and crow-foot adaptor, tighten the fuel pipe union nuts to the specified torque. Counterhold the unions on the pump and accumulator rail with an open-ended spanner, while tightening the union nuts **(see illustration).**

18 Reconnect the wiring connector at the pressure control valve on the rear of the fuel pump.

19 Reposition and secure the plastic wiring harness guide to the front of the engine, and reconnect any additional wiring disconnected for access.

20 Refit the filter mounting bracket or the filter assembly as applicable, to the engine and securely tighten the retaining bolts. Where applicable, locate the fuel filter back in position in the mounting bracket.

21 Remove the blanking plugs and reconnect the supply and return hose quick-release fittings at the fuel filter, and at the connections above the fuel pump. Secure the hoses with their respective retaining clips.

22 Refit the timing belt as described in Chapter 2C.

23 With everything reassembled and

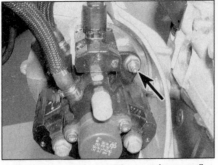

10.13b . . . and mounting nut (arrowed)

reconnected, and observing the precautions listed in Section 2, start the engine and allow it to idle. Check for leaks at the high-pressure fuel pipe unions with the engine idling. If satisfactory, increase the engine speed to 4000 rpm and check again for leaks. Take the car for a short road test and check for leaks once again on return. If any leaks are detected, obtain and fit another new high-pressure fuel pipe. **Do not** attempt to cure even the slightest leak by further tightening of the pipe unions.

24 Refit the engine cover on completion.

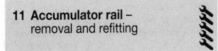

11 Accumulator rail – removal and refitting

Removal

 Warning: Refer to the information contained in Section 2 before proceeding.

Note: *A complete new set of high-pressure fuel pipes will be required for refitting.*

1 Disconnect the battery negative terminal (refer to *Disconnecting the battery* in the Reference Chapter).

2 Undo the four plastic nuts and lift off the engine cover.

3 Disconnect the wiring connectors at the fuel injectors and at the piston de-activator switch on the top of the fuel pump **(see illustrations).**

4 Undo the two nuts securing the plastic

10.17 Tighten the fuel pipe union nuts using a torque wrench and crow-foot adaptor

wiring harness guide to the cylinder head. Lift the guide off the two mounting studs and move it clear of the accumulator rail **(see illustration).** Disconnect any additional wiring connectors as necessary to enable the harness and guide assembly to be moved further for increased access.

5 Release the retaining clip and disconnect the crankcase ventilation hose from the cylinder head cover.

6 At the connections above the fuel pump, disconnect the fuel supply and return hose quick-release fittings using a small screwdriver to release the locking clip. Suitably plug or cover the open unions to prevent dirt entry.

7 Similarly disconnect the supply and return hose quick-release fittings at the fuel filter and plug or cover the open unions. Release the fuel hoses from the relevant retaining clips.

8 Thoroughly clean all the high-pressure fuel pipe unions on the accumulator rail, fuel pump and injectors. Using an open-ended spanner, unscrew the union nuts securing the high-pressure fuel pipe to the fuel pump and accumulator rail. Counterhold the unions on the pump and accumulator rail with a second spanner, while unscrewing the union nuts. Withdraw the high-pressure fuel pipe and plug or cover the open unions to prevent dirt entry.

9 Again using two spanners, hold the unions and unscrew the union nuts securing the high-pressure fuel pipes to the fuel injectors and accumulator rail **(see illustrations).** Withdraw the high-pressure fuel pipes and plug or cover the open unions to prevent dirt entry.

11.3a Disconnect the wiring connectors at the fuel injectors . . .

11.3b . . . and at the piston de-activator switch on top of the fuel pump

11.4 Undo the two nuts and lift off the plastic wiring harness guide

11.9a Using two spanners, unscrew the fuel pipe unions at the accumulator rail . . .

11.9b . . . and at each injector

10 Disconnect the wiring connectors at the fuel temperature sensor and fuel pressure sensor on the accumulator rail **(see illustration)**.
11 Undo the three bolts securing the accumulator rail to the cylinder head and withdraw the rail from its location **(see illustrations)**.
Caution: Do not attempt to remove the four high-pressure fuel pipe male unions from the accumulator rail. These parts are not available separately and if disturbed are likely to result in fuel leakage on reassembly.
12 Obtain a complete new set of high-pressure fuel pipes for refitting.

Refitting

13 Locate the accumulator rail in position, refit the three securing bolts and tighten to the specified torque.

14 Working on one fuel injector at a time, remove the blanking plugs from the fuel pipe unions on the accumulator rail and the relevant injector. Locate a new high-pressure fuel pipe over the unions and screw on the union nuts finger tight at this stage.
15 When all four fuel pipes are in place, hold the unions with a spanner and tighten the union nuts to the specified torque using a torque wrench and crow-foot adaptor **(see illustration)**.
16 Similarly, fit a new high-pressure fuel pipe to the fuel pump and accumulator rail, and tighten the union nuts to the specified torque.
17 Reconnect the fuel temperature sensor and fuel pressure sensor wiring connectors.
18 Remove the blanking plugs and reconnect the supply and return hose quick-release fittings at the fuel filter, and at the connections above the fuel pump. Secure the hoses with their respective retaining clips.

19 Reconnect the crankcase ventilation hose to the cylinder head cover.
20 Reposition the plastic wiring harness guide over the two mounting studs and secure with the retaining nuts.
21 Reconnect the fuel injector and pump piston de-activator switch wiring connectors, and reconnect any additional wiring disconnected for access.
22 Check that everything has been reconnected and secured with the relevant retaining clips then reconnect the battery negative terminal.
23 Observing the precautions listed in Section 2, start the engine and allow it to idle. Check for leaks at the high-pressure fuel pipe unions with the engine idling. If satisfactory, increase the engine speed to 4000 rpm and check again for leaks. Take the car for a short road test and check for leaks once again on return. If any leaks are detected, obtain and fit additional new high-pressure fuel pipes as required. **Do not** attempt to cure even the slightest leak by further tightening of the pipe unions.
24 Refit the engine cover on completion.

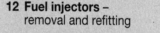

12 Fuel injectors –
removal and refitting

Note: *The following procedure describes the removal and refitting of the injectors as a complete set, however each injector may be removed individually if required. New copper washers, upper seals, injector clamp retaining nuts and a high-pressure fuel pipe will be required for each disturbed injector when refitting.*

Removal

⚠ **Warning: Refer to the information contained in Section 2 before proceeding.**

1 Carry out the operations described in Section 11, paragraphs 1 to 4.
2 At the connections above the fuel pump, disconnect the fuel supply and return hose quick-release fittings using a small screwdriver to release the locking clip. Suitably plug or cover the open unions to prevent dirt entry, then release the fuel hoses from the relevant retaining clips.
3 Thoroughly clean all the high-pressure fuel pipe unions on the fuel injectors and accumulator rail. Using two open-ended spanners, unscrew the union nuts securing the high-pressure fuel pipes to the fuel injectors and accumulator rail. Withdraw the high-pressure fuel pipes and plug or cover the open unions on the injectors and accumulator rail to prevent dirt entry. Note that a new high-pressure fuel pipe will be required for each removed injector when refitting.
4 Extract the retaining circlip and disconnect the leak-off pipe from each fuel injector **(see illustration)**.

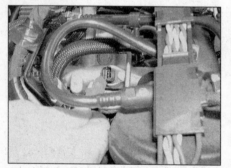

11.10 Disconnect the wiring connector at the fuel temperature sensor

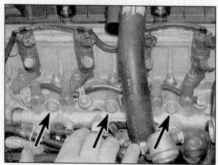

11.11a Undo the three accumulator rail retaining bolts (arrowed) . . .

11.11b . . . and withdraw the accumulator rail from the engine

11.15 Using a torque wrench and crow-foot adaptor, tighten the fuel pipe union nuts

12.4 Extract the circlip and disconnect the injector leak-off pipes

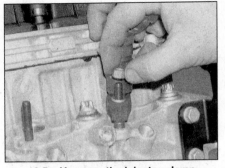

12.5a Unscrew the injector clamp retaining nut . . .

12.5b . . . and remove the washer

5 Unscrew the nut and remove the washer securing each injector clamp to its cylinder head stud **(see illustrations)**. Note that new clamp nuts will be required for refitting.

6 Withdraw the injectors, together with their clamps, from the cylinder head **(see illustration)**. Slide the clamp off the injector once it is clear of the mounting stud. If the injectors are a tight fit in the cylinder head and cannot be released, unscrew the mounting stud using a stud extractor and slide off the injector clamp. Using an open-ended spanner engaged with the clamp locating slot on the injector body, free the injector by twisting it and at the same time lifting it upwards.

7 Recover the injector clamp locating dowel from the cylinder head **(see illustration)**.

8 Remove the copper washer and the upper seal from each injector, or from the cylinder head if they remained in place during injector removal. New copper washers and upper seals will be required for refitting.

9 Examine each injector visually for any signs of obvious damage or deterioration. If any defects are apparent, renew the injector(s). *Caution: The injectors are manufactured to extremely close tolerances and must not be dismantled in any way. Do not unscrew the fuel pipe union on the side of the injector, or separate any parts of the injector body. Do not attempt to clean carbon deposits from the injector nozzle or carry out any form of ultra-sonic or pressure testing.*

10 If the injectors are in a satisfactory condition, plug the fuel pipe union (if not already done) and suitably cover the electrical element and the injector nozzle.

11 Prior to refitting, obtain new copper washers, upper seals, injector clamp retaining nuts and high-pressure fuel pipes for each removed injector.

Refitting

12 Locate a new upper seal on the body of each injector, and place a new copper washer on the injector nozzle **(see illustrations)**.

13 Refit the injector clamp locating dowels to the cylinder head.

14 Place the injector clamp in the slot on each injector body and refit the injectors to the cylinder head. Guide the clamp over the

mounting stud and onto the locating dowel as each injector is inserted.

15 Fit the washer and a new injector clamp retaining nut to each mounting stud. Tighten the nuts finger tight only at this stage.

16 Working on one fuel injector at a time, remove the blanking plugs from the fuel pipe unions on the accumulator rail and the relevant injector. Locate a new high-pressure fuel pipe over the unions and screw on the union nuts. Take care not to cross-thread the nuts or strain the fuel pipes as they are fitted. Once the union nut threads have started, tighten the nuts moderately tight only at this stage.

17 When all the fuel pipes are in place, tighten the injector clamp retaining nuts to the specified torque.

18 Using an open-ended spanner, hold each fuel pipe union in turn and tighten the union nut to the specified torque using a torque

wrench and crow-foot adaptor. Tighten all the disturbed union nuts in the same way.

19 Connect the leak-off pipes to each fuel injector and secure with the retaining circlips.

20 Remove the blanking plugs and reconnect the supply and return hose quick-release fittings at the connections above the fuel pump. Secure the hoses with their respective retaining clips.

21 Reposition the plastic wiring harness guide over the two mounting studs and secure with the retaining nuts.

22 Reconnect the fuel injector and pump piston de-activator switch wiring connectors, and reconnect any additional wiring disconnected for access.

23 Check that everything has been reconnected and secured with the relevant retaining clips then reconnect the battery negative terminal.

12.6 Withdraw the injectors, together with their clamps, from the cylinder head

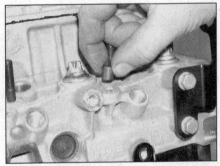

12.7 Recover the injector clamp locating dowel from the cylinder head

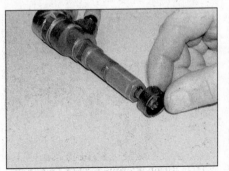

12.12a Locate a new upper seal on the body of each injector . . .

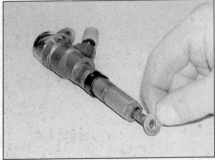

12.12b . . . and place a new copper washer on the injector nozzle

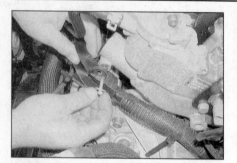

13.6 Release the plastic wiring harness guide for access to the crankshaft speed/position sensor

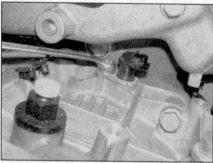

13.8 Slacken the bolt securing the sensor to the bellhousing

13.9 Turn the sensor body to clear the bolt and withdraw it from the bellhousing

24 Observing the precautions listed in Section 2, start the engine and allow it to idle. Check for leaks at the high-pressure fuel pipe unions with the engine idling. If satisfactory, increase the engine speed to 4000 rpm and check again for leaks. Take the car for a short road test and check for leaks once again on return. If any leaks are detected, obtain and fit additional new high-pressure fuel pipes as required. **Do not** attempt to cure even the slightest leak by further tightening of the pipe unions.

25 Refit the engine cover on completion.

---

13 Electronic control system components – testing, removal and refitting

Testing

1 If a fault is suspected in the electronic control side of the system, first ensure that all the wiring connectors are securely connected and free of corrosion. Ensure that the suspected problem is not of a mechanical nature, or due to poor maintenance; ie, check that the air cleaner filter element is clean, the engine breather hoses are clear and undamaged, and that the cylinder compression pressures are correct, referring to Chapters 1B and 2C for further information.

2 If these checks fail to reveal the cause of the problem, the vehicle should be taken to a Citroën dealer or suitably-equipped garage for testing. A diagnostic socket is located adjacent to the passenger compartment

13.13 Disconnect the camshaft position sensor wiring connector

fusebox in which a fault code reader or other suitable test equipment can be connected. By using the code reader or test equipment, the engine management ECU (and the various other vehicle system ECUs) can be interrogated, and any stored fault codes can be retrieved. This will allow the fault to be quickly and simply traced, alleviating the need to test all the system components individually, which is a time-consuming operation that carries a risk of damaging the ECU.

Removal and refitting

3 Before carrying out any of the following procedures, disconnect the battery negative terminal (refer to *Disconnecting the battery* in the Reference Chapter). Reconnect the battery on completion of refitting.

Electronic control unit (ECU)

Note: *If a new ECU is to be fitted, this work must be entrusted to a Citroën dealer. It is necessary to initialise the new ECU after installation, which requires the use of dedicated Citroën diagnostic equipment.*

4 Refer to the procedures contained in Chapter 4A, Section 13.

Crankshaft speed/position sensor

5 The crankshaft speed/position sensor is located at the top of the transmission bellhousing, directly above the engine flywheel. To gain access, remove the air cleaner assembly and air inlet ducts as described in Section 4.

6 Undo the retaining nuts and bolts and release the plastic wiring harness guide from its mountings **(see illustration)**.

13.17 Insert feeler blades bent through 90° through the sprocket to measure the camshaft position sensor air gap

7 Working below the coolant outlet housing, disconnect the wiring connector from the crankshaft speed/position sensor.

8 Slacken the bolt securing the sensor to the bellhousing **(see illustration)**. It is not necessary to remove the bolt completely as the sensor mounting flange is slotted.

9 Turn the sensor body to clear the mounting bolt, then withdraw the sensor from the bellhousing **(see illustration)**.

10 Refitting is reverse of the removal procedure ensuring the sensor retaining bolt is securely tightened.

Camshaft position sensor

11 The camshaft position sensor is mounted on the right-hand end of the cylinder head cover, directly behind the camshaft sprocket.

12 Remove the timing belt upper and inter-mediate covers as described in Chapter 2C.

13 Disconnect the sensor wiring connector **(see illustration)**.

14 Undo the retaining bolt and lift the sensor off the cylinder head cover.

15 To refit and adjust the sensor position, locate the sensor on the cylinder head cover and loosely refit the retaining bolt.

16 The air gap between the tip of the sensor and the target plate at the rear of the camshaft sprocket hub must be set to 1.2 mm, using feeler blades. Clearance for the feeler blades is limited with the timing belt and camshaft sprocket in place, but it is just possible if the feeler blades are bent through 90° so they can be inserted through the holes in the sprocket, to rest against the inner face of the target plate.

17 With the feeler blades placed against the target plate, move the sensor toward the sprocket until it just contacts the feeler blades. Hold the sensor in this position and tighten the retaining bolt **(see illustration)**.

18 With the gap correctly adjusted, reconnect the sensor wiring connector, then refit the timing belt upper and intermediate covers as described in Chapter 2C.

Accelerator pedal position sensor

19 The accelerator pedal position sensor is located on the side of the master cylinder reservoir mounting bracket.

20 Undo the two bolts and remove the sensor assembly from the mounting bracket.

21 Rotate the pedal position sensor quadrant, and release the accelerator inner cable from the quadrant **(see illustration)**. Withdraw the outer cable from the grommet in the pedal position sensor body.

22 Refitting is reverse of the removal procedure, but adjust the accelerator cable as described in Section 5 on completion.

Coolant temperature sensor

23 Refer to Chapter 3, Section 6.

Fuel temperature sensor

⚠️ *Warning: Refer to the information contained in Section 2 before proceeding.*

Note: *Do not remove the sensor from the accumulator rail unless there is a valid reason to do so. At the time of writing there was no information as to the availability of the sensor seal as a separate item. Consult a Citroën parts stockist for the latest information before proceeding.*

24 The fuel temperature sensor is located towards the right-hand end of the accumulator rail **(see illustration)**.

25 Undo the four plastic nuts and lift off the engine cover.

26 Disconnect the fuel temperature sensor wiring connector.

27 Thoroughly clean the area around the sensor and its location on the accumulator rail.

28 Suitably protect the components below the sensor and have plenty of clean rags handy. Be prepared for considerable fuel spillage.

29 Undo the retaining bolt and withdraw the sensor from the accumulator rail. Plug the opening in the accumulator rail as soon as the sensor is withdrawn.

30 Prior to refitting, if the original sensor is to be refitted, renew the sensor seal, where applicable (see the note at the start of this sub-Section).

31 Locate the sensor in the accumulator rail and refit the retaining bolt, tightened securely.

32 Refit the sensor wiring connector.

33 Observing the precautions listed in Section 2, start the engine and allow it to idle. Check for leaks at the fuel temperature sensor with the engine idling. If satisfactory, increase the engine speed to 4000 rpm and check again for leaks. Take the car for a short road test and check for leaks once again on return. If any leaks are detected, obtain and fit a new sensor.

34 Refit the engine cover on completion.

Air mass meter

35 The air mass meter is located in the flexible air inlet duct just behind the air cleaner lid.

36 Undo the four plastic nuts and lift off the engine cover.

37 Disconnect the wiring connector from the underside of the air mass meter.

38 Slacken the hose clips on each side of the air mass meter body.

13.21 Release the accelerator inner cable from the accelerator pedal position sensor quadrant

39 Lift the air cleaner assembly upward to release it from the support bracket then detach the air mass meter from the front inlet duct.

40 Withdraw the air mass meter from the rear inlet duct and remove it from the engine compartment. Suitably plug or cover the rear inlet duct using clean rag to prevent any dirt or foreign material from entering the turbocharger.

41 Refitting is reverse of the removal procedure.

Fuel pressure sensor

⚠️ *Warning: Refer to the information contained in Section 2 before proceeding.*

Note: *Citroën special tool (-).4220 TH (27 mm forked adaptor) or suitable equivalent will be required for this operation.*

42 The fuel pressure sensor is located centrally on the underside of the accumulator rail **(see illustration 13.24)**.

43 Undo the four plastic nuts and lift off the engine cover.

44 Release the retaining clip and disconnect the crankcase ventilation hose from the cylinder head cover.

45 Disconnect the fuel supply and return hose quick-release fittings at the fuel filter, using a small screwdriver to release the locking clip. Suitably plug or cover the open unions to prevent dirt entry. Release the fuel hoses from the relevant retaining clips.

46 Disconnect the fuel pressure sensor wiring connector.

47 Thoroughly clean the area around the sensor and its location on the accumulator rail.

48 Suitably protect the components below the sensor and have plenty of clean rags handy. Be prepared for considerable fuel spillage.

49 Using the Citroën special tool (or suitable alternative 27 mm forked adaptor) and a socket bar, unscrew the fuel pressure sensor from the base of the accumulator rail.

50 Obtain and fit a new sealing ring to the sensor prior to refitting.

51 Locate the sensor in the accumulator rail and tighten it to the specified torque using the special tool (or alternative) and a torque wrench.

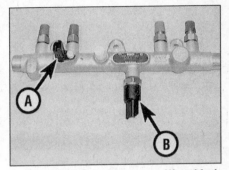
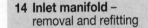

13.24 Fuel temperature sensor (A) and fuel pressure sensor (B) locations on the accumulator rail (shown removed for clarity)

52 Refit the sensor wiring connector.

53 Observing the precautions listed in Section 2, start the engine and allow it to idle. Check for leaks at the fuel pressure sensor with the engine idling. If satisfactory, increase the engine speed to 4000 rpm and check again for leaks. Take the car for a short road test and check for leaks once again on return. If any leaks are detected, obtain and fit another new sensor sealing ring.

54 Refit the engine cover on completion.

Fuel pressure control valve

55 The fuel pressure control valve is integral with the high-pressure fuel pump and cannot be separated.

Preheating system control unit

56 Refer to Chapter 5C.

EGR solenoid valve

57 Refer to Chapter 4C.

14 Inlet manifold – removal and refitting

Removal

Note: *Renew the manifold gasket when refitting.*

1 Remove the exhaust manifold as described in Section 15.

2 Undo the four bolts and four nuts securing the inlet manifolds flanges to the cylinder head **(see illustration)**. Recover the washers.

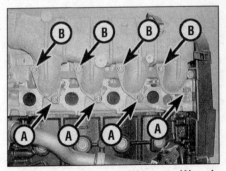

14.2 Inlet manifold retaining nuts (A) and bolts (B)

3 Lift the manifold off the cylinder head studs and recover the gasket **(see illustrations)**.

Refitting

4 Refitting is reverse of the removal procedure, bearing in mind the following points.

a) *Ensure that the manifold and cylinder head mating faces are clean, with all traces of old gasket removed.*

b) *Use a new gasket when refitting the manifold.*

c) *Ensure that all fixings and attachments are securely tightened.*

d) *Refit the exhaust manifold as described in Section 15.*

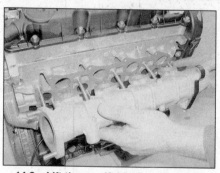

14.3a Lift the manifold off the cylinder head studs . . .

14.3b . . . and recover the gasket

15 Exhaust manifold – removal and refitting

Removal

Note: *The exhaust manifold is removed complete with the turbocharger and there is insufficient clearance to gain access to all the relevant attachments from either above or below with the engine in the car. Two alternatives are possible; either remove the complete engine/transmission unit from the car as described in Chapter 2E, or remove the front suspension subframe as described in Chapter 10. Both are involved operations and the course of action taken is largely dependent on the tools, equipment, skill and patience available.*

1 The following procedure is based on the assumption that the engine/transmission unit has been removed from the car. If the front suspension subframe has been removed instead, the operations are basically the same, but it may be necessary to disconnect and move aside certain additional items, and to be prepared for considerable manipulation to withdraw the components from the engine compartment.

2 If not already done, disconnect the battery negative terminal (refer to *Disconnecting the battery* in the Reference Chapter).

3 If the engine is in the car, remove the catalytic converter as described in Section 18.

4 Remove the turbocharger rear inlet and outlet ducts as described in Section 4.

5 Unscrew the union nut securing the turbocharger oil feed pipe to the cylinder block, then withdraw the pipe from its location **(see illustration)**.

6 Remove the filter from the end of the oil feed pipe, and examine it for contamination **(see illustration)**. Clean or renew if necessary.

7 Undo the two bolts securing the oil return pipe flange to the turbocharger. Separate the flange and recover the gasket **(see illustrations)**.

8 Remove the exhaust gas recirculation (EGR) valve and connecting pipe from the exhaust manifold as described in Chapter 4C.

9 Undo the eight exhaust manifold retaining nuts and recover the spacers from the studs **(see illustrations)**.

10 Undo the nut and bolt securing the base of the turbocharger to the support bracket on the cylinder block.

11 Withdraw the turbocharger and exhaust manifold off the mounting studs and remove the assembly from the engine. Recover the manifold gasket **(see illustrations)**.

15.5 Unscrew the turbocharger oil feed pipe union nut

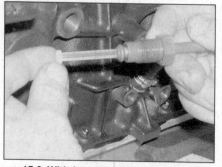

15.6 Withdraw the oil feed pipe and remove the filter

15.7a Undo the oil return pipe flange securing bolts (arrowed) . . .

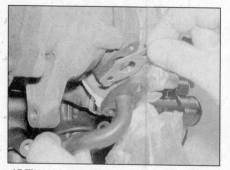

15.7b . . . separate the flange and recover the gasket

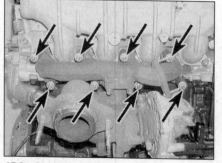

15.9a Undo the exhaust manifold retaining nuts (arrowed)

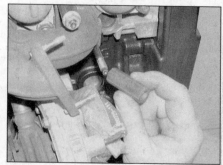

15.9b . . . and recover the spacers from the studs

Refitting

12 Refitting is a reverse of the removal procedure, bearing in mind the following points:

a) *Ensure that the manifold and cylinder head mating faces are clean, with all traces of old gasket removed.*

b) *Use new gaskets when refitting the manifold to the cylinder head and the oil return pipe flange to the turbocharger.*

c) *Tighten the exhaust manifold retaining nuts to the specified torque.*

d) *Refit the EGR valve and connecting pipe as described in Chapter 4C.*

e) *Refit the turbocharger rear inlet and outlet ducts as described in Section 4.*

f) *If the engine is in the car, refit the catalytic converter as described in Section 18.*

g) *Refit the engine/transmission unit or the front suspension subframe with reference to Chapter 2E or 10 as applicable.*

16 Turbocharger –
description and precautions

Description

1 The turbocharger increases engine efficiency by raising the pressure in the inlet manifold above atmospheric pressure. Instead of the air simply being sucked into the cylinders, it is forced in.

2 Energy for the operation of the turbocharger comes from the exhaust gas. The gas flows through a specially-shaped housing (the turbine housing) and, in so doing, spins the turbine wheel. The turbine wheel is attached to a shaft, at the end of which is another vaned wheel known as the compressor wheel. The compressor wheel spins in its own housing, and compresses the inlet air on the way to the inlet manifold.

3 Boost pressure (the pressure in the inlet manifold) is limited by a wastegate, which diverts the exhaust gas away from the turbine wheel in response to a pressure-sensitive actuator.

4 The turbo shaft is pressure-lubricated by an oil feed pipe from the main oil gallery. The shaft 'floats' on a cushion of oil. A drain pipe returns the oil to the sump.

Precautions

5 The turbocharger operates at extremely high speeds and temperatures. Certain precautions must be observed, to avoid premature failure of the turbo, or injury to the operator.

6 Do not operate the turbo with any of its parts exposed, or with any of its hoses removed. Foreign objects falling onto the rotating vanes could cause excessive damage, and (if ejected) personal injury.

7 Do not race the engine immediately after start-up, especially if it is cold. Give the oil a few seconds to circulate.

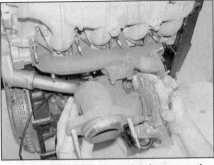

15.11a Withdraw the turbocharger and exhaust manifold off the mounting studs . . .

8 Always allow the engine to return to idle speed before switching it off – do not blip the throttle and switch off, as this will leave the turbo spinning without lubrication.

9 Allow the engine to idle for several minutes before switching off after a high-speed run.

10 Observe the recommended intervals for oil and filter changing, and use a reputable oil of the specified quality. Neglect of oil changing, or use of inferior oil, can cause carbon formation on the turbo shaft, leading to subsequent failure.

17 Turbocharger –
removal, inspection and refitting

Removal

1 Remove the exhaust manifold as described in Section 15. The turbocharger and exhaust manifold are removed from the engine as a complete assembly. The turbocharger can then be separated from the manifold on the bench as follows.

2 Undo the four bolts securing the exhaust outlet elbow to the turbocharger body and separate the elbow from the turbocharger **(see illustration)**.

3 Undo the three retaining nuts and lift the turbocharger off the manifold studs **(see illustration)**.

Inspection

4 With the turbocharger removed, inspect the housing for cracks or other visible damage.

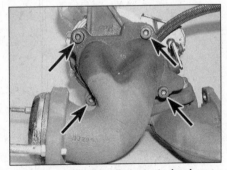

17.2 Exhaust outlet elbow-to-turbocharger retaining bolts (arrowed)

15.11b . . . and recover the gasket

5 Spin the turbine or the compressor wheel, to verify that the shaft is intact and to feel for excessive shake or roughness. Some play is normal, since in use, the shaft is 'floating' on a film of oil. Check that the wheel vanes are undamaged.

6 If oil contamination of the exhaust or induction passages is apparent, it is likely that turbo shaft oil seals have failed.

7 No DIY repair of the turbo is possible and none of the internal or external parts are available separately. If the turbocharger is suspect in any way a complete new unit must be obtained.

Refitting

8 Refitting is a reverse of the removal procedure, bearing in mind the following points:

a) *If a new turbocharger is being fitted, change the engine oil and filter. Also renew the filter in the oil feed pipe.*

b) *Prime the turbocharger by injecting clean engine oil through the oil feed pipe union before reconnecting the union.*

18 Exhaust system –
general information and component renewal

General information

1 The exhaust system consists of three sections comprising a front pipe with catalytic converter, an intermediate pipe, and a tailpipe.

17.3 Turbocharger-to-exhaust manifold retaining nuts (arrowed)

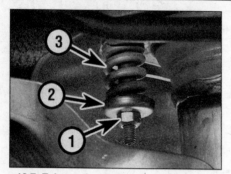

18.7 Exhaust front pipe-to-turbocharger securing nut (1), spring seat (2) and spring (3)

2 The front pipe-to-manifold joint is of the spring-loaded ball type, to allow for movement in the exhaust system, and the other joints are secured by clamping rings.
3 The system is suspended throughout its entire length by rubber mountings.

Removal

4 Each exhaust section can be removed individually, or alternatively, the complete system can be removed as a unit. Even if only one part of the system needs attention, it is often easier to remove the whole system and separate the sections on the bench.
5 To remove the system or part of the system, first jack up the front or rear of the car, and support it on axle stands (see *Jacking and vehicle support*). Alternatively, position the car over an inspection pit, or on car ramps.

Front pipe/catalytic converter

6 Slacken the clamping ring nut and bolt, and disengage the clamp from the intermediate pipe flange joint.
7 Slacken and remove the two nuts securing the front pipe to the turbocharger, and recover the spring cups and springs **(see illustration)**. Withdraw the bolts and remove the front pipe and catalytic converter from underneath the vehicle. Recover the wire-mesh gasket from the manifold joint.

Intermediate pipe

8 Slacken the clamping ring nuts and bolts, and disengage both clamps from the flange joints.
9 Release the pipe from its mounting rubber and remove it from underneath the vehicle.

Tailpipe

10 Slacken the tailpipe clamping ring nut and bolt, and disengage the clamp from the flange joint.
11 Unhook the tailpipe from its mounting rubbers, and remove it from the vehicle.

Complete system

12 Slacken and remove the two nuts securing the front pipe flange joint to the manifold, and recover the spring cups and springs. Remove the bolts, then free the system from its mounting rubbers and remove it from underneath the vehicle. Recover the wire-mesh gasket from the manifold joint.

Heat shield(s)

13 The heat shields are secured to the underside of the body by various nuts and bolts. Each shield can be removed once the relevant exhaust section has been removed. If a shield is being removed to gain access to a component located behind it, it may prove sufficient in some cases to remove the retaining nuts and/or bolts, and simply lower the shield, without disturbing the exhaust system.

Refitting

14 Each section is refitted by reversing the removal sequence, noting the following points:
a) Ensure that all traces of corrosion have been removed from the flanges, and renew all necessary gaskets.
b) Inspect the rubber mountings for signs of damage or deterioration, and renew as necessary.
c) Prior to assembling the spring-loaded joint, a smear of high-temperature grease should be applied to the joint mating surfaces.
d) On joints secured together by a clamping ring, apply a smear of exhaust system jointing paste to the flange joint, to ensure a gas-tight seal.
e) Prior to tightening the exhaust system fasteners, ensure that all rubber mountings are correctly located, and that there is adequate clearance between the exhaust system and vehicle underbody.

Chapter 4 Part C:
Emission control systems

Contents

Degrees of difficulty

Easy, suitable for novice with little experience	**Fairly easy,** suitable for beginner with some experience	**Fairly difficult,** suitable for competent DIY mechanic	**Difficult,** suitable for experienced DIY mechanic	**Very difficult,** suitable for expert DIY or professional

---

1 General information
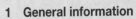

All petrol engines use unleaded petrol and have various other features built into the fuel system to help minimise harmful emissions. In addition, all engines are equipped with the crankcase emission control system described below, and are also equipped with a catalytic converter and an evaporative emission control system. 1.8 litre petrol engines also utilise a secondary air injection system to quickly bring the catalytic converter up to normal working temperature and are equipped with an exhaust gas recirculation (EGR) system.

The diesel engines are also designed to meet the strict emission requirements and are equipped with a crankcase emission control system and a catalytic converter. To further reduce exhaust emissions, diesel engines are also fitted with an exhaust gas recirculation (EGR) system.

The emission control systems function as follows.

Petrol engines

Crankcase emission control

To reduce the emission of unburned hydrocarbons from the crankcase into the atmosphere, the engine is sealed and the blow-by gases and oil vapour are drawn from inside the crankcase, through an oil separator, into the inlet tract to be burned by the engine during normal combustion.

Under all conditions the gases are forced out of the crankcase by the (relatively) higher crankcase pressure; if the engine is worn, the raised crankcase pressure (due to increased blow-by) will cause more of the flow to return under all manifold conditions.

Exhaust emission control

To minimise the amount of pollutants which escape into the atmosphere, all models are fitted with a catalytic converter in the exhaust system. The system is of the closed-loop type, in which one or two lambda sensors in the exhaust system provide the engine management ECU with constant feedback, enabling the ECU to adjust the air/fuel mixture ratio to provide the best possible conditions for the converter to operate.

The lambda sensor has a heating element built-in that is controlled by the ECU to quickly bring the sensor's tip to an efficient operating temperature. The sensor's tip is sensitive to oxygen and sends the ECU a varying voltage depending on the amount of oxygen in the exhaust gases; if the intake air/fuel mixture is too rich, the exhaust gases are low in oxygen so the sensor sends a low-voltage signal, the voltage rising as the mixture weakens and the amount of oxygen rises in the exhaust gases. Peak conversion efficiency of all major pollutants occurs if the intake air/fuel mixture is maintained at the chemically-correct ratio for the complete combustion of petrol of 14.7 parts (by weight) of air to 1 part of fuel (the 'stoichiometric' ratio). The sensor output voltage alters in a large step at this point, the ECU using the signal change as a reference point and correcting the intake air/fuel mixture accordingly by altering the fuel injector pulse width.

On early 1.6 litre engines, a single lambda sensor is used, located upstream of the catalytic converter. On later 1.6 litre engines, and all 1.8 litre engines, two lambda sensors are used, one upstream, and one downstream of the catalytic converter.

Evaporative emission control

To minimise the escape into the atmosphere of unburned hydrocarbons, an evaporative emission control system is fitted to all models. The fuel tank filler cap is sealed and a charcoal canister is mounted underneath the right-hand front wing to collect the petrol vapours generated in the tank when the car is parked. It stores them until they can be cleared from the canister (under the control of the engine management ECU) via the purge valve into the inlet tract to be burned by the engine during normal combustion.

To ensure that the engine runs correctly when it is cold and/or idling and to protect the catalytic converter from the effects of an over-rich mixture, the purge control valve(s) is/are not opened by the ECU until the engine has warmed-up, and the engine is under load; the valve solenoid is then modulated on and off to allow the stored vapour to pass into the inlet tract.

Secondary air injection

Note: *The secondary air injection system described below is also fitted to certain later 1.6 litre engines, however, no information on the system layout was available at the time of writing.*

1.8 litre engines are also equipped with a secondary air injection system. This system is designed to reduce exhaust emissions in the period between first starting the engine, and until the catalytic converter reaches operating (functioning) temperature. Introduction of air into the exhaust system during the initial start-up period, creates an 'afterburner' effect which quickly increases the temperature in the exhaust system front pipe, thus bringing the catalytic converter up to normal operating temperatures very quickly.

The system consists of an air pump, mounted under the front left-hand wheelarch, an air injection valve, mounted on the left-hand end of the cylinder head, and an interconnecting air hose.

The system operates for between 10 and 80 seconds after engine start-up, dependant on coolant temperature.

Exhaust gas recirculation system

An exhaust gas recirculation system is fitted to 1.8 litre engines. The system is designed to recirculate small quantities of exhaust gas into the inlet tract, and therefore into the combustion process. This process reduces the level of oxides of nitrogen present in the final exhaust gas which is released into the atmosphere.

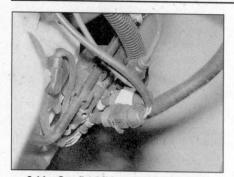

2.14a On all 1.6 litre petrol engines the lambda sensor wiring connectors are clipped onto the front of the transmission . . .

The volume of exhaust gas recirculated is controlled by vacuum supplied from the brake servo unit, via a solenoid valve.

A vacuum-operated valve located on the cylinder head is used to regulate the quantity of exhaust gas recirculated. The valve is operated by the vacuum supplied via the solenoid valve.

The system is controlled by the engine management ECU, which receives information on coolant temperature, engine load, and engine speed, via the coolant temperature sensor, throttle position sensor and crankshaft speed/position sensor respectively.

Diesel engines

Crankcase emission control

To reduce the emission of unburned hydrocarbons from the crankcase into the atmosphere, the engine is sealed and the blow-by gases and oil vapour are drawn from inside the crankcase, through a wire mesh oil separator, into the inlet tract to be burned by the engine during normal combustion.

Under all conditions the gases are forced out of the crankcase by the (relatively) higher crankcase pressure; if the engine is worn, the raised crankcase pressure (due to increased blow-by) will cause more of the flow to return under all manifold conditions.

Exhaust emission control

To minimise the level of exhaust pollutants released into the atmosphere, a catalytic converter is fitted in the exhaust system.

2.14b . . . and on later engines, also clipped to the side of the coolant outlet housing

The catalytic converter consists of a canister containing a fine mesh impregnated with a catalyst material, over which the hot exhaust gases pass. The catalyst speeds up the oxidation of harmful carbon monoxide, unburnt hydrocarbons and soot, effectively reducing the quantity of harmful products released into the atmosphere via the exhaust gases.

Exhaust gas recirculation system

This system is designed to recirculate small quantities of exhaust gas into the inlet tract, and therefore into the combustion process. This process reduces the level of oxides of nitrogen present in the final exhaust gas which is released into the atmosphere.

The volume of exhaust gas recirculated is controlled by vacuum supplied from the brake servo vacuum pump, via a solenoid valve controlled by the preheating system, in conjunction with the engine management ECU.

A vacuum-operated valve is fitted to the exhaust manifold, to regulate the quantity of exhaust gas recirculated. The valve is operated by the vacuum supplied via the solenoid valve.

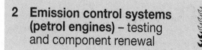

2   Emission control systems (petrol engines) – testing and component renewal

Crankcase emission control

1 The components of this system require no attention other than to check that the hose(s) are clear and undamaged at regular intervals.

Evaporative emission control

Testing

2 If the system is thought to be faulty, disconnect the hoses from the charcoal canister and purge control valve and check that they are clear by blowing through them. If the purge control valve(s) or charcoal canister are thought to be faulty, they must be renewed.

Charcoal canister renewal

3 The charcoal canister is located behind the right-hand front wing. To gain access to the canister, firmly apply the handbrake, then jack up the front of the car and support it securely on axle stands (see Jacking and vehicle support). The wheelarch plastic liner must now be removed. The liner is secured by screws and stud-type plastic clips along its upper and front edges. The clips can be removed using a forked type tool, or alternatively, with a large screwdriver (although there is a risk of breakage if the screwdriver method is used). Extract all the clips, then remove the liner centre section and front section from under the front wing. Note how the two sections overlap as you do this to aid refitting.

4 Slacken and remove the retaining bolt then free the canister from its mounting clamp and lower it out from underneath the wing. Mark the hoses for identification purposes.

5 Slacken the retaining clips then disconnect both hoses and remove the canister from the vehicle. Where the crimped-type hose clips are fitted, cut the clips and discard them, replace them with standard worm-drive hose clips on refitting. Where the hoses are equipped with quick-release fittings depress the centre collar of the fitting with a small flat-bladed screwdriver then detach the hose from the canister.

6 Refitting is a reverse of the removal procedure ensuring the hoses are correctly reconnected.

Purge valve(s) renewal

7 The purge valve is located on the right-hand side of the engine compartment below the washer reservoir filler neck.

8 Disconnect the battery negative terminal (refer to Disconnecting the battery in the Reference Chapter).

9 Depress the retaining clip and disconnect the wiring connector from the valve. Disconnect the hoses from either end of the valve then release the valve from its retaining clip or strap and remove it from the engine compartment, noting which way around it is fitted.

10 Refitting is a reversal of the removal procedure, ensuring the valve is fitted the correct way around and the hoses are securely connected.

Exhaust emission control

Testing

11 The performance of the catalytic converter can only be checked by measuring the exhaust gases using a good-quality, carefully-calibrated exhaust gas analyser. If access to such equipment can be gained, it should be connected and used according with the maker's instructions.

12 If the CO level at the tailpipe is too high, the vehicle should be taken to a Citroën dealer so that the complete engine management system can be thoroughly checked using the special diagnostic equipment. Once these have been checked and are known to be free from faults, the fault must be in the catalytic converter, which must be renewed.

Catalytic converter renewal

13 Refer to Chapter 4A, Section 16.

Lambda sensor(s) renewal

Note 1: *The lambda sensor is delicate and will not work if it is dropped or knocked, if its power supply is disrupted, or if any cleaning materials are used on it.*

Note 2: *Later 1.6 litre engines and all 1.8 litre engines are fitted with a 'downstream' lambda sensor located after the catalytic converter. Removal and refitting procedures are the same for both sensors.*

14 Trace the wiring back from the relevant lambda sensor, located in the exhaust manifold, or exhaust front pipe. Disconnect the wiring connectors and free the wiring from any relevant retaining clips or ties **(see illustrations)**.

15 Unscrew the sensor from its location and remove it, along with its sealing washer (**see illustrations**).

16 Refitting is a reverse of the removal procedure, using a new sealing washer. Prior to installing the sensor apply a smear of high temperature grease to the sensor threads. Ensure the sensor is securely tightened and that the wiring is correctly routed and in no danger of contacting either the exhaust system or engine.

Secondary air injection

Testing

17 The components of this system require no attention other than to check that the hose(s) and air pump air intake filter are clear and undamaged at periodic intervals.

18 Accurate testing of the system operation entails the use of diagnostic test equipment and should be entrusted to a Citroën dealer.

Air pump air intake filter cleaning

19 The air intake filter is contained in the air pump housing which is located under the left-hand side wheelarch.

20 Disconnect the battery negative terminal (refer to *Disconnecting the battery* in the Reference Chapter).

21 Remove the front bumper as described in Chapter 11. Remove the air cleaner assembly as described in Chapter 4A.

22 Disconnect the pump motor wiring connector then detach the air hose from the base of the pump (**see illustrations**).

23 Undo the nut securing the pump lower support bracket to the body (**see illustration**).

24 From within the engine compartment, slacken the two upper mounting nuts located on the body panel beneath the air cleaner location (**see illustration**).

25 From under the wheelarch, slide the unit rearwards to disengage the mounting nuts from their elongated slots, then remove the pump assembly from under the wing (**see illustration**).

26 Undo the central retaining bolt and lift off the pump housing cover (**see illustration**).

27 The air filter can now be withdrawn from the cover (**see illustration**). Wash the filter thoroughly and allow it to dry completely.

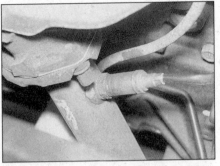

2.15a On early 1.6 litre engines the sensor is screwed into the top of the exhaust front pipe

2.15b On later 1.6 litre engines the upstream sensor is screwed into the exhaust manifold (shown with heat shield removed) . . .

2.15c . . . and the downstream sensor is screwed into the exhaust front pipe

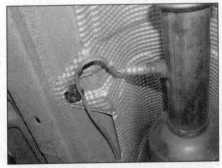

2.15d On 1.8 litre engines, the sensors are located either side of the catalytic converter (downstream sensor shown)

28 Refit the filter and pump housing cover, then refit the air pump assembly using a reverse of the removal procedure.

29 Refit the front bumper as described in Chapter 11, and the air cleaner as described in Chapter 4A.

2.22a Disconnect the air pump motor wiring connector . . .

2.22b . . . then detach the air hose from the base of the pump

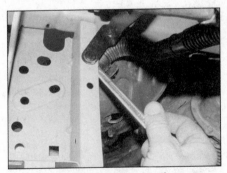

2.23 Undo the nut securing the pump lower support bracket to the body

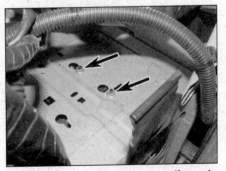

2.24 Slacken the two upper mounting nuts (arrowed) . . .

2.25 . . . then slide the unit rearwards to disengage the mounting nuts

2.26 Undo the retaining bolt and lift off the pump housing cover

2.27 The air filter can now be withdrawn from the cover

Air pump renewal

30 Proceed as described in paragraphs 20 to 25.

31 With the pump assembly removed, undo the three retaining nuts and remove the air pump from the mounting bracket.

32 Refitting is the reverse of the removal procedure.

33 With the pump assembly installed, refit the front bumper as described in Chapter 11, and the air cleaner as described in Chapter 4A.

Air injection valve renewal

34 Disconnect the battery negative terminal (refer to *Disconnecting the battery* in the Reference Section of this manual).

35 Undo the six screws and lift off the engine cover.

36 Disconnect the air inlet hose quick-release connector from the air injection valve at the left-hand end of the cylinder head **(see illustration)**.

37 Undo the two retaining bolts and carefully withdraw the valve from the cylinder head **(see illustration)**. Try not to damage the gasket as the valve is removed, otherwise it will be necessary to remove the coolant outlet housing to renew the gasket (see Chapter 3).

38 Refitting is the reverse of the removal procedure.

Exhaust gas recirculation

Testing

39 Testing of the system should be entrusted to a Citroën dealer.

EGR valve renewal

40 Disconnect the battery negative terminal (refer to *Disconnecting the battery* in the Reference Section of this manual).

41 Undo the six screws and lift off the engine cover.

42 Disconnect the wiring connector from the

EGR valve located on the coolant outlet housing at the left-hand end of the cylinder head.

43 Undo the two bolts and withdraw the valve from the housing **(see illustration)**. Remove the gasket and obtain a new gasket for refitting.

44 Clean all traces of old gasket from the mating faces of the EGR valve and coolant outlet housing.

45 Locate a new gasket in position with the word TOP uppermost **(see illustration)**.

46 Fit the valve and the retaining bolts and tighten the bolts securely.

47 Reconnect the wiring connector, refit the engine cover and reconnect the battery.

---

3 Emission control systems (diesel engines) – testing and component renewal

Crankcase emission control

1 The components of this system require no attention other than to check that the hose(s) are clear and undamaged at regular intervals.

Exhaust emission control

Testing

2 The performance of the catalytic converter can only be checked by measuring the exhaust gases using a good-quality, carefully-calibrated exhaust gas analyser. If access to such equipment can be gained, it should be connected and used according with the maker's instructions.

3 If the exhaust emissions are excessive, before assuming the catalytic converter is faulty, it is worth checking the problem is not due to a faulty injector(s), or other diesel fuel system fault. Refer to your Citroën dealer for further information.

Catalytic converter renewal

4 Refer to Chapter 4B, Section 18.

Exhaust gas recirculation

Testing

5 Testing of the system should be entrusted to a Citroën dealer.

EGR valve renewal

Note 1: *There is insufficient clearance to gain access to all the relevant EGR valve attachments from either above or below with the engine in the car. Two alternatives are possible; either remove the complete engine/transmission unit from the car as described in Chapter 2E, or remove the front suspension subframe as described in Chapter 10. Both are involved operations and the course of action taken is largely dependent on the tools, equipment, skill and patience available.*

Note 2: *On certain early engines the EGR pipe incorporated a heat exchanger. If this arrangement is encountered, the procedures*

2.36 Disconnect the air inlet hose from the secondary air injection valve

2.37 Undo the two bolts and carefully withdraw the air injection valve from the cylinder head

2.43 Undo the two bolts and withdraw the EGR valve from the coolant outlet housing

2.45 Locate a new EGR valve gasket in position with the word TOP uppermost

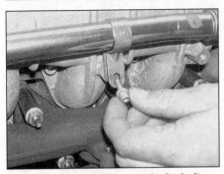

3.6 On diesel engines, undo the bolts securing the EGR pipe support clips to the inlet manifold . . .

3.7 . . . and the two nuts securing the EGR valve to the exhaust manifold

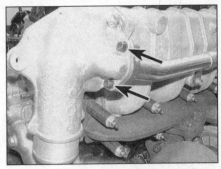

3.8a Undo the two bolts (arrowed) securing the EGR pipe to the inlet manifold elbow . . .

are the same as described below, but it will be necessary to drain the cooling system as described in Chapter 1B if the engine is in the car. Disconnect the coolant hoses at the heat exchanger after draining.

6 Undo the bolts securing the EGR pipe support clips to the inlet manifold **(see illustration)**.

7 Disconnect the vacuum hose, then undo the two nuts securing the EGR valve to the exhaust manifold **(see illustration)**.

8 Undo the two bolts securing the EGR pipe to the inlet manifold elbow. Withdraw the EGR valve and pipe assembly from the manifold and recover the gasket at the EGR pipe-to-inlet manifold flange **(see illustrations)**.

9 To separate the EGR pipe from the valve, remove the clip securing the upper flexible portion of the pipe to the valve. If the original crimped clip is still in place, cut it off; new clips are supplied by Citroën parts stockists with a screw clamp fixing. If a screw clamp type clip is fitted, undo the screw and manipulate the clip off the pipe.

10 Refitting is a reverse of the removal procedure, bearing in mind the following points:

a) Ensure that the EGR valve and exhaust manifold mating faces are clean.

b) Secure the EGR pipe with new screw clamp type clips, if crimped type clips were initially fitted.

c) Refit the engine/transmission unit or the front suspension subframe as described in Chapter 2E or 10, as applicable.

EGR solenoid valve renewal

11 The EGR solenoid valve is located in the right-hand rear corner of the engine compartment **(see illustration)**.

12 To remove the EGR solenoid valve, disconnect the two vacuum hoses and the wiring connector. Undo the mounting bracket nuts and remove the valve from the engine compartment.

13 Refitting is a reverse of the removal procedure.

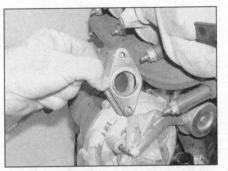

3.8b . . . then withdraw the valve and pipe assembly and recover the gasket at the EGR pipe flange

4 Catalytic converter –
general information
and precautions

1 The catalytic converter is a reliable and simple device which needs no maintenance in itself, but there are some facts of which an owner should be aware if the converter is to function properly for its full service life.

Petrol engines

a) DO NOT use leaded or lead replacement petrol (LRP) in a car equipped with a catalytic converter – the lead will coat the precious metals, reducing their converting efficiency and will eventually destroy the converter.

b) Always keep the ignition and fuel systems well-maintained in accordance with the manufacturer's schedule.

c) If the engine develops a misfire, do not drive the car at all (or at least as little as possible) until the fault is cured.

d) DO NOT push- or tow-start the car – this will soak the catalytic converter in unburned fuel, causing it to overheat when the engine does start.

e) DO NOT switch off the ignition at high engine speeds.

3.11 EGR solenoid valve location (arrowed)

f) DO NOT use fuel or engine oil additives – these may contain substances harmful to the catalytic converter.

g) DO NOT continue to use the car if the engine burns oil to the extent of leaving a visible trail of blue smoke.

h) Remember that the catalytic converter operates at very high temperatures. DO NOT, therefore, park the car in dry undergrowth, over long grass or piles of dead leaves after a long run.

i) Remember that the catalytic converter is FRAGILE – do not strike it with tools during servicing work.

j) In some cases a sulphurous smell (like that of rotten eggs) may be noticed from the exhaust. This is common to many catalytic converter-equipped cars and once the car has covered a few thousand miles the problem should disappear.

k) The catalytic converter, used on a well-maintained and well-driven car, should last for between 50 000 and 100 000 miles – if the converter is no longer effective it must be renewed.

Diesel engines

2 Refer to parts f, g, h and i of the petrol engine information given above.

Chapter 5 Part A:
Starting and charging systems

Contents

Degrees of difficulty

Easy, suitable for novice with little experience

Fairly easy, suitable for beginner with some experience

Fairly difficult, suitable for competent DIY mechanic

Difficult, suitable for experienced DIY mechanic

Very difficult, suitable for expert DIY or professional

Specifications

System type .... 12 volt, negative earth

Battery
Charge condition:
Poor .... 12.5 volts
Normal .... 12.6 volts
Good .... 12.7 volts

Alternator
Type .... Valeo or Bosch (depending on model)

Starter motor
Type .... Valeo or Bosch (depending on model)

---

1 General information and precautions

General information

The engine electrical system consists mainly of the charging and starting systems. Because of their engine-related functions, these components are covered separately from the body electrical devices such as the lights, instruments, etc (which are covered in Chapter 12). On petrol models refer to Part B for information on the ignition system, and on diesel models refer to Part C for information on the preheating system.

The electrical system is of the 12 volt negative earth type.

The battery is of the 'maintenance-free' (sealed for life) type and is charged by the alternator, which is belt-driven from the crankshaft pulley.

The starter motor is of the pre-engaged type incorporating an integral solenoid. On starting, the solenoid moves the drive pinion into engagement with the flywheel ring gear before the starter motor is energised. Once the engine has started, a one-way clutch prevents the motor armature being driven by the engine until the pinion disengages from the flywheel.

Precautions

Further details of the various systems are given in the relevant Sections of this Chapter. While some repair procedures are given, the usual course of action is to renew the component concerned. The owner whose interest extends beyond mere component renewal should obtain a copy of the *Automobile Electrical & Electronic Systems Manual*, available from the publishers of this manual.

It is necessary to take extra care when working on the electrical system to avoid damage to the various system electronic control units, and to avoid the risk of personal injury. In addition to the precautions given in *Safety first!* at the beginning of this manual, observe the following when working on the system:

Always remove rings, watches, etc, before working on the electrical system.

Even with the battery disconnected, capacitive discharge could occur if a component's live terminal is earthed through a metal object. This could cause a shock or nasty burn.

Do not reverse the battery connections. Components such as the alternator, electronic control units, or any other components having semi-conductor circuitry could be irreparably damaged.

If the engine is being started using jump leads and a slave battery, connect the batteries positive-to-positive and negative-to-negative (see 'Jump starting'). This also applies when connecting a battery charger.

Never disconnect the battery terminals, the alternator, any electrical wiring or any test instruments when the engine is running.

Do not allow the engine to turn the alternator when the alternator is not connected.

Never 'test' for alternator output by 'flashing' the output lead to earth.

Never use an ohmmeter of the type incorporating a hand-cranked generator for circuit or continuity testing.

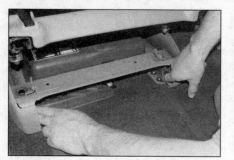

4.1 Move the front seat fully rearward then depress the locking catches located at the rear of the seat on each side

4.2 Tip the seat forward, release the locking clip on the top of the battery cover and lift off the cover

Always ensure that the battery negative terminal is disconnected when working on the electrical system.

Before using electric-arc welding equipment on the car, disconnect the battery, alternator and components such as the engine management and the ABS electronic control units to protect them from the risk of damage.

Several systems fitted to the vehicle require battery power to be available at all times, either to ensure their continued operation (such as the clock) or to maintain control unit memories or security codes which would be wiped if the battery were to be disconnected. To ensure that there are no unforeseen consequences of this action, Refer to 'Disconnecting the battery' in the Reference Chapter of this manual for further information.

2 Electrical fault finding – general information

Refer to Chapter 12.

3 Battery – testing and charging

Testing

1 With the 'sealed for life' maintenance-free battery fitted as original equipment, topping-

4.3 Battery quick-release positive terminal (left) and capped-nut type negative terminal (right)

up and testing of the electrolyte in each cell is not possible. The condition of the battery can therefore only be tested using a battery condition indicator or a voltmeter.

2 Certain models may be fitted with a 'Delco' type maintenance-free battery, with a built-in charge condition indicator. The indicator is located in the top of the battery casing, and indicates the condition of the battery from its colour. If the indicator shows green, then the battery is in a good state of charge. If the indicator turns darker, eventually to black, then the battery requires charging, as described later in this Section. If the indicator shows clear/yellow, then the electrolyte level in the battery is too low to allow further use, and the battery should be renewed.

Caution: Do not attempt to charge, load or jump start a battery when the indicator shows clear/yellow.

3 If testing the battery using a voltmeter, connect the voltmeter across the battery and compare the result with those given in the Specifications under 'charge condition'. The test is only accurate if the battery has not been subjected to any kind of charge for the previous six hours. If this is not the case, switch on the headlights for 30 seconds, then wait four to five minutes before testing the battery after switching off the headlights. All other electrical circuits must be switched off, so check that the doors and tailgate are fully shut when making the test.

4 If the voltage reading is less than 12.2 volts, then the battery is discharged, whilst a reading of 12.2 to 12.4 volts indicates a partially-discharged condition.

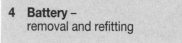

4.5 Battery clamp retaining stud and nut (arrowed)

5 If the battery is to be charged, remove it from the vehicle (see Section 4) and charge it as follows.

Charging

Note: *The following is intended as a guide only. Always refer to the manufacturer's recommendations (often printed on a label attached to the battery) before charging a battery.*

6 The time taken to charge a battery of this type is dependent on the extent of discharge, but it can take anything up to three days.

7 A constant voltage type charger is required, to be set, when connected, to 13.9 to 14.9 volts with a charger current below 25 amps. Using this method, the battery should be usable within three hours, giving a voltage reading of 12.5 volts, but this is for a partially discharged battery and, as mentioned, full charging can take considerably longer.

8 If the battery is to be charged from a fully discharged state (condition reading less than 12.2 volts), have it recharged by your Citroën dealer or local automotive electrician, as the charge rate is higher and constant supervision during charging is necessary.

4 Battery – removal and refitting

Note: *Refer to 'Disconnecting the battery' in the Reference Chapter of this manual before proceeding.*

Removal

1 The battery is located inside the car under the left-hand front seat. To gain access, move the front seat fully rearward then depress the locking catches located at the rear of the seat on each side **(see illustration)**.

2 Tip the seat forward then release the locking clip on the top of the battery cover. Lift off the cover for access to the battery **(see illustration)**.

3 Disconnect the lead at the battery negative (earth) terminal. Two possible types of battery negative terminal fixings may be encountered. With the first type, the lead is secured to a stud on the top of the terminal by means of a green coloured plastic-capped nut **(see illustration)**. On the second type a conventional fitting is used, secured in position by a clamp bolt and nut.

4 Remove the insulation cover (where fitted) and disconnect the positive terminal leads. The positive terminal fixings will either be one of the types described in paragraph 2 (except the plastic-capped nut will be coloured red), or of the quick-release type, whereby lifting the plastic insulation cover automatically releases the terminal clamp.

5 Unscrew the battery clamp rear retaining bolt, located under the seat base. Unscrew the nut on the retaining stud located in front of the battery and lift out the clamp **(see illustration)**.

6 Disconnect the vent hose on the side of the battery and lift the battery out of the engine compartment.

Refitting

7 Refitting is a reversal of removal, but smear petroleum jelly on the terminals when reconnecting the leads, and always reconnect the positive lead first, and the negative lead last. Ensure that the vent hose is reconnected to the battery.

5 Charging system – testing

Note: *Refer to the warnings given in 'Safety first!' and in Section 1 of this Chapter before starting work.*

1 If the ignition warning light fails to illuminate when the ignition is switched on, first check the alternator wiring connections for security. If satisfactory, check that the warning light bulb has not blown, and that the bulbholder is secure in its location in the instrument panel (see Chapter 12). If the light still fails to illuminate, check the continuity of the warning light feed wire from the alternator to the bulbholder. If all is satisfactory, the alternator is at fault and should be renewed or taken to an auto-electrician for testing and repair.

2 If the ignition warning light illuminates when the engine is running, stop the engine and check that the auxiliary drivebelt has not broken (see Chapter 1A or 1B) and that the alternator connections are secure. If all is so far satisfactory, have the alternator checked by an auto-electrician for testing and repair.

3 If the alternator output is suspect even though the warning light works correctly, the regulated voltage may be checked as follows.

4 Connect a voltmeter across the battery terminals and start the engine.

5 Increase the engine speed until the voltmeter reading remains steady; the reading should be approximately 12 to 13 volts, and no more than 14 volts.

6 Switch on as many electrical accessories (eg, the headlights, heated rear window and heater blower) as possible, and check that the alternator maintains the regulated voltage at around 13 to 14 volts.

7.4a Lift off the rubber covers . . .

7 If the regulated voltage is not as stated, the fault may be due to worn brushes, weak brush springs, a faulty voltage regulator, a faulty diode, a severed phase winding or worn or damaged slip rings. The alternator should be renewed or taken to an auto-electrician for testing and repair.

6 Alternator drivebelt – removal, refitting and tensioning

Refer to the procedure given for the auxiliary drivebelt in Chapter 1A or 1B.

7 Alternator – removal and refitting

Removal

1 Disconnect the battery negative terminal (refer to *Disconnecting the battery* in the Reference Chapter).

2 Remove the auxiliary drivebelt as described in Chapter 1A or 1B.

3 On 1.6 litre engine models, undo the retaining bolts and remove the heat shield at the rear of the alternator.

4 Remove the rubber covers from the alternator terminals, then unscrew the retaining nuts and disconnect the wiring from the rear of the alternator **(see illustrations)**.

7.4b . . . then undo the nuts (arrowed) and disconnect the wiring from the alternator

5 Unscrew the bolts securing the alternator to the upper mounting bracket **(see illustration)**. Note the location of any spacers and washers which may be fitted between the alternator and the mounting bracket.

6 Unscrew the alternator lower mounting bolts. Note that, where a long through-bolt is used to secure the alternator in position, the bolt does not need to be fully removed; the alternator can be disengaged from the bolt once it has been slackened sufficiently. On some models, it may be necessary to remove the drivebelt idler pulley to gain access to the alternator mounting bolts (depending on specification). On diesel engine models, the lower front mounting bolt also carries the auxiliary drivebelt idler pulley which can be left in position on the bolt as it is removed **(see illustrations)**.

7 Manoeuvre the alternator away from its mounting brackets and out of the engine bay.

Refitting

8 Refitting is a reversal of removal, tensioning the auxiliary drivebelt with reference to Chapter 1A or 1B, and ensuring that the alternator mountings are securely tightened.

8 Alternator – testing and overhaul

If the alternator is thought to be suspect, it should be removed from the vehicle and taken to an auto-electrician for testing. Most auto-

7.5 Unscrew the bolts securing the alternator to the upper mounting bracket

7.6a Unscrew the alternator lower mounting bolts

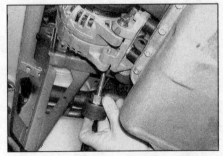

7.6b On diesel engine models, the lower front mounting bolt also carries the auxiliary drivebelt idler pulley

10.5 Unscrew the two nuts (arrowed) and disconnect the wiring from the rear of the starter motor

electricians will be able to supply and fit brushes at a reasonable cost. However, check on the cost of repairs before proceeding as it may prove more economical to obtain a new or exchange alternator.

9 Starting system – testing

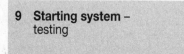

Note: *Refer to the precautions given in 'Safety first!' and in Section 1 of this Chapter before starting work.*

1 If the starter motor fails to operate when the ignition key is turned to the appropriate position, the following possible causes may be to blame.
   a) *The battery is faulty.*
   b) *The electrical connections between the switch, solenoid, battery and starter motor are somewhere failing to pass the necessary current from the battery through the starter to earth.*
   c) *The solenoid is faulty.*
   d) *The starter motor is mechanically or electrically defective.*

2 To check the battery, switch on the headlights. If they dim after a few seconds, this indicates that the battery is discharged – recharge (see Section 3) or renew the battery. If the headlights glow brightly, operate the ignition switch and observe the lights. If they dim, then this indicates that current is

10.7 Removing the starter motor from over the top of the transmission – 1.8 litre petrol engine models

reaching the starter motor, therefore the fault must lie in the starter motor. If the lights continue to glow brightly (and no clicking sound can be heard from the starter motor solenoid), this indicates that there is a fault in the circuit or solenoid – see following paragraphs. If the starter motor turns slowly when operated, but the battery is in good condition, then this shows that either the starter motor is faulty, or there is considerable resistance in the circuit.

3 If a fault in the circuit is suspected, disconnect the battery leads (including the earth connection to the body), the starter/solenoid wiring and the engine/transmission earth strap. Thoroughly clean the connections, and reconnect the leads and wiring, then use a voltmeter or test lamp to check that full battery voltage is available at the battery positive lead connection to the solenoid, and that the earth is sound. Smear petroleum jelly around the battery terminals to prevent corrosion – corroded connections are amongst the most frequent causes of electrical system faults.

4 If the battery and all connections are in good condition, check the circuit by disconnecting the ignition switch feed wire from the solenoid terminal. Connect a voltmeter or test lamp between the wire end and a good earth (such as the battery negative terminal), and check that the wire is live when the ignition switch is turned to the 'start' position. If it is, then the circuit is sound – if not the circuit wiring can be checked as described in Chapter 12.

5 The solenoid contacts can be checked by connecting a voltmeter or test lamp between the battery positive feed connection on the starter side of the solenoid, and earth. When the ignition switch is turned to the 'start' position, there should be a reading or lighted bulb, as applicable. If there is no reading or lighted bulb, the solenoid is faulty and should be renewed.

6 If the circuit and solenoid are proved sound, the fault must lie in the starter motor. In this event, it may be possible to have the starter motor overhauled by a specialist, but check on the cost of spares before proceeding, as it may prove more economical to obtain a new or exchange motor.

10 Starter motor – removal and refitting

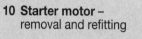

Removal

1 Disconnect the battery negative terminal (refer to *Disconnecting the battery* in the Reference Section of this manual).

2 So that access to the motor can be gained both from above and below, firmly apply the handbrake then jack up the front of the vehicle and support it on axle stands (see

Jacking and vehicle support). Remove the engine undertray.

3 Remove the air cleaner and air inlet ducts as described in Chapter 4A or 4B as necessary for access to the starter motor retaining bolts. It will also be necessary to release and move aside various cables and/or support brackets to provide sufficient clearance for removal.

4 On 1.8 litre petrol engine models, the starter motor is removed through the small gap between the underside of the inlet manifold and the upper edge of the transmission bellhousing. To do this it will be necessary to drain the cooling system as described in Chapter 1A and disconnect the two radiator hoses at the coolant outlet housing and thermostat cover.

5 Slacken and remove the two retaining nuts and disconnect the wiring from the starter motor solenoid. Recover the washers under the nuts **(see illustration)**.

6 Undo the three mounting bolts securing the starter motor to the transmission bellhousing, supporting the motor as the bolts are withdrawn. Recover the washers from under the bolt heads and note the locations of any wiring or hose brackets secured by the bolts.

7 Manoeuvre the starter motor out from underneath the engine, or from over the upper edge of the transmission, as applicable **(see illustration)**. Recover the locating dowel(s) from the starter motor/transmission (as applicable).

Refitting

8 Refitting is a reversal of removal, ensuring that the locating dowel(s) are correctly positioned. Also make sure that any wiring or hose brackets are in place under the bolt heads as noted prior to removal.

9 On 1.8 litre petrol engine models, refill the cooling system as described in Chapter 1A.

11 Starter motor – testing and overhaul

If the starter motor is thought to be suspect, it should be removed from the vehicle and taken to an auto-electrician for testing. Most auto-electricians will be able to supply and fit brushes at a reasonable cost. However, check on the cost of repairs before proceeding as it may prove more economical to obtain a new or exchange motor.

12 Ignition switch – removal and refitting

The ignition switch is integral with the steering column lock, and can be removed as described in Chapter 10.

13 Oil pressure warning light switch – removal and refitting

Removal

1 The switch is located at the front of the cylinder block, above the oil filter mounting, or in the oil filter housing. Note that on some models access to the switch may be improved if the vehicle is jacked up and supported on axle stands so that the switch can be reached from underneath (see *Jacking and vehicle support*). Remove the engine undertray after the vehicle is raised and supported.

2 Disconnect the battery negative terminal (refer to *Disconnecting the battery* in the Reference Chapter).

3 Remove the protective sleeve from the wiring plug (where applicable), then disconnect the wiring from the switch.

4 Unscrew the switch from the cylinder block, and recover the sealing washer. Be prepared for oil spillage, and if the switch is to be left removed from the engine for any length of time, plug the hole in the cylinder block.

Refitting

5 Examine the sealing washer for signs of damage or deterioration and if necessary renew.

6 Refit the switch, complete with washer, and tighten it securely. Reconnect the wiring connector.

7 Refit the engine undertray, lower the vehicle to the ground then check and, if necessary, top-up the engine oil as described in *Weekly checks*.

Notes

Chapter 5 Part B:
Ignition system (petrol engines)

Contents

Degrees of difficulty

Easy, suitable for novice with little experience 🔧	**Fairly easy,** suitable for beginner with some experience 🔧	**Fairly difficult,** suitable for competent DIY mechanic 🔧	**Difficult,** suitable for experienced DIY mechanic 🔧	**Very difficult,** suitable for expert DIY or professional 🔧

Specifications

General

System type	Static (distributorless) ignition system controlled by engine management ECU
Firing order	1-3-4-2 (No 1 cylinder at transmission end)
Spark plugs	See Chapter 1A Specifications
Ignition timing	Controlled by engine management ECU

Torque wrench setting	**Nm**	**lbf ft**
Knock sensor securing bolt	20	15

1 Ignition system – general information

The ignition system is integrated with the fuel injection system to form a combined engine management system under the control of one ECU (see Chapter 4A for further information). The ignition side of the system is of the static (distributorless) type, consisting of the ignition coils and spark plugs. The ignition coils are housed in a single unit mounted directly above the spark plugs. The coils are integral with the spark plug caps and are pushed directly onto the spark plugs, one for each plug. This removes the need for any HT leads connecting the coils to the plugs.

Under the control of the ECU, the ignition coils operate on the 'wasted spark' principle, ie, each spark plug sparks twice for every cycle of the engine, once during the compression stroke and once during the exhaust stroke. The spark voltage is greatest in the cylinder which is under compression; in the cylinder on its exhaust stroke, the compression is low and this produces a very weak spark which has no effect on the exhaust gases.

The ECU uses its inputs from the various sensors to calculate the required ignition advance setting and coil charging time, depending on engine temperature, load and speed. At idle speeds, the ECU varies the ignition timing to alter the torque characteristic of the engine, enabling the idle speed to be controlled. This system operates in conjunction with the idle speed stepper motor – see Chapter 4A for additional details.

A knock sensor is also incorporated into the ignition system. Mounted onto the cylinder block, the sensor detects the high-frequency vibrations caused when the engine starts to pre-ignite, or 'pink'. Under these conditions, the knock sensor sends an electrical signal to the ECU which in turn retards the ignition advance setting in small steps until the 'pinking' ceases.

2 Ignition system – testing

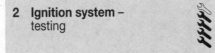

Warning: Voltages produced by an electronic ignition system are considerably higher than those produced by conventional ignition systems. Extreme care must be taken when working on the system with the ignition switched on. Persons with surgically-implanted cardiac pacemaker devices should keep well clear of the ignition circuits, components and test equipment.

If a fault appears in the engine management (fuel injection/ignition) system, first ensure that the fault is not due to a poor electrical connection or poor maintenance; ie, check that the air cleaner filter element is clean, the spark plugs are in good condition and correctly gapped, that the engine breather hoses are clear and undamaged, referring to Chapter 1A for further information. Also check that the accelerator cable is correctly adjusted as described in Chapter 4A. If the engine is running very roughly, check the compression pressures and the valve clearances as described in Chapter 2A or 2B, where applicable.

If these checks fail to reveal the cause of the problem the vehicle should be taken to a suitably-equipped Citroën dealer for testing. A wiring block diagnostic connector is incorporated in the engine management circuit into which a special electronic diagnostic tester can be plugged. The tester will locate the fault quickly and simply alleviating the need to test all the system components individually which is a time-consuming operation that carries a high risk of damaging the ECU.

The only ignition system checks which can be carried out by the home mechanic are those described in Chapter 1A relating to the spark plugs.

3.2a Disconnect the engine breather hose at the quick-release connections on the air cleaner air inlet duct . . .

3.2b . . . cylinder head cover . . .

3.2c . . . and inlet manifold

3.3 Unplug the wiring connector from the top of the ignition coil unit

3 Ignition coil unit –
removal, testing and refitting

Removal

1.6 litre engines

1 Disconnect the battery negative terminal (refer to *Disconnecting the battery* in the Reference Chapter).
2 Disconnect the engine breather hose at the quick-release connections on the air cleaner air inlet duct, cylinder head cover and inlet manifold **(see illustrations)**. Move the hose to one side.
3 Unplug the wiring connector from the top of the ignition coil unit **(see illustration)**.
4 Where applicable, unscrew the securing nut and remove radio suppresser from the right-

3.5 Remove the securing nuts and studs at each end of the ignition coil unit

hand end of the coil unit, together with its mounting bracket.
5 Undo the nut securing each end of the ignition coil unit to the mounting studs **(see illustration)**. Note that it is quite likely that the stud will be released with the nut.
6 Lift the ignition coil unit upwards off the mounting studs and at the same time carefully ease the HT extension pillars away from the tops of the spark plugs. Lift the unit off the plugs and withdraw it from the engine **(see illustration)**.

1.8 litre engines

7 Disconnect the battery negative terminal (refer to *Disconnecting the battery* in the Reference Chapter).
8 Undo the six screws and lift off the engine cover.
9 Disconnect the wiring connector at the left-hand end of the ignition coil unit. Undo the

3.6 Lift the ignition coil unit off the spark plugs

three retaining bolts and lift the coil unit upwards, off the spark plugs and from its location between the cylinder head covers.

Testing

10 The circuitry arrangement of the ignition coil unit on these engines is such that testing of an individual coil in isolation from the remainder of the engine management system is unlikely to prove effective in diagnosing a particular fault. Should there be any reason to suspect a faulty individual coil, the engine management system should be tested by a Citroën dealer using diagnostic test equipment (see Section 2).

Refitting

11 Refitting is a reversal of the relevant removal procedure ensuring the wiring connectors are securely reconnected.

4 Ignition timing –
checking and adjustment

1 There are no timing marks on the flywheel or crankshaft pulley. The timing is constantly being monitored and adjusted by the engine management ECU, and nominal values cannot be given. Therefore, it is not possible for the home mechanic to check the ignition timing.
2 The only way in which the ignition timing can be checked is using special electronic test equipment, connected to the engine management system diagnostic connector (refer to Chapter 4A for further information).

5 Knock sensor –
removal and refitting

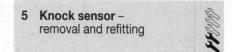

Removal

1 On 1.6 litre engines, the knock sensor is screwed into the rear face of the cylinder block, and on 1.8 litre engines, into the front face.
2 Disconnect the battery negative terminal (refer to *Disconnecting the battery* in the Reference Section of this manual).
3 Firmly apply the handbrake, then jack up the front of the vehicle and support it securely on axle stands (see *Jacking and vehicle support*). Remove the engine undertray.
4 Trace the wiring back from the sensor to its wiring connector, and disconnect it from the main loom.
5 Undo the sensor securing bolt and remove the sensor from the cylinder block.

Refitting

6 Refitting is a reversal of the removal procedure, ensuring that the sensor securing bolt is tightened to the specified torque.

Chapter 5 Part C:
Preheating system (diesel engines)

Contents

Degrees of difficulty

Easy, suitable for novice with little experience	Fairly easy, suitable for beginner with some experience	Fairly difficult, suitable for competent DIY mechanic	Difficult, suitable for experienced DIY mechanic	Very difficult, suitable for expert DIY or professional

Specifications

Glow plugs
Resistance (typical) . . . . Less than 1 ohm
Type . . . . See Chapter 1B Specifications

Torque wrench setting	Nm	lbf ft
Glow plugs	22	16

1 Preheating system – description and testing

Description

1 To assist cold starting, diesel engines are fitted with a preheating system, which consists of four glow plugs (one per cylinder), a preheating system control unit, a facia-mounted warning lamp, a coolant temperature sensor mounted on the coolant outlet housing, an ambient air temperature sensor mounted inside the preheating system control unit, and the associated electrical wiring.

2 The glow plugs are miniature electric heating elements, encapsulated in a metal case with a probe at one end and electrical connection at the other. Each combustion chamber has one glow plug threaded into it, with the tip of the glow plug probe positioned directly in line with incoming spray of fuel from the injectors. When the glow plug is energised, it heats up rapidly, causing the fuel passing over the glow plug probe to be heated to its optimum combustion temperature, ready for combustion. In addition, some of the fuel passing over the glow plugs is ignited and this helps to trigger the combustion process.

3 The preheating system begins to operate as soon as the ignition key is switched to the second position, but only if the engine coolant temperature is below 60°C. A facia-mounted warning lamp informs the driver that preheating is taking place. The lamp extinguishes when sufficient preheating has taken place to allow the engine to be started, but power will still be supplied to the glow plugs for a further period until the engine is started. If no attempt is made to start the engine, the power supply to the glow plugs is switched off after a period of time, to prevent battery drain and glow plug burn-out.

4 The glow plugs are operated by the preheating system control unit which in turn is controlled by the engine management system ECU. The ECU determines the necessary preheating and post-heating time based on inputs from the various system sensors.

5 Post-heating takes place after the ignition key has been released from the 'Start' position; the glow plugs continue to operate for at least a further 15 seconds, helping to improve fuel combustion whilst the engine is warming-up, resulting in quieter, smoother running and reduced exhaust emissions. The overall duration of the post-heating period is dependent on the coolant temperature and engine speed.

Testing

6 If the system malfunctions, testing is ultimately by substitution of known good units, but some preliminary checks may be made as follows.

7 Remove the engine cover and connect a voltmeter or 12 volt test lamp between the glow plug supply cable and earth (engine or vehicle metal). Make sure that the live connection is kept clear of the engine and bodywork.

8 Have an assistant switch on the ignition, and check that voltage is applied to the glow plugs. Note the time for which the warning light is lit, and the total time for which voltage is applied before the system cuts out. Switch off the ignition.

9 At an under-bonnet temperature of 20°C, typical times noted should be 5 or 6 seconds for warning light operation, followed by a further 10 seconds supply after the light goes out. Warning light time will increase with lower temperatures and decrease with higher temperatures.

10 If there is no supply at all, the control unit or associated wiring is at fault.

11 Disconnect the main supply cable and the interconnecting wire or strap from the top of the glow plugs. Be careful not to drop the nuts and washers. It may be necessary to move the wiring harness tray to one side after undoing the two retaining nuts and lower bolts, for access to No 4 glow plug.

12 Use a continuity tester, or a 12 volt test lamp connected to the battery positive terminal in the engine compartment positive cable terminal box, to check for continuity between each glow plug terminal and earth. The resistance of a glow plug in good condition is very low (less than 1 ohm), so if the test lamp does not light or the continuity tester shows a high resistance, the glow plug is certainly defective.

13 If an ammeter is available, the current draw of each glow plug can be checked. After an initial surge of 15 to 20 amps, each plug should draw 12 amps. Any plug which draws much more or less than this is probably defective.

14 As a final check, the glow plugs can be removed and inspected as described in the following Section. On completion, refit any components removed for access with reference to Chapter 4B.

2.2 Unscrew the nut (arrowed) and disconnect the glow plug supply cable

2.5 Unscrew the glow plug and remove it from the cylinder head

2 Glow plugs – removal, inspection and refitting

Removal

Caution: If the preheating system has just been energised, or if the engine has been running, the glow plugs will be very hot.

1 Disconnect the battery negative terminal (refer to *Disconnecting the battery* in the Reference Chapter).

2 Remove the engine cover then unscrew the two nuts and move the wiring harness tray to one side.

3 Unscrew the nut from the relevant glow plug terminal(s), and recover the washer(s). Note that the main supply cable is connected to Number 1 cylinder glow plug and an interconnecting wire is fitted between the four plugs **(see illustration)**.

4 Where applicable, carefully move any obstructing pipes or wires to one side to enable access to the relevant glow plug(s).

5 Unscrew the glow plug(s) and remove from the cylinder head **(see illustration)**.

Inspection

6 Inspect each glow plug for physical damage. Burnt or eroded glow plug tips can

be caused by a bad injector spray pattern. Have the injectors checked if this sort of damage is found.

7 If the glow plugs are in good physical condition, check them electrically using a 12 volt test lamp or continuity tester as described in the previous Section.

8 The glow plugs can be energised by applying 12 volts to them to verify that they heat up evenly and in the required time. Observe the following precautions.

a) Support the glow plug by clamping it carefully in a vice or self-locking pliers. Remember it will become red-hot.

b) Make sure that the power supply or test lead incorporates a fuse or overload trip to protect against damage from a short-circuit.

c) After testing, allow the glow plug to cool for several minutes before attempting to handle it.

9 A glow plug in good condition will start to glow red at the tip after drawing current for 5 seconds or so. Any plug which takes much longer to start glowing, or which starts glowing in the middle instead of at the tip, is defective.

Refitting

10 Refit by reversing the removal operations. Apply a smear of copper-based anti-seize

compound to the plug threads and tighten the glow plugs to the specified torque. Do not overtighten, as this can damage the glow plug element.

11 Refit any components removed for access.

3 Preheating system control unit – removal and refitting

Removal

1 The unit is located on the left-hand side of the engine compartment where it is mounted on the engine management ECU support tray.

2 Disconnect the battery negative terminal (refer to *Disconnecting the battery* in the Reference Chapter).

3 Unscrew the retaining nut securing the unit to the support tray **(see illustration)**.

4 Unscrew the two retaining nuts and free the main feed and supply wires from the base of the unit, then disconnect the wiring connector **(see illustration)**. Remove the unit from the engine compartment.

Refitting

5 Refitting is a reversal of removal, ensuring that the wiring connectors are correctly connected.

3.3 Unscrew the preheating system control unit retaining nut (arrowed) . . .

3.4 . . . then disconnect the main feed and supply wires and the wiring connector

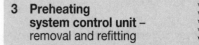

Chapter 6
Clutch

Contents

Degrees of difficulty

Easy, suitable for novice with little experience	**Fairly easy,** suitable for beginner with some experience	**Fairly difficult,** suitable for competent DIY mechanic	**Difficult,** suitable for experienced DIY mechanic	**Very difficult,** suitable for expert DIY or professional

Specifications

Type	Single dry disc with diaphragm spring, hydraulic or cable operation

Clutch operation

Right-hand drive models	Hydraulic
Left-hand drive models	Cable

Friction disc diameter

Petrol engine models	200 mm
Diesel engine models	228 mm

Torque wrench setting	**Nm**	**lbf ft**
Pressure plate retaining bolts	20	15

1 General information

The clutch consists of a friction disc, a pressure plate assembly, a release bearing and release fork; all of these components are contained in the large cast-aluminium alloy bellhousing, sandwiched between the engine and the transmission. The release mechanism is hydraulic on right-hand drive models utilising a master and slave cylinder, and mechanical on left-hand drive models, by means of a self-adjusting cable.

The friction disc is fitted between the engine flywheel and the clutch pressure plate, and is allowed to slide on the transmission input shaft splines.

The pressure plate assembly is bolted to the engine flywheel. When the engine is running, drive is transmitted from the crankshaft, via the flywheel, to the friction disc (these components being clamped securely together by the pressure plate assembly) and from the friction disc to the transmission input shaft.

To interrupt the drive, the spring pressure must be relaxed. This is done by means of the clutch release bearing, fitted concentrically around the transmission input shaft. The bearing is pushed onto the pressure plate assembly by means of the release fork actuated by the cable or clutch slave cylinder pushrod.

On models with a hydraulic clutch, the clutch pedal is connected to the clutch master cylinder by a short pushrod. The master cylinder is mounted on the engine side of the bulkhead in front of the driver and receives its hydraulic fluid supply from the brake master cylinder reservoir. Depressing the clutch pedal moves the piston in the master cylinder forwards, so forcing hydraulic fluid through the clutch hydraulic pipe to the slave cylinder. The piston in the slave cylinder moves forward on the entry of the fluid and actuates the clutch release fork by means of a short pushrod. The release fork pivots on its mounting stud, and the other end of the fork then presses the release bearing against the pressure plate spring fingers. This causes the springs to deform and releases the clamping force on the pressure plate.

Where a cable-operated clutch is fitted, at the transmission end the outer cable is retained by a fixed mounting bracket, and the inner cable is attached to the release fork.

Depressing the clutch pedal pulls the inner cable, allowing the release fork to pivot on its mounting stud and operate the release bearing in the same way as described for the hydraulic version.

On all models the clutch operating mechanism is self-adjusting, and no manual adjustment is required.

2 Clutch hydraulic system – bleeding

Warning: Hydraulic fluid is poisonous; wash off immediately and thoroughly in the case of skin contact, and seek immediate medical advice if any fluid is swallowed or gets into the eyes. Certain types of hydraulic fluid are inflammable, and may ignite when allowed into contact with hot components; when servicing any hydraulic system, it is safest to assume that the fluid IS inflammable, and to take precautions against the risk of fire as though it is petrol that is being handled. Hydraulic fluid is also an effective paint stripper, and will attack plastics; if any is spilt, it should be

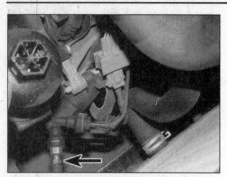

2.4 Clutch slave cylinder and bleed screw location (arrowed)

washed off immediately, using copious quantities of clean water. When topping-up or renewing the fluid, always use the recommended type, and ensure that it comes from a freshly-opened sealed container.

1 Obtain a clean jar, a suitable length of rubber or clear plastic tubing, which is a tight fit over the bleed screw on the clutch slave cylinder, and a tin of the specified hydraulic fluid. The help of an assistant will also be required. (If a one-man do-it-yourself bleeding kit for bleeding the brake hydraulic system is available, this can be used quite satisfactorily for the clutch also. Full information on the use of these kits may be found in Chapter 9.)

2 On diesel engine models, release the four plastic fasteners and lift off the engine cover.

3 Remove the filler cap from the brake master cylinder reservoir, and if necessary top-up the fluid. Keep the reservoir topped-up during subsequent operations.

4 Remove the dust cap from the slave cylinder bleed screw, located on the lower front facing side of the transmission **(see illustration)**.

5 Connect one end of the bleed tube to the bleed screw, and insert the other end of the tube in the jar containing sufficient clean hydraulic fluid to keep the end of the tube submerged.

6 Open the bleed screw half a turn and have your assistant depress the clutch pedal and then slowly release it. Continue this procedure until clean hydraulic fluid, free from air bubbles, emerges from the tube. Now tighten

the bleed screw at the end of a downstroke. Make sure that the brake master cylinder reservoir is checked frequently to ensure that the level does not drop too far, allowing air into the system.

7 Check the operation of the clutch pedal. After a few strokes it should feel normal. Any sponginess would indicate air still present in the system.

8 On completion remove the bleed tube and refit the dust cover. Top-up the master cylinder reservoir if necessary and refit the cap. Fluid expelled from the hydraulic system should now be discarded as it will be contaminated with moisture, air and dirt, making it unsuitable for further use.

3 Clutch master cylinder – removal and refitting

Note: *Before starting work, refer to the note at the beginning of Section 2 concerning the dangers of hydraulic fluid.*

Removal

1 Disconnect the battery negative terminal (refer to *Disconnecting the battery* in the Reference Chapter).

2 On 1.8 litre petrol engine models, and diesel engine models, firmly apply the handbrake, then jack up the front of the vehicle and support it securely on axle stands (see *Jacking and vehicle support*). Remove the engine undertray. The clutch master cylinder is located at the lower right-hand corner of the engine compartment bulkhead. Access is extremely limited from above, and only slightly better from below.

3 Using a forked type removal tool, release the stud-type plastic clips and remove the facia lower trim panel over the pedals on the driver's side.

4 Using a small screwdriver, release the slave cylinder pushrod end fitting from the clutch pedal **(see illustration)**.

5 To minimise hydraulic fluid loss, remove the brake master cylinder reservoir filler cap then tighten it down onto a piece of polythene to obtain an airtight seal.

6 Place absorbent rags under the clutch master cylinder and be prepared for hydraulic fluid loss.

7 Unscrew the union nut and disconnect the hydraulic pipe from the side of the master cylinder **(see illustration)**. Suitably plug or cap the pipe end to prevent further fluid loss and dirt entry.

8 Disconnect the hydraulic fluid supply hose and suitably plug or cap the hose end.

9 Undo the two retaining nuts, withdraw the master cylinder from the bulkhead and remove it from the engine compartment.

Refitting

10 Refitting the master cylinder is the reverse sequence to removal, bearing in mind the following points.

a) *Tighten all nuts and pipe unions securely.*

b) *Bleed the clutch hydraulic system as described in Section 2 on completion.*

4 Clutch slave cylinder – removal and refitting

Note: *Before starting work, refer to the note at the beginning of Section 2 concerning the dangers of hydraulic fluid.*

Removal

1 Disconnect the battery negative terminal (refer to *Disconnecting the battery* in the Reference Chapter).

2 To minimise hydraulic fluid loss, remove the brake master cylinder reservoir filler cap then tighten it down onto a piece of polythene to obtain an airtight seal.

3 Place absorbent rags under the clutch slave cylinder located on the lower front facing side of the transmission. Be prepared for hydraulic fluid loss.

4 Where necessary for access, release the wiring harness from the retaining clips and move the harness clear of the slave cylinder.

5 Unscrew the union nut and disconnect the hydraulic pipe from the side of the slave cylinder. Suitably plug or cap the pipe end to prevent further fluid loss and dirt entry.

6 Undo the two bolts securing the slave cylinder to the transmission, noting the correct fitted position of the cable and hose support bracket (where applicable). Withdraw the slave cylinder from the transmission and remove it from the engine compartment.

Refitting

7 Refitting the slave cylinder is the reverse sequence to removal, bearing in mind the following points.

a) *Tighten the mounting bolts and pipe union securely.*

b) *Bleed the clutch hydraulic system as described in Section 2 on completion.*

3.4 Using a small screwdriver, release the slave cylinder pushrod end fitting from the clutch pedal

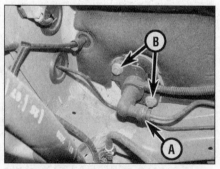

3.7 Clutch master cylinder hydraulic pipe union nut (A) and cylinder retaining nuts (B)

5.3 Disconnect the battery positive cables from the terminal box studs

5.5 Undo the retaining bolts (arrowed) and lift out the ECU support tray

5.8 Remove the facia lower trim panel above the pedals on the driver's side

5 Clutch cable – removal and refitting

Removal

1 Disconnect the battery negative terminal (refer to *Disconnecting the battery* in the Reference Chapter).

2 Remove the air cleaner and air inlet ducts as described in Chapter 4A or 4B as applicable.

3 Working in the engine compartment, lift up the covers on the battery positive cable terminal box and unscrew the nuts securing the battery cables to the terminal studs **(see illustration)**. Lift the cables off the studs and suitably label them for correct refitting.

4 Withdraw the engine management ECU from its location on the support tray and move it to one side.

5 Release the wiring harness from the retaining clips on the ECU support tray, then undo the retaining bolts and lift out the support tray **(see illustration)**.

6 Detach the clutch inner cable end fitting from the release fork on the transmission, then withdraw the outer cable end from the support bracket.

7 Release the outer cable from the cable guide bracket on the end of the transmission and withdraw the outer cable end fitting from the engine compartment bulkhead. Release the outer cable from any additional retaining clips in the engine compartment.

8 Working inside the car, extract the stud-type plastic clips using a forked type tool and remove the facia lower trim panel above the pedals on the driver's side **(see illustration)**.

9 Reach up and pull the end of the inner cable toward the pedal slightly, then slip the cable end out of the yoke on the pedal.

10 Return to the engine compartment, pull the cable through the bulkhead and remove it from the engine compartment.

11 Examine the cable, looking for worn end fittings or a damaged outer casing, and for signs of fraying of the inner cable. Check the cable's operation; the inner cable should move smoothly and easily through the outer casing. Remember that a cable that appears

serviceable when tested off the car may well be much heavier in operation when in its working position. Renew the cable if it shows signs of excessive wear or any damage.

Refitting

12 Apply a thin smear of multi-purpose grease to the cable end fitting, then pass the cable through the engine compartment bulkhead. Push the end fitting fully into position in the bulkhead aperture.

13 Hold the clutch pedal in its raised position and hook the inner cable end back into the pedal yoke.

14 Ensuring that the cable is correctly routed, position it in the guide bracket on the transmission and secure the cable with any additional retaining clips.

15 Locate the outer cable end in the transmission support bracket and connect the inner cable to the clutch release fork.

16 Depress the clutch pedal two or three times to settle the cable and operate the automatic adjuster.

17 Refit the facia lower trim panel and secure with the plastic clips.

18 Refit the engine management ECU support tray and secure with the retaining bolts. Attach the wiring harness to the retaining clips on the support tray.

19 Refit the ECU to the support tray then reconnect the battery cables to the terminal studs in the battery positive cable terminal box. Secure the cables with the retaining nuts securely tightened, then close the terminal box covers.

20 Refit the air cleaner and air inlet ducts as

6.7 Undo the nut from the clutch pedal pivot bolt (arrowed)

described in Chapter 4A or 4B as applicable, then reconnect the battery negative terminal.

6 Clutch pedal – removal and refitting

Removal

1 Disconnect the battery negative terminal (refer to *Disconnecting the battery* in the Reference Chapter).

2 Working inside the car, extract the stud-type plastic clips using a forked type tool and remove the facia lower trim panel above the pedals on the driver's side.

Right-hand drive models

3 Using a small screwdriver, release the slave cylinder pushrod end fitting from the clutch pedal **(see illustration 3.4)**.

Left-hand drive models

4 Detach the clutch inner cable end fitting from the release lever on the transmission.

5 Reach up and pull the end of the clutch inner cable toward the pedal slightly, then slip the cable end out of the yoke on the pedal.

All models

6 Detach the pedal helper spring end pieces and remove the helper spring from the pedal and pedal bracket.

7 Undo the nut from the clutch pedal pivot bolt and withdraw the bolt **(see illustration)**.

8 Remove the clutch pedal from the pedal bracket and recover the bush from the pedal pivot.

9 Check the condition of the pedal, pivot bush and helper spring assembly and renew any components as necessary.

Refitting

10 Lubricate the pedal pivot bolt with multi-purpose grease, then locate the pedal in the bracket and insert the pivot bolt. Refit the pivot bolt nut and tighten it securely.

11 Reconnect the helper spring to the pedal and pedal bracket.

Right-hand drive models

12 Refit the slave cylinder pushrod end fitting to the clutch pedal.

7.13 Fit the friction disc so that its spring hub assembly faces away from the flywheel

Left-hand drive models

13 Hold the clutch pedal in its raised position and hook the inner cable end back into the pedal yoke.

14 Reconnect the clutch inner cable end fitting to the transmission release fork.

All models

15 Depress the pedal two or three times and check the operation of the cable and clutch release mechanism.

16 Refit the facia lower trim panel and secure with the plastic clips.

17 Reconnect the battery negative terminal.

7	Clutch assembly – removal, inspection and refitting

Warning: Dust created by clutch wear and deposited on the clutch components may contain asbestos, which is a health hazard. DON'T blow it out with compressed air, nor inhale any of it. DO NOT use petrol or petroleum-based solvents to clean off the dust. Brake system cleaner or methylated spirit should be used to flush the dust into a suitable receptacle. After the clutch components are wiped clean with rags, dispose of the contaminated rags and cleaner in a sealed, marked container.

Note: *Although most friction materials no longer contain asbestos, it is safest to assume that some still do, and to take precautions accordingly.*

7.16 Using a clutch-aligning tool to centralise the friction disc

Removal

1 Unless the complete engine/transmission unit is to be removed from the car and separated for major overhaul (see Chapter 2D or 2E), the clutch can be reached by removing the transmission as described in Chapter 7.

2 Before disturbing the clutch, use chalk or a marker pen to mark the relationship of the pressure plate assembly to the flywheel.

3 Working in a diagonal sequence, slacken the pressure plate bolts by half a turn at a time, until spring pressure is released and the bolts can be unscrewed by hand.

4 Prise the pressure plate assembly off its locating dowels, and collect the friction disc, noting which way round the disc is fitted.

Inspection

Note: *Due to the amount of work necessary to remove and refit clutch components, it is considered good practice to renew the clutch friction disc, pressure plate assembly and release bearing as a matched set, even if only one of these is worn enough to require renewal. It is worth considering the renewal of the clutch components on a preventative basis if the engine and/or transmission have been removed for some other reason.*

5 When cleaning clutch components, read first the warning at the beginning of this Section; remove dust using a clean, dry cloth, and working in a well-ventilated atmosphere.

6 Check the friction disc facings for signs of wear, damage or oil contamination. If the friction material is cracked, burnt, scored or damaged, or if it is contaminated with oil or grease (shown by shiny black patches), the friction disc must be renewed.

7 If the friction material is still serviceable, check that the centre boss splines are unworn, that the torsion springs are in good condition and securely fastened, and that all the rivets are tight. If any wear or damage is found, the friction disc must be renewed.

8 If the friction material is fouled with oil, this must be due to an oil leak from the crankshaft left-hand oil seal, from the sump-to-cylinder block joint, or from the transmission input shaft. Renew the seal or repair the joint, as appropriate, as described in the relevant Part of Chapter 2 or 7, before installing the new friction disc.

9 Check the pressure plate assembly for obvious signs of wear or damage; shake it to check for loose rivets or worn or damaged fulcrum rings, and check that the drive straps securing the pressure plate to the cover do not show signs (such as a deep yellow or blue discoloration) of overheating. If the diaphragm spring is worn or damaged, or if its pressure is in any way suspect, the pressure plate assembly should be renewed.

10 Examine the machined bearing surfaces of the pressure plate and of the flywheel; they should be clean, completely flat, and free from scratches or scoring. If either is discoloured

from excessive heat, or shows signs of cracks, it should be renewed – although minor damage of this nature can sometimes be polished away using emery paper.

11 Check that the release bearing contact surface rotates smoothly and easily, with no sign of noise or roughness. Also check that the surface itself is smooth and unworn, with no signs of cracks, pitting or scoring. If there is any doubt about its condition, the bearing must be renewed.

Refitting

12 On reassembly, ensure that the bearing surfaces of the flywheel and pressure plate are completely clean, smooth, and free from oil or grease. Use solvent to remove any protective grease from new components.

13 Fit the friction disc so that its spring hub assembly faces away from the flywheel; there may be a marking showing which way round the disc is to be refitted (**see illustration**).

14 Refit the pressure plate assembly, aligning the marks made on dismantling (if the original pressure plate is re-used), and locating the pressure plate on its three locating dowels. Fit the pressure plate bolts, but tighten them only finger-tight, so that the friction disc can still be moved.

15 The friction disc must now be centralised, so that when the transmission is refitted, its input shaft will pass through the splines at the centre of the friction disc.

16 Centralisation can be achieved by passing a screwdriver or other long bar through the friction disc and into the hole in the crankshaft; the friction disc can then be moved around until it is centred on the crankshaft hole. Alternatively, a clutch-aligning tool can be used to eliminate the guesswork; these can be obtained from most accessory shops (**see illustration**).

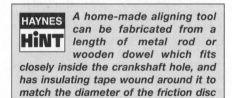

HAYNES HiNT *A home-made aligning tool can be fabricated from a length of metal rod or wooden dowel which fits closely inside the crankshaft hole, and has insulating tape wound around it to match the diameter of the friction disc splined hole.*

17 When the friction disc is centralised, tighten the pressure plate bolts evenly and in a diagonal sequence to the specified torque setting.

18 Apply a **thin** smear of molybdenum disulphide grease (Citroën recommend the use of Molykote BR2 Plus – available from your Citroën dealer) to the splines of the friction disc and the transmission input shaft, and also to the release bearing bore and release fork shaft.

19 Refit the transmission as described in Chapter 7.

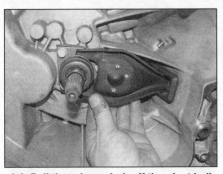

8.2 Pull the release fork off the pivot ball stud using hand pressure from behind the fork

8.3 Slide the release bearing off the guide tube and disengage the arms of the release fork

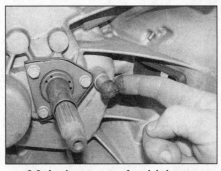

8.6 Apply a smear of molybdenum disulphide grease to the pivot ball stud

8 Clutch release mechanism – removal, inspection and refitting

Note: *Refer to the warning concerning the dangers of asbestos dust at the beginning of Section 7.*

Removal

1 Unless the complete engine/transmission unit is to be removed from the car and separated for major overhaul (see Chapter 2D or 2E), the clutch release mechanism can be reached by removing the transmission only, as described in Chapter 7.

2 With the transmission removed, pull the release fork off the pivot ball stud using hand pressure from behind the fork **(see illustration)**.

3 Slide the release bearing off the guide tube and disengage the arms of the release fork **(see illustration)**.

Inspection

4 Check that the release bearing contact surface rotates smoothly and easily, with no sign of noise or roughness, and that the surface itself is smooth and unworn, with no signs of cracks, pitting or scoring. If there is any doubt about its condition, the bearing must be renewed.

5 Check the bearing surfaces and points of contact on the release fork and pivot ball stud, renewing any component which is worn or damaged.

Refitting

6 Apply a smear of molybdenum disulphide grease to the pivot ball stud **(see illustration)**.

7 Insert the outer end of the release fork through the rubber boot in the side of the transmission bellhousing.

8 Engage the arms of the release fork with the release bearing collar, then slide the release bearing onto the guide tube.

8.9 Position the release fork over the ball pivot stud and push it firmly until it locks into place

9 Position the release fork over the ball pivot stud and push it firmly until it locks into place **(see illustration)**.

10 Refit the transmission as described in Chapter 7.

Chapter 7
Manual transmission

Contents

Degrees of difficulty

Easy, suitable for novice with little experience 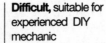	**Fairly easy,** suitable for beginner with some experience	**Fairly difficult,** suitable for competent DIY mechanic	**Difficult,** suitable for experienced DIY mechanic	**Very difficult,** suitable for expert DIY or professional

Specifications

General

Type	Manual, five forward speeds and reverse. Synchromesh on all speeds
Designation	BE4/5

Lubrication

Recommended oil type	Refer to *Lubricants and fluids*
Capacity	1.8 litres

Torque wrench settings

	Nm	lbf ft
Clutch cable bracket retaining bolts	18	13
Clutch release bearing guide sleeve bolts	12	9
Engine-to-transmission fixing bolts	50	37
Engine/transmission left-hand mounting components	Refer to Chapter 2A, 2B or 2C as applicable	
Lower suspension arm balljoint clamp bolt nut*	40	30
Oil drain plug	35	26
Oil filler/level plug	20	15
Reversing light switch	25	18
Right-hand driveshaft intermediate bearing retaining bolt nuts	17	13
Roadwheel bolts	85	63

New nuts must be used.

1 General information

The transmission is contained in a cast-aluminium alloy casing bolted to the engine's left-hand end, and consists of the gearbox and final drive differential – often called a transaxle.

Drive is transmitted from the crankshaft via the clutch to the input shaft, which has a splined extension to accept the clutch friction disc, and rotates in sealed ball-bearings. From the input shaft, drive is transmitted to the output shaft, which rotates in a roller bearing at its right-hand end, and a sealed ball-bearing at its left-hand end. From the output shaft, the drive is transmitted to the differential crownwheel, which rotates with the differential case and planetary gears, thus driving the sun gears and driveshafts. The rotation of the planetary gears on their shaft allows the inner roadwheel to rotate at a slower speed than the outer roadwheel when the car is cornering.

The input and output shafts are arranged side-by-side, parallel to the crankshaft and driveshafts, so that their gear pinion teeth are in constant mesh. In the neutral position, the output shaft gear pinions rotate freely, so that drive cannot be transmitted to the crownwheel.

Gear selection is via a centrally-mounted lever and cable-actuated selector mechanism. The transmission selector shaft causes the appropriate selector fork to move its respective synchro-sleeve along the shaft, to lock the gear pinion to the synchro-hub. Since the synchro-hubs are splined to the output shaft, this locks the pinion to the shaft, so that drive can be transmitted. To ensure that gearchanging can be made quickly and quietly, a synchromesh system is fitted to all forward gears, consisting of baulk rings and spring-loaded fingers, as well as the gear pinions and synchro-hubs. The synchromesh cones are formed on the mating faces of the baulk rings and gear pinions.

2.5a Undo the transmission drain plug using a square-section wrench . . .

2.5b . . . then remove the drain plug and collect the sealing washer

2.8 Refill the transmission slowly until the oil begins to trickle out of the orifice

2 Manual transmission – draining and refilling

Note: *A suitable square section wrench may be required to undo the transmission filler/level and drain plugs. These wrenches can be obtained from most motor factors or your Citroën dealer.*

HAYNES HiNT *It may be possible to use the square end fitting on a ratchet handle (as found in a typical socket set) to undo the plug.*

1 This operation is much quicker and more efficient if the car is first taken on a journey of sufficient length to warm the engine/transmission up to normal operating temperature.

2 Park the car on level ground, switch off the ignition and apply the handbrake firmly. To gain access to the filler/level plug, jack up the front and rear of the car and support it securely on axle stands (see *Jacking and vehicle support*). Note that the car must be level, to ensure accuracy when refilling and checking the oil level.

3 Remove the engine undertray, the left-hand front wheel, and the plastic wheelarch liner. The liner is secured by stud-type plastic clips along its upper and front edges which can be removed using a forked type tool. Extract all the clips, and remove the liner centre section

from under the front wing. It will be necessary to ease back the front section slightly to allow the front edge of the centre section to be released. Note how the two sections overlap, as you do this, to aid refitting.

4 Wipe clean the area around the filler/level plug, which is situated on the left-hand end of the transmission, next to the end cover. Unscrew the filler/level plug from the transmission and recover the sealing washer.

5 Position a suitable container under the drain plug (situated at the rear of transmission) and unscrew the plug. Allow the oil to drain completely into the container (see **illustrations**). If the oil is hot, take precautions against scalding.

6 Clean both the filler/level and the drain plugs, being especially careful to wipe any metallic particles off the magnetic inserts. Discard the original sealing washers; they should be renewed whenever they are disturbed.

7 When the oil has finished draining, clean the drain plug threads and those of the transmission casing, fit a new sealing washer and refit the drain plug, tightening it to the specified torque.

8 Refill the transmission slowly, through the filler/level plug orifice, until the oil begins to trickle out of the orifice (see **illustration**). Use only good-quality oil of the specified type (refer to *Lubricants and fluids*). To ensure that a correct level is established, wait until the initial trickle has stopped and allow the oil to settle within the transmission. Add a little more oil until a new trickle emerges; the level will be correct when the new flow ceases.

9 When the level is correct, fit a new sealing washer to the filler/level plug, refit the plug and tighten it to the specified torque.

10 Refit the wheelarch liner, engine undertray and roadwheel, then lower the car to the ground. Tighten the roadwheel bolts to the specified torque.

3 Gearchange cables – adjustment

Note: *The gearchange cables should be adjusted after any operation which entails disconnection of the cables at either the transmission end or the gear lever end. Adjustment is carried out by repositioning the balljoint end fittings at the transmission end of the cables.*

1 Citroën recommend the use of a gear lever positioning tool (special tool 9607-T) to lock the gear lever in the neutral position during the adjustment procedure. In practice, it was found that satisfactory adjustment could be carried out without the special tool, by aligning the gear lever mechanism visually and engaging the help of an assistant to hold the lever stationary in the aligned position.

2 Disconnect the battery negative terminal (refer to *Disconnecting the battery* in the Reference Chapter).

3 Remove the air cleaner assembly and air inlet ducts as described in Chapter 4A or 4B as applicable.

4 Remove the facia lower centre panel as described in Chapter 11.

5 Place the gear lever in the neutral position and ensure that the transmission is in neutral (if the cables have been disconnected from a previous operation).

6 Disconnect the two gearchange cable balljoint end fittings from the transmission selector levers. To do this, press the centre of the balljoint with your thumb and lift the fitting off the selector lever ball stud (see **illustration**). Do not use any tools to prise the end fittings free.

7 Turn the end fitting over and release the locking key securing the end fitting to the cable, using two thin screwdrivers (see **illustration**).

3.6 Press the centre of the cable balljoint end fitting with your thumb and lift the fitting off the selector lever ball stud

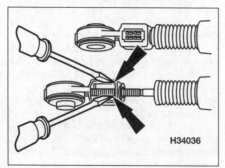

3.7 Release the end fitting locking key using two thin screwdrivers (arrowed)

8 With the locking key removed from each balljoint, refit the balljoints to the transmission selector levers.

9 From inside the car, observe the position of the horizontal selector shaft on the left-hand side of the gear lever base. The shaft must be parallel with the horizontal rib on the casting directly below the gear lever **(see illustration)**. The Citroën special tool engages with the rib and the selector shaft and holds the shaft in the correct position. In practice it was found that the gear lever automatically adopts this alignment with the cable locking keys released, due to the action of the detent springs.

10 With an assistant holding the gear lever in the correct position, refit the locking keys to the cable balljoint end fittings. The cable lengths should now be correct.

11 Check that it is possible to shift through all gears without encountering any tight spots. Check also that the travel of the gear lever is equal in each direction, ie, forward and backward, and left and right. If this is not the case, repeat the adjustment procedure.

12 When the adjustment is correct, refit the facia lower centre panel as described in Chapter 11.

13 Refit the air cleaner assembly and air inlet ducts as described in Chapter 4A or 4B, then reconnect the battery negative terminal.

---

4 Gearchange cables – removal and refitting

Removal

Note: *The two cables are removed as an assembly and cannot be individually separated.*

1 Disconnect the battery negative terminal (refer to *Disconnecting the battery* in the Reference Chapter).

2 Remove the facia lower centre panel as described in Chapter 11.

3 Using a screwdriver, release the wire locking clips, and disconnect the two gearchange inner cable end fittings from the linkage at the base of the gearchange lever **(see illustrations)**.

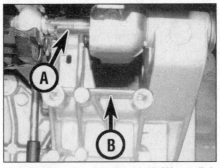

3.9 Position the selector shaft (A) parallel with the casting web (B)

4 Remove the heater air duct then disconnect both outer cables from their attachments on the gearchange mechanism base using a screwdriver to release the retaining clips **(see illustration)**.

5 Firmly apply the handbrake, then jack up the front of the vehicle and support it on axle stands (see *Jacking and vehicle support*).

6 Remove the engine undertray, then disconnect the engine/transmission rear mounting connecting link as described in the relevant Part of Chapter 2.

7 Remove the exhaust system front pipe and heat shield as described in Chapter 4A or 4B as applicable.

8 Undo the two nuts securing the gearchange cable closure plate to the bulkhead aperture.

9 Remove the air cleaner assembly and air inlet ducts as described in Chapter 4A or 4B.

10 Disconnect the two gearchange cable balljoint end fittings from the transmission selector levers. To do this, press the centre of the balljoint with your thumb and lift the fitting off the selector lever ball stud **(see illustration 3.6)**. Do not use any tools to prise the end fittings free.

11 Using circlip pliers, release the retaining clips and disconnect the two gearchange outer cables from the transmission mounting bracket.

12 Withdraw the cables through the bulkhead into the engine compartment and remove the assembly from the vehicle.

13 Inspect the cable assembly for signs of wear or damage, and for free movement of the inner cables in the outer sleeves. The

balljoint end fittings at the transmission end can be individually renewed, if necessary, but if any other wear or damage is noted, a complete cable assembly will have to be obtained.

Refitting

14 Refitting is a reversal of the removal procedure, noting the following points:

   a) *Prior to refitting the cables, check that the transmission selector levers are still in the neutral position.*

   b) *Tie the two cables together to make it easier to pass them through the bulkhead and into their correct locations.*

   c) *Apply a soapy water solution to the bulkhead aperture to assist entry of the cables at that point.*

   d) *With the cables connected at the gear lever end and at the transmission mounting bracket, carry out the adjustment procedure described in Section 3.*

   e) *With the cables correctly adjusted, refit the remainder of the removed components with reference to the Chapters indicated in the removal procedure.*

---

5 Gearchange lever assembly – removal and refitting

Removal

1 Carry out the operations described in Section 4, paragraphs 1 to 4.

2 Unclip the gearchange lever gaiter from the facia upper centre panel and feed the gaiter down the lever through the aperture.

3 Working up under the front of the gearchange lever assembly, undo the four bolts securing the mechanism base to the facia brackets.

4 Remove the assembly down and out from under the front of the facia **(see illustration)**.

5 Check the condition and operation of the linkage levers, end fittings, detent springs and pivot bushes. Renew any worn components as necessary.

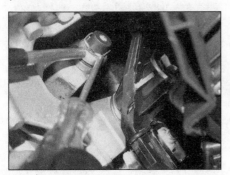

4.3a Release the wire locking clips using a screwdriver . . .

4.3b . . . and disconnect the two gearchange inner cable end fittings from the linkage

4.4 Disconnect the outer cables from their attachments on the gearchange mechanism base

5.4 Remove the gearchange lever assembly down and out from under the facia

Refitting

6 Refit the assembly to the facia and secure with the four bolts securely tightened. Relocate the gearchange lever gaiter into the facia upper centre panel.

6.2 Unbolt the flexible brake hose support bracket from the top of the swivel hub

6.3 Undo the nut and withdraw the lower suspension arm balljoint clamp bolt from the swivel hub

6.5 When the balljoint is released, remove the protector plate from the balljoint shank

7 Reconnect the gearchange cables to the mechanism base and gearchange linkage, then refit the heater air duct.
8 Adjust the cables as described in Section 3.
9 Refit the facia lower centre panel as described in Chapter 11, then reconnect the battery negative terminal.

---

6 Oil seals – renewal

Driveshaft oil seals

1 Drain the transmission oil as described in Section 2.
2 Unbolt the flexible brake hose support bracket from the top of the swivel hub, so as not to strain the brake hose during subsequent operations **(see illustration)**. Similarly, on models equipped with ABS, release the wheel sensor wiring harness from the bracket and from the support clip under the wheelarch.
3 Slacken and remove the nut, then withdraw the lower suspension arm balljoint clamp bolt from the swivel hub **(see illustration)**. Discard the nut – a new one must be used on refitting.
4 Tap a small chisel into the split on the swivel hub, to spread the hub slightly and allow the balljoint shank to be withdrawn. Pull the lower suspension arm downwards to release the balljoint shank from the swivel hub. To do this it will be necessary to use a long bar and block of wood which will engage

6.4a Spread the swivel hub by tapping a small chisel (arrowed) into the split . . .

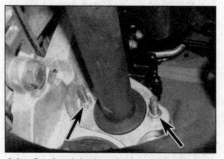

6.6a On the right-hand driveshaft, slacken the intermediate bearing retaining bolt nuts (arrowed) . . .

under the front subframe. Attach the bar to the suspension arm, preferably with a chain, or alternatively with a stout strap or rope **(see illustrations)**. Lever down on the bar to release the balljoint from the swivel hub.
5 Once the balljoint is free, remove the protector plate which is fitted to the balljoint shank, then proceed as described under the relevant sub-heading **(see illustration)**.

Right-hand seal

6 Loosen the two intermediate bearing retaining bolt nuts, then rotate the bolts through 90º so that their offset heads are clear of the bearing outer race **(see illustrations)**.
7 Carefully pull the swivel hub assembly outwards, and pull on the inner end of the driveshaft to free the intermediate bearing from its mounting bracket.
8 Once the driveshaft end is free from the transmission, support the inner end of the driveshaft to avoid damaging the constant velocity joints or gaiters.
9 Carefully prise the oil seal out of the transmission, using a large flat-bladed screwdriver **(see illustration)**.
10 Remove all traces of dirt from the area around the oil seal aperture, then apply a smear of grease to the outer lip of the new oil seal. Fit the new seal into its aperture, and drive it squarely into position using a small block of wood or suitable tubular drift (such as a socket), until it abuts its locating shoulder **(see illustrations)**.
11 Thoroughly clean the driveshaft splines, then apply a thin film of grease to the oil seal lips and to the driveshaft inner end splines.

6.4b . . . then pull the lower suspension arm downwards using a bar and chain or similar arrangement, pivoting on the subframe

6.6b . . . then turn the bolts through 90º to disengage their offset heads (arrowed) from the bearing (driveshaft removed for clarity)

6.9 Use a large flat-bladed screwdriver to prise the driveshaft oil seal out of position

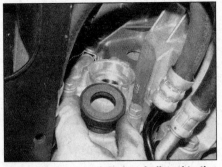

6.10a Fit the new right-hand oil seal to the transmission . . .

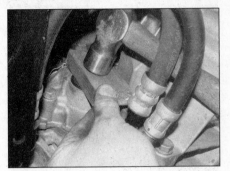

6.10b . . . and tap it into position using a small block of wood

12 Carefully locate the inner driveshaft splines with those of the differential sun gear, taking care not to damage the oil seal. Align the intermediate bearing with its mounting bracket, and push the driveshaft fully into position. If necessary, use a soft-faced mallet to tap the outer race of the bearing into position in the mounting bracket.

13 Ensure that the intermediate bearing is correctly seated, then rotate its retaining bolts back through 90° so that their offset heads are resting against the bearing outer race, and tighten the retaining nuts to the specified torque.

14 Engage the balljoint shank with the lower suspension arm, making sure the balljoint protector is correctly seated in the hub. Refit the clamp bolt and a new nut and tighten the nut to the specified torque.

15 Refit the flexible brake hose support bracket to the swivel hub and, where applicable, secure the ABS wheel sensor wiring to the bracket and clip.

16 Refill the transmission with the specified type and quantity of oil as described in Section 2.

Left-hand seal

17 Pull the swivel hub assembly outwards and withdraw the driveshaft inner constant velocity joint from the transmission. Support the driveshaft, to avoid damaging the constant velocity joints or gaiters.

18 Renew the oil seal as described above in paragraphs 9 to 11.

19 Carefully locate the inner constant velocity joint splines with those of the differential sun gear, taking care not to damage the oil seal, and push the driveshaft fully into position.

20 Carry out the operations described above in paragraphs 14 to 16.

Input shaft oil seal

21 Remove the transmission as described in Section 9, then remove the clutch release bearing as described in Chapter 6.

22 Undo the three bolts securing the clutch release bearing guide sleeve in position, and slide the guide sleeve off the input shaft, along with its O-ring or gasket, as applicable **(see illustrations)**. Recover any shims or thrustwashers which have stuck to the rear of

the guide sleeve, and refit them to the input shaft.

23 Carefully lever the oil seal out of the guide sleeve using a suitable flat-bladed screwdriver **(see illustration)**.

24 Before fitting a new seal, check the input shaft's seal rubbing surface for signs of burrs, scratches or other damage, which may have caused the seal to fail in the first place. It may be possible to polish away minor faults of this sort using fine abrasive paper; however, more serious defects will require the renewal of the input shaft. Ensure that the input shaft is clean and greased, to protect the seal lips on refitting.

25 Dip the new seal in clean oil, and fit it to the guide sleeve.

26 Fit a new O-ring or gasket (as applicable) to the rear of the guide sleeve, then carefully slide the sleeve into position over the input shaft **(see illustration)**. Refit the retaining

6.22a Undo the three release bearing guide sleeve retaining bolts . . .

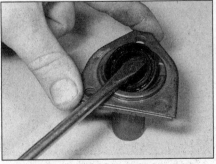

6.23 Removing the input shaft seal from the guide sleeve

bolts and tighten them to the specified torque setting.

27 Take the opportunity to inspect the clutch components, if not already done, then refit the release bearing (see Chapter 6). Finally, refit the transmission as described in Section 9.

<table><tr><td>**7**</td><td>**Reversing light switch –** testing, removal and refitting</td></tr></table>

Testing

1 The reversing light circuit is controlled by a plunger-type switch screwed into a recess in the upper front facing side of the transmission casing. If a fault develops, first ensure that the circuit fuse has not blown.

2 To test the switch, disconnect the wiring connector, and use a multimeter (set to the

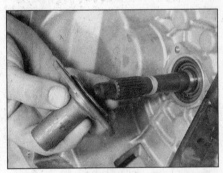

6.22b . . . and withdraw the guide sleeve from the input shaft

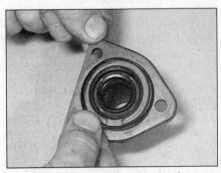

6.26 Fit a new O-ring/gasket (as applicable) to the rear of the guide sleeve

resistance function) or a battery-and-bulb test circuit to check that there is continuity between the switch terminals only when reverse gear is selected. If this is not the case, and there are no obvious breaks or other damage to the wires, the switch is faulty, and must be renewed.

Removal

3 To improve access to the switch, remove the air cleaner assembly and air inlet ducts as described in the relevant Part of Chapter 4.
4 Disconnect the wiring connector, then unscrew the switch from the transmission casing along with its sealing washer.

Refitting

5 Fit a new sealing washer to the switch, then screw it back into position in the top of the transmission housing and tighten it to the specified torque. Refit the wiring plug, and test the operation of the circuit. Refit any components removed for access.

8 Vehicle speed sensor – removal and refitting

Removal

1 Firmly apply the handbrake, then jack up the front of the car and support it on axle stands (see *Jacking and vehicle support*). The vehicle speed sensor is on the rear of the transmission housing, next to the inner end of the right-hand driveshaft.
2 Remove the engine undertray, then disconnect the wiring connector from the speed sensor.
3 Slacken and remove the retaining bolt, along with the heat shield (where fitted), and withdraw the speed sensor and driven pinion assembly from the transmission housing, along with its O-ring.
4 Examine the driven pinion for signs of

damage, and if evident, renew the speed sensor assembly. Renew the sealing O-ring as a matter of course.
5 If the driven pinion is worn or damaged, also examine the drive pinion in the transmission housing for similar signs.
6 To renew the drive pinion, first disengage the right-hand driveshaft from the transmission, as described in paragraphs 1 to 8 of Section 6. Undo the three retaining bolts, and remove the speed sensor extension housing from the transmission, along with its O-ring. Remove the drive pinion from the differential gear, and recover any adjustment shims from the gear **(see illustration)**.

Refitting

7 Where the drive pinion has been removed, refit the adjustment shims to the differential gear, then locate the drive pinion on the gear, ensuring it is correctly engaged in the gear slots **(see illustration)**. Fit a new O-ring to the rear of the extension housing, then refit the housing to the transmission and securely tighten its retaining bolts. Inspect the driveshaft oil seal for signs of wear, and renew if necessary. Refit the driveshaft to the transmission, with reference to Section 6.
8 Fit a new O-ring to the speed sensor assembly and refit it to the transmission, ensuring that the drive and driven pinions are correctly engaged.
9 Refit the retaining bolt and the heat shield (where fitted), and tighten the bolt. Reconnect the wiring connector to the speed sensor.
10 Refit the engine undertray and lower the vehicle to the ground.

9 Manual transmission – removal and refitting

Removal

1 Disconnect the battery negative terminal

(refer to *Disconnecting the battery* in the Reference Chapter).
2 Drain the transmission oil as described in Section 2, then refit the drain and filler plugs, tightening them to the specified torque.
3 Remove both driveshafts as described in Chapter 8.
4 Remove the air cleaner assembly and air inlet ducts as described in the relevant Part of Chapter 4.
5 Lift up the covers on the battery positive cable terminal box and unscrew the nuts securing the battery cables to the terminal studs. Lift the cables off the studs and suitably label them for correct refitting.
6 Withdraw the engine management ECU from its location on the support tray and move it to one side.
7 Release the wiring harness from the retaining clips on the ECU support tray, then undo the retaining bolts and lift out the support tray.
8 On models with a hydraulic clutch, where necessary for access, release the wiring harness from the retaining clips and move the harness clear of the clutch slave cylinder.
9 Release the hydraulic hose from its support bracket, then undo the two bolts securing the slave cylinder to the transmission. Note the correct fitted position of the cable and hose support bracket (where applicable). Withdraw the slave cylinder from the transmission and move it to one side of the engine compartment.
10 On models with a cable-operated clutch, detach the inner cable end fitting from the release fork on the transmission, then withdraw the outer cable end from the support bracket. Release the outer cable from the cable guide bracket on the end of the transmission.
11 Release the wiring harness, cables and hoses from the wiring harness support bracket on the coolant outlet housing. Undo the nuts and bolts securing the support bracket to the coolant outlet housing and remove the bracket.

8.6 Remove the speed sensor extension housing, O-ring and drive pinion from the transmission (transmission removed for clarity)

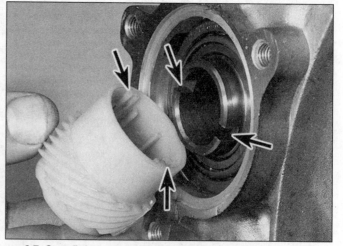

8.7 On refitting, ensure the drive pinion dogs are correctly engaged with the gear slots (arrowed)

12 Disconnect the wiring connectors at the following components/attachments:
 a) *Coolant temperature sensor.*
 b) *Reversing light switch.*
 c) *Vehicle speed sensor.*
 d) *Crankshaft sensor.*
 e) *Transmission earth strap.*

13 Disconnect the wiring from any additional switches/sensors as necessary, free the wiring loom from the retaining clips, and position it clear of the transmission.

14 Disconnect the two gearchange cable balljoint end fittings from the transmission selector levers. To do this, press the centre of the balljoint with your thumb and lift the fitting off the selector lever ball stud. Do not use any tools to prise the end fittings free.

15 Using circlip pliers, release the retaining clips and disconnect the two gearchange outer cables from their transmission mounting bracket.

16 Undo the three bolts securing the starter motor to the transmission. It is not necessary to remove the starter motor as long as it is released from the locating dowel(s).

17 Undo the retaining nuts and release the retaining clips securing the power steering pipes to the underside of the transmission (where applicable). Position the pipes clear of the transmission as far as possible.

18 Undo the retaining bolt(s), and remove the flywheel lower cover plate (where fitted) from the transmission.

19 Remove the vehicle speed sensor drive gear extension housing from the transmission as described in Section 8.

20 On 1.6 litre engine models, undo the bolt securing the exhaust front pipe to its transmission mounting bracket.

21 Undo the bolt securing the engine/transmission rear mounting connecting link to the bracket on the subframe.

22 Undo the bolts and remove the impact absorber from the rear of the differential housing.

23 Place a jack with a block of wood beneath the engine, to take the weight of the engine. Alternatively, attach a hoist or support bar to the engine lifting brackets, and just take the weight of the engine.

24 Place a jack and block of wood beneath the transmission, and raise the jack to take the weight of the transmission.

25 Slacken and remove the centre nut and washer from the left-hand engine/transmission mounting. Undo the two nuts securing the mounting to the support bracket, and remove the rubber mounting.

26 Remove the washer and spacer from the mounting stud, then unscrew the stud from the top of the transmission housing. Collect the large spacer plate from the mounting stud.

27 With the jack positioned beneath the transmission taking the weight, slacken and remove the remaining bolts securing the transmission housing to the engine. Note the correct fitted positions of each bolt, and the necessary brackets, as they are removed, to use as a reference on refitting. Make a final check that all components have been disconnected, and are positioned clear of the transmission so that they will not hinder the removal procedure.

28 With the bolts removed, move the trolley jack and transmission to the left, to free it from its locating dowels then pivot the differential end of the transmission upwards (to disengage it from the subframe).

29 Once the transmission is free, lower the jack and manoeuvre the unit out from under the car. Remove the locating dowels from the transmission or engine if they are loose, and keep them in a safe place.

Refitting

30 The transmission is refitted by a reversal of the removal procedure, bearing in mind the following points:
 a) *Apply a little high-melting-point grease (Citroën recommend the use of Molykote BR2 plus – available from your Citroën dealer) to the splines of the transmission input shaft. Do not apply too much, otherwise there is a possibility of the grease contaminating the clutch friction disc.*
 b) *Ensure that the locating dowels are correctly positioned prior to installation.*
 c) *Apply thread-locking fluid to the left-hand engine/transmission mounting stud threads, prior to refitting it to the transmission. Tighten the stud to the specified torque.*
 d) *Tighten all nuts and bolts to the specified torque (where given).*

 e) *Renew the driveshaft oil seals (Section 6), then refit the driveshafts (see Chapter 8).*
 f) *Adjust the gearchange cables as described in Section 3.*
 g) *On completion, refill the transmission with the specified type and quantity of lubricant, as described in Section 2.*

10 Manual transmission overhaul – general information

Overhauling a manual transmission is a difficult and involved job for the DIY home mechanic. In addition to dismantling and reassembling many small parts, clearances must be precisely measured and, if necessary, changed by selecting shims and spacers. Internal transmission components are also often difficult to obtain, and in many instances, extremely expensive. Because of this, if the transmission develops a fault or becomes noisy, the best course of action is to have the unit overhauled by a specialist repairer, or to obtain an exchange reconditioned unit.

Nevertheless, it is not impossible for the more experienced mechanic to overhaul the transmission, provided the special tools are available, and the job is done in a deliberate step-by-step manner, so that nothing is overlooked.

The tools necessary for an overhaul include internal and external circlip pliers, bearing pullers, a slide hammer, a set of pin punches, a dial test indicator, and possibly a hydraulic press. In addition, a large, sturdy workbench and a vice will be required.

During dismantling of the transmission, make careful notes of how each component is fitted, to make reassembly easier and more accurate.

Before dismantling the transmission, it will help if you have some idea what area is malfunctioning. Certain problems can be closely related to specific areas in the transmission, which can make component examination and replacement easier. Refer to the *Fault finding* Section in the Reference Section for more information.

Chapter 8
Driveshafts

Contents

Degrees of difficulty

Easy, suitable for novice with little experience	Fairly easy, suitable for beginner with some experience	Fairly difficult, suitable for competent DIY mechanic	Difficult, suitable for experienced DIY mechanic	Very difficult, suitable for expert DIY or professional

Specifications

Lubrication (overhaul only – see text)

Lubricant type/specification	Use only special grease supplied in sachets with gaiter kits – joints are otherwise pre-packed with grease and sealed

Lubricant quantity:
Outer CV joint	160 g
Inner CV joint	130 g

Torque wrench settings

	Nm	lbf ft
Anti-roll bar connecting link retaining nut*	40	30
Driveshaft retaining nut	320	236
Lower suspension arm balljoint retaining nuts	40	30
Right-hand driveshaft intermediate bearing retaining bolt nuts*	17	13
Roadwheel bolts	85	63

*New nuts must be used

1 General information

Drive is transmitted from the differential to the front wheels by means of two unequal-length driveshafts.

Both driveshafts are splined at their outer ends, to accept the wheel hubs, and are threaded so that each hub can be fastened by a large nut. The inner end of each driveshaft is splined, to accept the differential sun gear.

Constant velocity (CV) joints are fitted to each end of the driveshafts, to ensure the smooth and efficient transmission of power at all suspension and steering angles. The outer constant velocity joints are of the ball-and-cage type, with the inner constant velocity joints being of the tripod type.

On the right-hand side, due to the length of the driveshaft, the inner constant velocity joint is situated approximately halfway along the shaft's length, and an intermediate support bearing is mounted in the engine/transmission rear mounting bracket. The inner end of the driveshaft passes through the bearing (which prevents any lateral movement of the driveshaft inner end) and the inner constant velocity joint outer member.

2 Driveshafts – removal and refitting

Removal

Note: *Do not allow the vehicle to rest on its wheels with one or both driveshafts removed, as damage to the wheel bearing(s) may result. If moving the vehicle is unavoidable, temporarily insert the outer end of the driveshaft(s) in the hub(s) and tighten the hub nut(s): in this case, the inner end(s) of the driveshaft(s) must be supported, for example*

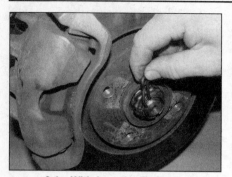

2.4a Withdraw the R-clip . . .

2.4b . . . and remove the locking cap from the driveshaft retaining nut

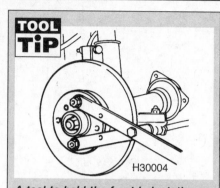

A tool to hold the front hub stationary whilst the driveshaft retaining nut is slackened can be fabricated from two lengths of steel strip (one long, one short) and a nut and bolt; the nut and bolt forming the pivot of a forked tool.

by suspending with string from the vehicle underbody. Do not allow the driveshaft to hang down under its own weight. New lower arm balljoint clamp bolt nuts and anti-roll bar connecting link nuts must be used on refitting.

1 Firmly apply the handbrake, then jack up the front of the car and support it securely on axle stands (see *Jacking and vehicle support*). Remove the appropriate front roadwheel.

2 Drain the transmission oil as described in Chapter 7.

3 On models equipped with ABS, trace the wiring connector back from the wheel sensor, freeing it from its retaining clips, and disconnect it at its wiring connector.

4 Withdraw the R-clip and remove the locking cap from the driveshaft retaining nut **(see illustrations)**.

5 To prevent rotation of the wheel hub as the driveshaft retaining nut is slackened, make up a holding tool and bolt the tool to the wheel hub using two wheel bolts **(see Tool Tip)**.

6 With the holding tool in place, slacken and remove the driveshaft retaining nut using a socket and long bar **(see illustration)**. Where necessary, support the socket on an axle stand to prevent it slipping off the nut. This nut is very tight; make sure that there is no risk of pulling the car off the axle stands as the nut is slackened.

7 Undo the nut and remove the washer securing the connecting link to the anti-roll bar. Swivel the connecting link to one side.

8 Slacken and remove the nut, then withdraw the lower suspension arm balljoint clamp bolt from the swivel hub. Discard the nut – a new one must be used on refitting **(see illustration)**.

9 Tap a small chisel into the split on the swivel hub, to spread the hub slightly and allow the balljoint shank to be withdrawn **(see illustration)**. Pull the lower suspension arm downwards to release the balljoint shank from the swivel hub. To do this it will be necessary to use a long bar and block of wood which will engage under the front subframe. Attach the bar to the suspension arm, preferably with a chain, or alternatively with a stout strap or rope. Lever down on the bar to release the balljoint from the swivel hub **(see illustration)**.

10 Once the balljoint is free, remove the protector plate which is fitted to the balljoint shank **(see illustration)**.

Left-hand driveshaft

11 Carefully pull the swivel hub assembly outwards, and withdraw the driveshaft outer constant velocity joint from the hub assembly **(see illustration)**. If necessary, the shaft can be tapped out of the hub using a soft-faced mallet.

12 Support the driveshaft, then withdraw the inner constant velocity joint from the transmission, taking care not to damage the driveshaft oil seal **(see illustration)**. Remove the driveshaft from the vehicle.

2.6 With the holding tool in place, slacken and remove the driveshaft retaining nut using a socket and long bar

2.8 Undo the nut and withdraw the lower suspension arm balljoint clamp bolt from the swivel hub

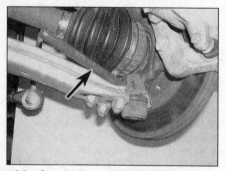

2.9a Spread the swivel hub by tapping a small chisel (arrowed) into the split . . .

2.9b . . . then pull the lower suspension arm downwards using a bar and chain or similar arrangement, pivoting on the subframe

2.10 When the balljoint is released, remove the protector plate from the balljoint shank

Right-hand driveshaft

13 Loosen the two intermediate bearing retaining bolt nuts, then rotate the bolts through 90°, so that their offset heads are clear of the bearing outer race **(see illustration)**.

14 Carefully pull the swivel hub assembly outwards, and withdraw the driveshaft outer constant velocity joint from the hub assembly. If necessary, the shaft can be tapped out of the hub using a soft-faced mallet.

15 Support the outer end of the driveshaft, then pull on the inner end of the shaft to free the shaft from the transmission, and the intermediate bearing from its mounting bracket **(see illustration)**. Remove the driveshaft from the vehicle.

Refitting

16 Before installing the driveshaft, examine the driveshaft oil seal in the transmission for signs of damage or deterioration and, if necessary, renew it as described in Chapter 7. (Having got this far it is worth renewing the seal as a matter of course.)

17 Thoroughly clean the driveshaft splines, and the apertures in the transmission and hub assembly. Apply a thin film of grease to the oil seal lips, and to the driveshaft splines and shoulders. Check that all gaiter clips are securely fastened.

Left-hand driveshaft

18 Offer up the driveshaft, and locate the joint splines with those of the differential sun gear, taking great care not to damage the oil seal. Push the joint fully into position.

19 Locate the outer constant velocity joint splines with those of the swivel hub, and slide the joint back into position in the hub.

20 Refit the protector plate to the lower arm balljoint then, using the method employed on removal, locate the balljoint shank in the swivel hub, ensuring that the lug on the protector plate is correctly located in the clamp split. Insert the balljoint clamp bolt (from the rear of the swivel hub), then fit the new retaining nut and tighten it to the specified torque.

21 Lubricate the inner face and threads of the driveshaft retaining nut with clean engine oil, and refit it to the end of the driveshaft. Use the method employed on removal to prevent the hub from rotating, and tighten the driveshaft retaining nut to the specified torque. Check that the hub rotates freely.

22 Engage the locking cap with the driveshaft nut so that one of its cut-outs is aligned with the driveshaft hole. Secure the cap in position with the R-clip.

23 Locate the connecting link on the anti-roll bar and refit the washer and a new retaining nut. Tighten the nut to the specified torque.

24 Where necessary, reconnect the ABS wheel sensor wiring connector, ensuring that the wiring is correctly routed and retained by all the necessary clips and ties.

25 Refill the transmission with the specified

2.11 Pull the swivel hub outwards, and withdraw the driveshaft outer constant velocity joint from the hub

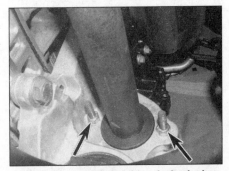

2.13 On the right-hand driveshaft, slacken the intermediate bearing retaining bolt nuts (arrowed), then turn the bolts through 90°

type and quantity of oil as described in Chapter 7.

26 On completion, refit the roadwheel, then lower the vehicle to the ground and tighten the roadwheel bolts to the specified torque.

Right-hand driveshaft

27 Check that the intermediate bearing rotates smoothly, without any sign of roughness or undue free play between its inner and outer races. If necessary, renew the bearing as described in Section 5.

28 Apply a smear of grease to the outer race of the intermediate bearing, then pass the inner end of the driveshaft through the bearing mounting bracket.

29 Carefully locate the inner driveshaft splines with those of the differential sun gear, taking care not to damage the oil seal. Align the intermediate bearing with its mounting bracket, and push the driveshaft fully into position. If necessary, use a soft-faced mallet to tap the outer race of the bearing into position in the mounting bracket.

30 Locate the outer constant velocity joint splines with those of the swivel hub, and slide the joint back into position in the hub.

31 Ensure that the intermediate bearing is correctly seated, then rotate its retaining bolts back through 90°, so that their offset heads are resting against the bearing outer race. Tighten the retaining nuts to the specified torque.

32 Carry out the operations described above in paragraphs 20 to 26.

2.12 Support the driveshaft, then withdraw the inner constant velocity joint from the transmission

2.15 Free the shaft inner end from the transmission, and the intermediate bearing from its mounting bracket

3 Driveshaft rubber gaiters – renewal

Outer joint

1 Remove the driveshaft from the car as described in Section 2.

2 Release the rubber gaiter outer retaining clip by cutting through it using a junior hacksaw **(see illustration)**. Spread the clip and remove it from the gaiter.

3 Release the rubber gaiter inner retaining clip using a screwdriver, then mark the position of the end of the gaiter on the driveshaft, using quick-drying paint **(see illustrations)**.

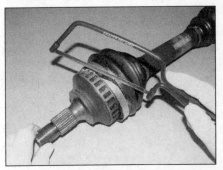

3.2 Release the rubber gaiter outer retaining clip by cutting through it with a hacksaw

3.3a Release the inner retaining clip using a screwdriver . . .

3.3b . . . then mark the position of the end of the gaiter on the driveshaft

3.4 Slide the gaiter down the shaft, then scoop out the excess grease

4 Slide the rubber gaiter down the shaft, to expose the outer constant velocity joint then scoop out the excess grease **(see illustration)**. It is advisable to wear disposable rubber gloves during this operation.

5 Hold the driveshaft and, using a mallet, sharply strike the edge of the outer joint to drive it off the end of the shaft **(see illustration)**. The joint is retained on the driveshaft by a circlip, and striking the joint in this manner forces the circlip into its groove, so allowing the joint to slide off.

6 Once the joint assembly has been removed, remove the circlip from the groove in the driveshaft splines, and discard it **(see illustration)**. A new circlip must be fitted on reassembly.

7 Withdraw the rubber gaiter from the driveshaft, and slide off the inner retaining clip.

8 With the constant velocity joint removed from the driveshaft, thoroughly clean the joint using paraffin, or a suitable solvent, and dry it thoroughly. Carry out a visual inspection of the joint.

9 Move the inner splined driving member from side-to-side, to expose each ball in turn at the top of its track. Examine the balls for cracks, flat spots, or signs of surface pitting.

10 Inspect the ball tracks on the inner and outer members. If the tracks have widened, the balls will no longer be a tight fit. At the same time, check the ball cage windows for wear or cracking between the windows.

11 If any of the constant velocity joint components are found to be worn or damaged, it will be necessary to renew the complete joint assembly (where available), or even the complete driveshaft (where no joint components are available separately). Refer to your Citroën dealer for further information

on parts availability. If the joint is in satisfactory condition, obtain a repair kit consisting of a new gaiter, circlip, retaining clips, and the correct type and quantity of grease.

12 To install the new gaiter, perform the operations shown **(see illustrations)**. Be sure to stay in order, and follow the captions carefully. Note that different types of gaiter retaining clips may be encountered, but the fitting procedures will be similar to those shown.

13 Check that the constant velocity joint moves freely in all directions, then refit the driveshaft to the car as described in Section 2.

Inner joint

14 Remove the driveshaft from the vehicle as described in Section 2.

15 Measure the distance between the inner edges of the driveshaft inner and outer rubber

3.5 Sharply strike the edge of the outer joint to drive it off the end of the shaft

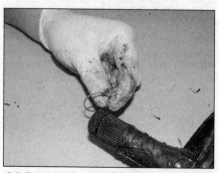

3.6 Remove the circlip from the groove in the driveshaft splines

3.12a Slide the new gaiter inner retaining clip on the driveshaft . . .

3.12b . . . followed by the new gaiter with the outer retaining clip in place

3.12c Locate a new circlip in the driveshaft groove . . .

3.12d . . . then compress the circlip using a cable tie

3.12e Use side-cutters to pull the cable tie as tight as possible, then cut off the end

3.12f Slide the CV joint onto the splines, and position the inner member up against the cable tie

3.12g Strike the end of the joint sharply to displace the cable tie and force the inner member over the circlip

3.12h With the joint in place, cut off the cable tie

3.12i Pack the joint with half the recommended quantity of grease . . .

3.12j . . . working it well into the ball tracks while twisting the joint

3.12k Fill the gaiter with the remaining grease . . .

3.12l . . . then slide the gaiter over the joint outer member, engaging it with the locating groove

3.12m Locate the gaiter inner end in the shaft groove or against the mark made on removal, slide the clip in place and compress the raised portion using pincers or side-cutters

gaiters and record this dimension for use when refitting (see illustration).

16 Release the rubber gaiter inner and outer retaining clips by cutting through them using a

junior hacksaw (see illustration). Spread the clips and remove them from the gaiter.

17 Withdraw the joint outer member from the tripod, and recover the spring and thrust cap

from inside the outer member (see illustrations). As the outer member is

3.12n Secure the gaiter outer retaining clip in the same way

3.15 Measure and record the distance between the inner edges of the driveshaft inner and outer gaiters

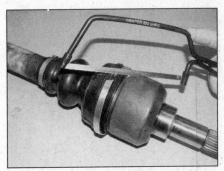

3.16 Release the gaiter retaining clips by cutting through them with a hacksaw

3.17a Withdraw the joint outer member from the tripod . . .

3.17b . . . and recover the spring and thrust cap from inside the outer member

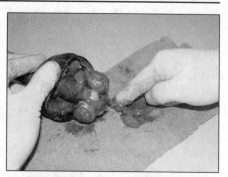

3.18 Wipe away as much grease as possible from the tripod and bearing rollers

3.19 Remove the tripod using a two- or three-legged hydraulic bearing puller or a press

3.22a Slide the new inner retaining clip and the gaiter onto the driveshaft

3.22b Mount the driveshaft in a vice, engage the tripod over the splines and tap it fully into position

withdrawn, check whether the tripod bearing rollers are staked to the tripod, or secured by circlips. If the rollers are not secured to the tripod, wrap adhesive tape around the rollers to hold them in position.

3.22c Using a small punch, stake the tripod to the driveshaft in three places

3.22e . . . working it well into the bearing rollers

18 Wipe away as much of the excess grease as possible from the tripod and bearing rollers **(see illustration)**. It is advisable to wear disposable rubber gloves during this operation.

3.22d Pack the tripod and the gaiter with half the recommended quantity of the grease . . .

3.22f Refit the spring and thrust cap to the outer member . . .

19 The tripod joint can now be removed using a two- or three-legged hydraulic bearing puller or a press. If a puller is being used, ensure that the legs of the puller are located behind the tripod, and not in contact with the joint rollers. If a press is being used, support the underside of the tripod, and press the driveshaft out of the joint **(see illustration)**.

20 With the tripod removed, slide the gaiter off the end of the driveshaft.

21 Thoroughly clean all the constant velocity joint components using paraffin, or a suitable solvent, and dry them thoroughly. Examine the tripod, bearing rollers and outer member for any signs of scoring or wear, and for smoothness of movement of the rollers on the tripod stems. If any of the components are found to be worn or damaged, it will be necessary to renew the complete joint assembly (where available), or even the complete driveshaft (where no joint components are available separately). Refer to your Citroën dealer for further information on parts availability. If the joint is in satisfactory condition, obtain a repair kit consisting of a new gaiter, retaining clips, and the correct type and quantity of grease.

22 To install the new gaiter, perform the operations shown **(see illustrations)**. Be sure to stay in order, and follow the captions carefully. Note that different types of gaiter retaining clips may be encountered, but the fitting procedures will be similar to those shown.

23 Check that the constant velocity joint moves freely in all directions, then refit the driveshaft to the car as described in Section 2.

3.22g . . . then pack the outer member with the remaining grease

3.22h Locate the outer member over the tripod and engage the gaiter with the outer member groove

3.22i Push the outer member fully into position over the tripod, while lifting the gaiter inner end to expel trapped air

3.22j Position the outer retaining clip over the gaiter and compress the raised portion using pincers or side-cutters

3.22k Position the gaiter inner end at the dimension recorded during removal, slip on the clip and compress the raised portion

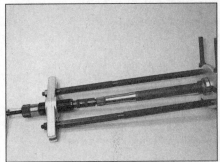

5.3 Using a long-reach bearing puller to remove the intermediate bearing from the right-hand driveshaft

4 Driveshaft overhaul – general information

1 If any of the checks described in *Road test* in Chapter 1A or 1B reveal possible wear in any driveshaft joint, carry out the following procedures to identify the source of the problem.

2 Firmly apply the handbrake, then jack up the front of the vehicle and support it securely on axle stands (see *Jacking and vehicle support*).

3 Referring to the information contained in Section 2, make up a tool to hold the wheel hub, and bolt the tool to the hub. Remove the R-clip and locking cap from the driveshaft retaining nut and use a torque wrench to check that the nut is securely fastened. Once tightened, refit the locking cap and R-clip. Repeat this check on the remaining driveshaft nut.

4 Road test the vehicle, and listen for a metallic clicking from the front as the vehicle

is driven slowly in a circle on full-lock. If a clicking noise is heard, this indicates wear in the outer constant velocity joint. This means that the joint must be renewed; reconditioning is not possible.

5 If vibration, consistent with road speed, is felt through the car when accelerating, there is a possibility of wear in the inner constant velocity joints.

6 To check the joints for wear, remove the driveshafts, then dismantle them as described in Section 3; if any wear or free play is found, the affected joint must be renewed. In some cases this may mean that the complete driveshaft assembly must be renewed, if the joints are not available separately. Refer to your Citroën dealer for information on the availability of driveshaft components.

5 Right-hand driveshaft intermediate bearing – renewal

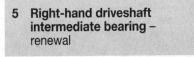

Note: *A suitable bearing puller will be*

required, to draw the bearing and collar off the driveshaft end.

1 Remove the right-hand driveshaft as described in Section 2 of this Chapter.

2 Check that the bearing outer race rotates smoothly and easily, without any signs of roughness or undue free play between the inner and outer races. If necessary, renew the bearing as follows.

3 Using a long-reach universal bearing puller, carefully draw the collar and intermediate bearing off the driveshaft inner end **(see illustration)**. Apply a smear of grease to the inner race of the new bearing, then fit the bearing over the end of the driveshaft. Using a hammer and suitable piece of tubing which bears only on the bearing inner race, tap the new bearing into position on the driveshaft, until it abuts the constant velocity joint outer member. Once the bearing is correctly positioned, tap the bearing collar onto the shaft until it contacts the bearing inner race.

4 Check that the bearing rotates freely, then refit the driveshaft as described in Section 2.

Chapter 9
Braking system

Contents

Degrees of difficulty

Easy, suitable for novice with little experience	Fairly easy, suitable for beginner with some experience	Fairly difficult, suitable for competent DIY mechanic	Difficult, suitable for experienced DIY mechanic	Very difficult, suitable for expert DIY or professional

Specifications

Front disc brakes
Caliper type . . . . Lucas C54
Disc diameter . . . . 266.0 mm
Disc thickness:
　New . . . . 20.4 mm
　Minimum thickness . . . . 18.4 mm
Maximum disc run-out . . . . 0.1 mm
Brake pad minimum thickness . . . . 2.0 mm

Rear drum brakes
Drum internal diameter:
　New . . . . 228.6 mm
　Maximum after machining . . . . 230.6 mm
Brake shoe minimum thickness . . . . 1.5 mm

Torque wrench settings	Nm	lbf ft
ABS hydraulic modulator retaining nuts	12	9
ABS wheel sensor retaining bolts*	8	6
Front brake caliper guide pin bolts*	27	20
Front brake caliper mounting bracket-to-swivel hub bolts*	105	77
Master cylinder-to-servo unit nuts	20	15
Rear brake pressure-regulating valve mounting bolt	27	20
Roadwheel bolts	85	63
Vacuum pump retaining nuts/bolts (diesel engine models)	25	18
Vacuum servo unit mounting nuts	23	17

*Use thread-locking compound

1 General information

The braking system is of the servo-assisted, dual-circuit hydraulic type. The arrangement of the hydraulic system is such that each circuit operates one front and one rear brake from a tandem master cylinder. Under normal circumstances, both circuits operate in unison. However, in the event of hydraulic failure in one circuit, full braking force will still be available at two wheels.

All models are fitted with ventilated front disc brakes and self-adjusting rear drum brakes. An Anti-lock Braking System (ABS) is fitted as standard to certain models, and is offered as an option on all other models (refer to Section 20 for further information on ABS operation).

The front disc brakes are actuated by single-piston sliding type calipers, which ensure that equal pressure is applied to each disc pad.

The rear drum brakes incorporate leading and trailing shoes, which are actuated by twin-piston wheel cylinders. A self-adjusting mechanism is incorporated, to automatically compensate for brake shoe wear. As the brake shoe linings wear, the footbrake operation automatically operates the adjuster mechanism, which effectively lengthens the shoe strut and repositions the brake shoes, to reduce the lining-to-drum clearance.

To prevent rear wheel lock-up during emergency braking, a load-sensitive pressure-regulating valve assembly is fitted into the hydraulic circuit to each rear brake. The valve is mounted on the underside of the vehicle at the rear and is attached to the rear suspension by means of an operating rod and spring. The valve measures the load on the rear of the vehicle via the movement of the rear suspension and regulates the hydraulic pressure applied to the rear brakes accordingly. On models equipped with ABS, the hydraulic pressure applied to the rear brakes is regulated by the ABS hydraulic modulator under all braking conditions. On these models, the separate mechanical pressure-regulating valve assembly is not used.

On all models, the handbrake provides an independent mechanical means of rear brake application.

On diesel engine models, there is insufficient vacuum in the inlet manifold to operate the braking system servo effectively at all times. To overcome this problem, a vacuum pump is fitted to the engine, to provide sufficient vacuum to operate the servo unit. The vacuum pump is mounted on the left-hand end of the cylinder head, and driven directly off the end of the camshaft.

Note: *When servicing any part of the system, work carefully and methodically; also observe scrupulous cleanliness when overhauling any part of the hydraulic system. Always renew* components *(in axle sets, where applicable) if in doubt about their condition, and use only genuine Citroën replacement parts, or at least those of known good quality. Note the warnings given in 'Safety first!' and at relevant points in this Chapter concerning the dangers of asbestos dust and brake hydraulic fluid.*

2 Hydraulic system – bleeding

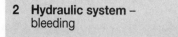

⚠ *Warning: Brake hydraulic fluid is poisonous; wash off immediately and thoroughly in the case of skin contact, and seek immediate medical advice if any fluid is swallowed or gets into the eyes. Certain types of hydraulic fluid are inflammable, and may ignite when allowed into contact with hot components; when servicing any hydraulic system, it is safest to assume that the fluid is inflammable, and to take precautions against the risk of fire as though it is petrol that is being handled. Hydraulic fluid is also an effective paint stripper, and will attack plastics; if any is spilt, it should be washed off immediately, using copious quantities of fresh water. Finally, it is hygroscopic (it absorbs moisture from the air) – old fluid may be contaminated and unfit for further use. When topping-up or renewing the fluid, always use the recommended type, and ensure that it comes from a freshly-opened sealed container.*

Note: *On models with a hydraulic clutch, it may be necessary to bleed that system; see Chapter 6.*

Models without ABS

General

1 The correct operation of any hydraulic system is only possible after removing all air from the components and circuit; this is achieved by bleeding the system.

2 During the bleeding procedure, add only clean, unused hydraulic fluid of the recommended type (see *Lubricants and fluids*); never re-use fluid that has already been bled from the system. Ensure that sufficient fluid is available before starting work.

2.14 Rear brake wheel cylinder dust cap (arrowed)

3 If there is any possibility of incorrect fluid being already in the system, the brake components and circuit must be flushed completely with uncontaminated, correct fluid, and new seals should be fitted to the various components.

4 If hydraulic fluid has been lost from the system, or air has entered because of a leak, ensure that the fault is cured before proceeding further.

5 Park the vehicle on level ground, switch off the engine and select first or reverse gear, then chock the wheels and release the handbrake.

6 Check that all pipes and hoses are secure, unions tight and bleed screws closed. Clean any dirt from around the bleed screws.

7 Unscrew the master cylinder reservoir cap, and top the master cylinder reservoir up to the MAX level line; refit the cap loosely, and remember to maintain the fluid level above the DANGER level line throughout the procedure, or there is a risk of further air entering the system.

8 There is a number of one-man, do-it-yourself brake bleeding kits currently available from motor accessory shops. It is recommended that one of these kits is used whenever possible, as they greatly simplify the bleeding operation, and also reduce the risk of expelled air and fluid being drawn back into the system. If such a kit is not available, the basic (two-man) method must be used, which is described in detail below.

9 If a kit is to be used, prepare the vehicle as described previously, and follow the kit manufacturer's instructions, as the procedure may vary slightly according to the type being used; generally, they are as outlined below in the relevant sub-section.

10 Whichever method is used, the same sequence must be followed (paragraphs 11 and 12) to ensure the removal of all air from the system.

Bleeding sequence

11 If the system has been only partially disconnected, and suitable precautions were taken to minimise fluid loss, it should be necessary only to bleed that part of the system (ie, the primary or secondary circuit).

12 If the complete system is to be bled, then it should be done working in the following sequence:
a) Right-hand rear brake.
b) Left-hand front brake.
c) Left-hand rear brake.
d) Right-hand front brake.

Basic (two-man) method

13 Collect a clean glass jar, a suitable length of plastic or rubber tubing which is a tight fit over the bleed screw, and a ring spanner to fit the screw. The help of an assistant will also be required.

14 Remove the dust cap from the first screw in the sequence **(see illustration)**. Fit the spanner and tube to the screw, place the other end of the tube in the jar, and pour in sufficient fluid to cover the end of the tube.

15 Ensure that the master cylinder reservoir fluid level is maintained above the DANGER level line throughout the procedure.

16 Have the assistant fully depress the brake pedal several times to build-up pressure, then maintain it on the final downstroke.

17 While pedal pressure is maintained, unscrew the bleed screw (approximately one turn) and allow the compressed fluid and air to flow into the jar. The assistant should maintain pedal pressure, following it down to the floor if necessary, and should not release it until instructed to do so. When the flow stops, tighten the bleed screw again, have the assistant release the pedal slowly, and recheck the reservoir fluid level.

18 Repeat the steps given in paragraphs 16 and 17 until the fluid emerging from the bleed screw is free from air bubbles. If the master cylinder has been drained and refilled, and air is being bled from the first screw in the sequence, allow approximately five seconds between cycles for the master cylinder passages to refill.

19 When no more air bubbles appear, tighten the bleed screw securely, remove the tube and spanner, and refit the dust cap. Do not overtighten the bleed screw.

20 Repeat the procedure on the remaining screws in the sequence, until all air is removed from the system and the brake pedal feels firm again.

Using a one-way valve kit

21 As their name implies, these kits consist of a length of tubing with a one-way valve fitted, to prevent expelled air and fluid being drawn back into the system; some kits include a translucent container, which can be positioned so that the air bubbles can be more easily seen flowing from the end of the tube.

22 The kit is connected to the bleed screw, which is then opened. The user returns to the driver's seat, depresses the brake pedal with a smooth, steady stroke, and slowly releases it; this is repeated until the expelled fluid is clear of air bubbles.

23 Note that these kits simplify work so much that it is easy to forget the master cylinder reservoir fluid level; ensure that this is maintained above the DANGER level line at all times.

Using a pressure-bleeding kit

24 These kits are usually operated by the reservoir of pressurised air contained in the spare tyre. However, note that it will probably be necessary to reduce the pressure to a lower level than normal; refer to the instructions supplied with the kit.

25 By connecting a pressurised, fluid-filled container to the master cylinder reservoir, bleeding can be carried out simply by opening each screw in turn (in the specified sequence), and allowing the fluid to flow out until no more air bubbles can be seen in the expelled fluid.

26 This method has the advantage that the large reservoir of fluid provides an additional safeguard against air being drawn into the system during bleeding.

27 Pressure-bleeding is particularly effective when bleeding 'difficult' systems, or when bleeding the complete system at the time of routine fluid renewal.

All methods

28 When bleeding is complete, and firm pedal feel is restored, wash off any spilt fluid, tighten the bleed screws, and refit their dust caps.

29 Check the hydraulic fluid level in the master cylinder reservoir, and top-up if necessary.

30 Discard any fluid that has been bled from the system; it will not be fit for re-use.

31 Check the feel of the brake pedal. If it feels at all spongy, air must still be present in the system, and further bleeding is required. Failure to bleed properly after a reasonable repetition of the bleeding procedure may be due to worn master cylinder seals.

Models with ABS

⚠️ **Warning: On models equipped with ABS, ensure that the ignition is switched off before starting the bleeding procedure, to avoid any possibility of voltage being applied to the hydraulic modulator before the bleeding procedure is completed. Ideally, the battery should be disconnected. If voltage is applied to the modulator before the bleeding procedure is complete, this will effectively drain the hydraulic fluid in the modulator, rendering the unit unserviceable. Do not, therefore, attempt to 'run' the modulator in order to bleed the brakes.**

32 A pressure-bleeding kit must be used for bleeding the hydraulic system on ABS models – see paragraphs 24 to 27.

33 Following the sequence given in paragraph 12, bleed each brake in turn until clean fluid, free of air bubbles, is seen to emerge. Pause between bleeding each brake to ensure that the fluid level in the reservoir is above the DANGER level.

34 When bleeding is complete, and firm pedal feel is restored, wash off any spilt fluid, tighten the bleed screws, and refit their dust caps.

35 Check the hydraulic fluid level in the master cylinder reservoir, and top-up if necessary.

36 Discard any fluid that has been bled from the system; it will not be fit for re-use.

37 Check the feel of the brake pedal. If it feels at all spongy, air must still be present in the system, and further bleeding is required.

⚠️ *Warning: Do not operate the vehicle if you are in doubt about the effectiveness of the braking system. If considerable air was present in the system prior to bleeding, it is possible for some of this air to remain trapped in the hydraulic modulator assembly. If the pedal continues to feel spongy after repeated bleedings, or if any of the brake system warning lights remain on, have the vehicle towed to a Citroën dealer to be bled with the use of Citroën diagnostic equipment.*

3 Hydraulic pipes and hoses – renewal

Note: *Before starting work, refer to the note at the beginning of Section 2 concerning the dangers of hydraulic fluid.*

1 If any pipe or hose is to be renewed, minimise fluid loss by first removing the master cylinder reservoir cap, then tightening it down onto a piece of polythene to obtain an airtight seal. Alternatively, flexible hoses can be sealed, if required, using a proprietary brake hose clamp; metal brake pipe unions can be plugged (if care is taken not to allow dirt into the system) or capped immediately they are disconnected. Place a wad of rag under any union that is to be disconnected, to catch any spilt fluid.

2 If a flexible hose is to be disconnected, unscrew the brake pipe union nut before removing the spring clip which secures the hose to its mounting bracket **(see illustration)**.

3 To unscrew the union nuts, it is preferable to obtain a brake pipe spanner of the correct size; these are available from most large motor accessory shops. Failing this, a close-fitting open-ended spanner will be required,

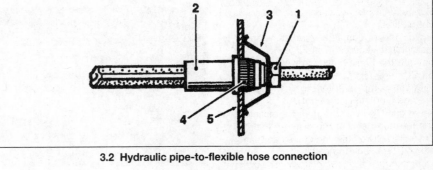

3.2 Hydraulic pipe-to-flexible hose connection

1 *Union nut*   3 *Spring clip support*   5 *Mounting bracket*
2 *Flexible hose*   4 *Splined end fitting*

though if the nuts are tight or corroded, their flats may be rounded-off if the spanner slips. In such a case, a self-locking wrench is often the only way to unscrew a stubborn union, but it follows that the pipe and the damaged nuts must be renewed on reassembly. Always clean a union and surrounding area before disconnecting it. If disconnecting a component with more than one union, make a careful note of the connections before disturbing any of them.

4 If a brake pipe is to be renewed, it can be obtained, cut to length and with the union nuts and end flares in place, from Citroën dealers. All that is then necessary is to bend it to shape, following the line of the original, before fitting it to the car. Alternatively, most motor accessory shops can make up brake pipes from kits, but this requires very careful measurement of the original, to ensure that the replacement is of the correct length. The safest answer is usually to take the original to the shop as a pattern.

5 On refitting, do not overtighten the union nuts. It is not necessary to exercise brute force to obtain a sound joint.

6 Ensure that the pipes and hoses are correctly routed, with no kinks, and that they are secured in the clips or brackets provided. After fitting, remove the polythene from the reservoir, and bleed the hydraulic system as described in Section 2. Wash off any spilt fluid, and check carefully for fluid leaks.

4 Front brake pads – renewal

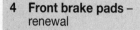

⚠ **Warning: Renew BOTH sets of front brake pads at the same time – NEVER renew the pads on only one wheel, as uneven braking may result. Note that the dust created by wear of the pads may contain asbestos, which is a health hazard. Never blow it out with compressed air, and don't inhale any of it. An approved filtering mask should be worn when working on the brakes. DO NOT use petrol or petroleum-based solvents to clean brake parts; use brake cleaner or methylated spirit only.**

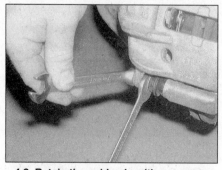

4.3 Retain the guide pin with a spanner while undoing the lower guide pin bolt

Note: *New guide pin bolts must be used on refitting.*

1 Apply the handbrake, then jack up the front of the vehicle and support it on axle stands (see *Jacking and vehicle support*). Remove the front roadwheels.

2 Push the piston into its bore by pulling the caliper outwards.

3 Where applicable, prise off the dust covers, then undo and remove the lower caliper guide pin bolt, using a slim open-ended spanner to prevent the guide pin itself from rotating **(see illustration)**. Discard the guide pin bolt – new bolts must be used on refitting.

4 Slacken the upper guide pin bolt, while holding the guide pin with the open-ended spanner as before. Pivot the caliper upwards off the brake pads, and tie the caliper to the suspension strut to hold it in this position **(see illustration)**.

5 Withdraw the two brake pads from the caliper mounting bracket noting their fitted positions if they are to be re-used (ie, inner and outer). Where fitted, recover the shim from the caliper piston, noting its correct fitted position **(see illustrations)**.

6 First measure the thickness of each brake pad's friction material. If either pad is worn at any point to the specified minimum thickness or less, all four pads must be renewed **(see illustration)**. Also, the pads should be renewed if any are fouled with oil or grease; there is no satisfactory way of degreasing friction material, once contaminated. If any of the brake pads are worn unevenly, or are fouled with oil or grease, trace and rectify the cause before reassembly. New brake pads

4.4 Slacken the upper guide pin bolt, and pivot the caliper upwards off the brake pads

and repair kits are available from Citroën dealers.

7 If the brake pads are still serviceable, carefully clean them using a clean, fine wire brush or similar, paying particular attention to the sides and back of the metal backing. Clean out the grooves in the friction material, and pick out any large embedded particles of dirt or debris. Carefully clean the pad locations in the caliper mounting bracket.

8 Prior to fitting the pads, check that the guide pins are free to slide easily in the caliper body/mounting bracket, and check that the rubber guide pin gaiters are undamaged. Brush the dust and dirt from the caliper and piston, but do not inhale it, as it is injurious to health. Inspect the dust seal around the piston for damage, and the piston for evidence of fluid leaks, corrosion or damage. If attention to any of these components is necessary, refer to Section 8.

9 If new brake pads are to be fitted, the caliper piston must be pushed back into the cylinder to make room for them; either use a G-clamp or similar tool, or use suitable pieces of wood as levers. Provided that the master cylinder reservoir has not been overfilled with hydraulic fluid, there should be no spillage, but keep a careful watch on the fluid level while retracting the piston. If the fluid level rises above the MAX level line at any time, the surplus should be syphoned off or ejected via a plastic tube connected to the bleed screw (see Section 2).

10 Install the pads in the caliper mounting bracket, ensuring that the friction material of each pad is against the brake disc, and that

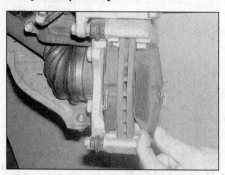

4.5a Withdraw the two brake pads from the caliper mounting bracket . . .

4.5b . . . and, where fitted, recover the shim from the caliper piston

4.6 Measuring brake pad friction material thickness

the pads are in their correct locations if the original pads are being re-used. Where fitted, locate the shim in place on the caliper piston.

11 Untie the caliper piston and carefully pivot it back down over the pads.

12 If not precoated, apply suitable thread locking compound to the threads of the two new guide pin bolts. Insert the lower bolt and tighten it to the specified torque. Hold the guide pin with the open-ended spanner as the guide pin bolt is tightened.

13 Remove the original upper guide pin bolt and fit the new bolt, tightening it to the specified torque. Where applicable, refit the dust covers to the guide pins.

14 Depress the brake pedal repeatedly, until the pads are pressed into firm contact with the brake disc, and normal (non-assisted) pedal pressure is restored.

15 Repeat the above procedure on the remaining front brake caliper.

16 Refit the roadwheels, then lower the vehicle to the ground and tighten the roadwheel bolts to the specified torque.

17 Finally, check the hydraulic fluid level in the master cylinder reservoir as described in *Weekly checks*.

18 Note that new pads will not give full braking efficiency until they have bedded-in. Be prepared for this, and avoid hard braking as far as possible for the first hundred miles or so after pad renewal.

5 Rear brake shoes – renewal

⚠️ *Warning: Brake shoes must be renewed on BOTH rear wheels at the same time – NEVER renew the shoes on only one wheel, as uneven braking may result. Also, the dust created by wear of the shoes may contain asbestos, which is a health hazard. Never blow it out with compressed air, and don't inhale any of it. An approved filtering mask should be worn when working on the brakes. DO NOT use petrol or petroleum-based solvents to clean brake parts; use brake cleaner or methylated spirit only.*

Note: *The components encountered may vary in detail, but the principles described in the following paragraphs are equally applicable to all models. Make a careful note of the fitted positions of all components before dismantling.*

1 Remove the brake drum as described in Section 7.

2 Working carefully, and taking the necessary precautions, remove all traces of brake dust from the brake drum, backplate and shoes.

3 Measure the thickness of the friction material of each brake shoe at several points; if either shoe is worn at any point to the specified minimum thickness or less, all four shoes must be renewed as a set. The shoes should also be renewed if any are fouled with

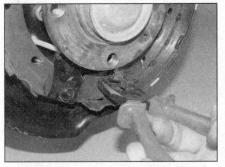
5.6 Disengage the lower return spring from the trailing shoe, unhook it from the leading shoe and lift out the spring

oil or grease; there is no satisfactory way of degreasing friction material, once contaminated.

4 If any of the brake shoes are worn unevenly, or fouled with oil or grease, trace and rectify the cause before reassembly.

5 Make a note of the correct fitted positions of the springs and adjuster strut, to use as a guide on reassembly.

6 Disengage the end of the lower return spring from the trailing shoe, unhook it from the leading shoe and lift out the spring **(see illustration)**.

7 Using pliers, depress the leading shoe retainer spring cup and turn it through 90°, while holding the retainer pin with your finger from the rear of the backplate. With the cup removed, lift off the spring, then withdraw the retainer pin **(see illustrations)**. Repeat this procedure for the retainer on the trailing shoe.

5.7a Depress the retainer spring cup and turn it through 90°, while holding the retainer pin from the rear of the backplate

8 Detach the handbrake cable end from the lever on the trailing shoe **(see illustration)**.

9 Disconnect the adjuster lever spring from the leading shoe and adjuster lever, then withdraw the adjuster lever **(see illustrations)**.

10 Lift the brake shoes off the lower pivot post and off the wheel cylinder pistons. Spread the shoes apart at the bottom and remove the adjuster strut, upper return spring and then the two brake shoes.

11 With the brake shoes removed, retain the wheel cylinder pistons in the wheel cylinder using a cable tie or a strong elastic band. Do not depress the brake pedal until the brakes are reassembled.

12 Withdraw the forked end from the adjuster strut, and carefully examine the assembly for signs of wear or damage. Pay particular attention to the threads and the knurled adjuster wheel, and renew if necessary.

5.7b With the cup removed, lift off the spring, then withdraw the retainer pin

5.8 Detach the handbrake cable end from the lever on the trailing shoe

5.9a Disconnect the adjuster lever spring (arrowed) . . .

5.9b . . . then withdraw the adjuster lever

5.17 Fit the upper return spring to the leading and trailing brake shoes

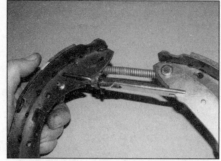

5.18 Engage the adjuster strut with the leading shoe and handbrake lever

5.20 Manoeuvre the partially assembled brake shoe assembly into position on the backplate

13 Check the condition of all return springs and renew any that show signs of distortion or other damage.

14 Peel back the rubber protective caps, and check the wheel cylinder for fluid leaks or other damage; check that both cylinder pistons are free to move easily. Refer to Section 9, if necessary, for information on wheel cylinder renewal.

15 Prior to installation, clean the backplate, and apply a thin smear of high-temperature brake grease or anti-seize compound to all those surfaces of the backplate which bear on the shoes, particularly the wheel cylinder pistons and lower pivot point. Do not allow the lubricant to foul the friction material.

16 Ensure that the handbrake lever stop-peg is correctly located against the edge of the trailing shoe, and that the return spring is in position.

17 Fit the upper return spring to its location in the leading and trailing brake shoes **(see illustration)**.

18 Screw in the adjuster wheel until the minimum strut length is obtained, then engage the strut with the leading shoe and handbrake lever **(see illustration)**.

19 Undo the two bolts securing the wheel cylinder to the brake backplate. Carefully ease the cylinder from its location until the bleed screw is clear of the backplate. Move the cylinder upwards as far as the hydraulic pipe will allow, to provide as much clearance between the cylinder and wheel hub as possible.

20 Manoeuvre the partially assembled brake shoe assembly into position on the backplate, and engage the brake shoes with the wheel cylinder pistons **(see illustration)**.

21 Feed the lower return spring behind the lower pivot post and connect one end to the leading brake shoe **(see illustration)**.

22 Hold the spring in place on the leading shoe and engage a screwdriver with the other end of the spring **(see illustration)**.

23 Pull the spring by means of the screwdriver until it just catches on the edge of its locating hole in the trailing shoe. Now engage the tip of the screwdriver with the end of the spring and pull it fully into place **(see illustration)**. Be prepared to have several attempts at this as there is very little working clearance behind the trailing shoe. Extreme patience is necessary!

24 Once the lower spring is connected, locate the brake shoes on the lower pivot post and at the same time ease the wheel cylinder back into its location. Refit the wheel cylinder retaining bolts and tighten them securely **(see illustration)**.

25 Position the adjuster lever on the leading shoe, ensuring that it locates behind the forked end of the adjuster strut. Reconnect the adjuster lever spring to the lever and leading shoe **(see illustration)**.

26 Reconnect the handbrake cable end to the handbrake lever on the trailing shoe.

27 Insert the leading brake shoe retainer pin through the backplate and place the spring on the pin. Hold the pin from behind, refit the cup and turn it through 90°. Repeat this procedure for the retainer on the trailing shoe, then tap the shoes to centralise them with the backplate.

5.21 Feed the lower return spring behind the pivot post and connect one end to the leading shoe

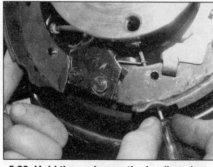

5.22 Hold the spring on the leading shoe and engage a screwdriver with the other end of the spring

5.23 Pull the spring until it catches on its locating hole, then pull it fully into place with the tip of a screwdriver

5.24 Locate the brake shoes on the lower pivot post and ease the wheel cylinder back into its location

5.25 Position the adjuster lever on the leading shoe and reconnect the spring

28 Using a screwdriver, turn the strut adjuster wheel to expand the shoes until the brake drum just slides over the shoes.

29 Refit the brake drum as described in Section 7.

30 Repeat the above procedure on the remaining rear brake.

31 Once both sets of rear shoes have been renewed, adjust the lining-to-drum clearance by repeatedly depressing the brake pedal. Whilst depressing the pedal, have an assistant listen to the rear drums, to check that the adjuster strut is functioning correctly; if so, a clicking sound will be emitted by the strut as the pedal is depressed.

32 Check and, if necessary, adjust the handbrake as described in Section 14.

33 On completion, check the hydraulic fluid level in the master cylinder as described in *Weekly checks*.

34 Note that new shoes will not give full braking efficiency until they have bedded-in. Be prepared for this, and avoid hard braking as far as possible for the first hundred miles or so after shoe renewal.

<table>
<tr><td>**6**</td><td>**Front brake disc –** inspection, removal and refitting</td><td></td></tr>
</table>

Note: *Before starting work, refer to the note at the beginning of Section 4 concerning the dangers of asbestos dust.*

Inspection

Note: *If either disc requires renewal, BOTH should be renewed at the same time, to ensure even and consistent braking. New brake pads should also be fitted.*

1 Apply the handbrake, then jack up the front of the car and support it on axle stands (see *Jacking and vehicle support*). Remove the appropriate front roadwheel.

2 Slowly rotate the brake disc so that the full area of both sides can be checked; remove the brake pads if better access is required to the inboard surface. Light scoring is normal in the area swept by the brake pads, but if heavy scoring or cracks are found, the disc must be renewed.

6.3 Using a micrometer to measure disc thickness

3 It is normal to find a lip of rust and brake dust around the disc's perimeter; this can be scraped off if required. If, however, a lip has formed due to excessive wear of the brake pad swept area, then the disc's thickness must be measured using a micrometer **(see illustration)**. Take measurements at several places around the disc, at the inside and outside of the pad swept area; if the disc has worn at any point to the specified minimum thickness or less, the disc must be renewed.

4 If the disc is thought to be warped, it can be checked for run-out. Either use a dial gauge mounted on any convenient fixed point while the disc is slowly rotated, or use feeler blades to measure (at several points all around the disc) the clearance between the disc and a fixed point, such as the caliper mounting bracket **(see illustration)**. If the measurements obtained are at the specified maximum or beyond, the disc is excessively warped, and must be renewed; however, it is worth checking first that the hub bearing is in good condition (Chapter 1A or 1B and/or 10). Also try the effect of removing the disc and turning it through 180º to reposition it on the hub; if the run-out is still excessive, the disc must be renewed.

5 Check the disc for cracks, especially around the wheel bolt holes, and any other wear or damage, and renew if necessary.

Removal

6 Remove the brake pads as described in Section 4.

7 Undo the two bolts securing the caliper mounting bracket to the swivel hub **(see**

6.4 Checking disc run-out using a dial gauge

illustration). Withdraw the mounting bracket, complete with caliper from the disc and swivel hub, and tie it to the front suspension coil spring, to avoid placing any strain on the fluid hose.

8 Use chalk or paint to mark the relationship of the disc to the hub, then remove the screws securing the brake disc to the hub, and remove the disc **(see illustrations)**. If it is tight, lightly tap its rear face with a hide or plastic mallet.

Refitting

9 Refitting is the reverse of the removal procedure, noting the following points:

a) Ensure that the mating surfaces of the disc and hub are clean and flat.

b) Align (if applicable) the marks made on removal, and securely tighten the disc retaining screws.

c) If a new disc has been fitted, use a suitable solvent to wipe any preservative coating from the disc before refitting the caliper.

d) Apply suitable thread locking compound to the threads of the caliper mounting bracket retaining bolts and tighten the bolts to the specified torque.

e) Refit the brake pads as described in Section 4.

f) Refit the roadwheel, then lower the vehicle to the ground and tighten the roadwheel bolts to the specified torque. On completion, repeatedly depress the brake pedal until normal (non-assisted) pedal pressure returns.

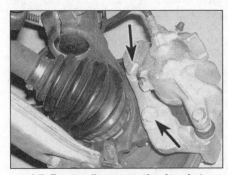

6.7 Front caliper mounting bracket retaining bolts (arrowed)

6.8a Undo the two retaining screws . . .

6.8b . . . and remove the front brake disc

7 Rear brake drum – removal, inspection and refitting

Note: *Before starting work, refer to the note at the beginning of Section 5 concerning the dangers of asbestos dust.*

Removal

1 Chock the front wheels, then jack up the rear of the vehicle and support it on axle stands (see *Jacking and vehicle support*). Remove the appropriate rear roadwheel and release the handbrake.

2 Remove the drum retaining screw(s).

3 It should now be possible to withdraw the brake drum by hand. It may be difficult to remove the drum due to the brake shoes binding on the inner circumference of the drum. If the brake shoes are binding, first check that the handbrake is fully released, then proceed as follows.

4 Turn the drum until one of the wheel bolt holes is positioned over the handbrake operating lever on the trailing shoe. This will be at approximately the 5 o'clock position on the left-hand rear brake, and the 7 o'clock position on the right-hand rear brake. Insert a screwdriver through the wheel bolt hole and move the handbrake operating lever towards the rear of the vehicle allowing the brake shoes to retract fully. It will be necessary to lift the lever slightly with the screwdriver so that the lever stop-peg can pass over the brake shoe web. The brake drum can now be withdrawn.

Inspection

Note: *If either drum requires renewal, BOTH should be renewed at the same time, to ensure even and consistent braking. New brake shoes should also be fitted.*

5 Working carefully, remove all traces of brake dust from the drum, but *avoid inhaling the dust, as it is injurious to health.*

6 Clean the outside of the drum, and check it for obvious signs of wear or damage, such as cracks around the roadwheel bolt holes; renew the drum if necessary.

7 Examine carefully the inside of the drum. Light scoring of the friction surface is normal, but if heavy scoring is found, the drum must be renewed. It is usual to find a lip on the drum's inboard edge which consists of a mixture of rust and brake dust; this should be scraped away, to leave a smooth surface which can be polished with fine (120- to 150-grade) emery paper. If, however, the lip is due to the friction surface being recessed by excessive wear, then the drum must be renewed.

8 If the drum is thought to be excessively worn, or oval, its internal diameter must be measured at several points using an internal micrometer. Take measurements in pairs, the second at right-angles to the first, and compare the two, to check for signs of ovality.

Provided that it does not enlarge the drum to beyond the specified maximum diameter, it may be possible to have the drum refinished by skimming or grinding; if this is not possible, the drums on both sides must be renewed. Note that if the drum is to be skimmed, BOTH drums must be refinished, to maintain a consistent internal diameter on both sides.

Refitting

9 If a new brake drum is to be installed, use a suitable solvent to remove any preservative coating that may have been applied to its interior. Note that it may also be necessary to shorten the adjuster strut length, by rotating the strut wheel, to allow the drum to pass over the brake shoes.

10 Ensure that the handbrake lever stop-peg is correctly repositioned against the edge of the brake shoe web, then locate the brake drum on the stub axle.

11 Refit and tighten the drum retaining screw(s).

12 Depress the footbrake several times to operate the self-adjusting mechanism.

13 Repeat the above procedure on the remaining rear brake assembly (where necessary), then check and, if necessary, adjust the handbrake cable as described in Section 14.

14 On completion, refit the roadwheel(s), then lower the vehicle to the ground and tighten the wheel bolts to the specified torque.

8 Front brake caliper – removal, overhaul and refitting

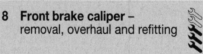

Note: *Before starting work, refer to the note at the beginning of Section 2 concerning the dangers of hydraulic fluid, and to the warning at the beginning of Section 4 concerning the dangers of asbestos dust.*
Note: *New guide pin bolts must be used on refitting.*

Removal

1 Apply the handbrake, then jack up the front of the vehicle and support it on axle stands (see *Jacking and vehicle support*). Remove the appropriate roadwheel.

2 Minimise fluid loss by first removing the master cylinder reservoir filler cap, and then tightening it down onto a piece of polythene, to obtain an airtight seal. Alternatively, use a brake hose clamp, a G-clamp or a similar tool to clamp the flexible hose.

3 Clean the area around the hydraulic fluid hose union on the caliper, then loosen the fluid hose union nut by half a turn.

4 Slacken and remove the upper and lower caliper guide pin bolts, using a slim open-ended spanner to prevent the guide pin itself from rotating. Discard the guide pin bolts – new bolts must be used on refitting. With the guide pin bolts removed, lift the caliper away

from the brake disc, then unscrew the caliper from the end of the brake hose. Note that the brake pads need not be disturbed, and can be left in position in the caliper mounting bracket.

Overhaul

5 The caliper can be overhauled after obtaining the relevant repair kit from a Citroën dealer. Ensure that the correct repair kit is obtained for the caliper being worked on. Note the locations of all components to ensure correct refitting, and lubricate the new seals using clean brake fluid. Follow the assembly instructions supplied with the repair kit.

Refitting

6 Screw the caliper body fully onto the flexible hydraulic fluid hose union, then check that the brake pads are still correctly fitted in the caliper mounting bracket.

7 Position the caliper over the brake pads. If the threads of the new guide pin bolts are not precoated with locking compound, apply a suitable locking compound to them. Fit the new lower guide pin bolt, then press the caliper into position and fit the new upper guide pin bolt. Tighten both the guide pin bolts to the specified torque, while retaining the guide pin with an open-ended spanner.

8 Tighten the hydraulic fluid hose union securely, then remove the brake hose clamp or polythene, where fitted, and bleed the hydraulic system as described in Section 2. Providing the precautions described were taken to minimise brake fluid loss, it should only be necessary to bleed the relevant front brake.

9 Depress the brake pedal repeatedly, until the pads are pressed into firm contact with the brake disc, and normal (non-assisted) pedal pressure is restored.

10 Refit the roadwheel, then lower the vehicle to the ground and tighten the roadwheel bolts to the specified torque.

9 Rear wheel cylinder – removal and refitting

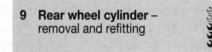

Note: *Before starting work, refer to the note at the beginning of Section 2 concerning the dangers of hydraulic fluid, and to the warning at the beginning of Section 5 concerning the dangers of asbestos dust.*

Removal

1 Remove the rear brake shoes as described in Section 5.

2 Minimise fluid loss by first removing the master cylinder reservoir filler cap, and then tightening it down onto a piece of polythene, to obtain an airtight seal. Alternatively, use a brake hose clamp, a G-clamp or a similar tool to clamp the flexible hose at the nearest convenient point to the wheel cylinder **(see illustration)**.

3 Wipe away all traces of dirt around the brake pipe union at the rear of the wheel cylinder, and unscrew the union nut **(see illustration)**. Carefully ease the pipe out of the wheel cylinder, and plug or tape over its end to prevent dirt entry. Wipe off any spilt fluid immediately.

4 Unscrew the two wheel cylinder retaining bolts from the rear of the backplate, and remove the cylinder, taking great care not to allow surplus hydraulic fluid to contaminate the brake shoe linings.

5 Note that it is not possible to overhaul the cylinder, since no components are available separately. If faulty, the complete wheel cylinder assembly must be renewed.

Refitting

6 The arrangement of the brake shoe components is such that the wheel cylinder must be released from the backplate to allow the shoes to be refitted. Follow the brake shoe refitting procedures contained in Section 5 then, with the wheel cylinder in position, proceed as follows.

7 Engage the brake pipe, and screw in the union nut two or three turns to ensure that the thread has started.

8 Insert the two wheel cylinder retaining bolts, and tighten them securely. Now fully tighten the brake pipe union nut.

9 Remove the clamp from the flexible brake hose, or the polythene from the master cylinder reservoir (as applicable).

10 Bleed the brake hydraulic system as described in Section 2. Providing suitable precautions were taken to minimise loss of fluid, it should only be necessary to bleed the relevant rear brake.

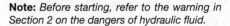

10 Master cylinder – removal and refitting

Note: *Before starting, refer to the warning in Section 2 on the dangers of hydraulic fluid.*

Removal

1 Minimise fluid loss by first removing the master cylinder reservoir filler cap, and then tightening it down onto a piece of polythene, to obtain an airtight seal.

2 Suitably cover the area below the master cylinder with absorbent rags and be prepared for escaping hydraulic fluid.

3 Wipe clean the area around the brake hydraulic pipe unions on the side of the master cylinder **(see illustration)**. Make a note of the correct fitted positions of the unions, then unscrew the union nuts and carefully withdraw the pipes. Plug or tape over the pipe ends and master cylinder orifices, to minimise fluid loss, and to prevent the entry of dirt into the system.

4 Disconnect the hydraulic fluid supply hose and suitably plug or cap the hose end.

5 Slacken and remove the two nuts securing

9.2 To minimise fluid loss, fit a brake hose clamp to the flexible hose

the master cylinder to the vacuum servo unit, then withdraw the unit from the servo.

6 Note that it is not possible to overhaul the master cylinder itself, since no internal components are available separately. If faulty, the complete cylinder assembly must be renewed.

Refitting

7 Fit the master cylinder to the servo unit, ensuring that the servo unit pushrod enters the master cylinder bore centrally. Refit the master cylinder mounting nuts, and tighten them to the specified torque.

8 Wipe clean the brake pipe unions, refit them to the master cylinder ports and tighten them securely.

9 Reconnect the hydraulic fluid supply hose.

10 Refill the master cylinder reservoir with new fluid, and bleed the complete hydraulic system as described in Section 2.

11 Vacuum servo unit (left-hand drive models) – testing, removal and refitting

Testing

1 To test the operation of the servo unit, depress the footbrake several times to exhaust the vacuum, then start the engine whilst keeping the pedal firmly depressed. As the engine starts, there should be a noticeable 'give' in the brake pedal as the vacuum builds-up. Allow the engine to run for at least two minutes, then switch it off. If the brake

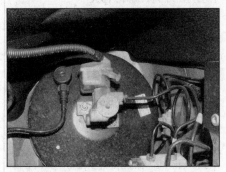

10.3 Master cylinder location on the front of the vacuum servo unit

9.3 Using a brake pipe spanner to unscrew the wheel cylinder union nut

pedal is now depressed it should feel normal, but further applications should result in the pedal feeling firmer, with the pedal stroke decreasing with each application.

2 If the servo does not operate as described, first inspect the servo unit check valve as described in Section 13. On diesel engine models, also check the operation of the vacuum pump as described in Section 23.

3 If the servo unit still fails to operate satisfactorily, the fault lies within the unit itself. Repairs to the unit are not possible – if faulty, the servo unit must be renewed.

Removal

4 Disconnect the battery negative terminal (refer to *Disconnecting the battery* in the Reference Chapter).

5 Remove the air cleaner assembly and air inlet ducts as described in the relevant Part of Chapter 4.

6 Remove the brake master cylinder reservoir filler cap, and tighten it down onto a piece of polythene, to obtain an airtight seal.

7 Suitably cover the area below the master cylinder with absorbent rags and be prepared for escaping hydraulic fluid.

8 Wipe clean the area around the brake hydraulic pipe unions on the side of the master cylinder. Make a note of the correct fitted positions of the unions, then unscrew the union nuts and carefully withdraw the pipes. Plug or tape over the pipe ends and master cylinder orifices, to minimise fluid loss, and to prevent the entry of dirt into the system.

9 Slacken and remove the two nuts securing the master cylinder to the vacuum servo unit, then withdraw the unit from the servo.

10 Withdraw the check valve from its rubber sealing grommet on the front face of the servo unit, using a pulling and twisting motion.

11 Working inside the car, extract the stud-type plastic clips, using a forked type tool, and remove the facia lower trim panel above the pedals on the driver's side.

12 Prise off the spring clip, then withdraw the clevis pin securing the servo unit pushrod to the brake pedal.

13 Disconnect the wiring connector from the stop-light switch above the brake pedal.

14 Undo the five nuts securing the pedal

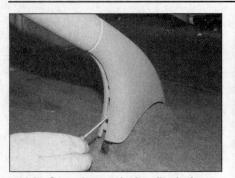

14.2a Spread apart the handbrake lever plastic trim . . .

bracket assembly to the bulkhead. Release the two lugs on the servo retaining plate located on either side of the pushrod rubber boot, then remove the pedal bracket assembly.

15 Spread open the servo retaining plate lugs located over the two diametrically opposite servo retaining studs. Return to the engine compartment and manoeuvre the servo unit from its location.

Refitting

16 Check the servo unit check valve sealing grommet for signs of damage or deterioration, and renew if necessary.
17 Locate the servo unit in position from within the engine compartment.
18 From inside the car, refit the pedal bracket assembly then secure the bracket and servo with the five retaining nuts tightened to the specified torque.
19 Reconnect the wiring connector to the stop-light switch.
20 Refit the servo unit pushrod-to-brake pedal clevis pin, and secure it in position with the spring clip.
21 Refit the facia lower trim panel and secure with the retaining clips.
22 Refit the servo unit check valve to its grommet in the servo.
23 Fit the master cylinder to the servo unit, ensuring that the servo unit pushrod enters the master cylinder bore centrally. Refit the master cylinder mounting nuts, and tighten them to the specified torque.
24 Wipe clean the brake pipe unions, refit them to the master cylinder ports and tighten them securely.

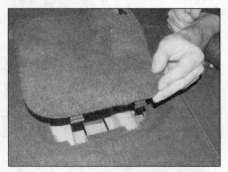

14.3 Unclip the carpet panel and lift the panel up and off the handbrake lever

14.2b . . . and remove the two sections of trim from the handbrake lever

25 Refit the air cleaner assembly and air inlet ducts as described in the relevant Part of Chapter 4.
26 On completion, reconnect the battery, start the engine, and check for air leaks at the check valve.

12 Vacuum servo unit (right-hand drive models) – testing, removal and refitting

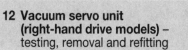

Testing

1 The procedures for testing the unit are as described for left-hand drive models in paragraphs 1 to 3 of Section 11.

Removal and refitting

2 On right-hand drive models, the servo unit is connected to the brake pedal by a cross-shaft assembly located behind the facia. To remove and refit the servo unit, the cross-shaft assembly must be removed, which entails the removal of the complete facia assembly and the heater/air conditioning air distribution unit. On models with air conditioning this also entails draining and refilling of the air conditioning refrigerant. These are extremely complex operations and are considered, in total, to be beyond the scope of this manual. For this reason, it is recommended that removal and refitting of the servo unit be entrusted to a Citroën dealer or suitably-equipped garage.

13 Vacuum servo unit check valve – removal, testing and refitting

Removal

1 Disconnect the battery negative terminal (refer to *Disconnecting the battery* in the Reference Chapter).
2 Remove the air cleaner assembly and air inlet ducts as described in the relevant Part of Chapter 4.
3 Withdraw the valve from its rubber sealing grommet in the servo unit, using a pulling and twisting motion. Remove the grommet from the servo.

4 Disconnect the vacuum pipe at the quick-release fitting on the inlet manifold or vacuum pump (as applicable), and remove the check valve and hose from the engine compartment.

Testing

5 Examine the check valve for signs of damage, and renew if necessary. The valve may be tested by blowing through it in both directions. Air should flow through the valve in one direction only – when blown through from the servo unit end of the valve. Renew the valve if this is not the case.
6 Examine the rubber sealing grommet and flexible vacuum hose for signs of damage or deterioration, and renew as necessary.

Refitting

7 Fit the sealing grommet into the servo unit.
8 Ease the check valve into position, taking care not to displace or damage the grommet.
9 Reconnect the vacuum pipe to the inlet manifold or vacuum pump (as applicable).
10 Refit the air cleaner assembly and air inlet ducts as described in the relevant Part of Chapter 4.
11 On completion, reconnect the battery, start the engine and check for air leaks at the check valve.

14 Handbrake – adjustment

1 To check the handbrake adjustment, first apply the footbrake firmly several times to establish correct shoe-to-drum clearance, then apply and release the handbrake several times to ensure that the self-adjust mechanism is fully adjusted. Applying normal moderate pressure, pull the handbrake lever to the fully-applied position, counting the number of clicks emitted from the handbrake ratchet mechanism. If adjustment is correct, there should be 5 clicks before the handbrake is fully applied. If this is not the case, adjust as follows.
2 Using a small screwdriver, carefully spread apart and remove the two sections of plastic trim at the base of the handbrake lever **(see illustrations)**.
3 Unclip the carpet panel surrounding the handbrake lever and lift the panel up and off the lever for access to the adjuster nut **(see illustration)**.
4 Chock the front wheels then jack up the rear of the vehicle and support it securely on axle stands (see *Jacking and vehicle support*).
5 Apply and release the handbrake four times.
6 With the handbrake set on the fifth notch of the ratchet mechanism, check that both rear wheels are locked. If not, tighten the handbrake adjusting nut until both rear wheels are locked **(see illustration)**. Once this is so, fully release the handbrake lever, and check that the rear wheels rotate freely. Check the adjustment by applying the handbrake fully,

counting the clicks from the handbrake ratchet and, if necessary, re-adjust.

7 When the adjustment is correct, refit the carpet and handbrake lever trim panels, then lower the vehicle to the ground.

15 Handbrake lever – removal and refitting

Removal

1 Carry out the operations described in paragraphs 2 and 3 of Section 14.

2 Ensure that the handbrake is released, then slacken the handbrake lever adjusting nut to obtain maximum free play in the cables. Disengage the inner cables from the handbrake lever equaliser plate.

3 Lift up the flaps of the carpet and undo the two handbrake lever retaining nuts each side **(see illustration)**. Remove the lever assembly from the vehicle.

Refitting

4 Refitting is a reversal of removal. Prior to refitting the carpet and handbrake lever trim panels, adjust the handbrake as described in Section 14.

16 Handbrake cables – removal and refitting

Removal

1 The handbrake cable consists of two sections, a right- and a left-hand section, which are linked to the lever by an equaliser plate. Each section can be removed individually.

2 Carry out the operations described in paragraphs 2 and 3 of Section 14.

3 Ensure that the handbrake is released, then slacken the handbrake lever adjusting nut to obtain maximum free play in the cables. Disengage relevant the inner cable from the handbrake lever equaliser plate.

4 Firmly chock the front wheels, then jack up the rear of the vehicle and support it on axle stands (see *Jacking and vehicle support*).

5 Where necessary, slacken and remove the retaining nuts, then release the exhaust system heat shield(s) from the vehicle underbody, to gain access to the front of the relevant handbrake cable. Free the front end of the outer cable from the body, and withdraw the cable from its support guide.

6 Working back along the length of the cable, free it from the fuel tank plastic clip and the wire support hooks on the underbody and trailing arm **(see illustration)**.

7 Remove the rear brake shoes from the relevant side as described in Section 5. Using pliers, carefully release the outer cable from the brake backplate, and remove it from underneath the vehicle **(see illustration)**.

14.6 Handbrake adjusting nut location (arrowed)

Refitting

8 Refitting is a reversal of the removal procedure, adjusting the handbrake as described in Section 14.

17 Rear brake pressure-regulating valve – removal and refitting

Removal

Note 1: *Before starting work, refer to the warning at the beginning of Section 2 concerning the dangers of hydraulic fluid.*

Note 2: *The rear brake pressure-regulating valve is only fitted to models without ABS.*

1 Firmly chock the front wheels, then jack up the rear of the vehicle and support it on axle stands (see *Jacking and vehicle support*). Remove the right-hand rear roadwheel.

2 Minimise fluid loss by first removing the master cylinder reservoir filler cap, and tightening it down onto a piece of polythene, to obtain an airtight seal.

3 Disconnect the lower end of the regulating valve operating rod from the bracket on the rear suspension.

4 Wipe clean the area around the brake pipe unions on the valve, and place absorbent rags beneath the pipe unions to catch any surplus fluid.

5 Unscrew the union nuts and carefully withdraw the brake pipes from the pressure-regulating valve. Plug or tape over the pipe ends and valve orifices, to minimise the loss

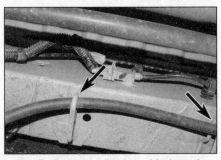

16.6 Free the handbrake cable from the wire support hooks (arrowed) on the underbody

15.3 Lift up the carpet flaps and undo the handbrake lever retaining nuts

of brake fluid, and to prevent the entry of dirt into the system.

6 Undo the bolt securing the valve to the mounting bracket and remove the assembly from under the car.

Refitting

7 Refitting is a reverse of the removal procedure, ensuring that the brake pipe union nuts are securely tightened. On completion, bleed the complete braking system as described in Section 2. If a new valve has been fitted, or if the adjusting nuts on the operating rod have been disturbed, the vehicle should be taken to a Citroën dealer for adjustment of the valve pressure settings.

18 Stop-light switch – removal, refitting and adjustment

Removal

1 The stop-light switch is located on the brake pedal bracket under the facia.

2 Extract the stud-type plastic clips, using a forked type tool, and remove the facia lower trim panel above the pedals on the driver's side.

3 Disconnect the wiring connector, then loosen the locking ring and unscrew the switch from the pedal bracket.

Refitting and adjustment

4 Screw the switch back into position in the mounting bracket, until the gap between the

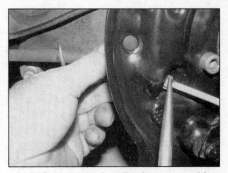

16.7 Release the handbrake outer cable from the brake backplate

21.18 Unscrew the nut and lift off the wheel sensor protective cover

end of the main body of the switch and the lug on the brake pedal is 2.0 to 3.0 mm.

5 Once the stop-light switch is correctly positioned, reconnect the wiring connector, and check the operation of the stop-lights. The stop-lights should illuminate after the brake pedal has travelled approximately 5.0 mm.

6 When the adjustment is correct, secure the switch with the locking ring and refit the facia lower trim panel

19 Handbrake 'on' warning light switch – removal and refitting

Removal

1 Carry out the operations described in paragraphs 2 and 3 of Section 14.

2 Disconnect the wiring connector and remove the switch from the frame of the handbrake lever assembly.

Refitting

3 Refitting is a reverse of the removal procedure.

20 Anti-lock braking system (ABS) – general information

ABS is available as an option on certain models covered by this manual, and is fitted as standard equipment on others. The

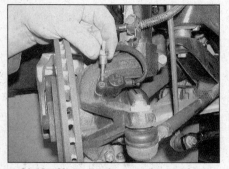

21.19a Unscrew the securing stud . . .

purpose of the system is to prevent the wheels locking during heavy braking. This is achieved by automatic release of the brake on the relevant wheel, followed by re-application of the brake. The system comprises an electronic control unit, a hydraulic modulator block, hydraulic solenoid valves (located in the modulator block), an electrically-driven fluid return pump, and four roadwheel sensors.

The solenoids (which control the fluid pressure to the calipers/wheel cylinders) are controlled by the electronic control unit, which itself receives signals from the wheel sensors. The wheel sensors monitor the speed of rotation of each wheel. By comparing these speed signals from the four wheels, the control unit can determine when a wheel is decelerating at an abnormal rate, compared to the speed of the vehicle. Using this information, the control unit can predict when a wheel is about to lock, and is able to reduce the fluid pressure to the brake on the relevant wheel to prevent it locking.

During normal operation, the system functions in the same way as a conventional non-ABS braking system.

21 Anti-lock braking system (ABS) components – removal and refitting

Modulator assembly

Note: *Before starting, refer to the note in Section 2 on the dangers of hydraulic fluid.*

Removal

1 Disconnect the battery negative terminal (refer to *Disconnecting the battery* in the Reference Chapter).

2 Remove the air cleaner and air inlet ducts as described in the relevant Part of Chapter 4.

3 Release the locking clip and disconnect the ECU wiring harness connector.

4 Minimise hydraulic fluid loss by first removing the master cylinder reservoir filler cap, then tightening it down onto a piece of polythene, to obtain an airtight seal.

5 Wipe clean the area around the brake pipe unions on the side of the modulator, and place absorbent rags beneath the pipe unions to catch any surplus fluid. Make a note of the

21.19b . . . and withdraw the front wheel sensor from the swivel hub

correct fitted positions of the unions, then unscrew the union nuts and carefully withdraw the pipes. Plug or tape over the pipe ends and modulator orifices to minimise the loss of fluid, and to prevent the entry of dirt into the system.

6 Undo the two retaining nuts, one on each side of the modulator, and remove the unit from the engine compartment.

Refitting

7 If a new modulator assembly is being fitted, it will be supplied prefilled with hydraulic fluid, and sealed with blanking plugs. Leave the plugs in position until just before connecting the brake pipes.

8 Locate the modulator in position and refit the two retaining nuts. Tighten the nuts to the specified torque.

9 Reconnect the brake pipes to their correct locations as noted during removal and tighten the union nuts securely.

10 Reconnect the ECU wiring connector.

11 Refit the air cleaner and air inlet ducts as described in the relevant Part of Chapter 4, then reconnect the battery.

12 Remove the polythene from the master cylinder reservoir and bleed the complete hydraulic system as described in Section 2.

Electronic control unit

13 The electronic control unit is removed with the modulator assembly as described previously. The ECU is an integral part of the modulator and the two components cannot be separated.

Front wheel sensor

Note: *Thread locking compound must be applied to the sensor securing stud on refitting.*

Removal

14 Disconnect the battery negative terminal (refer to *Disconnecting the battery* in the Reference Chapter).

15 Firmly apply the handbrake, then jack up the front of the car and support it securely on axle stands (see *Jacking and vehicle support*). Remove the relevant front roadwheel.

16 Unclip the wheel sensor wiring from the brackets on the suspension strut and inner wheelarch.

17 Trace the wiring back from the sensor, and separate the two halves of the wiring connector. Note the routing of the wiring to aid correct refitting.

18 Unscrew the retaining nut and lift off the wheel sensor protective cover **(see illustration)**.

19 Unscrew the securing stud, and withdraw the sensor from the swivel hub **(see illustrations)**.

Refitting

20 Refitting is a reversal of removal, noting the following points:

a) *Ensure that the mating faces of the sensor and the swivel hub are clean, and apply a*

*smear of high melting point brake grease
to the sensor location in the swivel hub
before refitting.*

b) *Ensure that the end face of the sensor is
clean.*

c) *Coat the threads of the sensor securing
stud with thread-locking compound and
tighten the stud to the specified torque.*

d) *Route the wiring as noted before removal.*

Rear wheel sensor

Note: *Thread-locking compound must be
applied to the sensor securing stud on
refitting.*

Removal

21 Chock the front wheels, then jack up the
rear of the vehicle and support it on axle
stands (see *Jacking and vehicle support*).
Remove the appropriate roadwheel.

22 Trace the wiring back from the sensor to
its wiring connector, then free the connector
from its retaining clip, and disconnect the
wiring from the main wiring loom.

23 Work back along the sensor wiring, and
free it from the retaining clips. Note the
routing of the wiring to aid correct refitting.

24 Slacken and remove the bolt securing the
sensor unit to the trailing arm, and remove the
sensor and lead assembly.

Refitting

25 Refitting is a reversal of removal, bearing
in mind the following points:

a) *Ensure that the mating faces of the sensor
and the trailing arm are clean, and apply a
smear of high melting point brake grease
to the sensor location in the trailing arm
before refitting.*

b) *Ensure that the end face of the sensor is
clean.*

c) *Coat the threads of the sensor securing*

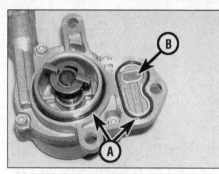

**22.5 Vacuum pump O-ring locations (A)
and gauze filter (B)**

*bolt with thread-locking compound and
tighten the stud to the specified torque.*

d) *Route the wiring as noted before removal.*

22 Vacuum pump (diesel engine models) – removal and refitting

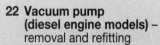

Note: *New O-rings must be used on refitting.*

Removal

1 Disconnect the battery negative terminal
(refer to *Disconnecting the battery* in the
Reference Chapter).

2 Remove the air cleaner assembly and air
inlet ducts as described in Chapter 4B.

3 Release the retaining clip and disconnect
the vacuum hose from the pump.

4 Slacken and remove the three bolts/nuts
and washers securing the pump to the left-
hand end of the cylinder head, then remove
the pump, along with its two O-rings. Discard
the O-rings – new ones must be used on
refitting. Check the condition of the gauze
filter at the rear of the pump and renew if
necessary.

Refitting

5 Fit new O-rings to the pump recesses, then
align the drive dog with the slot in the end of
the camshaft, and refit the pump to the
cylinder head, ensuring that the O-rings
remain correctly seated **(see illustration)**.

6 Refit the pump mounting bolts/nuts and
washers, and tighten them to the specified
torque.

7 Reconnect the vacuum hose to the pump,
and tighten its securing clip.

8 Refit the air cleaner assembly and air inlet
ducts as described in Chapter 4B, then
reconnect the battery

23 Vacuum pump (diesel engine models) – testing and overhaul

Testing

1 The operation of the braking system
vacuum pump can be checked using a
vacuum gauge.

2 Disconnect the vacuum pipe from the
pump, and connect the gauge to the pump
union using a suitable length of hose.

3 Start the engine and allow it to idle, then
measure the vacuum created by the pump. As
a guide, after one minute, a minimum of
approximately 500 mm Hg should be
recorded. If the vacuum registered is
significantly less than this, it is likely that the
pump is faulty. However, seek the advice of a
Citroën dealer before condemning the pump.

Overhaul

4 Overhaul of the vacuum pump is not
possible, since no components are available
separately for it. If faulty, the complete pump
assembly must be renewed.

Chapter 10
Suspension and steering

Contents

Degrees of difficulty

Easy, suitable for novice with little experience	Fairly easy, suitable for beginner with some experience	Fairly difficult, suitable for competent DIY mechanic	Difficult, suitable for experienced DIY mechanic	Very difficult, suitable for expert DIY or professional

Specifications

Steering
Power steering fluid type . . . .   See Lubricants and fluids

Front wheel alignment
Front wheel toe setting:
  Petrol engine models . . . .   2.0 ± 1.0 mm (0°18' ± 0.09') toe-in
  Diesel engine models . . . .   1.7 ± 1.0 mm (0°15' ± 0.09') toe-in

Roadwheels
Type . . . .   Pressed-steel or aluminium alloy (depending on model)
Size . . . .   6J x 15
Maximum run-out at rim . . . .   1.2 mm
Maximum eccentricity on tyre bead locating surface . . . .   0.8 mm

Tyre pressures . . . .   See end of Weekly checks

Torque wrench settings	Nm	lbf ft
Front suspension		
Anti-roll bar:		
Mounting clamp bolts	65	48
Connecting link securing nuts	40	30
Lower arm balljoint clamp bolt nut	40	30
Lower arm balljoint retaining nuts	50	37
Lower arm front pivot bolt	80	59
Lower arm rear pivot bush mounting bolts:		
8 mm bolt	35	26
10 mm bolt	65	48
Strut upper mounting bolts	25	18
Strut piston rod retaining nut	45	33
Strut-to-swivel hub bolt	45	33
Subframe mounting bolts	85	63

Torque wrench settings (continued)

	Nm	lbf ft
Rear suspension		
Rear axle mountings:		
Front mounting-to-body bolts	40	30
Rear mounting nuts	55	41
Rear hub nut:		
Nut with separate thrustwasher	275	203
Nut with integral thrustwasher	250	185
Shock absorber mounting nuts	110	81
Steering		
Power steering pump mounting bolts	22	16
Steering column mounting nuts/bolts	40	30
Steering column shaft-to-intermediate shaft universal joint		
pinch-bolt	23	17
Steering gear mounting bolts	80	59
Steering intermediate shaft-to-steering gear pinion universal joint		
pinch-bolt nut	23	17
Steering wheel nut	33	24
Track rod balljoint-to-swivel hub nut	40	30
Roadwheels		
Wheel bolts	85	63

1 General information

The independent front suspension is of the MacPherson strut type, incorporating coil springs and integral telescopic shock absorbers. The MacPherson struts are located by transverse lower suspension arms, which utilise rubber inner mounting bushes, and incorporate a balljoint at the outer ends. The front swivel hubs, which carry the wheel bearings, brake calipers and the hub/disc assemblies, are clamped to the MacPherson struts, and connected to the lower arms via the balljoints. A front anti-roll bar is fitted to all models. The anti-roll bar is rubber-mounted onto the subframe, and is attached to the front suspension struts by a connecting link on each side.

The rear suspension is of the independent trailing arm type, which consists of two trailing arms, linked by a tubular crossmember. Torsion bars linking the trailing arms are situated in front of and behind the crossmember, and a stabilizer bar linking the arms passes through the centre of the crossmember.

The complete rear axle assembly is mounted onto the vehicle underbody by four 'self-steering' rubber mountings. These mountings are designed to move slightly under extreme cornering forces. This movement of the rear axle assembly has the effect of actually turning the rear wheels slightly, to help steer the vehicle in the required direction. This improves the handling of the vehicle when cornering at high speeds.

The steering column has a universal joint fitted in the centre of its length, which is connected to an intermediate shaft having a second universal joint at its lower end. The lower universal joint is clamped to the steering gear pinion by means of a pinch-bolt.

The steering gear is mounted onto the front subframe, and is connected by two track rods, with balljoints at their outer ends, to the steering arms projecting rearwards from the swivel hubs. The track rods and balljoints are threaded, to facilitate toe setting adjustment.

Power-assisted steering is fitted as standard on all models. Hydraulic power for the steering system is provided by a pump, which is driven off the crankshaft pulley by the auxiliary drivebelt.

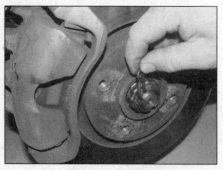

2.2a Withdraw the R-clip . . .

2.2b . . . and remove the locking cap from the driveshaft retaining nut

2 Front swivel hub assembly – removal and refitting

Note: *All Nyloc nuts disturbed on removal must be renewed as a matter of course. These nuts have threads which are precoated with locking compound (this is only effective once), and include the track rod balljoint nut, lower suspension arm balljoint clamp bolt nut, and the swivel hub clamp bolt nut. Suitable thread-locking compound will also be required for the brake caliper mounting bracket bolts.*

Removal

Caution: Do not allow the vehicle to rest on its wheels with one or both driveshafts disconnected from the swivel hubs, as damage to the wheel bearing(s) may result. If moving the vehicle is unavoidable, temporarily insert the outer end of the driveshaft(s) in the hub(s) and tighten the hub nut(s).

1 Chock the rear wheels, then firmly apply the handbrake. Jack up the front of the vehicle, and support it on axle stands (see *Jacking and vehicle support*). Remove the appropriate front roadwheel.

2 Withdraw the R-clip, and remove the locking cap from the driveshaft retaining nut **(see illustrations)**.

3 To prevent rotation of the wheel hub as the driveshaft retaining nut is slackened, make up a holding tool and bolt the tool to the wheel hub using two wheel bolts as described in Chapter 8, Section 2.

4 With the holding tool in place, slacken and remove the driveshaft retaining nut using a socket and long bar. Where necessary, support the socket on an axle stand to prevent it slipping off the nut. This nut is very tight; make sure that there is no risk of pulling the car off the axle stands as the nut is slackened.

5 Slacken and remove the bolt securing the wiring retaining bracket to the top of the swivel hub **(see illustration)**.

6 On models with ABS, remove the wheel sensor from the swivel hub as described in Chapter 9.

7 If the hub bearings are to be disturbed, remove the brake disc as described in Chapter 9. If not, unscrew the two bolts securing the brake caliper mounting bracket assembly to the swivel hub, and slide the caliper assembly off the disc. Using a piece of wire or string, tie the caliper to the front suspension coil spring, to avoid placing any strain on the hydraulic brake hose.

8 On all models, slacken and remove the nut securing the steering gear track rod balljoint to the swivel hub, and release the balljoint tapered shank using a balljoint separator.

9 Slacken and remove the nut, then withdraw the lower suspension arm balljoint clamp bolt from the swivel hub **(see illustration)**. Discard the nut – a new one must be used on refitting.

10 Tap a small chisel into the split on the swivel hub to spread the hub slightly, and allow the balljoint shank to be withdrawn **(see illustration)**. Pull the lower suspension arm downwards to release the balljoint shank from the swivel hub. To do this it will be necessary to use a long bar and block of wood which will engage under the front subframe. Attach the bar to the suspension arm, preferably with a chain, or alternatively with a stout strap or rope. Lever down on the bar to release the balljoint from the swivel hub **(see illustration)**.

11 Once the balljoint is free, remove the protector plate which is fitted to the balljoint shank **(see illustration)**.

12 Undo the nut and withdraw the swivel hub-to-suspension strut clamp bolt, noting that the bolt fits from the rear of the vehicle.

13 Tap a small chisel into the split on the swivel hub to spread the hub slightly. Free the swivel hub assembly from the end of the strut, then release it from the outer constant velocity joint splines, and remove it from the vehicle.

Refitting

14 Note that all Nyloc nuts disturbed on removal must be renewed as a matter of course. These nuts have threads which are precoated with locking compound (this is only effective once), and include the track rod balljoint nut, lower suspension arm balljoint clamp bolt nut, and the swivel hub clamp bolt nut.

15 Ensure that the driveshaft outer constant velocity joint and hub splines are clean, then slide the hub fully onto the driveshaft splines.

16 Slide the hub assembly fully onto the suspension strut, aligning the split in the hub clamp with the lug on the base of the strut. Also ensure that the stop bosses on the strut are in contact with the top surface of the swivel hub. Insert the swivel hub-to-suspension strut clamp bolt from the rear side

2.5 Remove the bolt securing the wiring retaining bracket to the swivel hub

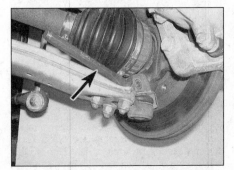

2.10a Spread the swivel hub by tapping a small chisel (arrowed) into the split . . .

of the strut, then fit a new nut to the clamp bolt, and tighten it to the specified torque **(see illustration)**.

17 Refit the protector plate to the lower arm balljoint then, using the method employed on removal, locate the balljoint shank in the swivel hub, ensuring that the lug on the protector plate is correctly located in the clamp split. Insert the balljoint clamp bolt (from the rear of the swivel hub), then fit the new retaining nut and tighten it to the specified torque.

18 Engage the track rod balljoint in the swivel hub, then fit a new retaining nut and tighten it to the specified torque.

19 Where necessary, refit the brake disc to the hub, referring to Chapter 9 for further information. Apply a suitable locking compound to the threads of the caliper mounting bracket bolts. Slide the caliper assembly into position over the disc, then fit

2.11 When the balljoint is released, remove the protector plate from the balljoint shank

2.9 Undo the nut and withdraw the lower suspension arm balljoint clamp bolt from the swivel hub

2.10b . . . then pull the lower suspension arm downwards using a bar and chain or similar arrangement, pivoting on the subframe

the mounting bolts and tighten them to the specified torque (see Chapter 9).

20 Where applicable, refit the ABS wheel sensor as described in Chapter 9.

21 Refit the wiring retaining bracket to the top of the swivel hub, and tighten its retaining bolt securely.

22 Lubricate the inner face and threads of the driveshaft retaining nut with clean engine oil, and refit it to the end of the driveshaft. Use the method employed on removal to prevent the hub from rotating, and tighten the drive-shaft retaining nut to the specified torque (see Chapter 8). Check that the hub rotates freely.

23 Engage the locking cap with the driveshaft nut so that one of its cut-outs is aligned with the driveshaft hole. Secure the cap with the R-clip.

24 Refit the roadwheel, then lower the vehicle to the ground and tighten the roadwheel bolts to the specified torque.

2.16 Ensure the swivel hub clamp is aligned with the lug (arrowed) on the strut prior to inserting the clamp bolt

3.3 Front hub bearing retaining circlip (arrowed)

3 Front hub bearings – renewal

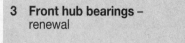

Note 1: *The bearing is a sealed, pre-adjusted and prelubricated, double-row roller type, and is intended to last the car's entire service life without maintenance or attention. Never overtighten the driveshaft nut beyond the specified torque wrench setting in an attempt to 'adjust' the bearing.*

Note 2: *A press will be required to dismantle and rebuild the assembly; if such a tool is not available, a large bench vice and spacers (such as large sockets) will serve as an adequate substitute. The bearing's inner races are an interference fit on the hub; if the inner race remains on the hub when it is pressed out of the hub carrier, a knife-edged bearing puller will be required to remove it. A new*

bearing retaining circlip must be used on refitting.

1 Remove the swivel hub assembly as described in Section 2.

2 Support the swivel hub securely on blocks or in a vice. Using a tubular spacer which bears only on the inner end of the hub flange, press the hub flange out of the bearing. If the bearing's outboard inner race remains on the hub, remove it using a bearing puller (see note above).

3 Extract the bearing retaining circlip from the inner end of the swivel hub assembly **(see illustration)**.

4 Where necessary, refit the inner race back in position over the ball cage, and securely support the inner face of the swivel hub. Using a tubular spacer which bears only on the inner race, press the complete bearing assembly out of the swivel hub.

5 Thoroughly clean the hub and swivel hub, removing all traces of dirt and grease, and polish away any burrs or raised edges which might hinder reassembly. Check both for cracks or any other signs of wear or damage, and renew them if necessary. Renew the circlip, regardless of its apparent condition.

6 On reassembly, apply a light film of oil to the bearing outer race and hub flange shaft, to aid installation of the bearing.

7 Securely support the swivel hub, and locate the bearing in the hub. Press the bearing fully into position, ensuring that it enters the hub squarely, using a tubular spacer which bears only on the bearing outer race.

8 Once the bearing is correctly seated, secure the bearing in position with the new

circlip, ensuring that it is correctly located in the groove in the swivel hub.

9 Securely support the outer face of the hub flange, and locate the swivel hub bearing inner race over the end of the hub flange. Press the bearing onto the hub, using a tubular spacer which bears only on the inner race of the hub bearing, until it seats against the hub shoulder. Check that the hub flange rotates freely, and wipe off any excess oil or grease.

10 Refit the swivel hub assembly as described in Section 2.

4 Front suspension strut – removal and refitting

Note: *All Nyloc nuts disturbed on removal must be renewed as a matter of course. These nuts have threads which are precoated with locking compound (this is only effective once), and include the swivel hub clamp bolt nut, and the anti-roll bar connecting link nut. Suitable spring compressor tools will be required for this operation.*

Removal

1 Chock the rear wheels, apply the handbrake, then jack up the front of the vehicle and support it on axle stands (see *Jacking and vehicle support*). Remove the appropriate roadwheel.

2 Remove the scuttle grille panel as described in Chapter 11, for access to the strut upper mounting bolts.

3 Slacken and remove the bolt securing the wiring retaining bracket to the top of the swivel hub.

4 Unclip the brake flexible hydraulic hose and any wiring from the strut.

5 Unscrew the nut (and recover the washer) securing the anti-roll bar connecting link to the strut, and position the link clear of the strut. Counterhold the link with an Allen key to prevent rotation as the nut is undone **(see illustration)**. Discard the nut – a new one must be used on refitting.

6 Undo the nut and withdraw the swivel hub-to-suspension strut clamp bolt, noting that the bolt fits from the rear of the strut. Discard the nut – a new one must be used on refitting **(see illustration)**.

7 The coil spring must now be compressed to enable the strut to be removed. Working under the wheelarch, fit suitable spring compressors to the spring and compress the spring sufficiently to enable the lower end of the strut to be disconnected from the swivel hub **(see illustration)**. Ensure that the compressors used are of a type that incorporate a method for positively locking them to the spring (usually by a small clamp bolt). Any other type may slip off or slide round the spring as they are tightened.

8 Tap a small chisel into the split on the swivel hub to spread the hub slightly, and allow the end of the strut to be withdrawn **(see illustration)**.

4.5 Unscrew the nut securing the anti-roll bar connecting link to the strut

4.6 Unscrew the nut and remove the swivel hub-to-suspension strut clamp bolt

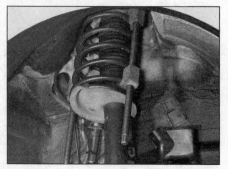

4.7 Coil spring compressors fitted to strut spring

4.8 Tap a small chisel (arrowed) into the split in the swivel hub to spread the hub

5.3 Unscrew the strut piston rod nut while counterholding the piston rod with a suitable Allen key

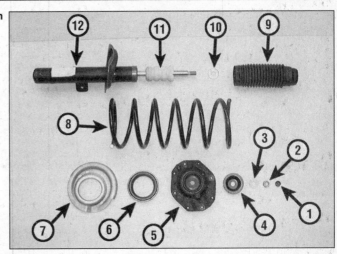

5.4 Front suspension strut components

1 Protective cap
2 Piston rod nut
3 Washer
4 Collar
5 Mounting plate
6 Bearing
7 Upper spring seat
8 Coil spring
9 Piston dust cover
10 Flat washer
11 Damper stop
12 Strut body

9 Slacken and remove the three suspension strut upper mounting bolts, then withdraw the strut from under the wheelarch.

Refitting

10 With the coil spring compressors in place, as during removal, manoeuvre the strut assembly into position, ensuring that the top mounting plate locating pin is correctly located in the corresponding hole in the body. Engage the lower end of the strut with the swivel hub, aligning the split in the hub with the lug on the base of the strut. Also ensure that the stop bosses on the strut are in contact with the top surface of the swivel hub.
11 Insert the strut upper mounting bolts, and tighten them to the specified torque.
12 Insert the swivel hub-to-suspension strut clamp bolt from the rear side of the strut. Fit a new nut to the clamp bolt, and tighten it to the specified torque.
13 Carefully slacken and then remove the spring compressors.
14 Refit the scuttle grille panel, referring to Chapter 11 if necessary.
15 Reconnect the anti-roll bar connecting link to the strut. Fit a new nut to the connecting link, and tighten it to the specified torque.
16 Refit the wiring retaining bracket to the top of the swivel hub, and clip the flexible hose and wiring to their locations on the strut.
17 Refit the roadwheel, then lower the vehicle to the ground and tighten the roadwheel bolts to the specified torque.

5 Front suspension strut – overhaul

⚠️ *Warning: Before attempting to dismantle the suspension strut, a suitable tool to hold the coil spring in compression must be obtained. Adjustable coil spring compressors which can be positively secured to the spring coils are readily available, and are recommended for this operation. Any attempt to dismantle the strut without such a tool is likely to result in damage or personal injury.*

1 With the strut removed from the car as described in Section 4, clean away all external dirt then mount the unit upright in a vice.
2 If not already in place, fit the spring compressors to the coils of the spring. Ensure that the compressors used are of a type that incorporate a method for positively locking them to the spring (usually by a small clamp bolt). Any other type may slip off or slide round the spring as they are tightened. Tighten the compressors until the load is taken off the spring seats.
3 Remove the protective cap then unscrew the piston rod nut, counterholding the piston rod with a suitable Allen key **(see illustration)**. Note that a new nut will be required for reassembly.

4 Remove the nut and washer, then lift off the collar, mounting plate, bearing, upper spring seat and flat washer. Remove the coil spring, then slide off the piston dust cover and rubber damper stop **(see illustration)**. The spring may remain in the compressed state ready for refitting to the strut. If the spring is to be renewed, release the compressors very gently and evenly until they can be removed and fitted to the new spring.
5 With the strut assembly now completely dismantled, examine all the components for wear, damage or deformation, and check the bearing for smoothness of operation. Renew any components as necessary.
6 Examine the strut body for signs of fluid leakage or damage, and the piston for signs of pitting or scoring. Test the operation of the strut, while holding it in an upright position, by moving the piston through a full stroke and then through short strokes of 50 to 100 mm. In both cases, the resistance felt should be smooth and continuous. If the resistance is jerky, or uneven, or if there is any visible sign of wear or damage, renewal is necessary.
7 If any doubt exists about the condition of the coil spring, carefully remove the spring compressors, and check the spring for distortion and signs of cracking. Renew the spring if it is damaged or distorted.
8 To reassemble the strut, follow the accompanying photos. Be sure to stay in order, and carefully read the captions **(see illustrations)**.

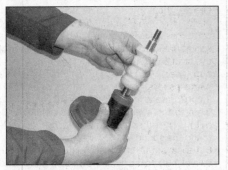

5.8a Pull the piston rod out as far as it will go and fit the damper stop

5.8b Fit the piston dust cover . . .

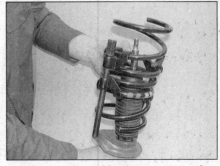

5.8c . . . followed by the compressed spring . . .

5.8d . . . ensuring that the end of the lower coil is located correctly in the lower seat

5.8e Place the flat washer in position . . .

5.8f . . . followed by the upper spring seat . . .

5.8g . . . bearing . . .

5.8h . . . and mounting plate

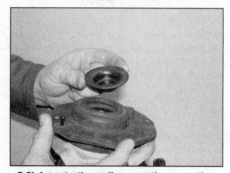

5.8i Locate the collar over the mounting plate . . .

5.8j . . . fit the upper washer . . .

5.8k . . . then fit and tighten the piston rod nut

9 Refit the strut to the car as described in Section 4 on completion of reassembly.

---

6 Front suspension lower arm – removal, overhaul and refitting

Note 1: *All Nyloc nuts disturbed on removal must be renewed as a matter of course. These nuts have threads which are precoated with locking compound (this is only effective once), and include the lower arm balljoint clamp bolt nut.*

Note 2: *Two different types of lower suspension arm may be encountered; type 1 being a steel pressing with a removable lower arm balljoint, and type 2 being a steel forging with fixed lower arm balljoint. The photos in this Section depict the type 1 suspension arm.*

Removal

1 Chock the rear wheels then jack up the front of the vehicle and support it on axle stands (see *Jacking and vehicle support*). Remove the appropriate front roadwheel.

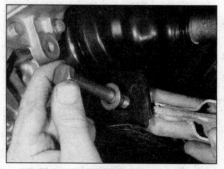

6.3 Remove the lower arm front pivot bolt . . .

2 Slacken and remove the nut, then withdraw the lower arm balljoint clamp bolt from the swivel hub. Discard the nut – a new one must be used on refitting.
3 Slacken and remove the lower arm front pivot bolt and nut. Recover the nut from its housing if it is loose **(see illustration)**.
4 Unscrew the two bolts securing the lower arm rear mounting bush to the subframe, noting that the larger bolt also secures the anti-roll bar mounting clamp (counterhold the nut if necessary) **(see illustration)**. Recover the nut from the top of the anti-roll bar mounting clamp.
5 Tap a small chisel into the split on the swivel hub to spread the hub slightly, and allow the balljoint shank to be withdrawn. Withdraw the inner end of the arm from the subframe and release the balljoint from the swivel hub. Remove the protector plate which is fitted to the balljoint shank.

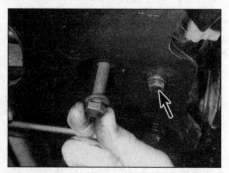

6.4 . . . and the two rear mounting bush bolts (second bolt arrowed) . . .

6 Manoeuvre the lower arm assembly out from underneath the vehicle **(see illustration)**.

Overhaul

Note: *If the lower arm balljoint on the type 1 suspension arm is to be renewed, new retaining nuts must be used on refitting.*

7 Thoroughly clean the lower arm and the area around the arm mountings, removing all traces of dirt and underseal if necessary, then check carefully for cracks, distortion or any other signs of wear or damage, paying particular attention to the pivot bushes, and renew components as necessary. Due to the number of special tools required (including a press), pivot bush renewal should be entrusted to a dealer or suitably-equipped garage.

8 Check that the lower arm balljoint moves freely, without any sign of roughness; check also that the balljoint dust cover shows no sign of deterioration, and is free from cracks and splits. If renewal is necessary (which is only possible on the type 1 suspension arm), slacken and remove its retaining bolts, and remove the balljoint from the arm. Fit the new balljoint, and insert its retaining bolts. Fit new nuts to the bolts, and tighten them to the specified torque.

9 Examine the shank of the lower arm pivot bolt for signs of wear or scoring, and renew if necessary.

Refitting

10 Manoeuvre the lower arm assembly into position, refit the protector plate to the lower arm balljoint, then locate the balljoint shank in the swivel hub. Ensure that the lug on the protector plate is correctly located in the clamp split.

11 Insert the balljoint clamp bolt (from the rear of the swivel hub), then fit the new retaining nut and tighten it to the specified torque.

12 Refit the front pivot bolt, tightening it finger-tight only. Ensure that the nut is located in its housing.

13 Refit the rear pivot bush retaining bolts and nut, ensuring that the bush bracket is located between the subframe and the anti-roll bar clamp. Tighten the fixings to the specified torque.

14 Refit the roadwheel, then lower the vehicle and tighten the roadwheel bolts to the specified torque. Rock the vehicle to settle the disturbed components, then tighten the lower arm front pivot bolt to the specified torque.

---

7 Front suspension lower arm balljoint – removal and refitting

Note 1: *Two different types of lower suspension arm may be encountered; type 1 being a steel pressing with a removable lower arm balljoint, and type 2 being a steel forging with fixed lower arm balljoint. The following*

6.6 . . . then remove the lower arm from the vehicle

procedures are applicable only to the type 1 lower suspension arm.

Note 2: *A new balljoint clamp bolt nut, and new balljoint securing nuts must be used on refitting.*

Removal

1 Chock the rear wheels then jack up the front of the vehicle and support it on axle stands (see *Jacking and vehicle support*). Remove the appropriate front roadwheel.

2 Slacken and remove the nut, then withdraw the lower suspension arm balljoint clamp bolt from the swivel hub. Discard the nut – a new one must be used on refitting.

3 Tap a small chisel into the split on the swivel hub to spread the hub slightly, and allow the balljoint shank to be withdrawn. Pull the lower suspension arm downwards to release the balljoint shank from the swivel hub. To do this it will be necessary to use a long bar and block of wood which will engage under the front subframe. Attach the bar to the suspension arm, preferably with a chain, or alternatively with a stout strap or rope. Lever down on the bar to release the balljoint from the swivel hub **(see illustration 2.10b)**.

4 Once the balljoint is free, remove the protector plate which is fitted to the balljoint shank.

5 Slacken and remove the three nuts, then withdraw the balljoint retaining bolts and remove the balljoint from the lower arm **(see illustrations)**. Discard the nuts – new ones must be used on refitting.

6 Check that the lower arm balljoint moves

freely, without any sign of roughness. Check also that the balljoint dust cover shows no sign of deterioration, and is free from cracks and splits. Renew worn or damaged components as necessary.

Refitting

7 Locate the balljoint in the end of the suspension arm, and insert the three retaining bolts. Fit new nuts to the bolts, and tighten them to the specified torque.

8 Refit the protector plate to the lower arm balljoint then, using the method employed on removal, locate the balljoint shank in the swivel hub, ensuring that the lug on the protector plate is correctly located in the clamp split. Insert the balljoint clamp bolt (from the rear of the swivel hub), then fit the new retaining nut and tighten it to the specified torque.

9 Refit the roadwheel, then lower the vehicle and tighten the roadwheel bolts to the specified torque.

---

8 Front suspension anti-roll bar – removal and refitting

Note: *All Nyloc nuts disturbed on removal must be renewed as a matter of course. These nuts have threads which are precoated with locking compound (this is only effective once), and include the anti-roll bar connecting link nuts, engine/transmission rear mounting bolt nut, and the intermediate shaft pinch-bolt nut (and pinch-bolt).*

Removal

1 Firmly apply the handbrake, then jack up the front of the car and support it securely on axle stands (see *Jacking and vehicle support*). Position the roadwheels in the straight-ahead position, then remove both front roadwheels.

2 Undo the nut and washer securing the left-hand connecting link to the anti-roll bar, and position the link clear of the bar **(see illustration)**. Repeat the procedure on the right-hand side.

3 Where applicable, unclip the clutch cable from the brackets on the subframe.

7.5a Remove the three retaining bolts . . .

7.5b . . . and remove the lower arm balljoint

8.2 Undo the nut and washer (arrowed) securing the left-hand connecting link to the anti-roll bar

4 Release the power steering fluid pipe support clips from the engine and transmission.

5 Working in the engine compartment, unscrew the securing nut from the intermediate shaft-to-steering gear pinion pinch-bolt, then carefully tap the pinch-bolt from the universal joint – discard the pinch-bolt and nut, new ones must be used on refitting. Pull off the metal clip securing the intermediate shaft to the pinion.

6 Make alignment marks on the universal joint and the steering gear pinion, then push the universal joint upwards to separate it from the pinion. Engage the steering lock to prevent the steering wheel from turning while the shaft is disconnected.

7 Unscrew the nut and remove the bolt securing the engine/transmission rear mounting connecting link to the mounting on the rear of the cylinder block.

8 Make a final check to ensure that all relevant pipes, hoses and wiring harnesses have been released and moved clear of the subframe to allow the rear of the subframe to be lowered.

9 Accurately measure and record the position of the subframe, both laterally and horizontally with respect to the chassis members and underbody. In practice, there will be marks made on the subframe by the retaining bolts and these can be used as a very accurate guide to correct location when refitting.

10 Slacken and remove the four subframe rear mounting bolts. Loosen the two subframe front mounting bolts by a few turns, until it is possible to lower the rear edge of the subframe approximately 65.0 mm. Wedge a block of wood between the rear of the subframe and the vehicle underbody to hold the subframe in this position.

11 Slacken the two anti-roll bar mounting clamp retaining bolts, and recover the nuts from the top of the clamps. Remove both clamps from the subframe.

12 Manoeuvre the anti-roll bar out from underneath the vehicle, and remove the mounting bushes from the bar.

13 Carefully examine the anti-roll bar components for signs of wear, damage or deterioration, paying particular attention to the mounting bushes. Renew worn components as necessary.

Refitting

14 Fit the rubber mounting bushes to the anti-roll bar, ensuring that the lugs on the inside of each bush engage with the corresponding cut-outs in the anti-roll bar. The bushes are correctly positioned when the alignment marks on the edges of the bushes are aligned with the paint marks on the anti-roll bar.

15 Offer up the anti-roll bar, and manoeuvre it into position on the subframe. Refit the mounting clamps, ensuring that their ends are correctly located in the hooks on the subframe, and refit the retaining bolts and nuts. Ensure that the bush markings are still aligned with the paint marks on the bar, then tighten the mounting clamp retaining bolts to the specified torque.

16 The remainder of the refitting is a reversal of the removal procedure, noting the following points:

a) All Nyloc nuts disturbed on removal must be renewed as a matter of course. These nuts have threads which are precoated with locking compound (this is only effective once), and include the anti-roll bar connecting link nuts, and the engine/transmission rear mounting bolt nut, and the intermediate shaft pinch-bolt nut (and pinch-bolt).

b) Ensure that the subframe is correctly positioned by using the measurements made during removal, or with reference to the marks made by the retaining bolts.

c) Tighten all nuts and bolts to the specified torque settings (where given).

d) Ensure that the metal clip is correctly refitted to the steering intermediate shaft universal joint and that the marks made on removal are aligned.

e) Fit a new intermediate shaft pinch-bolt and nut, ensuring that the lugs on the bolt engage with the cut-outs in the universal joint.

f) On completion have the front wheel alignment checked and where necessary adjusted (see Section 24).

9 Front suspension anti-roll bar connecting link – removal and refitting

Note: *New connecting link securing nuts must be used on refitting.*

Removal

1 Firmly apply the handbrake, then jack up the front of the car and support it securely on axle stands (see *Jacking and vehicle support*). Remove the appropriate front roadwheel.

2 Slacken and remove the upper and lower connecting link retaining nuts and washers, and remove the link from the vehicle.

3 Examine the connecting link for signs of damage, paying particular attention to the mounting bushes or balljoints (as applicable),

and renew the link if necessary. It is not possible to renew the bushes or balljoints separately. Note that the connecting link retaining nuts must be renewed as a matter of course.

Refitting

4 Refitting is a reversal of the removal procedure, using new retaining nuts and tightening them to the specified torque.

10 Front suspension subframe – removal and refitting

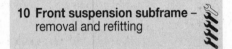

Note: *All Nyloc nuts disturbed on removal must be renewed as a matter of course. These nuts have threads which are precoated with locking compound (this is only effective once), and include the rear engine/transmission mounting bolt nuts and steering gear bolt nuts.*

Removal

1 Firmly apply the handbrake, then jack up the front of the car and support it securely on axle stands (see *Jacking and vehicle support*). Remove both front roadwheels.

2 Unscrew and remove the bolt securing the engine/transmission rear mounting connecting link to the mounting on the rear of the cylinder block. Remove the bolt securing the rear mounting link to the bracket on the subframe and withdraw the link **(see illustration)**.

3 Undo the bolt(s) securing the power steering fluid pipe(s) to the mounting bracket(s) on the subframe, and free the pipe(s) from any subframe retaining clips.

4 Slacken and remove the steering gear mounting bolts, and recover the nuts. Withdraw the mounting bolts, and recover the spacers from the subframe apertures. Secure the steering gear to the exhaust front pipe using a large cable tie or similar.

5 Slacken and remove the suspension lower arm front pivot bolt and nut on both sides. Recover the nut from its housing if it is loose.

6 Unscrew the two bolts securing the suspension lower arm rear mounting bush to the subframe on each side, noting that the larger bolt also secures the anti-roll bar mounting clamp (counterhold the nut if

10.2 Rear engine/transmission mounting connecting link attachments (arrowed)

necessary). Recover the nut from the top of each anti-roll bar mounting clamp.

7 Release the inner ends of both suspension lower arms from their locations in the subframe.

8 Place a jack and a suitable block of wood under the subframe to support the subframe as it is lowered.

9 Accurately measure and record the position of the subframe, both laterally and horizontally with respect to the chassis members and underbody. In practice, there will be marks made on the subframe by the retaining bolts and these can be used as a very accurate guide to correct location when refitting.

10 Slacken and remove the four rear subframe mounting bolts, and the two front bolts, then carefully lower the subframe assembly out of position and remove it from underneath the vehicle **(see illustrations)**. Ensure that the subframe assembly does not catch the power steering pipes as it is lowered out of position.

Refitting

11 Refitting is a reversal of the removal procedure, noting the following points:

a) *Ensure that the subframe is correctly positioned by using the measurements made during removal, or with reference to the marks made by the retaining bolts.*

b) *All Nyloc nuts disturbed on removal must be renewed as a matter of course. These nuts have threads which are precoated with locking compound (this is only effective once) and include the rear engine/transmission mounting bolt nuts and steering gear mounting bolt nuts.*

c) *Tighten all nuts and bolts to the specified torque settings (where given).*

d) *On completion have the front wheel alignment checked and where necessary adjusted (see Section 24).*

---

11 Rear hub assembly – removal and refitting

Note: *Do not remove the hub assembly unless it is absolutely necessary. A puller will be required to draw the hub assembly off the stub axle, and the hub bearing will be damaged by the removal procedure. A complete new hub assembly, hub nut, and a new hub cap must be used on refitting.*

Removal

1 Remove the relevant rear brake drum and, on models with ABS, the rear wheel sensor as described in Chapter 9.

2 Using a hammer and a large flat-bladed screwdriver, carefully tap and prise the cap out of the centre of the hub. Discard the cap – a new one must be used on refitting. Using a hammer and a chisel-nosed tool, tap up the staking securing the hub retaining nut to the groove in the stub axle.

3 Using a socket and long bar, slacken and

10.10a Front subframe left-hand rear mounting bolts (arrowed) . . .

10.10b . . . and front mounting bolt (arrowed)

remove the rear hub nut, and withdraw the thrustwasher (where fitted). Discard the hub nut – a new nut must used on refitting.

4 Using a puller, draw the hub assembly off the stub axle, along with the outer bearing. With the hub removed, use a bearing puller to draw the inner bearing inner race off the stub axle, then remove the flanged hub spacer, noting which way around it is fitted. On later models a plain spacer is used which can be fitted either way round.

5 With the hub removed, examine the stub axle shaft for signs of wear or damage. If stub axle shaft is worn, it will be necessary to renew the complete trailing arm, as the shaft is not available separately. Trailing arm renewal entails the use of numerous special tools and must be entrusted to a Citroën dealer.

6 Obtain a new hub assembly, hub nut and hub cap for refitting. Note that there are two different types of hub nut, one with a separate

thrustwasher, and one with an integral thrust-washer. The two types are interchangeable, but there is a different torque setting for each type.

Refitting

7 Lubricate the stub axle shaft with clean engine oil, then slide on the spacer, ensuring it is fitted the correct way round on early versions.

8 Slide the hub assembly onto the stub axle and tap it into position using a tubular drift.

9 Fit the thrustwasher (where applicable) then screw on the new nub nut. Do not use the separate thrustwasher if the new nut is of the type with an integral thrustwasher. Lubricate the threads and contact faces of the hub nut and tighten the nut to the specified torque according to type. Stake the nut firmly into the groove on the stub axle to secure it in position, then tap the new hub cap into place in the centre of the hub **(see illustrations)**.

11.9a Fit the thrustwasher (where applicable) and new hub nut, and tighten to the specified torque

11.9b Using a hammer and suitable punch . . .

11.9c . . . stake the hub nut firmly into the stub axle groove . . .

11.9d . . . then fit the new hub cap

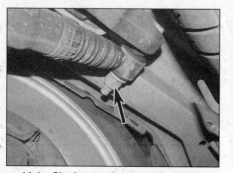

14.4a Slacken and remove the shock absorber upper mounting nut (arrowed) . . .

10 On completion, refit the brake drum and ABS wheel sensor (where applicable) as described in Chapter 9.

12 Rear hub bearings – renewal

Note: *The bearing is intended to last the car's entire service life without maintenance or attention. Never overtighten the hub nut beyond the specified torque setting in an attempt to 'adjust' the bearings.*

1 The rear hub bearing is integral with the rear hub, and it is not possible to renew the hub bearing separately. If the bearing is worn, the complete rear hub assembly must be renewed. See Section 11 for hub removal and refitting procedures.

13 Rear suspension components – general

Although it is possible to remove the rear suspension torsion bars, trailing arms and stabilizer bar independently of the complete rear axle assembly, it is essential to have certain special tools available to complete the work successfully.

Due to the complexity of the tasks, and the requirement for special tools to accurately set the suspension geometry on refitting, the removal and refitting of individual rear suspension components is considered to be

15.8 Unscrew the two brake inlet pipe union nuts at the brake pipe connecting block

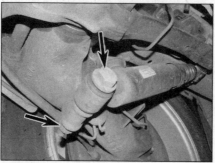

14.4b . . . and lower mounting nut and bolt (arrowed)

beyond the scope of DIY work, and should be entrusted to a Citroën dealer.

Procedures for removal and refitting of the rear shock absorbers, and the complete rear suspension assembly are given in Sections 14 and 15 respectively.

14 Rear shock absorber – removal, testing and refitting

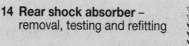

Note: *New shock absorber mounting nuts must be used on refitting.*

Removal

1 Chock the front wheels, then jack up the rear of the vehicle and support it on axle stands (see *Jacking and vehicle support*). Remove the relevant rear roadwheel.
2 Using a trolley jack, raise the trailing arm until the shock absorber is slightly compressed.
3 Unscrew the securing bolt, and detach the handbrake cable bracket from the trailing arm.
4 Slacken and remove the nuts and washers from both the upper and lower shock absorber mounting bolts **(see illustrations)**. Counterhold the bolts.
5 Withdraw the lower mounting bolt, noting which way round it is fitted, and manoeuvre the shock absorber out from underneath the vehicle.

Testing

6 Examine the shock absorber for signs of fluid leakage or damage. Test the operation of the shock absorber, while holding it in an upright position, by moving the piston through a full stroke and then through short strokes of 50 to 100 mm. In both cases, the resistance felt should be smooth and continuous. If the resistance is jerky, or uneven, or if there is any visible sign of wear or damage, renewal is necessary. Also check the rubber mounting bushes for damage and deterioration. Renew the complete unit if any damage or excessive wear is evident; the mounting bushes are not available separately. Inspect the shanks of the mounting bolts for signs of wear or damage, and renew as necessary.

Refitting

7 Prior to refitting the shock absorber, mount it upright in the vice, and operate it fully

through several strokes in order to prime it. Apply a smear of multi-purpose grease to both the shock absorber mounting bolts.
8 Manoeuvre the shock absorber into position, and insert the lower mounting bolt.
9 Place the washers in position then screw the new nuts onto the mounting bolts, but do not tighten the nuts at this stage.
10 Measure the distance between the shock absorber bolt head centres, and adjust the position of the jack under the trailing arm until a distance of 315.0 mm is obtained between the bolt centres. Tighten the shock absorber mounting nuts to the specified torque then remove the jack from under the trailing arm.
11 Refit the roadwheel, then lower the car to the ground and tighten the roadwheel bolts to the specified torque.

15 Rear axle assembly – removal and refitting

Removal

1 Disconnect the battery negative terminal (refer to *Disconnecting the battery* in the Reference Section of this manual).
2 Firmly chock the front wheels, then jack up the rear of the vehicle and support it on axle stands (see *Jacking and vehicle support*). Remove both rear roadwheels, then lower the spare wheel out from underneath the rear of the vehicle, and unhook the wheel carrier.
3 Remove the relevant exhaust system components and heat shield(s) as described in the relevant Part of Chapter 4.
4 Referring to Chapter 9, slacken the handbrake lever adjusting nut to obtain maximum free play in the handbrake cables, and disengage the inner cables from the handbrake lever equaliser plate.
5 From underneath the vehicle, work along the length of each handbrake cable, and free them from the retaining clips which secure them to the vehicle underbody. Note the routing of the cables to ensure correct refitting.
6 Where necessary, disconnect the ABS wheel sensors at the wiring connectors, and free them from any retaining clips.
7 To minimise brake hydraulic fluid loss, remove the master cylinder reservoir filler cap, and then tighten it down onto a piece of polythene, to obtain an airtight seal.
8 Wipe clean the area around the brake pipe connecting block and unscrew the union nuts of the two brake inlet pipes **(see illustration)**. Carefully withdraw the brake pipes from the connecting block and plug or cap the pipe ends and the connecting block orifices. Release the brake pipe leading from the connecting block to the left-hand rear brake from its clips on the underbody.
9 Make a final check that all necessary components have been disconnected and positioned so that they will not hinder the removal procedure, then position a trolley jack beneath the centre of the rear axle assembly.

17.4 Disconnect the wiring connector from the radio/cassette player remote control circuit board

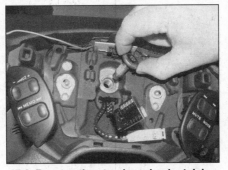

17.6 Remove the steering wheel retaining bolt and washer . . .

17.7 . . . and feed the wiring harness through the wheel as it is withdrawn

Raise the jack until it is supporting the weight of the axle.

10 Using a long-reach Torx bit, slacken and remove the rear axle rear mounting bolt on each side, accessible through the hole in the axle side-member just in front of the shock absorber upper mounting.

11 Slacken and remove the two retaining bolts securing each front mounting assembly to the underbody.

12 Lower the jack and axle assembly out of position, and remove it from underneath the car.

13 Examine the rear axle mountings for signs of damage or deterioration of the mounting rubber, and renew if necessary. Note that all four mountings should be renewed as a set; do not renew the mountings individually.

Refitting

14 Refitting is a reversal of the removal procedure, bearing in mind the following points:

a) Take care not to crush the brake pipes when positioning the axle assembly under the body.

b) Raise the rear axle assembly into position, and tighten the mounting retaining bolts to their specified torque settings.

c) Ensure that the brake pipes, handbrake cables and wiring (as applicable) are correctly routed, and retained by all the necessary retaining clips.

d) Tighten the brake pipe union nuts.

e) Reconnect and adjust the handbrake cables as described in Chapter 9.

f) Bleed the braking system hydraulic circuit as described in Chapter 9.

16 Vehicle ride height – checking

Checking of the vehicle ride height requires the use of Citroën special tools to accurately compress the suspension in a suspension checking bay.

The operation should be entrusted to a Citroën dealer, as it not possible to carry out checking accurately without the use of the appropriate tools.

17 Steering wheel – removal and refitting

Removal

1 Remove the air bag unit as described in Chapter 12.

2 Set the front wheels in the straight-ahead position, and release the steering lock by inserting the ignition key.

3 Slacken the steering wheel retaining bolt. Do not fully remove the bolt at this stage.

4 Where applicable, disconnect the wiring connector from the radio/cassette player remote control circuit board located in the slot at the top of the steering wheel **(see illustration)**.

5 Tap the wheel upwards near the centre, using the palm of your hand, or twist it from side-to-side, whilst pulling to release it from the shaft splines.

6 Once the wheel is released, remove the bolt then mark the steering wheel and steering column shaft in relation to each other **(see illustration)**.

7 Carefully withdraw the steering wheel, feeding the wiring harness for the air bag rotary connector and, where fitted, the radio/cassette player controls through the wheel as it is withdrawn **(see illustration)**.

Refitting

8 Refitting is a reversal of removal, noting the following points:

a) Ensure that the roadwheels are in the

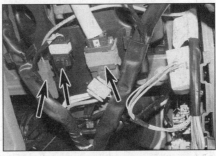

18.4 Disconnect the wiring connectors (arrowed) for the steering column controls and switches

straight-ahead position then align the two arrows on the face of the steering column rotary connector before fitting the steering wheel.

b) Make sure that the wiring is correctly routed through the wheel.

c) Align the marks made on removal, and tighten the retaining bolt to the specified torque.

d) Refit the air bag unit as described in Chapter 12.

18 Steering column – removal, inspection and refitting

Note: Where applicable, a new intermediate shaft-to-steering gear pinion nut and bolt must be used on refitting.

Removal

1 Disconnect the battery negative terminal (refer to Disconnecting the battery in the Reference Chapter).

2 Remove the steering wheel as described in Section 17.

3 Remove the facia lower side panel on the driver's side as described in Chapter 11.

4 Disconnect the wiring for the steering column controls and switches at the connectors under the centre of the column **(see illustration)**.

5 Unlock the catch and disconnect the wiring connector adjacent to the fuse/relay box **(see illustration)**. Check that any additional wiring connectors leading to the steering wheel components have been disconnected.

18.5 Unlock the catch and disconnect the wiring connector adjacent to the fuse/relay box

18.6 Remove the protective cover over the steering column universal joint

18.8 Unscrew the two lower steering column securing bolts (arrowed) . . .

18.9 . . . and the two upper steering column securing nuts (arrowed)

6 Release the retaining clips and remove the protective cover over the steering column universal joint **(see illustration)**.

7 Make alignment marks on the universal joint and the intermediate shaft, then unscrew the column-to-intermediate shaft pinch-bolt.

8 Unscrew the two lower steering column securing bolts **(see illustration)**.

9 Unscrew the two upper steering column securing nuts, and carefully withdraw the column from the vehicle **(see illustration)**.

10 To remove the intermediate shaft, proceed as follows. Note that on certain models, it will be necessary to jack up the front of the vehicle and support on axle stands (see *Jacking and vehicle support*) for access to the intermediate shaft-to-steering gear joint. On some models, the joint can be reached through the engine compartment.

a) *Unscrew the securing nut from the intermediate shaft-to-steering gear pinion pinch-bolt, then carefully tap the pinch-bolt from the universal joint – discard the pinch-bolt and nut, new ones must be used on refitting.*

b) *Pull off the metal clip securing the intermediate shaft to the pinion.*

c) *Make alignment marks on the universal joint and the steering gear pinion, then push the universal joint upwards to separate it from the pinion.*

d) *Release the shaft from the pinion splines, and remove it from the vehicle.*

Inspection

11 The steering column incorporates a telescopic safety feature. In the event of a front-end crash, the shaft collapses and prevents the steering wheel injuring the driver. Before refitting the steering column, examine the column and mountings for signs of damage and deformation, and renew as necessary.

12 Check the steering shaft for signs of free play in the column bushes, and check the universal joints for signs of damage or roughness in the joint bearings. If any damage or wear is found on the steering column universal joints or shaft bushes, the column must be renewed as an assembly.

13 Where disturbed, the intermediate shaft-to-steering gear pinch-bolt and nut must be renewed as a matter of course.

Refitting

14 Where removed, refit the intermediate shaft, engaging the universal joint with the steering gear drive pinion splines (align the marks made on removal). Ensure that the metal clip is correctly refitted to the intermediate shaft-to-steering gear universal joint, then fit a new pinch-bolt and nut, ensuring that the lugs on the bolt engage with the cut-outs in the universal joint. Tighten the nut to the specified torque.

15 Manoeuvre the steering column assembly into position then, aligning the marks made prior to removal, engage the universal joint with the intermediate shaft splines.

16 Fit the column over its mounting studs, and refit the steering column upper mounting nuts. Fit the lower mounting bolts and tighten the bolts and the nuts to the specified torque.

17 Refit the universal joint pinch-bolt and tighten the bolt to the specified torque. Refit the protective cover over the universal joint.

18 Reconnect the wiring connectors under the facia and secure them in position with the relevant clips.

19 Refit the facia lower side panel as described in Chapter 11.

20 Refit the steering wheel as described in Section 17.

19 Ignition switch/ steering column lock – removal and refitting

Removal

1 Disconnect the battery negative terminal (refer to *Disconnecting the battery* in the Reference Chapter).

2 Remove the facia lower side panel on the driver's side as described in Chapter 11.

3 Trace the wiring back from the ignition switch, and disconnect its wiring connectors under the facia.

4 Disconnect the wiring at the electronic immobiliser receiver on the ignition switch, then unclip and remove the receiver cover **(see illustration)**.

5 Slacken and remove the lock retaining screw and washer from the side of the lock.

6 With the ignition key inserted, turn the key

so that is aligned with the mark positioned between the A and M marks on the barrel.

7 Using a small flat-bladed screwdriver, depress the retaining lug on the side of the lock.

8 Withdraw the lock assembly from the steering column, and feed the wiring harness through the column tube.

Refitting

9 Feed the wiring harness through the column tube and locate the lock assembly in position. Check that the ignition key is still aligned with the mark positioned between the A and M marks, then push the lock firmly into place until the retaining lug engages.

10 Secure the lock with the retaining screw and washer, then refit the electronic immobiliser receiver. Reconnect the wiring connector to the immobiliser receiver.

11 Remove the ignition key and check that the steering lock functions correctly.

12 Reconnect the wiring connectors under the facia and secure them in position with the relevant clips.

13 Refit the facia lower side panel as described in Chapter 11.

20 Steering gear assembly – removal, overhaul and refitting

Note: *All Nyloc nuts disturbed on removal must be renewed as a matter of course. These nuts have threads which are precoated with locking compound (this is only effective once),*

19.4 Disconnect the wiring at the electronic immobiliser receiver on the ignition switch

and include the track rod balljoint nuts, steering gear mounting bolt nuts, and the intermediate shaft pinch-bolt nut.

Removal

1 Firmly apply the handbrake, then jack up the front of the vehicle and support on axle stands (see *Jacking and vehicle support*). Remove both front roadwheels.

2 Slacken and remove the nuts securing the steering gear track rod balljoints to the swivel hubs, and release the balljoint tapered shanks using a universal balljoint separator **(see illustration)**.

3 Unscrew the nut from the intermediate shaft-to-steering gear pinion pinch-bolt, then carefully tap the pinch-bolt from the universal joint – discard the pinch-bolt and nut, new ones must be used on refitting. Pull off the metal clip securing the intermediate shaft to the pinion.

4 Make alignment marks on the universal joint and the steering gear pinion, then push the universal joint upwards to separate it from the pinion.

5 Unscrew and remove the bolt securing the engine/transmission rear mounting connecting link to the mounting on the rear of the cylinder block.

6 Where applicable, unclip the clutch cable from the brackets on the subframe.

7 Undo the bolt(s) securing the power steering fluid pipe(s) to the mounting bracket(s) on the engine/transmission and subframe.

8 Accurately measure and record the position of the subframe, both laterally and horizontally with respect to the chassis members and underbody. In practice, there will be marks made on the subframe by the retaining bolts and these can be used as a very accurate guide to correct location when refitting.

9 Place a jack and a suitable block of wood under the front subframe to support the subframe as it is lowered.

10 Slacken and remove the four rear subframe mounting bolts, and the two front bolts, then carefully lower the subframe slightly.

11 Position a suitable container beneath the power steering gear assembly. Undo the bolt securing the fluid pipe flange plate to the rack housing and ease the flange plate from the rack. Allow the power steering fluid to drain into the container. When the fluid has finished draining, suitably cover the pipe ends and the orifices in the rack to prevent dirt ingress. Note that new O-rings will be required for the pipe ends for refitting.

12 Undo the two retaining screws (where fitted), then unclip the heat shield and remove it from the top of the steering gear assembly.

13 Undo the steering gear mounting bolts, and recover the nuts **(see illustration)**. Withdraw the mounting bolts, and recover the spacers from the subframe apertures.

14 Manoeuvre the steering gear out from under the right-hand wheelarch (right-hand drive models) or left-hand wheelarch (left-hand drive models).

Overhaul

15 Examine the steering gear assembly for signs of wear or damage, and check that the rack moves freely throughout the full length of its travel, with no signs of roughness or excessive free play between the steering gear pinion and rack. It is possible to overhaul the steering gear assembly housing components, but this task should be entrusted to a Citroën dealer. The only components which can be renewed easily by the home mechanic are the track rod balljoints (see Section 23).

16 Inspect all the steering gear fluid unions for signs of leakage, and check that all union nuts are securely tightened. Also examine the steering gear hydraulic ram for signs of fluid leakage or damage, and if necessary renew it.

Refitting

17 Note that all Nyloc nuts disturbed on removal must be renewed as a matter of course. These nuts have threads which are precoated with locking compound (this is only effective once), and include the track rod balljoint nuts, and the steering gear mounting bolt nuts.

18 Manoeuvre the steering gear assembly into position from the right-hand or left-hand side of the vehicle, as applicable.

19 Position the spacers in the subframe apertures, then insert the mounting bolts. Fit the new nuts onto the steering gear, then tighten the mounting bolts to the specified torque.

20 Clip the heat shield onto the top of the steering gear, and securely tighten its two retaining screws (where fitted).

21 Wipe clean the power steering pipes and locate new O-rings on the pipe ends. Locate the fluid pipe flange plate on the rack housing and secure with the retaining bolt.

22 Raise the jack and locate the subframe in position. Ensure that the subframe is correctly positioned by using the measurements made during removal, or with reference to the marks made by the retaining bolts. Fit the front and rear subframe retaining bolts and tighten to the specified torque.

23 Refit the power steering fluid pipe(s) to the mounting bracket(s) on the engine/transmission and subframe.

24 Where applicable, secure the clutch cable to the brackets on the subframe.

25 Refit the bolt securing the engine/transmission rear mounting link to the cylinder block and tighten to the specified torque (refer to the relevant Part of Chapter 2).

26 Engage the intermediate shaft universal joint with the steering gear pinion splines (align the marks made before removal). Ensure that the metal clip is correctly refitted to the intermediate shaft-to-steering gear universal joint, then fit a new pinch-bolt and nut, ensuring that the lugs on the bolt engage with the cut-outs in the universal joint. Tighten the nut to the specified torque.

20.2 Releasing a track rod balljoint using a balljoint separator

27 Engage the track rod balljoints in the swivel hubs, then fit a new retaining nut to each one. Tighten the nuts to the specified torque.

28 Make a final check that all cables, pipes and hoses are correctly routed, and are securely held by all the necessary retaining clips.

29 Refit the roadwheels, then lower the vehicle to the ground and tighten the roadwheel bolts to the specified torque.

30 Refill the fluid reservoir and bleed the hydraulic system as described in Section 21.

31 On completion have the front wheel alignment checked and, if necessary, adjusted (see Section 24).

21 Power steering system – bleeding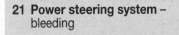

1 This procedure will only be necessary when any part of the hydraulic system has been disconnected.

2 Referring to *Weekly checks*, remove the fluid reservoir filler cap, and top-up with the specified fluid until the level is up to the Cold mark on the filler cap dipstick.

3 With the engine stopped, slowly move the steering from lock-to-lock approximately ten times to purge out the trapped air, then top-up the fluid until the level is again up to the Cold mark on the filler cap dipstick. Repeat this procedure until the fluid level in the reservoir does not drop any further.

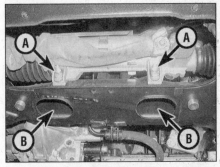

20.13 Undo the steering gear mounting bolts, and recover the nuts (A) and spacers (B) from the subframe apertures

22.7a Power steering fluid supply pipe support bracket attachment (arrowed) on 1.6 litre petrol engines . . .

22.10a Power steering pump rear mounting bolt (arrowed) . . .

22.7b . . . and on 1.8 litre petrol engines and diesel engines (arrowed)

22.10b . . . and front mounting bolts (arrowed)

4 Start the engine, and allow it to idle for two or three minutes without moving the steering wheel. Switch the engine off and, if necessary, top-up the fluid again, to the Cold mark on the dipstick.

5 Start the engine and slowly move the steering from lock-to-lock several times to purge out any remaining air in the system. Repeat this procedure until bubbles cease to appear in the fluid reservoir.

6 Once all traces of air have been removed from the power steering hydraulic system, turn the engine off and allow the system to cool. Once cool, check that the fluid level is up to the Cold mark on the dipstick, topping-up if necessary.

22 Power steering pump – removal and refitting

Removal

1 The power steering pump is mounted directly above the alternator at the front of the engine.

2 Remove the auxiliary drivebelt as described in the relevant Part of Chapter 1.

3 On diesel engine models, release the four plastic fasteners and remove the engine cover from the top of the engine.

4 On later 1.6 litre petrol engine models, unbolt and remove the heat shield at the rear of the power steering pump.

5 Using brake hose clamps, clamp both the supply and return hoses near the power

steering fluid reservoir. This will minimise fluid loss during subsequent operations.

6 Place absorbent rags beneath the fluid supply and return pipe and hose connections on the pump.

7 Undo the nut and bolt securing the fluid supply pipe to the support bracket located either at the rear of the pump, or adjacent to the cylinder head cover **(see illustrations)**.

8 Undo the union nut and disconnect the fluid supply pipe from the top of the pump. Move the pipe to one side and suitably cover the pipe end and the orifice in the pump to prevent dirt ingress.

9 Slacken the retaining clip, and disconnect the fluid return hose from the pump. If the original Citroën clip is still fitted, cut the clip and discard it; replace it with a standard worm-drive hose clip on refitting. Suitably cover the hose end and the orifice in the pump to prevent dirt ingress.

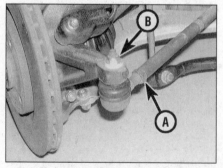

23.3 Track rod balljoint locknut (A) and balljoint-to-swivel hub retaining nut (B)

10 Undo the rear mounting bolt and the two front mounting bolts and withdraw the pump from the mounting bracket **(see illustrations)**. Access to the front mounting bolts can be gained through the holes in the pump pulley. If necessary move aside the washer bottle filler neck for increased clearance.

Refitting

11 Manoeuvre the pump into position, refit the pump mounting bolts and tighten them to the specified torque.

12 Reconnect the fluid supply pipe to the pump and securely tighten the union nut. Secure the pipe to the support bracket.

13 Refit the return hose to the pump, and securely tighten its retaining clip.

14 On diesel engine models, refit the engine cover. On later 1.6 litre petrol engine models, refit the heat shield to the rear of the pump.

15 Refit and tension the auxiliary drivebelt as described in Chapter 1A or 1B as applicable.

16 On completion, bleed the hydraulic system as described in Section 21.

23 Track rod balljoint – removal and refitting

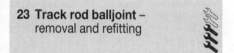

Note: *A new track rod end-to-swivel hub nut must be used on refitting.*

Removal

1 Apply the handbrake, then jack up the front of the vehicle and support it on axle stands (see *Jacking and vehicle support*). Remove the appropriate front roadwheel.

2 If the balljoint is to be re-used, use a straight-edge and a scriber, or similar, to mark its relationship to the track rod.

3 Hold the track rod, and unscrew the balljoint locknut by a quarter of a turn **(see illustration)**. Do not move the locknut from this position, as it will serve as a handy reference mark on refitting.

4 Slacken and remove the nut securing the track rod balljoint to the swivel hub, and release the balljoint tapered shank using a universal balljoint separator. Discard the nut – a new one must be used when refitting.

5 Counting the **exact** number of turns necessary to do so, unscrew the balljoint from the track rod.

6 Count the number of exposed threads between the end of the balljoint and the locknut, and record this figure. If a new balljoint is to be fitted, unscrew the locknut from the old balljoint.

7 Carefully clean the balljoint and the threads. Renew the balljoint if its movement is sloppy or too stiff, if excessively worn, or if damaged in any way; carefully check the stud taper and threads. If the balljoint dust cover is damaged, the complete balljoint assembly must be renewed; it is not possible to obtain the dust cover separately.

Refitting

8 If a new balljoint is to be fitted, screw the locknut onto its threads, and position it so that the same number of exposed threads are visible, as was noted prior to removal.

9 Screw the balljoint into the track rod by the number of turns noted on removal. This should bring the balljoint locknut to within a quarter of a turn from the end face of the track rod, with the alignment marks that were made on removal (if applicable) lined up. Hold the track rod and securely tighten the locknut.

10 Refit the balljoint shank to the swivel hub, then fit a new retaining nut and tighten it to the specified torque.

11 Refit the roadwheel, then lower the vehicle to the ground and tighten the roadwheel bolts to the specified torque.

12 On completion have the front wheel alignment checked, and if necessary, adjusted (see Section 24).

24 Wheel alignment and steering angles – general information

General

1 A car's steering and suspension geometry is defined in four basic settings – all angles are expressed in degrees (toe settings are also expressed as a measurement); the relevant settings are camber, castor, steering axis inclination, and toe-setting. With the exception of front wheel toe setting, none of these settings are adjustable, and in all cases, special equipment is necessary to check them. Note that the front wheel toe setting is often referred to as 'tracking' or 'front wheel alignment'.

Front wheel toe setting

2 Due to the special measuring equipment necessary to accurately check the front wheel toe setting, and the skill required to use it properly, checking and adjustment is best left to a Citroën dealer or suitably-equipped garage. Note that most tyre-fitting centres now possess sophisticated alignment equipment and will carry out the check and adjustment at minimal cost. The following is therefore provided as a guide to the procedure involved.

3 The front wheel toe setting is checked by measuring the distance between the front and rear inside edges of the roadwheel rims. Proprietary toe measurement gauges are available from larger motor accessory shops, although considering the infrequent use such equipment is likely to have, purchase may not prove cost effective. The toe setting adjustment is made by screwing the balljoints in or out of their track rods, to alter the effective length of the track rod assemblies.

4 For **accurate** checking, the vehicle **must** be at the kerb weight, ie, unladen and with a full tank of fuel.

5 Before starting work, check first that the tyre sizes and types are as specified, then check the tyre pressures and tread wear, the roadwheel run-out, the condition of the hub bearings, the steering wheel free play, and the condition of the front suspension components (Chapters 1A, 1B or 10). Correct any faults found.

6 Park the vehicle on level ground, check that the front roadwheels are in the straight-ahead position, then rock the rear and front ends to settle the suspension. Release the handbrake, and roll the vehicle backwards 1 metre, then forwards again, to relieve any stresses in the steering and suspension components.

7 Measure the distance between the front edges of the wheel rims and the rear edges of the rims. Subtract the front measurement from the rear measurement, and check that the result is within the specified range.

8 If adjustment is necessary, apply the handbrake, then jack up the front of the vehicle and support it securely on axle stands (see *Jacking and vehicle support*). Turn the steering wheel onto full-left lock, and record the number of exposed threads on the right-hand track rod balljoint. Now turn the steering onto full-right lock, and record the number of threads on the left-hand side. If there are the same number of threads visible on both sides, then subsequent adjustment should be made equally on both sides. If there are more threads visible on one side than the other, it will be necessary to compensate for this during adjustment. **Note:** *It is most important that after adjustment, the same number of threads are visible on each track rod balljoint.*

9 First clean the track rod balljoint threads; if they are corroded, apply penetrating fluid

24.11 Adjusting the front wheel toe setting

before starting adjustment. Release the rubber gaiter outboard clips (where necessary), and peel back the gaiters; apply a smear of grease to the inside of the gaiters, so that both are free, and will not be twisted or strained as their respective track rods are rotated.

10 Use a straight-edge and a scriber or similar to mark the relationship of each track rod to its balljoint then, holding each track rod in turn, unscrew its locknut slightly.

11 Alter the length of the track rods, bearing in mind the note made in paragraph 8. Screw them into or out of the balljoints, rotating the track rod using an open-ended spanner fitted to the flats provided. Shortening the track rods (screwing them into their balljoints) will reduce toe-in/increase toe-out **(see illustration)**.

12 When the setting is correct, hold the track rods and securely tighten the balljoint locknuts. Check that the balljoints are seated correctly, and count the exposed threads to check the length of both track rods. If they are not the same, then the adjustment has not been made equally, and problems will be encountered with tyre scrubbing in turns; also, the steering wheel spokes will no longer be horizontal when the wheels are in the straight-ahead position.

13 If the track rod lengths are the same, lower the vehicle to the ground and recheck the toe setting; re-adjust if necessary. When the setting is correct, securely tighten the track rod balljoint locknuts. Ensure that the rubber gaiters are seated correctly, and are not twisted or strained, and secure them in position with new retaining clips (where necessary).

Notes

Chapter 11
Bodywork and fittings

Contents

Degrees of difficulty

Easy, suitable for novice with little experience	**Fairly easy,** suitable for beginner with some experience	**Fairly difficult,** suitable for competent DIY mechanic	**Difficult,** suitable for experienced DIY mechanic	**Very difficult,** suitable for expert DIY or professional

---

1 General information

The bodyshell is made of pressed-steel sections, and is available in a five-door Hatchback version. Most components are welded together, but some use is made of structural adhesives. The front wings are bolted on.

The bonnet, doors and some other vulnerable panels are made of zinc-coated metal, and are further protected by being coated with an anti-chip primer prior to being sprayed.

Extensive use is made of plastic materials, mainly in the interior, but also in exterior components. The front and rear bumpers and the front grille are injection-moulded from a synthetic material which is very strong, yet light. Plastic components such as wheelarch liners are fitted to the underside of the vehicle, to improve the body's resistance to corrosion.

2 Maintenance – bodywork and underframe

The general condition of a vehicle's bodywork is the one thing that significantly affects its value. Maintenance is easy, but needs to be regular. Neglect, particularly after minor damage, can lead quickly to further deterioration and costly repair bills. It is important also to keep watch on those parts of the vehicle not immediately visible, for instance the underside, inside all the wheelarches, and the lower part of the engine compartment.

The basic maintenance routine for the bodywork is washing – preferably with a lot of water, from a hose. This will remove all the loose solids which may have stuck to the vehicle. It is important to flush these off in such a way as to prevent grit from scratching the finish. The wheelarches and underframe need washing in the same way, to remove any accumulated mud which will retain moisture and tend to encourage rust. Paradoxically enough, the best time to clean the underframe and wheelarches is in wet weather, when the mud is thoroughly wet and soft. In very wet weather, the underframe is usually cleaned of large accumulations automatically, and this is a good time for inspection.

Periodically, except on vehicles with a wax-based underbody protective coating, it is a good idea to have the whole of the underframe of the vehicle steam-cleaned, engine compartment included, so that a thorough inspection can be carried out to see what minor repairs and renovations are necessary. Steam-cleaning is available at many garages, and is necessary for the removal of the accumulation of oily grime, which sometimes is allowed to become thick in certain areas. If steam-cleaning facilities are not available, there are one or two excellent grease solvents available, which can be brush-applied; the dirt can then be simply hosed off. Note that these methods should not be used on vehicles with wax-based underbody protective coating, or the coating will be removed. Such vehicles should be inspected annually, preferably just prior to winter, when the underbody should be washed down, and any damage to the wax coating repaired using underseal. Ideally, a completely fresh coat should be applied. It would also be worth considering the use of wax-based protection for injection into door panels, sills, box sections, etc, as an additional safeguard against rust damage, where such protection is not provided by the vehicle manufacturer.

After washing paintwork, wipe off with a chamois leather to give an unspotted clear finish. A coat of clear protective wax polish will give added protection against chemical pollutants in the air. If the paintwork sheen has dulled or oxidised, use a cleaner/polisher combination to restore the brilliance of the shine. This requires a little effort, but such dulling is usually caused because regular washing has been neglected. Care needs to be taken with metallic paintwork, as a special non-abrasive cleaner/polisher is required to avoid damage to the finish. Always check that the door and ventilator opening drain holes and pipes are completely clear, so that water can be drained out. Brightwork should be treated in the same way as paintwork. Windscreens and windows can be kept clear of the smeary film which often appears, by the use of proprietary glass cleaner. Never use any form of wax or other body or chromium polish on glass.

3 Maintenance – upholstery and carpets

Mats and carpets should be brushed or vacuum-cleaned regularly, to keep them free of grit. If they are badly stained, remove them from the vehicle for scrubbing or sponging, and make quite sure they are dry before refitting. Seats and interior trim panels can be kept clean by wiping with a damp cloth and a proprietary upholstery cleaner. If they do become stained (which can be more apparent on light-coloured upholstery), use a little liquid detergent and a soft nail brush to scour the grime out of the grain of the material. Do not forget to keep the headlining clean in the same way as the upholstery. When using liquid cleaners inside the vehicle, do not over-wet the surfaces being cleaned. Excessive damp could get into the seams and padded interior, causing stains, offensive odours or even rot. If the inside of the vehicle gets wet accidentally, it is worthwhile taking some trouble to dry it out properly, particularly where carpets are involved.

Caution: Do not leave oil or electric heaters inside the vehicle for this purpose.

4 Minor body damage – repair

Repairs of minor scratches in bodywork

If the scratch is very superficial, and does not penetrate to the metal of the bodywork, repair is very simple. Lightly rub the area of the scratch with a paintwork renovator, or a very fine cutting paste, to remove loose paint from the scratch, and to clear the surrounding bodywork of wax polish. Rinse the area with clean water.

Apply touch-up paint to the scratch using a fine paint brush; continue to apply fine layers of paint until the surface of the paint in the scratch is level with the surrounding paintwork. Allow the new paint at least two weeks to harden, then blend it into the surrounding paintwork by rubbing the scratch area with a paintwork renovator or a very fine cutting paste. Finally apply wax polish.

Where the scratch has penetrated right through to the metal of the bodywork, causing the metal to rust, a different repair technique is required. Remove any loose rust from the bottom of the scratch with a penknife, then apply rust-inhibiting paint, to prevent the formation of rust in the future. Using a rubber or nylon applicator, fill the scratch with bodystopper paste. If required, this paste can be mixed with cellulose thinners, to provide a very thin paste which is ideal for filling narrow scratches. Before the stopper-paste in the scratch hardens, wrap a piece of smooth cotton rag around the top of a finger. Dip the finger in cellulose thinners, and quickly sweep it across the surface of the stopper-paste in the scratch; this will ensure that the surface of the stopper-paste is slightly hollowed. The scratch can now be painted over as described earlier in this Section.

Repairs of dents in bodywork

When deep denting of the vehicle's bodywork has taken place, the first task is to pull the dent out, until the affected bodywork almost attains its original shape. There is little point in trying to restore the original shape completely, as the metal in the damaged area will have stretched on impact, and cannot be reshaped fully to its original contour. It is better to bring the level of the dent up to a point which is about 3 mm below the level of the surrounding bodywork. In cases where the dent is very shallow anyway, it is not worth trying to pull it out at all. If the underside of the dent is accessible, it can be hammered out gently from behind, using a mallet with a wooden or plastic head. Whilst doing this, hold a suitable block of wood firmly against the outside of the panel, to absorb the impact from the hammer blows and thus prevent a large area of the bodywork from being 'belled-out'.

Should the dent be in a section of the bodywork which has a double skin, or some other factor making it inaccessible from behind, a different technique is called for. Drill several small holes through the metal inside the area – particularly in the deeper section. Then screw long self-tapping screws into the holes, just sufficiently for them to gain a good purchase in the metal. Now the dent can be pulled out by pulling on the protruding heads of the screws with a pair of pliers.

The next stage of the repair is the removal of the paint from the damaged area, and from an inch or so of the surrounding 'sound' bodywork. This is accomplished most easily by using a wire brush or abrasive pad on a power drill, although it can be done just as effectively by hand, using sheets of abrasive paper. To complete the preparation for filling, score the surface of the bare metal with a screwdriver or the tang of a file, or alternatively, drill small holes in the affected area. This will provide a really good 'key' for the filler paste.

To complete the repair, see the Section on filling and respraying.

Repairs of rust holes or gashes in bodywork

Remove all paint from the affected area, and from an inch or so of the surrounding 'sound' bodywork, using an abrasive pad or a wire brush on a power drill. If these are not available, a few sheets of abrasive paper will do the job most effectively. With the paint removed, you will be able to judge the severity of the corrosion, and therefore decide whether to renew the whole panel (if this is possible) or to repair the affected area. New body panels are not as expensive as most people think, and it is often quicker and more satisfactory to fit a new panel than to attempt to repair large areas of corrosion.

Remove all fittings from the affected area, except those which will act as a guide to the original shape of the damaged bodywork (eg headlight shells etc). Then, using tin snips or a hacksaw blade, remove all loose metal and any other metal badly affected by corrosion. Hammer the edges of the hole inwards, in order to create a slight depression for the filler paste.

Wire-brush the affected area to remove the powdery rust from the surface of the remaining metal. Paint the affected area with rust-inhibiting paint; if the back of the rusted area is accessible, treat this also.

Before filling can take place, it will be necessary to block the hole in some way. This can be achieved by the use of aluminium or plastic mesh, or aluminium tape.

Aluminium or plastic mesh, or glass-fibre matting, is probably the best material to use for a large hole. Cut a piece to the approximate size and shape of the hole to be filled, then position it in the hole so that its edges are below the level of the surrounding bodywork. It can be retained in position by several blobs of filler paste around its periphery.

Aluminium tape should be used for small or very narrow holes. Pull a piece off the roll, trim it to the approximate size and shape required, then pull off the backing paper (if used) and stick the tape over the hole; it can be overlapped if the thickness of one piece is insufficient. Burnish down the edges of the tape with the handle of a screwdriver or similar, to ensure that the tape is securely attached to the metal underneath.

Bodywork repairs – filling and respraying

Before using this Section, see the Sections on dent, minor scratch, rust holes and gash repairs.

Many types of bodyfiller are available, but generally speaking, those proprietary kits which contain a tin of filler paste and a tube of resin hardener are best for this type of repair; some can be used directly from the tube. A wide, flexible plastic or nylon applicator will be found invaluable for imparting a smooth and well-contoured finish to the surface of the filler.

Mix up a little filler on a clean piece of card or board – measure the hardener carefully (follow the maker's instructions on the pack), otherwise the filler will set too rapidly or too slowly. Using the applicator, apply the filler paste to the prepared area; draw the applicator across the surface of the filler to achieve the correct contour and to level the surface. As soon as a contour that approximates to the correct one is achieved, stop working the paste – if you carry on too long, the paste will become sticky and begin to 'pick-up' on the applicator. Continue to add thin layers of filler paste at 20-minute intervals, until the level of the filler is just proud of the surrounding bodywork.

Once the filler has hardened, the excess can be removed using a metal plane or file. From then on, progressively-finer grades of abrasive paper should be used, starting with a 40-grade production paper, and finishing with a 400-grade wet-and-dry paper. Always wrap the abrasive paper around a flat rubber, cork, or wooden block – otherwise the surface of the filler will not be completely flat. During the smoothing of the filler surface, the wet-and-dry paper should be periodically rinsed in water. This will ensure that a very smooth finish is imparted to the filler at the final stage.

At this stage, the 'dent' should be surrounded by a ring of bare metal, which in turn should be encircled by the finely 'feathered' edge of the good paintwork. Rinse the repair area with clean water, until all of the dust produced by the rubbing-down operation has gone.

Spray the whole area with a light coat of primer – this will show up any imperfections in the surface of the filler. Repair these imperfections with fresh filler paste or bodystopper, and once more smooth the surface with abrasive paper. If bodystopper is used, it can be mixed with cellulose thinners, to form a really thin paste which is ideal for filling small holes. Repeat this spray-and-repair procedure until you are satisfied that the surface of the filler, and the feathered edge of the paintwork, are perfect. Clean the repair area with clean water, and allow to dry fully.

The repair area is now ready for final spraying. Paint spraying must be carried out in a warm, dry, windless and dust-free atmosphere. This condition can be created artificially if you have access to a large indoor working area, but if you are forced to work in the open, you will have to pick your day very carefully. If you are working indoors, dousing the floor in the work area with water will help to settle the dust which would otherwise be in the atmosphere. If the repair area is confined to one body panel, mask off the surrounding panels; this will help to minimise the effects of a slight mismatch in paint colours. Bodywork fittings (eg chrome strips, door handles etc) will also need to be masked off. Use genuine masking tape, and several thicknesses of newspaper, for the masking operations.

Before commencing to spray, agitate the aerosol can thoroughly, then spray a test area (an old tin, or similar) until the technique is mastered. Cover the repair area with a thick coat of primer; the thickness should be built up using several thin layers of paint, rather than one thick one. Using 400 grade wet-and-dry paper, rub down the surface of the primer until it is really smooth. While doing this, the work area should be thoroughly doused with water, and the wet-and-dry paper periodically

rinsed in water. Allow to dry before spraying on more paint.

Spray on the top coat, again building up the thickness by using several thin layers of paint. Start spraying at the top of the repair area, and then, using a side-to-side motion, work downwards until the whole repair area and about 2 inches of the surrounding original paintwork is covered. Remove all masking material 10 to 15 minutes after spraying on the final coat of paint.

Allow the new paint at least two weeks to harden, then, using a paintwork renovator or a very fine cutting paste, blend the edges of the paint into the existing paintwork. Finally, apply wax polish.

Plastic components

With the use of more and more plastic body components by the vehicle manufacturers (eg bumpers. spoilers, and in some cases major body panels), rectification of more serious damage to such items has become a matter of either entrusting repair work to a specialist in this field, or renewing complete components. Repair of such damage by the DIY owner is not really feasible, owing to the cost of the equipment and materials required for effecting such repairs. The basic technique involves making a groove along the line of the crack in the plastic, using a rotary burr in a power drill. The damaged part is then welded back together, using a hot air gun to heat up and fuse a plastic filler rod into the groove. Any excess plastic is then removed, and the area rubbed down to a smooth finish. It is important that a filler rod of the correct plastic is used, as body components can be made of a variety of different types (eg polycarbonate, ABS, polypropylene).

Damage of a less serious nature (abrasions, minor cracks etc) can be repaired by the DIY owner using a two-part epoxy filler repair material. Once mixed in equal proportions, this is used in similar fashion to the bodywork filler used on metal panels. The filler is usually cured in twenty to thirty minutes, ready for sanding and painting.

If the owner is renewing a complete component himself, or if he has repaired it with epoxy filler, he will be left with the problem of finding a suitable paint for finishing which is compatible with the type of plastic used. At one time, the use of a universal paint was not possible, owing to the complex range of plastics encountered in body component applications. Standard paints, generally speaking, will not bond to plastic or rubber satisfactorily. However, it is now possible to obtain a plastic body parts finishing kit which consists of a pre-primer treatment, a primer and coloured top coat. Full instructions are normally supplied with a kit, but basically, the method of use is to first apply the pre-primer to the component concerned, and allow it to dry for up to 30 minutes. Then the primer is applied, and left to dry for about an hour before finally applying the special-coloured

top coat. The result is a correctly-coloured component, where the paint will flex with the plastic or rubber, a property that standard paint does not normally posses.

5 Major body damage – repair

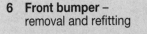

Where serious damage has occurred, or large areas need renewal due to neglect, it means that complete new panels will need welding-in, and this is best left to professionals. If the damage is due to impact, it will also be necessary to check completely the alignment of the bodyshell, and this can only be carried out accurately by a Citroën dealer, or accident repair specialist, using special jigs. If the body is left misaligned, it is primarily dangerous, as the car will not handle properly, and secondly, uneven stresses will be imposed on the steering, suspension and possibly transmission, causing abnormal wear, or complete failure, particularly to such items as the tyres.

6 Front bumper – removal and refitting

Note: *The help of an assistant is useful to support the bumper during the removal and refitting procedure.*

Removal

1 Firmly apply the handbrake, then jack up the front of the vehicle and support it securely on axle stands (see *Jacking and vehicle support*). Remove both front roadwheels.
2 Undo the screws securing the wheelarch liner to the underside of the bumper lower apron on each side. Release the stud-type retaining clips securing the wheelarch liner sections under the wheelarch and move the liner away from the bumper **(see illustrations)**. The stud-type clips can be removed using a forked type tool, or alternatively, with a large screwdriver (although there is a risk of breakage if the screwdriver method is used).

6.2a Undo the screws securing the wheelarch liner to the underside of the front bumper . . .

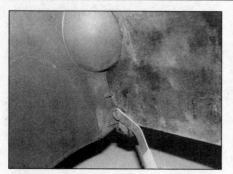

6.2b . . . release the stud-type retaining clips . . .

6.2c . . . and move the wheelarch liner away from the bumper

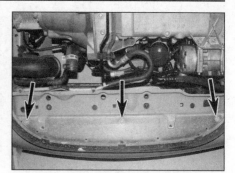

6.4 Undo the bolts (arrowed) securing the bumper lower apron to the body front crossmember

bolts each side securing the upper edge of the bumper to the front wing (see illustration).

6 At the front, undo the three bolts securing the upper edge of the bumper to the body upper crossmember (see illustration).

7 Lift the bumper off the pegs at each top corner adjacent to the headlights (see illustration).

8 Disengage the locating pegs along the top edge of the bumper on each side, then pull the bumper forward and carefully withdraw it from the front of the vehicle (see illustration).

9 To remove the impact absorber, undo the two nuts each side, and withdraw the impact absorber off the studs on the chassis side rails (see illustrations).

Refitting

10 Refitting is a reversal of removal, ensuring that the bumper correctly engages with the locating pegs each side as it is located in position.

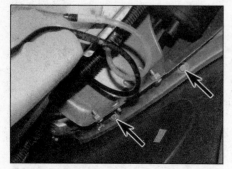

6.5 Undo the two bolts each side securing the upper edge of the bumper to the front wing

6.6 Undo the three bolts securing the upper edge of the bumper to the crossmember

3 On models with front foglights, reach up under the bumper and disconnect the wiring connectors at the rear of the bulbholder on each side.

4 Undo the three bolts securing the bumper lower apron to the body front crossmember (see illustration).

5 From under the wheelarch, undo the two

---

7 Rear bumper – removal and refitting

Note: The help of an assistant is useful to support the bumper during the removal and refitting procedure.

Removal

1 Chock the front wheels, then jack up the rear of the vehicle and support securely on axle stands (see Jacking and vehicle support).

2 Remove the rear light cluster on both sides as described in Chapter 12.

3 Remove the mud flap on each side by unscrewing the lower inner retaining screw, and the two screws on the rear edge of the wheelarch (see illustrations).

4 Undo the screw at the lower rear corner of the bumper on each side (see illustration).

5 From under the wheelarch, undo the bolt each side securing the front upper corner of the bumper to the rear wing (see illustration).

6 At the base of the rear light cluster aperture on each side, undo the nut securing the bumper to the rear wing (see illustration).

6.7 Lift the bumper off the pegs (arrowed) at each top corner

6.8 Pull the bumper forward and carefully remove it

6.9a Undo the two nuts each side (arrowed) . . .

6.9b . . . and remove the impact absorber

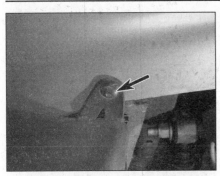

7.3a Remove the rear mud flap by unscrewing the lower inner retaining screw (arrowed)

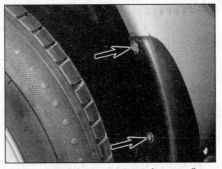

7.3b . . . and the two screws (arrowed) on the rear edge of the wheelarch

7.4 Undo the screw at the lower rear corner on each side

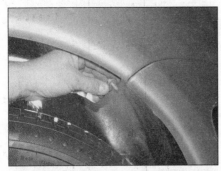

7.5 Undo the bolt each side securing the bumper front upper corner to the rear wing

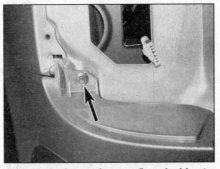

7.6 Undo the nut (arrowed) each side at the base of the rear light cluster aperture

7.7a Disengage the lug (arrowed) at the base of each light cluster . . .

7 Pull the bumper rearward and disengage the lug at the base of the rear light cluster, and the two plastic catches on each side **(see illustrations)**.

8 Using a small screwdriver, release the retaining catch each side, securing the upper edge of the bumper to the impact absorber **(see illustration)**.

9 Release the lug each side securing the lower edge of the bumper to the impact absorber, and carefully withdraw the bumper rearwards from its location **(see illustration)**.

10 To remove the impact absorber, undo the three bolts, one each side, and one in the centre, and withdraw the impact absorber from the vehicle **(see illustration)**.

Refitting

11 Refitting is a reversal of removal, ensuring that the bumper correctly engages with the lower lugs and side retaining catches as it is located in position.

8 Bonnet –
removal, refitting and adjustment

Removal

1 Open the bonnet and have an assistant support it, then, using a pencil or felt tip pen, mark the outline of each bonnet hinge relative to the bonnet, to use as a guide on refitting.

2 Slacken the upper, and unscrew the lower bonnet-to-hinge retaining bolts each side (see

illustration). With the help of the assistant, carefully lift the bonnet from the vehicle. Store the bonnet out of the way in a safe place.

3 Inspect the bonnet hinges for signs of wear

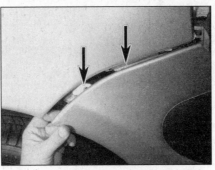

7.7b . . . and the two plastic catches (arrowed) on each side

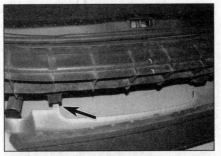

7.9 Release the lug (arrowed) each side securing the lower edge of the bumper to the impact absorber

and free play at the pivots, and if necessary renew. Each hinge is secured to the body by two bolts, accessible after removing the scuttle grille panel as described in Section 22.

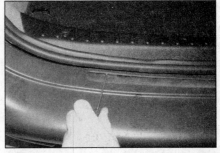

7.8 Release the retaining catch each side, securing the bumper to the impact absorber

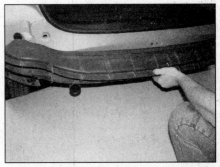

7.10 Undo the three bolts and withdraw the impact absorber

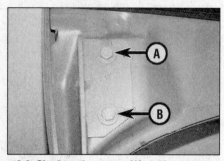

8.2 Slacken the upper (A), and unscrew the lower (B) bonnet-to-hinge retaining bolts

9.5 Remove the cover over the bonnet release cable entry point on the bulkhead

On refitting, apply a smear of multi-purpose grease to the hinges.

Refitting and adjustment

4 With the aid of an assistant, offer up the bonnet, engage the upper retaining bolts and loosely fit the lower bolts. Align the hinges with the marks made on removal, then tighten the retaining bolts securely.

5 Close the bonnet, and check for alignment with the adjacent panels. If necessary, slacken the hinge bolts and re-align the bonnet to suit. When correctly aligned, tighten the hinge bolts securely.

6 Once the bonnet is correctly aligned, check that the bonnet fastens and releases in a satisfactory manner. If adjustment is necessary, slacken the bonnet lock retaining bolts, and adjust the position of the lock to suit. Once the lock is operating correctly, securely tighten its retaining bolts.

11.2 Unscrew the locking ring and disconnect the door wiring connector

9.3 Bonnet release lever retaining bolt (arrowed)

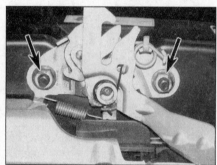

10.1 Bonnet lock assembly retaining nuts (arrowed)

9 Bonnet release cable – removal and refitting

Removal

1 Remove the front bumper as described in Section 6.

2 Remove the scuttle grille panel as described in Section 22.

3 Working under the facia on the left-hand side, unscrew the release lever bolt, and withdraw the lever assembly from its location (see illustration). Release the cable from the lever.

4 Working in the engine compartment, disconnect the end of the cable from the lock lever, then unclip the outer cable from the bracket on the lock body and from the clips on the radiator fan shroud and inner wing panel.

11.3 Unscrew the two bolts (arrowed) and disconnect the door check strap

5 Unclip and remove the plastic cover over the cable entry point on the bulkhead (see illustration).

6 Tie a length of string to the end of the cable in the passenger compartment, then carefully pull the cable through into the engine compartment. Untie the string from the end of the cable, and leave it in position to aid refitting.

7 Pull the cable out from under the headlight unit, noting its routing then remove the cable from the car.

Refitting

8 Locate the cable in position in the engine compartment, connecting it to the lock assembly and the relevant retaining clips.

9 Tie the end of the cable to the string, and pull it through into the vehicle interior.

10 Check that the bulkhead grommet is securely seated, then remove the string and connect the cable to the release lever. Refit the lever and secure with the retaining bolt.

11 Refit the plastic cover over the cable entry point on the bulkhead.

12 Refit the scuttle grille panel as described in Section 22, and the front bumper as described in Section 6.

10 Bonnet lock – removal and refitting

Removal

1 Unscrew the two nuts securing the lock assembly to the body upper crossmember (see illustration).

2 Withdraw the lock from the studs and disconnect the bonnet release cable from the lock lever.

Refitting

3 Refitting is a reversal of removal. On completion, check the operation of the lock and, if necessary, adjust the position of the lock within the elongated bolt holes to achieve satisfactory operation.

11 Door – removal, refitting and adjustment

Front door

Removal

1 Disconnect the battery negative terminal (refer to *Disconnecting the battery* in the Reference Chapter).

2 Open the door, then unscrew the locking ring and disconnect the door wiring connector from the socket in the front edge of the door or on the door pillar (see illustration).

3 Unscrew the two securing bolts, and disconnect the door check strap from the door pillar (see illustration).

11.4 Front door lower hinge pin (arrowed)

4 Ensure that the door is adequately supported, then unscrew the upper and lower hinge pins **(see illustration)**. Carefully lift the door from the vehicle.

12.1 Release the edge of the door mirror trim panel, disengage the clips and withdraw the panel

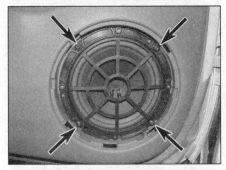

12.3a Undo the loudspeaker retaining screws (arrowed) . . .

12.4b . . . and withdraw the trim

Refitting

5 Refitting is a reversal of removal, but on completion, check the fit of the door in relation to the surrounding body panels, and if necessary adjust as follows:
a) Jack up the front of the vehicle, and support securely on axle stands (see 'Jacking and vehicle support').
b) Remove the roadwheel and wheelarch liner.
c) Close the door.
d) Using a suitable spanner through the wheelarch, loosen the bolts securing the door hinges to the body, and adjust the position of the door to provide a satisfactory fit. Tighten the bolts on completion.

Rear door

6 The procedure is as described for the front

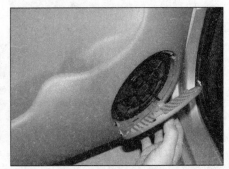

12.2 Carefully prise off the loudspeaker grille

12.3b . . . withdraw the speaker and disconnect the wiring

12.5 Undo the two screws located in the door pull handle

doors, but the hinge-to-body bolts are accessed for adjustment with the front door open.

12 Door inner trim panel – removal and refitting

Front door

Removal

1 Release the edge of the door mirror interior trim panel, disengage the retaining clips and withdraw the panel **(see illustration)**.
2 Carefully prise off the loudspeaker grille from the trim panel **(see illustration)**.
3 Undo the four loudspeaker retaining screws, withdraw the speaker and disconnect the wiring **(see illustrations)**.
4 Insert a small screwdriver into the hole on the front of the door pull handle. Release the retaining clip and withdraw the handle trim **(see illustrations)**.
5 Undo the two screws located in the door pull handle **(see illustration)**.
6 Undo the two screws located in the speaker aperture **(see illustration)**.
7 Using a suitable forked tool, work around the edge of the trim panel, and release the securing clips **(see illustration)**.
8 Pull the panel outwards, lift it up and remove it from the door **(see illustrations)**.

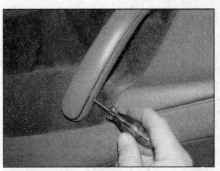

12.4a Release the door pull handle trim retaining clip . . .

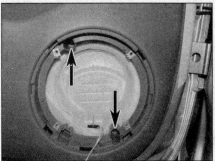

12.6 Undo the two screws located in the speaker aperture

12.7 Release the panel securing clips using a forked tool

12.8 Pull the panel outwards, lift it up and remove it from the door

12.10 Prise out the rear door upper interior finisher panel

12.11 Prise off the rear speaker grille

12.12a Undo the speaker retaining screws . . .

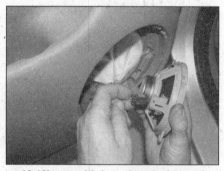

12.12b . . . withdraw the speaker and disconnect the wiring

Refitting

9 Before refitting, check whether any of the trim panel retaining studs were broken on removal. Renew the panel retaining studs as necessary, then refit the panel using a reversal of removal.

Rear door

Removal

10 Prise out the upper interior finisher panel at the rear of the door window **(see illustration)**.

11 Carefully prise off the speaker grille from the trim panel **(see illustration)**.
12 Undo the speaker retaining screws, withdraw the speaker and disconnect the wiring **(see illustrations)**.
13 Undo the two screws located in the speaker aperture **(see illustration)**.
14 On models with manual windows, pull the winder handle off the spindle, and then remove the spindle trim plate **(see illustration)**.
15 Insert a small screwdriver into the hole on the front of the door pull handle. Release the retaining clip and withdraw the handle trim **(see illustration)**.
16 Undo the two screws located in the door pull handle **(see illustration)**.
17 Using a suitable forked tool, work around the lower and side edges of the trim panel, and release the securing clips **(see illustration)**.

12.13 Undo the two screws located in the speaker aperture

12.14 Pull the window winder handle off the spindle, and remove the spindle trim plate

12.15 Release the retaining clip and withdraw the door pull handle trim

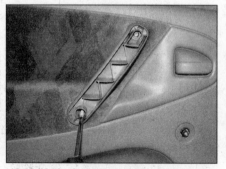

12.16 Undo the two screws located in the door pull handle

12.17 Release the panel lower and side securing clips using a forked tool

18 Pull the panel outwards, disengage the two lugs above the interior door handle and remove the panel from the door (see illustrations).

Refitting

19 Refitting is a reversal of removal, after first renewing any broken panel retaining studs as necessary.

13 Door handle and lock components – removal and refitting

Interior door handle

Removal

1 Remove the door inner trim panel, as described in Section 12.
2 Release the front edge of the handle from its location.

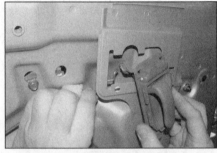

13.3 Disengage the interior handle locating lugs, rotate it through 90° and disconnect the link rod

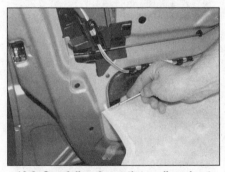

13.6 Carefully release the sealing sheet from the adhesive bead using a sharp knife

13.8 Release the wiring harness, then unclip and remove the lower protection shield

12.18a Disengage the two lugs above the interior door handle . . .

3 Slide the handle assembly towards the front of the door to disengage the rear locating lugs, rotate it through 90° and disconnect the link rod (see illustration).

Refitting

4 Refitting is a reversal of removal, but ensure that the link rod is correctly reconnected, and refit the inner trim panel (see Section 12).

Front door lock cylinder

Note: *A new door sealing sheet may be required on refitting.*

Removal

5 Remove the interior door handle as described previously.
6 Using a sharp knife, carefully release the plastic sealing sheet from the adhesive bead and remove the sheet from the door (see illustration). If care is taken, it may just be

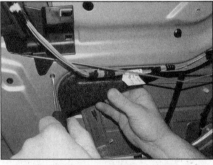

13.7a Undo the retaining screw . . .

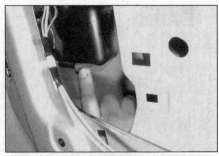

13.9 Depress the retaining plate and disengage the upper protection shield lower lug

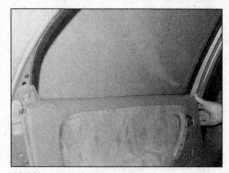

12.18b . . . and remove the trim panel from the door

possible to remove the sheet in one piece and re-use it when refitting.
7 Undo the retaining screw and remove the foam panel from the door (see illustrations).
8 Release the wiring harness clip from the lower plastic protection shield, then unclip and remove the shield (see illustration).
9 Depress the retaining plate at the base of the upper plastic protection shield and disengage the shield lower lug (see illustration).
10 Lower the shield to disengage its upper locating peg and remove the shield from the door (see illustration).
11 Extract the large retaining clip from the rear of the lock cylinder, then remove the lock cylinder from the outside of the door (see illustrations).

Refitting

12 Refitting is a reversal of removal, but

13.7b . . . and remove the foam panel from the door

13.10 Disengage the upper locating peg and remove the shield from the door

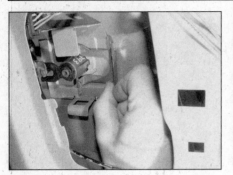

13.11a Extract the lock cylinder retaining clip . . .

13.11b . . . then remove the lock cylinder from the door

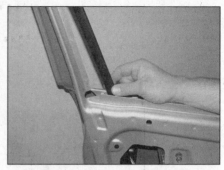

13.13 Withdraw the window guide channel for access to the door lock

ensure that the lock cylinder retaining clip is securely refitted. Fit a new sealing sheet to the door if the original was damaged in any way during removal. On completion, refit the door inner trim panel as described in Section 12.

Front door lock

Note: *A new door sealing sheet may be required on refitting.*

Removal

13 Remove the front door window glass as described in Section 14. With the glass removed, withdraw the rear part of the window guide channel from its location to gain access to the door lock **(see illustration)**.
14 Remove the door lock cylinder, as described previously in this Section.
15 Release the door lock link rod from the lever on the exterior handle **(see illustration)**.
16 Undo the three screws securing the lock

assembly to the edge of the door **(see illustration)**.
17 Release the interior handle link rod from the guide clips on the door, then lower the lock assembly and manipulate it out through the door aperture **(see illustration)**.
18 Disconnect the central locking motor wiring plug and remove the lock assembly **(see illustration)**.

Refitting

19 Refitting is a reversal of removal. Fit a new sealing sheet to the door if the original was damaged in any way during removal. On completion, refit the door inner trim panel as described in Section 12.

Front door exterior handle

Note 1: *A new door sealing sheet may be required for refitting.*
Note 2: *The exterior handle is riveted to the*

door. Ensure that new rivets of the correct size are available for refitting.

Removal

20 Carry out the operations described in paragraphs 6 to 10.
21 Remove the interior door handle as described previously.
22 Remove the front door window glass as described in Section 14. With the glass removed, withdraw the rear part of the window guide channel from its location to gain access to the handle.
23 Release the door lock link rod from the lever on the exterior handle.
24 Using a 6.0 mm diameter drill bit, drill off the rivet heads from the outside, and remove the handle from the door.

Refitting

25 Refitting is a reversal of removal, using new pop rivets to secure the handle. Fit a new sealing sheet to the door if the original was damaged in any way during removal. On completion, refit the inner trim panel as described in Section 12.

Rear door lock

Note: *A new door sealing sheet may be required on refitting.*

Removal

26 Remove the interior door handle as described previously.
27 Using a sharp knife, carefully release the plastic sealing sheet from the adhesive bead and remove the sheet from the door **(see illustration)**. If care is taken, it may just be

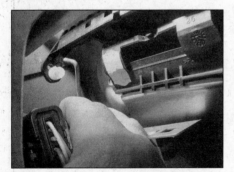

13.15 Release the door lock link rod from the exterior handle lever

13.16 Undo the three screws securing the lock assembly to the edge of the door

13.17 Manipulate the lock assembly out through the door aperture . . .

13.18 . . . and disconnect the wiring connector

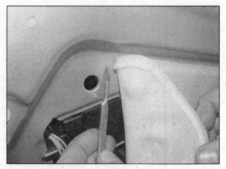

13.27 Using a sharp knife, carefully release the rear door plastic sealing sheet

13.29 Unclip and remove the plastic protection shield

13.30 Disengage the exterior handle link rod from the lever on the door lock

13.31 Disconnect the central locking motor wiring plug

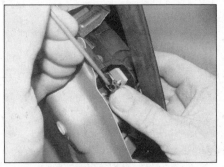

13.32 Disengage the interior handle link rod from the door lock lever

13.33a Undo the three securing screws . . .

13.33b . . . then manipulate the lock assembly out through the door aperture

possible to remove the sheet in one piece and re-use it when refitting.

28 Free the interior handle link rod from the guide clips on the door.

29 Release the wiring harness clip from the plastic protection shield, then unclip and remove the shield **(see illustration)**.

30 Disengage the exterior handle link rod from the lever on the door lock **(see illustration)**.

31 Disconnect the central locking motor wiring plug **(see illustration)**.

32 Disengage the interior handle link rod from the door lock lever **(see illustration)**.

33 Undo the three screws securing the lock assembly to the edge of the door, then manipulate the unit out through the door aperture **(see illustrations)**.

Refitting

34 Refitting is a reversal of removal. Fit a new

sealing sheet to the door if the original was damaged in any way during removal. On completion, refit the door inner trim panel as described in Section 12.

Rear door exterior door handle

Note 1: *A new door sealing sheet may be required for refitting.*
Note 2: *The exterior handle is riveted to the door. Ensure that new rivets of the correct size are available for refitting.*

Removal

35 Release the door lock link rod from the lever on the exterior handle.
36 Using a 6.0 mm diameter drill bit, drill off the rivet heads from the outside, and remove the handle from the door.

Refitting

37 Refitting is a reversal of removal, using new pop rivets to secure the handle. Fit a new

sealing sheet to the door if the original was damaged in any way during removal. On completion, refit the inner trim panel as described in Section 12.

14 Door window glass and regulator – removal and refitting

Front door window glass

Note: *A new door sealing sheet may be required on refitting.*

Removal

1 Remove the door inner trim panel as described in Section 12.
2 Using a sharp knife, carefully release the plastic sealing sheet from the adhesive bead and remove the sheet from the door. If care is taken, it may just be possible to remove the sheet in one piece and re-use it when refitting.
3 Remove the window glass interior and exterior waist seal from the door window aperture **(see illustration)**.
4 Position the window so the front attachment to the lifting channel is accessible through the loudspeaker aperture. Release the attachment lug on the lifting channel bracket from the locating hole in the window glass **(see illustration)**.
5 Reposition the window so that the rear attachment to the lifting channel is accessible through the main door aperture. Release the rear lifting channel attachment lug from the glass **(see illustration)**.

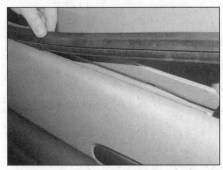

14.3 Remove the window glass waist seals from the door window aperture

14.4 Release the lug on the front lifting channel from the hole in the window glass

14.5 Reposition the window and release the lug on the rear lifting channel from the window glass

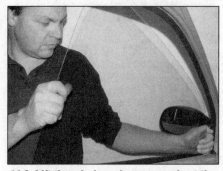

14.6 Lift the window glass upwards at the rear and remove it from the outside of the door

14.13 Release the three clips securing the regulator cable assembly to the door panel

6 Lift the window glass upwards at the rear and remove it from the outside of the door **(see illustration)**.

Refitting

7 Refitting is a reversal of removal, but fit a new sealing sheet to the door if the original was damaged in any way during removal. On completion, refit the inner trim panel as described in Section 12.

Front door window regulator

Removal

8 Remove the door inner trim panel as described in Section 12.

9 Using a sharp knife, carefully release the plastic sealing sheet from the adhesive bead and remove the sheet from the door. If care is taken, it may just be possible to remove the sheet in one piece and re-use it when refitting.

10 Position the window so the front attachment to the lifting channel is accessible through the loudspeaker aperture. Release the attachment lug on the lifting channel bracket from the locating hole in the window glass **(see illustration 14.4)**.

11 Reposition the window so that the rear attachment to the lifting channel is accessible through the main door aperture. Release the rear lifting channel attachment lug from the glass **(see illustration 14.5)**.

12 Slide the window up to the fully closed position and secure it in this position with masking tape over the top of the door frame.

13 Release the three clips securing the regulator cable assembly to the door panel **(see illustration)**.

14 Unscrew the two nuts securing the front of the regulator assembly to the door panel **(see illustration)**.

15 Unscrew the nuts securing the lower ends of the front and rear lifting channels to the door panel **(see illustration)**.

16 Slacken the bolts securing the upper ends of the front and rear lifting channels to the door panel **(see illustration)**.

17 Disconnect the window lift motor wiring plug, and manipulate the regulator assembly out through the door aperture **(see illustrations)**.

Refitting

18 Refitting is a reversal of removal.

Rear door window glass

Note: *A new door sealing sheet may be required on refitting.*

Removal

19 Remove the door inner trim panel as described in Section 12.

20 Using a sharp knife, carefully release the plastic sealing sheet from the adhesive bead and remove the sheet from the door. If care is taken, it may just be possible to remove the sheet in one piece and re-use it when refitting.

21 Undo the bolt securing the rear outer trim panel to the door. Using a forked tool, release the retaining clips and remove the panel from the door **(see illustrations)**.

22 Remove the window glass interior and exterior waist seal from the door window aperture **(see illustration)**.

23 Position the window so the attachment to the lifting channel is accessible through the door aperture. Release the attachment lug on the lifting channel bracket from the locating

14.14 Unscrew the regulator assembly front securing nuts (arrowed)

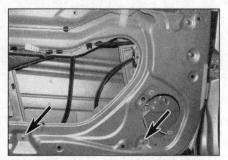

14.15 Unscrew the nuts (arrowed) securing the lower ends of the lifting channels to the door

14.16 Slacken the lifting channel upper securing bolts (rear bolt arrowed)

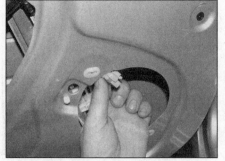

14.17a Disconnect the window lift motor wiring plug . . .

14.17b . . . and manipulate the regulator assembly out through the door aperture

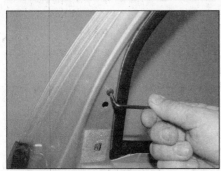

14.21a Undo the bolt securing the rear outer trim panel to the door . . .

14.21b . . . release the retaining clips using a forked tool . . .

14.21c . . . and remove the trim panel from the door

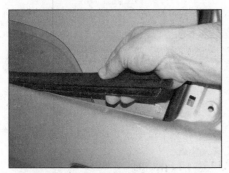

14.22 Remove the window glass waist seals from the door window aperture

14.23 Release the attachment lug on the lifting channel from the hole in the window glass

14.24 Withdraw the window glass guide channel from the door frame

hole in the window glass (see illustration).
24 Release the window glass guide channel from the door frame and withdraw the guide channel from the door (see illustration).
25 Lift the window glass upwards and remove it from the outside of the door (see illustration).

Refitting

26 Refitting is a reversal of removal, but fit a new sealing sheet to the door if the original was damaged in any way during removal. On completion, refit the inner trim panel as described in Section 12.

Rear door window regulator

Note: A new door sealing sheet may be required on refitting.

Removal

27 Remove the door inner trim panel as described in Section 12.
28 Using a sharp knife, carefully release the plastic sealing sheet from the adhesive bead and remove the sheet from the door. If care is taken, it may just be possible to remove the sheet in one piece and re-use it when refitting.
29 Position the window so the attachment to the lifting channel is accessible through the door aperture. Release the attachment lug on the lifting channel bracket from the locating hole in the window glass (see illustration 14.23).
30 Slide the window glass upwards by hand, and tape it to the top of the door frame to secure it in the raised position.
31 Slacken the upper nut, and undo the

lower nut securing the lifting channel to the door (see illustration).
32 Undo the three regulator securing nuts,

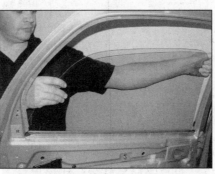

14.25 Lift the window glass upwards and remove it from the outside of the door

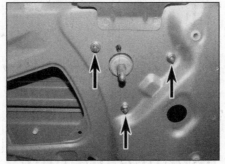

14.32a Undo the three regulator securing nuts (arrowed) . . .

release the two locating lugs and withdraw the regulator assembly out through the door aperture (see illustrations).

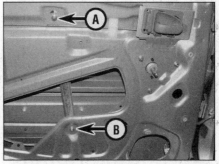

14.31 Slacken the lifting channel upper nut (A) and undo the lower nut (B)

14.32b . . . release the two locating lugs . . .

14.32c ... and withdraw the regulator assembly out through the door aperture

15.4 Disconnect the tailgate washer hose at the connection on the embellisher

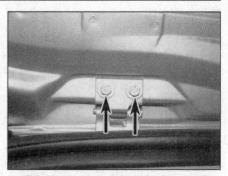

15.6 Unscrew the two bolts (arrowed) each side securing the hinges to the tailgate

15.10a Using a small screwdriver, release the support strut spring clip ...

15.10b ... and pull the support strut from its balljoint

8 Refitting is a reversal of removal, bearing in mind the following points:

a) If necessary, adjust the rubber buffers to obtain a good fit when the tailgate is shut.

b) If necessary, adjust the position of the tailgate lock and/or hinge bolts within their elongated holes to achieve satisfactory lock operation.

Support struts

Removal

9 Support the tailgate in the open position, with the help of an assistant, or using a stout piece of wood.
10 Using a small screwdriver, release the spring clip, and pull the support strut from its balljoint on the body (see illustrations).
11 Similarly, release the strut from the balljoint on the tailgate, and withdraw the strut from the vehicle.

Refitting

12 Refitting is a reversal of removal, but ensure the spring clips are correctly engaged.

Refitting

33 Refitting is a reversal of removal, but fit a new sealing sheet to the door if the original was damaged in any way during removal. On completion, refit the inner trim panel as described in Section 12.

---

15 Tailgate and support struts – removal and refitting

Tailgate

Removal

1 Disconnect the battery negative terminal (refer to *Disconnecting the battery* in the Reference Chapter).
2 Remove the tailgate trim panel as described in Section 25.

3 Disconnect the wiring harness connectors at the tailgate internal components, referring to the relevant procedures contained in Chapter 12. Release the grommet from the tailgate and withdraw the wiring harness.
4 Disconnect the tailgate washer hose at the connection on the embellisher (see illustration).
5 With the aid of an assistant, suitably support the tailgate, then prise out the support strut spring clips, and pull the struts from the balljoints on the tailgate.
6 Unscrew the two bolts each side securing the hinges to the tailgate, and carefully lift the tailgate from the vehicle (see illustration).

Refitting

7 If a new tailgate is to be fitted, transfer all serviceable components (lock mechanism, wiper motor, etc) to it, with reference to the relevant procedures in this Chapter, and in Chapter 12.

---

16 Tailgate lock components – removal and refitting

Tailgate lock

Removal

1 Remove the tailgate trim panel as described in Section 25.
2 Undo the two lock retaining screws, and the screw on the side of the lock assembly (see illustrations).
3 Withdraw the lock assembly through the tailgate aperture, disconnect the wiring connector and remove the lock (see illustration).

Refitting

4 Refitting is a reversal of removal, but adjust the tailgate lock striker as necessary to obtain satisfactory closure.

Tailgate lock striker

Removal

5 Undo the screws and remove the tailgate

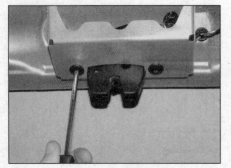

16.2a Undo the two tailgate lock retaining screws ...

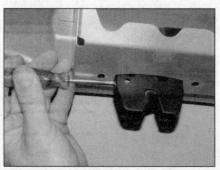

16.2b ... and the screw on the side of the lock assembly

aperture lower panel (see Section 25) for access to the striker plate retaining bolts.

6 Mark the position of the striker on the body, for use when refitting. Unscrew the two securing bolts, and remove the striker from the body **(see illustration)**.

Refitting

7 Refitting is a reversal of removal. Before tightening the securing bolts, the position of the striker should be altered (the securing bolt holes are elongated) until satisfactory lock operation is obtained. Use the marks made prior to removal, if appropriate.

17 Central locking components – removal and refitting

Control unit

1 The central locking system is controlled by the Built-in Systems Interface (BSI) which is the vehicle central computer controlling the main body electrical system functions. The unit is located under the facia adjacent to the steering column. Refer to Chapter 12 for further information.

2 Should any problems be experienced with the operation of the central locking system or any of the other functions controlled by the BSI, the vehicle should be taken to a Citroën dealer for diagnostic investigation.

Door lock motor

3 The motor is integral with the door lock assembly. Removal and refitting of the lock assembly is described in Section 13.

Tailgate lock motor

4 Removal of the tailgate lock motor is described as part of the tailgate lock removal and refitting procedure described in Section 16.

Remote control transmitter

Battery renewal

5 When the remote control transmitter battery is nearing the end of its usable life, an audible signal will be emitted from within the vehicle, accompanied by a message on the instrument panel multifunction screen. The battery should then be renewed with a type CR 1620 (3 volt) battery as follows.

6 Using a small screwdriver, carefully prise the two halves of the transmitter apart, and remove the battery.

7 Fit the new battery and clip the transmitter back together.

Initialisation

8 To initialise the unit after renewing the battery, switch on the ignition and depress one of the buttons on the remote control transmitter.

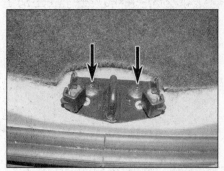

16.3 Withdraw the lock through the tailgate aperture and disconnect the wiring connector

18 Exterior mirrors and mirror glass – removal and refitting

Mirror assembly

Removal

1 Disconnect the battery negative terminal (refer to *Disconnecting the battery* in the Reference Chapter).

2 Release the edge of the door mirror interior trim panel, disengage the retaining clips and remove the panel **(see illustration)**.

3 Place a cloth over the upper edge of the door inner trim panel, to prevent the mirror securing screws falling inside the panel if you

18.2 Release the door mirror trim panel, disengage the clips and remove the panel

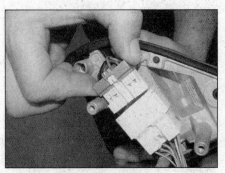

18.4a Separate the two halves of the wiring connector . . .

16.6 Unscrew the two securing bolts (arrowed) and remove the tailgate striker from the body

drop them. Remove the three mirror securing screws, then withdraw the mirror from the door **(see illustration)**.

4 Separate the two halves of the wiring connector then, using a small screwdriver, release the retaining catch and release the wiring connector from the mirror frame **(see illustrations)**. Remove the mirror assembly from the vehicle.

Refitting

5 Refitting is a reversal of removal.

Mirror glass

Removal

6 Working through the gap at the outer edge of the mirror glass, using a screwdriver,

18.3 Undo the mirror securing screws (arrowed) then withdraw the mirror from the door

18.4b . . . then release the retaining catch and remove the wiring connector from the mirror frame

18.6a To remove the mirror glass, spread the legs of the internal spring clip apart to release the glass . . .

18.6b . . . as shown here with the glass removed

18.8 Refit the spring clip to the mirror glass, ensuring the clip is correctly located in the slots

release the ends of the spring clip which secures the glass to the mirror body **(see illustrations)**.

7 Withdraw the glass, and disconnect the wiring connector.

Refitting

8 Refit the ends of the spring clip to the rear of the mirror glass, ensuring the clip is correctly located in the slots in the rear of the mirror glass **(see illustration)**.

9 Push the mirror glass into the mirror until the spring clip locks into position in the mirror adjuster groove.

19 Windscreen, tailgate and fixed side window glass – general information

These areas of glass are secured by the tight fit of the weatherstrip in the body aperture, and are bonded in position with a special adhesive. Renewal of such fixed glass is a difficult, messy and time-consuming task, which is considered beyond the scope of the home mechanic. It is difficult, unless one has plenty of practice, to obtain a secure, waterproof fit. Furthermore, the task carries a high risk of breakage; this applies especially to the laminated glass windscreen. In view of this, owners are strongly advised to have this sort of work carried out by one of the many specialist windscreen fitters.

For those possessing the necessary skills and equipment to carry out this task, some

preliminary removal of the vehicle interior trim and associated components is necessary, as follows, referring to the procedures contained in the Sections and Chapters indicated.

Windscreen

1 Remove both wiper arms (Chapter 12).
2 Remove the scuttle grille panel (Section 22 of this Chapter).
3 Remove the windscreen pillar trim on both sides (Section 25 of this Chapter).
4 Remove the sun visors.

Front fixed side window

5 Remove the windscreen pillar trim on the side concerned (Section 25 of this Chapter).

Rear fixed side window

6 Remove the rear quarter trim panel (Section 25 of this Chapter).

Tailgate window

7 Remove the tailgate trim panel as described in Section 25 of this Chapter.

20 Sunroof – general information

The factory-fitted sunroof is of the electric tilt/slide type.

Due to the complexity of the sunroof mechanism, considerable expertise is required to repair, renew or adjust the sunroof components successfully. Removal of the roof

first requires the headlining to be removed, which is a tedious operation, and not a task to be undertaken lightly. Any problems with the sunroof should be referred to a Citroën dealer.

21 Body exterior fittings – removal and refitting

Bonnet grille panel

Removal

1 Open the bonnet and undo the four grille panel retaining screws **(see illustration)**.
2 Release the two retaining catches each side and withdraw the grille panel from the bonnet **(see illustrations)**.

Refitting

3 Refitting is a reversal of removal.

Wheelarch liners/mud shields

4 The wheelarch liners and mud shields are secured by a combination of self-tapping screws, and stud-type clips. Removal is self-evident, and the clips can be released using a forked-shaped tool. The specific removal procedure is normally included in the relevant removal procedure for the components concerned.

Body trim strips & badges

5 The various body trim strips and badges are held in position with a special adhesive

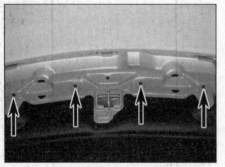

21.1 Undo the grille panel retaining screws (arrowed)

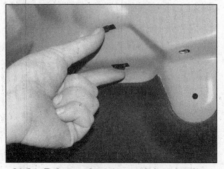

21.2a Release the two retaining catches each side . . .

21.2b . . . and withdraw the grille panel from the bonnet

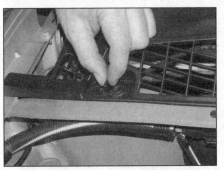

22.3 Release the scuttle grille panel fasteners by turning them through 90°

22.4a Pull the scuttle panel downwards to release the upper retaining clips . . .

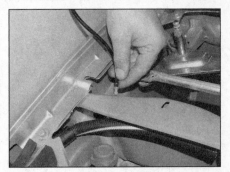

22.4b . . . then disconnect the windscreen washer hose

membrane. Removal requires the trim/badge to be heated, to soften the adhesive, and then cut away from the surface. Due to the high risk of damage to the vehicle paintwork during this operation, it is recommended that this task should be entrusted to a Citroën dealer.

22 Scuttle grille panel – removal and refitting

Removal

1 Open the bonnet and support it in the highest position.
2 Remove the windscreen wiper arms as described in Chapter 12.
3 Release the two outer, and the single centre retaining fasteners by turning them through 90° **(see illustration)**.

4 Pull the scuttle panel downwards to release the upper retaining clips, then disconnect the windscreen washer hose and remove the panel **(see illustrations)**.

Refitting

5 Refitting is a reversal of removal.

23 Seats – removal and refitting

Front seats

⚠ *Warning: The front seats are equipped with side air bags built into the outer sides of the seats. Refer to Chapter 12 for the precautions which should be observed when dealing with an air bag system. Do not tamper with*

the air bag unit in any way, and do not attempt to test any air bag system components. Note that the air bag is triggered if the mechanism is supplied with an electrical current (including via an ohmmeter), or if the assembly is subjected to a temperature of greater than 100°C.

Removal

1 De-activate the air bag system as described in Chapter 12 before attempting to remove the seat.
2 Move the seat fully rearwards.
3 Unclip and remove the seat rear trim panel and take out the storage tray from under the seat **(see illustrations)**.
4 Disconnect the wiring connector located at the centre of the front seat rail **(see illustration)**.
5 Remove the bolts (one bolt on each side) securing the front of the seat frame to the floor **(see illustration)**.
6 Move the seat fully forwards.
7 Remove the bolts (one bolt on the outer frame, and two on the inner frame) securing the rear of the seat frame to the floor **(see illustration)**.
8 Lift the seat and frame assembly from the vehicle and, where applicable, recover any washers and spacer plates from the floor.

Refitting

9 Refitting is a reversal of removal, but observe the following precautions before reconnecting the battery.
 a) Ensure that there are no occupants in the vehicle, and that there are no loose objects around the vicinity of the seats.

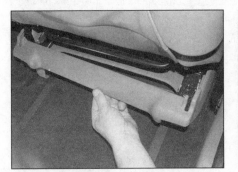

23.3a Unclip and remove the front seat rear trim panel . . .

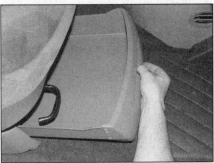

23.3b . . . and take out the storage tray from under the seat

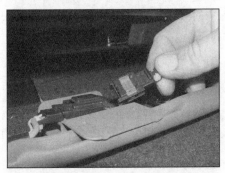

23.4 Disconnect the wiring connector at the centre of the front seat rail

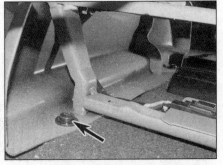

23.5 Seat frame front mounting bolt (arrowed)

23.7 Seat frame inner rear securing bolts (arrowed)

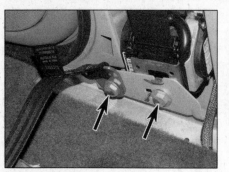

24.5 Undo the seat belt lower anchor bolt and the inertia reel anchor bolt (arrowed)

24.6 Slip the seat belt out of its upper guide and withdraw the inertia reel from the door pillar

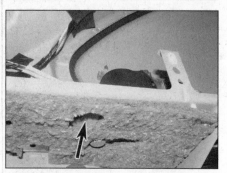

24.9 Undo the rear seat belt inertia reel retaining bolt (arrowed)

b) *Ensure that the ignition is switched off then reconnect the battery negative terminal.*

c) *Open the driver's door and switch on the ignition. Check that the air bag warning light illuminates briefly then extinguishes.*

d) *Switch off the ignition.*

e) *If the air bag warning light does not operate as described in paragraph c), consult a Citroën dealer before driving the vehicle.*

Rear seats

Removal

10 Remove the headrest then lift the lever at the side of the seat and fold the seat back onto the seat cushion. Push the seat back fully down to lock it in this position.

11 Lift the bar at the rear of the seat to release the rear securing points and tilt the seat assembly forward at an angle of 45°. Lift the seat up to disengage the front anchorages and remove the seat from the vehicle.

Refitting

12 Refitting is a reversal of removal.

---

24 Seat belt components – removal and refitting

Note: *Record the positions of the washers and spacers on the seat belt anchors, and ensure they are refitted in their original positions.*

Front seat belt

⚠️ **Warning: The front seat belt inertia reels are equipped with a pyrotechnic pretensioner mechanism. Refer to the air bag system precautions contained in Chapter 12 which apply equally to the seat belt pretensioners. Do not tamper with the inertia reel pretensioner unit in any way, and do not attempt to test the unit. Note that the unit is triggered if the mechanism is supplied with an electrical current (including via an ohmmeter), or if the assembly is subjected to a temperature of greater than 100°C.**

Removal

1 De-activate the air bag system (which will also de-activate the pyrotechnic pretensioner mechanism) as described in Chapter 12 before attempting to remove the seatbelt.

2 If desired, to improve access, remove the relevant front seat as described in Section 23.

3 Remove the centre pillar trim panels as described in Section 25.

4 Disconnect the wiring connector from the inertia reel pretensioner unit.

5 Undo the seat belt lower anchor bolt and the inertia reel anchor bolt, and recover the washers **(see illustration)**.

6 Slip the seat belt out of its upper guide and withdraw the inertia reel from the door pillar **(see illustration)**. Remove the seat belt assembly from the vehicle.

Refitting

7 Refitting is a reversal of removal, but

observe the following precautions before reconnecting the battery.

a) *Ensure that there are no occupants in the vehicle, and that there are no loose objects around the vicinity of the seats.*

b) *Ensure that the ignition is switched off then reconnect the battery negative terminal.*

c) *Open the driver's door and switch on the ignition. Check that the air bag warning light illuminates briefly then extinguishes.*

d) *Switch off the ignition.*

e) *If the air bag warning light does not operate as described in paragraph c), consult a Citroën dealer before driving the vehicle.*

Rear seat belts

Removal

8 Remove the parcel shelf support, rear quarter trim panel and luggage compartment lower side panel, on the relevant side, as described in Section 25.

9 From the underside of the body side member, undo the inertia reel retaining bolt **(see illustration)**. Note the locations of any washers and spacers on the bolt, then remove the inertia reel.

Refitting

10 Refitting is a reversal of removal, but ensure that any washers and spacers are positioned as noted before removal, and tighten the mounting bolts securely.

---

25 Interior trim – removal and refitting

Door inner trim

1 Refer to Section 12.

Windscreen pillar trim

Removal

2 Prise the weatherstrip from the front door aperture in the vicinity of the pillar trim **(see illustration)**.

3 Carefully prise the trim away from the pillar at the sides and top to release the retaining clips **(see illustration)**.

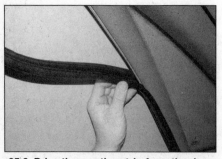

25.2 Prise the weatherstrip from the door aperture in the vicinity of the windscreen pillar trim

25.3 Prise the trim away from the pillar at the sides and top

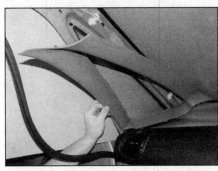

25.4 Lift the trim up to disengage the lower lugs and remove it from the vehicle

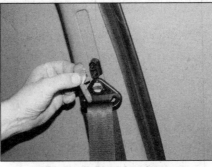

25.6a Unclip the trim plate . . .

25.6b . . . then undo the front seat belt upper anchor bolt

25.7a Pull the top and sides of the centre pillar upper panel from the pillar to release the clips . . .

25.7b . . . then lift it up to disengage it from the lower panel

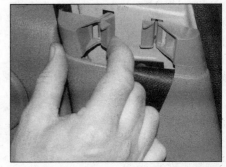

25.8 Depress the retaining tags and pull the lower panel from the pillar at the top

4 Lift the trim up to disengage the lower locating lugs and remove it from the vehicle (see illustration).

Refitting

5 Refitting is a reversal of removal, but ensure that all retaining clips are fully engaged and that the weatherstrip is fully seated.

Centre pillar trim

Removal

6 Unclip the trim plate, then undo the seat belt upper anchor bolt (see illustrations).
7 Pull the top and sides of the upper panel from the pillar to release the securing clips, lift it up to disengage it from the lower panel and remove it from the vehicle (see illustrations).
8 Depress the upper retaining tags and pull the lower panel from the pillar at the top (see illustration).
9 Lift the panel upwards to disengage the two lower locating lugs and remove the panel from the vehicle (see illustration).

Refitting

10 Refitting is a reversal of removal, but ensure that all retaining clips are fully engaged.

Parcel shelf support

Removal

11 If working on the right-hand side, release the holding strap and remove the shopping trolley.
12 Remove the trim cap then undo the rear seat belt lower anchor bolt (see illustration).

13 Undo the three screws (left-hand side) or four screws (right-hand side) securing the centre of the parcel shelf support to the body side-member (see illustration).

25.9 Lift the panel up to disengage the two lower locating lugs (arrowed)

25.13 Undo the parcel shelf support centre retaining screws

14 Disengage the parcel shelf clips from the rear quarter trim panel and withdraw the shelf from its location (see illustration).
15 Disconnect the wiring connectors from

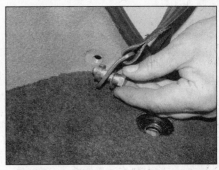

25.12 Remove the trim cap and undo the rear seat belt lower anchor bolt

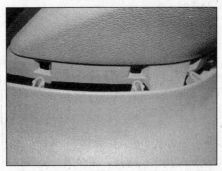

25.14 Disengage the parcel shelf support clips from the rear quarter trim panel

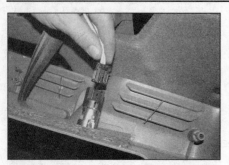

25.15a Where applicable, disconnect the wiring connectors from the accessories socket . . .

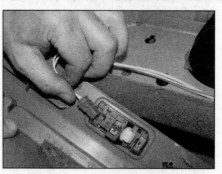

25.15b . . . and interior light . . .

25.15c . . . then feed the seat belt through the parcel shelf support aperture

25.18 Pull the top and sides of the rear quarter trim panel from the body to release the securing clips

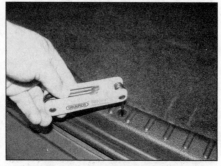

25.21 Undo the screws and remove the luggage compartment scuff plate

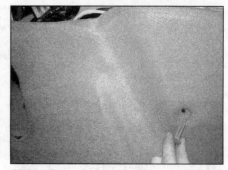

25.23a Remove the plastic screw from the front of the luggage compartment lower side panel . . .

the accessories socket and interior light (as applicable). Feed the seat belt through the aperture and remove the parcel shelf support from the vehicle (see illustrations).

Refitting

16 Refitting is a reversal of removal, but ensure that all retaining clips are fully engaged and that the seat belt lower anchor bolt is securely tightened.

Rear quarter trim

Removal

17 Remove the parcel shelf support as described previously.
18 Pull the top and sides of the panel from the body to release the securing clips and remove it from the vehicle (see illustration).

Refitting

19 Refitting is a reversal of removal, but ensure that all retaining clips are fully engaged. With the panel in place, refit the parcel shelf support as described previously.

Luggage area lower side trim

Removal

20 Remove the rear quarter trim panel as described previously.
21 Prise the weatherstrip from the bottom of the tailgate aperture, then undo the screws and remove the luggage compartment scuff plate (see illustration).
22 If working on the left-hand side, on vehicles with a satellite navigation system, remove the storage bin cover. Undo the three

bolts securing the navigation unit to the body side-member. Withdraw the unit and disconnect the wiring connectors.
23 Remove the plastic screw located at the front of the panel, then extract the two stud-type clips at the top, and the clip at the rear, using a forked type tool (see illustrations).
24 Withdraw the panel at the top, lift it up to release the base and remove the panel from the vehicle (see illustration).

Refitting

25 Refitting is a reversal of removal, but ensure that all retaining clips are fully engaged. With the side panel in place, refit the rear quarter trim panel as described previously.

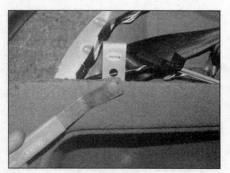

25.23b . . . then extract the stud-type clips at the top . . .

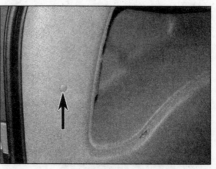

25.23c . . . and at the rear (arrowed) using a forked type tool

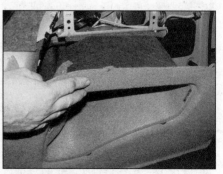

25.24 Withdraw the panel at the top then lift it up to release the base

25.27 Remove the ventilation grille from the tailgate trim panel

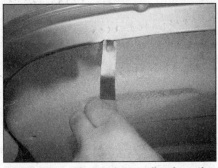

25.28 Extract the stud-type clips from the periphery of the tailgate trim panel

25.29 Pull the panel away at the top corners to release the clips, then remove the panel

Tailgate trim

Removal

26 Open the tailgate and remove the parcel shelf.

27 Remove the ventilation grille from the centre of the tailgate trim panel **(see illustration)**.

28 Using a forked type tool, extract the stud-type clips from the periphery of the tailgate **(see illustration)**.

29 Pull the panel away from the tailgate at the top corners to release the retaining clips, then remove the panel from the tailgate **(see illustration)**.

Refitting

30 Refitting is a reversal of removal, but ensure that all retaining clips are fully engaged.

Carpets

General

31 The carpets consist of three sections – a front and rear passenger compartment section which is actually a two-piece false floor panel with the carpet bonded to it, and a luggage compartment section which is a conventional carpet.

False floor rear section removal

32 Remove the battery as described in Chapter 5A.

33 Remove the front seats as described in Section 23.

34 Remove the facia lower centre panel as described in Section 26.

35 Remove the centre pillar trim panels as described previously in this Section.

36 Prise the weatherstrip from the bottom of the front and rear door apertures.

37 Using a small screwdriver, carefully spread apart and remove the two sections of plastic trim at the base of the handbrake lever.

38 Unclip the carpet panel surrounding the handbrake lever and lift the panel up and off the lever.

39 Undo the screw at the front of the left-hand and right-hand rear passenger air vents and remove both air vents.

40 Undo the screws at the rear edge of the false floor and the screw adjacent to the right-hand air vent location.

41 Lift the floor up and remove it from the vehicle.

False floor front section removal

42 Remove the false floor rear section as described previously.

43 Working under the facia, undo the retaining bolt and release the bonnet release lever from its location.

44 Undo the two screws on the driver's side, located on each side of the rubber foot protection mat. Undo the two screws on the passenger's side in the same location.

45 On the passenger's side release the retaining clip located at the upper outer edge of the floor. On the driver's side, release the retaining lug located adjacent to the heater/air conditioning unit below the pedals.

46 Lift the floor up and remove it from the vehicle.

False floor refitting

47 Refitting is a reversal of removal, referring to the relevant Sections and Chapters of this manual as indicated during removal.

Luggage area carpet removal

48 Remove the rear seats as described in Section 23.

49 Prise the weatherstrip from the bottom of the tailgate aperture, then undo the screws and remove the luggage compartment scuff plate.

50 Prise the weatherstrip from the bottom of the door apertures.

51 Undo the screws at the rear edge of the false floor rear section, release the carpet, and remove it from the vehicle.

Luggage area carpet refitting

52 Refitting is a reversal of removal.

Headling

Note: *Headlining removal requires considerable skill and experience if it is to be carried out without damage, and is therefore best entrusted to a Citroën dealer or bodywork specialist. A general overview of the procedure is given below for those with the expertise to attempt the operation on a DIY basis.*

53 The headlining is clipped and glued to the roof, and can be withdrawn only once all fittings such as the grab handles, courtesy lights, sun visors, sunroof (if fitted), pillar trim panels, and associated additional panels have been removed. The door, tailgate and sunroof aperture weatherstrips will also have to be prised clear and any additional screws and clips removed. Once the headlining attachments are released, the adhesive bonding in the centre panels must be broken using a hot air gun and spatula, starting at the front and working rearwards.

54 When refitting, a coat of neoprene adhesive (available from Citroën dealers) must be applied to the centre panels in the locations noted during removal. Position the headlining carefully and refit all components disturbed during removal. Clean the headlining with soap and water or white spirit on completion.

26 Facia panel components – removal and refitting

Upper centre panel

Removal

1 Remove the radio/cassette player as described in Chapter 12.

2 Unclip the gearchange lever gaiter from its location in the centre panel **(see illustration)**.

3 Undo the two panel securing screws located on either side of the gearchange lever.

26.2 Unclip the gearchange lever gaiter from the facia upper centre panel

26.4a Withdraw the lower edge and the sides of the upper centre panel from the facia . . .

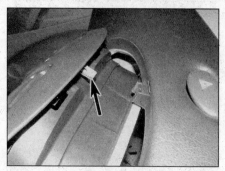

26.4b . . . then disengage the upper centre locating tag (arrowed)

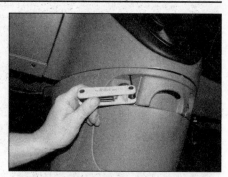

26.8 Undo the facia lower centre panel retaining screw at the top of the cigarette lighter aperture

26.9 Withdraw the trim blank and remove the similar screw on the other side

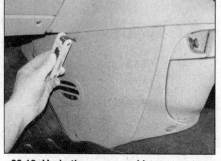

26.10 Undo the upper and lower screws from both sides of the panel

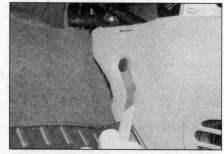

26.11 Using a forked type tool, extract the stud-type clip from the rear of the panel on both sides

4 Withdraw the lower edge and the sides of the centre panel from the facia, then disengage the upper centre locating tag (see illustrations). Remove the centre panel from the vehicle.

Refitting

5 Refitting is a reversal of removal.

Lower centre panel

6 Disconnect the battery negative terminal (refer to *Disconnecting the battery* in the Reference Chapter).
7 On right-hand drive models, undo the two screws and remove the driver's footrest from the base of the lower centre panel.
8 Remove the cigarette lighter element and undo the screw at the top of the cigarette lighter aperture (see illustration).
9 Withdraw the trim blank and remove the similar screw on the other side (see illustration).
10 Undo the upper and lower screws from both sides of the panel (see illustration).

11 Using a forked type removal tool, extract the stud-type clip from the rear of the panel on both sides (see illustration).
12 Withdraw the panel from its location and disconnect the wiring connectors from the ashtray illumination bulbholder and from the cigarette lighter (see illustrations). Remove the facia lower centre panel from the vehicle.

Refitting

13 Refitting is a reversal of removal.

Steering column shrouds

Removal

14 Unscrew the two lower steering column shroud securing screws. Unclip and lift off the upper shroud, then remove the lower shroud (see illustrations).

26.12a Withdraw the panel from its location . . .

26.12b . . . and disconnect the wiring connectors from the ashtray illumination bulbholder . . .

26.12c . . . and from the cigarette lighter

26.14a Unscrew the two lower steering column shroud securing screws (arrowed) . . .

26.14b . . . unclip and lift off the upper shroud, then remove the lower shroud

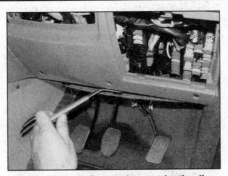

26.18a Extract the stud-type plastic clips using a forked type tool . . .

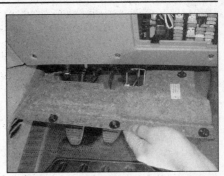

26.18b . . . and remove the lower trim panel above the pedals on the driver's side

26.19 Undo the three screws securing the lower edge of the facia lower side panel

26.21a Withdraw the lower part of the panel from the facia . . .

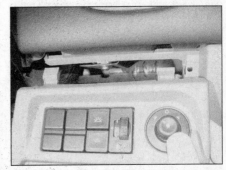

26.21b . . . and disengage the two upper locating lugs

Refitting

15 Refitting is a reversal of removal.

Lower side panel

Removal

16 Remove the steering column shrouds as described previously in this Section.
17 Remove the fuse/relay box cover.
18 Extract the stud-type plastic clips, using a forked type tool, and remove the lower trim panel above the pedals on the driver's side (see illustrations).
19 Undo the three screws securing the lower edge of the panel to the facia (see illustration).
20 Undo the screw in the fuse/relay box cover aperture, and the screw below the steering column height adjuster lever.

21 Withdraw the lower part of the panel from the facia, and disengage the two upper locating lugs (see illustrations).
22 Disconnect the wiring connectors from the panel switches, noting their locations for refitting (see illustration).

Refitting

23 Refitting is a reversal of removal.

Instrument surround

Removal

24 Using a small screwdriver, carefully release the surround from the retaining clips on each side, then remove the surround from the instrument panel (see illustrations).

Refitting

25 Refitting is a reversal of removal.

Glovebox

Removal

26 Disconnect the battery negative terminal (refer to *Disconnecting the battery* in the Reference Chapter).
27 Undo the three screws at the base of the glovebox lid, and remove the lid from the glovebox (see illustrations).
28 Undo the nut and remove the washer from the facia lower mounting bracket below the glovebox (see illustration).
29 Undo the eight screws securing the glovebox to the facia and withdraw the glovebox from its location (see illustration).
30 Disconnect the wiring connector from the glovebox light and remove the glovebox from the facia (see illustration).

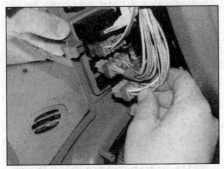

26.22 Disconnect the wiring connectors from the panel switches, noting their locations for refitting

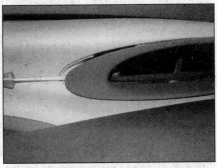

26.24a Using a small screwdriver, release the instrument panel surround from the retaining clips each side . . .

26.24b . . . then remove the surround from the instrument panel

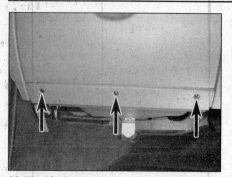

26.27a Undo the three screws (arrowed) at the base of the glovebox lid . . .

26.27b . . . and remove the lid from the facia

26.28 Undo the nut and remove the washer from the facia lower mounting bracket

26.29 Undo the screws securing the glovebox to the facia and withdraw the glovebox

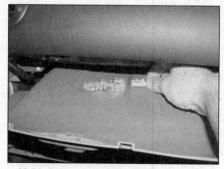

26.30 Disconnect the wiring connector from the glovebox light and remove the glovebox

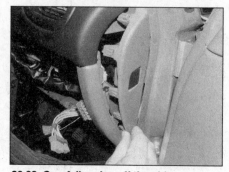

26.38 Carefully prise off the side covers at each end of the facia

Refitting

31 Refitting is a reversal of removal.

Complete facia assembly

Note: *This is an involved operation entailing the removal of numerous components and assemblies, and the disconnection of a multitude of wiring connectors. Make notes on the location of all disconnected wiring, or attach labels to the connectors, to avoid confusion when refitting.*

Removal

32 Disconnect the battery negative terminal (refer to *Disconnecting the battery* in the Reference Chapter).

33 Remove the windscreen pillar trim on both sides as described in Section 25.

34 Extract the stud-type plastic clips, using a forked type tool, and remove the lower trim panel from the footwell on both sides.

35 Remove the following facia panels as described previously in this Section:

a) *Facia upper centre panel.*
b) *Facia lower centre panel.*
c) *Facia lower side panel.*
d) *Instrument panel surround.*

36 Remove the steering wheel as described in Chapter 10.

37 Remove the instrument panel, steering column combination switches and the radio/cassette player as described in Chapter 12.

38 Using a small screwdriver, carefully prise off the side covers at each end of the facia. Disconnect the air bag disable switch wiring

connector from the side cover on the passenger's side **(see illustration)**.

39 Undo the two facia side retaining bolts each side accessible through the side cover apertures **(see illustration)**.

40 Undo the nut and remove the washer from the facia lower mounting bracket below the glovebox **(see illustration)**.

41 Undo the two screws located at the base of the radio/cassette player aperture **(see illustration)**.

42 Undo the bolts securing the front and rear strengthening braces at the left-hand side of the heater air distribution housing **(see illustrations)**. Remove the two braces.

43 Undo the lower bolt securing the right-hand strengthening brace to the floor bracket **(see illustration)**.

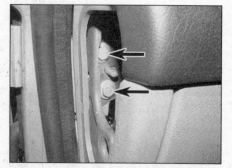

26.39 Undo the two facia side retaining bolts (arrowed) on each side

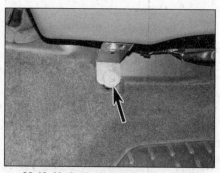

26.40 Undo the nut and remove the washer from the facia lower mounting bracket

26.41 Undo the two screws located at the base of the radio/cassette player aperture

26.42a Undo the bolts and remove the front (arrowed) . . .

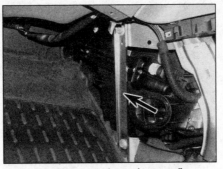

26.42b . . . and rear (arrowed) strengthening braces on the left-hand side

26.43 Undo the lower bolt (arrowed) securing the right-hand strengthening brace to the floor bracket

44 In the lower centre of the facia, undo the screw securing the facia bracket to the heater air distribution housing **(see illustration)**.

45 Working as described in Chapter 10, Section 18, undo the steering column upper mounting nuts and lower mounting bolts and lower the column from its location. Note that it is not necessary to disconnect the steering column universal joint.

46 Undo the two bolts from the underside of the steering column mounting bracket **(see illustration)**.

47 Undo the four screws securing the heater/ventilation control unit to the facia Lift the unit up to disengage the two lower locating lugs, then feed it back into the aperture.

48 Insert a long screwdriver through the facia side cover apertures and lift the ends of the locating brackets off the mounting lugs **(see illustration)**. Carefully ease the facia from the bulkhead, and disconnect the remaining wiring connectors. Withdraw the facia fully from its location and remove it from the vehicle **(see illustration)**.

Refitting

49 Refitting is a reversal of removal ensuring that all wiring is correctly reconnected and all mountings securely tightened.

26.44 Undo the screw (arrowed) securing the facia bracket to the heater air distribution housing

26.46 Undo the two bolts (arrowed) from the underside of the steering column mounting bracket

26.48a Lift the ends of the facia side locating brackets (arrowed) off the mounting lugs . . .

26.48b . . . then ease the facia from the bulkhead, and disconnect the remaining wiring connectors

Chapter 12
Body electrical systems

Contents

Degrees of difficulty

Easy, suitable for novice with little experience	**Fairly easy,** suitable for beginner with some experience	**Fairly difficult,** suitable for competent DIY mechanic	**Difficult,** suitable for experienced DIY mechanic	**Very difficult,** suitable for expert DIY or professional

Specifications

General

System type .... 12 volt negative earth

Bulbs

	Type	Wattage
Headlights (dip/main beam)	H4 (anti UV type)	60/55
Front foglight	H1	55
Front sidelights	Push-fit	5
Direction indicator light	Bayonet	21
Direction indicator side repeater	Push-fit	5
Stop/tail light	Bayonet	21/5
Rear foglight	Bayonet	21
Reversing light	Bayonet	21
Number plate light	Push-fit	5
High-level stop-light	Push-fit	5
Interior lights	Push fit	6
Luggage compartment light	Push fit	5
Glovebox light	Push fit	5

1 General information and precautions

Warning: Before carrying out any work on the electrical system, read through the precautions given in 'Safety first!' at the beginning of this manual, and in Chapter 5A.

The electrical system is of 12 volt negative earth type. Power for the lights and all electrical accessories is supplied by a lead-acid type battery, which is charged by the alternator.

Many of the body electrical systems are controlled by individual electronic control units (ECUs) and these are in turn controlled by a main ECU known as a Built-in Systems Interface (BSI). The various ECUs and the BSI exchange data with each other via a multiplex network. The multiplex network is a two-wire system linking the BSI with the system ECUs and is termed by Citroën as a 'Comfort Van' network. Essentially this means that the BSI and the ECUs controlling the 'comfort' systems in the vehicle, ie, the air conditioning system, the electronic instrument panel, the satellite navigation system (where fitted), and radio/cassette/CD player, are all inter-connected via a Vehicle Area Network (VAN).

An ECU connected to the multiplex network only directly receives some of the data needed for it to operate, with the remaining data being supplied by the other ECUs on the network. Because the ECUs share information via the network, several ECUs can control the operation of the same system. Also, one ECU can control several systems in an autonomous manner. The BSI is the manager of this information interchange as well as also being responsible for the control of certain vehicle systems itself. The BSI has a full diagnostic capability whereby any fault in any of the ECUs on the multiplex network can be traced using diagnostic equipment connected to the vehicle diagnostic connector.

This Chapter covers repair and service procedures for the various electrical components not associated with the engine. Information on the battery, alternator and starter motor can be found in Chapter 5A.

It should be noted that, prior to working on any component in the electrical system, the battery negative terminal should first be disconnected, to prevent the possibility of electrical short-circuits.

Caution: Before proceeding, refer to 'Disconnecting the battery' in the Reference Chapter for further information.

2 Electrical fault finding – general information

Note: *Refer to the precautions given in 'Safety first!' and in Section 1 of this Chapter before starting work. The following tests relate to testing of the main electrical circuits, and should not be used to test delicate electronic circuits (such as engine management systems or anti-lock braking systems), particularly where an electronic control unit is used.*

General

1 A typical electrical circuit consists of an electrical component, any switches, relays, motors, fuses, fusible links or circuit breakers related to that component, and the wiring and connectors which link the component to both the battery and the chassis. To help to pinpoint a problem in an electrical circuit, wiring diagrams are included at the end of this Chapter.

2 Before attempting to diagnose an electrical fault, first study the appropriate wiring diagram, to obtain a more complete understanding of the components included in the particular circuit concerned. The possible sources of a fault can be narrowed down by noting whether other components related to the circuit are operating properly. If several components or circuits fail at one time, the problem is likely to be related to a shared fuse or earth connection.

3 Electrical problems usually stem from simple causes, such as loose or corroded connections, a faulty earth connection, a blown fuse, a melted fusible link, or a faulty relay. Visually inspect the condition of all fuses, wires and connections in a problem circuit before testing the components. Use the wiring diagrams to determine which terminal connections will need to be checked, in order to pinpoint the trouble-spot.

4 The basic tools required for electrical fault finding include a circuit tester or voltmeter (a 12 volt bulb with a set of test leads can also be used for certain tests); a self-powered test light (sometimes known as a continuity tester); an ohmmeter (to measure resistance); a battery and set of test leads; and a jumper wire, preferably with a circuit breaker or fuse incorporated, which can be used to bypass suspect wires or electrical components. Before attempting to locate a problem with test instruments, use the wiring diagram to determine where to make the connections.

5 To find the source of an intermittent wiring fault (usually due to a poor or dirty connection, or damaged wiring insulation), a 'wiggle' test can be performed on the wiring. This involves wiggling the wiring by hand, to see if the fault occurs as the wiring is moved. It should be possible to narrow down the source of the fault to a particular section of wiring. This method of testing can be used in conjunction with any of the tests described in the following sub-Sections.

6 Apart from problems due to poor connections, two basic types of fault can occur in an electrical circuit – open-circuit, or short-circuit.

7 Open-circuit faults are caused by a break somewhere in the circuit, which prevents current from flowing. An open-circuit fault will prevent a component from working, but will not cause the relevant circuit fuse to blow.

8 Short-circuit faults are normally caused by a breakdown in wiring insulation, which allows a feed wire to touch either another wire, or an earthed component such as the bodyshell. This allows the current flowing in the circuit to 'escape' along an alternative route, usually to earth. As the circuit does not now follow its original complete path, it is known as a 'short' circuit. A short-circuit fault will normally cause the relevant circuit fuse to blow.

Finding an open-circuit

9 To check for an open-circuit, connect one lead of a circuit tester or voltmeter to either the negative battery terminal or a known good earth.

10 Connect the other lead to a connector in the circuit being tested, preferably nearest to the battery or fuse.

11 Switch on the circuit, bearing in mind that some circuits are live only when the ignition switch is moved to a particular position.

12 If voltage is present (indicated either by the tester bulb lighting or a voltmeter reading, as applicable), this means that the section of the circuit between the relevant connector and the battery is problem-free.

13 Continue to check the remainder of the circuit in the same fashion.

14 When a point is reached at which no voltage is present, the problem must lie between that point and the previous test point with voltage. Most problems can be traced to a broken, corroded or loose connection.

Finding a short-circuit

15 To check for a short-circuit, first disconnect the load(s) from the circuit (loads are the components which draw current from a circuit, such as bulbs, motors, heating elements, etc).

16 Remove the relevant fuse from the circuit, and connect a circuit tester or voltmeter to the fuse connections.

17 Switch on the circuit, bearing in mind that some circuits are live only when the ignition switch is moved to a particular position.

18 If voltage is present (indicated either by the tester bulb lighting or a voltmeter reading, as applicable), this means that there is a short-circuit.

19 If no voltage is present, but the fuse still blows with the load(s) connected, this indicates an internal fault in the load(s).

Finding an earth fault

20 The battery negative terminal is connected to 'earth' – the metal of the engine/transmission and the car body – and most systems are wired so that they only receive a positive feed, the current returning via the metal of the car body. This means that the component mounting and the body form part of that circuit. Loose or corroded mountings can therefore cause a range of electrical faults, ranging from total failure of a circuit, to a puzzling partial fault. In particular, lights may shine dimly (especially when another circuit sharing the same earth point is in operation), motors (eg, wiper motors or the radiator cooling fan motor) may run slowly, and the operation of one circuit may have an apparently-unrelated effect on another. Note that earth straps are used between certain components, such as the engine/transmission and the body, usually where there is no metal-to-metal contact between components, due to flexible rubber mountings, etc.

21 To check whether a component is properly earthed, disconnect the battery, and connect one lead of an ohmmeter to a known good earth point. Connect the other lead to the wire or earth connection being tested. The resistance reading should be zero; if not, check the connection as follows.

22 If an earth connection is thought to be faulty, dismantle the connection, and clean back to bare metal both the bodyshell and the wire terminal or the component earth connection mating surface. Be careful to remove all traces of dirt and corrosion, then use a knife to trim away any paint, so that a clean metal-to-metal joint is made. On reassembly, tighten the joint fasteners securely; if a wire terminal is being refitted, use serrated washers between the terminal and the bodyshell, to ensure a clean and secure connection. When the connection is remade, prevent the onset of corrosion in the future by applying a coat of petroleum jelly or silicone-based grease, or by spraying on (at regular intervals) a proprietary ignition sealer or water-dispersant lubricant.

3 Fuses and relays – general information

Fuses

1 Fuses are designed to break a circuit when a predetermined current is reached, in order to protect the components and wiring which could be damaged by excessive current flow. Any excessive current flow will be due to a fault in the circuit, usually a short-circuit (see Section 2).

2 The main fuses are located in the interior fuse/relay box located in the facia on the driver's side, and in the engine compartment fuse/relay box on the left-hand side of the engine compartment.

3 For access to the interior fuses, pull the fuse/relay box cover from the facia. For access to the engine compartment fuses, lift off the cover over the fuse/relay box **(see illustrations)**.

3.3a For access to the fuses, remove the cover from the interior fuse/relay box . . .

3.3b . . . and engine compartment fuse/relay box

3.6 Using the plastic tool provided in the fuse/relay box to pull a fuse from its location

4 A blown fuse can be recognised from its melted or broken wire.

5 To remove a fuse, first ensure that the relevant circuit is switched off.

6 Using the plastic tool provided in the fuse/relay box, pull the fuse from its location **(see illustration)**.

7 Spare fuses are provided in the blank terminal positions in the fuse/relay box.

8 Before renewing a blown fuse, trace and rectify the cause, and always use a fuse of the correct rating. Never substitute a fuse of a higher rating, or make temporary repairs using wire or metal foil; more serious damage, or even fire, could result.

9 Note that the fuses are colour-coded as follows. Refer to the wiring diagrams for details of the fuse ratings and the circuits protected:

Colour	Rating
Orange	*5A*
Red	*10A*
Blue	*15A*
Yellow	*20A*
Clear or white	*25A*
Green	*30A*

10 Additional 'maxi-fuses' are located in the engine compartment fuse/relay box. These are generally known as 'fusible links' and carry a heavy current for the major vehicle circuits. Fusible links do not normally blow, but if they do, this indicates a major circuit failure or short-circuit.

Relays

11 A relay is an electrically-operated switch, which is used for the following reasons:
  a) *A relay can switch a heavy current remotely from the circuit in which the current is flowing, allowing the use of lighter-gauge wiring and switch contacts.*
  b) *A relay can receive more than one control input, unlike a mechanical switch.*
  c) *A relay can have a timer function – for example, the intermittent wiper relay.*

12 Most of the relays are located in the interior fuse/relay box, or in the engine compartment fuse/relay box. Depending on model and equipment fitted, further relays may be located on, or adjacent to, the components they control.

13 If a circuit or system controlled by a relay develops a fault, and the relay is suspect, operate the system. If the relay is functioning, it should be possible to hear it 'click' as it is energised. If this is the case, the fault lies with the components or wiring of the system. If the relay is not being energised, then either the relay is not receiving a main supply or a switching voltage, or the relay itself is faulty. Testing is by the substitution of a known good unit, but be careful – while some relays are identical in appearance and in operation, others look similar but perform different functions.

14 To remove a relay, first ensure that the relevant circuit is switched off. In most cases, the relay can then simply be pulled out from the socket, and pushed back into position. Note, however, that with the ever increasing standardisation of vehicle wiring and electrical system components, many relays are now 'welded' in position in their relevant circuit boards for ease of manufacture. This means that the relays are soldered in place and cannot be individually removed. If faulty, the complete circuit board or relay housing must be renewed as an assembly. Changes of this nature occur regularly during the course of vehicle production and are not normally documented by the vehicle manufacturer. Therefore, if a relay appears reluctant to come free from its location, consider that it may be of the welded type and consult a Citroën dealer for the latest information.

4 Switches – removal and refitting

Note: *Disconnect the battery negative terminal before removing any switch, and reconnect the terminal after refitting the switch. Refer to 'Disconnecting the battery' in the Reference Chapter.*

Ignition switch

1 Refer to Chapter 10.

Steering wheel switches

2 Remove the driver's air bag unit as described in Section 20.

3 Disconnect the wiring connector from the steering wheel switches circuit board located in the slot at the top of the steering wheel.

4 Withdraw the circuit board and switches from their locations in the steering wheel, and remove them together from the wheel **(see illustrations)**

5 Refit the switch assembly using a reversal of removal, then refit the air bag unit as described in Section 20.

Steering column switches

6 Remove the steering wheel as described in Chapter 10.

7 Remove the steering column shrouds as described in Chapter 11, Section 26.

8 Remove the air bag rotary connector as described in Section 20.

4.4a Withdraw the circuit board and switches from their locations in the steering wheel . . .

4.4b . . . and remove them from the wheel

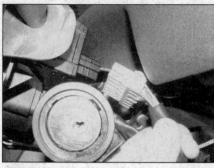

4.9 Disconnect the wiring connectors at the rear of the steering column switches

4.10 Undo the three screws (arrowed) and remove the switch housing from the column

4.14a Remove the centre facia mounted switches from the upper sides . . .

4.14b . . . top . . .

4.14c . . . and lower sides of the facia

9 Disconnect the wiring connectors at the rear of the steering column switches **(see illustration)**.

10 Undo the three screws securing the switch housing to the steering column and remove the housing from the column **(see illustration)**.

11 The relevant switch can now be removed from the housing after unscrewing the two retaining screws.

12 Refitting is a reversal of removal.

Facia-mounted switches

Centre switches

13 Remove the facia upper centre panel as described in Chapter 11.

14 Using a small screwdriver, carefully prise up the relevant switch to release the retaining clips, or alternatively push the switch out from behind **(see illustrations)**.

15 Disconnect the wiring plug and remove the switch from the facia.

16 Refitting is a reversal of removal.

Driver's side switches

17 Remove the facia lower side panel as described in Chapter 11.

18 Depress the retaining catches at the rear of the switch(es) and remove the switch(es) from the panel **(see illustrations)**.

19 Refitting is a reversal of removal.

5	Bulbs (exterior lights) – renewal

General

1 Whenever a bulb is renewed, note the following points:

a) Disconnect the battery negative terminal before starting work. Refer to 'Disconnecting the battery' in the Reference Chapter.

b) Remember that, if the light has just been in use, the bulb may be extremely hot.

c) Always check the bulb contacts and holder, ensuring that there is clean metal-to-metal contact between the bulb and its live(s) and earth. Clean off any corrosion or dirt before fitting a new bulb.

d) Wherever bayonet-type bulbs are fitted (see Specifications), ensure that the live contact(s) bear firmly against the bulb contact.

e) Always ensure that the new bulb is of the correct rating, and that it is completely clean before fitting it; this applies particularly to headlight/foglight bulbs (see below).

Headlight

2 Working in the engine compartment, disconnect the wiring plug from the rear of the headlight bulb **(see illustration)**.

3 Remove the protective rubber cover from the rear of the headlight bulb **(see illustration)**.

4 Release the spring clip ends and withdraw the bulb **(see illustrations)**.

5 When handling the new bulb, use a tissue or clean cloth to avoid touching the glass with the fingers; moisture and grease from the skin can cause blackening and rapid failure of this type of bulb. If the glass is accidentally touched, wipe it clean using methylated spirit.

6 Install the new bulb, ensuring that its locating tabs are correctly seated in the light

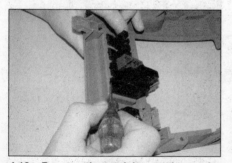

4.18a Depress the retaining catches at the rear of the facia lower side panel switch(es) . . .

4.18b . . . and remove the switch(es) from the panel

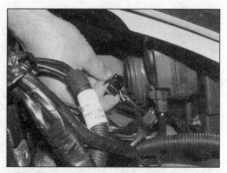

5.2 Disconnect the wiring plug from the rear of the headlight bulb

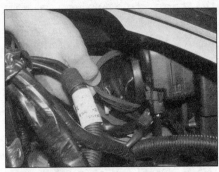

5.3 Remove the protective rubber cover from the rear of the bulb

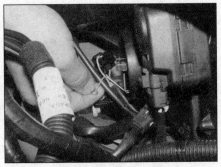

5.4a Release the spring clip ends . . .

5.4b . . . and withdraw the headlight bulb

5.8 Twist the sidelight bulbholder anti-clockwise and withdraw it from the headlight unit

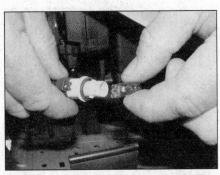

5.9 The sidelight bulb is a push-fit in the bulbholder

5.12 Remove the bayonet fit direction indicator bulb from the bulbholder

cut-outs. Secure the bulb in position with the spring clip.
7 Refit the rubber cover, and reconnect the wiring plug.

Front sidelight

8 Twist the sidelight bulbholder anti-clock-wise, then withdraw it from the side of the headlight unit **(see illustration)**.
9 The bulb is a push-fit in the bulbholder **(see illustration)**.
10 Refitting is the reverse of the removal procedure, ensuring that the bulbholder seal is in good condition.

Front direction indicator

11 Twist the bulbholder anti-clockwise to release it from the upper rear of the headlight unit.
12 The bulb is a bayonet fit in the bulbholder **(see illustration)**.
13 Refitting is a reversal of the removal procedure.

Front indicator side repeater

14 Push the light unit towards the front of the car, release the rear of the unit from the front wing, and withdraw the light unit **(see illustration)**.
15 Withdraw the bulbholder from the light unit and remove the bulb from the bulbholder **(see illustrations)**.
16 Refitting is a reversal of the removal procedure.

Front foglight

17 Firmly apply the handbrake, then jack up

the front of the vehicle and support it securely on axle stands (see *Jacking and vehicle support*). Remove the relevant front roadwheel.
18 Undo the screws securing the wheelarch

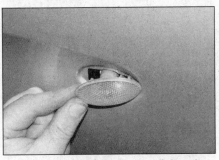

5.14 Push the side repeater light unit towards the front of the car and disengage it at the rear

5.15b . . . and remove the bulb from the bulbholder

liner to the underside of the bumper lower apron. Release the stud-type retaining clips securing the wheelarch liner sections under the wheelarch and move the liner away from the bumper **(see illustration)**. The stud-type

5.15a Withdraw the bulbholder from the light unit . . .

5.18 Release the wheelarch liner for access to the front foglight

5.19 Turn the bulbholder a quarter turn to release it from the light unit

5.20 Remove the foglight bulb from the bulbholder

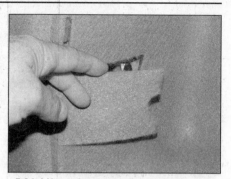

5.24 Lift up the carpet flap for access to the rear light cluster

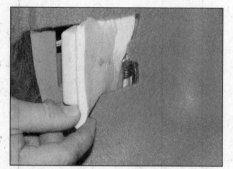

5.25 Withdraw the foam insulation pad from the access aperture

5.26 Using a screwdriver, depress the light unit lower retaining spring clip

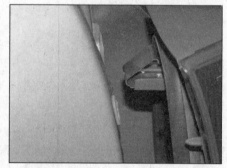

5.27 Withdraw the unit at the bottom and release the upper retaining spring clip

clips can be removed using a forked type tool, or alternatively, with a large screwdriver (although there is a risk of breakage if the screwdriver method is used).

19 Reach up under the bumper and turn the bulbholder a quarter turn to release it from the light unit **(see illustration)**.

20 Remove the bulb from the bulbholder **(see illustration)**.

21 When handling the new bulb, use a tissue or clean cloth to avoid touching the glass with the fingers; moisture and grease from the skin can cause blackening and rapid failure of this type of bulb. If the glass is accidentally touched, wipe it clean using methylated spirit.

22 Install the new bulb, and refit the bulbholder.

23 Secure the wheelarch liner back in position, refit the roadwheel and lower the

vehicle to the ground. Tighten the wheel bolts to the specified torque (see Chapter 10 Specifications).

Rear light cluster

24 Working in the luggage compartment, remove the storage bin cover, then lift up the carpet flap for access to the rear of the light unit **(see illustration)**.

25 Withdraw the foam insulation pad from the access aperture **(see illustration)**

26 Insert a screwdriver through the access aperture and depress the light unit lower retaining spring clip **(see illustration)**.

27 Withdraw the light unit at the bottom and pull the unit downwards to release the upper retaining spring clip **(see illustration)**.

28 Disconnect the wiring connector and remove the light unit **(see illustrations)**.

29 Squeeze the plastic retaining tags

together and remove the bulbholder from the light unit **(see illustration)**.

30 Turn the relevant bayonet fit bulb a quarter turn and remove it from the bulbholder **(see illustration)**.

31 Fit the new bulb then refit the bulbholder to the light unit. Reconnect the wiring connector.

32 Engage the light unit upper spring clip with the body, then push the bottom of the light unit into position until the lower spring clip locks into place.

33 Refit the foam pad and carpet flap, then refit the storage bin cover.

High-level stop-light

34 Open the tailgate and press on the sides of the stop-light cover to release the cover **(see illustration)**.

35 Press the tabs of the bulbholder retaining

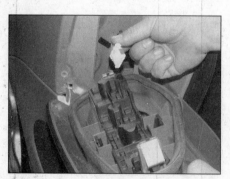

5.28 Disconnect the wiring connector and remove the light unit

5.29 Squeeze the plastic retaining tags together and remove the bulbholder

5.30 Turn the relevant bayonet fit bulb a quarter turn and remove it from the bulbholder

5.34 Press on the sides of the high-level stop-light cover to release the cover

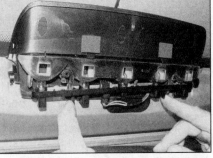

5.35 Press the tabs of the bulbholder retaining clips and withdraw the bulbholder

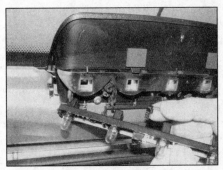

5.36 Disconnect the wiring connector and remove the bulbholder

clips and withdraw the bulbholder from the light unit **(see illustration)**.

36 Disconnect the wiring connector and remove the bulbholder **(see illustration)**.

37 The bulbs are a push-fit in the bulbholder **(see illustration)**.

38 Refitting is a reversal of the removal procedure.

Number plate light

39 Using a suitable screwdriver, release the tag on the side of the lens and lift the lens off the light unit **(see illustrations)**.

40 Withdraw the push-fit bulb from the light unit **(see illustration)**.

41 Refitting is a reversal of removal.

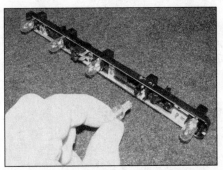

5.37 The bulbs are a push-fit in the bulbholder

5.39a Release the tag on the side of the number plate lens . . .

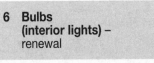

6 Bulbs (interior lights) – renewal

General

1 Refer to Section 5, paragraph 1.

Courtesy/map reading light

2 Using a small screwdriver, carefully prise the courtesy light lens from the light unit **(see illustration)**.

3 Withdraw the push-fit bulb from the light unit **(see illustration)**.

4 Refitting is a reversal of removal.

Luggage compartment light

5 Using a small screwdriver, carefully prise

5.39b . . . and lift the lens off the light unit

the luggage compartment light unit from the trim panel **(see illustration)**.

6 Withdraw the bulbholder from the light unit, then withdraw the push-fit bulb from the bulbholder **(see illustrations)**.

5.40 Withdraw the push-fit bulb from the light unit

7 Refitting is a reversal of removal.

Glovebox light

8 Open the glovebox, then carefully prise out the light unit.

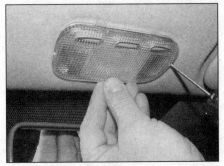

6.2 Carefully prise the courtesy light lens from the light unit

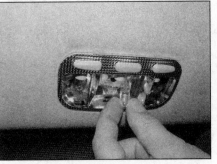

6.3 Withdraw the push-fit bulb from the light unit

6.5 Carefully prise the luggage compartment light unit from the trim panel

6.6a Withdraw the bulbholder from the light unit . . .

6.6b . . . then withdraw the push-fit bulb from the bulbholder

6.9 Withdraw the push-fit glovebox light bulb from the light unit

6.12 Pull off the knob from the air recirculation control lever

6.13a Carefully prise the control knobs off their spindles . . .

6.13b . . . and recover the small spring and detent plunger from the rear of the knob

9 Withdraw the push-fit bulb from the light unit **(see illustration)**.

10 Refitting is a reversal of removal.

Heater/ventilation control lights

11 Remove the heater ventilation control unit as described in Chapter 3.

12 Pull off the knob from the air recirculation control lever **(see illustration)**.

13 Using a small screwdriver, carefully prise the control knobs off their spindles. As the knobs are released, recover the small spring and detent plunger from the rear of the knob **(see illustrations)**.

14 Release the plastic catches and separate the two halves of the control unit **(see illustration)**.

15 Remove the relevant push-fit bulb from the printed circuit board **(see illustration)**.

16 Refitting is a reversal of removal.

Instruments/warning lights

17 Remove the instrument panel as described in Section 9.

18 Using pointed-nose pliers, twist the relevant bulbholder anti-clockwise to remove it from the rear of the panel **(see illustration)**.

19 Remove the push-fit bulb from the bulbholder **(see illustration)**.

20 On completion, refit the instrument panel with reference to Section 9.

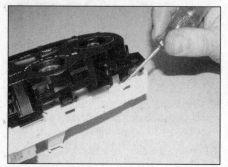

6.14 Release the catches and separate the two halves of the control unit

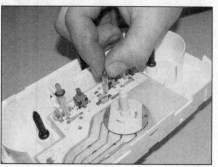

6.15 Remove the relevant push-fit bulb from the printed circuit board

6.18 Twist the relevant bulbholder anti-clockwise to remove it from the rear of the instrument panel

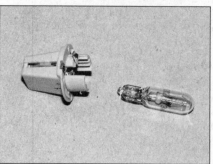

6.19 Remove the push-fit bulb from the bulbholder

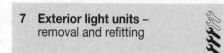

7	**Exterior light units –** removal and refitting

Note: *Disconnect the battery negative terminal before removing any light unit, and reconnect the terminal after refitting the unit. Refer to 'Disconnecting the battery' in the Reference Chapter.*

7.2 Undo the retaining screw at the base of the headlight unit

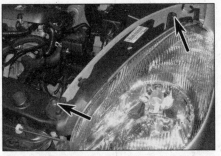

7.3 Undo the upper and lower retaining screws (arrowed) on the side of the headlight unit

7.4 Release the upper plastic locating tag and withdraw the headlight from its location

7.9 Undo the bolts securing the foglight support frame to the foglight and bumper

7.10a Lift off the support frame . . .

7.10b . . . then remove the foglight from the bumper

Headlight

Removal

1 Remove the front bumper as described in Chapter 11.

2 Undo the retaining screw at the base of the headlight unit, below the edge of the front wing **(see illustration)**.

3 Undo the upper and lower retaining screws on the side of the headlight unit in the bonnet closure channel **(see illustration)**.

4 Release the upper plastic locating tag and withdraw the headlight from its location **(see illustration)**.

5 Disconnect the wiring connectors and remove the headlight unit.

Refitting

6 Refitting is a reversal of removal, but on completion have the headlight beam alignment checked at the earliest opportunity.

Front indicator side repeater

7 The procedure is described as part of the bulb renewal procedure in Section 5.

Front foglight

Removal

8 Remove the front bumper as described in Chapter 11.

9 From the rear of the bumper, undo the bolts securing the foglight support frame to the foglight and bumper **(see illustration)**.

10 Lift off the support frame, then remove the foglight from the bumper **(see illustrations)**.

Refitting

11 Refitting is a reversal of removal.

Rear light cluster

12 The procedure is described as part of the bulb renewal procedure in Section 5.

High-level stop-light

Removal

13 Remove the stop-light bulbholder as described in Section 5.

14 Undo the two screws and remove the light unit from the tailgate **(see illustration)**.

Refitting

15 Refitting is a reversal of removal.

Number plate light

Removal

16 Using a suitable screwdriver, release the tag on the side of the number plate light lens and lift the lens off the light unit.

17 Open the tailgate and remove the ventilation grille from the centre of the tailgate trim panel.

18 Working through the ventilation grille aperture, push the relevant number plate light unit out from its location **(see illustrations)**.

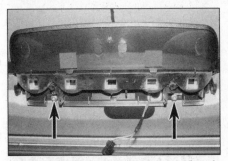

7.14 Undo the two screws (arrowed) and remove the high-level stop-light unit from the tailgate

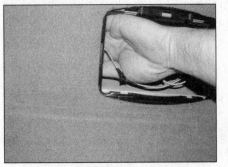

7.18a Working through the ventilation grille aperture . . .

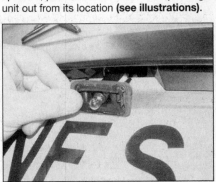

7.18b . . . push the relevant number plate light unit out from its location

9.2a Carefully release the instrument panel surround from the retaining clips on each side . . .

9.2b . . . then remove the surround from the instrument panel

9.3a Undo the screw (arrowed) located at each end of the instrument panel . . .

9.3b . . . and withdraw the panel from the facia

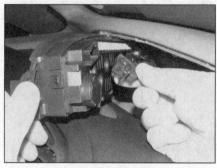

9.4 Disconnect the wiring connectors and remove the instrument panel

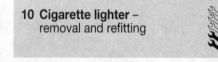

10 Cigarette lighter – removal and refitting

19 Disconnect the wiring connector and remove the light unit.

Refitting

20 Refitting is a reversal of removal.

8 Headlight beam alignment – general information

1 Accurate adjustment of the headlight beam is only possible using optical beam-setting equipment, and this work should therefore be carried out by a Citroën dealer or suitably-equipped workshop.
2 Each headlight unit is equipped with a five-position vertical beam adjuster unit – this can be used to adjust the headlight beam to compensate for the relevant load which the vehicle is carrying. The adjuster units are operated by a switch on the facia side panel. The adjusters should be positioned as follows according to the load being carried in the vehicle:

Position 0 Front seats occupied
            (1 or 2 people)
Position – Front or rear seats occupied
            (3 people)
Position 1 Front and rear seats occupied
            (5 people)
Position 2 Front and rear seats occupied
            and luggage compartment fully-
            loaded
Position 3 Driver's seat occupied and
            luggage compartment fully-
            loaded

3 Be sure to reset the adjustment if the vehicle load is altered.

9 Instrument panel – removal and refitting

Note: *If a new instrument panel is to be fitted, this work must be entrusted to a Citroën dealer. It is necessary to initialise the new instrument panel after installation which requires the use of dedicated Citroën diagnostic equipment.*

Removal

1 Disconnect the battery negative terminal (refer to *Disconnecting the battery* in the Reference Chapter).
2 Using a small screwdriver, carefully release the instrument panel surround from the retaining clips on each side, then remove the surround from the instrument panel **(see illustrations)**.
3 Undo the screw located at each end of the panel and withdraw the panel from the facia **(see illustrations)**.
4 Disconnect the wiring connectors and remove the instrument panel from the facia **(see illustration)**.
5 Renewal of the illumination and warning light bulbs is described in Section 6. The remainder of the instrument panel is a sealed assembly and cannot be dismantled.

Refitting

6 Refitting is a reversal of removal.

Removal

1 Disconnect the battery negative terminal (refer to *Disconnecting the battery* in the Reference Chapter).
2 Remove the facia lower centre panel as described in Chapter 11.
3 Pull out the lighter element, release the internal tangs and push out the metal insert.

Refitting

4 Refitting is a reversal of removal.

11 Horn – removal and refitting

Removal

1 Disconnect the battery negative terminal (refer to *Disconnecting the battery* in the Reference Chapter).
2 Remove the front bumper as described in Chapter 11.
3 Disconnect the wiring plug from the horn, then unscrew the securing nut, and withdraw the horn from its bracket **(see illustration)**.

Refitting

4 Refitting is a reversal of removal.

11.3 Horn wiring connector (A) and retaining nut (B)

12.3 Lift up the wiper arm spindle nut cover, then slacken and remove the spindle nut

12.4 Release the wiper arm from the spindle using a small puller

4 Disconnect the wiring connector from the wiper motor.
5 Drill out the rivets securing the motor mounting bracket to the tailgate **(see illustration)**.
6 Withdraw the motor assembly from the tailgate.

Refitting

7 Refitting is a reversal of removal, using new rivets to secure the motor in position.

12 Wiper arm –
removal and refitting

Removal

1 Operate the wiper motor, then switch it off so that the wiper arm(s) return to the at-rest position.
2 Stick a piece of masking tape to the window, along the edge of the wiper blade, to use as an alignment aid on refitting.
3 Lift up the wiper arm spindle nut cover, then slacken and remove the spindle nut **(see illustration)**.
4 Using a small puller, release the wiper arm from the spindle and remove the arm **(see illustration)**.

Refitting

5 Ensure that the wiper arm and spindle splines are clean and dry, then refit the arm to the spindle, aligning the wiper blade with the tape fitted on removal.
6 Refit the spindle nut, tightening it securely, and clip the nut cover back into position.

13 Windscreen wiper components –
removal and refitting

Removal

1 Disconnect the battery negative terminal (refer to *Disconnecting the battery* in the Reference Chapter).
2 Remove the wiper arms as described in Section 12.
3 Remove the scuttle grille panel as described in Chapter 11.
4 Undo the two bolts securing the motor mounting plate to the centre of the scuttle **(see illustration)**.
5 Undo the bolt at each end securing the linkage to the scuttle mounting brackets **(see illustration)**.
6 Disconnect the motor wiring connector, and manipulate the motor/linkage assembly from the scuttle **(see illustration)**.

Refitting

7 Refitting is a reversal of removal.

14 Rear window wiper motor –
removal and refitting

Note: *New wiper motor securing rivets will be required for refitting.*

Removal

1 Disconnect the battery negative terminal (refer to *Disconnecting the battery* in the Reference Chapter).
2 Remove the wiper arm as described in Section 12.
3 Remove the tailgate trim panel as described in Chapter 11, Section 25.

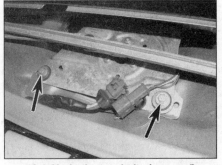

13.4 Undo the two bolts (arrowed) securing the windscreen wiper motor mounting plate to the centre of the scuttle

13.6 Disconnect the wiring connector, and manipulate the motor/linkage assembly from the scuttle

15 Windscreen/rear window washer system components
– removal and refitting

Washer fluid reservoir

Removal

1 Disconnect the battery negative terminal (refer to *Disconnecting the battery* in the Reference Chapter).
2 Working in the engine compartment, unscrew the filler neck from the reservoir.
3 Firmly apply the handbrake, then jack up the front of the vehicle and support it securely on axle stands (see *Jacking and vehicle support*). Remove the right-hand roadwheel.
4 Undo the screws securing the right-hand wheelarch liner to the underside of the bumper lower apron. Release the stud-type retaining clips securing the wheelarch liner sections under the wheelarch and move the liner away from the bumper. The stud-type

13.5 Undo the bolt (arrowed) at each end securing the linkage to the scuttle mounting brackets

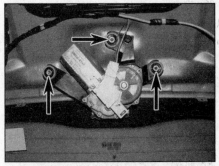

14.5 Tailgate wiper motor bracket securing rivets (arrowed)

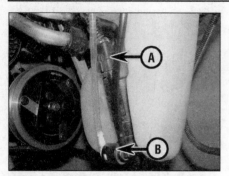

15.5 Washer pump wiring connector (A) and fluid supply pipes (B)

clips can be removed using a forked type tool, or alternatively, with a large screwdriver (although there is a risk of breakage if the screwdriver method is used).

5 Disconnect the wiring plug from the washer pump located in the reservoir **(see illustration)**.

6 Disconnect the supply pipe(s) from the washer pump. Be prepared for fluid spillage if there is still fluid in the reservoir.

7 Slacken and remove the reservoir retaining nuts, then lower the reservoir out from underneath the wheelarch.

Refitting

8 Refitting is a reversal of removal.

Washer pump

Note: *Prior to removing the pump, empty the contents of the reservoir, or be prepared for fluid spillage.*

Removal

9 Carry out the operations described previously in paragraphs 1 to 6, with the exception of paragraph 2.

10 Carefully ease the pump out of its sealing grommet.

Refitting

11 Refitting is a reversal of removal.

16 Radio/cassette player – removal and refitting

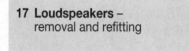

Note: *Once the battery has been disconnected, the radio/cassette unit cannot be re-activated until the appropriate security code has been entered.*

Removal

1 Disconnect the battery negative terminal (refer to *Disconnecting the battery* in the Reference Chapter).

2 Using a small screwdriver, lift up the screw covers located at each side of the radio/cassette player **(see illustration)**.

3 Undo the two screws now exposed, securing the radio/cassette player to the facia **(see illustration)**.

4 Withdraw the unit from its location and disconnect the aerial lead and the wiring connectors at the rear **(see illustrations)**.

Refitting

5 Reconnect the wiring connectors and the

aerial lead to the rear of the unit, then locate the unit in the facia.

6 Refit the two retaining screws and close the screw covers.

7 Reconnect the battery negative terminal, then enter the appropriate code to activate the unit.

17 Loudspeakers – removal and refitting

Door mounted speakers

Removal

1 Disconnect the battery negative terminal (refer to *Disconnecting the battery* in the Reference Chapter).

2 Prise the loudspeaker grille from the door trim panel **(see illustration)**.

3 Undo the screws, then withdraw the loudspeaker and disconnect the wiring plug **(see illustrations)**.

Refitting

4 Refitting is a reversal of removal.

Facia-mounted speakers

Removal

5 Disconnect the battery negative terminal (refer to *Disconnecting the battery* in the Reference Chapter).

6 Prise the speaker grille from its location on the top of the facia.

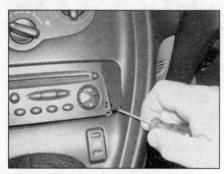

16.2 Lift up the screw covers located at each side of the radio/cassette player

16.3 Undo the screws now exposed, securing the radio/cassette player to the facia

16.4a Withdraw the unit and disconnect the aerial lead . . .

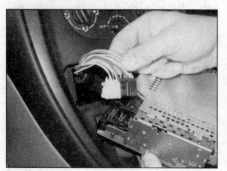

16.4b . . . and the wiring connectors at the rear

17.2 Prise the loudspeaker grille from the door trim panel

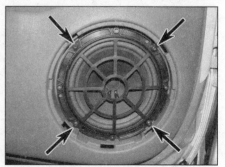

17.3a Undo the speaker retaining screws . . .

7 Turn the speaker a quarter turn and lift it from the facia. Disconnect the wiring connector and remove the speaker.

Refitting

8 Refitting is a reversal of removal.

18 Anti-theft system and engine immobiliser – general information

All models in the range are equipped as standard with a transponder-operated remote control central locking system incorporating an electronic engine immobiliser function. An anti-theft alarm system is only available as an aftermarket accessory.

The electronic engine immobiliser is operated by the transponder fitted to the ignition key, in conjunction with an analogue module fitted around the ignition switch. The system is controlled by the Built-in Systems Interface unit (see Section 1).

When the ignition key is inserted in the switch and turned to the ignition 'on' position, the control module sends a preprogrammed recognition code signal to the analogue module on the ignition switch. If the recognition code signal matches that of the transponder on the ignition key, an unlocking request signal is sent to the engine management ECU allowing the engine to be started. If the ignition key signal is not recognised, the engine management system remains immobilised.

When the ignition is switched off, a locking signal is sent to the ECU and the engine is immobilised until the unlocking request signal is again received.

The recognition code is programmed into the system during manufacture and is contained on a confidential card supplied with the vehicle. The card should be kept in a safe place – never in the vehicle. The confidential card will be required if any work is to be carried out on the system by a Citroën dealer, or if new keys are required.

19 Air bag system – general information, precautions and system de-activation

General information

A driver's and passenger's air bag are fitted as standard equipment on all models. The driver's air bag is located in the steering wheel centre pad and the passenger's air bag is located above the glovebox in the facia. Side air bags are also standard equipment and are located in the front seats.

The system is armed only when the ignition is switched on, however, a reserve power source maintains a power supply to the system in the event of a break in the main electrical supply. The steering wheel and facia

17.3b . . . then withdraw the speaker and disconnect the wiring plug

air bags are activated by a 'g' sensor (deceleration sensor), and controlled by an electronic control unit located under the centre of the facia. The side air bags are activated by severe side impact and operate independently of the main system and of each other. A separate electrical supply and control unit is provided for each side air bag.

The air bags are inflated by a gas generator, which forces the bag out from its location in the steering wheel, facia or seat back frame.

Precautions

⚠️ *Warning: The following precautions must be observed when working on vehicles equipped with an air bag system, to prevent the possibility of personal injury.*

General precautions

The following precautions **must** be observed when carrying out work on a vehicle equipped with an air bag:

a) *Do not disconnect the battery with the engine running.*

b) *Before carrying out any work in the vicinity of the air bag, removal of any of the air bag components, or any welding work on the vehicle, de-activate the system as described in the following sub-Section.*

c) *Do not attempt to test any of the air bag system circuits using test meters or any other test equipment.*

d) *If the air bag warning light comes on, or any fault in the system is suspected, consult a Citroën dealer without delay.* **Do not** *attempt to carry out fault diagnosis, or any dismantling of the components.*

When handling an air bag

a) *Transport the air bag by itself, bag upward.*

b) *Do not put your arms around the air bag.*

c) *Carry the air bag close to the body, bag outward.*

d) *Do not drop the air bag or expose it to impacts.*

e) *Do not attempt to dismantle the air bag unit.*

f) *Do not connect any form of electrical equipment to any part of the air bag circuit.*

When storing an air bag unit

a) *Store the unit in a cupboard with the air bag upward.*

b) *Do not expose the air bag to temperatures above 80ºC.*

c) *Do not expose the air bag to flames.*

d) *Do not attempt to dispose of the air bag – consult a Citroën dealer.*

e) *Never refit an air bag which is known to be faulty or damaged.*

De-activation of air bag

The system must be de-activated before carrying out any work on the air bag components or surrounding area:

a) *Switch on the ignition and check the operation of the air bag warning light on the instrument panel. The light should illuminate when the ignition is switched on, then extinguish.*

b) *Switch off the ignition.*

c) *Remove the ignition key.*

d) *Switch off all electrical equipment.*

e) *Disconnect the battery negative terminal (refer to 'Disconnecting the battery' in the Reference Chapter).*

f) *Insulate the battery negative terminal and the end of the battery negative lead to prevent any possibility of contact.*

g) *Wait for at least two minutes before carrying out any further work. Wait at least ten minutes if the air bag warning light did not operate correctly.*

Activation of air bag

To activate the system on completion of any work, proceed as follows:

a) *Ensure that there are no occupants in the vehicle, and that there are no loose objects around the vicinity of the seats.*

b) *Ensure that the ignition is switched off then reconnect the battery negative terminal.*

c) *Open the driver's door and switch on the ignition. Check that the air bag warning light illuminates briefly then extinguishes.*

d) *Switch off the ignition.*

e) *If the air bag warning light does not operate as described in paragraph c), consult a Citroën dealer before driving the vehicle.*

20 Air bag system components – removal and refitting

⚠️ *Warning: Refer to the precautions given in Section 19 before attempting to carry out work on any of the air bag components.*

General

1 The air bag sensors are integral with the electronic control unit.

2 Any suspected faults with the air bag system should be referred to a Citroën dealer – under no circumstances attempt to carry out

20.8 Gently pull the driver's air bag unit from the centre of the steering wheel

20.9 Carefully unclip the wiring connector from the air bag unit and disconnect the earth lead (where fitted)

20.16a Withdraw the rotary connector from the steering column . . .

20.16b . . . feeding the wiring harness through the stalk switch bracket

any work other than removal and refitting of the front air bag unit(s) and/or the rotary connector, as described in the following paragraphs.

Electronic control units

3 The main ECU is located under the lower front section of the facia and is accessible after removal of the facia lower centre panel as described in Chapter 11. Each of the side air bags has its own control unit, fitted under the false floor, adjacent to the centre door pillar (Chapter 11, Section 25).

Driver's air bag unit

Removal

4 The air bag unit is an integral part of the steering wheel centre boss.
5 De-activate the air bag system as described in Section 19.
6 Move the steering wheel as necessary for access to the two air bag unit securing screws. The screws are located at the rear of the steering wheel boss.
7 Remove the two air bag unit securing screws.
8 Gently pull the air bag unit from the centre of the steering wheel **(see illustration)**.

9 Carefully unclip the wiring connector from the air bag unit (use the fingers only, and pull the connector upward from the air bag unit) **(see illustration)**. Where fitted, disconnect the additional earth lead from the air bag unit.
10 If the air bag unit is to be stored for any length of time, refer to the storage precautions given in Section 19.

Refitting

11 Refitting is a reversal of removal, bearing in mind the following points:
a) Do not strike the air bag unit, or expose it to impacts during refitting.
b) On completion of refitting, activate the air bag system as described in Section 19.

Air bag rotary connector

Removal

12 Remove the air bag unit, as described previously in this Section.
13 Remove the steering wheel as described in Chapter 10.
14 Remove the steering column shrouds as described in Chapter 11, Section 26.
15 Trace the rotary connector wiring back to the connectors below the steering column and disconnect the wiring.

16 Unscrew the three securing screws, and withdraw the rotary connector from the steering column, feeding the wiring harness through the stalk switch bracket **(see illustrations)**. Note the routing of the wiring harness.

Refitting

17 Refitting is a reversal of removal, bearing in mind the following points:
a) Ensure that the rotary connector is centralised by aligning the marks on the rotary connector body and the rotating centre part prior to refitting. Instructions for centralising the unit are also provided on a label on the face of the unit.
b) Ensure that the roadwheels are in the straight-ahead position before refitting the rotary connector and steering wheel.
c) Before refitting the steering column shrouds, ensure that the rotary connector wiring harness is correctly routed as noted before removal.
d) Refit the steering wheel as described in Chapter 10, and refit the air bag unit as described previously in this Section.

Passenger's air bag unit

Removal

18 The passenger's air bag is fitted to the upper part of the facia, above the glovebox.
19 De-activate the air bag system as described in Section 19.
20 Remove the glovebox as described in Chapter 11, Section 26.
21 Undo the two bolts each side securing the air bag mounting bracket to the facia.
22 Disconnect the wiring connector and remove the air bag and mounting bracket from the facia.
23 Undo the four nuts and separate the air bag from the mounting bracket.
24 If the air bag unit is to be stored for any length of time, refer to the storage precautions given in Section 19.

Refitting

25 Refitting is a reversal of removal, bearing in mind the following points:
a) Do not strike the air bag unit, or expose it to impacts during refitting.
b) On completion of refitting, activate the air bag system as described in Section 19.

Side air bag units

26 The side air bags are located internally within the front seat back and no attempt should be made to remove them. Any suspected problems with the side air bag system should be referred to a Citroën dealer.

CITROËN XSARA PICASSO 2000 to 2002 wiring diagrams

Diagram 1

Key to symbols

Bulb	
Switch	
Multiple contact switch (ganged)	
Fuse/fusible link and current rating	F5 30A
Resistor	
Variable resistor	
Connecting wires	
Plug and socket contact	
Item no.	2
Pump/motor	M
Earth point and location	E12
Gauge/meter	
Diode	
Wire splice or soldered joint	
Solenoid actuator	
Light emitting diode (LED)	
Wire colour (brown with black tracer)	Br/Sw
Screened cable	

Dashed outline denotes part of a larger item, containing in this case an electronic or solid state device.
2 - unspecified connector pin 2.
2Br 1 - Connector Brown 2, pin 1.

Earth points

E1	Earthing strap, battery to body	E9	RH dashboard
E2	Engine LH side	E10	LH seat crossmember
E3	LH wing	E11	RH seat crossmember
E4	LH dashboard	E12	RH rear corner
E5	LH wing front	E13	RH wing front
E6	Dashboard middle	E14	Near engine fusebox
E7	RH rear	E15	Engine LH side
E8	LH rear	E16	LH wing

Key to circuits

Diagram 1	Information for wiring diagrams
Diagram 2	Front and rear wash/wipe, BSI, cigarette lighter and horn
Diagram 3	Central locking, airbag and heated rear window
Diagram 4	Interior lights, headlights, sidelights, licence plate light and tail lights
Diagram 5	Headlight levelling, brake light, powered mirrors and reverse lights
Diagram 6	Direction indicator lights, hazard warning, foglights, sunroof and ABS
Diagram 7	Electric windows and radio
Diagram 8	Air conditioning, heater and engine cooling (NFV, 6FZ engine only)
Diagram 9	Engine cooling (RHY engine), coolant heater (RHY engine) and fuel burning coolant heater (RHY engine)
Diagram 10	Starting and charging, diesel pre-heating and engine cooling with A/C (NFV, 6FZ engines)
Diagram 11	Engine management system (NFV engine)
Diagram 12	Engine management system (6FZ engine)
Diagram 13	Engine management system (RHY engine)
Diagram 14	Instrument module

Fuse table

Engine fuse box

Fuses	Rating	Circuit protected
MF1	70A	BSI supply, windscreen wiper, heated rear screen, central locking
MF2	70A	Fan
MF3	60A	Fan (RHY w/out A/C)
MF4	60A	ABS
F5	20A	Horn
F6	30A	Dipped beam relay
F7	30A	Cooling fan
MF8	70A	Passenger fuse box
MF9	50A	BSI supply, direction indicators, electric windows, sun roof, VAN+, rear wiper, A/C
MF10	40A	Lighting control
MF12	70A	Ignition switch
MF13	40A	Diagnostic socket
F14	20A	Heated seats
MF15	20A	BSI supply, windscreen wiper, heated rear screen, central locking
MF16	40A	Passenger fuse box
MF17	30A	Additional heater burner
F20	10A	Cooling fan relay
F22	25A	Direction indicators
F23	15A	ABS
F24	5A	Engine management, heater unit, relay 3
F25	15A	Fuel pump
F26	40A	Double relay
F27	30A	Double relay
F28	10A	Carburettor/throttle housing heater
F29	30A-5A	Air pump, Additional heater burner
F30	10A	RH front fog light
F31	10A	LH front fog light
F32	10A	Speed sensor, reverse light, relay 3
F33	15A	Coolant temp unit, diagnostic socket, engine coolant level switch
F34	5A	Oxygen sensor, EGR valve, canister purge solenoid valve

Passenger fuse box

Fuses	Rating	Circuit protected
F1	Shunt	Airbag control module
F3	5A	Clutch switch
F4	5A	BSI supply
F5	10A	Brake light switch, instrument module
F6	5A	Hazard warning light switch
F7	5A	BSI supply
F8	10A	Coolant temp unit, interior lights, instrument module
F9	5A	Boot light
F10	5A	Navigation system
F13	20A	Heated seats
F14	15A	Accessory socket
	30A	Caravan socket
F15	20A	Rear electric windows
F16	40A	Electric window
F17	15A	Radio
F19	5A	Rear fog lights
F22	10A	Glove box light, interior lights, vanity mirror light
F23	20A	Cigarette lighter
F24	15A	Radio
F26	5A	Electric mirrors
F27	10A	BSI supply
F29	10A	LH main beam
F30	10A	RH main beam
F31	10A	LH dipped beam
F32	10A	RH dipped beam
F33	10A	Headlight levelling motor
F34	10A	LH sidelights, licence plate lights, VV interface, rotary connector
F35	10A	RH sidelights
F36	15A	Additional heating
F37	5A	Daytime running lights
F38	5A	Pressostat
F40	40A	A/C blower

H32549

Wire colours

Br	Brown	**Gr**	Gray
Bg	Beige	**Or**	Orange
Bl	Blue	**Pk**	Pink
Ro	Red	**Pu**	Purple
Ge	Yellow	**Sw**	Black
Gn	Green	**Ws**	White

Key to items

1 Battery
2 Engine fuse box
3 Interior fuse box
4 Ignition switch
5 Built-in System Interface
6 Vehicle speed sensor
7 Windscreen wiper motor
8 Washer pump
9 Wash/wipe switches
10 Rear wiper motor
11 Accessory socket
12 Cigarette lighter
13 Horn switch
14 Horn

Diagram 2

MTS
H32550

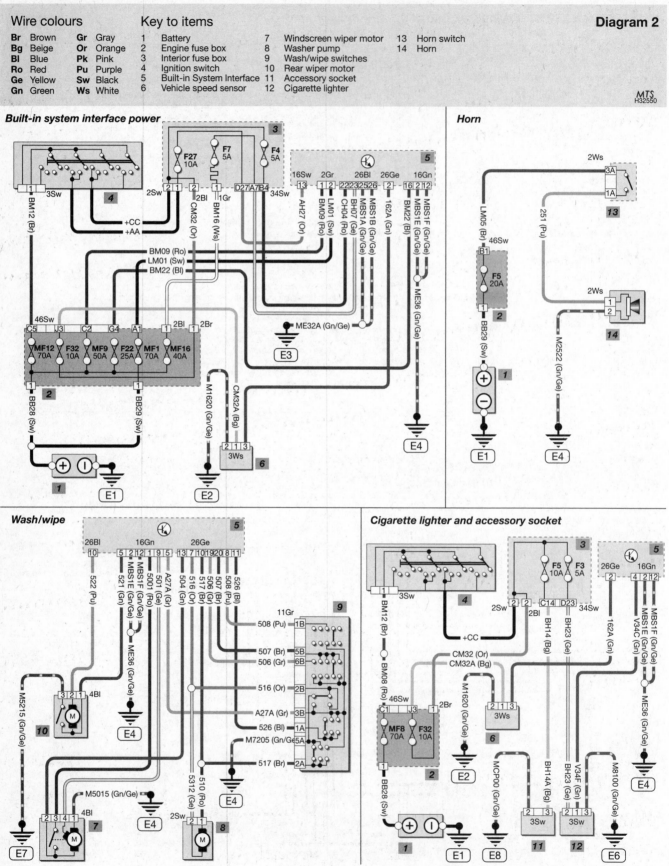

Built-in system interface power

Horn

Wash/wipe

Cigarette lighter and accessory socket

Wire colours

Br	Brown	**Gr**	Gray
Bg	Beige	**Or**	Orange
Bl	Blue	**Pk**	Pink
Ro	Red	**Pu**	Purple
Ge	Yellow	**Sw**	Black
Gn	Green	**Ws**	White

Key to items

1 Battery
2 Engine fuse box
3 Interior fuse box
4 Ignition switch
5 Built-in System Interface
15 Tailgate motor
16 Tailgate lock switch

17 Inertia switch
18 LH rear door lock motor
19 LH front door lock motor
20 RH front door lock motor
21 RH rear door lock motor
22 Door lock switch
23 Airbag control module

24 RH side airbag
25 LH side airbag
26 Drivers airbag
27 Clock spring
28 Passenger airbag
29 Airbag sensor
30 Drivers pretensionner

31 Passenger pretensionner
32 Passenger airbag override switch
33 Airbag sensor
34 Diagnostic socket
35 Heated rear screen
36 Heater controls

Diagram 3

MTS
H32551

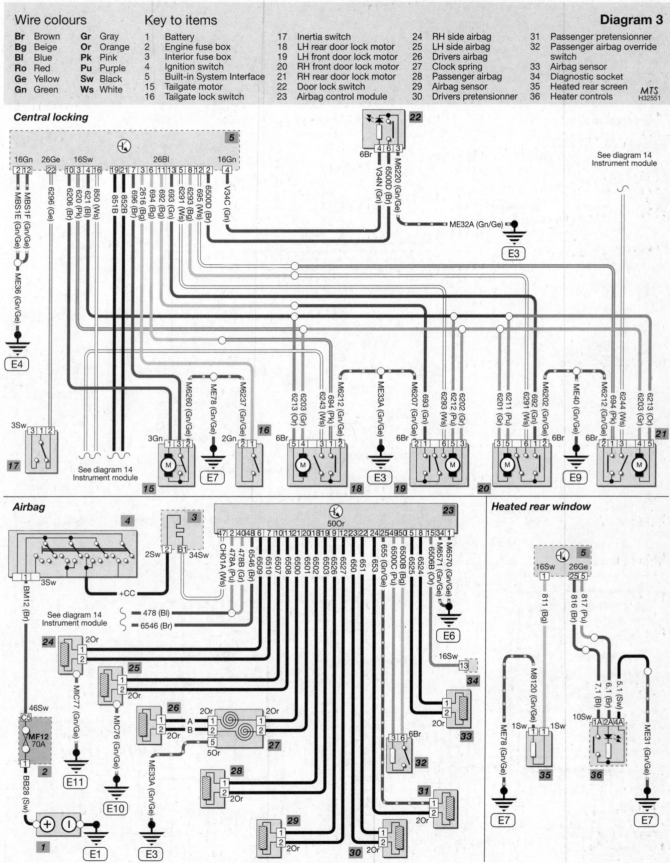

Central locking

Airbag

Heated rear window

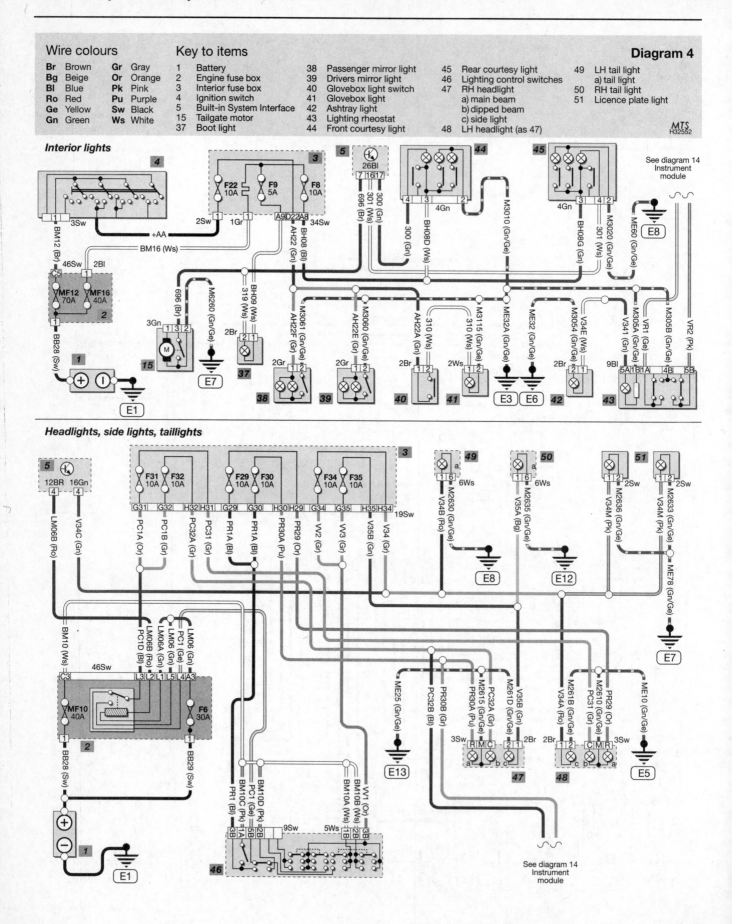

Wire colours

Br	Brown	**Gr**	Gray
Bg	Beige	**Or**	Orange
Bl	Blue	**Pk**	Pink
Ro	Red	**Pu**	Purple
Ge	Yellow	**Sw**	Black
Gn	Green	**Ws**	White

Key to items

1 Battery
2 Engine fuse box
3 Interior fuse box
4 Ignition switch
5 Built-in System Interface
15 Tailgate motor
37 Boot light
38 Passenger mirror light
39 Drivers mirror light
40 Glovebox light switch
41 Glovebox light
42 Ashtray light
43 Lighting rheostat
44 Front courtesy light
45 Rear courtesy light
46 Lighting control switches
47 RH headlight
a) main beam
b) dipped beam
c) side light
48 LH headlight (as 47)
49 LH tail light
a) tail light
50 RH tail light
51 Licence plate light

Diagram 4

MTS
H32552

Interior lights

See diagram 14
Instrument module

Headlights, side lights, taillights

See diagram 14
Instrument module

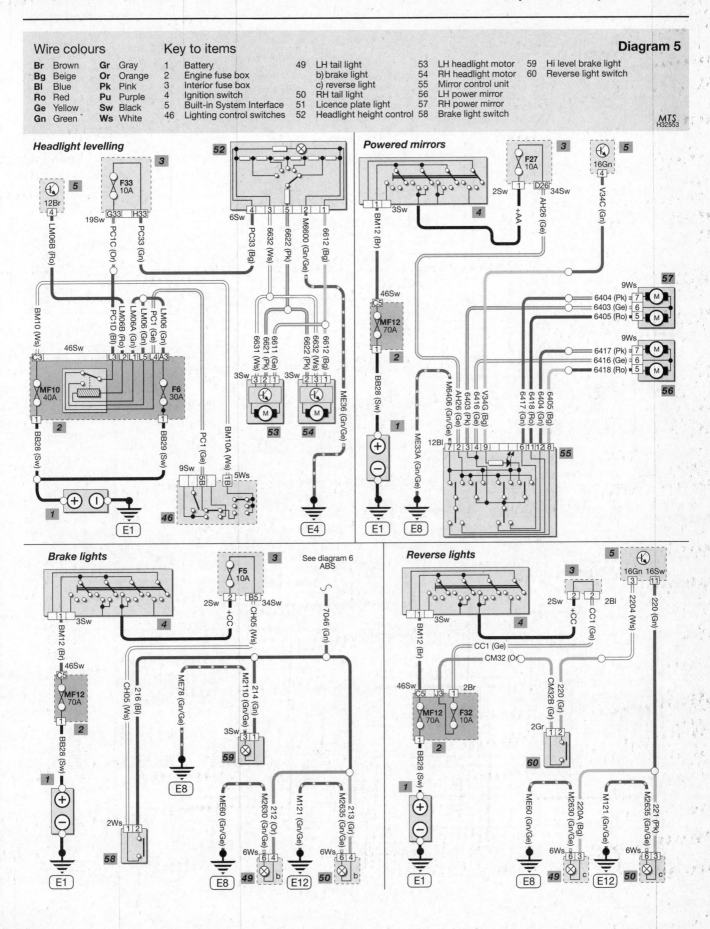

Diagram 5

Wire colours

Br	Brown	Gr	Gray
Bg	Beige	Or	Orange
Bl	Blue	Pk	Pink
Ro	Red	Pu	Purple
Ge	Yellow	Sw	Black
Gn	Green	Ws	White

Key to items

1 Battery
2 Engine fuse box
3 Interior fuse box
4 Ignition switch
5 Built-in System Interface
46 Lighting control switches

49 LH tail light
   b) brake light
   c) reverse light
50 RH tail light
51 Licence plate light
52 Headlight height control

53 LH headlight motor
54 RH headlight motor
55 Mirror control unit
56 LH power mirror
57 RH power mirror
58 Brake light switch

59 Hi level brake light
60 Reverse light switch

MTS
H32553

Headlight levelling

Powered mirrors

Brake lights

See diagram 6
ABS

Reverse lights

Wire colours

Br	Brown	Gr	Gray
Bg	Beige	Or	Orange
Bl	Blue	Pk	Pink
Ro	Red	Pu	Purple
Ge	Yellow	Sw	Black
Gn	Green	Ws	White

Key to items

1	Battery	47	RH headlight	61	Hazard warning switch
2	Engine fuse box		d) direction indicator	62	LH side direction indicator
3	Interior fuse box	48	LH headlight (as 47)		
4	Ignition switch		d) direction indicator	63	RH side direction indicator
5	Built-in System Interface	49	LH tail light		
34	Diagnostic socket		d) direction indicator	64	LH front fog light
46	Lighting control switches		e) fog light	65	RH front fog light
		50	RH tail light (as 49)	66	Sun roof motor

67	Sun roof switch
68	End of travel switch
69	Sun roof motor
70	ABS module
71	LH front brake sensor
72	RH front brake sensor
73	LH rear brake sensor
74	RH rear brake sensor

Diagram 6

MTS H32554

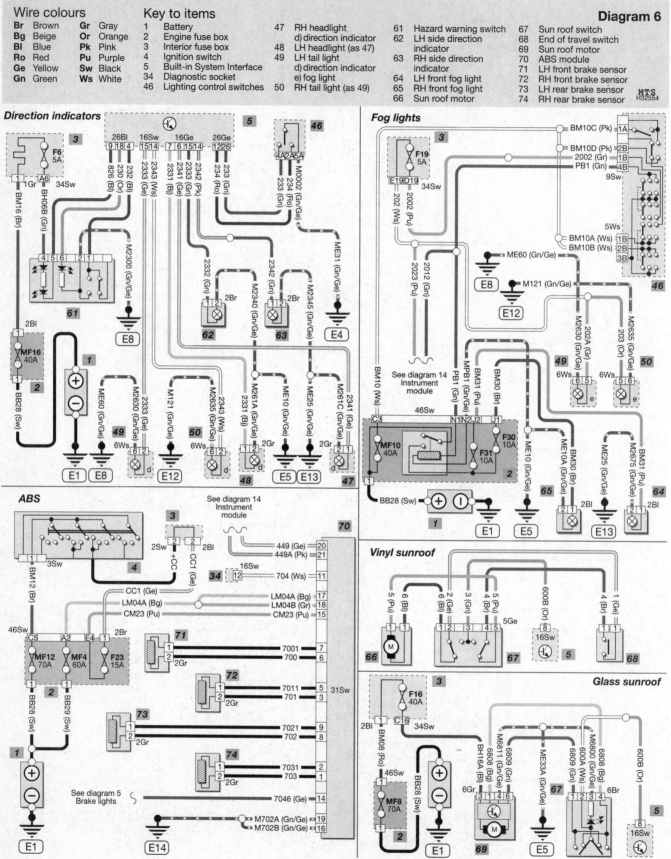

Direction indicators

Fog lights

ABS

Vinyl sunroof

Glass sunroof

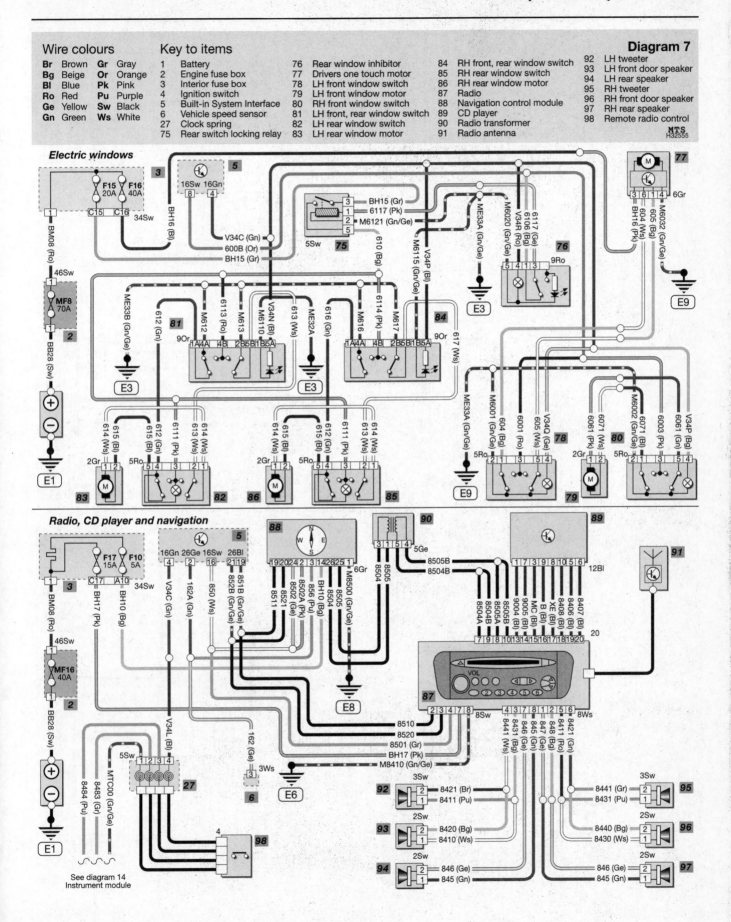

Wire colours

Br	Brown	**Gr**	Gray
Bg	Beige	**Or**	Orange
Bl	Blue	**Pk**	Pink
Ro	Red	**Pu**	Purple
Ge	Yellow	**Sw**	Black
Gn	Green	**Ws**	White

Key to items

1 Battery
2 Engine fuse box
3 Interior fuse box
4 Ignition switch
5 Built-in System Interface
6 Vehicle speed sensor
27 Clock spring
75 Rear switch locking relay

76 Rear window inhibitor
77 Drivers one touch motor
78 LH front window switch
79 LH front window motor
80 RH front window switch
81 LH front, rear window switch
82 LH rear window switch
83 LH rear window motor

84 RH front, rear window switch
85 RH rear window switch
86 RH rear window motor
87 Radio
88 Navigation control module
89 CD player
90 Radio transformer
91 Radio antenna

92 LH tweeter
93 LH front door speaker
94 LH rear speaker
95 RH tweeter
96 RH front door speaker
97 RH rear speaker
98 Remote radio control

Diagram 7

MTS
H32555

Electric windows

Radio, CD player and navigation

See diagram 14
Instrument module

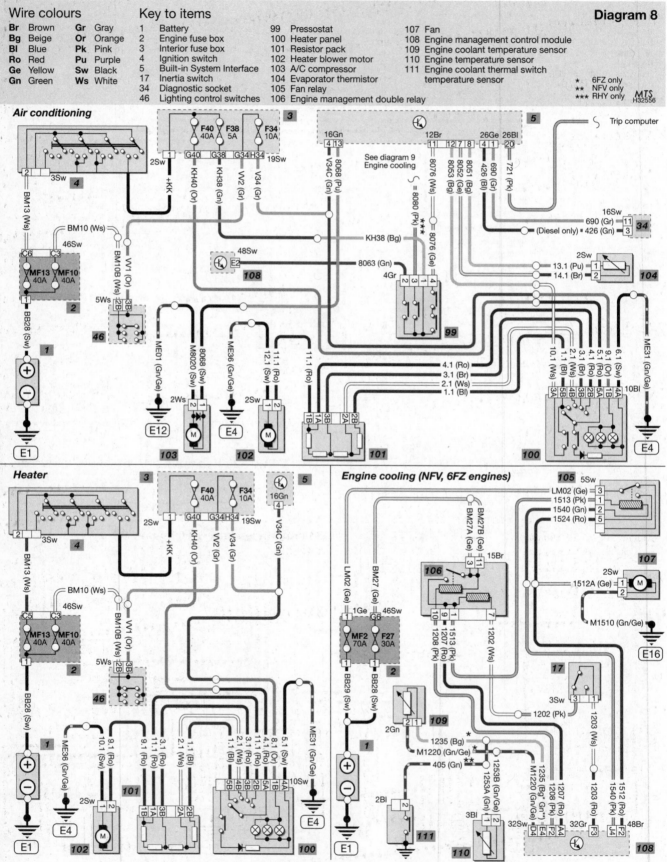

Diagram 8

Wire colours

Br	Brown	Gr	Gray
Bg	Beige	Or	Orange
Bl	Blue	Pk	Pink
Ro	Red	Pu	Purple
Ge	Yellow	Sw	Black
Gn	Green	Ws	White

Key to items

1 Battery
2 Engine fuse box
3 Interior fuse box
4 Ignition switch
5 Built-in System Interface
17 Inertia switch
34 Diagnostic socket
46 Lighting control switches

99 Pressostat
100 Heater panel
101 Resistor pack
102 Heater blower motor
103 A/C compressor
104 Evaporator thermistor
105 Fan relay
106 Engine management double relay

107 Fan
108 Engine management control module
109 Engine coolant temperature sensor
110 Engine temperature sensor
111 Engine coolant thermal switch
   temperature sensor

★   6FZ only
★★   NFV only
★★★ RHY only

MTS
H32556

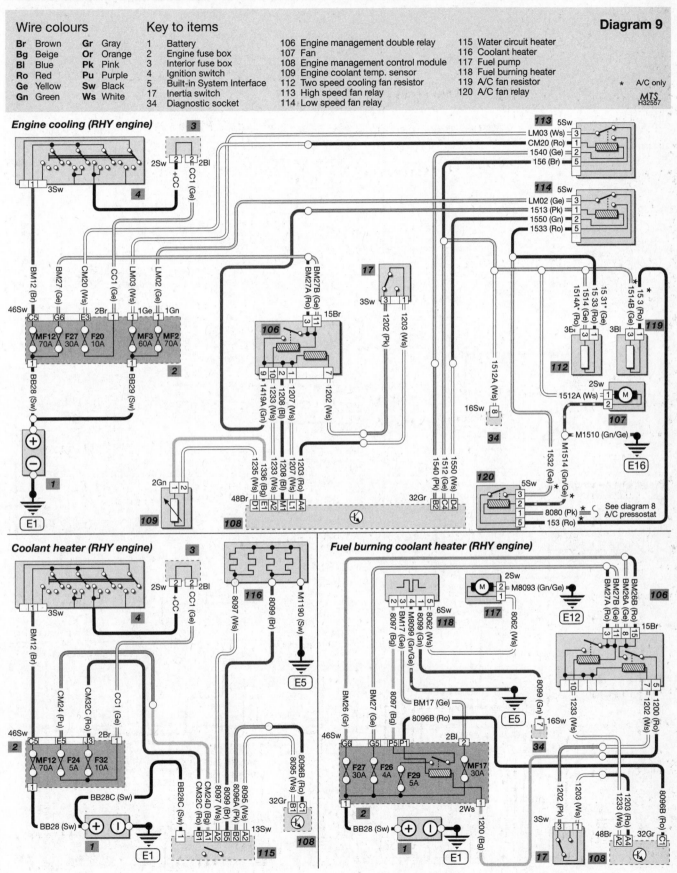

Wire colours

Br	Brown	**Gr**	Gray
Bg	Beige	**Or**	Orange
Bl	Blue	**Pk**	Pink
Ro	Red	**Pu**	Purple
Ge	Yellow	**Sw**	Black
Gn	Green	**Ws**	White

Key to items

1 Battery
2 Engine fuse box
3 Interior fuse box
4 Ignition switch
5 Built-in System Interface
17 Inertia switch
34 Diagnostic socket

106 Engine management double relay
107 Fan
108 Engine management control module
109 Engine coolant temp. sensor
112 Two speed cooling fan resistor
113 High speed fan relay
114 Low speed fan relay

115 Water circuit heater
116 Coolant heater
117 Fuel pump
118 Fuel burning heater
119 A/C fan resistor
120 A/C fan relay

* A/C only

Diagram 9

MTS
H32557

Engine cooling (RHY engine)

Coolant heater (RHY engine)

Fuel burning coolant heater (RHY engine)

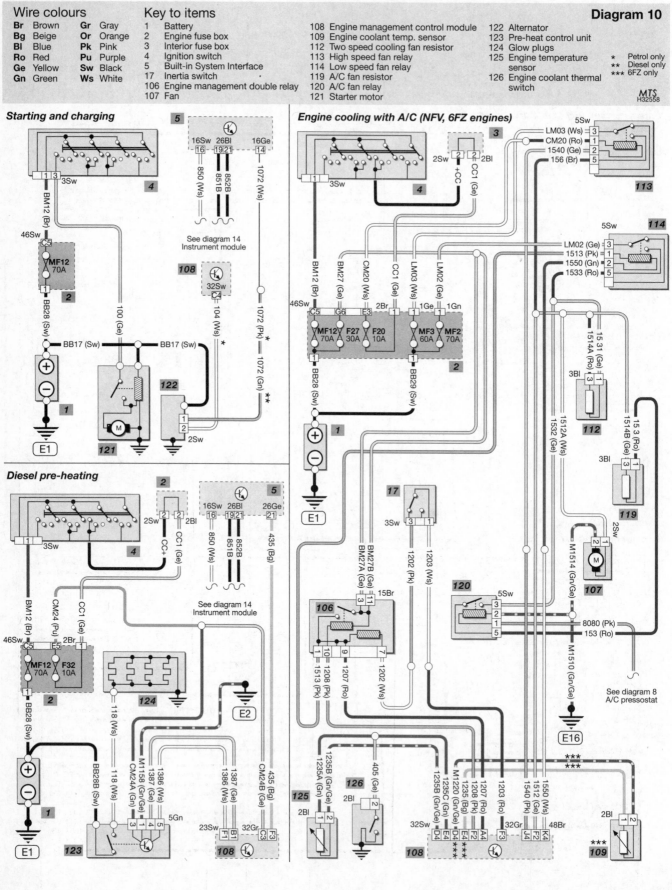

Wire colours

Br	Brown	Gr	Gray
Bg	Beige	Or	Orange
Bl	Blue	Pk	Pink
Ro	Red	Pu	Purple
Ge	Yellow	Sw	Black
Gn	Green	Ws	White

Key to items

1 Battery
2 Engine fuse box
3 Interior fuse box
4 Ignition switch
5 Built-in System Interface
17 Inertia switch
106 Engine management double relay
107 Fan
108 Engine management control module
109 Engine coolant temp. sensor
112 Two speed cooling fan resistor
113 High speed fan relay
114 Low speed fan relay
119 A/C fan resistor
120 A/C fan relay
121 Starter motor
122 Alternator
123 Pre-heat control unit
124 Glow plugs
125 Engine temperature sensor
126 Engine coolant thermal switch

* Petrol only
** Diesel only
*** 6FZ only

Diagram 10

MTS
H32558

Starting and charging

Engine cooling with A/C (NFV, 6FZ engines)

Diesel pre-heating

See diagram 14
Instrument module

See diagram 8
A/C pressostat

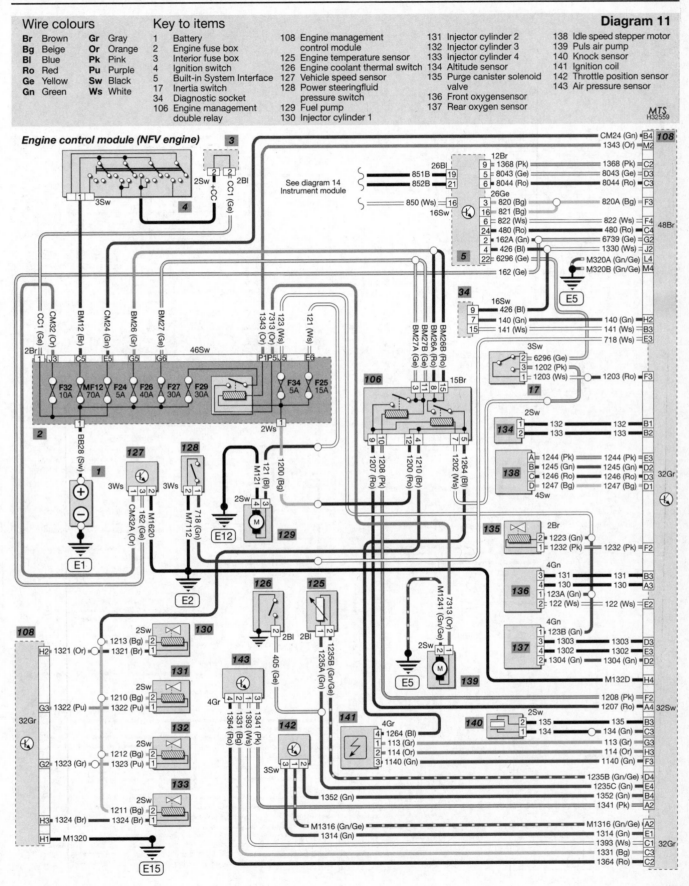

Diagram 11

Wire colours

Br	Brown	Gr	Gray
Bg	Beige	Or	Orange
Bl	Blue	Pk	Pink
Ro	Red	Pu	Purple
Ge	Yellow	Sw	Black
Gn	Green	Ws	White

Key to items

1 Battery
2 Engine fuse box
3 Interior fuse box
4 Ignition switch
5 Built-in System Interface
17 Inertia switch
34 Diagnostic socket
106 Engine management double relay
108 Engine management control module
125 Engine temperature sensor
126 Engine coolant thermal switch
127 Vehicle speed sensor
128 Power steeringfluid pressure switch
129 Fuel pump
130 Injector cylinder 1
131 Injector cylinder 2
132 Injector cylinder 3
133 Injector cylinder 4
134 Altitude sensor
135 Purge canister solenoid valve
136 Front oxygensensor
137 Rear oxygen sensor
138 Idle speed stepper motor
139 Puls air pump
140 Knock sensor
141 Ignition coil
142 Throttle position sensor
143 Air pressure sensor

MTS
H32559

Engine control module (NFV engine)

Wire colours

Br	Brown	**Gr**	Gray
Bg	Beige	**Or**	Orange
Bl	Blue	**Pk**	Pink
Ro	Red	**Pu**	Purple
Ge	Yellow	**Sw**	Black
Gn	Green	**Ws**	White

MTS
H32560

Key to items

1 Battery
2 Engine fuse box
3 Interior fuse box
4 Ignition switch
5 Built-in System Interface
17 Inertia switch
34 Diagnostic socket
106 Engine management
   double relay
108 Engine management
   control module
109 Engine coolant temp. sensor
127 Vehicle speed sensor
128 Power steering fluid
   pressure switch
129 Fuel pump
130 Injector cylinder 1
131 Injector cylinder 2

132 Injector cylinder 3
133 Injector cylinder 4
134 Engine speed sensor
135 Purge canister solenoid valve
136 Front oxygen sensor
137 Rear oxygen sensor
138 Idle speed stepper motor
139 Pulse air pump
140 Knock sensor

141 Ignition coil
142 Throttle position sensor
143 Air pressure sensor
144 Throttle body heater
145 EGR valve
146 Cylinder reference sensor
161 Induction air temperature
   sensor

Diagram 12

Engine control module (6FZ engine)

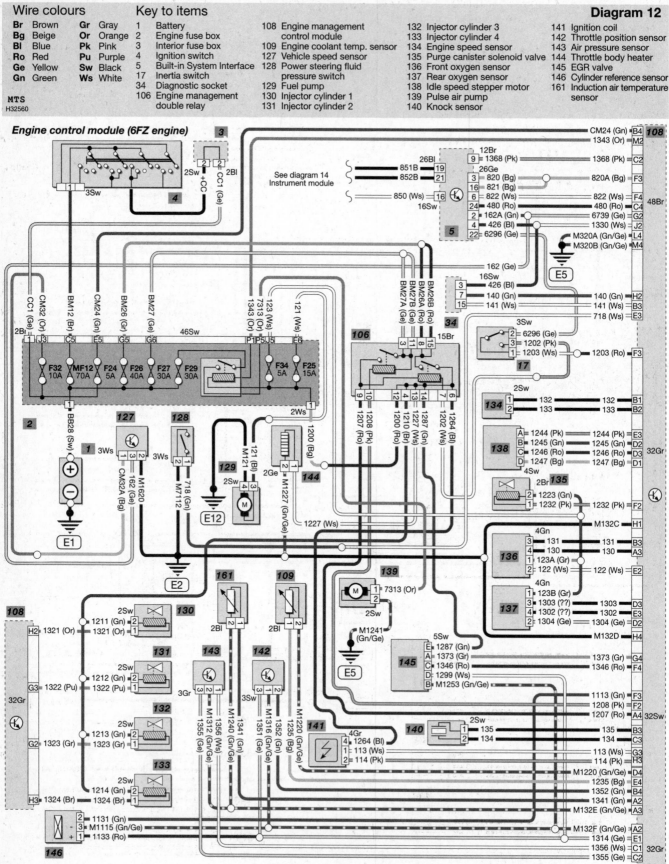

Wire colours

Br Brown **Gr** Gray
Bg Beige **Or** Orange
Bl Blue **Pk** Pink
Ro Red **Pu** Purple
Ge Yellow **Sw** Black
Gn Green **Ws** White

MTS
H32561

Key to items

1 Battery
2 Engine fuse box
3 Interior fuse box
4 Ignition switch
5 Built-in System Interface
17 Inertia switch
34 Diagnostic socket

106 Engine management double relay
108 Engine management control module
109 Engine coolant temp. sensor
127 Vehicle speed sensor
129 Fuel pump

130 Injector cylinder 1
131 Injector cylinder 2
132 Injector cylinder 3
133 Injector cylinder 4
134 Altitude sensor
145 EGR valve
146 Cylinder reference sensor
147 Immobiliser switch

148 Clutch pedal switch
149 Throttle position sensor
150 High pressure regulator
151 EGR with butterfly valve
152 Diesel injection pump
153 Diesel thermistor
154 High pressure sensor
155 Airflow sensor

Diagram 13

Engine control module (RHY engine)

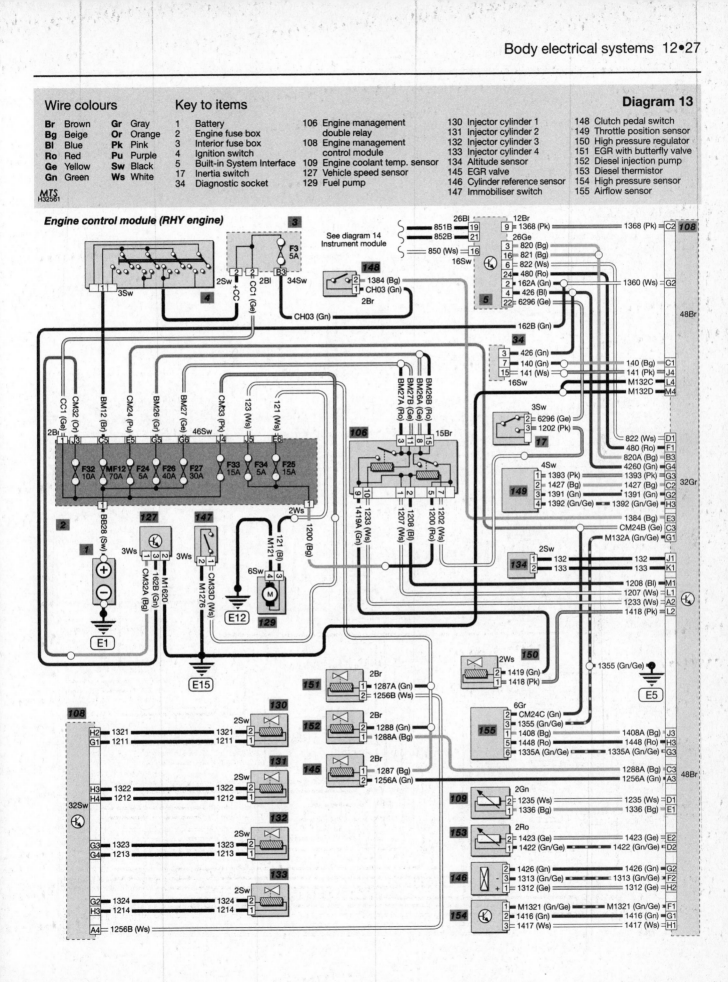

Wire colours

Br	Brown	**Gr**	Gray
Bg	Beige	**Or**	Orange
Bl	Blue	**Pk**	Pink
Ro	Red	**Pu**	Purple
Ge	Yellow	**Sw**	Black
Gn	Green	**Ws**	White

Key to items

1 Battery
2 Engine fuse box
3 Interior fuse box
4 Ignition switch
5 Built-in System Interface
129 Fuel pump

156 Instrument module
157 Engine coolant level switch
158 Oil pressure switch
159 Brake fluid level switch
160 Handbrake switch

Diagram 14

MTS
H32582

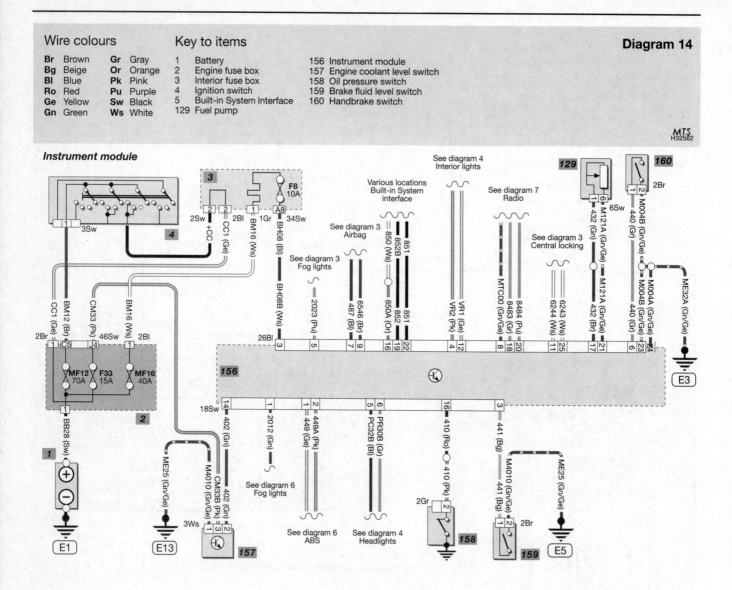

Instrument module

Dimensions and weights

Note: *All figures are approximate, and may vary according to model. Refer to manufacturer's data for exact figures.*

Dimensions

Overall length	4276 mm
Overall width (including mirrors)	2000 mm
Overall height (unladen)	1637 mm
Wheelbase	2760 mm

Weights

Kerb weight	1240 to 1300 kg*
Maximum gross vehicle weight	1790 to 1850 kg*
Maximum roof rack load	80 kg
Maximum towing weight (unbraked trailer)**	650 to 685 kg
Maximum towing weight (braked trailer)**	900 to 1300 kg*
Maximum trailer nose weight	80 kg*

Depending on model and specification.
**Refer to Citroën dealer for exact recommendations.*

Conversion factors

Length (distance)

Inches (in)	x 25.4	= Millimetres (mm)	x 0.0394	=	Inches (in)
Feet (ft)	x 0.305	= Metres (m)	x 3.281	=	Feet (ft)
Miles	x 1.609	= Kilometres (km)	x 0.621	=	Miles

Volume (capacity)

Cubic inches (cu in; in³)	x 16.387	= Cubic centimetres (cc; cm³)	x 0.061	=	Cubic inches (cu in; in³)
Imperial pints (Imp pt)	x 0.568	= Litres (l)	x 1.76	=	Imperial pints (Imp pt)
Imperial quarts (Imp qt)	x 1.137	= Litres (l)	x 0.88	=	Imperial quarts (Imp qt)
Imperial quarts (Imp qt)	x 1.201	= US quarts (US qt)	x 0.833	=	Imperial quarts (Imp qt)
US quarts (US qt)	x 0.946	= Litres (l)	x 1.057	=	US quarts (US qt)
Imperial gallons (Imp gal)	x 4.546	= Litres (l)	x 0.22	=	Imperial gallons (Imp gal)
Imperial gallons (Imp gal)	x 1.201	= US gallons (US gal)	x 0.833	=	Imperial gallons (Imp gal)
US gallons (US gal)	x 3.785	= Litres (l)	x 0.264	=	US gallons (US gal)

Mass (weight)

Ounces (oz)	x 28.35	= Grams (g)	x 0.035	=	Ounces (oz)
Pounds (lb)	x 0.454	= Kilograms (kg)	x 2.205	=	Pounds (lb)

Force

Ounces-force (ozf; oz)	x 0.278	= Newtons (N)	x 3.6	=	Ounces-force (ozf; oz)
Pounds-force (lbf; lb)	x 4.448	= Newtons (N)	x 0.225	=	Pounds-force (lbf; lb)
Newtons (N)	x 0.1	= Kilograms-force (kgf; kg)	x 9.81	=	Newtons (N)

Pressure

Pounds-force per square inch (psi; lbf/in²; lb/in²)	x 0.070	= Kilograms-force per square centimetre (kgf/cm²; kg/cm²)	x 14.223	=	Pounds-force per square inch (psi; lbf/in²; lb/in²)
Pounds-force per square inch (psi; lbf/in²; lb/in²)	x 0.068	= Atmospheres (atm)	x 14.696	=	Pounds-force per square inch (psi; lbf/in²; lb/in²)
Pounds-force per square inch (psi; lbf/in²; lb/in²)	x 0.069	= Bars	x 14.5	=	Pounds-force per square inch (psi; lbf/in²; lb/in²)
Pounds-force per square inch (psi; lbf/in²; lb/in²)	x 6.895	= Kilopascals (kPa)	x 0.145	=	Pounds-force per square inch (psi; lbf/in²; lb/in²)
Kilopascals (kPa)	x 0.01	= Kilograms-force per square centimetre (kgf/cm²; kg/cm²)	x 98.1	=	Kilopascals (kPa)
Millibar (mbar)	x 100	= Pascals (Pa)	x 0.01	=	Millibar (mbar)
Millibar (mbar)	x 0.0145	= Pounds-force per square inch (psi; lbf/in²; lb/in²)	x 68.947	=	Millibar (mbar)
Millibar (mbar)	x 0.75	= Millimetres of mercury (mmHg)	x 1.333	=	Millibar (mbar)
Millibar (mbar)	x 0.401	= Inches of water (inH₂O)	x 2.491	=	Millibar (mbar)
Millimetres of mercury (mmHg)	x 0.535	= Inches of water (inH₂O)	x 1.868	=	Millimetres of mercury (mmHg)
Inches of water (inH₂O)	x 0.036	= Pounds-force per square inch (psi; lbf/in²; lb/in²)	x 27.68	=	Inches of water (inH₂O)

Torque (moment of force)

Pounds-force inches (lbf in; lb in)	x 1.152	= Kilograms-force centimetre (kgf cm; kg cm)	x 0.868	=	Pounds-force inches (lbf in; lb in)
Pounds-force inches (lbf in; lb in)	x 0.113	= Newton metres (Nm)	x 8.85	=	Pounds-force inches (lbf in; lb in)
Pounds-force inches (lbf in; lb in)	x 0.083	= Pounds-force feet (lbf ft; lb ft)	x 12	=	Pounds-force inches (lbf in; lb in)
Pounds-force feet (lbf ft; lb ft)	x 0.138	= Kilograms-force metres (kgf m; kg m)	x 7.233	=	Pounds-force feet (lbf ft; lb ft)
Pounds-force feet (lbf ft; lb ft)	x 1.356	= Newton metres (Nm)	x 0.738	=	Pounds-force feet (lbf ft; lb ft)
Newton metres (Nm)	x 0.102	= Kilograms-force metres (kgf m; kg m)	x 9.804	=	Newton metres (Nm)

Power

Horsepower (hp)	x 745.7	= Watts (W)	x 0.0013	=	Horsepower (hp)

Velocity (speed)

Miles per hour (miles/hr; mph)	x 1.609	= Kilometres per hour (km/hr; kph)	x 0.621	=	Miles per hour (miles/hr; mph)

Fuel consumption*

Miles per gallon, Imperial (mpg)	x 0.354	= Kilometres per litre (km/l)	x 2.825	=	Miles per gallon, Imperial (mpg)
Miles per gallon, US (mpg)	x 0.425	= Kilometres per litre (km/l)	x 2.352	=	Miles per gallon, US (mpg)

Temperature

Degrees Fahrenheit = (°C x 1.8) + 32   Degrees Celsius (Degrees Centigrade; °C) = (°F - 32) x 0.56

It is common practice to convert from miles per gallon (mpg) to litres/100 kilometres (l/100km), where mpg x l/100 km = 282

Spare parts are available from many sources, including maker's appointed garages, accessory shops, and motor factors. To be sure of obtaining the correct parts, it will sometimes be necessary to quote the vehicle identification number. If possible, it can also be useful to take the old parts along for positive identification. Items such as starter motors and alternators may be available under a service exchange scheme – any parts returned should be clean.

Our advice regarding spare parts is as follows.

Officially-appointed garages

This is the best source of parts which are peculiar to your car, and which are not otherwise generally available (eg, badges, interior trim, certain body panels, etc). It is also the only place at which you should buy parts if the vehicle is still under warranty.

Accessory shops

These are very good places to buy materials and components needed for the maintenance of your car (oil, air and fuel filters, light bulbs, drivebelts, greases, brake pads, tough-up paint, etc). Components of this nature sold by a reputable shop are of the same standard as those used by the car manufacturer.

Besides components, these shops also sell tools and general accessories, usually have convenient opening hours, charge lower prices, and can often be found close to home. Some accessory shops have parts counters where components needed for almost any repair job can be purchased or ordered.

Motor factors

Good factors will stock all the more important components which wear out comparatively quickly, and can sometimes supply individual components needed for the overhaul of a larger assembly (eg, brake seals and hydraulic parts, bearing shells, pistons, valves). They may also handle work such as cylinder block reboring, crankshaft regrinding, etc.

Tyre and exhaust specialists

These outlets may be independent, or members of a local or national chain. They frequently offer competitive prices when compared with a main dealer or local garage, but it will pay to obtain several quotes before making a decision. When researching prices, also ask what 'extras' may be added – for instance fitting a new valve and balancing the wheel are both commonly charged on top of the price of a new tyre.

Other sources

Beware of parts or materials obtained from market stalls, car boot sales or similar outlets. Such items are not invariably sub-standard, but there is little chance of compensation if they do prove unsatisfactory. In the case of safety-critical components such as brake pads, there is the risk not only of financial loss, but also of an accident causing injury or death.

Second-hand components or assemblies obtained from a car breaker can be a good buy in some circumstances, but his sort of purchase is best made by the experienced DIY mechanic.

Modifications are a continuing and unpublicised process in vehicle manufacture, quite apart from major model changes. Spare parts manuals and lists are compiled upon a numerical basis, the individual vehicle identification numbers being essential for correct identification of the part concerned. When ordering spare parts, always give as much information as possible. Quote the car model, year of manufacture, VIN and engine numbers as appropriate.

The Vehicle Identification Number (VIN) plate is located at the base of the central door pillar on the right-hand side (see illustration). Additional identification numbers for weight information, paint codes, chassis numbers, and details of the vehicle which are required by law for export to certain countries are also provided, and their locations are shown in the illustration.

The vehicle identification (chassis) number is stamped into the body, along the top edge of the scuttle panel on the right-hand side, and can be viewed with the bonnet open. On some models, the chassis number may also be etched into the windscreen and window glass.

The engine identification numbers are situated on the front face of the cylinder block, either on a plate, or stamped directly to the centre, or side, of the block face. The engine code is located on the first line of the engine number sequence – eg, 6FZ.

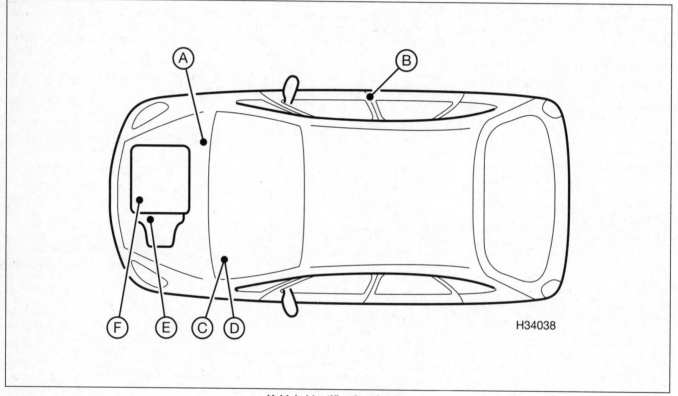

H34038

Vehicle identification details

A Chassis number
B VIN plate

C Manufacturer's modification
   reference number
D Body paint colour code

E Transmission number
F Engine number

Whenever servicing, repair or overhaul work is carried out on the car or its components, observe the following procedures and instructions. This will assist in carrying out the operation efficiently and to a professional standard of workmanship.

Joint mating faces and gaskets

When separating components at their mating faces, never insert screwdrivers or similar implements into the joint between the faces in order to prise them apart. This can cause severe damage which results in oil leaks, coolant leaks, etc upon reassembly. Separation is usually achieved by tapping along the joint with a soft-faced hammer in order to break the seal. However, note that this method may not be suitable where dowels are used for component location.

Where a gasket is used between the mating faces of two components, a new one must be fitted on reassembly; fit it dry unless otherwise stated in the repair procedure. Make sure that the mating faces are clean and dry, with all traces of old gasket removed. When cleaning a joint face, use a tool which is unlikely to score or damage the face, and remove any burrs or nicks with an oilstone or fine file.

Make sure that tapped holes are cleaned with a pipe cleaner, and keep them free of jointing compound, if this is being used, unless specifically instructed otherwise.

Ensure that all orifices, channels or pipes are clear, and blow through them, preferably using compressed air.

Oil seals

Oil seals can be removed by levering them out with a wide flat-bladed screwdriver or similar implement. Alternatively, a number of self-tapping screws may be screwed into the seal, and these used as a purchase for pliers or some similar device in order to pull the seal free.

Whenever an oil seal is removed from its working location, either individually or as part of an assembly, it should be renewed.

The very fine sealing lip of the seal is easily damaged, and will not seal if the surface it contacts is not completely clean and free from scratches, nicks or grooves. If the original sealing surface of the component cannot be restored, and the manufacturer has not made provision for slight relocation of the seal relative to the sealing surface, the component should be renewed.

Protect the lips of the seal from any surface which may damage them in the course of fitting. Use tape or a conical sleeve where possible. Lubricate the seal lips with oil before fitting and, on dual-lipped seals, fill the space between the lips with grease.

Unless otherwise stated, oil seals must be fitted with their sealing lips toward the lubricant to be sealed.

Use a tubular drift or block of wood of the appropriate size to install the seal and, if the seal housing is shouldered, drive the seal down to the shoulder. If the seal housing is unshouldered, the seal should be fitted with its face flush with the housing top face (unless otherwise instructed).

Screw threads and fastenings

Seized nuts, bolts and screws are quite a common occurrence where corrosion has set in, and the use of penetrating oil or releasing fluid will often overcome this problem if the offending item is soaked for a while before attempting to release it. The use of an impact driver may also provide a means of releasing such stubborn fastening devices, when used in conjunction with the appropriate screwdriver bit or socket. If none of these methods works, it may be necessary to resort to the careful application of heat, or the use of a hacksaw or nut splitter device.

Studs are usually removed by locking two nuts together on the threaded part, and then using a spanner on the lower nut to unscrew the stud. Studs or bolts which have broken off below the surface of the component in which they are mounted can sometimes be removed using a stud extractor. Always ensure that a blind tapped hole is completely free from oil, grease, water or other fluid before installing the bolt or stud. Failure to do this could cause the housing to crack due to the hydraulic action of the bolt or stud as it is screwed in.

When tightening a castellated nut to accept a split pin, tighten the nut to the specified torque, where applicable, and then tighten further to the next split pin hole. Never slacken the nut to align the split pin hole, unless stated in the repair procedure.

When checking or retightening a nut or bolt to a specified torque setting, slacken the nut or bolt by a quarter of a turn, and then retighten to the specified setting. However, this should not be attempted where angular tightening has been used.

For some screw fastenings, notably cylinder head bolts or nuts, torque wrench settings are no longer specified for the latter stages of tightening, "angle-tightening" being called up instead. Typically, a fairly low torque wrench setting will be applied to the bolts/nuts in the correct sequence, followed by one or more stages of tightening through specified angles.

Locknuts, locktabs and washers

Any fastening which will rotate against a component or housing during tightening should always have a washer between it and the relevant component or housing.

Spring or split washers should always be renewed when they are used to lock a critical component such as a big-end bearing retaining bolt or nut. Locktabs which are folded over to retain a nut or bolt should always be renewed.

Self-locking nuts can be re-used in non-critical areas, providing resistance can be felt when the locking portion passes over the bolt or stud thread. However, it should be noted that self-locking stiffnuts tend to lose their effectiveness after long periods of use, and should then be renewed as a matter of course.

Split pins must always be replaced with new ones of the correct size for the hole.

When thread-locking compound is found on the threads of a fastener which is to be re-used, it should be cleaned off with a wire brush and solvent, and fresh compound applied on reassembly.

Special tools

Some repair procedures in this manual entail the use of special tools such as a press, two or three-legged pullers, spring compressors, etc. Wherever possible, suitable readily-available alternatives to the manufacturer's special tools are described, and are shown in use. In some instances, where no alternative is possible, it has been necessary to resort to the use of a manufacturer's tool, and this has been done for reasons of safety as well as the efficient completion of the repair operation. Unless you are highly-skilled and have a thorough understanding of the procedures described, never attempt to bypass the use of any special tool when the procedure described specifies its use. Not only is there a very great risk of personal injury, but expensive damage could be caused to the components involved.

Environmental considerations

When disposing of used engine oil, brake fluid, antifreeze, etc, give due consideration to any detrimental environmental effects. Do not, for instance, pour any of the above liquids down drains into the general sewage system, or onto the ground to soak away. Many local council refuse tips provide a facility for waste oil disposal, as do some garages. If none of these facilities are available, consult your local Environmental Health Department, or the National Rivers Authority, for further advice.

With the universal tightening-up of legislation regarding the emission of environmentally-harmful substances from motor vehicles, most vehicles have tamperproof devices fitted to the main adjustment points of the fuel system. These devices are primarily designed to prevent unqualified persons from adjusting the fuel/air mixture, with the chance of a consequent increase in toxic emissions. If such devices are found during servicing or overhaul, they should, wherever possible, be renewed or refitted in accordance with the manufacturer's requirements or current legislation.

OIL CARE
FOLLOW THE CODE

OIL BANK LINE
0800 66 33 66
www.oilbankline.org.uk

Note: It is antisocial and illegal to dump oil down the drain. To find the location of your local oil recycling bank, call this number free.

FRONT

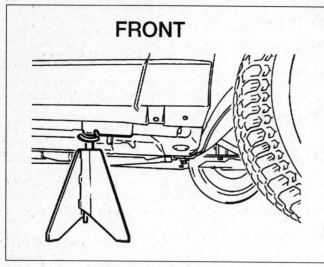

Location points for axle stands – front

REAR

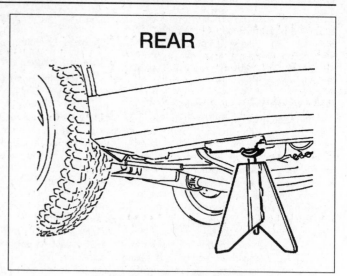

Location points for axle stands – rear

The jack supplied with the vehicle should only be used for changing the roadwheels – see *Wheel changing* at the front of this manual. When carrying out any other kind of work, raise the vehicle using a hydraulic (or 'trolley') jack, and always supplement the jack with axle stands at the vehicle jacking points.

When using a hydraulic jack or axle stands, always position the jack head or axle stand head under one of the relevant jacking points in the ridge on the underside of the sill **(see illustrations)**.

To raise the front of the vehicle, position the jack with an interposed block of wood underneath the centre of the front subframe **(see illustration)**. **Do not** jack the vehicle under the sump, or any of the steering or suspension components.

To raise the rear of the vehicle, position the jack head underneath the centre of the rear axle tubular crossmember **(see illustration)**. **Do not** attempt to raise the vehicle with the jack positioned underneath the spare wheel, as the vehicle floor will almost certainly be damaged.

Never work under, around, or near a raised vehicle, unless it is adequately supported in at least two places.

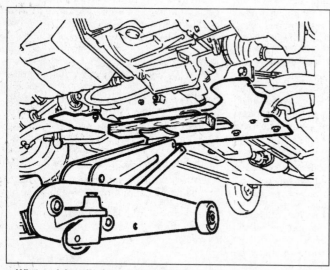

When raising the front of the vehicle, locate the jack under the centre of the front subframe

Note the use of the block of wood placed on the jack head

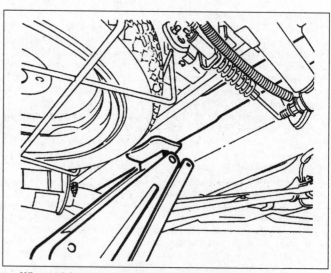

When raising the rear of the vehicle, position the jack head underneath the rear axle tubular crossmember

Numerous systems fitted to the vehicle require battery power to be available at all times, either to ensure their continued operation (such as the clock) or to maintain control unit memories which would be erased if the battery were to be disconnected. Whenever the battery is to be disconnected therefore, first note the following, to ensure that there are no unforeseen consequences of this action:

a) *First, on any vehicle with central locking, it is a wise precaution to remove the key from the ignition, and to keep it with you, so that it does not get locked in if the central locking should engage accidentally when the battery is reconnected.*

b) *The majority of models covered in this manual are equipped with a Citroën anti-theft alarm system. When reconnecting the battery after disconnection, the alarm may be automatically activated. If so, use the remote transmitter to turn off the alarm, or turn off the alarm manually by switching on the ignition. To fully reactivate the system once the battery is reconnected, lock then unlock the vehicle using the remote transmitter; the alarm will be functional again the next time the vehicle is locked with the remote transmitter.*

c) *If a security-coded audio unit is fitted, and the unit and/or the battery is disconnected, the unit will not function again on reconnection until the correct security code is entered. Details of this procedure, which varies according to the*

unit fitted, *are given in the vehicle owner's handbook. Ensure you have the correct code before you disconnect the battery. If you do not have the code or details of the correct procedure, but can supply proof of ownership and a legitimate reason for wanting this information, a Citroën dealer may be able to help.*

d) *On all engines, the engine management electronic control unit is of the 'self-learning' type, meaning that as it operates, it also monitors and stores the settings which give optimum engine performance under all operating conditions. When the battery is disconnected, these settings are lost and the ECU reverts to the base settings programmed into its memory at the factory. On restarting, this may lead to the engine running/idling roughly for a short while, until the ECU has relearned the optimum settings. This process is best accomplished by taking the vehicle on a road test (for approximately 15 minutes), covering all engine speeds and loads, concentrating mainly in the 2500 to 3500 rpm region.*

e) *On all models, when reconnecting the battery after disconnection, switch on the ignition and wait 10 seconds to allow the electronic vehicle systems to stabilise and re-initialise.*

Devices known as 'memory-savers' (or 'code-savers') can be used to avoid some of the above problems. Precise details vary according to the device used. Typically, it is plugged into the cigarette lighter, and is connected by its own wires to a spare battery; the vehicle's own battery is then disconnected from the electrical system, leaving the 'memory-saver' to pass sufficient current to maintain audio unit security codes and any other memory values, and also to run permanently-live circuits such as the clock.

⚠️ *Warning: Some of these devices allow a considerable amount of current to pass, which can mean that many of the vehicle's systems are still operational when the main battery is disconnected. If a 'memory saver' is used, ensure that the circuit concerned is actually 'dead' before carrying out any work on it.*

Disconnecting the negative (earth) lead

1 The battery is located inside the car under the left-hand front seat. To gain access, move the front seat fully rearward then depress the locking catches located at the rear of the seat on each side **(see illustration)**.

2 Tip the seat forward then release the locking clip on the top of the battery cover. Lift off the cover for access to the battery **(see illustration)**.

3 Disconnect the lead at the battery negative (earth) terminal. Two possible types of battery negative terminal fixings may be encountered. With the first type, the lead is secured to a stud on the top of the terminal by means of a green coloured plastic-capped nut **(see illustration)**. On the second type a conventional fitting is used, secured in position by a clamp bolt and nut.

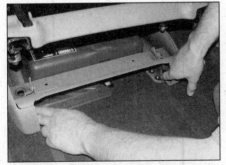

Move the front seat fully rearward then depress the locking catches located at the rear of the seat on each side

Tip the seat forward, release the locking clip on the top of the battery cover and lift off the cover

Battery quick-release positive terminal (left) and capped-nut type negative terminal (right)

Introduction

A selection of good tools is a fundamental requirement for anyone contemplating the maintenance and repair of a motor vehicle. For the owner who does not possess any, their purchase will prove a considerable expense, offsetting some of the savings made by doing-it-yourself. However, provided that the tools purchased meet the relevant national safety standards and are of good quality, they will last for many years and prove an extremely worthwhile investment.

To help the average owner to decide which tools are needed to carry out the various tasks detailed in this manual, we have compiled three lists of tools under the following headings: *Maintenance and minor repair*, *Repair and overhaul*, and *Special*. Newcomers to practical mechanics should start off with the *Maintenance and minor repair* tool kit, and confine themselves to the simpler jobs around the vehicle. Then, as confidence and experience grow, more difficult tasks can be undertaken, with extra tools being purchased as, and when, they are needed. In this way, a *Maintenance and minor repair* tool kit can be built up into a *Repair and overhaul* tool kit over a considerable period of time, without any major cash outlays. The experienced do-it-yourselfer will have a tool kit good enough for most repair and overhaul procedures, and will add tools from the *Special* category when it is felt that the expense is justified by the amount of use to which these tools will be put.

Maintenance and minor repair tool kit

The tools given in this list should be considered as a minimum requirement if routine maintenance, servicing and minor repair operations are to be undertaken. We recommend the purchase of combination spanners (ring one end, open-ended the other); although more expensive than open-ended ones, they do give the advantages of both types of spanner.

☐ *Combination spanners:*
Metric - 8 to 19 mm inclusive
☐ *Adjustable spanner - 35 mm jaw (approx.)*
☐ *Spark plug spanner (with rubber insert) - petrol models*
☐ *Spark plug gap adjustment tool - petrol models*
☐ *Set of feeler gauges*
☐ *Brake bleed nipple spanner*
☐ *Screwdrivers:*
Flat blade - 100 mm long x 6 mm dia
Cross blade - 100 mm long x 6 mm dia
Torx - various sizes (not all vehicles)
☐ *Combination pliers*
☐ *Hacksaw (junior)*
☐ *Tyre pump*
☐ *Tyre pressure gauge*
☐ *Oil can*
☐ *Oil filter removal tool*
☐ *Fine emery cloth*
☐ *Wire brush (small)*
☐ *Funnel (medium size)*
☐ *Sump drain plug key (not all vehicles)*

Repair and overhaul tool kit

These tools are virtually essential for anyone undertaking any major repairs to a motor vehicle, and are additional to those given in the *Maintenance and minor repair* list. Included in this list is a comprehensive set of sockets. Although these are expensive, they will be found invaluable as they are so versatile - particularly if various drives are included in the set. We recommend the half-inch square-drive type, as this can be used with most proprietary torque wrenches.

The tools in this list will sometimes need to be supplemented by tools from the *Special* list:

☐ *Sockets (or box spanners) to cover range in previous list (including Torx sockets)*
☐ *Reversible ratchet drive (for use with sockets)*
☐ *Extension piece, 250 mm (for use with sockets)*
☐ *Universal joint (for use with sockets)*
☐ *Flexible handle or sliding T "breaker bar" (for use with sockets)*
☐ *Torque wrench (for use with sockets)*
☐ *Self-locking grips*
☐ *Ball pein hammer*
☐ *Soft-faced mallet (plastic or rubber)*
☐ *Screwdrivers:*
Flat blade - long & sturdy, short (chubby), and narrow (electrician's) types
Cross blade – long & sturdy, and short (chubby) types
☐ *Pliers:*
Long-nosed
Side cutters (electrician's)
Circlip (internal and external)
☐ *Cold chisel - 25 mm*
☐ *Scriber*
☐ *Scraper*
☐ *Centre-punch*
☐ *Pin punch*
☐ *Hacksaw*
☐ *Brake hose clamp*
☐ *Brake/clutch bleeding kit*
☐ *Selection of twist drills*
☐ *Steel rule/straight-edge*
☐ *Allen keys (inc. splined/Torx type)*
☐ *Selection of files*
☐ *Wire brush*
☐ *Axle stands*
☐ *Jack (strong trolley or hydraulic type)*
☐ *Light with extension lead*
☐ *Universal electrical multi-meter*

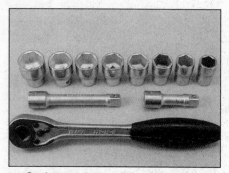

Sockets and reversible ratchet drive

Brake bleeding kit

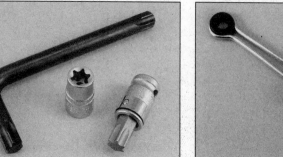

Torx key, socket and bit

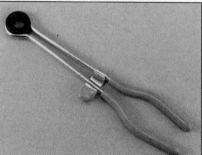

Hose clamp

Angular-tightening gauge

Special tools

The tools in this list are those which are not used regularly, are expensive to buy, or which need to be used in accordance with their manufacturers' instructions. Unless relatively difficult mechanical jobs are undertaken frequently, it will not be economic to buy many of these tools. Where this is the case, you could consider clubbing together with friends (or joining a motorists' club) to make a joint purchase, or borrowing the tools against a deposit from a local garage or tool hire specialist. It is worth noting that many of the larger DIY superstores now carry a large range of special tools for hire at modest rates.

The following list contains only those tools and instruments freely available to the public, and not those special tools produced by the vehicle manufacturer specifically for its dealer network. You will find occasional references to these manufacturers' special tools in the text of this manual. Generally, an alternative method of doing the job without the vehicle manufacturers' special tool is given. However, sometimes there is no alternative to using them. Where this is the case and the relevant tool cannot be bought or borrowed, you will have to entrust the work to a dealer.

☐ Angular-tightening gauge
☐ Valve spring compressor
☐ Valve grinding tool
☐ Piston ring compressor
☐ Piston ring removal/installation tool
☐ Cylinder bore hone
☐ Balljoint separator
☐ Coil spring compressors (where applicable)
☐ Two/three-legged hub and bearing puller
☐ Impact screwdriver
☐ Micrometer and/or vernier calipers
☐ Dial gauge
☐ Stroboscopic timing light
☐ Dwell angle meter/tachometer
☐ Fault code reader
☐ Cylinder compression gauge
☐ Hand-operated vacuum pump and gauge
☐ Clutch plate alignment set
☐ Brake shoe steady spring cup removal tool
☐ Bush and bearing removal/installation set
☐ Stud extractors
☐ Tap and die set
☐ Lifting tackle
☐ Trolley jack

Buying tools

Reputable motor accessory shops and superstores often offer excellent quality tools at discount prices, so it pays to shop around.

Remember, you don't have to buy the most expensive items on the shelf, but it is always advisable to steer clear of the very cheap tools. Beware of 'bargains' offered on market stalls or at car boot sales. There are plenty of good tools around at reasonable prices, but always aim to purchase items which meet the relevant national safety standards. If in doubt, ask the proprietor or manager of the shop for advice before making a purchase.

Care and maintenance of tools

Having purchased a reasonable tool kit, it is necessary to keep the tools in a clean and serviceable condition. After use, always wipe off any dirt, grease and metal particles using a clean, dry cloth, before putting the tools away. Never leave them lying around after they have been used. A simple tool rack on the garage or workshop wall for items such as screwdrivers and pliers is a good idea. Store all normal spanners and sockets in a metal box. Any measuring instruments, gauges, meters, etc, must be carefully stored where they cannot be damaged or become rusty.

Take a little care when tools are used. Hammer heads inevitably become marked, and screwdrivers lose the keen edge on their blades from time to time. A little timely attention with emery cloth or a file will soon restore items like this to a good finish.

Working facilities

Not to be forgotten when discussing tools is the workshop itself. If anything more than routine maintenance is to be carried out, a suitable working area becomes essential.

It is appreciated that many an owner-mechanic is forced by circumstances to remove an engine or similar item without the benefit of a garage or workshop. Having done this, any repairs should always be done under the cover of a roof.

Wherever possible, any dismantling should be done on a clean, flat workbench or table at a suitable working height.

Any workbench needs a vice; one with a jaw opening of 100 mm is suitable for most jobs. As mentioned previously, some clean dry storage space is also required for tools, as well as for any lubricants, cleaning fluids, touch-up paints etc, which become necessary.

Another item which may be required, and which has a much more general usage, is an electric drill with a chuck capacity of at least 8 mm. This, together with a good range of twist drills, is virtually essential for fitting accessories.

Last, but not least, always keep a supply of old newspapers and clean, lint-free rags available, and try to keep any working area as clean as possible.

Micrometers

Dial test indicator ("dial gauge")

Strap wrench

Compression tester

Fault code reader

This is a guide to getting your vehicle through the MOT test. Obviously it will not be possible to examine the vehicle to the same standard as the professional MOT tester. However, working through the following checks will enable you to identify any problem areas before submitting the vehicle for the test.

Where a testable component is in borderline condition, the tester has discretion in deciding whether to pass or fail it. The basis of such discretion is whether the tester would be happy for a close relative or friend to use the vehicle with the component in that condition. If the vehicle presented is clean and evidently well cared for, the tester may be more inclined to pass a borderline component than if the vehicle is scruffy and apparently neglected.

It has only been possible to summarise the test requirements here, based on the regulations in force at the time of printing. Test standards are becoming increasingly stringent, although there are some exemptions for older vehicles.

An assistant will be needed to help carry out some of these checks.

The checks have been sub-divided into four categories, as follows:

1 Checks carried out **FROM THE DRIVER'S SEAT**

2 Checks carried out **WITH THE VEHICLE ON THE GROUND**

3 Checks carried out **WITH THE VEHICLE RAISED AND THE WHEELS FREE TO TURN**

4 Checks carried out on **YOUR VEHICLE'S EXHAUST EMISSION SYSTEM**

---

1 Checks carried out **FROM THE DRIVER'S SEAT**

Handbrake

☐ Test the operation of the handbrake. Excessive travel (too many clicks) indicates incorrect brake or cable adjustment.

☐ Check that the handbrake cannot be released by tapping the lever sideways. Check the security of the lever mountings.

Footbrake

☐ Depress the brake pedal and check that it does not creep down to the floor, indicating a master cylinder fault. Release the pedal, wait a few seconds, then depress it again. If the pedal travels nearly to the floor before firm resistance is felt, brake adjustment or repair is necessary. If the pedal feels spongy, there is air in the hydraulic system which must be removed by bleeding.

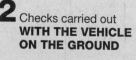

☐ Check that the brake pedal is secure and in good condition. Check also for signs of fluid leaks on the pedal, floor or carpets, which would indicate failed seals in the brake master cylinder.

☐ Check the servo unit (when applicable) by operating the brake pedal several times, then keeping the pedal depressed and starting the engine. As the engine starts, the pedal will move down slightly. If not, the vacuum hose or the servo itself may be faulty.

Steering wheel and column

☐ Examine the steering wheel for fractures or looseness of the hub, spokes or rim.

☐ Move the steering wheel from side to side and then up and down. Check that the steering wheel is not loose on the column, indicating wear or a loose retaining nut. Continue moving the steering wheel as before, but also turn it slightly from left to right.

☐ Check that the steering wheel is not loose on the column, and that there is no abnormal

movement of the steering wheel, indicating wear in the column support bearings or couplings.

Windscreen, mirrors and sunvisor

☐ The windscreen must be free of cracks or other significant damage within the driver's field of view. (Small stone chips are acceptable.) Rear view mirrors must be secure, intact, and capable of being adjusted.

290mm

☐ The driver's sunvisor must be capable of being stored in the "up" position.

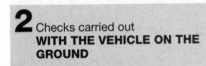

Seat belts and seats

Note: *The following checks are applicable to all seat belts, front and rear.*

☐ Examine the webbing of all the belts (including rear belts if fitted) for cuts, serious fraying or deterioration. Fasten and unfasten each belt to check the buckles. If applicable, check the retracting mechanism. Check the security of all seat belt mountings accessible from inside the vehicle.

☐ Seat belts with pre-tensioners, once activated, have a "flag" or similar showing on the seat belt stalk. This, in itself, is not a reason for test failure.

☐ The front seats themselves must be securely attached and the backrests must lock in the upright position.

Doors

☐ Both front doors must be able to be opened and closed from outside and inside, and must latch securely when closed.

2 Checks carried out WITH THE VEHICLE ON THE GROUND

Vehicle identification

☐ Number plates must be in good condition, secure and legible, with letters and numbers correctly spaced – spacing at (A) should be at least twice that at (B).

☐ The VIN plate and/or homologation plate must be legible.

Electrical equipment

☐ Switch on the ignition and check the operation of the horn.

☐ Check the windscreen washers and wipers, examining the wiper blades; renew damaged or perished blades. Also check the operation of the stop-lights.

☐ Check the operation of the sidelights and number plate lights. The lenses and reflectors must be secure, clean and undamaged.

☐ Check the operation and alignment of the headlights. The headlight reflectors must not be tarnished and the lenses must be undamaged.

☐ Switch on the ignition and check the operation of the direction indicators (including the instrument panel tell-tale) and the hazard warning lights. Operation of the sidelights and stop-lights must not affect the indicators - if it does, the cause is usually a bad earth at the rear light cluster.

☐ Check the operation of the rear foglight(s), including the warning light on the instrument panel or in the switch.

☐ The ABS warning light must illuminate in accordance with the manufacturers' design. For most vehicles, the ABS warning light should illuminate when the ignition is switched on, and (if the system is operating properly) extinguish after a few seconds. Refer to the owner's handbook.

Footbrake

☐ Examine the master cylinder, brake pipes and servo unit for leaks, loose mountings, corrosion or other damage.

☐ The fluid reservoir must be secure and the fluid level must be between the upper (**A**) and lower (**B**) markings.

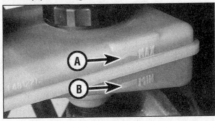

☐ Inspect both front brake flexible hoses for cracks or deterioration of the rubber. Turn the steering from lock to lock, and ensure that the hoses do not contact the wheel, tyre, or any part of the steering or suspension mechanism. With the brake pedal firmly depressed, check the hoses for bulges or leaks under pressure.

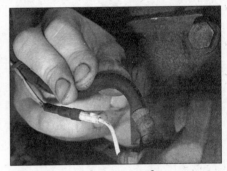

Steering and suspension

☐ Have your assistant turn the steering wheel from side to side slightly, up to the point where the steering gear just begins to transmit this movement to the roadwheels. Check for excessive free play between the steering wheel and the steering gear, indicating wear or insecurity of the steering column joints, the column-to-steering gear coupling, or the steering gear itself.

☐ Have your assistant turn the steering wheel more vigorously in each direction, so that the roadwheels just begin to turn. As this is done, examine all the steering joints, linkages, fittings and attachments. Renew any component that shows signs of wear or damage. On vehicles with power steering, check the security and condition of the steering pump, drivebelt and hoses.

☐ Check that the vehicle is standing level, and at approximately the correct ride height.

Shock absorbers

☐ Depress each corner of the vehicle in turn, then release it. The vehicle should rise and then settle in its normal position. If the vehicle continues to rise and fall, the shock absorber is defective. A shock absorber which has seized will also cause the vehicle to fail.

Exhaust system

☐ Start the engine. With your assistant holding a rag over the tailpipe, check the entire system for leaks. Repair or renew leaking sections.

3 Checks carried out **WITH THE VEHICLE RAISED AND THE WHEELS FREE TO TURN**

Jack up the front and rear of the vehicle, and securely support it on axle stands. Position the stands clear of the suspension assemblies. Ensure that the wheels are clear of the ground and that the steering can be turned from lock to lock.

Steering mechanism

☐ Have your assistant turn the steering from lock to lock. Check that the steering turns smoothly, and that no part of the steering mechanism, including a wheel or tyre, fouls any brake hose or pipe or any part of the body structure.

☐ Examine the steering rack rubber gaiters for damage or insecurity of the retaining clips. If power steering is fitted, check for signs of damage or leakage of the fluid hoses, pipes or connections. Also check for excessive stiffness or binding of the steering, a missing split pin or locking device, or severe corrosion of the body structure within 30 cm of any steering component attachment point.

Front and rear suspension and wheel bearings

☐ Starting at the front right-hand side, grasp the roadwheel at the 3 o'clock and 9 o'clock positions and rock gently but firmly. Check for free play or insecurity at the wheel bearings, suspension balljoints, or suspension mountings, pivots and attachments.

☐ Now grasp the wheel at the 12 o'clock and 6 o'clock positions and repeat the previous inspection. Spin the wheel, and check for roughness or tightness of the front wheel bearing.

☐ If excess free play is suspected at a component pivot point, this can be confirmed by using a large screwdriver or similar tool and levering between the mounting and the component attachment. This will confirm whether the wear is in the pivot bush, its retaining bolt, or in the mounting itself (the bolt holes can often become elongated).

☐ Carry out all the above checks at the other front wheel, and then at both rear wheels.

Springs and shock absorbers

☐ Examine the suspension struts (when applicable) for serious fluid leakage, corrosion, or damage to the casing. Also check the security of the mounting points.

☐ If coil springs are fitted, check that the spring ends locate in their seats, and that the spring is not corroded, cracked or broken.

☐ If leaf springs are fitted, check that all leaves are intact, that the axle is securely attached to each spring, and that there is no deterioration of the spring eye mountings, bushes, and shackles.

☐ The same general checks apply to vehicles fitted with other suspension types, such as torsion bars, hydraulic displacer units, etc. Ensure that all mountings and attachments are secure, that there are no signs of excessive wear, corrosion or damage, and (on hydraulic types) that there are no fluid leaks or damaged pipes.

☐ Inspect the shock absorbers for signs of serious fluid leakage. Check for wear of the mounting bushes or attachments, or damage to the body of the unit.

Driveshafts (fwd vehicles only)

☐ Rotate each front wheel in turn and inspect the constant velocity joint gaiters for splits or damage. Also check that each driveshaft is straight and undamaged.

Braking system

☐ If possible without dismantling, check brake pad wear and disc condition. Ensure that the friction lining material has not worn excessively, (A) and that the discs are not fractured, pitted, scored or badly worn (B).

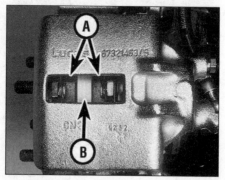

☐ Examine all the rigid brake pipes underneath the vehicle, and the flexible hose(s) at the rear. Look for corrosion, chafing or insecurity of the pipes, and for signs of bulging under pressure, chafing, splits or deterioration of the flexible hoses.

☐ Look for signs of fluid leaks at the brake calipers or on the brake backplates. Repair or renew leaking components.

☐ Slowly spin each wheel, while your assistant depresses and releases the footbrake. Ensure that each brake is operating and does not bind when the pedal is released.

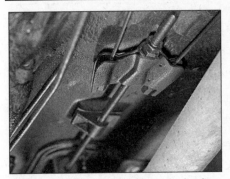

☐ Examine the handbrake mechanism, checking for frayed or broken cables, excessive corrosion, or wear or insecurity of the linkage. Check that the mechanism works on each relevant wheel, and releases fully, without binding.

☐ It is not possible to test brake efficiency without special equipment, but a road test can be carried out later to check that the vehicle pulls up in a straight line.

Fuel and exhaust systems

☐ Inspect the fuel tank (including the filler cap), fuel pipes, hoses and unions. All components must be secure and free from leaks.

☐ Examine the exhaust system over its entire length, checking for any damaged, broken or missing mountings, security of the retaining clamps and rust or corrosion.

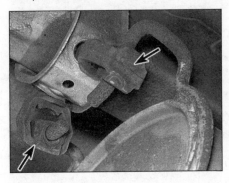

Wheels and tyres

☐ Examine the sidewalls and tread area of each tyre in turn. Check for cuts, tears, lumps, bulges, separation of the tread, and exposure of the ply or cord due to wear or damage. Check that the tyre bead is correctly seated on the wheel rim, that the valve is sound and properly seated, and that the wheel is not distorted or damaged.

☐ Check that the tyres are of the correct size for the vehicle, that they are of the same size and type on each axle, and that the pressures are correct.

☐ Check the tyre tread depth. The legal minimum at the time of writing is 1.6 mm over at least three-quarters of the tread width. Abnormal tread wear may indicate incorrect front wheel alignment.

Body corrosion

☐ Check the condition of the entire vehicle structure for signs of corrosion in load-bearing areas. (These include chassis box sections, side sills, cross-members, pillars, and all suspension, steering, braking system and seat belt mountings and anchorages.) Any corrosion which has seriously reduced the thickness of a load-bearing area is likely to cause the vehicle to fail. In this case professional repairs are likely to be needed.

☐ Damage or corrosion which causes sharp or otherwise dangerous edges to be exposed will also cause the vehicle to fail.

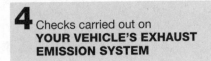

4 Checks carried out on **YOUR VEHICLE'S EXHAUST EMISSION SYSTEM**

Petrol models

☐ Have the engine at normal operating temperature, and make sure that it is in good tune (ignition system in good order, air filter element clean, etc).

☐ Before any measurements are carried out, raise the engine speed to around 2500 rpm, and hold it at this speed for 20 seconds. Allow the engine speed to return to idle, and watch for smoke emissions from the exhaust tailpipe. If the idle speed is obviously much too high, or if dense blue or clearly-visible black smoke comes from the tailpipe for more than 5 seconds, the vehicle will fail. As a rule of thumb, blue smoke signifies oil being burnt (engine wear) while black smoke signifies unburnt fuel (dirty air cleaner element, or other carburettor or fuel system fault).

☐ An exhaust gas analyser capable of measuring carbon monoxide (CO) and hydrocarbons (HC) is now needed. If such an instrument cannot be hired or borrowed, a local garage may agree to perform the check for a small fee.

CO emissions (mixture)

☐ At the time of writing, for vehicles first used between 1st August 1975 and 31st July 1986 (P to C registration), the CO level must not exceed 4.5% by volume. For vehicles first used between 1st August 1986 and 31st July 1992 (D to J registration), the CO level must not exceed 3.5% by volume. Vehicles first

used after 1st August 1992 (K registration) must conform to the manufacturer's specification. The MOT tester has access to a DOT database or emissions handbook, which lists the CO and HC limits for each make and model of vehicle. The CO level is measured with the engine at idle speed, and at "fast idle". The following limits are given as a general guide:

At idle speed -
CO level no more than 0.5%
At "fast idle" (2500 to 3000 rpm) -
CO level no more than 0.3%
(Minimum oil temperature 60ºC)

☐ If the CO level cannot be reduced far enough to pass the test (and the fuel and ignition systems are otherwise in good condition) then the carburettor is badly worn, or there is some problem in the fuel injection system or catalytic converter (as applicable).

HC emissions

☐ With the CO within limits, HC emissions for vehicles first used between 1st August 1975 and 31st July 1992 (P to J registration) must not exceed 1200 ppm. Vehicles first used after 1st August 1992 (K registration) must conform to the manufacturer's specification. The MOT tester has access to a DOT database or emissions handbook, which lists the CO and HC limits for each make and model of vehicle. The HC level is measured with the engine at "fast idle". The following is given as a general guide:

At "fast idle" (2500 to 3000 rpm) -
HC level no more than 200 ppm
(Minimum oil temperature 60ºC)

☐ Excessive HC emissions are caused by incomplete combustion, the causes of which can include oil being burnt, mechanical wear and ignition/fuel system malfunction.

Diesel models

☐ The only emission test applicable to Diesel engines is the measuring of exhaust smoke density. The test involves accelerating the engine several times to its maximum unloaded speed.

Note: *It is of the utmost importance that the engine timing belt is in good condition before the test is carried out.*

☐ The limits for Diesel engine exhaust smoke, introduced in September 1995 are:
Vehicles first used before 1st August 1979:
Exempt from metered smoke testing, but must not emit "dense blue or clearly visible black smoke for a period of more than 5 seconds at idle" or "dense blue or clearly visible black smoke during acceleration which would obscure the view of other road users".
Non-turbocharged vehicles first used after 1st August 1979: 2.5m⁻¹
Turbocharged vehicles first used after 1st August 1979: 3.0m⁻¹

☐ Excessive smoke can be caused by a dirty air cleaner element. Otherwise, professional advice may be needed to find the cause.

Engine

- Engine fails to rotate when attempting to start
- Engine rotates, but will not start
- Engine difficult to start when cold
- Engine difficult to start when hot
- Starter motor noisy or excessively-rough in engagement
- Engine starts, but stops immediately
- Engine idles erratically
- Engine misfires at idle speed
- Engine misfires throughout the driving speed range
- Engine hesitates on acceleration
- Engine stalls
- Engine lacks power
- Engine backfires
- Oil pressure warning light on with engine running
- Engine runs-on after switching off
- Engine noises

Cooling system

- Overheating
- Overcooling
- External coolant leakage
- Internal coolant leakage
- Corrosion

Fuel and exhaust systems

- Excessive fuel consumption
- Fuel leakage and/or fuel odour
- Excessive noise or fumes from exhaust system

Clutch

- Pedal travels to floor – no pressure or very little resistance
- Clutch fails to disengage (unable to select gears)
- Clutch slips (engine speed rises, with no increase in vehicle speed)
- Judder as clutch is engaged
- Noise when depressing or releasing clutch pedal

Transmission

- Noisy in neutral with engine running
- Noisy in one particular gear
- Difficulty engaging gears
- Jumps out of gear
- Vibration
- Lubricant leaks

Driveshafts

- Clicking or knocking noise on turns (at slow speed on full-lock)
- Vibration when accelerating or decelerating

Braking system

- Vehicle pulls to one side under braking
- Noise (grinding or high-pitched squeal) when brakes applied
- Excessive brake pedal travel
- Brake pedal feels spongy when depressed
- Excessive brake pedal effort required to stop vehicle
- Judder felt through brake pedal or steering wheel when braking
- Brakes binding
- Rear wheels locking under normal braking

Suspension and steering systems

- Vehicle pulls to one side
- Wheel wobble and vibration
- Excessive pitching and/or rolling around corners, or during braking
- Wandering or general instability
- Excessively-stiff steering
- Excessive play in steering
- Lack of power assistance
- Tyre wear excessive

Electrical system

- Battery will not hold a charge for more than a few days
- Ignition/no-charge warning light stays on with engine running
- Ignition/no-charge warning light fails to come on
- Lights inoperative
- Instrument readings inaccurate or erratic
- Horn inoperative, or unsatisfactory in operation
- Windscreen/tailgate wipers failed, or unsatisfactory in operation
- Windscreen/tailgate washers failed, or unsatisfactory in operation
- Electric windows inoperative, or unsatisfactory in operation
- Central locking system inoperative, or unsatisfactory in operation

Introduction

The vehicle owner who does his or her own maintenance according to the recommended service schedules should not have to use this section of the manual very often. Modern component reliability is such that, provided those items subject to wear or deterioration are inspected or renewed at the specified intervals, sudden failure is comparatively rare. Faults do not usually just happen as a result of sudden failure, but develop over a period of time. Major mechanical failures in particular are usually preceded by characteristic symptoms over hundreds or even thousands of miles. Those components which do occasionally fail without warning are often small and easily carried in the vehicle.

With any fault-finding, the first step is to decide where to begin investigations. This may

be obvious, but some detective work may be necessary. The owner who makes half a dozen haphazard adjustments or replacements may be successful in curing a fault (or its symptoms), but will be none the wiser if the fault recurs, and ultimately may have spent more time and money than was necessary. A calm and logical approach will be found to be more satisfactory in the long run. Always take into account any warning signs that may have been noticed in the period preceding the fault – power loss, high or low gauge readings, unusual smells, etc – and remember – failure of components such as fuses or spark plugs may only be pointers to some underlying fault.

The pages which follow provide an easy-reference guide to the more common problems which may occur during the

operation of the vehicle. These problems and their possible causes are grouped under headings denoting various components or systems, such as Engine, Cooling system, etc. The Chapter which deals with the problem is shown in brackets, but in some instances it will be necessary to refer to the specific Chapter Part, depending on model or system, as applicable. Some problems may be more obvious, such as loose or disconnected wiring, and in these instances a Chapter reference may not be given as the problem can be simply overcome by dealing with the fault as it stands. Whatever the problem, certain basic principles apply. These are as follows:

Verify the fault. This is simply a matter of being sure that you know what the symptoms are before starting work. This is particularly important if you are investigating a fault for someone else, who may not have described it very accurately.

Don't overlook the obvious. For example, if the vehicle won't start, is there fuel in the tank? (Don't take anyone else's word on this particular point, and don't trust the fuel gauge either!) If an electrical fault is indicated, look for loose or broken wires before digging out the test gear.

Cure the disease, not the symptom. Substituting a flat battery with a fully-charged one will get you off the hard shoulder, but if the underlying cause is not attended to, the new battery will go the same way. Similarly, changing oil-fouled spark plugs for a new set will get you moving again, but remember that the reason for the fouling (if it wasn't simply an incorrect grade of plug) will have to be established and corrected.

Don't take anything for granted. Particularly, don't forget that a 'new' component may itself be defective (especially if it's been rattling around in the boot for months), and don't leave components out of a fault diagnosis sequence just because they are new or recently-fitted. When you do finally diagnose a difficult fault, you'll probably realise that all the evidence was there from the start.

Engine

Engine fails to rotate when attempting to start

☐ Battery terminal connections loose or corroded (*Weekly checks*).
☐ Battery discharged or faulty (Chapter 5).
☐ Broken, loose or disconnected wiring in the starting circuit (Chapter 5).
☐ Defective starter solenoid (Chapter 5).
☐ Defective starter motor (Chapter 5).
☐ Starter pinion or flywheel ring gear teeth loose or broken (Chapters 2 and 5).
☐ Engine earth strap broken or disconnected.

Engine rotates, but will not start

☐ Fuel tank empty.
☐ Battery discharged (engine rotates slowly) (Chapter 5).
☐ Battery terminal connections loose or corroded (*Weekly checks*).
☐ Broken, loose or disconnected wiring in the ignition circuit – petrol engine models (Chapters 1 and 5).
☐ Worn, faulty or incorrectly-gapped spark plugs – petrol engine models (Chapter 1).
☐ Preheating system faulty – diesel engine models (Chapter 5).
☐ Fuel injection or engine management system fault (Chapter 4).
☐ Ignition key not recognised by anti-theft system (Chapter 12)
☐ Major mechanical failure (eg camshaft drive) (Chapter 2).

Engine difficult to start when cold

☐ Battery discharged (Chapter 5).
☐ Battery terminal connections loose or corroded (*Weekly checks*).
☐ Worn, faulty or incorrectly-gapped spark plugs – petrol engine models (Chapter 1).
☐ Preheating system faulty – diesel models (Chapter 5).
☐ Fuel injection or engine management system fault (Chapter 4).
☐ Other ignition system fault – petrol engine models (Chapters 1 and 5).
☐ Low cylinder compressions (Chapter 2).

Engine difficult to start when hot

☐ Air filter element dirty or clogged (Chapter 1).
☐ Fuel injection or engine management system fault (Chapter 4).
☐ Low cylinder compressions (Chapter 2).

Starter motor noisy or excessively-rough in engagement

☐ Starter pinion or flywheel ring gear teeth loose or broken (Chapters 2 and 5).
☐ Starter motor mounting bolts loose or missing (Chapter 5).
☐ Starter motor internal components worn or damaged (Chapter 5).

Engine starts, but stops immediately

☐ Loose or faulty electrical connections in the ignition circuit – petrol engine models (Chapters 1 and 5).
☐ Vacuum leak at the throttle housing or inlet manifold – petrol engine models (Chapter 4).
☐ Blocked injector/fuel injection system fault – petrol engine models (Chapter 4).

Engine idles erratically

☐ Air filter element clogged (Chapter 1).
☐ Vacuum leak at the throttle housing, inlet manifold or associated hoses – petrol engine models (Chapter 4).
☐ Worn, faulty or incorrectly-gapped spark plugs – petrol engine models (Chapter 1).
☐ Uneven or low cylinder compressions (Chapter 2).
☐ Camshaft lobes worn (Chapter 2).
☐ Timing belt incorrectly fitted (Chapter 2).
☐ Blocked injector/fuel injection system fault (Chapter 4).

Engine misfires at idle speed

☐ Worn, faulty or incorrectly-gapped spark plugs – petrol engine models (Chapter 1).
☐ Vacuum leak at the throttle housing, inlet manifold or associated hoses – petrol engine models (Chapter 4).
☐ Blocked injector/fuel injection system fault (Chapter 4).
☐ Uneven or low cylinder compressions (Chapter 2).
☐ Disconnected, leaking, or perished crankcase ventilation hoses (Chapter 4).

Engine misfires throughout the driving speed range

☐ Fuel filter choked (Chapter 1).
☐ Fuel pump faulty, or delivery pressure low (Chapter 4).
☐ Fuel tank vent blocked, or fuel pipes restricted (Chapter 4).
☐ Vacuum leak at the throttle housing, inlet manifold or associated hoses – petrol engine models (Chapter 4).
☐ Worn, faulty or incorrectly-gapped spark plugs – petrol engine models (Chapter 1).
☐ Faulty ignition coil unit – petrol engine models (Chapter 5).
☐ Uneven or low cylinder compressions (Chapter 2).
☐ Blocked injector/fuel injection system fault (Chapter 4).

Engine (continued)

Engine hesitates on acceleration

- ☐ Worn, faulty or incorrectly-gapped spark plugs – petrol engine models (Chapter 1).
- ☐ Vacuum leak at the throttle housing, inlet manifold or associated hoses (Chapter 4).
- ☐ Blocked injector/fuel injection system fault (Chapter 4).

Engine stalls

- ☐ Vacuum leak at the throttle housing, inlet manifold or associated hoses – petrol engine models (Chapter 4).
- ☐ Fuel filter choked (Chapter 1).
- ☐ Fuel pump faulty, or delivery pressure low – petrol engine models (Chapter 4).
- ☐ Fuel tank vent blocked, or fuel pipes restricted (Chapter 4).
- ☐ Blocked injector/fuel injection system fault (Chapter 4).

Engine lacks power

- ☐ Timing belt incorrectly fitted or adjusted (Chapter 2).
- ☐ Fuel filter choked (Chapter 1).
- ☐ Fuel pump faulty, or delivery pressure low (Chapter 4).
- ☐ Uneven or low cylinder compressions (Chapter 2).
- ☐ Worn, faulty or incorrectly-gapped spark plugs – petrol engine models (Chapter 1).
- ☐ Vacuum leak at the throttle housing, inlet manifold or associated hoses – petrol engine models (Chapter 4).
- ☐ Blocked injector/fuel injection system fault (Chapter 4).
- ☐ Brakes binding (Chapters 1 and 9).
- ☐ Clutch slipping (Chapter 6).

Engine backfires

- ☐ Timing belt incorrectly fitted or adjusted (Chapter 2).
- ☐ Vacuum leak at the throttle housing, inlet manifold or associated hoses – petrol engine models (Chapter 4).
- ☐ Blocked injector/fuel injection system fault (Chapter 4).

Oil pressure warning light on with engine running

- ☐ Low oil level, or incorrect oil grade (Weekly checks).
- ☐ Faulty oil pressure warning light switch (Chapter 5).
- ☐ Worn engine bearings and/or oil pump (Chapter 2).
- ☐ High engine operating temperature (Chapter 3).
- ☐ Oil pressure relief valve defective (Chapter 2).
- ☐ Oil pick-up strainer clogged (Chapter 2).

Engine runs-on after switching off

- ☐ Excessive carbon build-up in engine (Chapter 2).
- ☐ High engine operating temperature (Chapter 3).
- ☐ Fuel injection or engine management system fault (Chapter 4).

Engine noises

Pre-ignition (pinking) or knocking during acceleration or under load

- ☐ Ignition or engine management system fault (Chapters 1 and 5).
- ☐ Incorrect grade of spark plug – petrol engine models (Chapter 1).
- ☐ Incorrect grade of fuel (Chapter 1).
- ☐ Vacuum leak at the throttle housing, inlet manifold or associated hoses – petrol engine models (Chapter 4).
- ☐ Excessive carbon build-up in engine (Chapter 2).
- ☐ Blocked injector/fuel injection system fault (Chapter 4).

Whistling or wheezing noises

- ☐ Leaking inlet manifold or throttle housing gasket – petrol engine models (Chapter 4).
- ☐ Leaking exhaust manifold gasket or pipe-to-manifold joint (Chapter 4).
- ☐ Leaking vacuum hose (Chapters 4, 5 and 9).
- ☐ Blowing cylinder head gasket (Chapter 2).

Tapping or rattling noises

- ☐ Worn valve gear or camshaft (Chapter 2).
- ☐ Ancillary component fault (coolant pump, alternator, etc) (Chapters 3, 5, etc).

Knocking or thumping noises

- ☐ Worn big-end bearings (regular heavy knocking, perhaps less under load) (Chapter 2).
- ☐ Worn main bearings (rumbling and knocking, perhaps worsening under load) (Chapter 2).
- ☐ Piston slap (most noticeable when cold) (Chapter 2).
- ☐ Ancillary component fault (coolant pump, alternator, etc) (Chapters 3, 5, etc).

Cooling system

Overheating

- ☐ Insufficient coolant in system (Weekly checks).
- ☐ Thermostat faulty (Chapter 3).
- ☐ Radiator core blocked, or grille restricted (Chapter 3).
- ☐ Electric cooling fan or thermoswitch faulty (Chapter 3).
- ☐ Pressure cap faulty (Chapter 3).
- ☐ Engine management system fault (Chapters 1 and 5).
- ☐ Inaccurate coolant temperature sensor (Chapter 3).
- ☐ Airlock in cooling system (Chapter 1).

Overcooling

- ☐ Thermostat faulty (Chapter 3).
- ☐ Inaccurate coolant temperature sensor (Chapter 3).

External coolant leakage

- ☐ Deteriorated or damaged hoses or hose clips (Chapter 1).
- ☐ Radiator core or heater matrix leaking (Chapter 3).
- ☐ Pressure cap faulty (Chapter 3).
- ☐ Coolant pump seal leaking (Chapter 3).
- ☐ Boiling due to overheating (Chapter 3).
- ☐ Core plug leaking (Chapter 2).

Internal coolant leakage

- ☐ Leaking cylinder head gasket (Chapter 2).
- ☐ Cracked cylinder head or cylinder bore (Chapter 2).

Corrosion

- ☐ Infrequent draining and flushing (Chapter 1).
- ☐ Incorrect coolant mixture or inappropriate coolant type (Chapter 1).

Fuel and exhaust systems

Excessive fuel consumption

☐ Air filter element dirty or clogged (Chapter 1).
☐ Fuel injection or engine management system fault (Chapter 4).
☐ Ignition system fault – petrol engine models (Chapters 1 and 5).
☐ Tyres under-inflated (*Weekly checks*).
☐ Brakes binding (Chapters 1 and 9).

Fuel leakage and/or fuel odour

☐ Damaged or corroded fuel tank, pipes or connections (Chapter 4).

Excessive noise or fumes from exhaust system

☐ Leaking exhaust system or manifold joints (Chapters 1 and 4).
☐ Leaking, corroded or damaged silencers or pipe (Chapters 1 and 4).
☐ Broken mountings causing body or suspension contact (Chapter 1).

Clutch

Pedal travels to floor – no pressure or very little resistance

☐ Broken clutch cable – where applicable (Chapter 6).
☐ Air in clutch hydraulic system – where applicable (Chapter 6).
☐ Faulty clutch master or slave cylinder – where applicable (Chapter 6).
☐ Broken clutch release bearing or fork (Chapter 6).
☐ Broken diaphragm spring in clutch pressure plate (Chapter 6).

Clutch fails to disengage (unable to select gears)

☐ Clutch friction plate on transmission input shaft splines (Chapter 6).
☐ Clutch friction plate sticking to flywheel or pressure plate (Chapter 6).
☐ Faulty pressure plate assembly (Chapter 6).
☐ Clutch release mechanism worn or incorrectly assembled (Chapter 6).

Clutch slips (engine speed rises, with no increase in vehicle speed)

☐ Clutch friction plate linings excessively worn (Chapter 6).
☐ Clutch friction plate linings contaminated with oil or grease (Chapter 6).
☐ Faulty pressure plate or weak diaphragm spring (Chapter 6).

Judder as clutch is engaged

☐ Clutch friction plate linings contaminated with oil or grease (Chapter 6).
☐ Clutch friction plate linings excessively worn (Chapter 6).
☐ Clutch cable sticking or frayed – where applicable (Chapter 6).
☐ Faulty or distorted pressure plate or diaphragm spring (Chapter 6).
☐ Worn or loose engine/transmission mountings (Chapter 2).
☐ Clutch friction plate hub or transmission input shaft splines worn (Chapter 6).

Noise when depressing or releasing clutch pedal

☐ Worn clutch release bearing (Chapter 6).
☐ Worn or dry clutch pedal bushes (Chap-ter 6).
☐ Faulty pressure plate assembly (Chapter 6).
☐ Pressure plate diaphragm spring broken (Chapter 6).
☐ Broken clutch friction plate cushioning springs (Chapter 6).

Transmission

Noisy in neutral with engine running

☐ Input shaft bearings worn (noise apparent with clutch pedal released, but not when depressed) (Chapter 7).*
☐ Clutch release bearing worn (noise apparent with clutch pedal depressed, possibly less when released) (Chapter 6).

Noisy in one particular gear

☐ Worn, damaged or chipped gear teeth (Chapter 7).*

Difficulty engaging gears

☐ Clutch fault (Chapter 6).
☐ Worn or damaged gear linkage (Chapter 7).
☐ Incorrectly-adjusted gear linkage (Chap-ter 7).
☐ Worn synchroniser units (Chapter 7).*

Jumps out of gear

☐ Worn or damaged gear linkage (Chapter 7).
☐ Worn synchroniser units (Chapter 7).*
☐ Worn selector forks (Chapter 7).*

Vibration

☐ Lack of oil (Chapter 1).
☐ Worn bearings (Chapter 7).*

Lubricant leaks

☐ Leaking driveshaft oil seal (Chapter 7).
☐ Leaking housing joint (Chapter 7).*
☐ Leaking input shaft oil seal (Chapter 7).

Although the corrective action necessary to remedy the symptoms described is beyond the scope of the home mechanic, the above information should be helpful in isolating the cause of the condition, so that the owner can communicate clearly with a professional mechanic.

Driveshafts

Clicking or knocking noise on turns (at slow speed on full-lock)

☐ Lack of constant velocity joint lubricant, possibly due to damaged gaiter (Chapter 8).
☐ Worn outer constant velocity joint (Chapter 8).

Vibration when accelerating or decelerating

☐ Worn inner constant velocity joint (Chapter 8).
☐ Bent or distorted driveshaft (Chapter 8).
☐ Worn driveshaft intermediate bearing (Chapter 8).

Braking system

Note: *Before assuming that a brake problem exists, make sure that the tyres are in good condition and correctly inflated, that the front wheel alignment is correct, and that the vehicle is not loaded with weight in an unequal manner. Apart from checking the condition of all pipe and hose connections, any faults occurring on the anti-lock braking system should be referred to a Citroën dealer for diagnosis.*

Vehicle pulls to one side under braking

☐ Worn, defective, damaged or contaminated brake pads/shoes on one side (Chapters 1 and 9).
☐ Seized or partially-seized front brake caliper/wheel cylinder piston (Chapters 1 and 9).
☐ A mixture of brake pad/shoe lining materials fitted between sides (Chapters 1 and 9).
☐ Brake caliper or backplate mounting bolts loose (Chapter 9).
☐ Worn or damaged steering or suspension components (Chapters 1 and 10).

Noise (grinding or high-pitched squeal) when brakes applied

☐ Brake pad or shoe friction lining material worn down to metal backing (Chapters 1 and 9).
☐ Excessive corrosion of brake disc or drum. May be apparent after the vehicle has been standing for some time (Chapters 1 and 9).
☐ Foreign object (stone chipping, etc) trapped between brake disc and caliper (Chapters 1 and 9).

Excessive brake pedal travel

☐ Inoperative rear brake self-adjust mechanism (Chapters 1 and 9).
☐ Faulty master cylinder (Chapter 9).
☐ Air in hydraulic system (Chapters 1 and 9).
☐ Faulty vacuum servo unit (Chapter 9).

Brake pedal feels spongy when depressed

☐ Air in hydraulic system (Chapters 1 and 9).
☐ Deteriorated flexible rubber brake hoses (Chapters 1 and 9).
☐ Master cylinder mounting nuts loose (Chapter 9).
☐ Faulty master cylinder (Chapter 9).

Excessive brake pedal effort required to stop vehicle

☐ Faulty vacuum servo unit (Chapter 9).
☐ Disconnected, damaged or insecure brake servo vacuum hose (Chapter 9).
☐ Primary or secondary hydraulic circuit failure (Chapter 9).
☐ Seized brake caliper or wheel cylinder piston(s) (Chapter 9).
☐ Brake pads or brake shoes incorrectly fitted (Chapters 1 and 9).
☐ Incorrect grade of brake pads or brake shoes fitted (Chapters 1 and 9).
☐ Brake pads or brake shoe linings contaminated (Chapters 1 and 9).

Judder felt through brake pedal or steering wheel when braking

☐ Excessive run-out or distortion of discs/drums (Chapters 1 and 9).
☐ Brake pad or brake shoe linings worn (Chapters 1 and 9).
☐ Brake caliper or brake backplate mounting bolts loose (Chapter 9).
☐ Wear in suspension or steering components or mountings (Chapters 1 and 10).

Brakes binding

☐ Seized brake caliper or wheel cylinder piston(s) (Chapter 9).
☐ Incorrectly-adjusted handbrake mechanism (Chapter 9).
☐ Faulty master cylinder (Chapter 9).

Rear wheels locking under normal braking

☐ Rear brake shoe linings contaminated (Chapters 1 and 9).
☐ Faulty brake pressure regulator (Chapter 9).

Suspension and steering

Note: *Before diagnosing suspension or steering faults, be sure that the trouble is not due to incorrect tyre pressures, mixtures of tyre types, or binding brakes.*

Vehicle pulls to one side

- ☐ Defective tyre (*Weekly checks*).
- ☐ Excessive wear in suspension or steering components (Chapters 1 and 10).
- ☐ Incorrect front wheel alignment (Chapter 10).
- ☐ Damage to steering or suspension components (Chapter 1).

Wheel wobble and vibration

- ☐ Front roadwheels out of balance (vibration felt mainly through the steering wheel) (Chapters 1 and 10).
- ☐ Rear roadwheels out of balance (vibration felt throughout the vehicle) (Chapters 1 and 10).
- ☐ Roadwheels damaged or distorted (Chapters 1 and 10).
- ☐ Faulty or damaged tyre (*Weekly checks*).
- ☐ Worn steering or suspension joints, bushes or components (Chapters 1 and 10).
- ☐ Wheel bolts loose (Chapters 1 and 10).

Excessive pitching and/or rolling around corners, or during braking

- ☐ Defective shock absorbers (Chapters 1 and 10).
- ☐ Broken or weak spring and/or suspension part (Chapters 1 and 10).
- ☐ Worn or damaged anti-roll bar or mountings (Chapter 10).

Wandering or general instability

- ☐ Incorrect front wheel alignment (Chapter 10).
- ☐ Worn steering or suspension joints, bushes or components (Chapters 1 and 10).
- ☐ Roadwheels out of balance (Chapters 1 and 10).
- ☐ Faulty or damaged tyre (*Weekly checks*).
- ☐ Wheel bolts loose (Chapters 1 and 10).
- ☐ Defective shock absorbers (Chapters 1 and 10).

Excessively-stiff steering

- ☐ Broken or incorrectly-adjusted auxiliary drivebelt (Chapter 1).
- ☐ Faulty power steering pump (Chapter 10).
- ☐ Lack of steering gear lubricant (Chapter 10).
- ☐ Seized track rod end balljoint or suspension balljoint (Chapters 1 and 10).
- ☐ Incorrect front wheel alignment (Chap-ter 10).
- ☐ Steering rack or column bent or damaged (Chapter 10).

Excessive play in steering

- ☐ Worn steering column intermediate shaft universal joint (Chapter 10).
- ☐ Worn steering track rod balljoints (Chapters 1 and 10).
- ☐ Worn rack-and-pinion steering gear (Chapter 10).
- ☐ Worn steering or suspension joints, bushes or components (Chapters 1 and 10).

Lack of power assistance

- ☐ Broken or incorrectly-adjusted auxiliary drivebelt (Chapter 1).
- ☐ Incorrect power steering fluid level (*Weekly checks*).
- ☐ Restriction in power steering fluid hoses (Chapter 1).
- ☐ Faulty power steering pump (Chapter 10).
- ☐ Faulty rack-and-pinion steering gear (Chapter 10).

Tyre wear excessive

Tyre treads exhibit feathered edges

- ☐ Incorrect toe setting (Chapter 10).

Tyres worn in centre of tread

- ☐ Tyres over-inflated (*Weekly checks*).

Tyres worn on inside and outside edges

- ☐ Tyres under-inflated (*Weekly checks*).

Tyres worn on inside or outside edges

- ☐ Incorrect camber/castor angles (wear on one edge only) (Chapter 10).
- ☐ Worn steering or suspension joints, bushes or components (Chapters 1 and 10).
- ☐ Excessively-hard cornering.
- ☐ Accident damage.

Tyres worn unevenly

- ☐ Tyres/wheels out of balance (*Weekly checks*).
- ☐ Excessive wheel or tyre run-out (Chapter 1).
- ☐ Worn shock absorbers (Chapters 1 and 10).
- ☐ Faulty tyre (*Weekly checks*).

Electrical system

Note: *For problems associated with the starting system, refer to the faults listed under 'Engine' earlier in this Section.*

Battery won't hold a charge for more than a few days

- [ ] Battery defective internally (Chapter 5).
- [ ] Battery terminal connections loose or corroded (*Weekly checks*).
- [ ] Auxiliary drivebelt worn or incorrectly adjusted (Chapter 1).
- [ ] Alternator not charging at correct output (Chapter 5).
- [ ] Alternator or voltage regulator faulty (Chapter 5).
- [ ] Short-circuit causing continual battery drain (Chapters 5 and 12).

Ignition/no-charge warning light stays on with engine running

- [ ] Auxiliary drivebelt broken, worn, or incorrectly adjusted (Chapter 1).
- [ ] Alternator brushes worn, sticking, or dirty (Chapter 5).
- [ ] Alternator brush springs weak or broken (Chapter 5).
- [ ] Internal fault in alternator or voltage regulator (Chapter 5).
- [ ] Broken, disconnected, or loose wiring in charging circuit (Chapter 5).

Ignition/no-charge warning light fails to come on

- [ ] Warning light bulb blown (Chapter 12).
- [ ] Broken, disconnected, or loose wiring in warning light circuit (Chapter 12).
- [ ] Alternator faulty (Chapter 5).

Lights inoperative

- [ ] Bulb blown (Chapter 12).
- [ ] Corrosion of bulb or bulbholder contacts (Chapter 12).
- [ ] Blown fuse (Chapter 12).
- [ ] Faulty relay (Chapter 12).
- [ ] Broken, loose, or disconnected wiring (Chapter 12).
- [ ] Faulty switch (Chapter 12).

Instrument readings inaccurate or erratic

- [ ] Faulty instrument panel/multifunction screen (Chapter 12).

Fuel or temperature gauges give no reading

- [ ] Faulty gauge sender unit (Chapters 3 and 4).
- [ ] Wiring open-circuit (Chapter 12).
- [ ] Faulty instrument panel/multifunction screen (Chapter 12).

Fuel or temperature gauges give continuous maximum reading

- [ ] Faulty gauge sender unit (Chapters 3 and 4).
- [ ] Wiring short-circuit (Chapter 12).
- [ ] Faulty instrument panel/multifunction screen (Chapter 12).

Horn inoperative, or unsatisfactory in operation

Horn operates all the time

- [ ] Horn push either earthed or stuck down (Chapter 12).
- [ ] Horn cable-to-horn push earthed (Chapter 12).

Horn fails to operate

- [ ] Blown fuse (Chapter 12).
- [ ] Cable or cable connections loose, broken or disconnected (Chapter 12).
- [ ] Faulty horn (Chapter 12).

Horn emits intermittent or unsatisfactory sound

- [ ] Cable connections loose (Chapter 12).
- [ ] Horn mountings loose (Chapter 12).
- [ ] Faulty horn (Chapter 12).

Windscreen/tailgate wipers failed, or unsatisfactory in operation

Wipers fail to operate, or operate very slowly

- [ ] Wiper blades stuck to screen, or linkage seized or binding (Chapters 1 and 12).
- [ ] Blown fuse (Chapter 12).
- [ ] Cable or cable connections loose, broken or disconnected (Chapter 12).
- [ ] Faulty relay (Chapter 12).
- [ ] Faulty wiper motor (Chapter 12).

Wiper blades sweep over too large or too small an area of the glass

- [ ] Wiper arms incorrectly positioned on spindles (Chapter 1).
- [ ] Excessive wear of wiper linkage (Chapter 12).
- [ ] Wiper motor or linkage mountings loose or insecure (Chapter 12).

Wiper blades fail to clean the glass effectively

- [ ] Wiper blade rubbers worn or perished (*Weekly checks*).
- [ ] Wiper arm tension springs broken, or arm pivots seized (Chapter 12).
- [ ] Insufficient windscreen washer additive to adequately remove road film (*Weekly checks*).

Windscreen/tailgate washers failed, or unsatisfactory in operation

One or more washer jets inoperative

- [ ] Blocked washer jet.
- [ ] Disconnected, kinked or restricted fluid hose (Chapter 12).
- [ ] Insufficient fluid in washer reservoir (*Weekly checks*).

Washer pump fails to operate

- [ ] Broken or disconnected wiring or connections (Chapter 12).
- [ ] Blown fuse (Chapter 12).
- [ ] Faulty washer switch (Chapter 12).
- [ ] Faulty washer pump (Chapter 12).

Washer pump runs for some time before fluid is emitted from jets

- [ ] Faulty one-way valve in fluid supply hose.

Electric windows inoperative, or unsatisfactory in operation

Window glass will only move in one direction

- [ ] Faulty switch (Chapter 12).

Window glass slow to move

- [ ] Regulator seized or damaged, or in need of lubricant (Chapter 11).
- [ ] Door internal components or trim fouling regulator (Chapter 11).
- [ ] Faulty motor (Chapter 11).

Window glass fails to move

- [ ] Blown fuse (Chapter 12).
- [ ] Faulty relay (Chapter 12).
- [ ] Broken or disconnected wiring or connections (Chapter 12).
- [ ] Faulty motor (Chapter 11).

Electrical system (continued)

Central locking system inoperative, or unsatisfactory in operation

Complete system failure

- [ ] Blown fuse (Chapter 12).
- [ ] Faulty relay (Chapter 12).
- [ ] Broken or disconnected wiring or connections (Chapter 12).
- [ ] Faulty control unit (Chapter 11).

Latch locks but will not unlock, or unlocks but will not lock

- [ ] Faulty master switch (Chapter 12).
- [ ] Broken or disconnected latch operating rods or levers (Chapter 11).
- [ ] Faulty relay (Chapter 12).
- [ ] Faulty control unit (Chapter 11).

One solenoid/motor fails to operate

- [ ] Broken or disconnected wiring or connections (Chapter 12).
- [ ] Faulty solenoid/motor (Chapter 11).
- [ ] Broken, binding or disconnected latch operating rods or levers (Chapter 11).
- [ ] Fault in door latch (Chapter 11).

A

ABS (Anti-lock brake system) A system, usually electronically controlled, that senses incipient wheel lockup during braking and relieves hydraulic pressure at wheels that are about to skid.

Air bag An inflatable bag hidden in the steering wheel (driver's side) or the dash or glovebox (passenger side). In a head-on collision, the bags inflate, preventing the driver and front passenger from being thrown forward into the steering wheel or windscreen.

Air cleaner A metal or plastic housing, containing a filter element, which removes dust and dirt from the air being drawn into the engine.

Air filter element The actual filter in an air cleaner system, usually manufactured from pleated paper and requiring renewal at regular intervals.

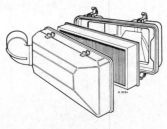

Air filter

Allen key A hexagonal wrench which fits into a recessed hexagonal hole.

Alligator clip A long-nosed spring-loaded metal clip with meshing teeth. Used to make temporary electrical connections.

Alternator A component in the electrical system which converts mechanical energy from a drivebelt into electrical energy to charge the battery and to operate the starting system, ignition system and electrical accessories.

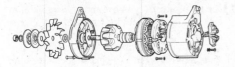

Alternator (exploded view)

Ampere (amp) A unit of measurement for the flow of electric current. One amp is the amount of current produced by one volt acting through a resistance of one ohm.

Anaerobic sealer A substance used to prevent bolts and screws from loosening. Anaerobic means that it does not require oxygen for activation. The Loctite brand is widely used.

Antifreeze A substance (usually ethylene glycol) mixed with water, and added to a vehicle's cooling system, to prevent freezing of the coolant in winter. Antifreeze also contains chemicals to inhibit corrosion and the formation of rust and other deposits that would tend to clog the radiator and coolant passages and reduce cooling efficiency.

Anti-seize compound A coating that reduces the risk of seizing on fasteners that are subjected to high temperatures, such as exhaust manifold bolts and nuts.

Anti-seize compound

Asbestos A natural fibrous mineral with great heat resistance, commonly used in the composition of brake friction materials. Asbestos is a health hazard and the dust created by brake systems should never be inhaled or ingested.

Axle A shaft on which a wheel revolves, or which revolves with a wheel. Also, a solid beam that connects the two wheels at one end of the vehicle. An axle which also transmits power to the wheels is known as a live axle.

Axle assembly

Axleshaft A single rotating shaft, on either side of the differential, which delivers power from the final drive assembly to the drive wheels. Also called a driveshaft or a halfshaft.

B

Ball bearing An anti-friction bearing consisting of a hardened inner and outer race with hardened steel balls between two races.

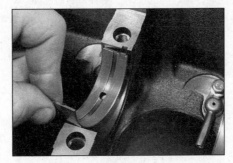

Bearing

Bearing The curved surface on a shaft or in a bore, or the part assembled into either, that permits relative motion between them with minimum wear and friction.

Big-end bearing The bearing in the end of the connecting rod that's attached to the crankshaft.

Bleed nipple A valve on a brake wheel cylinder, caliper or other hydraulic component that is opened to purge the hydraulic system of air. Also called a bleed screw.

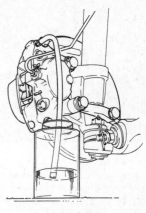

Brake bleeding

Brake bleeding Procedure for removing air from lines of a hydraulic brake system.

Brake disc The component of a disc brake that rotates with the wheels.

Brake drum The component of a drum brake that rotates with the wheels.

Brake linings The friction material which contacts the brake disc or drum to retard the vehicle's speed. The linings are bonded or riveted to the brake pads or shoes.

Brake pads The replaceable friction pads that pinch the brake disc when the brakes are applied. Brake pads consist of a friction material bonded or riveted to a rigid backing plate.

Brake shoe The crescent-shaped carrier to which the brake linings are mounted and which forces the lining against the rotating drum during braking.

Braking systems For more information on braking systems, consult the *Haynes Automotive Brake Manual.*

Breaker bar A long socket wrench handle providing greater leverage.

Bulkhead The insulated partition between the engine and the passenger compartment.

C

Caliper The non-rotating part of a disc-brake assembly that straddles the disc and carries the brake pads. The caliper also contains the hydraulic components that cause the pads to pinch the disc when the brakes are applied. A caliper is also a measuring tool that can be set to measure inside or outside dimensions of an object.

Camshaft A rotating shaft on which a series of cam lobes operate the valve mechanisms. The camshaft may be driven by gears, by sprockets and chain or by sprockets and a belt.

Canister A container in an evaporative emission control system; contains activated charcoal granules to trap vapours from the fuel system.

Canister

Carburettor A device which mixes fuel with air in the proper proportions to provide a desired power output from a spark ignition internal combustion engine.

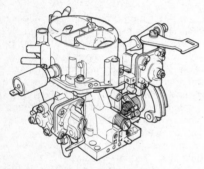

Carburettor

Castellated Resembling the parapets along the top of a castle wall. For example, a castellated balljoint stud nut.

Castellated nut

Castor In wheel alignment, the backward or forward tilt of the steering axis. Castor is positive when the steering axis is inclined rearward at the top.

Catalytic converter A silencer-like device in the exhaust system which converts certain pollutants in the exhaust gases into less harmful substances.

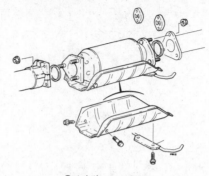

Catalytic converter

Circlip A ring-shaped clip used to prevent endwise movement of cylindrical parts and shafts. An internal circlip is installed in a groove in a housing; an external circlip fits into a groove on the outside of a cylindrical piece such as a shaft.

Clearance The amount of space between two parts. For example, between a piston and a cylinder, between a bearing and a journal, etc.

Coil spring A spiral of elastic steel found in various sizes throughout a vehicle, for example as a springing medium in the suspension and in the valve train.

Compression Reduction in volume, and increase in pressure and temperature, of a gas, caused by squeezing it into a smaller space.

Compression ratio The relationship between cylinder volume when the piston is at top dead centre and cylinder volume when the piston is at bottom dead centre.

Constant velocity (CV) joint A type of universal joint that cancels out vibrations caused by driving power being transmitted through an angle.

Core plug A disc or cup-shaped metal device inserted in a hole in a casting through which core was removed when the casting was formed. Also known as a freeze plug or expansion plug.

Crankcase The lower part of the engine block in which the crankshaft rotates.

Crankshaft The main rotating member, or shaft, running the length of the crankcase, with offset "throws" to which the connecting rods are attached.

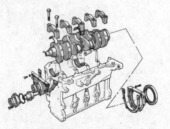

Crankshaft assembly

Crocodile clip See Alligator clip

D

Diagnostic code Code numbers obtained by accessing the diagnostic mode of an engine management computer. This code can be used to determine the area in the system where a malfunction may be located.

Disc brake A brake design incorporating a rotating disc onto which brake pads are squeezed. The resulting friction converts the energy of a moving vehicle into heat.

Double-overhead cam (DOHC) An engine that uses two overhead camshafts, usually one for the intake valves and one for the exhaust valves.

Drivebelt(s) The belt(s) used to drive accessories such as the alternator, water pump, power steering pump, air conditioning compressor, etc. off the crankshaft pulley.

Accessory drivebelts

Driveshaft Any shaft used to transmit motion. Commonly used when referring to the axleshafts on a front wheel drive vehicle.

Driveshaft

Drum brake A type of brake using a drum-shaped metal cylinder attached to the inner surface of the wheel. When the brake pedal is pressed, curved brake shoes with friction linings press against the inside of the drum to slow or stop the vehicle.

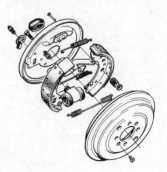

Drum brake assembly

E

EGR valve A valve used to introduce exhaust gases into the intake air stream.

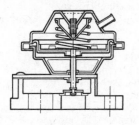

EGR valve

Electronic control unit (ECU) A computer which controls (for instance) ignition and fuel injection systems, or an anti-lock braking system. For more information refer to the *Haynes Automotive Electrical and Electronic Systems Manual*.

Electronic Fuel Injection (EFI) A computer controlled fuel system that distributes fuel through an injector located in each intake port of the engine.

Emergency brake A braking system, independent of the main hydraulic system, that can be used to slow or stop the vehicle if the primary brakes fail, or to hold the vehicle stationary even though the brake pedal isn't depressed. It usually consists of a hand lever that actuates either front or rear brakes mechanically through a series of cables and linkages. Also known as a handbrake or parking brake.

Endfloat The amount of lengthwise movement between two parts. As applied to a crankshaft, the distance that the crankshaft can move forward and back in the cylinder block.

Engine management system (EMS) A computer controlled system which manages the fuel injection and the ignition systems in an integrated fashion.

Exhaust manifold A part with several passages through which exhaust gases leave the engine combustion chambers and enter the exhaust pipe.

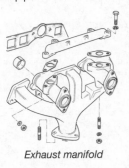

Exhaust manifold

F

Fan clutch A viscous (fluid) drive coupling device which permits variable engine fan speeds in relation to engine speeds.

Feeler blade A thin strip or blade of hardened steel, ground to an exact thickness, used to check or measure clearances between parts.

Feeler blade

Firing order The order in which the engine cylinders fire, or deliver their power strokes, beginning with the number one cylinder.

Flywheel A heavy spinning wheel in which energy is absorbed and stored by means of momentum. On cars, the flywheel is attached to the crankshaft to smooth out firing impulses.

Free play The amount of travel before any action takes place. The "looseness" in a linkage, or an assembly of parts, between the initial application of force and actual movement. For example, the distance the brake pedal moves before the pistons in the master cylinder are actuated.

Fuse An electrical device which protects a circuit against accidental overload. The typical fuse contains a soft piece of metal which is calibrated to melt at a predetermined current flow (expressed as amps) and break the circuit.

Fusible link A circuit protection device consisting of a conductor surrounded by heat-resistant insulation. The conductor is smaller than the wire it protects, so it acts as the weakest link in the circuit. Unlike a blown fuse, a failed fusible link must frequently be cut from the wire for replacement.

G

Gap The distance the spark must travel in jumping from the centre electrode to the side

Adjusting spark plug gap

electrode in a spark plug. Also refers to the spacing between the points in a contact breaker assembly in a conventional points-type ignition, or to the distance between the reluctor or rotor and the pickup coil in an electronic ignition.

Gasket Any thin, soft material - usually cork, cardboard, asbestos or soft metal - installed between two metal surfaces to ensure a good seal. For instance, the cylinder head gasket seals the joint between the block and the cylinder head.

Gasket

Gauge An instrument panel display used to monitor engine conditions. A gauge with a movable pointer on a dial or a fixed scale is an analogue gauge. A gauge with a numerical readout is called a digital gauge.

H

Halfshaft A rotating shaft that transmits power from the final drive unit to a drive wheel, usually when referring to a live rear axle.

Harmonic balancer A device designed to reduce torsion or twisting vibration in the crankshaft. May be incorporated in the crankshaft pulley. Also known as a vibration damper.

Hone An abrasive tool for correcting small irregularities or differences in diameter in an engine cylinder, brake cylinder, etc.

Hydraulic tappet A tappet that utilises hydraulic pressure from the engine's lubrication system to maintain zero clearance (constant contact with both camshaft and valve stem). Automatically adjusts to variation in valve stem length. Hydraulic tappets also reduce valve noise.

I

Ignition timing The moment at which the spark plug fires, usually expressed in the number of crankshaft degrees before the piston reaches the top of its stroke.

Inlet manifold A tube or housing with passages through which flows the air-fuel mixture (carburettor vehicles and vehicles with throttle body injection) or air only (port fuel-injected vehicles) to the port openings in the cylinder head.

J

Jump start Starting the engine of a vehicle with a discharged or weak battery by attaching jump leads from the weak battery to a charged or helper battery.

L

Load Sensing Proportioning Valve (LSPV) A brake hydraulic system control valve that works like a proportioning valve, but also takes into consideration the amount of weight carried by the rear axle.

Locknut A nut used to lock an adjustment nut, or other threaded component, in place. For example, a locknut is employed to keep the adjusting nut on the rocker arm in position.

Lockwasher A form of washer designed to prevent an attaching nut from working loose.

M

MacPherson strut A type of front suspension system devised by Earle MacPherson at Ford of England. In its original form, a simple lateral link with the anti-roll bar creates the lower control arm. A long strut - an integral coil spring and shock absorber - is mounted between the body and the steering knuckle. Many modern so-called MacPherson strut systems use a conventional lower A-arm and don't rely on the anti-roll bar for location.

Multimeter An electrical test instrument with the capability to measure voltage, current and resistance.

N

NOx Oxides of Nitrogen. A common toxic pollutant emitted by petrol and diesel engines at higher temperatures.

O

Ohm The unit of electrical resistance. One volt applied to a resistance of one ohm will produce a current of one amp.

Ohmmeter An instrument for measuring electrical resistance.

O-ring A type of sealing ring made of a special rubber-like material; in use, the O-ring is compressed into a groove to provide the sealing action.

O-ring

Overhead cam (ohc) engine An engine with the camshaft(s) located on top of the cylinder head(s).

Overhead valve (ohv) engine An engine with the valves located in the cylinder head, but with the camshaft located in the engine block.

Oxygen sensor A device installed in the engine exhaust manifold, which senses the oxygen content in the exhaust and converts this information into an electric current. Also called a Lambda sensor.

P

Phillips screw A type of screw head having a cross instead of a slot for a corresponding type of screwdriver.

Plastigage A thin strip of plastic thread, available in different sizes, used for measuring clearances. For example, a strip of Plastigage is laid across a bearing journal. The parts are assembled and dismantled; the width of the crushed strip indicates the clearance between journal and bearing.

Plastigage

Propeller shaft The long hollow tube with universal joints at both ends that carries power from the transmission to the differential on front-engined rear wheel drive vehicles.

Proportioning valve A hydraulic control valve which limits the amount of pressure to the rear brakes during panic stops to prevent wheel lock-up.

R

Rack-and-pinion steering A steering system with a pinion gear on the end of the steering shaft that mates with a rack (think of a geared wheel opened up and laid flat). When the steering wheel is turned, the pinion turns, moving the rack to the left or right. This movement is transmitted through the track rods to the steering arms at the wheels.

Radiator A liquid-to-air heat transfer device designed to reduce the temperature of the coolant in an internal combustion engine cooling system.

Refrigerant Any substance used as a heat transfer agent in an air-conditioning system. R-12 has been the principle refrigerant for many years; recently, however, manufacturers have begun using R-134a, a non-CFC substance that is considered less harmful to the ozone in the upper atmosphere.

Rocker arm A lever arm that rocks on a shaft or pivots on a stud. In an overhead valve engine, the rocker arm converts the upward movement of the pushrod into a downward movement to open a valve.

Rotor In a distributor, the rotating device inside the cap that connects the centre electrode and the outer terminals as it turns, distributing the high voltage from the coil secondary winding to the proper spark plug. Also, that part of an alternator which rotates inside the stator. Also, the rotating assembly of a turbocharger, including the compressor wheel, shaft and turbine wheel.

Runout The amount of wobble (in-and-out movement) of a gear or wheel as it's rotated. The amount a shaft rotates "out-of-true." The out-of-round condition of a rotating part.

S

Sealant A liquid or paste used to prevent leakage at a joint. Sometimes used in conjunction with a gasket.

Sealed beam lamp An older headlight design which integrates the reflector, lens and filaments into a hermetically-sealed one-piece unit. When a filament burns out or the lens cracks, the entire unit is simply replaced.

Serpentine drivebelt A single, long, wide accessory drivebelt that's used on some newer vehicles to drive all the accessories, instead of a series of smaller, shorter belts. Serpentine drivebelts are usually tensioned by an automatic tensioner.

Serpentine drivebelt

Shim Thin spacer, commonly used to adjust the clearance or relative positions between two parts. For example, shims inserted into or under bucket tappets control valve clearances. Clearance is adjusted by changing the thickness of the shim.

Slide hammer A special puller that screws into or hooks onto a component such as a shaft or bearing; a heavy sliding handle on the shaft bottoms against the end of the shaft to knock the component free.

Sprocket A tooth or projection on the periphery of a wheel, shaped to engage with a chain or drivebelt. Commonly used to refer to the sprocket wheel itself.

Starter inhibitor switch On vehicles with an automatic transmission, a switch that prevents starting if the vehicle is not in Neutral or Park.

Strut See MacPherson strut.

T

Tappet A cylindrical component which transmits motion from the cam to the valve stem, either directly or via a pushrod and rocker arm. Also called a cam follower.

Thermostat A heat-controlled valve that regulates the flow of coolant between the cylinder block and the radiator, so maintaining optimum engine operating temperature. A thermostat is also used in some air cleaners in which the temperature is regulated.

Thrust bearing The bearing in the clutch assembly that is moved in to the release levers by clutch pedal action to disengage the clutch. Also referred to as a release bearing.

Timing belt A toothed belt which drives the camshaft. Serious engine damage may result if it breaks in service.

Timing chain A chain which drives the camshaft.

Toe-in The amount the front wheels are closer together at the front than at the rear. On rear wheel drive vehicles, a slight amount of toe-in is usually specified to keep the front wheels running parallel on the road by offsetting other forces that tend to spread the wheels apart.

Toe-out The amount the front wheels are closer together at the rear than at the front. On front wheel drive vehicles, a slight amount of toe-out is usually specified.

Tools For full information on choosing and using tools, refer to the *Haynes Automotive Tools Manual*.

Tracer A stripe of a second colour applied to a wire insulator to distinguish that wire from another one with the same colour insulator.

Tune-up A process of accurate and careful adjustments and parts replacement to obtain the best possible engine performance.

Turbocharger A centrifugal device, driven by exhaust gases, that pressurises the intake air. Normally used to increase the power output from a given engine displacement, but can also be used primarily to reduce exhaust emissions (as on VW's "Umwelt" Diesel engine).

U

Universal joint or U-joint A double-pivoted connection for transmitting power from a driving to a driven shaft through an angle. A U-joint consists of two Y-shaped yokes and a cross-shaped member called the spider.

V

Valve A device through which the flow of liquid, gas, vacuum, or loose material in bulk may be started, stopped, or regulated by a movable part that opens, shuts, or partially obstructs one or more ports or passageways. A valve is also the movable part of such a device.

Valve clearance The clearance between the valve tip (the end of the valve stem) and the rocker arm or tappet. The valve clearance is measured when the valve is closed.

Vernier caliper A precision measuring instrument that measures inside and outside dimensions. Not quite as accurate as a micrometer, but more convenient.

Viscosity The thickness of a liquid or its resistance to flow.

Volt A unit for expressing electrical "pressure" in a circuit. One volt that will produce a current of one ampere through a resistance of one ohm.

W

Welding Various processes used to join metal items by heating the areas to be joined to a molten state and fusing them together. For more information refer to the *Haynes Automotive Welding Manual*.

Wiring diagram A drawing portraying the components and wires in a vehicle's electrical system, using standardised symbols. For more information refer to the *Haynes Automotive Electrical and Electronic Systems Manual*.

Note: *References throughout this index are in the form "Chapter number" • "Page number"*

Notes

Notes

Haynes Manuals – The Complete UK Car List

Title	Book No.
ALFA ROMEO Alfasud/Sprint (74 - 88) up to F *	0292
Alfa Romeo Alfetta (73 - 87) up to E *	0531
AUDI 80, 90 & Coupe Petrol (79 - Nov 88) up to F	0605
Audi 80, 90 & Coupe Petrol (Oct 86 - 90) D to H	1491
Audi 100 & 200 Petrol (Oct 82 - 90) up to H	0907
Audi 100 & A6 Petrol & Diesel (May 91 - May 97) H to P	3504
Audi A3 Petrol & Diesel (96 - May 03) P to 03	4253
Audi A4 Petrol & Diesel (95 - 00) M to X	3575
Audi A4 Petrol & Diesel (01 - 04) X to 54	4609
AUSTIN A35 & A40 (56 - 67) up to F *	0118
Austin/MG/Rover Maestro 1.3 & 1.6 Petrol (83 - 95) up to M	0922
Austin/MG Metro (80 - May 90) up to G	0718
Austin/Rover Montego 1.3 & 1.6 Petrol (84 - 94) A to L	1066
Austin/MG/Rover Montego 2.0 Petrol (84 - 95) A to M	1067
Mini (59 - 69) up to H *	0527
Mini (69 - 01) up to X	0646
Austin/Rover 2.0 litre Diesel Engine (86 - 93) C to L	1857
Austin Healey 100/6 & 3000 (56 - 68) up to G *	0049
BEDFORD CF Petrol (69 - 87) up to E	0163
Bedford/Vauxhall Rascal & Suzuki Supercarry (86 - Oct 94) C to M	3015
BMW 316, 320 & 320i (4-cyl) (75 - Feb 83) up to Y *	0276
BMW 320, 320i, 323i & 325i (6-cyl) (Oct 77 - Sept 87) up to E	0815
BMW 3- & 5-Series Petrol (81 - 91) up to J	1948
BMW 3-Series Petrol (Apr 91 - 99) H to V	3210
BMW 3-Series Petrol (Sept 98 - 03) S to 53	4067
BMW 520i & 525e (Oct 81 - June 88) up to E	1560
BMW 525, 528 & 528i (73 - Sept 81) up to X *	0632
BMW 5-Series 6-cyl Petrol (April 96 - Aug 03) N to 03	4151
BMW 1500, 1502, 1600, 1602, 2000 & 2002 (59 - 77) up to S *	0240
CHRYSLER PT Cruiser Petrol (00 - 03) W to 53	4058
CITROËN 2CV, Ami & Dyane (67 - 90) up to H	0196
Citroën AX Petrol & Diesel (87 - 97) D to P	3014
Citroën Berlingo & Peugeot Partner Petrol & Diesel (96 - 05) P to 55	4281
Citroën BX Petrol (83 - 94) A to L	0908
Citroën C15 Van Petrol & Diesel (89 - Oct 98) F to S	3509
Citroën C3 Petrol & Diesel (02 - 05) 51 to 05	4197
Citroën CX Petrol (75 - 88) up to F	0528
Citroën Saxo Petrol & Diesel (96 - 04) N to 54	3506
Citroën Visa Petrol (79 - 88) up to F	0620
Citroën Xantia Petrol & Diesel (93 - 01) K to Y	3082
Citroën XM Petrol & Diesel (89 - 00) G to X	3451
Citroën Xsara Petrol & Diesel (97 - Sept 00) R to W	3751
Citroën Xsara Picasso Petrol & Diesel (00 - 02) W to 52	3944
Citroën ZX Diesel (91 - 98) J to S	1922
Citroën ZX Petrol (91 - 98) H to S	1881
Citroën 1.7 & 1.9 litre Diesel Engine (84 - 96) A to N	1379
FIAT 126 (73 - 87) up to E *	0305
Fiat 500 (57 - 73) up to M *	0090
Fiat Bravo & Brava Petrol (95 - 00) N to W	3572
Fiat Cinquecento (93 - 98) K to R	3501
Fiat Panda (81 - 95) up to M	0793
Fiat Punto Petrol & Diesel (94 - Oct 99) L to V	3251
Fiat Punto Petrol (Oct 99 - July 03) V to 03	4066
Fiat Regata Petrol (84 - 88) A to F	1167
Fiat Tipo Petrol (88 - 91) E to J	1625
Fiat Uno Petrol (83 - 95) up to M	0923
Fiat X1/9 (74 - 89) up to G *	0273
FORD Anglia (59 - 68) up to G *	0001
Ford Capri II (& III) 1.6 & 2.0 (74 - 87) up to E *	0283
Ford Capri II (& III) 2.8 & 3.0 V6 (74 - 87) up to E	1309

Title	Book No.
Ford Cortina Mk I & Corsair 1500 ('62 - '66) up to D*	0214
Ford Cortina Mk III 1300 & 1600 (70 - 76) up to P *	0070
Ford Escort Mk I 1100 & 1300 (68 - 74) up to N *	0171
Ford Escort Mk I Mexico, RS 1600 & RS 2000 (70 - 74) up to N *	0139
Ford Escort Mk II Mexico, RS 1800 & RS 2000 (75 - 80) up to W *	0735
Ford Escort (75 - Aug 80) up to V *	0280
Ford Escort Petrol (Sept 80 - Sept 90) up to H	0686
Ford Escort & Orion Petrol (Sept 90 - 00) H to X	1737
Ford Escort & Orion Diesel (Sept 90 - 00) H to X	4081
Ford Fiesta (76 - Aug 83) up to Y	0334
Ford Fiesta Petrol (Aug 83 - Feb 89) A to F	1030
Ford Fiesta Petrol (Feb 89 - Oct 95) F to N	1595
Ford Fiesta Petrol & Diesel (Oct 95 - Mar 02) N to 02	3397
Ford Fiesta Petrol & Diesel (Apr 02 - 05) 02 to 54	4170
Ford Focus Petrol & Diesel (98 - 01) S to Y	3759
Ford Focus Petrol & Diesel (Oct 01 - 05) 51 to 05	4167
Ford Galaxy Petrol & Diesel (95 - Aug 00) M to W	3984
Ford Granada Petrol (Sept 77 - Feb 85) up to B *	0481
Ford Granada & Scorpio Petrol (Mar 85 - 94) B to M	1245
Ford Ka (96 - 02) P to 52	3570
Ford Mondeo Petrol (93 - Sept 00) K to X	1923
Ford Mondeo Petrol & Diesel (Oct 00 - Jul 03) X to 03	3990
Ford Mondeo Petrol & Diesel (July 03 - 07) 03 to 56	4619
Ford Mondeo Diesel (93 - 96) L to N	3465
Ford Orion Petrol (83 - Sept 90) up to H	1009
Ford Sierra 4-cyl Petrol (82 - 93) up to K	0903
Ford Sierra V6 Petrol (82 - 91) up to J	0904
Ford Transit Petrol (Mk 2) (78 - Jan 86) up to C	0719
Ford Transit Petrol (Mk 3) (Feb 86 - 89) C to G	1468
Ford Transit Diesel (Feb 86 - 99) C to T	3019
Ford 1.6 & 1.8 litre Diesel Engine (84 - 96) A to N	1172
Ford 2.1, 2.3 & 2.5 litre Diesel Engine (77 - 90) up to H	1606
FREIGHT ROVER Sherpa Petrol (74 - 87) up to E	0463
HILLMAN Avenger (70 - 82) up to Y	0037
Hillman Imp (63 - 76) up to R *	0022
HONDA Civic (Feb 84 - Oct 87) A to E	1226
Honda Civic (Nov 91 - 96) J to N	3199
Honda Civic Petrol (Mar 95 - 00) M to X	4050
Honda Civic Petrol & Diesel (01 - 05) X to 55	4611
Honda Jazz (01 - Feb 08) 51 - 57	4735
HYUNDAI Pony (85 - 94) C to M	3398
JAGUAR E Type (61 - 72) up to L *	0140
Jaguar MkI & II, 240 & 340 (55 - 69) up to H *	0098
Jaguar XJ6, XJ & Sovereign; Daimler Sovereign (68 - Oct 86) up to D	0242
Jaguar XJ6 & Sovereign (Oct 86 - Sept 94) D to M	3261
Jaguar XJ12, XJS & Sovereign; Daimler Double Six (72 - 88) up to F	0478
JEEP Cherokee Petrol (93 - 96) K to N	1943
LADA 1200, 1300, 1500 & 1600 (74 - 91) up to J	0413
Lada Samara (87 - 91) D to J	1610
LAND ROVER 90, 110 & Defender Diesel (83 - 07) up to 56	3017
Land Rover Discovery Petrol & Diesel (89 - 98) G to S	3016
Land Rover Discovery Diesel (Nov 98 - Jul 04) S to 04	4606
Land Rover Freelander Petrol & Diesel (97 - Sept 03) R to 53	3929
Land Rover Freelander Petrol & Diesel (Oct 03 - Oct 06) 53 to 56	4623
Land Rover Series IIA & III Diesel (58 - 85) up to C	0529
Land Rover Series II, IIA & III 4-cyl Petrol (58 - 85) up to C	0314

Title	Book No.
MAZDA 323 (Mar 81 - Oct 89) up to G	1608
Mazda 323 (Oct 89 - 98) G to R	3455
Mazda 626 (May 83 - Sept 87) up to E	0929
Mazda B1600, B1800 & B2000 Pick-up Petrol (72 - 88) up to F	0267
Mazda RX-7 (79 - 85) up to C *	0460
MERCEDES-BENZ 190, 190E & 190D Petrol & Diesel (83 - 93) A to L	3450
Mercedes-Benz 200D, 240D, 240TD, 300D & 300TD 123 Series Diesel (76 - 85)	1114
Mercedes-Benz 250 & 280 (68 - 72) up to L *	0346
Mercedes-Benz 250 & 280 123 Series Petrol (Oct 76 - 84) up to B *	0677
Mercedes-Benz 124 Series Petrol & Diesel (85 - Aug 93) C to K	3253
Mercedes-Benz C-Class Petrol & Diesel (93 - Aug 00) L to W	3511
MGA (55 - 62) *	0475
MGB (62 - 80) up to W	0111
MG Midget & Austin-Healey Sprite (58 - 80) up to W *	0265
MINI Petrol (July 01 - 05) Y to 05	4273
MITSUBISHI Shogun & L200 Pick-Ups Petrol (83 - 94) up to M	1944
MORRIS Ital 1.3 (80 - 84) up to B	0705
Morris Minor 1000 (56 - 71) up to K	0024
NISSAN Almera Petrol (95 - Feb 00) N to V	4053
Nissan Almera & Tino Petrol (Feb 00 - 07) V to 56	4612
Nissan Bluebird (May 84 - Mar 86) A to C	1223
Nissan Bluebird Petrol (Mar 86 - 90) C to H	1473
Nissan Cherry (Sept 82 - 86) up to D	1031
Nissan Micra (83 - Jan 93) up to K	0931
Nissan Micra (93 - 02) K to 52	3254
Nissan Primera Petrol (90 - Aug 99) H to T	1851
Nissan Stanza (82 - 86) up to D	0824
Nissan Sunny Petrol (May 82 - Oct 86) up to D	0895
Nissan Sunny Petrol (Oct 86 - Mar 91) D to H	1378
Nissan Sunny Petrol (Apr 91 - 95) H to N	3219
OPEL Ascona & Manta (B Series) (Sept 75 - 88) up to F *	0316
Opel Ascona Petrol (81 - 88)	3215
Opel Astra Petrol (Oct 91 - Feb 98)	3156
Opel Corsa Petrol (83 - Mar 93)	3160
Opel Corsa Petrol (Mar 93 - 97)	3159
Opel Kadett Petrol (Nov 79 - Oct 84) up to B	0634
Opel Kadett Petrol (Oct 84 - Oct 91)	3196
Opel Omega & Senator Petrol (Nov 86 - 94)	3157
Opel Rekord Petrol (Feb 78 - Oct 86) up to D	0543
Opel Vectra Petrol (Oct 88 - Oct 95)	3158
PEUGEOT 106 Petrol & Diesel (91 - 04) J to 53	1882
Peugeot 205 Petrol (83 - 97) A to P	0932
Peugeot 206 Petrol & Diesel (98 - 01) S to X	3757
Peugeot 206 Petrol & Diesel (02 - 06) 51 to 06	4613
Peugeot 306 Petrol & Diesel (93 - 02) K to 02	3073
Peugeot 307 Petrol & Diesel (01 - 04) Y to 54	4147
Peugeot 309 Petrol (86 - 93) C to K	1266
Peugeot 405 Petrol (88 - 97) E to P	1559
Peugeot 405 Diesel (88 - 97) E to P	3198
Peugeot 406 Petrol & Diesel (96 - Mar 99) N to T	3394
Peugeot 406 Petrol & Diesel (Mar 99 - 02) T to 52	3982
Peugeot 505 Petrol (79 - 89) up to G	0762
Peugeot 1.7/1.8 & 1.9 litre Diesel Engine (82 - 96) up to N	0950
Peugeot 2.0, 2.1, 2.3 & 2.5 litre Diesel Engines (74 - 90) up to H	1607
PORSCHE 911 (65 - 85) up to C	0264

* Classic reprint

All the products featured on this page are available through most motor accessory shops, cycle shops and book stores. Our policy of continuous updating and development means that titles are being constantly added to the range. For up-to-date information on our complete list of titles, please telephone: (UK) +44 1963 442030 • (USA) +1 805 498 6703 • (Sweden) +46 18 124016 • (Australia) +61 3 9763 8100

CL23.12/07

Preserving Our Motoring Heritage

<
The Model J Duesenberg
Derham Tourster.
Only eight of these
magnificent cars were
ever built – this is the
only example to be found
outside the United States
of America

Almost every car you've ever loved, loathed or desired is gathered under one roof at the Haynes Motor Museum. Over 300 immaculately presented cars and motorbikes represent every aspect of our motoring heritage, from elegant reminders of bygone days, such as the superb Model J Duesenberg to curiosities like the bug-eyed BMW Isetta. There are also many old friends and flames. Perhaps you remember the 1959 Ford Popular that you did your courting in? The magnificent 'Red Collection' is a spectacle of classic sports cars including AC, Alfa Romeo, Austin Healey, Ferrari, Lamborghini, Maserati, MG, Riley, Porsche and Triumph.

A Perfect Day Out

Each and every vehicle at the Haynes Motor Museum has played its part in the history and culture of Motoring. Today, they make a wonderful spectacle and a great day out for all the family. Bring the kids, bring Mum and Dad, but above all bring your camera to capture those golden memories for ever. You will also find an impressive array of motoring memorabilia, a comfortable 70 seat video cinema and one of the most extensive transport book shops in Britain. The Pit Stop Cafe serves everything from a cup of tea to wholesome, home-made meals or, if you prefer, you can enjoy the large picnic area nestled in the beautiful rural surroundings of Somerset.

>
John Haynes O.B.E.,
Founder and
Chairman of the
museum at the wheel
of a Haynes Light 12.

<
Graham Hill's Lola
Cosworth Formula 1
car next to a 1934
Riley Sports.

The Museum is situated on the A359 Yeovil to Frome road at Sparkford, just off the A303 in Somerset. It is about 40 miles south of Bristol, and 25 minutes drive from the M5 intersection at Taunton.
Open 9.30am - 5.30pm (10.00am - 4.00pm Winter) 7 days a week, *except Christmas Day, Boxing Day and New Years Day*
Special rates available for schools, coach parties and outings Charitable Trust No. 292048